Uncertainty in Strategic Decision Making

Richard J. Arend

Uncertainty in Strategic Decision Making

Analysis, Categorization, Causation and Resolution

{uncertainty's everything logo ©}

palgrave
macmillan

Richard J. Arend
University of Southern Maine
Portland, ME, USA

ISBN 978-3-031-48552-7   ISBN 978-3-031-48553-4 (eBook)
https://doi.org/10.1007/978-3-031-48553-4

© The Editor(s) (if applicable) and The Author(s), under exclusive license to Springer Nature Switzerland AG 2024

This work is subject to copyright. All rights are solely and exclusively licensed by the Publisher, whether the whole or part of the material is concerned, specifically the rights of translation, reprinting, reuse of illustrations, recitation, broadcasting, reproduction on microfilms or in any other physical way, and transmission or information storage and retrieval, electronic adaptation, computer software, or by similar or dissimilar methodology now known or hereafter developed.
The use of general descriptive names, registered names, trademarks, service marks, etc. in this publication does not imply, even in the absence of a specific statement, that such names are exempt from the relevant protective laws and regulations and therefore free for general use.
The publisher, the authors, and the editors are safe to assume that the advice and information in this book are believed to be true and accurate at the date of publication. Neither the publisher nor the authors or the editors give a warranty, expressed or implied, with respect to the material contained herein or for any errors or omissions that may have been made. The publisher remains neutral with regard to jurisdictional claims in published maps and institutional affiliations.

This Palgrave Macmillan imprint is published by the registered company Springer Nature Switzerland AG
The registered company address is: Gewerbestrasse 11, 6330 Cham, Switzerland

Paper in this product is recyclable.

*To my Family and Friends,
...and for all those who try to make the unknowns
more beneficially known, and the knowns
less disinformationally unknown.*

Acknowledgments

Many thanks to Ruth, Damon, and Holly for their love and support. Gratitude to the 909, 416, 905, 604, 207, and the +31 for their inspiration and humor. Thanks to my former instructors and students for their lessons. Appreciation to USM and L.L. Bean for the academic chair, and to Palgrave Macmillan for their publishing support. All errors, pop culture references, and snide remarks remain our own.

Contents

1 Overview of This Book on Strategic Decision-Making Under Uncertainty   1
  Why This Book on Uncertainty?   1
  Notable Takes on Uncertainty   5
  Further Preliminaries   6
  More Notable Takes on Uncertainty   8
  Uncertainty as Good or Bad or Both?   9
    Examples of the Bads of Uncertainty   10
    Examples of the Goods of Uncertainty   10
    Effective Management of Uncertainty   11
  Our Perspective (Business-Based, Applying Western/Democratic Values)   11
  Delineation from Risk (and Probability)   13
    Hence, Non-Mathematicalness   14
  The Heterogeneity of Uncertainty   14
  Decision-Making and Knowns   15
    Creating the Decision-Making Model   15
    Complications   16
  Big Questions   18
  Philosophy of Science   20
  Goals   22
  Resistance (…Is Eventually Futile)   23
  Why This Book Now   25
  Plan of Analysis   25
  References   28

2   *Confusion* over Uncertainty in Decision-Making   33
Why Clarity Is Important   34
What Confusion Exists   35
What Terms Are Confused   35
Sources of Confusion   37
How to Unconfuse   38
References   40

3   *Definitions* of Uncertainty (for Decision-Making)   43
Why Definitional Precision Is Important   44
Classic Definitions   44
Uncertainty as the Inability to Assign Probabilities   45
Uncertainty as Unknown Cause-and-Effect Relationships   46
Uncertainty-as-Unpredictability   46
Knight's Definition of Uncertainty   47
Ellsberg's Definition of Ambiguity   48
Alternative Definitions of Uncertainty   48
    Uncertainty as Unknowability   49
    Uncertainty as Novelty   49
    Uncertainty as Non-Optimizability   50
    Uncertainty as Doubt   50
Contrasts to Full Information   50
The Amount of Uncertainty Question   51
The Epistemological Question   52
References   54

4   *Sources* of Uncertainty (in Decision-Making)   59
Why the Causes of Uncertainties are Important   60
Reminder—How a Cause's Symptoms Can Manifest in a Decision to Make it Non-Optimizable   60
Sources of Uncertainty Related to the Problem Itself   62
Sources in the Problem Characteristics   63
    Novelty/Uniqueness   63
    Complexity of Phenomena   63
    Non-linear Dynamic Systems and Chaos   64
    Ill-Defined Problems   65
    Relationships with Time   65
    Other (Pointed) Issues   65
Sources in the Problem's External Context (Exogenous to the Decision-Maker)   66

New Technology	66
The Inherent Randomness of Nature	67
Luck [as Randomness for Humans]	67
Inconsistent (Often Rivalrous) External Human Behaviors	68
Dynamic Aspects of Inconsistent External Human Behaviors (as Unpredictable Reactions)	69
Conflicting External Reports	70
Sources in the Problem's Internal Context (Endogenous to the Decision-Maker)	71
Change and Its Consequences (Inside)	71
Communications Issues	71
Personal Artefacts and Choices	72
Biases and Errors in Statistical Analysis	72
Blissful Ignorance and Dangerous Implicit Assumptions	73
Limits of Analysis	73
General Limits to Problem Analysis	74
Laws and Regulations	74
Measurement Error	75
Computational Limits over Current Facts	75
Mathematical Limits	76
System-atic Errors	76
Incomplete Modeling	77
Empirical Non-Verifiability	78
Organizational Limits to Problem Analysis	79
Lack of Investigatory Time	79
Lack of Other Investigatory Resources	79
Human Limits	79
Lack of Control	80
Individual Limits to Problem Analysis	80
Lack of Expertise	80
Epistemic Issues/Decision-Maker Weakness	81
References	83
5 ***Span of Effects* of Uncertainty (in Decision-Making)**	89
The Impacts of Uncertainty	89
Impacts on Entities	90
On Survival	90
On Feelings	91

	On Challenges	92
	On Organization	95
	On Compensation for Experiencing Uncertainty	97
	On Rational Behaviors and Choices	98
	Impacts on Entity Reactions	100
	On Behaviors to Reduce or Accept Uncertainty	100
	On Behaviors to Explore or Exploit Uncertainty	103
	Impacts on Understanding	105
	Impacts on Theorizing	106
	Impacts on Lab Studies	108
	Impacts on Communications and Measures	108
	References	111
6	*Negative Effects* of Uncertainty (on Decision-Making)	115
	Costly Uncertainties	115
	Negative Effects of Uncertainty	117
	Drivers of Negative Effects	120
	Contexts for Negative Effects	120
	Dealing with Negative Effects	121
	References	124
7	*Positive Effects* of Uncertainty (on Decision-Making)	127
	The Existential Positive Effects of Uncertainty	127
	Uncertainty as a Signal of Potential Rewards	129
	Conceptual Benefits from Uncertainty	130
	Real Benefits from Uncertainty	131
	Conditions for Benefits	132
	Who Benefits	133
	References	135
8	*Optimal* Uncertainty (in Decision-Making)	137
	Why a Goldilocksian 'Amount' of Uncertainty Can Exist	138
	At What Level of Analysis?	139
	For What Ends?	139
	How to Generate It	141
	References	142
9	*Measures* of Uncertainty (in Decision-Making)	145
	The Importance of Measuring Uncertainty and Its Characteristics	146
	Approaches to Measurement	148

	Practical Measures	148
	Conceptual Measures	151
	Immeasurability	152
	References	154
10	**Multi-Dimensionality** of Uncertainty	155
	Why Uncertainty Is Multi-Dimensional	156
	Which Dimensions?	157
	Bases for These Dimensions	159
	Dealing with Multi-Dimensionality	162
	References	164
11	Uncertainty's Connections to *Entrepreneurship*	167
	Why Uncertainty Connects to Entrepreneurship	167
	Which Uncertainties and Activities?	170
	Drivers of the Entrepreneurship Connection	171
	The Context of the Entrepreneurship Connection	172
	Managing the Entrepreneurship Connection	173
	References	176
12	Uncertainty's Connections to *Strategy*	179
	Why Uncertainty Connects to Strategy	179
	Uncertainty and Theories of the Firm (and of Firm Rents)	181
	Top Management's Focus on Uncertainty	182
	Uncertainty and Contracting	183
	Deeper into Uncertainty	184
	Drivers of the Strategy Connection	184
	The Context of the Strategy Connection	185
	Uncertainties and Activities	186
	Managing the Strategy Connection	187
	References	188
13	Uncertainty's Connections to *Creativity, Art, and Music*	193
	Connecting Uncertainty to Creativity	194
	Connecting Uncertainty to Art and Music	196
	Why the Connections Exist	197
	Philosophical Questions Raised	199
	References	200

14 Uncertainty's Connections to *Spirituality/Religion* 203
Connecting Uncertainty to Spirituality and Religion 204
Connecting Spirituality to Decision-Making
under Uncertainty 206
Importance of Uncertainty in Religion 206
Drivers of Uncertainty in Religion 208
Offering Some Balance 208
References 211

15 Uncertainty's Connections to Curiosity, Neurobiology, and Evolution 213
Connecting Uncertainty to Curiosity 213
Connecting Uncertainty to Neurobiology 215
Connecting Uncertainty to Cognition 217
Connecting Uncertainty to Evolution 220
Drivers of the Connections 224
Philosophical Implications 225
References 227

16 Past Failures to Engage with Uncertainty 231
Identifying the Failures to Engage 232
Drivers of the Failures 236
Why Probability-Based Approaches Fail 240
  How That Failure Extends to Subjective Expected Utility 242
Alternatives 243
References 244

17 *A New Typology* of Uncertainty (for Decision-Making) 247
Introduction to a New Typology 248
Reminders About the Main Assumption and Definition 249
The Plan for This Chapter 250
Past Uncertainty Types and Labels 250
  Incomplete Information 251
  Knightian Uncertainty 252
  Ellsbergian Ambiguity 254
  Ignorance 256
  Aleatory Uncertainty 257
  Unknown Unknowns 258
  Equivocality 260
  Vagueness 260

Epistemic Uncertainty	261
Other Potential Types	263
The New Primary Typology	263
Cleaning Up the Minor Issues Involved	266
The Relevant Secondary Typology	268
Step One—Assessing the Background Facts	268
State Uncertainty/ Uncertainty about the Present Reality	269
Uncertainty about the Past	270
Step Two—Understanding the Goals	270
Step Three—Identifying the Stakeholders	271
Step Four—Recognizing All Possible Relevant Options/ Choices	271
Step Five—Identifying All Possible Outcomes (Relevant to the Choices)	272
Step Six—Calculating the (Monetary) Payoffs of the Outcomes	273
Step Seven—Considering the Ethics and Values of the Outcomes [separated from Goals]	274
Step Eight—Calculating the (Overall) Worth of the Outcomes [Utilities]	275
Step Nine—Assigning Probabilities to the Uncontrollable Outcome-Affecting Events	275
Step Ten—Including Any Timing Issues Involved in the Process	276
Step Eleven—Applying the Relevant Constraints	276
A Line of Demarcation in the Decision-Making Process	277
Step Twelve—Identifying the Dynamic Links in the Extended Process	277
Step Thirteen—Assessing the Dynamics of Competition	278
Unknown Effects on Rival Targets	278
Unknown Responses of Targets	279
Unknown Target Intensions	279
Unknown Target Decision Constraints	280
A Tertiary Typology	281
Dimensions of Specifying What Is Uncertain	282
Dimensions of Specifying Why the Uncertainty Exists	287
Dimensions of Specifying Where the Uncertainty Exists	287
Revisiting a Selection of Uncertainty Sources to Highlight the Separation from Types	288

    Measurement Uncertainty   288
    Model Uncertainty   288
    Environmental Uncertainty   289
    Endogenous Uncertainty and Knowable Unknowns   289
    Supplement on Knightian Uncertainty Issues   291
    Knight's Model as a Theory of Rents   292
    The Three Dangers of the Knightian Model   293
        The Premise Danger   293
        The Implication Danger   296
        The Definition Danger   298
    Discussion   300
    References   302

18 ***Best Treatments and Approaches* to Uncertainty Types (in Decision-Making)**   313
    Introduction to Uncertainty Treatment   314
    Part One—Treating the Treatable Uncertainties   317
    Bucket One—Uncovering Unknowns via Discovery, Search, and Monitoring   319
    Bucket Two—Uncovering Unknowns via Experimentation, Experience, Analysis, and Modeling   322
        Experimentation   323
        Sensemaking and Modeling   324
        Experience and Alertness   325
        Inference from Big Data   326
        Other Active Learning Approaches   327
    Bucket Three—Uncovering Unknowns via Influencing the Outcome Through Social Construction and Preemption   328
    Bucket Four—Uncovering Unknowns via Scenarios and Simulations   329
    Bucket Five—Uncovering Unknowns via Adapting to Outcomes Through Flexibility, Options and Robustness   332
    Bucket Six—Uncovering Unknowns via Sharing the Burden with Cooperation and Insurance, or Through Diversification   335
    Part Two—Addressing the Untreatable Uncertainties (the Unknown-and-Unknowables)   338
        A Shift in Mentality   339
        The Four Approaches   339

Bucket A-One—Addressing the Untreatable by Bearing the Irreducible Uncertainty	341
Bucket A-Two—Addressing the Untreatable by Changing the Goal	343
Heuristics in General	343
Conditions for Heuristic Use	344
Dangers of Heuristics	346
Types and Examples of Heuristics	346
Acting 'As If' the Unknown Is Known	349
Acting on the Knowns Alone	352
Altering the Knowns to Reduce Harms	352
Modeling What Is Known	352
Applying Information-Gap Theory	353
Bucket A-Two-Plus—Addressing the Untreatable by Changing the Goal to a Relative One	353
Bucket A-Three—Addressing the Untreatable by Changing the Focal Entity	354
Playing No-Regrets, Conservative Moves	355
Following Available Standard Procedures and Norms	355
Expressing Dissatisfaction or Doubt	356
Ignoring, Suppressing, or Denying the Uncertainty	356
Trying to Delay the Decision or Action	356
Avoiding the Uncertainty	357
Bucket A-Four—Addressing the Untreatable by Altering the Game	357
Part Three—Processing Issues in Decision Uncertainty Treatment/Approach	359
The Awareness of Uncertainties	360
Prioritization	361
Context Matters—Big and Small	361
The Costs of Addressing Uncertainties	364
Combining Approaches	365
On the Offense—Creating Uncertainties	366
References	368

19 Conclusions of the Analysis of Uncertainty (as Everything)   381
   Summary   382
   Implications   382

	Philosophical and Scientific Issues	383
	Future Work	388
	(Almost) Final Thoughts	389
	References	391
20	***Supplement* on the Impact of Artificial Intelligence on Uncertainty**	**393**
	Why This Supplement (Now)?	394
	Summary of AI's Impacts on Uncertainties	395
	The Relevant Impact of AI Itself	397
	AI the Good	398
	AI the Bad	398
	The Uncertainties in the AI Box	400
	Mitigating Those (Treatable) Internal AI Uncertainties	401
	Estimating Those Uncertainties in AI	402
	Main Implications	403
	Wrapping IT Up—the Real and the F.ai.k	405
	References	407
Uncertainty Literature		**409**
Index		**447**

List of Figures

Fig. 1.1	Chapter flow	26
Fig. 17.1	The possible unknowns (underlying uncertainty)	249
Fig. 17.2	A logical path from unknowns to a new primary typology of uncertainties	265
Fig. 18.1	Flowchart of triaging uncertainty	316

List of Tables

Table 3.1	Alternative definitions of uncertainty	45
Table 4.1	The possible sources of uncertainty	61
Table 5.1	The span of uncertainty's effects	90
Table 6.1	Possible negative effects of uncertainty	116
Table 7.1	Possible positive effects of uncertainty	128
Table 9.1	Measuring uncertainty	147
Table 17.1	New primary typology of uncertainty	266
Table 17.2	New secondary typology of uncertainty	269
Table 17.3	New tertiary typology breakdown on the main dimensions of the known factor's unknown characteristic value to consider	283
Table 17.4	Examples of what could be unknown in the business decision context	286

CHAPTER 1

Overview of This Book on Strategic Decision-Making Under Uncertainty

Why This Book on Uncertainty?

That uncertainty is elemental, everywhere, everything, and existentially connected to all human activity is the thesis of this book. Uncertainty is not just fundamental to business, but to all decision-making, especially of the strategic kind. Every significant choice a firm makes is

© The Author(s), under exclusive license to Springer Nature Switzerland AG 2024
R. J. Arend, *Uncertainty in Strategic Decision Making*,
https://doi.org/10.1007/978-3-031-48553-4_1

done under uncertainty—under the condition of incomplete information (whether also often supplemented by bias, bounded rationality, error, miscommunication and opportunism, or not) (Courtney et al., 2013).

The fact that there is no go-to reference material for such decisions is the reason for this book. There are just too many definitions, terms, labels, and misrepresentations of concepts that say they capture uncertainty in the literature. And, when uncertainty is considered incomplete information that lies 'beyond risk'—i.e., that involves the types of unknowns that preclude the optimization of a decision—the recent management literature has come up short. Clarity is necessary to move our understanding of this phenomenon forward. We hope to bring that clarity through the contents of this book.

What differentiates this book from the many others that have spoken to decision-making under uncertainty are three main things:

1. A *more holistic approach* to uncertainty and the influence it has on business and other human activity. [Given our thesis, we believe that the bigger picture provides the Reader with a greater understanding of the possible opportunities available for addressing uncertainty.]
2. A *unique focus on the types of uncertainty that ensure decisions cannot be optimized- as -given*. [These are the more difficult types to study, the types that have been overlooked, but the ones with the greatest potential for impact, in business and in society.] (This means we do not deal with risk or its equivalents—as embodied in quantified subjective beliefs, expected utilities, and so on. There is no math here (in the main text). We don't calculate learning—by Bayesian updating or otherwise.)
3. A *new typological angle*—one based primarily on the treatability of the uncertainties in such decisions, and a *new, related categorization of appropriate treatments and approaches* for those uncertainty types. [Given that our goal is to improve the outcomes of such decisions, starting with a triage mentality prior to diagnosing the specific issues and recommending remedies is appropriate, but has yet to be done in the literature.]

Why is uncertainty everything? Well, it forms a basis of our entertainment (e.g., in the forms of tension, mystery, and gambles), our psychoses (e.g., in the form of anxiety), our religions (e.g., as a basis for faith), our relationships (e.g., as a basis for trust), our sciences (e.g., in the form of explorable unknowns), our politics (e.g., in the form of ambiguity-as-unaccountability), and so much more (e.g., Packard et al., 2017). Arguably, it is even the precursor (and yet also the driver) for evolution: a precursor because evolutionary adaptation would be unnecessary if all were known; and, a driver in terms of the randomness of mutation and even selection. In business, it is the reason why entrepreneurship (Knight, 1921) and strategic planning occur. In government, emergency management exists because of the uncertainties within society and between it and nature (Bammer & Smithson, 2008).

Scholars have attempted to explain how the mind weighs uncertainty for centuries; moreso from the eighteenth century on (Hertwig et al., 2019). Why? Because science exists to make the uncertain-as-the-unknown more known. Science is about investigating phenomena of human interest with the goal of gaining control over those phenomena, and if not control then predictive power, and if not that then greater understanding toward control or prediction. Why? Because with control or prediction, fewer resources are required to reach a goal and more goals are attainable. Any species gaining such benefits is more likely to survive, and so that 'scientific mindset' is an evolved drive to try to reach out further into the future with greater knowledge of what will occur.

We frame this scientific drive into uncertainty in a specific way—*as affecting our decision-making*. Why? Because decision-making is a well-understood process, and one we do many times a day, consciously and not. It involves everything from understanding a phenomenon of interest (and our interest in it), to modeling it as actionable by us, to making a choice, and finally to acting upon it. (Depending on the dynamics involved, it may also then include observing the outcome and learning from the experience.)

The main assumption we make here is that *sometimes a decision is non-optimizable* because a factor, or the value of a characteristic of that factor, is unknowable at the time the decision must be made (Mousavi & Gigerenzer, 2017). When the factor is important to the phenomenon that we intend to act upon, then it affects the decision process significantly (e.g., identifying the goals, outcomes, or options) because the expected value of every possible relevant choice cannot be computed, and so the identification of a maximized expected outcome path is not possible. It is these cases of non-optimization that we are interested in. Why? Because these are the [only] decisions where new advantages can [theoretically] emerge. Approaching such decisions better offers a way for organizations to experience greater gains and fewer losses than their rivals.

The study of decision-making under uncertainty is especially relevant today because uncertainty has reached an unfortunate peak of ubiquity. In a world increasingly characterized by placing self-interested beliefs over objective facts, where plausible alternative stories (often of the conspiracy kind) are deployed as wedges of doubt, and where disinformation is so widely and cheaply (thank you AI !?) dispersed, uncertainty reigns. And with that, danger rises—for democracy and for any other truth-based governance or living system; in that world, it is violence that is the determining factor for outcomes rather than rationality. That is not a good world. So, it is very important to study uncertainty—most especially with an eye on ensuring that as rational a decision-making approach as possible is used (i.e., where the economically and ethically efficient choice is identified and acted upon). However, at present, we only '*see through a glass, darkly*' (1 Corinthians 13:12). So, we need to bring the unknowns—the uncertainties—to light. That is only done through science; progress otherwise is simply a myth (Gray, 2002).

At present, there is an insufficient understanding on how to deal with decision-making under uncertainty (Halpern, 2003). While a variety of tools and approaches for making those decisions have been put forward, there is no comparative overview (Marchau et al., 2019). So, uncertainty remains a major research and policy challenge, for specific issues and for the larger agenda (Bammer & Smithson, 2008). For example, there is still no useful guide on when to spend effort on reducing uncertainty rather than understanding, accepting, and managing it; some have noted that an investigation of methods for the latter requires a book on its own (Bammer & Smithson, 2008). That, hopefully, is this book here.

Every day provides new discoveries about uncertainties and their many forms and meanings; so much so that new methods may be required to model them (Taylor, 2003). We believe that the 'science of uncertainty' forms the basis for the sciences of the future (Stewart, 2019). And we hope this book leads one step further in that inquiry.

Notable Takes on Uncertainty

Many scholars have provided quotes about uncertainty; we provide a representative sample here (and elsewhere) to provide some feel for how it has been interpreted over time and across contexts—as important, challenging, ever-present, and even humbling, to humankind:

I know that I know nothing—Socrates

Prediction is very difficult, especially about the future—Bohr

People inhabit isolated islands of certainty in an ocean of uncertainty—Arendt (1958)

I risk, therefore I am, I venture therefore I am, I suffer therefore I am—Beck (2009)

The only danger from the unknown is in our turning our backs to it—Baker (1976)

We can never say how complete our information is at any point—Runde (1990)

The world has always been uncertain, and will always be part of the human condition—Hertwig et al. (2019)

Incomplete knowledge is the key property and condition of many real work choices—Arrow (1951)

The idea of the future, pregnant with an infinity of possibilities, is thus more fruitful than the future itself, and this is why we find more charm in hope that in possession, in dreams than in reality—Bergson (1913)

The world is in fact filled with terrifying uncertainty, and it is a tribute to the dauntless and objectively insane optimism of the human species that we, most of the time, are fairly cheerful about it—Costikyan (2013)

The challenge of decision-making under severe uncertainty is as old as thinking and as current as each moment's passing thought—Ben-Haim (2001)

Uncertainty isn't just a sign of human ignorance, it is what the world is made of—Stewart (2019)

Hence, for long-term decision-making, deep uncertainties are in most cases a given—Marchau et al. (2019)

We have seen that practically all human activity, even that of the purest routine character, is in some manner and degree forward looking and involves meeting unexpected—Knight (1921)

Uncertainty is a fundamental—and unavoidable—feature of daily life—Halpern (2003)

I guess we'll never fuckin' know—Poutyface (2021)

Further Preliminaries

Although uncertainty has been used as a catch-all in the business literature to cover everything from quantified risk to complete ignorance, our use of the term in this book will follow Knight's (1921) delineation. Uncertainty is *not* risk; it extends beyond it to the unknowns that make decisions non-optimizable and events uninsurable. While we look at a variety of approaches to such a challenging context, this is not a book about how to reduce uncertainty to risk (e.g., as based on subjective beliefs); instead, we consider our/true/interesting *uncertainty as irreducible uncertainty*. When we assume something is unknowable, we mean it is unknowable to all (i.e., that subjective beliefs are highly unreliable). Given that there are several articles and books on standard risk, as well as on subjective belief-based risk, but few if any on irreducible uncertainty (at least for a century), we focus on that here.

The other main delineation we make is one of convenience (and often a standard one taken when studying uncertainty)—*we assume an objective reality exists*. We do so because the theoretical analysis is cleaner. Regardless, we understand that real decisions are made by human beings, done under subjective realities. We consider those many subjective (e.g., neurobiological, psychological, and sociological) issues separately for clarity. We understand the limitations of so doing (e.g., the reduction of a person-centric holistic analysis); but, at this point in studying decision-making under uncertainty, we are willing to make that sacrifice to speed progress.

So, to be clear to the Reader, this is also not a book focused on how individuals can mitigate the subjective uncertainties that they (alone) feel or generate (knowingly or not).

We understand that every decision involves both objective facts and subjective beliefs (Bernstein, 1996). As such, that means the 'world'—as a social construction—then consists of multiple realities (Berger & Luckmann, 1966). But, that is *not* an easily analyzable world. As soon as any element of subjectivity is attached (e.g., to the probabilities or to the valuation of a decision's outcomes) then no objectively correct solutions are available (Kay & King, 2020). That is a situation we wish to avoid. Instead, we wish to apply logic, and that implies staying in hypothetically-realistic—objectively framed—worlds. Given that the accounts of how people perceive and respond to uncertainty are sparse in many disciplines (Bammer & Smithson, 2008), and we wish to be more holistic in terms of subject matter here, it again makes sense to keep the analysis objective. We understand the critique regarding this choice, regardless if it is at its core somewhat tired. (Yes, the point that there is no such thing as objective truth may be fashionable, but it is hardly new—as 2500 years ago Protagoras declared '*man is the measure of all things*'. The postmodern version of it seems pitifully just the latest fad in such anthropocentrism [Gray, 2002].) Further, one could argue that it is flawed as well, given that the game of doubting everything itself presupposes an objective certainty (Rouvray, 1997).

We follow Knight (1921)—and the many other scholars who followed—in taking this objective reality perspective. Limiting the analysis to a rational grounds of choice is the best approach at this time. For clarity of exposition, we describe uncertain contexts in terms of true (objective) uncertainty, rather than in terms of perceived uncertainty. We take a normative approach; a micro-economic, game-theoretical approach (i.e., that policy-makers, scientific experts, and the law [see putative performance] all also emphasize—see Roeser, 2019; Marchau et al., 2019). But, again, we understand that real decision-makers act on estimates, intuitions, and routines and not high-level reasoning over verified facts (Mousavi & Gigerenzer, 2014), which means that there are further tools needed to deal with such non-rationality when decisions under uncertainty arise (Hertwig et al., 2019).

By taking a rationalist perspective, we avoid having to deal with the complex issues involving human limitations (at least to begin with). We understand that such bounds exist, in perception, computation, communication, and so on (e.g., Kay & King, 2020; Kozyreva & Hertwig, 2021; Simon, 1990), and specifically when it comes to dealing with uncertainty (Schoemaker, 2002). Humans have myopic eyes, timid souls, overconfident attitudes, and often lazy dispositions (Schoemaker, 2002). They make decisions under uncertainty often limited by cognitive capacity, time, and other resources (Bammer & Smithson, 2008). We try to consider many of these issues secondarily to the primary challenge of dealing with non-optimizable decisions—which is our focus here. It is a sufficiently difficult challenge alone. [Opening it fully up to the myriad of ways that subjectivity and bounded rationality could come into play in the many steps of the decision process (e.g., involving all the how's of each step—like how do possible uncontemplated events affect actors' feelings and thoughts—see Dosi & Egidi, 1991) would take many books. It also opens the causes of non-optimal decisions up to further possibilities, such as non-stationarity and a co-dependence of the context with the non-idealized agent (Dosi & Egidi, 1991).]

We believe that the best way to deal with the primary challenge is to structure uncertainty in a way to gain some control over its dimensionality in order to move toward addressing it. This starts with a triage mentality of understanding the kinds of uncertainties that are treatable (based on their knowability status). This involves a taxonomy of uncertainties, one that distinguishes between good and bad types (Bammer & Smithson, 2008). Many scholars believe that such investigation needs to occur (e.g., Aggarwal & Mohanty, 2022; Machina & Siniscalchi, 2014), and so we provide it in the chapters following.

More Notable Takes on Uncertainty

Many scholars have commented on the (recent) *importance of uncertainty*, and we share a select few for perspective and effect now:

> The importance of uncertainty is virtually unquestioned—Townsend et al. (2020)

> Perhaps because we are so clearly hostage to enormous uncertainties, even to the extent that we cannot be sure about our own long-term survival as a species, we all tend to strive after certainties—Rouvray (1997)

The volatility of stock and bond prices is evidence of the frequency with which the expected fails to happen and investors turn out to be wrong—Bernstein (1996)

Nobel Prize winner Fermi bet on whether the 1945 [atomic bomb] test explosion would destroy the world—Kay and King (2020)

Uncertainties challenge the central claim of science: that all problems are presumed to be solvable by research—Tannert et al. (2007)

It is first essential to understand deep uncertainty, which is ubiquitous in the innovation economy—Teece et al. (2016)

We are now experiencing a whole new level of uncertainty, as questions only the virus can answer complicate the outlook—*Federal Reserve Chairman Jerome Powell*

Although our intellect always longs for clarity and certainty, our nature often finds uncertainty fascinating—*Carl von Clausewtiz*

An optimist is someone who thinks the future is uncertain—Barrow (1998)

UNCERTAINTY AS GOOD OR BAD OR BOTH?

Uncertainty, in the broadest sense, is neither good nor bad; it is its management that determines the levels and distribution of the associated costs and benefits (Ben-Haim, 2001). Most often—for non-strategic, everyday decisions—the relevant uncertainty is neutral. It is a residual noise that has reasonable bounds that people can tolerate; as such, people retain the necessary experience and knowledge sufficient to think confidently about the future (Bammer & Smithson, 2008). Because of that attitude, relatively little effort has gone into studying uncertainty seriously, at least until relatively recently (Bammer & Smithson, 2008). And, it is about time, given it is becoming more apparent that uncertainty can have significant impacts on behavior. It can be disabling (e.g., when embodied as a taboo); but, it can also be enabling (e.g., by giving decision-makers freedom to explore when existing knowledge is weak).

Examples of the Bads of Uncertainty

When uncertainty is generated with intent, then like any tool it can be used for bad. Terrorists create fear and uncertainty with the aim—at best—of achieving a political goal (Bammer & Smithson, 2008). Repressive regimes use disinformation and propaganda to retain power, making their subjects uncertain about what is real and more accepting of costly falsehoods. Politicians bluster and lie to win. Lawyers tell stories to create reasonable doubt for guilty clients. And, so on.

At a more basic level, uncertainty has created the need for certainty that itself might be considered as one of humanism's pathologies. In its most unhealthy form, that need for certainty in the face of uncertainty explains fundamentalism—which has often been leveraged for violent, discriminatory purposes in human history. Humans simply have a lust for certitude (Towler, 1984). It is a very strong—often too strong—desire for order, for meaning, and ultimately for control (Bammer & Smithson, 2008). It manifests itself in the human need to make sense of surprises, to think counterfactually about bad outcomes, and to prognosticate about the future. It is a fundamental drive to free oneself from the tyranny of doubt (Bradac, 2001). Why? Because it is an evolved trait. It is natural because we've always had to survive in an uncertain world (Stewart, 2019). But, it is a futile quest. More knowledge will not make us free; that is a false dream—one not based on science, but on an illusion that we can become masters of our own destinies (Gray, 2002).

Examples of the Goods of Uncertainty

When uncertainty is generated with intent, it can also be used for good. For example, it can be used as a basis for artistic creativity, and as a core of the enjoyment of extreme sports (Bammer & Smithson, 2008).

When it is sought out and borne voluntarily, it is the basis for entrepreneurship, innovation, and scientific discovery (e.g., Knight, 1921; Schumpeter, 1932).

Effective Management of Uncertainty

The management of uncertainty partly determines whether its impact is contained or catastrophic. As such, there is great interest in policies for effectively addressing deeply uncertain conditions and developments. Decision-makers are increasingly confronted with challenges—both threats and opportunities—where not all uncertainties can be mitigated, and if ignored, could appear in worse and unignorable forms in the future (Marchau et al., 2019). If not ignored, the questions over whether and how to act in the face of uncertainty remain difficult, given few criteria presently exist for doing so (e.g., regarding how much and what kinds of uncertainties can be tolerated) (Bammer & Smithson, 2008).

The management of uncertainty depends on both what the decision-maker knows and what they do not know. In some management systems and organizational routines, there may be formally or informally set boundaries that determine which uncertainties are ignored or banished, rightly or wrongly (Bammer & Smithson, 2008). In practice, the management of uncertainty is likely part art and part science (Bammer & Smithson, 2008). (On the science part, there are new fields, like 'futures', that are building a body of knowledge for understanding the drivers of an unpredictable future.)

The management of uncertainty not only involves identifying it and responding to its presence—sometimes voluntarily and sometimes not—but also involves (as alluded to above) its intended (and sometimes initially unintended) generation. Modern society continuously generates new uncertainties, not because of its defeats but because of its triumphs (Beck, 2009); such new uncertainties are the product of more and better scientific knowledge. Consider CFCs (chlorofluorocarbons), which began use in 1930s, were only considered dangerous in 1970s, with a hole then being caused in the ozone layer in 1985; it raises the question of how much such a lack of knowledge of unintended consequences of new scientific breakthroughs the world can afford? (Beck, 2009).

OUR PERSPECTIVE (BUSINESS-BASED, APPLYING WESTERN/DEMOCRATIC VALUES)

We consider decision-making primarily from a business/economic perspective. It is arguably a cleaner analysis (relative to alternatives like politics, military, or the arts) because the value-maximization is easier to understand and more accessible. It is also a perspective that is global, competitive, visible, and involves a level(ish) playing field. More people are voluntarily involved in it than the alternatives (e.g., as decision-makers and stakeholders). The perspective is widely studied. Business involves more than just zero-sum games, is exposed to a near-full range of uncertainties, and considers a near-full range of approaches for addressing them. [We note 'near-full' because there are some things business cannot do that, say, a government can.] No strategic decision taken by a business is made under complete information (as each such decision involves an unpredictable future, most often complicated by other decision-makers with unknown motives and resources). The unknowability of focal factors or their values is assumed in many cases. *Strategic decisions* are those non-routine choices that involve significant performance implications and irreversible resource allocations; they are the ones that organizations take time and effort to get right. So, like Simon (1972), we also assign a much larger role to the irreducible uncertainty that has a crucial impact on business decision-making processes (Kozyreva & Hertwig, 2021).

Unless otherwise stated, we assume free markets and voluntary participation of all involved parties in a relevant transaction. We assume that truth matters, fairness matters, and ('western') ethical principles matter (e.g., rights, justice, professional standards, and so on). We assume an objective measure of uncertainty exists, that decision-makers desire better (e.g., higher-value) outcomes over worse, that decision-makers are ideally rational and 'neutral' (e.g., not ambiguity-averse), with the understanding that real decision-makers can be biased, subjective, manipulative, manipulated, and limited. The objectivity assumption helps the analysis in several ways: First, we can separate the objective from the subjective issues in decision-making under uncertainty, where the latter are often idiosyncratic, hidden, and complex. Second, we can separate the analysis here from the mathematics-based subjective expected utility (SEU) approaches. Given we do not believe SEU is a valid approach (because, in reality, humans do not hold beliefs over probabilities and other relevant factors that are comprehensive, let alone consistent), this assumption eliminates the issue of comparing subjective utilities as well. Nevertheless, we do understand that decision-making in the face of uncertainty is a ubiquitous problem confronted by individuals in their day-to-day economic lives, and, as such, involves outcomes based on many factors including ability, temperament, and sheer luck (MacLeod & Pingle, 2000).

Delineation from Risk (and Probability)

Uncertainty is not risk (Knight, 1921; Teece et al., 2016); therefore, probability theory does not apply. Decisions under uncertainty differ from decisions under risk (Mousavi & Gigerenzer, 2014), even though beliefs concerning uncertainties are often expressed as odds (Tversky & Kahneman, 1974). Under risk, incumbent firms can apply standard operating procedures, diversification, planning, and insurance to effectively deal with those decisions; under uncertainty, they cannot, and that opens the markets to entrepreneurs (e.g., through new ventures). Under the uncertainty considered here, critical information pertaining to one or more steps of the decision process (e.g., outcome probability estimation; alternative choice identification) is unavailable. In such situations, probability theory and statistics can no longer provide the best solution; often inductive tools (e.g., heuristics) are considered instead (Mousavi & Gigerenzer, 2014).

Situations of uncertainty often concern unique or unprecedented events and situations; in such singular events there is no valid basis for classifying instances, and so objective probabilistic or statistical calculations do not apply.[1] As such, uncertainty is liberated from calculation altogether (Hertwig et al., 2019). This is perhaps appropriate, given probability is not the best candidate for modeling the true fabric of nature (Ben-Haim, 2001). The debate over whether uncertainty can be overcome—by converting it to risk through the application of sufficient time, resources, and intelligence—or whether it remains a constant and inevitable part of life continues in business, science, religion, and even mathematics [given Gödel's incompleteness theorem] (Bammer & Smithson, 2008). We leave it for future work.

Uncertainty, not risk, is ubiquitous in the innovation economy (Teece et al., 2016). In these areas and others, nobody knows how to calculate a numerical probability value (Lipshitz & Strauss, 1997). The world is inherently uncertain; to pretend otherwise creates more uncertainties and risks (Kay & King, 2020).

---

[1] Note that even the probability distributions used in classical statistical mechanics are purely fictitious, given in that realm an enormous number of complex and highly differentiated situations arise so that the laws of probability theory do not accurately depict physical realities (Rouvray, 1997).

Hence, Non-Mathematicalness

Uncertainty is not risk; uncertainty violates the necessary premises for such optimization calculations and that is why we do not 'do math' in (the main text of) this book. There are many journal papers, simulations, books, and laboratory studies that draw upon probability theory or that try to explain human behavior in the face of various perceived uncertainties in some numerical manner; that is not what we do here.

We believe that our approach is more appropriate to the uncertainties we study. We also believe that such an approach is more readable, understandable, general, and convenient. (We avoid mathematical tricks for converting uncertainties because such tricks involve assumptions, assumptions that would be highly questionable when factors are unknown and unknowable [Gilboa, 2009].) We stick with logic as our method of analysis.

THE HETEROGENEITY OF UNCERTAINTY

A primary challenge of dealing with uncertainty is grappling with its heterogeneity; there are not only many separable types of uncertainty, but also many different labels for the same types. The latter causes needless confusion and impedes the progress of the study of uncertainties. For example, if we cannot apply the divide-and-conquer method because the 'divisions' keep being redrawn, then there is no conquering. At present, there are just too many versions of what uncertainty is supposed to encompass; in finance it is a term synonymous with volatility or variance, in management it is often used to describe risk or the product of complexity, and so on. In fact, much of the battle between schools of decision theorists involves the concept of uncertainty (Ben-Haim, 2001).

There is value, then, in providing clarity. With one universally accepted typology of uncertainties, we can reduce miscommunication about decision characteristics, we can catalogue which approaches do and do not work for each type (to use as a reference), and we can more effectively study any one type (which can then be used as a benchmark for studying what occurs when more than one type is involved in a decision). An agreed-upon typology can also be useful in better understanding how to generate specific uncertainties (and how to control any potential consequences in deploying them) (Bammer & Smithson, 2008). With a solid typology, we can determine who is best in an organization (or in an economy) to deal with a specific uncertainty. Given that people differ in their capacities and motivations to perceive, assess, and act upon any one decision, and that specific uncertainties can affect one or more of these steps, then identifying which uncertainties are present will likely help in choosing better agents to ensure a more desirable outcome from a given decision problem (Knight, 1921).

DECISION-MAKING AND KNOWNS

This book is about how to make better decisions under uncertainty. Thus, the idea and process of decision-making are baked into our approach. The decision-making paradigm is also used to categorize uncertainties (i.e., as a secondary logic).

To apply the decision-making lens, we necessarily assume that some things are known (even though at least one thing—i.e., the uncertainty—is not) about the problem, including that the unknown is impeding the optimization of the decision. Further, we assume a decision-making process is appropriate (e.g., one that involves things like options, goals, outcomes, probabilities, payoffs, and so on).

Uncertainty causes decision-making to be challenging, even agonizing (Kuhlthau, 1993). It forms a block between what is known (e.g., verifiable information) and what to do to make things better. It sometimes generates surprises that, in hindsight, could have been predictable given we almost never 'know nothing' about a situation of interest (Kay & King, 2020). In order to improve decision-making under uncertainty, one thing we need to do is consider the process and structure of decision-making itself, rather than simply the outcomes (Ben-Haim, 2001; Kay & King, 2020). We do so when we present our typology and the approaches to those newly identified types of uncertainty.

Creating the Decision-Making Model

We take a logical, rational, normative approach to the decision-making process here, acknowledging alternatives perspectives exist (e.g., those based solely on studying real behaviors, and identifying routines and heuristics) (Gigerenzer & Gaissmaier, 2011).

We assume that a situation arises that requires attention. There is an awareness that a decision must be made and a motivation to begin the process. We assume that the capability to carry out that process is present, and that it is feasible to do so in the time and with the resources available.

The process then begins with the gathering of facts (here, we assume these are objectively truths relevant to the decision problem). The goal of the decision-maker is identified. The stakeholders (and their interests) are identified.

The decision can then be modeled as connecting choices to outcomes (Ghirardato, 2001). The possible choices are identified. The possible outcomes are identified. For each outcome, the net payoffs and utilities of interest are calculated (when available). The probabilities of such outcomes are determined (when available).

Constraints and ethical considerations are identified. The choice that maximizes the expected level of the goal, accounting for constraints and other applicable considerations is then identified so that the decision problem can be solved and closed.

This is a somewhat static and ideal version of the process. In the literature, the process is characterized in various ways. For example, a decision problem involves a utility function, a set of possible outcomes, a set of acts that produce consequences in those worlds, that set of consequences, and a set of probabilities of those consequences being produced by those acts (Halpern, 2003). Another version of the decision problem involves a matrix where the rows designate acts, columns designate states of the world, and cell entries designate outcomes; this representation provides a distinction between acts over which the decision-maker has control, and states, over they have no control (Gilboa, 2009). Yet another version of the decision problem involves the selection of some option from the consideration set by assessing its association with some subset of possible outcomes, where the selection is made so as to lead to a desired outcome (or to avoid an undesired one) with high likelihood (Packard et al., 2017). As a counter to these versions, others have argued that there is no universal format for a decision problem; instead, one has to grope along in the darkness caused by incomplete information (Ben-Haim, 2001).

Complications

As alluded to, the ideal process can be interrupted (at any stage) by the presence of an unknown. It can be an unknown goal, outcome, payoff, option, constraint, utility, stakeholder, probability, and something else. Such unknowns are often attributed to some capricious mechanism, normally called nature (Yager, 1999). Regarding unknown possible outcomes (*aka* states of the world), it seems difficult to imagine that any agent could construct an appropriate and complete possible-worlds model when she is unlikely to know what all the possibilities are (especially in large, complex domains). [Note that using a catch-all outcome category such as 'something unexpected happens' is not a viable 'hack' when it comes to making decisions because no payoff can be associated with such a category (Halpern, 2003).] Regarding unknown outcome probabilities, it also seems difficult to imagine that these are available for entirely new or unique events, even when all possible outcomes can be imagined. It seems even worse for more specific, detailed decision problems, because the more that information is sought (e.g., in spatial, temporal, or other empirical terms) then the more likely there are to be gaps in knowledge, making precise probabilistic predictions impossible (Bradley & Steele, 2015).

Besides the direct issues with possible unknowns and gaps, the simple decision process gets much more messy when complexities in the form of multiplicity are involved—e.g., from multiple time periods (dynamics), from the effects of multiple sentient, reactive parties (rather than simply nature), and from having to juggle multiple goals (for robustness).

Consider the added dynamics of many decision processes—where, in-between (sub)decisions, there is feedback and time for reflection and learning (e.g., updating knowledge). In such cases, decision-makers (agents) continually obtain new information and then update their knowledge pool; how this is done depends in part on how uncertainty is represented (Halpern, 2003). (For example, consider a world where any of 1000 people can have a virus; that can be modeled as 2^{1000} possible worlds or simply a percentage or a hazard rate, but where the first is incomputable.) In dynamic situations, decisions can help sort out a vague and unclear situation through feedback (Ben-Haim, 2001). However, the systematic acquisition, evaluation, and application of such information-gathering is costly and should be considered when initiating and continuing such a process that has limited benefits (some of which may simply exist in the power of that extra knowledge) (Ben-Haim, 2001).

Consider the added stakeholders (e.g., rivals) of many decision processes—where the actions and reactions of separate but interdependent parties need to be taken into account when making choices. In decision theory, it is common to distinguish among three domains (Bradley &

Steele, 2015): The first is *individual decision theory—which is our benchmark in this book, and concerns a one-shot decision problem of a single entity that faces an uncertainty*. The second is *game theory*—which focuses on decisions involving strategic interaction among separate entities whose rationality is modelable (we comment on such cases, but this is not our focus given the infinite variations possible). The third is *social choice theory*—which concerns how a number of entities (e.g., people) may collectively think and act (we also comment on such a case, but this is also not our focus).

Finally, also consider the added goals (e.g., in addition to achieving the highest possible payoff with lowest possible loss) imposed on many decision-makers. This imposition is actually more common for decisions made under uncertainty—i.e., that they are robust to many possibilities, and responsive to both adverse and favorable aspects of the uncertainties involved (Ben-Haim, 2001). Such decision-making is challenging in reality; so much so that some scholars believe that it involves both skill and art (e.g., to write a contract that covers as many contingencies as possible—Halpern, 2003).

BIG QUESTIONS

The study of decision-making under uncertainty—especially under non-optimizability (as we do here)—raises some big questions. *What does the realization that a decision cannot be optimized due to the presence of uncertainty mean to decision-making, to business, and to humanity?* To some it signals opportunity (Knight, 1921), to many it signals a threat, and to others it means very little (e.g., that business-as-usual continues in the form of muddling, groping, satisficing, and otherwise adapting along). There is often initial chaos, but what it ultimately means for humanity remains shrouded in an impenetrable cloak of obscurity (Rouvray, 1997). That initial chaos arises because, when complete knowledge of the future and of the past is an impossibility, then questions over how representative the information we have at hand arise even to the point that we then doubt what our current reality is (Bernstein, 1996).

So, the question of *what is going on here?* is an important one to start the analysis for any decision (Kay & King, 2020). Being able to legitimately answer that question has changed over the history of studying uncertainty, and enormously so from when statistics first became well-understood (Ben-Haim, 2001). Yet, we remain challenged in doing that, at least in terms of describing the source, nature, and effects of the uncertainties we confront in business and elsewhere (Packard et al., 2017; Stewart, 2019). Sometimes so much so that problems can seem so underspecified that they appear like mysteries, ones that have no rulebook (Kay & King, 2020). Under such circumstances, agents often apply automatic (*System 1*—Kahneman, 2011) rather than analytical (*System 2*) responses; they apply heuristics rather than stepping through the full, rational decision process (Hodgson, 2011).

As we begin to better understand uncertainty, then we also begin to better understand our limits, and that is uncomfortable. It is uncomfortable because it raises some tough realizations and questions. We realize that in many important areas of human interest—from business to medicine to catastrophic events—the gap between what we know and what we need to know is substantial and growing (Ben-Haim, 2001). We realize that some uncertainties possess the destructive force of war (Beck, 2009). We realize that the frontiers of the doable are beginning to lag further behind those of the conceivable (Barrow, 1998). We realize that our understanding of the workings of economic systems requires a much deeper engagement with the meaning and significance of uncertainty, and perhaps even of the nature of knowledge itself (Nash, 2003). And, we begin to wonder whether are ultimately capable of such engagement in light of the great impacts our current decisions (e.g., over the environment; over AI; over privacy rights) are making (Kay & King, 2020).

We must realize that the world is not as the Enlightenment thinkers had hoped. Rather, it appears that increasing our knowledge about the world (e.g., by discovering new chemicals and their possible commercial uses) simply generates new forms of uncertainty—many of which have incalculable effects (Beck, 2009). We can see such dangers in the sloppy determination of the hazardousness of products, their proliferation, and negative impacts they have had throughout history to today (e.g., in PFAS 'forever' chemicals). Perhaps, if such impacts had a personal or culturally visible and immediate effect (e.g., in itchiness), the treatment of such uncertainties would not be so cavalier (Beck, 2009). Even when we do focus on better understanding the nature of uncertainties specifically (rather than simply gaining more knowledge about a given problem), the effect is often not a reduction in uncertainty. For example, research often reveals *further sensitivities* to uncertainty characteristics than previously considered (e.g., as seen when individuals adjust their preferences under ambiguity to what the sources are of that ambiguous information—Aggarwal & Mohanty, 2022).

PHILOSOPHY OF SCIENCE

Big questions raise the need to invoke the philosophy of science—to clarify the terminological soup involved. Our intended *ontology is one of objectivity*; we assume objective reality exists—a standard assumption in this literature. This influences our *epistemology—that knowledge exists as theoretical truths* (rather than assuming it exists as somewhat problematic alternatives like justified true beliefs). Again, this is done to simplify the analysis of a complex subject matter (and, it is also standard in this literature). Our *methodology is logic* (supported by observation based on past research). And, of course, we assume that uncertainties exist (i.e., that there are separable types of unknowns that make decisions non-optimizable).

Science is the study of phenomena of interest to humanity with the goal of control, and if not control then prediction, and if not prediction then a greater understanding of the phenomenon that could lead to control or prediction. As such, in some sense, science is a game of information efficiency—a search for compressions of strings of data into briefer encodings that contain the same information. However, there is no way in which a general string of symbols can be proved incompressible, and therefore one can never know when the 'ultimate' theory is found (Barrow, 1998). Science is a never-ending endeavor (because uncertainties will always exist). Knowledge will never be complete, and so research can do no more than produce partial stories of what is happening, meaning that science, in some regard, is not so much about facts but about strong beliefs (Tannert et al., 2007). While humanity may wish to achieve the highest degree of certainty possible, in the words of the philosopher Bertrand Russell, it is valuable to remember that '*[i]n science, we find all grades of certainty short of the highest*' (Rouvray, 1997). Uncertainties that are both ineradicable and consequential are now even accepted in physics; while, in practical endeavors, we have accepted (for quite some time) that many uncertainties are realistically irreducible due to the costs, time, or politics involved (Bammer & Smithson, 2008).

Regardless of the real constraints that uncertainties have on scientific inquiry—at least in terms of knowing fully 'what is going on'—there is no shortage of approaches available for thinking about the impacts of those uncertainties. For example, counterfactual reasoning and scenario-planning explore alternative possibilities (Halpern, 2003), while probabilistic functionalism is a model of the human cognition where one operates in an environment full of uncertainties under internal epistemic constraints (Kozyreva & Hertwig, 2021). And, at the other end of the spectrum, there are approaches like system modeling that sacrifice the inclusion of uncertainty to provide a more general understanding of a given decision problem first (Ben-Haim, 2001).

When it comes to addressing uncertainties, one issue is *at what level?* The level of analysis issue is interesting for several reasons, including whether uncertainty needs to be considered holistically or whether insights are possible at different echelons in the hierarchy. For example, the physicist Feynman separates those levels humorously, when he states that there are many things he does not know anything about, such as whether it means anything to ask why we're here; he does not have to know that answer, or feel frightened about 'not knowing things' more generally, in order to try to know specific things (about previously unknown characteristics of physical systems) (Hertwig et al., 2019). At the other end of that attitude, other scholars have lamented that uncertainty is an Achilles' heel of any holistic approach—that the inability to predict today what will be discovered tomorrow can be a major impediment to the comprehensive modeling or management of things like individual or collective behaviors (Ben-Haim, 2001).

We conclude this section with a more philosophical concern—about the possible impossibility of dealing with uncertainty (given several scholars have raised it). For example, Hertwig et al. (2019) agonize that establishing a science in the Aristotelian sense of certain truths seems impossible. Halpern (2003) wonders how it could be possible to represent uncertainty when part of the uncertainty is about the set of possible worlds (that is unknown under uncertainty). Postmodernists don't seem to have an answer regardless of whether they propose that their relativism works better as a strange acceptance of the fact that we cannot claim to have the ultimate truth; and, in denying that the natural world exists independently of their beliefs about it, they arrogantly reject any limit on human ambitions, claiming that nothing exists unless it appears in human consciousness—which seems incredibly dangerous given there are so many things that are surprising to us, continuously, and harmfully. So, it would appear that currently there is no accepted structure within which to discuss uncertainty (Bammer & Smithson, 2008). We need a common language as start to addressing that, which is what this book intends to provide.

Goals

The goal of this book is to improve decision-making under uncertainty, with a focus on the types of uncertainty that too many have so far shied away from. We believe a path forward is by both understanding the many ways that uncertainties can affect humanity and by determining how to treat those different uncertainties through categorizing them clearly (and in a manner where it can become obvious which treatments and approaches should and should not work for each type).

This path is responsive to the various calls in the literature that include: calls for the classification of uncertainties (Rowe, 1994; Walker et al., 2003); calls for classifications of methodologies for addressing uncertainties (Bammer & Smithson, 2008; Rowe, 1994); calls for a clearer terminology for uncertainties (Walker et al., 2003); calls for a new systematic view of uncertainty (Hertwig et al., 2019); calls for the identification of sources of uncertainties (Rowe, 1994); and, calls for the ethical understanding of uncertainty (Gray, 2002; Tannert et al., 2007). This path may even provide new insights into existing, complex phenomena. For example, if synergies are defined as the unpredicted behavior of whole systems based on the behavior of their parts (Halpern, 2003), a better understanding of such surprises may come from a better typology of such uncertainties. And, if learning can be expressed as the process of updating an uncertainty model (Ben-Haim, 2001), then perhaps a better understanding of approaches to uncovering unknowns can help with such models and updating.

We engage this path with some understanding of the scope of the challenge involved. Reducing uncertainty is an effortful and costly business (Bernstein, 1996). Under uncertainty, there are countless ways to do the wrong thing in a given situation, or to do the right thing at the wrong time or in the wrong place, all while the number of ways to even approximate a fitting response is vanishingly small (Hertwig et al., 2019). Humankind's record of understanding uncertainties in complex systems has been pitiful, and marred with retrospective distortions, and there is nothing to indicate that we have gotten better at it over time (Taleb, 2012). It just seems that science, while increasing human power, also magnifies the flaws in human nature and in its capacity for understanding and compassion; so, even with that greater power, the human animal remains the same highly inventive, yet predatory and most-destructive of species (Gray, 2002). All that said, perhaps part of the task is to accept that we have to learn to live rigorously with some uncertainties, and *'bridges need not fall down in the attempt'* (Ben-Haim, 2001).

At this point, it is useful to remember that uncertainty can be good. We need uncertainty to make the games we play fun (Costikyan, 2013); games are a prime example of an anti-fragile product (Taleb, 2012). Uncertainty about each other makes humans human—interesting, autonomous entities who have individual discretion, and who provide surprise and invention to each other. Uncertainty in our environments often makes the world interesting, providing wonder and hope for better tomorrows. Uncertainty provides room for entrepreneurship, innovation, and scientific progress (Gray, 2002). Awareness of uncertainty—in terms of one's own ignorance—is the essence of wisdom (Socrates). It provokes improvements to processes—as the analysis of outcome variance (Ben-Haim, 2001). It is at the core of the strong human drive to explore, experiment, and model things in the natural world, as well as to improve our dealings with other beings, human and otherwise (Bammer & Smithson, 2008).

Resistance (...Is Eventually Futile)

The resistance to seriously addressing uncertainty has been effective until recently. The idea of non-optimizability is hard for people to accept, especially academics. It evokes an almost visceral defensive reaction. This is because accepting non-optimizability is seen as 'anti-scientific'—given it questions the (false) promises that science can conquer all, that no unknown can remain unknown, and that human ingenuity has no limits. That defensive reaction has meant that such 'questioning' work—the research that acknowledges unknowability and non-optimizability—has been unpublishable in the past. In its place has been an almost relentless series of ways that convert, almost magically, the unknowable into the knowable, the uncertain into the risky, the unoptimizable into the optimizable. Whether by infusing (often special) people with super-powers that allow them to make credible subjective estimates of missing probabilities (upon no valid basis) or to intuitively judge the unknowable successfully or to control the future through sheer effort and spunk, the pages of top business and economics journals have been filled with mathematical and verbal tricks to get to a 'right' (but false) answer in the face of deep uncertainty.

The alternative, of course, is bad for the scientific/academic brand. The alternative is much harder to evaluate. So, if we can all agree to bury our heads so as not to acknowledge the unknowable, the uncertain, and the non-optimizable, perhaps it will all go away? But, it has not (and it cannot). The truth 'does out' regardless of how much we fake like we know the unknowable with elaborate equations, models, simulations, scenarios, and post-mortem analyses. Yes, it makes both academics and practitioners look like 'we' do not have the answers, but that is readily apparent by looking around (at the state of the world now). It is unfortunate that it has taken such a long time to get to the point where uncertainty must be considered much more seriously, because in the meantime, much too much confusion has been sown (e.g., by poor terminology).

A large part of the delay is that decision-makers have a difficult time admitting '*I don't know*' (Kay & King, 2020). Economists (and stock markets) most often react to unpredictability with angst or even panic (Hodgson, 2011). As such, many of humanity's oldest institutions are tributes to the need for 'make-believe' in positive certainties—as embodied in our religions, laws, and governments (Gray, 2002). Exploitative consequences can lurk behind the mantle of uncertainty, of not knowing, and of the inability to know, and so uncertainty has remained something about which we are only too ready to deceive ourselves is less present than it is (Beck, 2009). For example, in classical rationality, there is no room for uncertainty (e.g., in the form of unanticipated consequences); we happily deceive ourselves even in our academic pursuits for the sake of saying we know something, like how to set a benchmark based on this unreal world that assumes the condition of 'what if everything was known?' (Kozyreva & Hertwig, 2021). But, such models have limits, especially in prediction (Hodgson, 2011); and, perhaps their better use is in explaining (rather than solving) a problem in such circumstances. Finally, there has even been resistance to better understanding (and possibly reducing) uncertainties based on how that might negatively affect privacy, autonomy, and the maintenance of religious faith (Bammer & Smithson, 2008). It is time to conquer that resistance and move forward.

Why This Book Now

So, returning to the reason for why this book now—we can add several reasons: First, the firehose of materials that have not actually addressed uncertainty but rather converted it into something else (something that is [falsely] optimizable) seems to now be sputtering, or at least is being more understood for the limited value it offers. Second, it takes a book to provide a holistic account of uncertainty, and to argue for a new typology that is linked to possible approaches for different uncertainty types (i.e., neither can be done in an academic journal article). Third, sadly at present there are few journals (read: editors and reviewers) who would be comfortable with an analysis of non-optimizable problems. Fourth, because there is demand for such an analysis given the more recent interest in shocks, black swans, 100-year events that are happening frequently, uncontrolled technologies like AI, and the fashionable revisiting of Knight's (1921) classic work a century later, let alone the worldwide impacts of pandemics (that often begin with scientists having no name for the disease, no idea of the cause or clinical course or long-term implications or spreading mechanics of the disease or when its infectiousness commences or finishes for a patient, or about immunity, or how to test for it, let alone a way to its clear-cut diagnosis, all the while when they have to make real decisions under those unknowns) (Bammer & Smithson, 2008).

Plan of Analysis

The next nineteen chapters provide a (semi-)holistic[2] overview of uncertainty, its ubiquity, and impact, connecting it to relevant human activities, and building toward a better understanding of making decisions under its influence through the presentation of a new typology and an assessment of the approaches that should and should not work for the main types. Figure 1.1 depicts the flow of our analysis.

---

[2] No one book can provide a complete and substantive review of the full set of ways that uncertainty has touched every scientific and practical field. While we provide a review of a subset of these, some directly and some only indirectly connected to business, we acknowledge that we forego many, many more (e.g., in psychology, marketing, sociology, medicine, climatology, law, and more). We can only hope that our peers in these fields follow suit in bringing more clarity to decision-making under uncertainty in their respective areas in the near future.

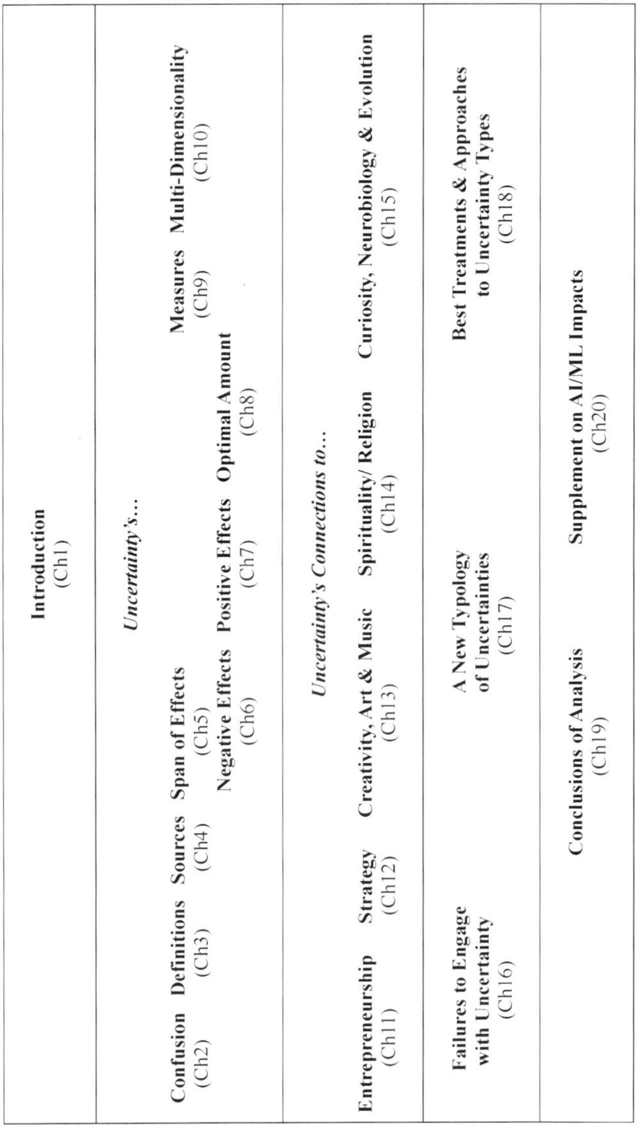

Introduction
(Ch1)

Uncertainty's...

Confusion	Definitions	Sources	Span of Effects			Measures	Multi-Dimensionality
(Ch2)	(Ch3)	(Ch4)	(Ch5)			(Ch9)	(Ch10)
			Negative Effects	Positive Effects	Optimal Amount		
			(Ch6)	(Ch7)	(Ch8)		

Uncertainty's Connections to...

Entrepreneurship	Strategy	Creativity, Art & Music	Spirituality/Religion	Curiosity, Neurobiology & Evolution
(Ch11)	(Ch12)	(Ch13)	(Ch14)	(Ch15)

Failures to Engage with Uncertainty	A New Typology of Uncertainties	Best Treatments & Approaches to Uncertainty Types
(Ch16)	(Ch17)	(Ch18)

Conclusions of Analysis	Supplement on AI/ML Impacts
(Ch19)	(Ch20)

Fig. 1.1 Chapter flow

The seven early chapters (2–8) define the uncertainties of interest and discuss them from emergence to impacts. Chapter 2 explains the confusion over uncertainty. Chapter 3 defines uncertainty (considering alternatives). Chapter 4 describes the main sources of uncertainties with an eye on treatment. Chapter 5 lays out the range of uncertainty's impacts. Chapter 6 focuses on the negative effects while Chapter 7 focuses on the positive effects. Chapter 8 discusses whether there can be an optimal amount of uncertainty.

The next two chapters flesh out two important characteristics of uncertainty. Chapter 9 considers the various measures of uncertainties in the relevant literatures. Chapter 10 delves into the potential multi-dimensionalities of uncertainty.

The middle five chapters (11–15) connect uncertainty to a wide range of interesting human activities. Chapter 11 considers the connections—existential and otherwise—to entrepreneurship. Chapter 12 describes the connections to strategic management. Chapter 13 reflects on the connections to creativity, art, and music. Chapter 14 explores the connections—existential and otherwise—to religion and spirituality. Chapter 15 examines the connections to curiosity, and the possible underlying neurological and evolutionary mechanisms.

The final chapters (16–20) traverse from the avoidance to the confrontation of the various types of uncertainties. Chapter 16 explains the past failures in seriously engaging with uncertainty. Chapter 17 argues a new typology of uncertainties relevant to decision-making. Chapter 18 explores the various ways to treat and address uncertainties, explaining which do and do not work for the newly categorized types. Chapter 19 concludes, summing up the path taken, and proposing further work into this fascinating phenomenon. Chapter 20 is a supplement, updating the contents to the impacts of artificial intelligence.

Summary
A book—this book—is needed to provide clarity and understanding to uncertainty and to improve decision-making under it. We provide a path for so doing by considering the expanse of uncertainty—in order to more fully appreciate its width, depth, types, range of impacts, and existential connections to most human activities—and by applying a divide-and-conquer push where we categorize the types of uncertainty in a clear and

logical way, a categorization that is then leveraged to identify the treatments and approaches that are applicable to those types (and which are not). We cut through the confusing literature in so doing, exposing false claims, and clarifying the terminology and premises.

Why uncertainty matters:

- Uncertainty *is* everything, so we need to better understand how it is existentially linked to most human activities and why it is ubiquitous in our lives.
- Uncertainty has been recognized as an important issue over time, by many scholars, yet remains poorly understood.
- Uncertainty is linked to big questions in science, philosophy, and business, especially regarding what to do when a decision is non-optimizable.

What uncertainty means for business and policy:

- If it is everywhere, and it is important to living, then it is important to business—to make better decisions to generate better products for society while reducing costs and harms
- Given it can eliminate an incumbent's advantages (as no standard operating procedure or insurance can optimize a decision under the kind of uncertainty considered here), it is a source of entry for new ventures and innovation
- It is not risk, and should not be treated as insurable; it must be addressed in novel ways.

References

Aggarwal, D., & Mohanty, P. (2022). Influence of imprecise information on risk and ambiguity preferences: Experimental evidence. *Managerial and Decision Economics*, 43(4), 1025–1038.
Arendt, H. (1958). *The human condition*. University of Chicago Press.
Arrow, K. J. (1951). *Social choice and individual values*. Wiley.
Baker, E. (1976). *Klynt's Law: A novel*. Houghton Mifflin Harcourt Press.
Bammer, G., & Smithson, M. (2008). Understanding uncertainty. *Integration Insights*, 7(1), 1–7.
Barrow, J. D. (1998). *Impossibility: The limits of science and the science of limits*. Oxford University Press on Demand.
Beck, U. (2009). *World at risk*. Polity.

Ben-Haim, Y. (2001). Decision trade-offs under severe info-gap uncertainty. *ISIPTA* (June), 32–39.
Berger, P., & Luckmann, T. (1966). *The social construction of reality*. Penguin Book.
Bergson, H. (1913). *Time and free will: An essay on the immediate date of consciousness*. Dover Publications.
Bernstein, P. L. (1996). *Against the gods: The remarkable story of risk*. Wiley.
Bradac, J. J. (2001). Theory comparison: Uncertainty reduction, problematic integration, uncertainty management, and other curious constructs. *Journal of Communication, 51*(3), 456–476.
Bradley, R., & Steele, K. (2015). Making climate decisions. *Philosophy Compass, 10*(11), 799–810.
Costikyan, G. (2013). *Uncertainty in games*. MIT Press.
Courtney, H., Lovallo, D., & Clarke, C. (2013). Deciding how to decide. *Harvard Business Review, 91*(11), 62–70.
Dosi, G., & Egidi, M. (1991). Substantive and procedural uncertainty: An exploration of economic behaviours in changing environments. *Journal of Evolutionary Economics, 1*, 145–168.
Ghirardato, P. (2001). Coping with ignorance: Unforeseen contingencies and non-additive uncertainty. *Economic Theory, 17*, 247–276.
Gigerenzer, G., & Gaissmaier, W. (2011). Heuristic decision making. *Annual Review of Psychology, 62*, 451–482.
Gilboa, I. (2009). *Theory of decision under uncertainty*. Cambridge University Press.
Gray, J. (2002). *Straw dogs: Thoughts on humans and other animals*. Farrar.
Halpern, J. Y. (2003). *Reasoning about uncertainty*. MIT Press.
Hertwig, R., Pleskac, T. J., & Pachur, T. (2019). *Taming uncertainty*. MIT Press.
Hodgson, G. M. (2011). The eclipse of the uncertainty concept in mainstream economics. *Journal of Economic Issues, 45*(1), 159–176.
Kahneman, D. (2011). *Thinking, fast and slow*. Macmillan.
Kay, J. A., & King, M. A. (2020). *Radical uncertainty*. Bridge Street Press.
Knight, F. H. (1921/1964). *Risk, uncertainty and profit*. Augustus M. Kelley.
Kozyreva, A., & Hertwig, R. (2021). The interpretation of uncertainty in ecological rationality. *Synthese, 198*(2), 1517–1547.
Kuhlthau, C. C. (1993). A principle of uncertainty for information seeking. *Journal of Documentation, 49*(4), 339–355.
Lipshitz, R., & Strauss, O. (1997). Coping with uncertainty: A naturalistic decision-making analysis. *Organizational Behavior and Human Decision Processes, 69*(2), 149–163.

Machina, M. J., & Siniscalchi, M. (2014). Ambiguity and ambiguity aversion. In *Handbook of the Economics of Risk and Uncertainty* (Vol. 1, 729–807). North-Holland.

MacLeod, W. B., & Pingle, M. (2000). An experiment on the relative effects of ability, temperament and luck on search with uncertainty [University of Southern California Law School, Olin Research paper 00–12].

Marchau, V. A., Walker, W. E., Bloemen, P. J., & Popper, S. W. (2019). *Decision making under deep uncertainty: From theory to practice*. Springer Nature.

Mousavi, S., & Gigerenzer, G. (2014). Risk, uncertainty, and heuristics. *Journal of Business Research*, 67(8), 1671–1678.

Mousavi, S., & Gigerenzer, G. (2017). Heuristics are tools for uncertainty. *Homo Oeconomicus*, 34(4), 361–379.

Nash, S. J. (2003). On pragmatic philosophy and Knightian uncertainty. *Review of Social Economy*, 61(2), 251–272.

Packard, M. D., Clark, B. B., & Klein, P. G. (2017). Uncertainty types and transitions in the entrepreneurial process. *Organization Science*, 28(5), 840–856.

Poutyface. (2021). *Never fuckin know*. Island Records.

Roeser, S. (2019). Emotional responses to luck, risk, and uncertainty. In *The Routledge handbook of the philosophy and psychology of luck* (pp. 356–364). Routledge.

Rouvray, D. H. (1997). The treatment of uncertainty in the sciences. *Endeavour*, 21(4), 154–158.

Rowe, W. D. (1994). Understanding uncertainty. *Risk Analysis*, 14(5), 743–750.

Runde, J. (1990). Keynesian uncertainty and the weight of arguments. *Economics & Philosophy*, 6(2), 275–292.

Schoemaker, P. J. (2002). *Profiting from uncertainty: Strategies for succeeding no matter what the future brings*. Simon & Schuster.

Schumpeter, J. (1932). Development. *Journal of Economic Literature*, 18, 104–116.

Simon, H. A. (1972). Theories of bounded rationality. *Decision and Organization*, 1(1), 161–176.

Simon, H. A. (1990). Invariants of human behavior. *Annual Review of Psychology*, 41(1), 1–20.

Stewart, I. (2019). *Do dice play god?: The mathematics of uncertainty*. Hachette UK.

Taleb, N. N. (2012). *Antifragile: How to live in a world we don't understand*. Allen Lane.

Tannert, C., Elvers, H. D., & Jandrig, B. (2007). The ethics of uncertainty: In the light of possible dangers, research becomes a moral duty. *EMBO Reports*, 8(10), 892–896.

Taylor, C. R. (2003). The role of risk versus the role of uncertainty in economic systems. *Agricultural Systems, 75*(2–3), 251–264.

Teece, D., Peteraf, M., & Leih, S. (2016). Dynamic capabilities and organizational agility: Risk, uncertainty, and strategy in the innovation economy. *California Management Review, 58*(4), 13–35.

Towler, R. (1984). *The need for certainty: A sociological study of conventional religion.* Routledge & Kegan Paul.

Townsend, D. M., Hunt, R. A., Beal, D. J., & hyeong Jin, J. (2020). Venturing into the unknown: A meta-analytic assessment of uncertainty in entrepreneurship research. *Academy of Management Proceedings.*

Tversky, A., & Kahneman, D. (1974). Judgment under uncertainty: Heuristics and biases. *Science, 185,* 1124–1131.

Walker, W. E., Harremoës, P., Rotmans, J., Van Der Sluijs, J. P., Van Asselt, M. B., Janssen, P., & Krayer von Krauss, M. P. (2003). Defining uncertainty: A conceptual basis for uncertainty management in model-based decision support. *Integrated Assessment, 4*(1), 5–17.

Yager, R. R. (1999). A game-theoretic approach to decision making under uncertainty. *Intelligent Systems in Accounting, Finance & Management, 8*(2), 131–143.

CHAPTER 2

Confusion over Uncertainty in Decision-Making

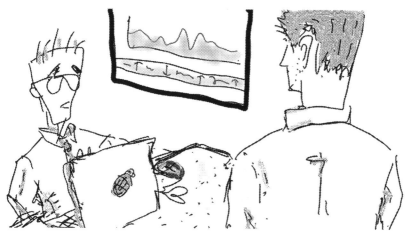

Just a ball of confusion. Oh yeah, that's what the world is today.—*The Temptations (1970)*

WHY CLARITY IS IMPORTANT

Without clarity, decisions lead to disastrous actions. This bodes poorly for decisions made under uncertainty because the use and understanding of the concept of uncertainty has not been, and continues to not be, clear. There are thousands of published academic papers referencing uncertainty, and yet there remains a lack of convergence on the concept; there is not only inconsistency across the different papers but often even within the same paper on what is described as uncertainty and what is actually measured or modeled. As such, the uncertainty construct can be considered both overused and misused, especially when it refers to all manner of unknownness (Townsend et al., 2018). The term uncertainty is too commonly used, so much so that parties with different definitions simply (and mistakenly) assume the other parties know what is being referred to, and so there is often insufficient attention paid to rigorously and explicitly describing the concept and its operationalization when communicating about it (Milliken, 1987).

The lack of clarity over uncertainty is likely more problematic than the widespread use of the term uncertainty suggests. When a term not only covers multiple variants of a condition (i.e., of unknownness) but is also central to strategic decision-making and entrepreneurial activity, then the scope for 'damage' due to confusion, imprecision, misuse, and miscommunication is significant (Packard et al., 2017). It is because the different variants—arising from different philosophies, theories, and models—suggest different approaches (Feduzi et al., 2012) causing dangerous confusion over which applies (i.e., as a misidentified variant can lead to an inappropriate treatment being applied). When the possibility of any such misapplication for any one decision involving uncertainty is multiplied by the number of decisions that involve uncertainty—theoretically being most of them—then the danger is even more grave. Further still, when a non-trivial proportion of those decisions, due to the nature of uncertainty, can involve sizeable benefits (e.g., entrepreneurial opportunities) or catastrophic harms (e.g., irreversible global warming), the enormity of the need for clarity is immense.

What Confusion Exists

To summarize, to this day there remains a significant lack of agreement on what uncertainty is and how to model it in theory and in practice (Townsend et al., 2018). There are as many conceptualizations of uncertainty as treatments of it (Lipshitz & Strauss, 1997). Alternative theories use the same language of uncertainty, although different types of uncertainty are implicated, and starkly different behavioral assumptions are used (Leiblein et al., 2018). Even a century after the explicit delineation of uncertainty from risk by Knight (1921), its identification, description, and operationalization are confused. Uncertainty, as a construct, is still plagued by conflicting and imprecise definitions, inconsistent and tautological measures, and significant conflations with variants of unknownness from risk to ignorance (Townsend et al., 2018).

Thus, what exists is confusion over uncertainty in terms of: its definition(s) [from an umbrella level down to different types and subtypes]; the valid measures available at such levels and the better approaches to deal with those variants; the possible sources of it; the possible effects of it; the possible relationships it has with other fields of study; the identification of possible beneficiaries, victims and decision-makers involved; the possible uses of (and ways to create) it; the possible interactions it can have with other constructs (especially those that amplify its effects); and, other strategic issues (e.g., the constraints—like temporal or spatial—the decisions involving it can have). This book explores these areas of confusion in order to provide clarity.

What Terms Are Confused

Many terms relevant to uncertainty lack clarity. For illustration, we consider three categories here: *definitions* (at the umbrella level and some popular variants); alternative bases for *measures* of prediction; and, related *mathematical concepts*.

Both at the general—umbrella—level and at the level of major types, terminology remains less-than-clear. Lipshitz and Strauss (1997) compiled a list of alternative ways that uncertainty has been captured and defined in the literature, for example, as: risk; ambiguity; the inability to act deterministically; a paucity of information; turbulence; equivocality; conflict; and, ignorance (Townsend et al., 2018). Even established variants of uncertainty like *Knightian uncertainty* are confused—both by academics and by practitioners. To the latter, Taleb (2007) observes that individual decision-makers confront Knightian risk and uncertainty in the same way. To the former, it appears that a non-trivial proportion of the strategic management literature uses the terms as synonyms despite their clear and famous delineation by Knight (1921) now over a century ago (Magnani & Zucchella, 2018). And, although Ellsberg's (1961) famous experiments clearly defined what ambiguity is, strategic management often confuses it with risk, uncertainty, or a mixture of both (O'Reilly & Tushman, 2008). Other well-established concepts like luck are similarly confused with risk and uncertainty, especially when the importance of positive or negative outcomes is considered (Roeser, 2019).

Besides specific types of uncertainty being confused, the terminology that describes the bases from which beliefs over outcome predictions are formed lacks clarity. For example, often conflated are the separate concepts of the *confidence* that a decision-maker has in their judgment versus the *likelihood* that their judgment is correct (the latter being the primary belief and the former a belief about that). Then, mixing subjective and objective ideas, there is a *confidence* based on a review of evidence and the views of experts over an estimate of an event occurring. There is also a *likelihood* of the event based on facts and logical inference (Kay & King, 2020). Adding to that terminological ambiguity, there is also the observed *frequency* of past related events that can be used for predictions. When the same term represents different degrees and bases for an estimate, then confusion abounds, and any precision over which uncertainties are at play is lost.

Lastly, the terms chosen by academics to describe succinct mathematical forms of uncertainty too often bump up against how such terms are used naturally by practitioners. Examples include the academically delineated but often naturally synonymous *possibility and probability*, *fuzzy (sets) versus fuzziness*, and *chaos (theory) versus chaotic-in-nature*. That theory-versus-practice terminological confusion being noted, even academics can disagree on some theoretical distinctions being 'too clean' (e.g., Knight's delineation between uncertainty and risk being based on insurability) to be translated effectively into practice, where reality often reveals fuzziness (e.g., about what actually gets insured versus what does not and why) (Feduzi et al., 2012).

Sources of Confusion

There are several major sources of confusion. These range from the characteristics of the uncertainty concept itself to the characteristics of the decision-maker.

One problematic characteristic of uncertainty is its *everythingness*—in that it involves many dimensions that can be unknown. Not readily being able to nail down what things are unknown (with one or a small number of terms)—whether it be related to the actions, outcomes, actors, or greater context of the focal decision problem—leads to the lack of construct clarity. As such, the label of uncertainty is ubiquitous, being used by both practitioners and scholars as a synonym for too wide a range of different unknownnesses (Townsend et al., 2018).

Another problematic characteristic of uncertainty lies its very nature of being unknown—which makes the boundary of whatever it is actually referring to more difficult to identify, the phenomenon involved less stable, and its scope less measurable. But, when attempts are made to contain it (e.g., with an ergodic assumption), the conception of uncertainty can then become too limited, which overly restricts the study of the phenomenon (Fontana & Gerrard, 2004). For example, when uncertainty-as-unpredictability is only attributed to the question of free will (even though other factors often contribute to observed randomness), then mistaken conclusions and prescriptions are likely to be drawn (Gilboa, 2009).

When we speak to every strategic decision being made based on incomplete information, we are implicitly referring to the unknowns at that level of analysis—e.g., the inability to peek into the minds and lives of the stakeholders involved, whether consumers, rivals, suppliers, regulators, or employees. But, confusion over uncertainty can also arise from questions over the level of analysis involved. For example, when a business problem is considered (in a very deep dive) down at the subatomic scale, the uncertainty-as-unpredictability described in quantum theory applies. So, a question may arise over at what level of analysis does the uncertainty matter/exist (for the focal decision)? In this book, we have described that level—where the unknown makes the decision non-optimizable (as given). In reality, the level is often obvious in terms of the focus of the decision problem (e.g., as dealing with demand, or technology, or weather, and so on). The correct level is problem-unique (and based on whether, at that level, it can affect the optimal choice in a significant way).

Besides issues with uncertainty's unusual characteristics, practical factors often drive confusion when uncertainty exists. Uncertainty's presence often increases the occurrence of biases, miscommunications, exploitative uses of information gaps, and disinformation of and by decision-makers. Just the fact that terms are ill-defined but ubiquitous has the effect of multiplying that confusion through the dispersion of multiple, overlapping, and conflicting concepts. Added to that mix, decision-makers often meet potential crises (that arise due to uncertainty) with incompetence, and even willful blindness, and so make such situations even more bewildering to stakeholders (Kay & King, 2020).

The idiosyncratic (non-repeated) nature of many decisions made under uncertainty also adds to confusion. Singular problems—and the specific uncertainties that drive them—make identification, understanding, and learning about such phenomena more difficult, limiting any insights that can be gleaned from them. This effect is observed in the real world—e.g., in the odds for gambles of repeated events being much fairer than for single-shot events (Kay & King, 2020).

Even at a higher—philosophical—level, uncertainty appears unresolved. Basic ontological, epistemological, and methodological questions—e.g., over what is reality, knowledge, truth, free will, and so on—involve what is uncertain, what is unknown, and what is unknowable. Such questions often lead to *rabbit holes* of unending debates that have little impact on practice, but still hold interest to select academic outlets. Such big questions can be considered the 'ultimate' theoretical drivers of confusion over uncertainty.

How to Unconfuse

The direct, logical approach to address such confusion is to provide clarity in the form of some framework based on the study of the phenomenon itself. However, in today's world, unconfusing a subject does not simply involve providing a reasonable framework, it must then be sold effectively (i.e., in order to counter the inroads that alternative answers and misplaced questions [e.g., involving what-about-isms] have on adoption).

A market-driven approach would involve studying how, when, and why the intended audience (of decision-makers) is confused in order to address the biggest identified factors, their perceived sources, and any requested resolutions.

Other approaches are less direct. For example, one could use textual analysis of written confusion over uncertainty (and of any patterns of convergence to clarity) to learn which specific factors improve and worsen that confusion in order to come up with mechanisms to manipulate to lessen it. Or, one could perhaps base policies on observations of when and how people gamble in order to inform how framing and other contextual cues can reduce specific confusions surrounding risk and uncertainty (Kay & King, 2020).

We take the direct approach here. This book focuses on arguing a proper typology of uncertainty; proper as being based on *a relevant structure—the logic of decision-making*. That typology seeks to provide a mutually exclusive and collectively exhaustive (MECE), parsimonious, and practical categorization in order to clarify the uncertainty construct (in all its relevant forms). The selling of this framework is dependent on others (and, so is practically unlikely in the near future). It requires adoption and, to some degree, enforcement. Stakeholders will need to voluntarily agree on definitions and dimensions. Editors and reviewers (as well as authors and educators) will need to comply and help enforce the consistency of terminological use. Then, it will be incumbent upon scholars to ensure that the constructs are accurate, intelligible, utilizable, and meaningful (Townsend et al., 2018); however, given the competition for attention in this subject area, any such unified efforts are only hopeful if not questionable. (That said, if 'we' could come to some consensus [on definitions, terms, and types] then making the historic corrections and clarifications [of them] can be [easily] done, as it has never been easier and more feasible given the digital versions of past research exist to be easily corrected or retracted.)

We finish up this analysis of confusion with a question about whether the perspective that we have assumed so far in this chapter—that confusion is bad—now needs to be discussed. There is an argument that uncertainty-related confusion can be good. Confusion can be beneficial in real life—to help in reaching agreement among parties (when each believe a privately useful interpretation of an ambiguous term is correct), to delay painful choices, to escape accountability, to place doubt in a rival's mind, and so forth. The confusion of uncertainty may even be harnessed to inspire creative exploration, for example, in design (e.g., along with other principles like variety and complexity—see Kuhlthau, 1993). Despite the fact that confusion can be privately beneficial in specific circumstances, it is almost always harmful to society (due to the many inefficiencies it generates) and so we stand by our assumption that it is bad (in the case of uncertainty).

> **Summary**
> Cutting through the confusion over uncertainty is important to anyone trying to understand the unknowns they face when they have to identify it, communicate about it, act on it, or decide given it. It is also important to those hoping to exploit the confusion surrounding uncertainty for their own private gains. Such confusion arises from characteristics of concept itself as well as from the people dealing with it. While that confusion can provide some specific private benefits, it is almost always harmful to society due to the inefficiencies involved (e.g., from resource misallocations, miscommunications, distrust, and so on). Unfortunately, the relevant literature has not been helpful in cutting through the confusion; rather, it has mostly added to the redundant, overlapping, and contradictory mess of terminology about uncertainty that exists today.
>
> Why confusion matters:
>
> - It leads to costs and harms that are unnecessary.
> - It slows down the progress of studying and understanding uncertainty
>
> What confusion means for business and policy:
>
> - There is untapped value in clarifying the terminology (e.g., definitions and typology) relevant to uncertainty.
> - Such clarification is—in theory—easy to propose, and even cheap to implement (given digital records); but, it requires a legitimate standards-setting body to get done (in a timely manner).
> - There is no legitimate barrier to getting this (clarification) done (despite the many powerful illegitimate ones).

REFERENCES

Ellsberg, D. (1961). Risk, ambiguity, and the savage axioms. *The Quarterly Journal of Economics, 75*(4), 643–669.

Fontana, G., & Gerrard, B. (2004). A Post Keynesian theory of decision making under uncertainty. *Journal of Economic Psychology, 25*(5), 619–637.

Feduzi, A., Runde, J., & Zappia, C. (2012). De Finetti on the insurance of risks and uncertainties. *The British Journal for the Philosophy of Science, 63*(2), 329–356.

Gilboa, I. (2009). *Theory of decision under uncertainty*. Cambridge University Press.
Kay, J. A., & King, M. A. (2020). *Radical uncertainty*. Bridge Street Press.
Knight, F. H. (1921/1964). *Risk, uncertainty and profit*. Augustus M. Kelley.
Kuhlthau, C. C. (1993). A principle of uncertainty for information seeking. *Journal of Documentation, 49*(4), 339–355.
Leiblein, M. J., Reuer, J. J., & Zenger, T. (2018). What makes a decision strategic? *Strategy Science, 3*(4), 558–573.
Lipshitz, R., & Strauss, O. (1997). Coping with uncertainty: A naturalistic decision-making analysis. *Organizational Behavior and Human Decision Processes, 69*(2), 149–163.
Magnani, G., & Zucchella, A. (2018). Uncertainty in entrepreneurship and management studies: A systematic literature review. *International Journal of Business and Management, 13*(3), 98–133.
Milliken, F. J. (1987). Three types of perceived uncertainty about the environment: State, effect, and response uncertainty. *Academy of Management Review, 12*(1), 133–143.
O'Reilly, C. A., III., & Tushman, M. L. (2008). Ambidexterity as a dynamic capability: Resolving the innovator's dilemma. *Research in Organizational Behavior, 28*, 185–206.
Packard, M. D., Clark, B. B., & Klein, P. G. (2017). Uncertainty types and transitions in the entrepreneurial process. *Organization Science, 28*(5), 840–856.
Roeser, S. (2019). Emotional responses to luck, risk, and uncertainty. In *The Routledge handbook of the philosophy and psychology of luck* (pp. 356–364). Routledge.
Taleb, N. N. (2007). *The black swan: The impact of the highly improbable*. Random House.
Townsend, D. M., Hunt, R. A., McMullen, J. S., & Sarasvathy, S. D. (2018). Uncertainty, knowledge problems, and entrepreneurial action. *Academy of Management Annals, 12*(2), 659–687.

CHAPTER 3

Definitions of Uncertainty (for Decision-Making)

The beginning of wisdom is the definition of terms—*Socrates*

Why Definitional Precision Is Important

Logical persuasion and compelling arguments require a clear and careful definition of terms; a fact recognized by fields such as mathematics, physics, and economics, as well as by many theorists (e.g., Hobbes; Pascal). Without the solid foundation provided by a deep, common understanding of a focal term—its definition—nothing of any predictive or relational substance can be built or tested (e.g., empirically). When such a definition does not exist, too much room is left to exploit—with post hoc exceptions, excuses, and hand-waving reinterpretations of verbiage—such that any outcome can be justified; and, when any outcome can be justified then nothing is explained. Without precision, chaos.

Unfortunately, there is no consensus on the definition of uncertainty (e.g., Kozyreva & Hertwig, 2021; Rapp & Olbrich, 2020), or even on the single correct world-as-context to use (Halpern, 2003). One reason is that some believe it is unmeasurable (Keynes, 1937). Another reason is that others believe it is not an independent condition; instead, it is considered to be a property of the system constituted by the decision-maker and their environment (Kozyreva & Hertwig, 2021). As such, (too) many representations of uncertainty have been described in the literature (Halpern, 2003). Table 3.1 summarizes the main definitions in the relevant literature.

Classic Definitions

The three most common definitions of uncertainty—at least as cited by organization theorists—are: uncertainty being *an inability to assign probabilities* to the likelihood of future events (e.g., Duncan, 1972; Pennings, 1981; Pennings & Tripathi, 1978; Pfeffer & Salancik, 1978); uncertainty being *the lack of information about cause-effect* relationships (e.g., Duncan, 1972; Lawrence & Lorsch, 1967); and, uncertainty being *the inability to accurately predict* the outcomes of a decision (e.g., Downey & Slocum, 1975; Duncan, 1972; Hickson et al., 1971; Schmidt & Cummings, 1976).

Table 3.1 Alternative definitions of uncertainty

'Type'	Definition(s)
Classic	*An inability to assign probabilities (to a known set of outcomes)* *A lack of information over cause-and-effect relationships* *An inability to predict the outcomes of a decision*
Knightian	*Not risk. Involving uninsurable future states (because some possible states are unknown, or the probabilities of future states are unknown and unknowable). Involving irreducible unknowns*
Ellsbergian (Ambiguity)	*A subset of Knightian Uncertainty where the (non-trivial) range of possible values is known but the distribution of those values is unknown and unknowable*
Other	*Unknowability; irreducible unknowns involved prior to decision point* *Novelty (so, providing no legitimate reference point for a subjective probability estimate)* *Doubt (as a subjective/affect-based assessment)*
...for this Book	*The cause of the non-optimizability of a decision (which covers any unknown part[s] of a decision, including probabilities, options, outcome states, facts, and so on) such that the expected or point values for all relevant choice-outcome combinations cannot be calculated prior to the decision point*

UNCERTAINTY AS THE INABILITY TO ASSIGN PROBABILITIES

The first common definition appears to be the most popular (noting some variation). For example, Magnani and Zucchella (2018) understand uncertainty as, at best, the impossibility of assigning objective probabilities to every possible known outcome, and, at worst, not being able to do so to collections of those outcomes. Hodgson (2011) and others (e.g., Etner et al., 2012; Feduzi et al., 2012; Fontana & Gerrard, 2004; Hastie, 2001; Hertwig et al., 2019) also align the concept of uncertainty with when events (e.g., decision outcomes; possible losses) entail incalculable probability assignments. More bluntly, Keynes (1937: p. 214) spoke to uncertainty as when '*there is no scientific basis on which to form any calculable probability whatever. We simply do not know*'. Others are similarly succinct, defining uncertainty as involving unknowns that cannot be described by probabilities (Kay & King, 2020). Some are careful to separate unknown probabilities of known events from unknown events themselves (e.g., Mousavi & Gigerenzer, 2014). Some are careful to separate the event probabilities as being unknown versus as being un-meaningful (Raiffa & Luce, 1957).[1]

UNCERTAINTY AS UNKNOWN CAUSE-AND-EFFECT RELATIONSHIPS

The second common definition focuses more on process—understanding how a phenomenon works—rather than on product—whether probabilities can be meaningfully assigned to the outcomes. Milliken (1987) speaks to this regarding incomplete knowledge of relevant interrelationships. Fontana and Gerrard (2004) speak to this in terms of underlying process structures that are unstable or unknown. The relationship between means and ends is simply unclear (Nash, 2003). Even if the direction of a change is relatively well-known, uncertainty may still exist if the magnitude and probability of consequences cannot be accurately estimated or the receptors at play precisely identified. So, there is a wide range of ways in which the cause-and-effect relationships may be unclear, especially in more complex systems and decisions. Some scholars have gone so far as to label high levels of that unclearness as *ignorance*—e.g., when even the broad directions of change are unknown and relationships not understood (e.g., Bammer & Smithson, 2008).

UNCERTAINTY-AS-UNPREDICTABILITY

The third common definition is also wider of range than the first; but, it is narrower than the second. Milliken (1987) also refers to this definition when she associates uncertainty with unforeseeableness —an inability to accurately predict due to a lack of information or an inability to discern between relevant and irrelevant data (Duncan, 1972; Galbraith, 1973, 1977; Griffin & Grote, 2020; Grote, 2009; Lipshitz & Strauss, 1997). Fontana and Gerrard (2004) find fundamental uncertainty in cases where relevant future possible outcomes are unclear (e.g., where one cannot compare the present to anything previously experienced). Such departures from determinism lie at the core of uncertainty (Gigerenzer & Gaissmaier,

---

[1] Regardless of this definition by some scholars—i.e., where probabilities are impossible or meaningless to assign—there are others who try to assign a version of those probabilities nonetheless. Versions include: sets of probability measures; Dempster-Shafer belief functions; possibility measures; ranking functions; and, plausibility measures.

2011; Walker et al., 2003). This form of uncertainty—the ignorance of the consequences of the various options—is one of the most discussed in the decision-making literature (Hansson, 1996).

The set of possible worlds—across which it is impossible to predict where the outcome will land—is one way to quantitatively assess a decision-maker's uncertainty (Halpern, 2003).[2] That measure breaks, however, when the decision-maker admits that there could exist *other* possible worlds—unknown ones—in which the outcome could land, in what would be a 'higher' level of uncertainty (Kay & King, 2020). Note that when such unknown possible worlds exist, then it is logically implied that their probabilities of being landed in are also unknown (and unknowable).

There are variants on the unforeseeableness or alternative-worlds conceptualizations (underlying unpredictability). For example, some conceive uncertainty when a decision-maker cannot distinguish between alternative possible worlds (Ben-Haim, 2001). Others find uncertainty in the unforeseeable elements in the markets or in organizations (Magnani & Zucchella, 2018; Miles & Snow, 1978; Pfeffer & Salancik, 1978; Schoemaker, 2002). Hodgson (2011) sees uncertainty as not only unpredictableness but unquantifiableness as well.

KNIGHT'S DEFINITION OF UNCERTAINTY

Related to the first common definition is the concept of *Knightian* uncertainty. Knight (1921) distinguished uncertainty from risk through a test of insurability. Uncertainty involves *a priori* irreducible unknowns (McGrath, 1999) and is thus uninsurable because no immediate market pricing mechanisms exist that include unforeseen eventualities (Townsend et al., 2018). By contrast, risks are insurable (e.g., through grouping) and thus involve regular business activities. Knight (1921) argued that uncertainty explains entrepreneurial profit—not as a reward for risk-taking but as motivation for accepting the role of decision-making and action-executing under uncertainty.

---

[2] That said, such a measure is subjective in the sense that it is dependent on a decision-maker's perceptions (and judgments and assumptions) rather than any objective assessment of the situation.

In practical terms, risk occurs when the distribution of possible outcomes is known (e.g., through experience, statistics, or cause-and-effect structure). For uncertainty, this is not true (e.g., because the decision problem is to a high degree unique and consequently includes unmeasurable unknowns). For Knight (1921), uncertainty must be dealt with using judgment and opinion rather than scientific knowledge (because knowledge is incomplete about both the present and the future—Nash, 2003). Many scholars explicitly express understanding, if not agreement, on Knight's (1921) definition and distinction of uncertainty (e.g., Boyd, 2012; Keynes, 1937; McMullen & Shepherd, 2006; Posner, 2004; Sunstein, 2007). Knightian uncertainty appears to be the basis for the first common definition—where no meaningful probabilities can be assigned to possible outcomes of a decision.

Ellsberg's Definition of Ambiguity

Also related to the first common definition of uncertainty is the concept of *Ellsbergian ambiguity*. Ellsberg (1961) described decision-making under ambiguity in a series of hypothetical urn-based experiments where the relevant probabilities (e.g., for a gamble) were unknown but bounded for ambiguity; by contrast, those probabilities were known for risk (Epstein, 1999). The aversion of real decision-makers to ambiguous problems differs from that induced by risk; and, several potential explanations for that ambiguity aversion have been considered (e.g., Gilboa & Schmeidler, 1989). Returning to the first common definition of uncertainty, Ellsberg's ambiguity provides a subtype, where the probabilities of possible outcomes are unknown, but are also finitely bounded in value.

Alternative Definitions of Uncertainty

Besides the three common definitions of uncertainty (and their variants), several other definitions deserve consideration. These retain the core concept of incomplete information (of some sort), but vary in their scope (e.g., generality) and focus (e.g., measure; subjectivity). We consider four such alternatives below for illustration.

Uncertainty as Unknowability

At the largest scope and least focus is the definition of uncertainty as dealing with unknowns, and unknowability (e.g., Kay & King, 2020; Ramoglou, 2021). This has important effects on decision-making because when factors are unknown—as when an organization's knowledge cannot be identified explicitly—then the proper allocation of resources is impossible (Spender, 2006). Uncertainty can embody a lack of knowledge about the choices available, their outcomes, or the value of those outcomes (or some combination of those unknowns) (Conrath, 1967; Dequech, 1999; Milliken, 1987). In economics, uncertainty is more associated with a lack of knowledge over the possible future states (Arrow, 1974; Hirshleifer & Riley, 1979; Koopmans, 1957; Machina, 1987; Magnani & Zucchella, 2018; Milgrom & Roberts, 1982). Keynes (1937) describes such situations as when the theory of probability is useless (Hertwig et al., 2019).

Uncertainty can involve various forms of unknowns. This embodiment of uncertainty-as-inadequate-knowledge has been around since the ancient Greeks debated epistemology. Risk can be seen as dealing with estimable (and controllable) unknowns, and uncertainty as dealing with the uncontrollable ones (Marchau et al., 2019). In terms of the latter, some focus on the unknown unknowns—like the surprises that innovation brings (e.g., Taleb, 2007; Teece et al., 2016). Some focus on the known unknowns, and others categorize phenomena by whether the unknowability (e.g., about the decision-making context) is objective or subjective (Miller, 2012; Townsend et al., 2018). We consider these variants when we review and analyze the types of uncertainty that exist (later in this book).

Uncertainty as Novelty

At a more specific focus is the definition of uncertainty as novelty—and, specifically, the kind that Knight (1921) refers to as 'conditions that are unique to the point of lacking antecedents' (Scoblic, 2020). Due to such uniqueness, these can be uninsurable situations because, besides lacking precedents, they may lack other necessary properties that satisfy the mathematics of probabilities (Mousavi & Gigerenzer, 2014). In such situations, any existing rules no longer apply as new ones are invented (Teece et al., 2016), making the prediction of outcomes difficult, if not impossible. The chaotic reactions and consequences that occur in the short-term when technological breakthroughs begin commercialization, or when new contagious and deadly diseases begin to spread, exemplify the effects of this uncertainty-as-novelty characterization.

Uncertainty as Non-Optimizability

A definition with a wide scope but a narrow acid-test of applicability involves uncertainty as generating a state of (theoretical) non-optimizability. Note that this is different from plain mathematical intractability; it is more than dealing with defined complex structures, non-linearities, or functional discontinuities. Those can be practically optimized through numerical or simulation-based methods. This is also different than situations where it is the limits of the decision-maker that inhibit the identification of better-to-best solutions. Uncertainty arrests the rational analysis of the problem (Spender, 1983); it prohibits methods to compute each choice's expected value across possible outcomes and so makes it impossible to determine preferred actions.

Uncertainty as Doubt

A definition with a relatively wide scope but a more subjective perspective characterizes uncertainty as a state of doubt (e.g., Ben-Haim, 2001). This is embodied when the decision-maker does not know what to do or even what to believe the true state of the world is (Bradley & Drechsler, 2014). It delays or blocks action (Lipshitz & Strauss, 1997). When situations lack accessible analogies, decision-makers feel doubt about any visions of how the future will play out (Scoblic, 2020). Uncertainty occurs when the individual doubts that their own knowledge, cognitive abilities, and work environment can support their thinking to successfully address the problem at hand (Kuhlthau, 1993).

CONTRASTS TO FULL INFORMATION

Another way to define something is through contrast. Uncertainty has often been defined in that (indirect) way—essentially as the opposite of (full) knowledge or as the counterpart of (complete) information (e.g., Ben-Haim, 2001). Some have even dichotomized economics into two such contrasting paradigms—one dealing with knowable realities and the other with unknowable realities (Davidson, 1996). In theory and in practice there are many ways that information is not *full*. Game theory differentiates *incomplete* information from *imperfect* information; incompleteness occurs, for example, when one player does not know the one type of the other player from a known set of possible types, whereas imperfection occurs when players act simultaneously and so none knows what decision the others made prior to making their own. Games of imperfect information are common, and they have 'best' solutions (when player rationality is assumed). Games of incomplete information have calculable best solutions for each possible case (e.g., for each known player type), but not necessarily for the overall choice (unless one assumes a reasonable belief over the probabilities covering those cases).

There are many other ways that knowledge can be missing, including: in the description of how the current problem arose; in what the current problem is; and, in what the outcomes will be for any decision made about the problem (Dewey, 1915; Dosi & Egidi, 1991; Nash, 2003). In most real situations, the decision-maker lacks much of the information that is neatly provided in standard textbook cases (Hansson, 1996), such as demand curves, rival costs, and so on (Ben-Haim, 2001). Besides relevant information being absent, often in reality it is also unobtainable (Rowe, 1994). In reality, then, people almost always make decisions on partial information—knowing some facts but not all facts to make an optimal decision (Dequech, 1999; Langlois & Cosgel, 1993). (Some label that partial information as *vagueness* when it involves not knowing which of a range of values is correct—e.g., Bammer & Smithson, 2008.)

This contrast of full to partial information can be used as one measure of uncertainty—being the gap in information between what is known and the minimum that needs to be known to make an optimal decision (Ben-Haim, 2001; Mack, 1971). Alternatively, it can be used as a 'triggered' exposition—where uncertainty exists with any deviation from a completely deterministic understanding of the relevant problem and its system (e.g., Walker et al., 2003).

The Amount of Uncertainty Question

Is uncertainty a dichotomous concept (uninsurable versus insurable) or, as the information-gap-based measure suggests, a continuum of conditions that differ in their distance from absolute certainty (i.e., full information)? To the latter, this may be useful to know if (and really only if) the different levels have different impacts and/or require different approaches to address them. If the problem is non-optimizable, then does it really matter how non-optimizable it is if one only cares about optimization?

That question aside, there are those who believe that the range of knownness does matter, at least for a range that spans from certainty to risk to uncertainty to complete ignorance (e.g., Hertwig et al., 2019; Hmieleski et al., 2015; Raiffa & Luce, 1957; Magnani & Zucchella, 2018; Meijer et al., 2006; Samsami et al., 2015). With such an extended range (that includes conditions that are 'not uncertainty') it is easier to make the argument that the continuum is interesting as it does cover points that involve very different degrees of skill, expertise, and judgment to address effectively (Miller, 2007).

Drawing on the idea that more (valid) information is better than less, it certainly may be valuable to understand just *how much* is uncertain, especially when it is not just quantity (e.g., how many possible future states do we not know about?) but also variety (e.g., is it just probabilities of known outcomes that we don't know, or are other items also unknown like the range of choices available?). To the latter, it may be possible—if the uncertainties are independent—to address them differently (and simultaneously) for a more effective management of the problem (although this is not guaranteed). We consider such questions later in this book.

THE EPISTEMOLOGICAL QUESTION

If uncertainty is defined as the lack of knowledge or as the antithesis of knowledge, then it is important to know just what is meant by the term *knowledge* (e.g., Halpern, 2003; Knight, 1921). *What exactly does it mean to 'know' something?* That is the main question debated in the realm of *epistemology*. (It is a subject that Knight [1921] spends considerable energy analyzing and clarifying in his seminal work on uncertainty because to be uncertain one must understand what *knowing* is so that *not knowing* is itself a meaningful state to investigate.) Knowledge is often understood as awareness of, familiarity with, or understanding about some specific thing. There are several types of knowledge, including: Propositional knowledge is about facts—knowing what. Procedural knowledge is about skills—knowing how. Acquaintance knowledge is about objects—knowing about. *A priori* knowledge is about what is known independent of, and before, experience—as in rationalist deduction. *A posteriori* knowledge is about what is known through experience—as in empirical discovery.

Epistemology considers more than simply what knowledge is (e.g., a *justified true belief*—a standard definition, but where each of those three terms is also debated). It also considers questions about the sources of knowledge (e.g., perception [direct and indirect] versus reason), the nature of knowledge, and the structure of knowledge (e.g., as built upon premises about senses or about nature). Books are needed to adequately cover this philosophical area (that has yet to be resolved). This book is not one of them. This book focuses on ways that things are not known, and how to deal with that. However, it should be noted that such philosophical debates—those related to the nature of uncertainty—can spill upward (i.e., to ontological issues [regarding what the nature of *reality* is—perhaps as only subjective—which can affect what is meant by what is unknown across subjects]) as well as downward (e.g., to methodology [as to how knowledge—and in whole or in part—could or should be measured]). To make progress on decision-making under uncertainty, we have assumed an explicit epistemology—*that knowledge exists as theoretical truths*.

Summary

Many definitions of uncertainty exist; too many. Several share commonalities. Few are precise. What is needed is a set of precise definitions for each type of uncertainty; a set that is mutually exclusive and collectively exhaustive [MECE] of the possible types. And, a set that is as consistent with the literature (especially the empirical work) as possible. Currently, there are too many overlaps and too many gaps. We have had over a century of such 'mucking about' in terminology without much progress; that must change. The endless epistemological debates must be sidestepped (e.g., about what knowledge is and is not) so that real progress can be made on better understanding uncertainty.

Why definitions matter:

- Without precise definitions, there is chaos and inefficiency; we cannot focus and catalogue better approaches, tested solutions, and further gaps related to uncertainty
- To manage, one must measure; but to measure, one must first define what is at stake
- While the epistemological debate rages over what knowledge is, not much progress has been made on what unknowledge is—i.e., what uncertainty is, what forms it takes, and how to address it; this is a

> failure of science because unknowledge is perhaps more ubiquitous (and important in our lives) as knowledge
>
> What definitions mean for business and policy:
>
> - Practical applications of uncertainty (e.g., in mitigating or creating it) require precision, which does not exist without proper definitions
> - The more precise definitions, and the more MECE the set of definitions, the greater the progress that can be made on understanding and treating uncertainties by firms and institutions (and, the more efficiently a firm and the economy can run).

References

Arrow, K. J. (1974). *Limited knowledge and economic analysis*. University of Illinois at Urbana-Champaign's Academy for Entrepreneurial Leadership Historical Research Reference in Entrepreneurship. SSRN.

Bammer, G., & Smithson, M. (2008). Understanding uncertainty. *Integration Insights, 7*(1), 1–7.

Ben-Haim, Y. (2001). Decision trade-offs under severe info-gap uncertainty. *ISIPTA* (June), 32–39.

Boyd, W. (2012). Genealogies of risk: Searching for safety, 1930s–1970s. *Ecology Law Quarterly, 39*, 895–987.

Bradley, R., & Drechsler, M. (2014). Types of uncertainty. *Erkenntnis, 79*, 1225–1248.

Conrath, D. W. (1967). Organizational decision making behavior under varying conditions of uncertainty. *Management Science, 13*(8), B-487.

Davidson, P. (1996). Reality and economic theory. *Journal of Post Keynesian Economics, 18*(4), 479–508.

Dequech, D. (1999). Expectations and confidence under uncertainty. *Journal of Post Keynesian Economics, 21*(3), 415–430.

Dewey, J. (1915). The logic of judgements of practice. *Journal of Philosophy, 12*(1), 505–510.

Dosi, G., & Egidi, M. (1991). Substantive and procedural uncertainty: An exploration of economic behaviours in changing environments. *Journal of Evolutionary Economics, 1*, 145–168.

Downey, H. K., & Slocum, J. W. (1975). Uncertainty: Measures, research, and sources of variation. *Academy of Management Journal, 18*(3), 562–578.

Duncan, R. B. (1972). Characteristics of organizational environments and perceived environmental uncertainty. *Administrative Science Quarterly, 17*(3), 313–327.

Ellsberg, D. (1961). Risk, ambiguity, and the savage axioms. *The Quarterly Journal of Economics, 75*(4), 643–669.

Epstein, L. G. (1999). A definition of uncertainty aversion. *Review of Economic Studies, 66,* 579–608.

Etner, J., Jeleva, M., & Tallon, J. M. (2012). Decision theory under ambiguity. *Journal of Economic Surveys, 26*(2), 234–270.

Feduzi, A., Runde, J., & Zappia, C. (2012). De Finetti on the insurance of risks and uncertainties. *The British Journal for the Philosophy of Science, 63*(2), 329–356.

Fontana, G., & Gerrard, B. (2004). A post Keynesian theory of decision making under uncertainty. *Journal of Economic Psychology, 25*(5), 619–637.

Galbraith, J. (1973). *Designing complex organizations.* Addison-Wesley.

Galbraith, J. (1977). *Organizational design.* Addison-Wesley.

Gigerenzer, G., & Gaissmaier, W. (2011). Heuristic decision making. *Annual Review of Psychology, 62,* 451–482.

Gilboa, I., & Schmeidler, D. (1989). Maxmin expected utility with non-unique prior. *Journal of Mathematical Economics, 18*(2), 141–153.

Griffin, M. A., & Grote, G. (2020). When is more uncertainty better? A model of uncertainty regulation and effectiveness. *Academy of Management Review, 45*(4), 745–765.

Grote, G. (2009). *Management of uncertainty: Theory and application in the design of systems and organizations.* Springer.

Halpern, J. Y. (2003). *Reasoning about uncertainty.* MIT Press.

Hansson, S. O. (1996). Decision making under great uncertainty. *Philosophy of the Social Sciences, 26*(3), 369–386.

Hastie, R. (2001). Problems for judgment and decision making. *Annual Review of Psychology, 52*(1), 653–683.

Hertwig, R., Pleskac, T. J., & Pachur, T. (2019). *Taming uncertainty.* MIT Press.

Hickson, D. J., Hinings, C. R., Lee, C. A., Schneck, R. E., & Pennings, J. M. (1971). A strategic contingencies' theory of intraorganizational power. *Administrative Science Quarterly, 16*(2), 216–229.

Hirshleifer, J., & Riley, J. G. (1979). The analytics of uncertainty and information-an expository survey. *Journal of Economic Literature, 17*(4), 1375–1421.

Hmieleski, K. M., Carr, J. C., & Baron, R. A. (2015). Integrating discovery and creation perspectives of entrepreneurial action: The relative roles of founding CEO human capital, social capital, and psychological capital in contexts of risk versus uncertainty. *Strategic Entrepreneurship Journal, 9*(4), 289–312.

Hodgson, G. M. (2011). The eclipse of the uncertainty concept in mainstream economics. *Journal of Economic Issues, 45*(1), 159–176.

Kay, J. A., & King, M. A. (2020). *Radical uncertainty*. Bridge Street Press.

Keynes, J.M. (1937 [1973]). The general theory of employment. In *The collected writings of John Maynard Keynes* (Vol. 14, pp. 109–123). Macmillan, Cambridge University Press for the Royal Economic Society.

Knight, F. H. (1921/64). *Risk, uncertainty and profit*. Augustus M. Kelley.

Koopmans, T. C. (1957). *Three essays on the state of economic science*. McGraw Hill.

Kozyreva, A., & Hertwig, R. (2021). The interpretation of uncertainty in ecological rationality. *Synthese, 198*(2), 1517–1547.

Kuhlthau, C. C. (1993). A principle of uncertainty for information seeking. *Journal of Documentation, 49*(4), 339–355.

Langlois, R. N., & Cosgel, M. M. (1993). Frank Knight on risk, uncertainty, and the firm: A new interpretation. *Economic Inquiry, 31*(3), 456–465.

Lawrence, P. R. & Lorsch, J.W. (1967). Differentiation and integration in complex organizations. *Administrative Science Quarterly, 12*, 1–47.

Lipshitz, R., & Strauss, O. (1997). Coping with uncertainty: A naturalistic decision-making analysis. *Organizational Behavior and Human Decision Processes, 69*(2), 149–163.

Machina, M. J. (1987). Choice under uncertainty: Problems solved and unsolved. *Journal of Economic Perspectives, 1*(1), 121–154.

Mack, R. P. (1971). *Planning on uncertainty*. John Wiley.

Magnani, G., & Zucchella, A. (2018). Uncertainty in entrepreneurship and management studies: A systematic literature review. *International Journal of Business and Management, 13*(3), 98–133.

Marchau, V. A., Walker, W. E., Bloemen, P. J. & Popper, S. W. (2019). *Decision making under deep uncertainty: From theory to practice*. Springer Nature.

McGrath, R. G. (1999). Falling forward: Real options reasoning and entrepreneurial failure. *Academy of Management Review, 24*(1), 13–30.

McMullen, J. S., & Shepherd, D. A. (2006). Entrepreneurial action and the role of uncertainty in the theory of the entrepreneur. *Academy of Management Review, 31*(1), 132–152.

Meijer, I. S., Hekkert, M. P., Faber, J., & Smits, R. E. (2006). Perceived uncertainties regarding socio-technological transformations: Towards a framework. *International Journal of Foresight and Innovation Policy, 2*(2), 214–240.

Miles, R. E., & Snow, C. C. (1978). *Organizational strategy, structure and process*. McGraw-Hill.

Milgrom, P., & Roberts, J. (1982). Limit pricing and entry under incomplete information: An equilibrium analysis. *Econometrica, 50*(2), 443–459.

Miller, A. I. (Ed.). (2012). *Sixty-two years of uncertainty: Historical, philosophical, and physical inquiries into the foundations of quantum mechanics* (Vol. 226). Springer Science & Business Media.

Miller, K. D. (2007). Risk and rationality in entrepreneurial processes. *Strategic Entrepreneurship Journal*, 1(1–2), 57–74.

Milliken, F. J. (1987). Three types of perceived uncertainty about the environment: State, effect, and response uncertainty. *Academy of Management Review*, 12(1), 133–143.

Mousavi, S., & Gigerenzer, G. (2014). Risk, uncertainty, and heuristics. *Journal of Business Research*, 67(8), 1671–1678.

Nash, S. J. (2003). On pragmatic philosophy and knightian uncertainty. *Review of Social Economy*, 61(2), 251–272.

Pennings, J. M., & Tripathi, R. C. (1978). The organization-environment relationship: Dimensional versus typological viewpoints. In L. Karpik (Ed.), *Organization and environment* (pp. 171–195). Sage.

Pennings, J. M. (1981). Strategically interdependent organizations. In P. C. Nystrom & W. H. Starbuck (Eds.), *Handbook of organizational design* (Vol. 1, pp. 433–455). Oxford University Press.

Pfeffer, J., & Salancik, G. R. (1978). *The external control of organizations: A resource dependence perspective*. Harper & Row Publishers.

Posner, R. A. (2004). *Catastrophe: Risk and response*. Oxford University Press.

Raiffa, L., & Luce, R.D. (1957). *Games and decisions: Introduction and critical survey*. Wiley.

Ramoglou, S. (2021). Knowable opportunities in an unknowable future? On the epistemological paradoxes of entrepreneurship theory. *Journal of Business Venturing*, 36(2), 106090.

Rapp, D. J., & Olbrich, M. (2020). On entrepreneurial decision logics under conditions of uncertainty: An attempt to advance the current debate. *Journal of Innovation and Entrepreneurship*, 9(1), 21.

Rowe, W. D. (1994). Understanding uncertainty. *Risk Analysis*, 14(5), 743–750.

Samsami, F., Hosseini, S. H. K., Kordnaeij, A., & Azar, A. (2015). Managing environmental uncertainty: From conceptual review to strategic management point of view. *International Journal of Business and Management*, 10(7), 215–229.

Schmidt, S. M., & Cummings, L. L. (1976). Organizational environment, differentiation and perceived environmental uncertainty. *Decision Sciences*, 7, 447–467.

Schoemaker, P. J. (2002). *Profiting from uncertainty: strategies for succeeding no matter what the future brings*. Simon & Schuster.

Scoblic, J. P. (2020). Learning from the future. *Harvard Business Review*, 98(4), 38–47.

Spender, J. -C. (1983). The business policy problem and industry recipes. *Advances in Strategic Management, 2*, 211–229.

Spender, J. -C. (2006). *Knightian uncertainty and its resolution as institutionalized practice* (v9 Working Paper).

Sunstein, C. R. (2007). *Worst-case scenarios*. Harvard University Press.

Taleb, N. N. (2007). *The black swan: The impact of the highly improbable*. Random House.

Teece, D., Peteraf, M., & Leih, S. (2016). Dynamic capabilities and organizational agility: Risk, uncertainty, and strategy in the innovation economy. *California Management Review, 58*(4), 13–35.

The Temptations. (1970). *Ball of confusion*. Gordy (Motown) Label (Written by N. Whitfield and B. Strong).

Townsend, D. M., Hunt, R. A., McMullen, J. S., & Sarasvathy, S. D. (2018). Uncertainty, knowledge problems, and entrepreneurial action. *Academy of Management Annals, 12*(2), 659–687.

Walker, W. E., Harremoës, P., Rotmans, J., Van Der Sluijs, J. P., Van Asselt, M. B., Janssen, P., & Krayer von Krauss, M. P. (2003). Defining uncertainty: A conceptual basis for uncertainty management in model-based decision support. *Integrated Assessment, 4*(1), 5–17.

CHAPTER 4

Sources of Uncertainty (in Decision-Making)

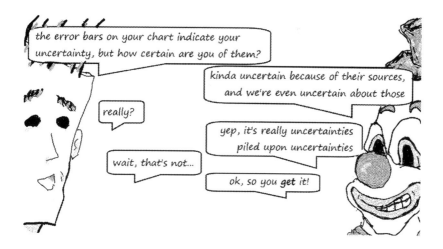

Why the Causes of Uncertainties are Important

With a deeper understanding of the sources of uncertainty comes more possibilities to treat it now and in the future. With knowledge of the causes, it is often easier to predict or control the uncertainties that result. At a minimum, when the drivers are identified, then there is a possibility of monitoring or measuring them to study how, when, where, why, and for whom the resulting uncertainties are produced. In this chapter, we consider a myriad of potential causes of uncertainties—from outside and inside the affected decision-maker's realm—and then attempt to group them in order to provide greater clarity to this part of the uncertainty story.

It is in this chapter that we begin thinking in earnest about the appropriate way(s) to categorize uncertainties. We do so in this book in terms of the treatability of the various types of uncertainty, and in this chapter we do so in terms of the treatability of possible causes. We start with the question of whether any of the causes are unknown. We do this because if that is the case then it makes 'their' treatment impossible (i.e., the treatment of both the cause and the uncertainty itself). If the unknowableness of the cause is the first division of that categorization, then the secondary divisions involve only known causes of uncertainties. (We note that for any one decision, or any one uncertainty involved in that decision, it is possible for there to be *multiple* causes).

In terms of known possible causes, we divide these into two groups—those concerning the decision problem itself, and those concerning the limits of its analysis. For each group, there are three subgroups (and several sub-subgroups). In terms of the causes related to the problem itself, we consider those arising from the characteristics of the problem, from relevant exogenous sources, and from relevant endogenous sources. In terms of the causes related to the limits of the problem's analysis, we consider those that are general, those that arise at the organizational level, and those that arise at the individual (decision-maker) level. Table 4.1 depicts the groups and items of the main causes of uncertainty.

Reminder—How a Cause's Symptoms Can Manifest in a Decision to Make it Non-Optimizable

It is useful to recall that we are looking at causes of uncertainties that appear as unknown factors that impede moving from one decision process

Table 4.1 The possible sources of uncertainty

Sources Related to the Problem Itself	...in the Problem's Characteristics	novelty/uniqueness complexity non-linear, dynamic systems and chaos ill-definition issues with the relationship with time/intertemporal choice other (e.g., impossible problems)
	...in the Problem's External (to Decision-Maker) Context	new technologies inherent randomness of nature 'luck' (randomness *for* humans) inconsistent (often rivalrous) external human behaviors ...the dynamic aspects of such behaviors conflicting external reports
	...in the Problem's Internal (to Decision-Maker) Context	change and its consequences (inside) communications issues individual/decision-maker artefacts and choices biases, and errors in statistical analysis blissful ignorance and dangerous implicit assumptions
Sources Related to the Limits of Analysis	General Limits	laws and regulations measurement error computational limits over current facts mathematical limits 'system'-atic errors incomplete modeling empirical non-verifiability
	Organizational Limits	lack of investigatory time lack of other investigatory resources

(continued)

Table 4.1 (continued)

Individual Limits	human/employee/agency limits lack of control lack of expertise epistemic issues/decision-maker weaknesses

step to the next—i.e., we are looking at the causes of incompletely known goals, options, outcomes, probabilities, payoffs, and more[1]. For example, sources of imprecise information can induce probability imprecision (Aggarwal & Mohanty, 2022). Our limited imaginations to conjure possible future states may make it impossible to attribute to them any probability (Dequech, 2011). Our limited measurement presence may miss when extreme outcomes are much more frequent than expected and affect our understanding of the problem context (Kay & King, 2020). Our inability to notice possible differences in the spatial or temporal location of outcomes may affect the completeness in our modeling of the problem (Hertwig et al., 2019). Parts of an economic system in which we transact may be hidden, creating uncertainties in exchange relationships (Adobor, 2006). The timing of a decision may be unclear due to the complex dynamics of the underlying system (Hertwig et al., 2019). And, so on.

SOURCES OF UNCERTAINTY RELATED TO THE PROBLEM ITSELF

We forge ahead with our analysis now under the assumption that *the possible causes of the focal uncertainties are known*[2]. We are set to explore those in a logical manner starting with the sources related to the problem

---

[1] Note that one source can affect multiple decision steps; for example, if some cause impedes the identification of choices, then it also impedes the identification of outcomes under those missing choices and more.

[2] Note that this implies those possible causes are known at the 'highest' level of analysis where a final diagnosis of treatability can be made; we are not considering going down the rabbit holes of causes of causes of causes (e.g., if the cause is a lack of expertise, that can be treated; the reason for that lack of expertise is not needed to treat its current effect).

itself. These can be classified into three groups: We start with the decision problem's characteristics—i.e., the kinds of characteristics that can generate uncertainties. We keep these as general as possible at this point, understanding that any specific characteristic (or cause) would need to be examined in greater depth once a specific decision problem was provided. We then move on to the sources that are exogenous—external to the decision-maker—that create uncertainties in the problem. We finish up with the sources that are endogenous—internal to the decision-maker—that create uncertainties in the problem.

Sources in the Problem Characteristics

Uncertainties often arise when a problem is not simple or clear—when it is difficult to understand what it is or how it works. Problem characteristics that are likely to generate such uncertainties include: novelty; complexity; non-linear dynamics and chaos; ill-definition; an unusual relationship with time; and, other more pointed issues.

Novelty/Uniqueness

When a problem is new or unique then there is often no basis for certainty about its possible outcomes, their probabilities, the options to influence them, and so on. Such uncertainties can arise when a paradigm shift occurs that alters axioms (Dosi & Egidi, 1991). The novelty can be brought about by a newly emerging technology—in the form of ignorance about its possible applications (Kapoor & Klueter, 2021). Such novelty violates the Savage framework—as there is no mutually exclusive, collectively exhaustive state space given; instead, these initially unique problems can involve many unforeseen contingencies (Bradley & Drechsler, 2014).

Complexity of Phenomena

Theoretically (i.e., with super-rational agents), complexity alone should not create uncertainty. Practically, it often does because real decision-makers cannot keep track of all the interactions that can occur in the complex systems that some problems embody. Such complexity generates uncertainty (e.g., in terms of causal indeterminacy—Packard & Clark,

2020), not risk (Mousavi & Gigerenzer, 2014). Many real complex interactions are not only *a priori* irreducible, but the uncertainty associated with them is often increased *ex post* because of unforeseen consequences of operating in those contexts (Townsend et al., 2018). Indeed, irreducible uncertainties can arise out of the intrinsic limits to predictability that occur when dealing with complex systems (Marchau et al., 2019).

Complexity can be seen in intractable problems like the *traveling salesman* and other like *NP* mathematical challenges (Barrow, 1998). It can also be seen in entrepreneurial opportunities, where it has been argued that the existence of any one viable opportunity is unknowable because of the 'indefinitely large number' of interacting ingredients that create it (Ramoglou, 2021).

Complexity itself can arise from a range of social and organizational sources. For example, it can arise from the aggregation of factors that are influenced by a large number of interacting micro-level actions of various agents (Townsend et al., 2018). It may even arise from the interconnections of systems of problems (e.g., relating to illicit drug use) and the impossibility of knowing everything (e.g., due to privacy concerns) (Bammer & Smithson, 2008). Or, it may arise due to the interaction of different sources of uncertainty in a pooled, sequential, or reciprocal way (Kapoor & Klueter, 2021).

Even trying to model such complex problems—e.g., as searches over interdependent landscapes—can imply a catastrophe, as simulated decision-makers face growing numbers of factors and greater interdependence among them (Fleming, 2001).

Non-linear Dynamic Systems and Chaos

Non-linearities are difficult to model and thus to predict (Rowe, 1994). The hyper-sensitivity of chaotic systems to initial conditions makes those systems practically impossible to predict as well. However, such entropic and chaotical systems do exist in nature, always generating uncertainty (Stewart, 2019). Non-linear dynamics invoke irreducible uncertainties (Bammer & Smithson, 2008). Further, the 'other' chaos—as an absence of rules (rather than as a type of mathematical system)—also creates uncertainty in the economy (Porter, 1980; Taylor, 2003). Such chaos— as seen in today's global innovation economy where existing rules are being changed while entirely new rules are being invented—brings unpredictability and even irreducible ignorance for firms and investors (Faber & Faber, 2012; Teece et al., 2016).

Ill-Defined Problems

A problem that is incompletely described often creates uncertainties that impede its optimization. A state of doubt arises often from an incomplete situation that leads to perplexity, confusion, and hesitation (Kuhlthau, 1993). When it is not even clear what the decision is all about, when the scope of the decision is indeterminate, or what it is supposed to solve is undefined, then ambiguity and uncertainty occur (Bammer & Smithson, 2008; Hansson, 1996; Mousavi & Gigerenzer, 2017). This can happen when a client/principal's directions are vague or uninformed, when predicates are ill-defined, when rules are implicit, and when relationships are unclear (e.g., Samsami et al., 2015). Such problems are ill-structured or afflicted by structural defects (Adam & Witte, 1979).

Relationships with Time

Uncertainty has an existential relationship with time (i.e., as in: no future, no past, then no uncertainty) (Bernstein, 1996). Given there is a future, time exists, and any delay between a choice and its feedback increases the scope for further uncertainties to arise (i.e., in terms of time for other events to occur that affect the focal outcome). As such, uncertainty is pervasive in problems with intertemporal choice—like *the marshmallow test* (Hertwig et al., 2019; Samsami et al., 2015). Time is the dominant factor in gambling; delay, real or not, generates risk and uncertainty (Bammer & Smithson, 2008; Nosal & Ordoñez, 2016).

Other (Pointed) Issues

There are other, more specific, and pointed issues possible with a problem that can generate uncertainties. At the most basic level, a lack of information about the problem can lead to substantive uncertainty (Packard et al., 2017). For example, there exists a number of well-known 'undecidable problems' in computational theory—those arising out of our own constructed languages of logic, mathematics, topology, and so forth. There are also the 'impossible challenges' that can be given by bad actors to others as some form of punishment—e.g., to write a 'golden rule' (for riches), to prove a negative, or to provide an implementable solution for a situation that is unlikely to have one (e.g., a feasible path to world peace).

SOURCES IN THE PROBLEM'S EXTERNAL CONTEXT (EXOGENOUS TO THE DECISION-MAKER)

Some problems involving uncertainty are created due to various external forces, often observed in the form of disruption or shock (Knight, 1921; O'Connor & Rice, 2013). Such external sources that do so include: innovations (Teece et al., 2016); the inherent randomness of nature and luck; inconsistent human behaviors and reactions (Dequech, 2003, 2011); and, getting conflicting outside information. At present, there is no theory for dealing with such shocks (Bradley & Drechsler, 2014).

New Technology

Uncertainties are common in interdependent economies experiencing rapid technological progress (Teece et al., 2016). Radical innovation generates high levels of uncertainty (Eggers & Park, 2018; O'Connor & Rice, 2013) because the new technologies involved entail discontinuities in input-output knowledge, in costs, in processes, and in commercializable products (Schoemaker, 2002; Wernerfelt & Karnani, 1987). New technologies involve significant uncertainties regarding whether and when their potentials may be realized (Kapoor & Klueter, 2021). And, such technologies are even more rampant now due to compressed new product development and adoption cycles.

Any one technological change can generate a wide range of possible entrepreneurial opportunities, many of which are unknown to firms (Shane, 2000). The more radical technologies can even transform existing markets and industries in unpredictable ways, or create completely new ones (O'Connor & Rice, 2013).

New technology also creates uncertainties in terms of the timing (e.g., the delay) and range (e.g., in size, location, or audience) of their impacts (Dattee et al., 2018). Such uncertainties involve the adoption and diffusion of new technologies, the level of market and customer acceptance, and competitors' strategic reactions (Fleming, 2001; Rosenberg, 1996). These uncertainties persist despite models of such events, like the product life-cycle archetype, models that may be useful as educational tools but are poor in prediction (Anderson & Tushman, 1990; Fleming, 2001; Klepper, 1997).

Even the processes that generate the new technologies involve significant uncertainties. For example, such uncertainties may be found in inventors' search processes with unfamiliar components and their untried combinations (Fleming, 2001).

All that said, it is useful to acknowledge that new technologies can also act to reduce some uncertainties (e.g., related to complexity, process, origins, and cause-and-effect relationships) by providing cheaper and faster access to data, testing, simulation and statistical analysis (Dosi & Egidi, 1991).

The Inherent Randomness of Nature

True randomness (e.g., not draws from a known distribution) generates uncertainty; and, nature often provides such randomness (Rowe, 1994). A characteristic of nature—entropy—captures the idea that there are more ways to pass from order to disorder than vice versa (Barrow, 1998). Uncertainty is a primary and inherent feature of nature. In many cases, no amount of knowledge can make events predictable because the system itself doesn't know what it is going to do. As the physicist Feynman remarked—*if you think you understand quantum mechanics, you don't understand quantum mechanics* (Stewart, 2019). This inherent randomness often spills over into issues with the attempted (and imperfect) measurements of such systems, as the inevitable variability in doing so ends up contributing to additional uncertainty in further dimensions (Rowe, 1994).

Luck [as Randomness for Humans]

Besides the randomness that affects many focal problems, sometimes that outside randomness works with a decision-maker more specifically. That is often labeled as *luck*; it is unpredictable and not probabilistic. For example, it may 'explain' why one inventor is successful over another who has similar skills and puts in similar effort. And, through what is a stochastic process, some lucky people possess valuable information that others do not have and so can make better decisions (Nelson & Winter, 1982; Shane, 2000).

Inconsistent (Often Rivalrous) External Human Behaviors

The actions of our fellow humans are often hard to predict because we cannot see into their minds, hearts, or other organs and spirits that may affect their behaviors from one minute to the next (Dosi & Egidi, 1991). Given many problems have more to do with people rather than physics (and as our knowledge of the hard sciences progresses), human interactions are an ever more important source of uncertainties to consider (Bernstein, 1996). As Newton has remarked—*I can calculate the movement of stars, but not the madness of men* (Stewart, 2019). Similarly, Knight harbored so many doubts about the rationality of human beings, to believe that measuring their behaviors would be academically useless (Bernstein, 1996).

At present, humans appear unaccountable for generating uncertainty-filled threats to each other for their own benefit (e.g., through global warming; pollution; toxic chemicals; AI-generated disinformation; radiation; and, so on). At best, it seems that authoring an uncertain threat is only impermissible when it can be identified and then proven that inadequate due care was taken to insulate others from potential harm (Szentkirályi, 2020), which is not often. Instead, the capability to generate unforeseeable changes to others is seen as a strength (Dosi & Egidi, 1991). (A strength that, fairly, can also be used for 'good'—as in creating ambiguity in language to speed negotiations or to create entertainment through irony [Bradac, 2001]).

Forms of these uncertainties—involving interdependencies with others—are formalized in game theory. Outside of *Folk* theorems, however, most games can be solved (i.e., in that they have less than infinite possible stable outcomes), at least in terms of what occurs when rational players choose (e.g., as calculable [Nash] equilibrium outcomes). So, expected values can be computed in such simplified models even when there is uncertainty over the intensions and actions of others (Bernstein, 1996). That provides one idealized benchmark. In reality, much of the information needed to solve these games is hidden or questionable; because people lie, as does nature (e.g., in camouflage), in order to control others (Stewart, 2019).

When departing from the rational behaviors modeled in game theory, uncertainties arise from interdependent players who are ignorant, inconsistent, or irrational (Brafman & Brafman, 2008; Rowe, 1994). Free will makes prediction difficult (Barrow, 1998), especially when it means that people will accept sweeping claims when there is no serious evidence to support them, or worse, that people will readily embrace irrational beliefs even when there's clear evidence against those (Stewart, 2019). Social pressures (e.g., the pressure not to stand out) can even create doubt-as-uncertainty where none had existed or needs to (Brafman & Brafman, 2008). When these things happen, nature, even with its many vagaries, appears much more dependable than a group of people trying to make up their minds about something (Bernstein, 1996).

These human-based uncertainties are only exacerbated by increased globalization (where we interact more with people who are even less-known to us than before). Whipsawing regulatory changes and growing stock market volatilities highlight the impacts (Schoemaker, 2002). In practice, these sources of uncertainty need to be understood in terms of both their possible objective and subjective (i.e., perceived) impacts on society (Berger & Luckmann, 1966), in addition to both their micro-level impacts and how those add up to potential macro-level ones (e.g., the prospect of wide-ranging war) (Keynes, 1937; Townsend et al., 2018). Doing so is a great challenge, however, given changing political agendas and societal values, the limited access to data, and any fragmentation of responsibilities in agencies that would have the budget to do it (Bammer & Smithson, 2008). On the brighter side, when the interactions with others are repeated, it is sometimes possible to either detect patterns of behavior or to build trust in order to reduce the uncertainties they bring to a problem (Adobor, 2006).

Dynamic Aspects of Inconsistent External Human Behaviors (as Unpredictable Reactions)

When the problem includes dynamics—multiple time periods, at least some of which involve other parties reacting to the decision-maker's actions or to uncertainties—then there are further issues to consider (e.g., more uncertainties over when, where, how, who, what, and why outsiders will affect the relevant outcomes). As military strategist von Clausewitz noted—*war does not work in a mathematical way because it is radically uncertain, reflexive and a collective activity* (Kay & King, 2020).

Continuing interactions with other sentient beings (for good or bad) cause a cascading and sometimes exponential increase in options, making predictability impossible (Packard et al., 2017). When the agents being predicted can react (and exploit those predictions), the probability of a correct forecast can drop dramatically (Barrow, 1998). For example, when governments cannot commit to *not* providing bailouts (i.e., leaving some residual uncertainty in the market), then banks may take excessive risks and generate crises (and further uncertainties) (Nosal & Ordoñez, 2016).

Even when the action-reaction cycle is not combative, uncertainties can grow over time rather than lessen. Actions to generate knowledge to reduce uncertainty can result in basic breakthroughs in technology—ones that then create the disequilibrium conditions characterized by new uncertainties (some of which have social benefits in the form of new products) (Taylor, 2003). Reactions to problems generate innovation, new routines, and new uncertainties for decision-makers and for others (Dosi & Egidi, 1991). Sometimes the reaction to problems is to try an insulate the system from the uncertain environment (Samsami et al., 2015); but, even then, when that system is pushed toward its limits of efficiency it often becomes highly sensitive to disturbances and so when the insulation is inevitably breached, the price paid is often in the form of a costly surprise (e.g., as when the supply chains broke disastrously for some during the pandemic) (Barrow, 1998).

Conflicting External Reports

Uncertainty can be caused by conflicts of opinion. When the gap of consensus is sufficiently large, then one or more items remain unknown in the decision process (e.g., the range of possible outcomes), making that problem unoptimizable. Such uncertainties are more likely to emerge when the relevant evidence for the phenomenon is unreliable and conflicting (Aggarwal & Mohanty, 2022; Einhorn & Hogarth, 1986; Frisch & Baron, 1988).

Such conflicts often arise with complex systems because those are more likely to involve a variety of stakeholders with different perspectives on what the system is, what the goals are, and even what the problem is that they are trying to solve (Marchau et al., 2019). Different people may reasonably (or unreasonably) arrive at different interpretations of the same problem or even the same set of 'facts' (Kay & King, 2020). On the unreasonable side, some problems elicit a maelstrom of deception and disinformation, due to power struggles, miscommunications, and secrecy (Bammer & Smithson, 2008); the resulting uncertainties can provide opportunities for a sudden rise of influence of an interest group, and so muddying the waters over the 'facts' can be useful. For example, some of the uncertainties over climate change have arisen due to disagreement of experts—some of whom could be argued to harbor ulterior motives (Bradley & Steele, 2015). Even when such motives are not expected to exist, the underlying information imprecision can lead experts to disagree. This conflict can be seen in some non-life insurance decisions where experts often clash over the probability of an event occurring (e.g., related to global warming) because of the lack of a large, reliable historical data base on such events (Cabantous, 2007). Sometimes, even when there is agreement at the expert level, fragmentation and a lack of coordination across relevant policy sectors may make it look like there is not.

SOURCES IN THE PROBLEM'S INTERNAL CONTEXT (ENDOGENOUS TO THE DECISION-MAKER)

We as decision-makers can be a significant source of a problem's apparent uncertainties due to our own sometimes unpredictable behaviors that create gaps, conflicts, errors, and misunderstandings in the process. To begin with, we have incomplete knowledge simply due to our bounded cognitive capacities (Hayek, 1948; Magnani & Zucchella, 2018). Even the origin and nature of consciousness and sensation that drives our cognition is unknown (Barrow, 1998).

Change and Its Consequences (Inside)

Any kind of significant change (including predictable change) can bring about uncertainty in people, that then generates new uncertainty over how they react (Kay & King, 2020; Rock, 2008), whether those people reside in our organization or outside of it. Being aware of the changing trends and goals may be a first step in helping control this source of uncertainty that arises in our organizations as they process decision problems (Bammer & Smithson, 2008).

Communications Issues

Uncertainties can arise from within due to ambiguities, noise, misinterpretations, and misrepresentations in communicating knowledge within the organization (unintentionally or not). They can occur with the sender, the receiver, or the lines of communications themselves. Line degradation occurs with distance, potentially causing uncertainty (Bammer &

Smithson, 2008). Member (i.e., sender or receiver) participation may also be unknown (Stager, 1967). Even in the animal kingdom and within the same species, communications are not actually used to disseminate the truth, but instead to maximize personal fitness (Barrow, 1998). Often, it is the mode of communication that can create uncertainties—such as the ambiguities found in most languages (e.g., with words and phrases having multiple meanings) (Kay & King, 2020). And, even with words alone, there are concerns—given that food labels and terminologies can be misused and cause confusion (Hertwig et al., 2019; Rowe, 1994).

Personal Artefacts and Choices

Decision-maker idiosyncrasies and self-interests can be sources of uncertainty. A decision-maker's tools can be unknown or produce unpredictable results (Hertwig et al., 2019). Decision-making delays, especially underexplained ones, can create uncertainties (Bammer & Smithson, 2008). Government officials and their committees have been shown to be quite skilled in avoiding clear, measurable goals and targets—intentionally generating ambiguities for private gain (e.g., in terms of deniability should something go wrong). As well, the more-entrepreneurial actors often want to find or generate uncertainties as a means to create opportunities and freedoms for themselves (Bammer & Smithson, 2008).

Biases and Errors in Statistical Analysis

Uncertainty can emerge from self-serving research, from using intentionally biased sources, or simply from sloppy work. Most published research findings are 'essentially false' (Ioannidis, 2005) because they are not replicated in subsequent studies; replication rates are below 50 percent in economics, even when the original studies are based on large datasets. That rate is likely much worse when studies—many in management and most in entrepreneurship—are based on proprietary data (Kay & King, 2020). Researchers tend to report only positive and significant results because other results are not publishable (and this has proven problematic in the past for tobacco and pharmaceutical product related studies). Unless *all* trials are reported, claims of statistical significance are essentially meaningless. But, all trials will never be reported because people do not pursue lines of research that do not appear to produce significant results (Kay & King, 2020). Even when unintentional, the act of sampling data from a population, especially when its distribution is not fully understood, can result in misrepresentative outcomes and add uncertainty to the problem (Einhorn & Hogarth, 1986).

Blissful Ignorance and Dangerous Implicit Assumptions

Sadly, sometimes uncertainty comes from simply not wanting to know the dangers, or the possible outcomes, or even the range of options available, of a likely decision or issue (often because it would hurt a different goal, usually one involving self-protection). Sometimes termed 'closed ignorance' or 'nescience', this choice entails an absence of knowledge, often self-imposed (Gross, 2007). Closed ignorance results from rejecting or ignoring available knowledge, which has been referred to as the '*Galileo effect*' (Tannert et al., 2007). An intentional lack of awareness about the consequences of a decision has often been used to try to escape responsibility (e.g., as a form of plausible deniability) (Samsami et al., 2015). So, such inattention can be rational or irrational in nature (Kay & King, 2020). Non-knowing has many terms, such as willful ignorance, the conscious inability to know, and reflected non-knowing (Beck, 2009).

Uncertainty can also be caused by decision-makers holding dangerous, often implicit, assumptions about the information they source (e.g., about the good intentions of the people that they manage and monitor). Take the case of TSCA's Toxic Release Inventory—here, government regulators not only permit emitters to self-report their own chemical substance release data, but they also limit the number of chemicals requiring reports of emission to only 60 of the 80,000 substances in use (the latter of which remain largely untested by regulators!) (Shrader-Frechette, 2007; Szentkirályi, 2020). Whether this is a frightening example of regulatory capture, or a result of short-sighted budget allocations, several alarming uncertainties about public health appear to be involved.

LIMITS OF ANALYSIS

Besides the uncertainties that relate to the problem itself (and its decision-maker), there are a myriad of uncertainties that arise from the *limits* that exist on analyzing the problem. These can be roughly grouped by specificity, from general to those limits more connected to the organization and then to those limits more connected to the individual decision-maker. We acknowledge that the grouping is imperfect, with some overlap (e.g., because organizational limits may affect the individual and vice versa). Such limits involve those imposed by nature itself, directly and indirectly (Barrow, 1998).

General Limits to Problem Analysis

General limits involve contextual issues that apply to many organizations, such as privacy laws. These limits impinge on the decision-maker's ability to obtain complete information, sometimes resulting in having unknowns in one or more steps of the decision process, making that decision unoptimizable.

Laws and Regulations

Laws and regulations limit the types and amounts of information available to decision-makers, creating unknowns. Further, changes in them can cause uncertainty, as can the unpredictability of when and what kind of changes occur. Still further, there are also uncertainties about the decisions on when to apply those laws and regulations and against whom by the prosecutors and plaintiffs involved.

Besides creating limits on information-gathering, laws and regulations create uncertainty about those limits themselves. Given that how laws and regulations are written and interpreted is not always clear, even when precedents exist (e.g., *Roe v. Wade* in the US), ambiguity over what those limits actually are often remains. The trial process (that is supposed to apply those laws and clarify the limits) can also be open to a wide range of uncertainties involving jury behavior, judicial rulings, witness reliability, and conflicting evidence.

For businesses, in the US, Common Law State Tort can affect an organization's ability to gain, maintain, or lose market share (or even go bankrupt) as it affects the relationships between free enterprise and the consumer (Krumbein, 2012). In addition to uncertainties about that law, firms are also subject to competition law (e.g., through the Sherman Antitrust Act) that helps ensure that they do not act in ways to gain an unfair advantage or that abuse any market power that they may accrue. As such, the authors and enforcers of such laws produce significant uncertainties for those governed under them, especially when strategic moves are contemplated (e.g., product bundling; mergers; joint ventures; and, so on) (Hertwig et al., 2019).

Measurement Error

Much of the data we gather for making decisions is affected by the precision with which it is measured. Errors in measurement caused by limits in our technology can create unknowns, or at least doubts in what we believe we know, that affect decision steps. We are bounded by the instruments we use to gather information (including our own senses and cognition) and that can produce or exacerbate uncertainties. What we know is always separated from what is real by our brains; there exists an unbreachable gap between what we can know about a thing and what it actually is (Barrow, 1998). The resulting imprecision can produce the kind of ambiguity that challenges decision-making (Du & Budescu, 2005; Kuhn & Budescu, 1996). Further, that gap often comes in the form of information that is received too late, that is irrelevant, or that is inaccurate—the kind of information that in many cases increases uncertainty (Bammer & Smithson, 2008).

We are limited in the measurements we can take and that affects the level of analysis we can get to. In terms of the ultimate origin of natural forces and the nature of matter, we are barred from observation. These facts are ultimately hidden from us because they require the ability to extrapolate down to infinitesimally small sizes and to identify all the forces that act there. By definition (of physical properties), such abilities are unavailable (Barrow, 1998).

As an example of error assessment, simply consider the algebra behind the total number of errors that exist when two agents are tasked with finding them: the number of unfound errors equals the product of the number found only by Jack and the number found only by Jill divided by the number found by them both. Leveraging this equation, we can work out some interesting conditions: when the overlap of found errors is below 41 percent then the number of unfound errors is greater than the number found; and, even when the overlap is 90 percent, the proportion of unfound errors is about 38 percent of those found. In other words, even using multiple error checkers to increase accuracy, error rates can still remain significantly high (with the related uncertainty persisting).

Computational Limits over Current Facts

Most decisions require knowledge about current conditions, if not past ones (e.g., as a basis for relative computations). Unfortunately, the veracity of that knowledge is sometimes in doubt. For example, historic narratives are often false, self-serving, biased, and otherwise limited; relying on them as a basis for computing outcomes may be questionable (Kay & King, 2020). Given a worse state of technology in the past, including that related to measurement instruments, the possibility of errors in past state conditions can give rise to further uncertainty (Rowe, 1994). Poor knowledge of the past may also put into question any causal relationships we believe exist now in a current system, the one that affects the new decision (Kay & King, 2020). Holes in our past knowledge also reduce our awareness of present facts and uncertainties (Shane, 2000).

Mathematical Limits

Mathematics has progressed sufficiently far to prove that it has limits to what it can do both theoretically (see Gödel) and practically (e.g., most solutions to equations of greater than degree 4 are not algebraically tractable; and, some problems have no algorithmic solution—Rapp & Olbrich, 2020). So now any attempt at the complete understanding of a mathematical problem entails two prongs of attack: one to determine whether a solution is possible and, two, if so, to find any explicit solutions (Barrow, 1998). When no solution is possible, an unknown exists that could affect what a decision step needs (e.g., as a viable option or a possible outcome) in order to optimize the problem.

System-atic Errors

Limits to understanding and analysis also arise from the system that the decision problem involves. Although simplifying real systems into 'small world' models helps with general understanding, the exercise is most often useless for forecasting. Uncertainty, besides arising from the decision-maker or the surrounding context alone, can also emerge from the mind–environment system and others (Kozyreva & Hertwig, 2021; Todd & Gigerenzer, 2012).

Dynamic systems limit understanding. When change is sufficiently fast, such systems are never completely understood in the moment of a decision (Marchau et al., 2019). The non-stationarity of some systems makes forecasting hopeless, as there is no underlying model or probability distribution to discover (Kay & King, 2020). For stochastic discontinuous systems, it is impossible to reconstruct what occurred using time regression, and often those unknowns linger (Rowe, 1994). Adding reactions by sentient agents to the workings of those systems makes uncertainty worse. For example, new technologies spur discontinuous changes in prices, demand volumes, and competition, which is then worsened by changes in individual preferences, expectations, and investments to exploit or leapfrog that technology (Kay & King, 2020), creating more unknowns. Sometimes inflection points result, and that can accelerate uncertainties as firms feel pressure to change without much planning—where their own resource discontinuities can then challenge the progress of such endeavors (O'Connor & Rice, 2013; Teece et al., 2016).

Tightly linked systems in time or function also limit control and knowledge and can lead to uncertainty. Intertemporal choice—in terms of the ability to delay change in the system—can add to uncertainty of when impacts are felt (Hertwig et al., 2019). Uncertainties can escalate from small deviations to larger and wider effects when functional linkages are tight and sensitive (Brafman & Brafman, 2008), limiting the ability to identify and treat them along the way. In many systems, the people involved operate in multiple worlds, where each world is molded by contextual factors intertwined with the very act of engaging in it, limiting the understanding of any one system and creating the possibility that factors will be unknown when making decisions involving that system (Bammer & Smithson, 2008).

Incomplete Modeling

We are often limited in the modeling of the phenomena underlying a decision problem. This can come from our doubts about the model's content, as well as from the finite and imperfect modeling tools we have available.

When we are unsure about which factors should be in the model, of the causes or the effects or the logic in the model, or its bounds, then unknowns are likely to arise in the decision process (Einhorn & Hogarth, 1986). The exclusion of factors as we translate a reality into a model will always occur. Even for mathematics, incompleteness is an issue. For example, arithmetic truth was something apparently too large to be ensnared by any formal system of rules, as Gödel revealed by logically proving that there were things that could not be proved (Barrow, 1998). When mathematicians discovered that Euclid's geometry of flat surfaces was not the sole logically consistent geometry but instead one of many, the idea of absolute truth was questioned. From such proofs and discoveries grew several varieties of relativism about our understanding of the world, resulting in the realization that even the concept of truth was not absolute. Essentially, it was determined that what was false in one model of a phenomenon could be true in another, making its 'true' state unknown (Barrow, 1998).

Modeling logic also limits our knowledge. When one sets up a system of rules of reasoning, then one is, by definition, placing limitations on what one counts as being true; and, given any one model is limited, so is the extent of what is known (Barrow, 1998). The nature of knowledge—as logical or mathematical models—imposes limits in terms of the unexpected properties and restrictions on its full exploration. There is no such thing as complete truthful knowledge, as it cannot be rigorously defined in the same order of language used to express it (Barrow, 1998). Having gaps in our information—unknowns—may affect the decision process. Ways around that have been proposed—such as to make such gaps fuzzy. Fuzzy set theory provides a way to deal with that kind of model imprecision (e.g., Rouvray, 1997).

Modeling real phenomena, such as major innovation projects, is often limited by a range of issues that are difficult to assess and capture, such: as strategic ambiguity (Zahra, 2008); varied organizational interpretive lenses (Dougherty & Hardy, 1996); competency gaps (Danneels, 2002; O'Connor & Rice (2013); and, poorly defined roles, responsibilities, policies, management rights, and property rights (Bammer & Smithson, 2008). Such gaps generate unknowns.

Empirical Non-Verifiability

In order to best understand a (real) problem, we have to empirically investigate it. Often, however, we cannot measure everything, due to issues of time, distance, non-interference, miniaturization, and so on. In such cases, we can theorize general cause-and-effect relationships, but precise factors and outcomes will then remain unknown (Ben-Haim, 2001). And, even if one of the researcher can know something, its verification (by others) may be impossible due to the limits of our communications. Such irreducible ignorance may arise from the ways in which we conceive the phenomena, make discoveries, and communicate such new knowledge (Faber et al., 1992). Empirical verifiability requires that any other trained scientist can replicate the initial findings, and sometimes that is impossible due to the uniqueness of the phenomenon, or the quality of the measurement tools, or the ambiguities of common (and even scientific) language (Wittgenstein, 1971).

Organizational Limits to Problem Analysis

Besides the general limits on the analysis of decision problems, further limits may be imposed by the characteristics of the organization contemplating the problem. For example, there may be a lack of investigatory time and resources, a lack of expertise or training for the employees, or a lack of control over the situation (where, in theory for an ideal firm, such items should not be lacking).

Lack of Investigatory Time

Real organizations face limited schedules and opportunities to investigate a problem prior to having to make a decision on it. Such temporal limits increase the chances that factors in the decision steps will be unknown (like the full set of options available or the full set of outcomes possible) when actions need to be taken.

Lack of Other Investigatory Resources

Besides a lack of time, real organizations face resource constraints. What the organization wants to know about the problem (even if it fully knew that) may not be what it can discover in the allotted time, given the allotted personnel, equipment, and budget (Packard & Clark, 2020). As such, pertinent factors will likely remain unknown when a decision has to be made. To think that everything that can be done will be done in a real organization is a pipedream; many things that are achievable in principle are not in practice due to the financial costs and the level of expertise involved, let alone the laws of thermodynamics (Barrow, 1998).

Human Limits

Even if time, tools, and budget are sufficient to understand the problem, the participants in the focal organization do have limits to their involvement due to contextual issues like culture, training, reporting structure, politics, communications systems, and motivation (e.g., through compensation). For example, governments faced significant uncertainties at the onset of the last financial crisis due to policy-makers being limited in their capacities to acquire and rapidly process information about the scope and severity of the problems due to many factors, including those related to their specific departments and their workings (Nosal & Ordoñez, 2016). Information-gap uncertainties can occur anywhere along the organization's hierarchy and even be caused by managerial inattention at any one level of reporting (Ben-Haim, 2001).

Lack of Control

Bureaucracies often produce a real, perceived, or exploitable lack of control for those employees in them. Being able to shirk responsibility in the steps of decision-making (e.g., in information-gathering or verification), or simply having the goal-determiners separated from the decision-makers separated from the action-implementors limits the effort, consistency and quality of the understanding of factors in a problem, and hence, also the amount of unknowns that can impede the decision (Dosi & Egidi, 1991).

INDIVIDUAL LIMITS TO PROBLEM ANALYSIS

Besides the general limits and those imposed by the characteristics of the affected organization, further limits to analyzing the problem may arise due to issues involving the individual decision-maker(s) conducting the process. These individual limits are often labeled *epistemic* in nature in terms of the uncertainties that they can generate; these limits can be due to a lack of expertise or other personal or human weaknesses.

Lack of Expertise

Not every person approaches the skill of a theoretically idealized decision-maker; most individuals lack some knowledge regarding a strategic decision that could impede its optimization. Uncertainty can be attributed to a lack of expertise or a lack of access to needed information in such cases (Aggarwal & Mohanty, 2022; Dequech, 2011; Samsami et al., 2015; Spender, 2006). Uncertainty can be considered as the difference between the amount of information required to make the right decision and the amount of information already possessed by the focal individual.

That gap itself is often caused by novelty. For example, due to the emergence of a new technology (Kapoor & Klueter, 2021). New experiences sometimes cannot be assimilated into the existing system of constructs in an individual's mind, and that can result in feelings of confusion and doubt which can increase when further new information is inconsistent and incompatible with existing constructs (Kuhlthau, 1993). In such cases of novelty, the future is often considered unpredictable because the entirety of the ingredients necessary for desirable outcomes is also unknowable by the decision-maker (Ramoglou, 2021).

Even when not caused by novelty, and outside of any organizational influence, the lack of individual expertise is a common phenomenon in decision-making. Consider day-traders: in the context of voluntarily investing in stock markets, these amateur individual investors face relevant missing information in a myriad of forms and still make decisions under uncertainty (although structured, most often non-strategic ones with known and rapid feedback mechanisms) (Aggarwal & Mohanty, 2022).

The level of expertise required to make effective strategic decisions often lies outside any one individual in specialized knowledge that is socially distributed across many employees (Berger & Luckmann, 1966). Such expertise can be technical, cultural, or even ethical (Bradley & Steele, 2015). But, there is no guarantee that such expertise, even when available within an organization, will be transmitted to the decision-maker in a truthful and timely manner. Note also that a lack expertise can be a cause of uncertainty both when there is too little and too much information (Bammer & Smithson, 2008).

Epistemic Issues/Decision-Maker Weakness

Individual decision-makers are host to a variety of other limitations on problem analysis besides any particular lack of expertise. Humans have weak input, throughput, and output processes that cause variation and surprise in evaluating and processing a problem. Although we may believe that we are rational, we are much more prone to irrational behavior than we realize, and situations in which this occurs are everywhere (Brafman & Brafman, 2008). For example, epistemic limitations occur often in climate-related decisions (Bradley & Steele, 2015).

We have input limitations due to our bounded senses and the ways we perceive and process the information that they provide (Hansson, 1994). We are often unable to recognize and interpret the relevant information even when it is available (Dosi & Egidi, 1991). We are a bundle of sensations that cannot know the actual reality lying behind those experiences (Gray, 2002).

We have throughput—computational—limitations due to the very narrow bandwidth of our brains (e.g., in working memory and conscious data processing) (e.g., Dosi & Egidi, 1991; Packard et al., 2017). We often apply a diagnosis bias where we put blinders on to all evidence that contradicts our initial thinking, which is a very bad way of dealing with uncertain situations (Brafman & Brafman, 2008). Worse, we often base such diagnoses on an excessive attention to prior, often subjective and unfounded, probabilities (Kay & King, 2020). We suffer from vulnerable preferences and expectations, mistaken inferences, and missed contingencies in our analyses (Heiner, 1983). We are easily overwhelmed when confronted by complexity, dynamism, or stochasticity (Packard & Clark, 2020). What results has been characterized as bounded rationality (Simon, 1955)—a rationalized form of irrational choice (Hertwig et al., 2019)—that is evident even when uncertainty does not exist.

We also have output limitations—which create uncertainties in outcomes; when we doubt our ability to execute (differentially) across alternatives then that affects the choice. Uncertainty can arise due to issues like our limited capacity for accuracy, speed, and span in implementing our planned choices (Knight, 1921).

Further, even when uncertainty is not isolated to the decision-maker or their environment (when it is not solely 'epistemic' or 'aleatory'— Bammer & Smithson, 2008), it can emerge from the interaction of the two—as 'ecological' (Hertwig et al., 2019).

Summary
Much of the relevant research remains agnostic about the sources of uncertainty, focusing on its embodiment alone (Fleming, 2001; Klepper, 1996; Nelson & Winter, 1982). That is bad, given it ignores opportunities to treat the causes and not just the symptoms of uncertainties. There are many possible sources; and, these can be roughly differentiated based on whether they are related to the specific problem (and its characteristics and processing) or to the limitations in dealing with any problem.

(Subgrouping can be based on the entity involved, such as the individual decision-maker or their organization.) Studying the possible drivers of uncertainty provides insights on where to look for them and how they change over time; such insights help with determining whether treating those sources is a worthwhile approach for addressing current and future uncertainties.

Why drivers of uncertainty matter:

- Being able to separate the unintentional from the intentional sources can lead to better accountability for the harms that the consequent uncertainties cause
- Being able to differentiate the sources is useful given they entail different treatments (with some being untreatable)

What the drivers of uncertainty mean for business and policy:

- For the endogenous sources, finding better ways to organize to minimize their impacts
- For the endogenous sources, identifying which rivals are more likely to suffer from them and exploiting that difference
- Identifying the sources that new technologies may feasibly address provides useful targeting information for funded R&D.

References

Adam, D., & Witte, T. (1979). Merkmale der Planung in gut-und schlechtstrukturierten Planungssituationen. *Das Wirtschaftsstudium, 8*(1), 380–386.

Adobor, H. (2006). Optimal trust? Uncertainty as a determinant and limit to trust in inter-firm alliances. *Leadership & Organization Development Journal, 27*(7), 537–553.

Aggarwal, D., & Mohanty, P. (2022). Influence of imprecise information on risk and ambiguity preferences: Experimental evidence. *Managerial and Decision Economics, 43*(4), 1025–1038.

Anderson, P., & Tushman, M. L. (1990). Technological discontinuities and dominant designs: A cyclical model of technological change. *Administrative Science Quarterly, 35*(4), 604–633.

Bammer, G., & Smithson, M. (2008). Understanding uncertainly. *Integration Insights, 7*(1), 1–7.

Barrow, J. D. (1998). *Impossibility: The limits of science and the science of limits.* Oxford University Press on Demand.

Beck, U. (2009). *World at risk.* Polity.

Ben-Haim, Y. (2001). Decision trade-offs under severe info-gap uncertainty. *ISIPTA* (June), 32–39.
Berger, P. & Luckmann, T. (1966). *The social construction of reality*. Penguin Book.
Bernstein, P. L. (1996). *Against the gods: The remarkable story of risk*. Wiley.
Bradac, J. J. (2001). Theory comparison: Uncertainty reduction, problematic integration, uncertainty management, and other curious constructs. *Journal of Communication, 51*(3), 456–476.
Bradley, R., & Drechsler, M. (2014). Types of uncertainty. *Erkenntnis, 79*, 1225–1248.
Bradley, R., & Steele, K. (2015). Making climate decisions. *Philosophy Compass, 10*(11), 799–810.
Brafman, O., & Brafman, R. (2008). *Sway: The irresistible pull of irrational behavior*. Doubleday Business.
Cabantous, L. (2007). Ambiguity aversion in the field of insurance: Insurers' attitude to imprecise and conflicting probability estimates. *Theory and Decision, 62*(3), 219–240.
Danneels, E. (2002). The dynamics of product innovation and firm competences. *Strategic Management Journal, 23*(12), 1095–1121.
Dattée, B., Alexy, O., & Autio, E. (2018). Maneuvering in poor visibility: How firms play the ecosystem game when uncertainty is high. *Academy of Management Journal, 61*(2), 466–498.
Dequech, D. (2003). Uncertainty and economic sociology: A preliminary discussion. *American Journal of Economics and Sociology, 62*(3), 509–532.
Dequech, D. (2011). Uncertainty: a typology and refinements of existing concepts. *Journal of Economic Issues, 45*(3), 621–640.
Dosi, G., & Egidi, M. (1991). Substantive and procedural uncertainty: an exploration of economic behaviours in changing environments. *Journal of Evolutionary Economics, 1*, 145–168.
Dougherty, D., & Hardy, C. (1996). Sustained product innovation in large, mature organizations: Overcoming innovation-to-organization problems. *Academy of Management Journal, 39*(5), 1120–1153.
Du, N., & Budescu, D. V. (2005). The effects of imprecise probabilities and outcomes in evaluating investment options. *Management Science, 51*(12), 1791–1803.
Eggers, J. P., & Park, K. F. (2018). Incumbent adaptation to technological change: The past, present, and future of research on heterogeneous incumbent response. *Academy of Management Annals, 12*(1), 357–389.
Einhorn, H. J., & Hogarth, R. M. (1986). Decision making under ambiguity. *Journal of Business, 59*(4), S225–S250.

Faber, M., Manstetten, R., & Proops, J. L. (1992). Humankind and the environment: An anatomy of surprise and ignorance. *Environmental Values, 1*(3), 217–241.

Faber, M. H., & Faber, M. H. (2012). Uncertainty modeling. *Statistics and Probability Theory: In Pursuit of Engineering Decision Support,* 43–84.

Fleming, L. (2001). Recombinant uncertainty in technological search. *Management Science, 47*(1), 117–132.

Frisch, D., & Baron, J. (1988). Ambiguity and rationality. *Journal of Behavioral Decision Making, 1*(3), 149–157.

Gray, J. (2002). *Straw dogs: Thoughts on humans and other animals.* Farrar.

Gross, M. (2007). The unknown in process: Dynamic connections of ignorance, non-knowledge and related concepts. *Current Sociology, 55*(5), 742–759.

Hansson, S. O. (1994). *Decision theory: A brief introduction.* Department of Philosophy and the History of technology, Royal Institute of Technology.

Hansson, S. O. (1996). Decision making under great uncertainty. *Philosophy of the Social Sciences, 26*(3), 369–386.

Hayek, F. A. (1948). The meaning of competition. *Econ Journal Watch, 13,* 360–372.

Heiner, R. A. (1983). The origin of predictable behavior. *The American Economic Review, 73*(4), 560–595.

Hertwig, R., Pleskac, T. J., & Pachur, T. (2019). *Taming uncertainty.* MIT Press.

Ioannidis, J. P. (2005). Why most published research findings are false. *PLoS Medicine, 2*(8), e124.

Kapoor, R., & Klueter, T. (2021). Unbundling and managing uncertainty surrounding emerging technologies. *Strategy Science, 6*(1), 62–74.

Kay, J. A., & King, M. A. (2020). *Radical uncertainty.* Bridge Street Press.

Keynes, J. M. (1937 [1973]). The general theory of employment. In *The collected writings of John Maynard Keynes* (Vol. 14, pp. 109–123). Macmillan, Cambridge University Press for the Royal Economic Society.

Klepper, S. (1996). Entry, exit, growth, and innovation over the product life cycle. *The American Economic Review, 86*(3)562-583.

Klepper, S. (1997). Industry life cycles. *Industrial and Corporate Change, 6*(1), 145–182.

Knight, F.H. (1921/64). *Risk, uncertainty and profit.* Augustus M. Kelley.

Kozyreva, A., & Hertwig, R. (2021). The interpretation of uncertainty in ecological rationality. *Synthese, 198*(2), 1517–1547.

Krumbein, J. (2012). *Two invisible hands and optimal uncertainty.* SSRN 2034000.

Kuhlthau, C. C. (1993). A principle of uncertainty for information seeking. *Journal of Documentation, 49*(4), 339–355.

Kuhn, K. M., & Budescu, D. V. (1996). The relative importance of probabilities, outcomes, and vagueness in hazard risk decisions. *Organizational Behavior and Human Decision Processes, 68*(3), 301–317.

Magnani, G., & Zucchella, A. (2018). Uncertainty in entrepreneurship and management studies: A systematic literature review. *International Journal of Business and Management, 13*(3), 98–133.

Marchau, V. A., Walker, W. E., Bloemen, P. J. & Popper, S. W. (2019). *Decision making under deep uncertainty: from theory to practice*. Springer Nature.

Mousavi, S., & Gigerenzer, G. (2014). Risk, uncertainty, and heuristics. *Journal of Business Research, 67*(8), 1671–1678.

Mousavi, S., & Gigerenzer, G. (2017). Heuristics are tools for uncertainty. *Homo Oeconomicus, 34*(4), 361–379.

Nelson, R. R., & Winter, S. G. (1982). *An evolutionary theory of economic change*. Belknap Press/Harvard University Press.

Nosal, J. B., & Ordonez, G. (2016). Uncertainty as commitment. *Journal of Monetary Economics, 80*, 124–140.

O'Connor, G. C., & Rice, M. P. (2013). A comprehensive model of uncertainty associated with radical innovation. *Journal of Product Innovation Management, 30*, 2–18.

Packard, M. D., & Clark, B. B. (2020). On the mitigability of uncertainty and the choice between predictive and nonpredictive strategy. *Academy of Management Review, 45*(4), 766–786.

Packard, M. D., Clark, B. B., & Klein, P. G. (2017). Uncertainty types and transitions in the entrepreneurial process. *Organization Science, 28*(5), 840–856.

Porter, M. E. (1980). *Competitive strategy: Techniques for analyzing industries and competitors*. Free Press.

Ramoglou, S. (2021). Knowable opportunities in an unknowable future? On the epistemological paradoxes of entrepreneurship theory. *Journal of Business Venturing, 36*(2), 106090.

Rapp, D. J., & Olbrich, M. (2020). On entrepreneurial decision logics under conditions of uncertainty: An attempt to advance the current debate. *Journal of Innovation and Entrepreneurship, 9*(1), 21.

Rock, D. (2008). SCARF: A brain-based model for collaborating with and influencing others. *NeuroLeadership Journal, 1*(1), 44–52.

Rosenberg, N. (1996). Uncertainty and technological change. In R. Landau, T. Taylor, & G. Wright (Eds.), *The mosaic of economic growth*. Stanford University Press.

Rouvray, D. H. (1997). The treatment of uncertainty in the sciences. *Endeavour, 21*(4), 154–158.

Rowe, W. D. (1994). Understanding uncertainty. *Risk Analysis, 14*(5), 743–750.

Samsami, F., Hosseini, S. H. K., Kordnaeij, A., & Azar, A. (2015). Managing environmental uncertainty: From conceptual review to strategic management point of view. *International Journal of Business and Management*, 10(7), 215–229.

Schoemaker, P. J. (2002). *Profiting from uncertainty: Strategies for succeeding no matter what the future brings*. Simon & Schuster.

Shane, S. (2000). Prior knowledge and the discovery of entrepreneurial opportunities. *Organization Science*, 11(4), 448–469.

Shrader-Frechette, K. (2007). *Taking action, saving lives: Our duties to protect environmental and public health*. Oxford University Press.

Simon, H. A. (1955). A behavioral model of rational choice. *The Quarterly Journal of Economics*, 69(1), 99–118.

Spender, J. -C. (2006). *Knightian uncertainty and its resolution as institutionalized practice* (v9 Working Paper).

Stager, P. (1967). Conceptual level as a composition variable in small-group decision making. *Journal of Personality and Social Psychology*, 5(2), 152–161.

Stewart, I. (2019). *Do dice play god?: The mathematics of uncertainty*. Hachette UK.

Szentkirályi, L. (2020). Luck has nothing to do with It: Prevailing uncertainty and responsibilities of due care. *Ethics, Policy & Environment*, 23(3), 261–280.

Tannert, C., Elvers, H. D., & Jandrig, B. (2007). The ethics of uncertainty: In the light of possible dangers, research becomes a moral duty. *EMBO Reports*, 8(10), 892–896.

Taylor, C. R. (2003). The role of risk versus the role of uncertainty in economic systems. *Agricultural Systems*, 75(2–3), 251–264.

Teece, D., Peteraf, M., & Leih, S. (2016). Dynamic capabilities and organizational agility: Risk, uncertainty, and strategy in the innovation economy. *California Management Review*, 58(4), 13–35.

Todd, P. M. & Gigerenzer, G. E. (2012). *Ecological rationality: Intelligence in the world*. Oxford University Press.

Townsend, D. M., Hunt, R. A., McMullen, J. S., & Sarasvathy, S. D. (2018). Uncertainty, knowledge problems, and entrepreneurial action. *Academy of Management Annals*, 12(2), 659–687.

Wernerfelt, B., & Karnani, A. (1987). Competitive strategy under uncertainty. *Strategic Management Journal*, 8(2), 187–194.

Wittgenstein, L. (1971). *Tractatus Logico-Philosophicu*. Routledge & Kegan Paul.

Zahra, S. A. (2008). The virtuous cycle of discovery and creation of entrepreneurial opportunities. *Strategic Entrepreneurship Journal*, 2(3), 243–257.

CHAPTER 5

Span of Effects of Uncertainty (in Decision-Making)

THE IMPACTS OF UNCERTAINTY

Uncertainty has significant effects on any entity that recognizes it, especially humans and their organizations. It affects their decisions and actions, their feelings and learnings, their fellow beings, and their

Table 5.1 The span of uncertainty's effects

In Terms of Uncertainty's Behavioral Impacts	...directly on an entity's:	survival feelings challenges organizing & organizations compensation (for experiencing uncertainty) rational behaviors and choices
	...on human reactions:	in our behaviors to reduce or accept uncertainty in our behaviors to explore or exploit uncertainty
In Terms of How Humans Deal with Uncertainty's Impacts	...regarding human understanding ...regarding theorizing ...regarding lab studies ...regarding communications and measures	

contexts. Different uncertainties affect humans in different ways when these separate types (of uncertainty) can be identified (Fontana & Gerrard, 2004). And, even when 'we' are not directly involved in the uncertainties, we tend to treat others who are involved differently—often relatively worse than if they were not subject to such uncertainty (Bammer & Smithson, 2008). In other words, uncertainty has wide-ranging, significant, and sometimes surprising, effects on humankind. Table 5.1 depicts the span of effects, from those directly felt by entities to what the reactions are, and then to the various ways humankind has tried to understand uncertainty as a result.

IMPACTS ON ENTITIES

Uncertainty only matters to beings that purposefully decide actions. The importance of how that matters ranges from the existential to the trivial.

On Survival

Uncertainty is ubiquitous; it is a pervasive feature of the environment in which people and organizations must adapt to to survive (Cyert & March, 1963; Griffin & Grote, 2020; Thompson, 1967). Simply put, humans live in an uncertain world, a world facing a doubtful continued existence. And, all the sciences that should help reduce such doubts are themselves perfused with uncertainties. In fact, certainty (*aka* complete information) about anything is unattainable (Rouvray, 1997). Small initial differences can generate massive disparities in survival outcomes in uncertain decision environments (Crawford et al., 2015), and humankind confronts an increasingly uncertain environment due to climate change (Bradley & Steele, 2015). Besides its effects on species survival, uncertainty has effects on economic and venture survival; for example, in providing openings for new ventures to displace incumbents (Taylor, 2003). Even technologies and tools like artificial intelligence (AI) do not have the ability to address many of the deepest uncertainties (see Chapter 20); in fact, such tools may themselves pose a threat to human survival. Humans (ourselves) remain the primary entity with the skills to synthesize both the qualitative and quantitative information to make sense of an ill-defined and complex context, regardless of whether we decide to apply those skills or not (Kay & King, 2020).

On Feelings

Uncertainty manifests itself in many ways in the minds of decision-makers, often through a myriad of feelings. Uncertainty has been defined as a cognitive feeling that encompasses subjective experiences of wonder, doubt, or being unsure (Clore, 1992; Schwarz & Clore, 1996). It is experienced when one is conscious about a lack of knowledge or understanding over pertinent issues related to oneself, others, or different aspects of the environment (Jordan et al., 2012; Kaur & Dasgupta, 2018; Smithson, 1989). Uncertainty is something we all feel emotionally, and for good evolutionary reasons (Kay & King, 2020). We both feel the uncertainty and the need to do something about it (Knight, 1921). These feelings are mostly negative, but some can be positive.

Humans fear anything that they cannot subject to their will, including uncertainty (Gray, 2002). We hate uncertainty, even though life and business are inherently uncertain (Schoemaker, 2002). Uncertainty often has a detrimental effect on the well-being and mental health of CEOs, managers, and entrepreneurs (Millar et al., 2018). Much of that arises from the anxiety about uncertain outcomes (Rowe, 1994). Others feel the horror of ambiguity, or the futility of trying to deal with the unknown (Beck, 2009). The range of negative feelings and metaphors toward uncertainty is wide, and includes: blindness or obstructed vision; straying from the path; being in the wilderness; being the prey; having an internal war; helplessness and impotence; being stuck; insecurity and fear; shiftiness; crippling; demotivating; anxiety-creating; and, debilitating (Bammer & Smithson, 2008). Negative emotions are not 'simply bad', they also have bad consequences. Such emotions can destroy the self-control needed for rationality; for example, to the point where decision-makers can: become unable to understand fully what they are dealing with; have trouble recognizing how much information is enough and how much is too much; and, pay excessive attention to low-probability, high-drama events (Bernstein, 1996).

However, uncertainty's impacts on human feelings are not all negative. Surprise is often considered a good emotion, usually stemming from ignorance, and deriving from outcomes not foreseen as possible or at all (Faber et al., 1992). Such surprise is the basis for humor and for stimulating musical and visual artistry. That kind of uncertainty-induced feeling is akin to health or food as a source of inspiration, and is associated with artistic freedom (Bammer & Smithson, 2008).

In the end, we as humans must accept uncertainty and the feelings it generates within us. We must accept that we are not the authors of our lives, given that nearly everything that is most important on our paths is unchosen (Gray, 2002).

On Challenges

'*We live on an island of knowledge surrounded by a sea of ignorance. As our island of knowledge grows, so does the shore of our ignorance*' (Wheeler, 1992). The concept of uncertainty has been around for millennia—from at least Socrates and Plato—and so those shores are long, presenting many challenges to humankind (Tannert et al., 2007). Our lives are plagued by uncertainty; the world we live in remains fundamentally unpredictable (Bradac, 2001; Pressman & Choi, 1997). As such, it is a fundamental truth that humankind is denied ultimate security (Beck, 2009). The list of everything that might go wrong in the future, however unlikely, is infinite, making that future incalculable (Kay & King, 2020). Even in our most basic sciences, like physics, there is a need to include a *god-of-the-gaps* (e.g., in the Heisenberg Principle) to cover uncertainty (Barrow, 1998). And, our optimism in science to close those gaps implies that we are currently quite ignorant, and that we will be repeatedly and profoundly surprised in the future. Because of this uncertainty, most decision-makers confront significant incomplete information that will affect their choices and the outcomes (Marchau et al., 2019). Given that uncertainty (i.e., the wall of uninsurable unknowns), the primary challenge for human life becomes deciding what to do and how to do it regardless—making doing the right things more important than doing things right (Teece et al., 2016).

The challenge of uncertainty is mainly future-looking. What matters more is anticipating the future (to predict and control phenomena) rather than analyzing the past (to understand them) (Kay & King, 2020). Past and present conditions operate mostly as grounds for prediction (Knight, 1921). Uncertainty forces us to look the unexpected in the eye, but that is quite difficult given one cannot expect the unexpected (Beck, 2009). That said, decision-making—as a phenomenon—differs from ignorance in that 'we' do have some knowledge available upon which to draw; we possess some minimal awareness that a judgment must be made even though we may not possess certitude over either the relevant factors or the likely consequences of action (Townsend et al., 2018). We still must decide and do, often without the ability or motivation to obtain, sift, and integrate the relevant information that may be widely and unequally distributed 'out there' (Kay & King, 2020). A further challenge then is to instill confidence nonetheless to the stakeholders—to those affected by the decision—that such decisions are being made rationally and responsibly even in the face of such uncertainty (O'Malley, 2000).

In real life, decision-makers can never access complete information. For example, chaos theory reveals that, even for a moderately complex deterministic system, all the information feasibly gatherable will simply not suffice to give a complete prediction (Gilboa, 2009). So, it is as true of business as of other spheres of activity, that action must be taken according to opinion because knowledge is only partial (Knight, 1921). Indeed, most problems we confront in life are not well-defined (i.e., there is no clean dichotomy between known and unknown, deterministic and random) and so they do not have single analytic solutions (Kay & King, 2020). Further, many of the strategic problems we face are novel—our progress creates new uncertainties where historic knowledge is unlikely to apply. '... *the more characteristic economic problems are problems of change, of growth and retrogression, and of fluctuation. The extent to which these can be reduced into scientific terms is rather limited; for at every stage in an economic process new things are happening, things which have not happened before'* (Hicks, 1979: x–xi). As a result, there will be things that we will not see, events that we will not record, and many possibilities that we will not be able to rule out (Barrow, 1998). Entropy, chaos, complexity, and dynamics will always limit our knowledge (Stewart, 2019). And, that is likely to produce a growing danger, as with greater the situational uncertainty, not only is there less chance of recognizing the right situation in which to select an action, but also there is more chance of not detecting the wrong situation for selecting it (Beckert, 1996).

Defaulting to a probability-based analysis is unlikely to be the answer. Neoclassical economic decision theories were never designed to address uncertainty (Simon, 1979); the probabilistic reasoning that undergirds such theories breaks down in the presence of uncertainty (Shackle, 1955). The real world is a 'large' world, involving decisions in which some relevant information is unknown, violating the conditions for rational decision theory (Gigerenzer & Gaissmaier, 2011). Economic theory simply cannot maintain the maximizing assumption convincingly in the face of uncertainty; this is because agents cannot anticipate the possible outcomes of a decision nor assign probabilities to them (Beckert, 1996).

There are few answers to the challenges of uncertainty because there are too few relevant tools (because the challenge of addressing uncertainty [as 'not risk'] has been ignored for so long). For too long, the intelligence and effort necessary to cope with world of radical uncertainty has been underestimated and undernourished (Kay & King, 2020). And, whatever has been used in place has not been adequate. For example, Tetlock's study of geopolitical forecasters revealed how poor they were, with the higher profile ones faring worse (Kay & King, 2020). Uncertainty creates innumerable challenges for even the most skilled organizational actors; they simply cannot adequately comprehend and predict the consequences of their actions (Huang & Pearce, 2015). As such, uncertainty remains important and ubiquitous, but poorly understood (Stewart, 2019).

Complicating the challenge of uncertainty is the fact that in business, as well as in many situations in life, decisions are made in a game with relative stakes—i.e., where rivals are also making decisions under uncertainty. While the uncertainty of the future makes it difficult to strategize by identifying effective courses of action, the decision-maker does not suffer alone. Instead of being judged in absolute terms, the decision often only needs to be better than the rival's to be deemed adequate by the market (Scoblic, 2020).

For all humans, however, this is a game played throughout our lifetimes. Handling uncertainty is challenging for learners and is often difficult, but it is an important experience that can improve later decision-making and how one deals with unforeseen outcomes (Jordan et al., 2012; Kaur & Dasgupta, 2018). All of us are uncertain, to varying degrees, about much of the future, much of the past, and even much of the present. The feeling of that may diminish over time, through experience and some ability to avoid or address it (partially), but uncertainty is everywhere and cannot be escaped.

Even if we do somehow get better at playing the current uncertainty-infused game, it is a game that undeviatingly changes in the next round. As we make progress in building out our island of knowledge, the shores of our ignorance only grow longer. New forms of social and economic organization end up producing new risks and uncertainties (Kozyreva & Hertwig, 2021). Any knowledge we gain over physical processes is imperfect and constantly changing; and, any knowledge we think we have over social processes is illusory, given it depends not only on what people do (publicly) but also on (the unobservable, unverifiable, and unstable possibilities of) what people think (Kay & King, 2020).

On Organization

Uncertainty significantly affects humankind in the many ways it organizes. The argument has even been made that firms-as-organizations would not need to exist without uncertainty. Indeed, the rise of capitalism needed two things—bookkeeping and risk-taking—the latter being more precisely expressed as forecasting under uncertainty (Bernstein, 1996). Even Simon concludes that, absent uncertainties, there is neither need nor place for a theory of administration (Spender, 2006). The human capacity to manage uncertainty and our appetite to take it on are primary drivers of our economic system (Bernstein, 1996). In fact, uncertainty is critical not only to business enterprise but also to the kind of liberal (democratic) freedoms that support the (free) markets in which they operate (O'Malley, 2000).

Uncertainty creates opportunities for new ventures, and new profits for those who would bear it and save others from doing so. Without uncertainty there is no entrepreneurial activity (Knight, 1921). Profit only emerges from acting in the face of the kind of uncertainty that cannot be insured nor capitalized nor salaried. Profitable opportunities arise out of the inherent, absolute unpredictability of things, often resulting from the kind of human activity that cannot be anticipated (i.e., where any probability calculation with regard to them is impossible and meaningless). The receipt of profit in a particular case may be argued to be the result of 'superior judgment' (Knight, 1921). That said, in any one individual case, there is no way of telling good judgment from good luck. More generally, uncertainty is the root problem for managers and for the theory of the firm (Spender, 2006). Fundamentally, organized activity transforms the uncertainties of human opinion and action into measurable probabilities (e.g., over the judgment and capacity of the manager-as-decision-maker) (Knight, 1921). Organizations transform a problem that involves many uncertainties (e.g., about technology, demand, regulation, and so on) into a much simpler problem that involves an investor's (or employee's) beliefs in the firm's management (e.g., where history-based probabilistic risk is more appropriate).

Not only is uncertainty important for entrepreneurship (i.e., defined as pursuing new opportunities in the face of incomplete information), it is important in terms of transactions costs (i.e., contracting) and a primary reason why hierarchies exist (rather than only spot markets). Contractual incompleteness is ultimately a matter of uncertainty—about future events and about the other party (Langlois & Cosgel, 1993). Firms—as organized hierarchies that allow close employee monitoring and, thereby, the management of incomplete, long-term, employment contracts—exist only because they provide transactional environments that lower information and control losses; they simply deal better than spot markets with uncertainty, and the informational failures (e.g., opportunism) that exist in the real world (Spender, 2006). Uncertainty is the basis for a (Coasian) theory of the firm—i.e., when information is incomplete regarding productive inputs, making bargains hard to strike because information is asymmetrical, it makes sense to keep those bargained activities within the firm (so they are made versus bought).

While it is important to recognize that the firm form, and new firms, each exist because of uncertainty, the relationship is not just a theoretically foundational one. For example, it also involves some tricky optimization. A major challenge for a firm is to not take on more uncertainty than it needs to in order to generate the returns it seeks (Bernstein, 1996). As well, uncertainty generates several roles for managers—where some managers need to be good at foresight, others good at making judgments in the light of uncertainty and that foresight, others in taking action given the uncertainty and judgments, and yet others in leading employees into such unstable contexts (Knight, 1921).

Besides having an impact on organizing business, uncertainty presents challenges to organizing society. For example, a large part of the legal system is organized to deal with uncertainty—with court proceedings being the most systematic (and yet quite flawed) process we have for reaching decisions under conditions of imperfect knowledge (Kay & King, 2020).

Uncertainty even has a significant impact on how we, as individuals, organize ourselves. We often pre-organize (and pre-commit) our lives around a particular future scenario to which we aspire (e.g., a career; a relationship), and that investment puts us 'at risk' because the outcomes of such scenarios are uncertain (Dimov, 2016).

On Compensation for Experiencing Uncertainty

Uncertainty has an impact on the rewards for those willing to bear it, one based on the price paid by those willing to purchase the products generated by those willing to bear that uncertainty. Uncertainty means that markets will be incomplete (Kay & King, 2020) and, so, profits will be available as the prices cleared rise above the average costs of production. That impact of uncertainty—in terms of offering potential significant benefits to those bearing it—is the engine that powers innovation; indeed, the monetary and non-monetary rewards from being an innovator are a powerful draw to action.

Knight argued that, absent uncertainty, there is *no* compelling explanation for profit (Beckert, 1996; Spender, 2006). Society pays higher prices for goods whose production involves uncertainty (and their subsequent deficient supply) than for goods of the opposite character (Knight, 1921). A conventional view then may be to regard uncertainty-bearing as repugnant and irksome, with profit being the reward for assuming that burden. Essentially, society pays those firms for their sacrifice of assuming uncertainty, doing so through higher prices for goods in whose production it is a factor; those higher prices being the result of the restricted supply of those goods because rivals are deterred from entering markets by their unwillingness to assume the same uncertainty (Knight, 1921).

On Rational Behaviors and Choices

Uncertainty impacts real human decisions and actions, not simply human feelings. So much so that arguably, through decision-making, rationality itself is existentially linked to uncertainty. Whether a decision is viewed as rational or not is largely determined by the uncertainty surrounding that decision (e.g., Hansen, 1972; Meyer & Sathi, 1985). When there is no uncertainty, rationality can be assessed on how well the decision is optimized (e.g., in terms of choosing the option with the highest expected value or utility). When uncertainty exists, being able to assess rationality after the decision but prior to the outcome is difficult. This is because of information asymmetries that may exist between the assessor and the decision-maker that may only be revealed after the outcome (e.g., where the decision-maker was using strategic dishonesty to gain an advantage). So, when uncertainty exists, assessment usually waits until the outcome is revealed. When the outcome is positive, the rationality may be seen as either good judgment or good luck (Knight, 1921). Often, though, when the uncertainty is well-understood by the assessor, judgment is withheld—i.e., where the context is *arational* and no third-party verifiable justification for a decision choice existed (i.e., as it was uninsurable and doubted by others).

To be clear, in sufficiently uncertain contexts, there is no rational best choice, regardless of how that choice is spun *after* that uncertainty is resolved. Outside of 'small' worlds (i.e., artificial economic games), there is no basis for rationality; radical uncertainty is simply fatal to rationality (Kay & King, 2020). It is impossible to make good decisions in the face of true uncertainty (Marchau et al., 2019), impossible to deduce rational strategies under a given goal of utility optimization or profit maximization (Beckert, 1996). Reality is the 'large' world, where some relevant information is unknown and the future is uncertain, violating the conditions for rational decision theory (Gigerenzer & Gaissmaier, 2011). It leads to questions about how to deal with unforeseen contingencies—how to take into account, when making a decision today, the things that can happen that the decision-maker cannot even conceive of (Etner et al., 2012). Reality is not puzzle-solving, where the assumptions are completely specified (and modeled as such by the decision-maker); reality is a mystery that involves not being able to describe all possible events or their relative probabilities (Kay & King, 2020). The kind of uncertainty that rules out rational choice can arise in any part of a real decision; for example, the events which are relevant for the results of possible choices may be left out of the description of the state space, actions which are available at a future date may be excluded from consideration in the initial choice set, or outcomes may not reflect the decision-maker's eventual tastes (Ghirardato, 2001). Uncertainty can also arise out of a moderately complex system when it is combined with a decision-maker's bounded rationality (Marchau et al., 2019). And, even when the real question is known, the range of possible answers may essentially be unbounded, rendering rationality via the math of probability inapplicable (Kay & King, 2020). Reality is also dynamic, so even if an initial decision can be made rationally, the list of hypotheses for the sequel to its enactment can be a black box containing unknowns that cannot be tackled rationally (Shackle, 1966).

If uncertainty rules out rational behavior, then what behaviors do result from it? Research indicates the risk-taking and uncertainty-bearing behaviors that do occur appear inconsistent with axiomatic rationality; and, it is these behaviors that drive the central dynamics of capitalist society (Kay & King, 2020). Humans act upon estimates rather than inferences, and upon judgment and intuition rather than reasoning, for the most part, when confronted with uncertainty (Knight, 1921). Empirical evidence also reveals that uncertainty (in the form of ambiguity) affects judgments and choices (Einhorn & Hogarth, 1986) differently and separately from the effects of risk (e.g., recorded as ambiguity aversion—Ellsberg, 1961). Such effects of uncertainty have been studied for some time, dating back at least to Wald (1950), and have more recently become a significant concern of decision theory (Manski, 2000). For example, it has been shown that in situations of uncertainty, behavior is affected not only by the degree of uncertainty but also its source (Fontana & Gerrard, 2004). And, this effect on decision behavior is not just isolated to 'true' forms of uncertainty; it can arise when people apply intuition (poorly) to problems of well-defined but dynamic probability, like the *Monty Hall problem* (Kay & King, 2020). In other words, uncertainty—in many forms—can affect decision-making behaviors and choices in many ways.

Uncertainty can trigger bad decision-making behaviors. For example, it can trigger the use of uninformed priors to fill in the gaps left by true unknowns; those priors may be the result of ideology or arrogance (i.e., an inability to recognize the limits of one's knowledge) but that is often hidden from stakeholders (Kay & King, 2020). What, unfortunately, feeds such behaviors is a society that punishes decision-makers from expressing (honest) uncertainty (Kay & King, 2020). When that punishment is doled out, it can prove dangerous (e.g., as it can lead to science losing the public's trust, a free press being suppressed, and identity politics growing). Honesty, including about the limits of knowledge, needs to be the best policy for decision-making (and, not just in theory).

Uncertainty makes it difficult to be rational even when we want to be. And, reality is even more harsh because many decision environments do not allow for rational thought even when computational tools are applicable. Some of the most important decisions must be made under complex, confusing, indistinct, or frightening conditions—with no time to consult the laws of probability (Bernstein, 1996). In reality, there is often more information that we don't know than we do know when it comes to the most critical decisions involving unknowns (Rowe, 1994). And, often those unknowns arise from 'us'—from the complexity of our social reality (Dequech, 2003)—where, ironically, we are trying to predict how others make decisions (in their non-rational ways) under conditions of uncertainty.

If uncertainty precludes rationality, then what is a second-best (or even minimally logical) approach to apply? The preclusion of rationality implies that the search for an optimal way to choose among undominated actions must ultimately fail. The best remaining normative analysis is then to identify the undominated actions (Manski, 2000) and try to assess them using other 'relevant' criteria. This may be unsatisfying, but it is a valuable exercise, especially when further details—perhaps available with greater specification now or in the future—can potentially shift the problem from one of uncertainty to one of risk.

IMPACTS ON ENTITY REACTIONS

As we have explored so far, uncertainty affects primary actors directly—their feelings, organization, behaviors, and more. Uncertainty also impacts their reactions and those affected by the primary actors (e.g., the secondary actors who may be involved in creating that uncertainty).

On Behaviors to Reduce or Accept Uncertainty

Humankind has had to deal with uncertainty, mostly in a reactive stance, throughout its history. For centuries, uncertainty was simply considered as 'the will of the gods'. So, when humanity did take control of society by separating it from the realm of the divine, it seemed initially frustrating just to place it at the mercy of chance (*aka* mathematical probabilities) (Bernstein, 1996). Fortunately, businesses and institutions leveraged that new representation to move society forward by taming some of that 'chance' (e.g., using insurance, financial markets, optimization methods, innovations, scientific research, information-sharing technology, and so on).

Probability theory gave rise to the establishment of markets in risk (Kay & King, 2020). In the seventeenth century, Pascal initiated probability theory over a question of a bet, and it grew to include complexities like compound probabilities. From it sprang the fundamental concept of expected value, underlying a significant branch of optimization logic (and insurance). As long as there are (sufficiently similar) repeated events, where the outcome is not manipulable, such logic solves previously paralyzing decisions, thus allowing fair investment (i.e., where expected returns compensate for putting treasure at risk) to encourage action. Probability theory allows the decision-maker to act 'as if' the focal uncertainty can be estimated, so that outcomes can be envisioned, and theoretically 'better' choices can be made and acted upon.

Probability theory allows humanity to bound some of its (minor) 'irreducible uncertainties'. For example, instead of working out the underlying cause-and-effect of roll of a die or flip of a coin (or other randomizing device), that 'uncertainty' can be converted into a probability of occurring—a risk (Knight, 1921). In those cases, ignorance of the future is due to practical indeterminateness of nature itself, and we can appeal to the law of large numbers to distribute the outcomes and to make them calculable when the focal events repeat themselves (Knight, 1921).

But, even when such 'uncertainty' is reduced to probability, especially in a newer context, suspicion remains over the legitimacy of that reduction. Rational people do not act until they have sufficient confidence in the narrative provided; humans are not natural probability theorists or Bayesians (Kay & King, 2020). For example, rational people will decline to participate in a proposed wager when they do not have perfect information, and especially when the information that they do have differs from that held by others—like the party offering the wager (Kay & King, 2020)—entertainment value aside (e.g., in the cases of carnival games, 'homer'-like sports betting, and so on). One reason (besides not wanting to be a 'sucker' to a con) is that, under conditions of radical uncertainty, subjective probabilities are necessarily sensitive to trivial information and details of problem specification, and so it makes little sense to act on them (Kay & King, 2020). Real people often have solid instincts in such situations.

In the face of uncertainty, real people do not optimize because they know they cannot (Kay & King, 2020). Instead, the natural reaction is to try to reduce the uncertainty because it is aversive. It is aversive to strategy, operations, organizational behavior, and psychology. Even where embracing it is key—for entrepreneurship, innovation, and creativity—uncertainty reduction remains an important driver of behavior (Griffin & Grote, 2020). In fact, in business, the desire for liquidity and the urge to cement future arrangements by legally enforceable agreements, each testify to the significant worry about uncertainty that affects firms' decision-making (Bernstein, 1996).

Uncertainty reduction is often pursued through the aggressive search for more information, especially when the uncertainty is asymmetric. Luckily, there is a free press to do some of that heavy lifting when others fail to find important information. For example, the now-infamous firm *Theranos* was only exposed—their actual uncertainties revealed—when journalists asked penetrating questions that its board and investors did not, to burst the bubble of one (misleading) narrative (Kay & King, 2020). Other entities that search primarily to reduce uncertainty also exist, including those involved in basic science. But, such searching involves costs, which fortunately society is willing to bear because the costs of continued uncertainty seem higher. Another way to reduce uncertainty is through large-scale organization and institutionalization of various forms—e.g., where governments act to insure its communities, at least partially, against various extreme outcomes (like natural disasters) (Knight, 1921).

When uncertainty cannot be reduced through information-seeking, then several other approaches to dealing with it are observed. One approach is to simplify the situation and rely on minimal-step rules—*heuristics*—that apply to the information given and have had some success in the past. Another way is to fight fire with fire—choosing a creative solution that adds uncertainty to the outcome (Dequech, 2003). Often what is observed (e.g., applying a heuristic) is *not* the outcome of a conscious process. The opinions upon which humans act in everyday affairs, even those which govern the decisions of responsible business managers, have little similarity with conclusions reached by an exhaustive analysis based upon accurate measurements; in everyday life, choices are mostly subconscious (Knight, 1921).

A more passive reaction to the identified presence of a given uncertainty is simply to *monitor* the relevant events for signs of the 'expectedly' worst (e.g., high negative-impact) outcomes. In a world of radical uncertainty, we cannot act in anticipation of every unlikely possibility, and so we select a set of potential disasters to monitor—relying on judgment and experience—in order to provide some (minimal) cushion to act prior to the realized devastation (e.g., acting through evacuating people and moving emergency assets into the targeted area) (Kay & King, 2020). Unfortunately, for some events, such monitoring can couple us to them and influence the outcomes in ways that are only partially predictable or knowable, essentially aggravating the level of uncertainty to which we need to react (Barrow, 1998).

Another somewhat passive reaction is to rely on others—experts—to reduce the uncertainty to risk. However, this is often unwise, as history has shown. For example, of the 207 recessions pre-2016, the *IMF* (through its *World Economic Outlook*) predicted none of them. Regardless, the demand for forecasts remains frustratingly high (Kay & King, 2020). Indeed, such consulting—that which (falsely) quantifies uncertainty—is increasingly fashionable, however, even though we know, theoretically, that uncertainty eschews prediction (Hodgson, 2011).

A final reaction to uncertainty is to 'hide' in the hoped-for safety of its theoretical study. Science provides one refuge from uncertainty, promising the miracle of freedom from thought (Gray, 2002). There may be comfort in the fact that science regularly uncovers possibilities more unusual than any fiction-writer has yet imagined, even when such discoveries also lead to more questions and greater uncertainties to consider in the future (Barrow, 1998). That one step forward with two steps back process can still appear to feel like progress because of that initial forward inertia, though, and sometimes that is what humanity requires for some feeling of comfort to go on.

On Behaviors to Explore or Exploit Uncertainty

An argument can be made that the dividing line between humanity's (reactive) past and its (more active) modernity has been its 'mastery' of uncertainty, or at least of risk, through math and science. Humankind is much less comfortable being at 'the whim of the gods' and much more comfortable (and confident) in its attempts to tame nature's unknowns (Bernstein, 1996). In the latter framework, we believe that we can better choose when to take on uncertainty and when to avoid it; and, we can even create it and exploit it.

One way to treat any instance of economic uncertainty is as a choice between a smaller reward more-confidently anticipated and a larger one less-confidently anticipated (Knight, 1921); in that perspective, there are often options available to firms for avoiding 'greater' uncertainties. So, for some firms, a tactic of robust *satisficing* may help in protecting against pernicious surprises while achieving critical outcomes; but, it will come at the cost of not being able to exploit favorable surprises to facilitate windfall outcomes (Marchau et al., 2019). Because opportunities are unknown until discovered (Shane, 2000), the firms that do not choose to bear the uncertainty of such discovery efforts when others do will be less likely to find entrepreneurial success; they will simply not profit from indeterminacy when others do (Shackle, 1966).

In terms of making that choice to take action to discover new information, there are some interesting patterns of human behavior. Individuals who experience uncertainty below a preferred level engage in exploration and then harness the opportunities from any subsequent discoveries, while individuals who experience uncertainty above a preferred level of uncertainty instead default to exploiting existing knowledge (Griffin & Grote, 2020). To pursue such discovery, firms usually structure themselves to be more flexible—e.g., their investments are more short-term and their fixed costs are reduced in favor of variable costs. This is especially important when the number of uncertainties is high, the range of outcomes is broad, and the firm lacks a source of competitive advantage (Samsami et al., 2015).

If one chooses to bear uncertainty—or even simply risk—it is important to remember that, for any one specific occurrence, the outcome can be quite bad. There may be comfort, at least from probability theory, that such bad outcomes will be balanced out by good ones over time (or repetition), but that is cold comfort 'in the moment'. Life is mostly made up of uncertainties, and the conditions under which a loss in any one case may be compensated by other cases are bafflingly complex (at least, relative to a simple set of gambles in a lab experiment). So, it is important that when one does choose to confront a given situation involving uncertainty, that one should deal with it on own its merits as an isolated case (Knight, 1921).

While there are some interesting choices on reacting to uncertainty by exploring it, perhaps the choices involving exploiting uncertainty—especially when it is used on others—has even more interesting issues to consider (e.g., ethical issues). Like any other 'tool', uncertainty can be used for good or for bad. In the good category, artists, musicians, novelists, film-makers, and game-designers all use uncertainty to create surprise, suspense, and healthy mental challenges for their appreciative audiences (Costikyan, 2013). In the bad category, uncertainty can be used as a weapon to dominate or manipulate others (Bammer & Smithson, 2008) especially in governing and politics (e.g., with disinformation, with terror, and through the sowing of distrust in established entities).

Impacts on Understanding

As we have described, uncertainty affects human behaviors, feelings, actions, and reactions. At a more cognitive level, it also affects 'our' understandings of the natural world and of each other. We think to decide, as every decision starts by thinking about 'what it is that is going on here', which is difficult to address under uncertainty (Kay & King, 2020). It leads to the (regressive) problem of determining what to do when we do not know what is best to do because of uncertainty (Beckert, 1996). As pointed out previously, it even raises the question of what rationality—or rational understanding—entails in a radically uncertain world (Kay & King, 2020). To counter uncertainty, we search for greater knowledge to understand our world, where knowledge is defined by the *certainty* that focal phenomena are real and possess specific characteristics (Berger & Luckmann, 1966). Because of that definition of knowledge, it is no surprise that uncertainty lies at the center of many disciplines and branches of science (Kozyreva & Hertwig, 2021). Unfortunately, however, we can never defeat uncertainty—we can never know that we know everything even if we ever do (Barrow, 1998). (Even in business, it is often difficult to know, in the moment what is real and what is not, as investors in *FTX* may attest to, due to the uncertainties involved and created by those in such markets.)

Impacts on Theorizing

One way to improve our understanding of uncertainty is to theorize more about it. In fact, such efforts have had a foundational impact on commerce as we know it. In some ways, the first attempts to conceptualize uncertainty defined the first scholars of management (Samsami et al., 2015). From them emerged a wide range of organizational theories—including theories of the firm and its behaviors—to incorporate various types of uncertainty as analytical constructs (e.g., Townsend et al., 2018). There has been (at least) a century of related work done in the hope that uncertainty would provide the core of the new economic theory (Bernstein, 1996), some of which has been accomplished in the *Austrian School* of economics (Beckert, 1996). Ultimately, however, such theories—or at least their practical applications—will be limited because access to important information will always be restricted (e.g., due to privacy, complexity, competition, and so on). Regardless, there is a large group of economic phenomena connected with imperfect knowledge that can be further illuminated by such theorizing (Knight, 1921).

In economics, theorizing usually means identifying the likely outcome—the equilibrium of the phenomenon. However, when agents are uncertain about the future state of affairs, they cannot, in a dynamic economy, make decisions that lead to equilibria outcomes (Beckert, 1996). Under uncertainty, it is *ex ante* impossible to determine whether a chosen means is rational or irrational for optimization. Further, even searching for more information that would help with that determination is costly, and the marginal utility of an investment in that information cannot be determined. Consequently, a decision-maker cannot allocate resources rationally between competing ends because they cannot determine the opportunity costs *ex ante*. It becomes inevitable under such uncertainty that wrong decisions will be made on the basis of wrong assumptions, ensuring that reaching an equilibrium is impossible (Beckert, 1996). Uncertainty, then, represents a fundamental challenge to economic theory—as it not only complicates the decision-making processes, but also calls into question the optimizing assumption itself that would provide an equilibrium solution (Beckert, 1996).

Besides economics, uncertainty affects our understanding of phenomena well beyond those local and artificial realms. For example, *cosmology* is the science that extrapolates into the unknown, arguably the most (Barrow, 1998); and, it uses uncertainty as an exploratory, hypothesis-development device (and, as that science progresses toward more powerful equipment, it then tests those hypotheses to further its understanding of space). While uncertainty offers opportunities for more research and information-gathering (to mitigate it) in some fields, it also can deny humanity feasible ways to link that progress *across* scientific fields. In practice, our updating of any knowledge remains far from smoothly percolating into a completely linked system of ideas (e.g., parts of biology are not linked well with biochemical studies of the origin of life) (Barrow, 1998). One reason for this frustrating lack of coordination is that uncertainty presents itself in different fields with very different nuances, and sometimes leads to conflicting approaches (Magnani & Zucchella, 2018). Uncertainty even denies us the ability to predict when cause-and-effect can be identified, at least at some level; for example, due to unknown factor values in chaotic systems, even with the relevant Laws of Nature known, we are still not guaranteed to discern the outcomes of those laws (Barrow, 1998). The limits to science are clear—we will never be able to get all the facts that we need to put into some possible future 'universal' formula (Barrow, 1998). Note that such a realization has been relatively recent; only post-WW1 does it appear that mathematicians and philosophers started to admit that reality encompassed entire sets of circumstances that people had never contemplated before. Research began to seriously seek for ways of conducting a systematic analysis of the unexpected, but not without the understanding that the journey would be never-ending (Bernstein, 1996).

One stop on that journey was the introduction of *non-binary logic*. The foundations of a three-valued logic were laid in the 1920s; the basic idea argued was that statements were not necessarily true or false, but could also be uncertain (Rouvray, 1997). This innovation changed science dramatically—as it effectively generated a scale of *degrees of truthfulness* (Rouvray, 1997). The idea of imprecise probability assignments presented a serious alternative to the standard probabilistic model, one that could benefit formal approaches to epistemology and philosophy of science in the future (Romeijn & Roy, 2014). Such basic science 'stops on the journey' gave rise to the remarkable interdisciplinary interest in uncertainty and its kindred topics of risk, complexity, and unpredictability more recently (Kozyreva & Hertwig, 2021).

Another way to adjust our understanding of uncertainty, besides through deductive theorizing, is through inductive theorizing—observing the behaviors of people confronting uncertainty to better understand its effects. We need to ask how humans think and act in 'large' worlds where they can only have imperfect knowledge (Kay & King, 2020). While some of that can be done in a lab setting—in 'small' worlds where right and wrong answers can be identified for comparison—such research must *not* end there (Kay & King, 2020).

Impacts on Lab Studies

Controlled experiments are one way to better understand human behavior in the face of uncertainty; the results of such experiments may provide some reference points and inspiration for field work (e.g., regarding measurable biases and aversions, and the identification of heuristics). However, lab work faces substantial criticism due to the limitations involved in representing actual uncertainties. Many lab experiments are devoid of meaningful context; they tell us little about 'large' worlds, where behavior is driven by the purpose of the activity (e.g., counting basketball passes or searching for a gorilla—see https://www.youtube.com/watch?v=vJG698U2Mvo). Simply put, lab-based 'small' world problems do *not* present a definition of rationality relevant to 'large' worlds, where there are no well-defined solutions (Kay & King, 2020).

Impacts on Communications and Measures

The understanding of any phenomenon, to be valuable, needs to be communicated and shared. Often, to do so effectively, it also needs to be based on things that others can verify (i.e., it needs measures). These requirements apply to the understanding of uncertainty as well, if not even more so, because of its special nature. Where one cannot measure, one's knowledge is meager and unsatisfactory, which presents a challenge to fields where uncertainties loom large (e.g., in the social sciences) (Kay & King, 2020). Where one cannot effectively communicate, one ends up with secrets—which are seen as unknowns to others, unknowns that render mutually beneficial decisions impossible (Bammer & Smithson, 2008).

Communication is about transferring knowledge. In fact, information has been defined in terms of transferred knowledge that reduces uncertainty. In other words, even the concept of information has an existential relationship with uncertainty (just like so many other socially-constructed concepts). Any communicative act provides information *only* when it reduces ignorance or uncertainty about the state of things under consideration (Garner, 1962). Information occurs only when there is some *a priori* uncertainty, with the amount of that information determined by the amount of the uncertainty (Garner, 1962). In other words, we can actually measure information in terms of the decrease in uncertainty realized (Garner, 1962). The uncertainty principle for the fundamental theory of information flow is built on those ideas (Kuhlthau, 1993).

Communications can break down, however, when uncertainty is involved. For example, if uncertainty is so high that it is impossible to create a meaningful vision by the potential messengers to enlist prospective stakeholders (e.g., because the messengers cannot gain sufficient visibility or legitimacy) then even initiating communications is impossible (Dattée et al., 2018). So, communication is not just about the information itself, but also about the confidence in the message and messenger. Confidence in the message is jointly determined by the uncertainty perception and the receiver's uncertainty aversion (Dequech, 1999). Many factors, including the medium used, can affect the confidence in the messenger. Understanding these real-world influences on the effectiveness of communication is important to designing information systems and services. Such designs need to enable people to move from uncertainty to understanding quickly, clearly, and with trust, especially as 'our' information world becomes more and more one that threatens its inhabitants with being in a perpetual state of uncertainty (Kuhlthau, 1993).

Unfortunately, even clear communication about risks and uncertainties does not stop harmful human behaviors. For example, legal gambling—a situation in which participants know that they are expected to lose to the house (as odds are often legally required to be posted)—still involves, worldwide, over 10-trillion USD worth of voluntary exchange (Stewart, 2019), with a significant proportion of that essentially being a tax on the poor.

Also, unfortunately, in contexts of uncertainty, honest messengers are bound to show their ignorance—whether openly stated or not—mostly to their, and society's, detriment. While, theoretically, if one does not know something (completely), the best answer is a truthful one—admitting to what they do not know (Kay & King, 2020). However, how one does this without losing the trust of their recipients, especially when the void of knowledge can be filled with unaccountable disinformation by less-honest others, is not straightforward (as some experiences with the Covid-19 messaging appeared to have indicated). We—as academics and society—need to work harder on this, so that the information we do have is not twisted and lost on rather stupid frictions and fictions (e.g., often tossed up by grifters playing a different game altogether). In other words, uncertainty not only presents a rather harsh set of direct challenges to us, but then human psychology often appears to exacerbate them. As it stands, however, this conflict between truth-finding (as neutral, objective, uncertainty reduction) and power-grabbing (as tactical uncertainty application) is likely to provide the main storyline to humankind's eventual success or failure.

Summary
The span of uncertainty's impacts is wide; and, its effects are often deep. There are positive, neutral, and negative impacts. There are direct impacts on entities (e.g., on individuals and their organizations) of many kinds (e.g., on feelings and on behaviors), as well as on how those entities react. There are even effects on how 'we' then deal with uncertainty more broadly (e.g., through increased theorizing). Those who better understand and control such impacts are likely to have greater influence in our world.

Why the span of uncertainty's impacts matters:

- Understanding the measures and sites of those impacts provides a better way to prioritize the uncertainties that need to be addressed
- Understanding human reactions to uncertainties (and the impacts of those uncertainties) provides a way to mitigate the systemic errors those behaviors can entail
- Understanding the potential impacts on our communications provides a basis for more robust designs for informational transfer

What uncertainty's potential impacts mean for business and policy:

- Understanding the impacts can provide a better way to allocate resources for affecting those impacts
- Given some uncertainty aversion exists in people, there may be opportunities to exploit or mitigate it; given some demand for uncertainty also exists, there may be opportunities to leverage and satisfy it for the appropriate audiences

- Given the effects of uncertainty on communications, especially involving new policies (and especially as information gets updated, as with a pandemic), more work is needed on the impacts identified to increase the trust in truthful messaging while reducing the harms of generated-uncertainty-as-disinformation

REFERENCES

Bammer, G., & Smithson, M. (2008). Understanding uncertainty. *Integration Insights, 7*(1), 1–7.

Barrow, J. D. (1998). *Impossibility: The limits of science and the science of limits*. Oxford University Press on Demand.

Beck, U. (2009). *World at risk*. Polity.

Beckert, J. (1996). What is sociological about economic sociology? Uncertainty and the embeddedness of economic action. *Theory and Society, 25*, 803–840.

Berger, P., & Luckmann, T. (1966). *The social construction of reality*. Penguin Book.

Bernstein, P. L. (1996). *Against the gods: The remarkable story of risk*. Wiley.

Bradac, J. J. (2001). Theory comparison: Uncertainty reduction, problematic integration, uncertainty management, and other curious constructs. *Journal of Communication, 51*(3), 456–476.

Bradley, R., & Steele, K. (2015). Making climate decisions. *Philosophy Compass, 10*(11), 799–810.

Clore, G. L. (1992). Cognitive phenomenology: Feelings and the construction of judgment. In L. L. Martin & A. Tesser (Eds.), *The construction of social judgments* (pp. 133–163). Erlbaum.

Costikyan, G. (2013). *Uncertainty in games*. MIT Press.

Crawford, G. C., Aguinis, H., Lichtenstein, B., Davidsson, P., & McKelvey, B. (2015). Power law distributions in entrepreneurship: Implications for theory and research. *Journal of Business Venturing, 30*(5), 696–713.

Cyert, R. M., & March, J. G. (1963). *A behavioral theory of the firm*. Prentice-Hall.

Dattée, B., Alexy, O., & Autio, E. (2018). Maneuvering in poor visibility: How firms play the ecosystem game when uncertainty is high. *Academy of Management Journal, 61*(2), 466–498.

Dequech, D. (1999). Expectations and confidence under uncertainty. *Journal of Post Keynesian Economics, 21*(3), 415–430.

Dequech, D. (2003). Uncertainty and economic sociology: A preliminary discussion. *American Journal of Economics and Sociology, 62*(3), 509–532.

Dimov, D. (2016). Toward a design science of entrepreneurship. In *Models of start-up thinking and action: Theoretical, empirical and pedagogical approaches* (18, 1–31). Emerald Group Publishing Limited.
Einhorn, H. J., & Hogarth, R. M. (1986). Decision making under ambiguity. *Journal of Business*, 59(4), S225–S250.
Ellsberg, D. (1961). Risk, ambiguity, and the Savage axioms. *The Quarterly Journal of Economics*, 75(4), 643–669.
Etner, J., Jeleva, M., & Tallon, J. M. (2012). Decision theory under ambiguity. *Journal of Economic Surveys*, 26(2), 234–270.
Faber, M., Manstetten, R., & Proops, J. L. (1992). Humankind and the environment: An anatomy of surprise and ignorance. *Environmental Values*, 1(3), 217–241.
Fontana, G., & Gerrard, B. (2004). A Post Keynesian theory of decision making under uncertainty. *Journal of Economic Psychology*, 25(5), 619–637.
Garner, W. R. (1962). *Uncertainty and structure as psychological concepts*. Wiley.
Ghirardato, P. (2001). Coping with ignorance: Unforeseen contingencies and non-additive uncertainty. *Economic Theory*, 17, 247–276.
Gigerenzer, G., & Gaissmaier, W. (2011). Heuristic decision making. *Annual Review of Psychology*, 62, 451–482.
Gilboa, I. (2009). *Theory of decision under uncertainty*. Cambridge University Press.
Gray, J. (2002). *Straw dogs: Thoughts on humans and other animals*. Farrar.
Griffin, M. A., & Grote, G. (2020). When is more uncertainty better? A model of uncertainty regulation and effectiveness. *Academy of Management Review*, 45(4), 745–765.
Hansen, F. (1972). *Consumer choice behavior: A cognitive theory*. The Free Press.
Hodgson, G. M. (2011). The eclipse of the uncertainty concept in mainstream economics. *Journal of Economic Issues*, 45(1), 159-176.
Hicks, J. R. (1979). *Causality in economics*. Basil Blackwell.
Huang, L., & Pearce, J. L. (2015). Managing the unknowable: The effectiveness of early-stage investor gut feel in entrepreneurial investment decisions. *Administrative Science Quarterly*, 60(4), 634–670.
Jordan, M. E., Schallert, D. L., Park, Y., Lee, S., Chiang, Y. H. V., Cheng, A. C. J., ... Lee, H. (2012). Expressing uncertainty in computer-mediated discourse: Language as a marker of intellectual work. *Discourse Processes*, 49(8), 660–692.
Kaur, N. & Dasgupta, C. (2018). Types of uncertainty and collaborative uncertainty management strategies evidenced during the engineering design process. In *International Conference on Computers in Education* (pp. 175–180).
Kay, J. A., & King, M. A. (2020). *Radical uncertainty*. Bridge Street Press.
Knight, F. H. (1921). *Risk, uncertainty and profit*. Augustus M. Kelley.

Kozyreva, A., & Hertwig, R. (2021). The interpretation of uncertainty in ecological rationality. *Synthese, 198*(2), 1517–1547.
Kuhlthau, C. C. (1993). A principle of uncertainty for information seeking. *Journal of Documentation, 49*(4), 339–355.
Langlois, R. N., & Cosgel, M. M. (1993). Frank Knight on risk, uncertainty, and the firm: A new interpretation. *Economic Inquiry, 31*(3), 456–465.
Magnani, G., & Zucchella, A. (2018). Uncertainty in entrepreneurship and management studies: A systematic literature review. *International Journal of Business and Management, 13*(3), 98–133.
Manski, C. F. (2000). Identification problems and decisions under ambiguity: Empirical analysis of treatment response and normative analysis of treatment choice. *Journal of Econometrics, 95*(2), 415–442.
Marchau, V. A., Walker, W. E., Bloemen, P. J., & Popper, S. W. (2019). *Decision making under deep uncertainty: from theory to practice*. Springer Nature.
Meyer, R. J., & Sathi, A. (1985). A multi-attribute model of consumer choice during product learning. *Marketing Science, 4*(1), 41–61.
Millar, C. C., Groth, O., & Mahon, J. F. (2018). Management innovation in a VUCA world: Challenges and recommendations. *California Management Review, 61*(1), 5–14.
O'Malley, P. (2000). Uncertain subjects: Risks, liberalism and contract. *Economy and Society, 29*(4), 460–484.
Pressman, S., & Choi, Y. B. (1997). Paradigms, conventions and the entrepreneur: A review article and response. *American Journal of Economics and Sociology, 56*(1), 51–68.
Romeijn, J. W., & Roy, O. (2014). Radical uncertainty: Beyond probabilistic models of belief. *Erkenntnis, 79*, 1221–1223.
Rowe, W. D. (1994). Understanding uncertainty. *Risk Analysis, 14*(5), 743–750.
Rouvray, D. H. (1997). The treatment of uncertainty in the sciences. *Endeavour, 21*(4), 154–158.
Samsami, F., Hosseini, S. H. K., Kordnaeij, A., & Azar, A. (2015). Managing environmental uncertainty: From conceptual review to strategic management point of view. *International Journal of Business and Management, 10*(7), 215–229.
Schoemaker, P. J. (2002). *Profiting from uncertainty: Strategies for succeeding no matter what the future brings*. Simon & Schuster.
Schwarz, N., & Clore, G. L. (1996). Feelings and phenomenal experiences. In E. T. Higgins & A. Kruglanski (Eds.), *Social psychology: Handbook of basic principles* (pp. 433–465). Guilford.
Scoblic, J. P. (2020). Learning from the future. *Harvard Business Review, 98*(4), 38–47.
Shackle, G. L. S. (1955). *Uncertainty in Economics*. Cambridge University Press.

Shackle, G. L. S. (1966). Policy, poetry and success. *The Economic Journal, 76*(304), 755–767.
Shane, S. (2000). Prior knowledge and the discovery of entrepreneurial opportunities. *Organization Science, 11*(4), 448–469.
Simon, H. A. (1979). Rational decision making in business organizations. *American Economic Review, 69*(4), 493–513.
Smithson, M. (1989). *Ignorance and uncertainty: Emerging paradigms*. Springer Verlag.
Spender, J.-C. (2006). Knightian uncertainty and its resolution as institutionalized practice [v9 Working Paper].
Stewart, I. (2019). *Do Dice Play God? The mathematics of uncertainty*. Hachette UK.
Thompson, J. (1967). *Organizations in action*. McGraw-Hill.
Tannert, C., Elvers, H. D., & Jandrig, B. (2007). The ethics of uncertainty: In the light of possible dangers, research becomes a moral duty. *EMBO Reports, 8*(10), 892–896.
Taylor, C. R. (2003). The role of risk versus the role of uncertainty in economic systems. *Agricultural Systems, 75*(2–3), 251–264.
Teece, D., Peteraf, M., & Leih, S. (2016). Dynamic capabilities and organizational agility: Risk, uncertainty, and strategy in the innovation economy. *California Management Review, 58*(4), 13–35.
Townsend, D. M., Hunt, R. A., McMullen, J. S., & Sarasvathy, S. D. (2018). Uncertainty, knowledge problems, and entrepreneurial action. *Academy of Management Annals, 12*(2), 659–687.
Wald, A. (1950). *Statistical decision functions*. Wiley.
Wheeler, J. A. (1992). [Quoted in Scientific American, December, 1992, p. 20]

CHAPTER 6

Negative Effects of Uncertainty (on Decision-Making)

Costly Uncertainties

Why do people hate uncertainty?—because they hate the idea of losses (Bernstein, 1996). Uncertainty involves many kinds of possible real and psychological costs; for example, to the latter, the aversion to ambiguity

© The Author(s), under exclusive license to Springer Nature Switzerland AG 2024
R. J. Arend, *Uncertainty in Strategic Decision Making*,
https://doi.org/10.1007/978-3-031-48553-4_6

Table 6.1 Possible negative effects of uncertainty

Uncertainty's costliness is seen in many real and possible forms, including:

- the non-optimizability of decision problems
- market failures (and the resulting inefficiencies)
- costs arising from dealing with it (e.g., possibly causing additional uncertainties)
- realized harms (as negative outcomes that were unprepared for)
- doubt, anxiety and despair
- miscommunications
- mistrust
- unaccountability

is driven by a decision-maker's feelings of incompetence (Tversky & Fox, 1995). Taleb (2012) labels 'things' that experience real costs from uncertainty as *fragile*. Overall, in most circumstances, uncertainty is not considered a 'good' thing (Costikyan, 2013). Table 6.1 depicts the main negative effects of uncertainty that are described in more detail below.

In lab studies, and the real world, uncertainty is so associated with harm that people will pay significantly to avoid it; for example, in experiments, subjects will pay over 70 percent of the expected value of an alternative *un*ambiguous choice just to avoid the ambiguous one (Becker & Brownson, 1964). Even when given a choice among ambiguous options, subjects will pay a premium for the one involving a smaller range of possible outcomes (Becker & Brownson, 1964). In the real world, one rough measure of what people are willing to pay to avoid uncertainty is indicated by what they are willing to pay to simply avoid basic risks—i.e., as seen in the various forms of insurance invested in. (Noting that insurance industries, savings accounts, and pension plans comprise significant parts of any [western] economy.)

Again referencing risk as a (very) rough guide to the effect of uncertainty's possible downsides, prospect theory describes a significant observed bias to downside exposure for most individual decision-makers (Kahneman & Tversky, 1979). As such, their decision weights are much higher for downside possibilities (Kay & King, 2020) when outcomes span a range including benefits and harms. In short, humans are wired for pronounced sensitivity to the costs of uncertainties.

That said, such sensitivities can be unfortunately repressed in some organizational cultures and through some routinizations, most often with deleterious effects. For example, with the *NASA Challenger* disaster, several painfully overconfident statements about the probabilities of malfunctions were provided that disguised the real uncertainties, hiding the need to seriously address them (Kay & King, 2020).

It is that failure to identify and address uncertainties that too often results in the worst (or at least the most regrettable) costs; hopefully, such cases serve as warnings going forward given the current threats humanity faces (e.g., from global warming, terrorism, nuclear proliferation, saber-rattling, and political polarization). Those threats are especially dangerous when they add to uncertainties by supplying disinformation and by questioning the few facts that may be available in new situations. To the latter, exploiting an already dangerous situation by suggesting that any current absence of corroborating evidence of harm or of unreasonable risk of harm (e.g., from global warming) somehow equates to evidence of the benign nature of an uncertain threat (Szentkirályi, 2020) seems criminal. When it comes to threats from 'existential-level' uncertainties, the absence of evidence of possible downsides is absolutely not evidence of their absence. While arguing it may score quick political points (and garner lobbyist funding from polluting industries), it is simply irresponsible; instead, such uncertainties (e.g., about climate change) need to be analyzed and addressed based on their potential negative impacts and irreversibility (Bradley & Steele, 2015). It would be useful to remember that under conditions of true uncertainty that one possible consequence is defined by *catastrophic* failure (Ben-Haim, 2001).

NEGATIVE EFFECTS OF UNCERTAINTY

The discerning and definitional feature of uncertainty in this book is a negative one—i.e., uncertainty renders impossible the optimization of a decision problem. It causes an informational market failure and that, by definition, entails costly-to-society inefficiencies.

Uncertainty is costly whether firms try to account for its impacts or whether they do not. When they do recognize a focal uncertainty and try to reduce it through gathering new information, that new information can actually worsen the knowledge problem for decision-makers by exposing more unknowns, more complications, and greater downside possibilities (Townsend et al., 2018). And, when they don't, decision-makers often suffer, for example, by unknowingly directing their assets inefficiently with over-investments in exploitation of present products rather than with exploration of new ones (Lampert et al., 2020). Even choosing to ignore the uncertainty offers no escape, as the resultant decisions are likely to fail; and, even if they do succeed, the firm will then be incapable of seizing any opportunities that arise (Marchau et al., 2019).

In other words, under uncertainty, most approaches to strategizing, including traditional ones, can be dangerous (Courtney et al., 1997). Underestimating and under-addressing uncertainty leads to strategic plans that neither defend against threats nor take advantage of opportunities generated by that uncertainty (Courtney et al., 1997). Further, actually taking action under such conditions entails high opportunity costs (Shackle, 1955; Townsend et al., 2020).

Uncertainty not only means not knowing the future, it also often involves not knowing everything about the present or the past. That additional lack of knowledge is usually also costly. For example, it limits our ability to learn; making the repetition of mistakes more likely and the repetition of successes less so. And, if we ignore the past unknowns and apply hindsight anyways, for example, by mislabeling 'luck' as 'good judgment' in cases of successful outcomes, we are likely to be disappointed (Kay & King, 2020). Under uncertainty, we know that good decisions have possible bad outcomes and that bad decisions have possible good outcomes, and so it is a mistake to judge the quality of decisions solely on outcomes alone. Thus, one bad outcome should not discredit a method of addressing an uncertainty. Ignoring that logic can lead to escalations of commitments to bad-but-so-far-lucky methods (and abandonments of good-but-so-far-unlucky methods). So, under uncertainty, it is important to challenge prevailing methods when the stakes are high (Kay & King, 2020).

Over and above the costs uncertainty entails because of unknown factors of the past, present, and future, it can generate further costs involving 'what should be known'. A greater manifestation of unknowns breeds greater doubt, and that makes communications more challenging. At high levels of uncertainty, people are often unwilling to try to build trust (Adobor, 2006). And, when trust declines (as unknowns make opportunism easier and its possible downsides worse—Adobor, 2006), even transferring knowledge becomes less efficient (increasing the monetarily costs) and feelings of discomfort increase, including among co-workers and business partners (increasing the non-monetarily costs) (Stewart, 2019).

Uncertainty is considered a negative cognitive state, a state that often causes harmful affective symptoms like anxiety and self-doubt. When confronted by uncertainty—as a lack of understanding, a gap in meaning, or a limitation in a focal construct—'our' natural response is to feel anxious and then to seek more information to alleviate that feeling. Symptoms like confusion and frustration are associated with the vague, unclear thoughts about the focal unknown that arise as the information search process begins (Kuhlthau, 1993). And, as the decision involving the uncertainty becomes more imminent, the human ability to analyze that uncertainty decreases. Sometimes, decision-makers freeze and are unable to work (Bammer & Smithson, 2008). One reason is that uncertainty arouses an emotional response that dominates the human analytical approach (Rowe, 1994). Those emotional responses are to the fear of the unwanted possible consequences, but also to indignation (Roeser, 2019); such responses include feeling a lack of control.

Beyond the strategic and affective negative consequences of uncertainty, there lies another important one—one that has been growing in danger recently—that of *unaccountability*. Unfortunately, under the common conditions of uncertainty—when future outcomes are unforeseeable and probabilities of harm inestimable—it is much more difficult to hold culpable the entities that do take actions that end up harming others (Szentkirályi, 2020). This appears as both a moral and a legal issue. The core argument for culpability being that to act in a manner that places others in the way of potential but uncertain harm is to wrongfully disregard their interests and their capacity for self-determination (Szentkirályi, 2020). Thus, failing to exercise due care—whatever that may be in contexts of uncertainties like global warming—is to commit wrongdoing. The bottom line is that *uncertainty cannot be used as a means to escape the responsibility* of that care (although it appears it has been a historically successful one) especially when an entity is actively creating that uncertainty (e.g., finding new uses for the 'forever chemical' toxins that have uncertain future harms). It is what the creation of the uncertain threat implies about the relationship between the threat-creator and the potential victims (i.e., it implies a reckless disregard of their interests) that violates their autonomy (Szentkirályi, 2020)—a violation that needs to be better deterred and punished in the future.

Drivers of Negative Effects

The drivers of uncertainty's realized objective harms are the standard economic drivers of such negative effects. However, they entail an additional element—i.e., incomplete information about whether those harms can or will occur (e.g., whether a component generated in the manufacture of a firm's product will be found to be toxic in the future—be a negative externality—and then whether the firm will be held liable). Given the focus of this book is on strategic decisions—those involving significant potential upsides and downsides—the drivers are a special set. They can be known to be able to produce a wide range of possible benefits and harms, or not known to (i.e., that can be a surprise until revealed), at the time of the decision. In other words, the driver's cause-and-effect may not be fully understood, and its outcome not usefully predictable or controllable. When revealed, however, the driver will end up being a standard mechanism that destroys or (unfairly) transfers value in the economy (e.g., a negative externality; a regulatory loophole; a grift; an exploited information asymmetry; an abuse of market power).

What the drivers involve (e.g., the technologies behind the negative externalities), who the drivers involve (e.g., regulators; rivals; nature), and why they may be unknown (e.g., disinformation), are questions that generate an infinite range of specific possible embodiments of those drivers. The drivers may be human-based (e.g., involving the decision-maker, rivals, business partners, customers, and so on) or non-human-based (e.g., involving nature), be in the realm of physics, chemistry, genetics, neuroscience, politics, sociology, psychology, or some combination of these, or something else. To the former, the negative effects of those drivers may even be made larger because uncertainties are often *not* put into the hands of those who have the best capacity to handle them (Kay & King, 2020). Further ways that uncertainty's negative effects can be worsened, regardless of their driver, involve poor problem specification, misunderstandings of relevant historic outcomes and their causes, and a lack of appreciation of any base rates involved (Kay & King, 2020).

Contexts for Negative Effects

The focus of this book is on decision-making under uncertainty, and moreso, on those decisions that are strategically interesting; as such, the real possibility of significant negative effects is implied. In fact, most contexts where uncertainty exists involve possible costs and harms. That said, contexts that are more likely to involve greater negative effects entail: limited upsides (e.g., where benefits must be shared, or are capped by regulation) without symmetrical limits to the downsides; larger downside ranges in ambiguity-as-range problems; greater 'accelerator' issues—conditions that allow for expanding one negative outcome, like having more than one uncertainty involved, or having those uncertainties be interdependent; and, larger difficulties in justifying *ex post* the choices originally made should bad outcomes occur (e.g., in terms of any reputational damages that follow).

One of the most famous contexts for consideration of the negative effects of uncertainty relates to entrepreneurial activity (Knight, 1921). Dangers (like total venture failure) are very apparent when entrepreneurs confront *a priori* objective unknowns that they cannot explain or wish away. Those potential negative effects impact the venture regardless of whether the entrepreneurs remain ignorant of them or not (Townsend et al., 2020). Further, it is always possible that even good actions taken by entrepreneurs will be offset by the impact of uncertainty on the venture's performance, making outcome-based assessments of them questionable (Venkataraman, 1997).

Of course, not all decisions are equally endangered by uncertainty. It depends on the known unknown and the stakes involved (if these are known). It may also depend on the granularity of the decision—the more that the specifics can be considered, like options, outcomes, probabilities, payoffs, values, and so on, the greater the opportunity to debate how uncertainty can have negative effects (Bradley & Steele, 2015).

Dealing with Negative Effects

The myriad of ways to address various forms of uncertainty is covered later in this book. (Many of those ways, by default, are then also potential ways to deal with the possible negative effects of such uncertainties.) That said, it is advised to avoid any voluntary uncertainties when these are deemed unattractive (e.g., when the judgment is that the downsides dominate the upsides). If not avoidable, then actions that can limit the downsides of the uncertainties—with external protections (e.g., bankruptcy regulations; limited liability; not holding residual rights...)—or that can at least reduce the downside ranges (i.e., for decisions involving ambiguity in terms of bounded outcomes or their probabilities) are recommended when feasible. Otherwise, actions that limit 'domino' effects (e.g., that decouple one uncertainty from another or that deleverage outcomes) are potentially wise investments.

Regarding voluntary uncertainties—for example, when decision-makers create it—it is worthwhile to consider the worst-cases (i.e., the very negative effect scenarios). This consideration has been termed *knowledge-enabled destruction*, and it emerges from the apocalyptic hypothesis that technologically-progressive societies never progress far beyond the time when they create the means to destroy themselves (Barrow, 1998). Humanity's instinctive desires for discovery and the trappings of success stop us retreating from our advances, while political systems prevent effective regulations, and financial systems induce myopia; combined, that is a recipe for generating greater and greater destructive uncertainty.

The better our technologies become in ordering nature's randomness and departing from thermal equilibrium, the greater the pent-up hazards, whether foreseeable or not, and the greater the irreversibility of any disastrous outcomes arising from those departures (Barrow, 1998). When that is accompanied by a declining knowledge (or trust) of the sciences underlying new products by end-users and by powerful political figures, the likelihood of such disasters becomes inevitable. And, that is not even speaking to the military issues of such scientific progress; where, if history is preamble, the power of new technologies will certainly be used to commit atrocious crimes (Gray, 2002).

Not to belabor the potential negatives, but we know that even the costs of uncertainty reduction—when unknowns can be made more known over time—are great, not just in terms of resources, but also (sadly) in terms of what more knowledge (and less uncertainty) can lead to. It can lead to boredom and vice—where we observe that a great deal of time (and of the economy) is focused on (not very productive) entertainment (Gray, 2002). And, when that knowledge is not widely shared, it can also lead to abuses of the power by those holding superior information. Further, when we actually do try to make unknowables known, we are likely to fail; our instincts are often wrong (about estimating unknown probabilities—Schoemaker, 2002), and it has been shown that real decision-makers do not actually carry around subjective probabilities for everything, let alone have consistent preferences over lotteries involving those (e.g., the 9/11 attacks had little probability attached to them prior to occurring—Kay & King, 2020). Humans, including experts in specific decisions and events, regularly suffer from failures of imagination. As such, it must be acknowledged that there may be many negative effects of uncertainties that cannot be fully dealt with ahead of time.

> **Summary**
> Uncertainty can generate a wide range and depth of costs and harms, to a wide swath of victims (i.e., from individuals to organizations to communities to economies to the environment). Uncertainties can generate new costs, increase existing costs, and lower existing benefits. Once the uncertainty is revealed, the driver of any realized harms can be categorized within the standard set of economic causes of inefficiencies; prior to that revelation, it is often difficult to do so (e.g., due to the nature of unknown unknowns). There are few contexts where proactive moves can be attempted to mitigate possible downsides. As technologies get more powerful, and power gets more concentrated, humanity must get better at assessing the negative impacts of uncertainties, and identifying and treating the uncertainties themselves, or face annihilation.
>
> Why the negative effects of uncertainty matter:
>
> - For some decision problems, these effects can be severe and irreversible, and so these need to be identified and treated seriously
> - Progress (especially in novel technologies [like AI] where uncertainties are greater) needs to be assessed not just for the possible benefits but for the possible costs (and their distributions), and proper restraints applied
> - When the possible negative impacts can be mitigated—e.g., because the uncertainties are being generated (e.g., disinformation)—they need to be, and with harsh and speedy effect
>
> What the negative effects of uncertainty mean for business and policy:
>
> - Measuring the growth of possible downsides (along multiple dimensions, including reversibility) needs to start in order to better assess trends and prioritize investments in addressing these problems
> - Advanced nations have reached a period where 'most' people work to entertain/distract/amuse other people by inventing new vices and creating novel experiences as antidotes for boredom (Gray, 2002); but while the demand and money might be there, the dangers of such nonknowledge pursuits are unknown (and likely large)
> - There is no commerce if humanity ceases to exist; it is in business's long- (medium-?) term interest to help with pricing in the

> negative externalities, improving liability laws, and raising the level of the morality relating to new technology's exploitation of human neurological responses

References

Adobor, H. (2006). Optimal trust? Uncertainty as a determinant and limit to trust in inter-firm alliances. *Leadership & Organization Development Journal*, 27(7), 537–553.

Bammer, G., & Smithson, M. (2008). Understanding uncertainty. *Integration Insights*, 7(1), 1–7.

Barrow, J. D. (1998). *Impossibility: The limits of science and the science of limits*. Oxford University Press on Demand.

Becker, S. W., & Brownson, F. O. (1964). What price ambiguity? Or the role of ambiguity in decision-making. *Journal of Political Economy*, 72(1), 62–73.

Ben-Haim, Y. (2001). Decision trade-offs under severe info-gap uncertainty. *ISIPTA* (June) (pp. 32–39).

Bernstein, P. L. (1996). *Against the gods: The remarkable story of risk*. Wiley.

Bradley, R., & Steele, K. (2015). Making climate decisions. *Philosophy Compass*, 10(11), 799–810.

Costikyan, G. (2013). *Uncertainty in games*. MIT Press.

Courtney, H., Kirkland, J., & Viguerie, P. (1997). Strategy under uncertainty. *Harvard Business Review*, 75(6), 67–79.

Gray, J. (2002). *Straw dogs: Thoughts on humans and other animals*. Farrar.

Kahneman, D., & Tversky, A. (1979). Prospect theory. *Econometrica*, 47, 263–292.

Kay, J. A., & King, M. A. (2020). *Radical uncertainty*. Bridge Street Press.

Knight, F. H. (1921/64). *Risk, uncertainty and profit*. Augustus M. Kelley.

Kuhlthau, C. C. (1993). A principle of uncertainty for information seeking. *Journal of Documentation*, 49(4), 339–355.

Lampert, C. M., Kim, M., & Polidoro, F., Jr. (2020). Branching and anchoring: Complementary asset configurations in conditions of Knightian uncertainty. *Academy of Management Review*, 45(4), 847–868.

Marchau, V. A., Walker, W. E., Bloemen, P. J., & Popper, S. W. (2019). *Decision making under deep uncertainty: from theory to practice*. Springer Nature.

Roeser, S. (2019). Emotional responses to luck, risk, and uncertainty. In *The Routledge handbook of the philosophy and psychology of luck* (pp. 356–364). Routledge.

Rowe, W. D. (1994). Understanding uncertainty. *Risk Analysis*, 14(5), 743–750.

Schoemaker, P. J. (2002). *Profiting from uncertainty: Strategies for succeeding no matter what the future brings*. Simon & Schuster.
Shackle, G. L. S. (1955). *Uncertainty in economics*. Cambridge University Press.
Stewart, I. (2019). *Do dice play God? The mathematics of uncertainty*. Hachette UK.
Szentkirályi, L. (2020). Luck has nothing to do with it: Prevailing uncertainty and responsibilities of due care. *Ethics, Policy & Environment, 23*(3), 261–280.
Taleb, N. N. (2012). *Antifragile: How to live in a world we don't understand*. Allen Lane.
Townsend, D. M., Hunt, R. A., McMullen, J. S., & Sarasvathy, S. D. (2018). Uncertainty, knowledge problems, and entrepreneurial action. *Academy of Management Annals, 12*(2), 659–687.
Townsend, D. M., Hunt, R. A., Beal, D. J., & Hyeong Jin, J. (2020). Venturing into the unknown: A meta-analytic assessment of uncertainty in entrepreneurship research. *Academy of Management Proceedings*.
Tversky, A., & Fox, C. R. (1995). Weighing risk and uncertainty. *Psychological Review, 102*(2), 269–283.
Venkataraman, S. (1997). The distinctive domain of entrepreneurship research: An editor's perspective. In J. Katz & R. Brockhaus (Eds.), *Advances in entrepreneurship, firm emergence and growth* (Vol. 3, pp.119–138). JAI Press.

CHAPTER 7

Positive Effects of Uncertainty (on Decision-Making)

The Existential Positive Effects of Uncertainty

Uncertainty provides freedom. Freedom to pursue entrepreneurial activities (Bernstein, 1996). Freedom to choose. And, freedom to imagine better futures (Shackle, 1979). Uncertainty, as embodied in humans, evidences our free will, for good and for bad. For good in terms of our creative products. (And for bad, in terms of our unpredictability, irrationality, and guileful opportunism.) Table 7.1 depicts the many embodiments of the good impacts of uncertainty that we describe in more detail below.

Major theories of competitive advantage draw upon uncertainty as a necessary condition. The resource-based view [RBV] models firms as making decisions about resources and capabilities under necessary uncertainty about their values (Barney, 1986). Entrepreneurial activity has an existential relationship with uncertainty in Knight's (1921) model. Transaction costs economics [TCE] models unknowns about agent and partner behaviors (i.e., their opportunism), making the holding of residual rights (i.e., all the things that are not insurable) of great import. In other words, in many cases (and perhaps the most interesting cases), *for profits to exist*—the profits that drive innovation and the possibility of higher standards of living—*uncertainty must be present* (or pursued).

Progress is not possible without uncertainty (Beck, 2009). Uncertainty is a fundamental force that has led to the discovery of 'new' worlds, and the creation of new markets, products, services, and organizational forms. Uncertainty is needed for mystery, perhaps even for a meaningful life (Bernstein, 1996).

Table 7.1 Possible positive effects of uncertainty

Uncertainty's benefits are found in many real and possible forms, including:

- as freedom and free will
- as creativity and technological progress
- as a randomizer for sampling
- as a means to control chaotic systems
- as antifragility
- as synergy
- as a requirement for trust-building
- as curiosity
- as entrepreneurship/ innovation / new entry
- as entertainment
- as forging institutions
- as renewing organizational structure
- as hope

And, from a different perspective, uncertainty—as embodied in variability—is also the requirement for 'structures' to be defined and to evolve (Garner, 1962). (If everything was the same, or static, or even completely predictable, there would be less-to-no need for systems that require interesting organizational forms.) When you consider most products, each has a well-defined shell or boundary (e.g., a plastic casing); that structure protects its workings from the variations and unknowns of the outside (e.g., rain, dust, static) while protecting mostly known others from those workings (e.g., from electric shock, loud noise, fast-moving parts). Structures arise because of uncertainties; they arise to help us control for them. And, in many cases, such structures are beneficial to human progress (e.g., for safety, security, and the ability to survive in otherwise harsh environments—like outer-space).

UNCERTAINTY AS A SIGNAL OF POTENTIAL REWARDS

Uncertainty signals potential rewards; not only from taking on decisions that others won't and winning (Knight, 1921), but also from learning new information and from gaining experience (e.g., Griffin & Grote, 2020). By actively seeking out and confronting uncertainty, firms (and individuals like entrepreneurs) can create and/or identify new opportunities for value creation.

Of course, such actions are not without direct costs, in addition to the possible losses from making the wrong choices. The uncertainty embodies an informational market imperfection—one that offers possible benefits to those who either choose luckily (e.g., by guessing correctly the unknown's value and acting on that), or who bear the unknown at a cost to reveal its true value privately and can then use that informational advantage to reap gains over those costs (or, who can somehow find naïve others to bear the uncertainty at a cost below the fee of that 'insurance'). In any case, such firms are 'unusual' by definition. Knight (1921) posits this unusualness can be embodied in the form of 'entrepreneurial judgment'—seemingly a shorthand for an informational advantage (whether objective or subjective).

The point is that, while uncertainty often signals a potential for benefits, in order for it to be attractive to bear, additional conditions are often required. As an analogy, for the case of risk-like volatility, a financial (or real) *option* is valuable because it fulfills such conditions (i.e., its downside is limited while its upside is not, while its cost is known). In the case of uncertainty, more work needs to be done to identify the conditions (and tools and signals) that both entice real entrepreneurs to bear it and that make such a choice theoretically attractive.

Conceptual Benefits from Uncertainty

Besides Knight's (1921) theoretical entrepreneurial benefits arising from uncertainty, others, including Ellsberg, have illustrated cases where decision-makers see uncertainties—like ambiguity—as being conceptually favorable (Becker & Brownson, 1964; Townsend et al., 2020). Heiner (1983) argues that when a gap exists between a decision-maker's competence and the difficulty of the problem to be solved, for example as caused by uncertainty, institutions (and their rules) are constructed to restrict the flexibility of choices (Denzau & North, 1994). So, uncertainty can favor beneficial institution-building; and, it can also favor healthy renewal within existing organizations. Uncertainty opens up the possibility for new actors to gain power and improve frames and structures in an organization (Kaplan, 2008).

In terms of conceiving of a more balanced perspective about uncertainty, it begins with acknowledging that there are two contrasting consequences of uncertainty—possible catastrophic failure and possible windfall success (Ben-Haim, 2001). But, these are not weighed equally by real decision-makers due to a number of factors (e.g., loss aversion; overconfidence; framing; and, so on). More conceptual and lab work is needed to better understand how such factors should and do interact (e.g., by canceling or intensifying each other).

Like any source of market failure, uncertainty promises theoretical upsides to those either brave or desperate enough, or who believe that they are informationally-advantaged enough, to bear it. While businesses and governments have been successful in providing instruments to people to take on risks (e.g., in options, insurance, and other diversification techniques), they have been less successful—*ex ante*—in providing instruments to take on uncertainties; this is because better conceptualizations of uncertainty have been lacking. More work is needed there, not just to cover downsides, but also to spread upsides when they occur (e.g., so those who see windfalls do not then leverage them into market power).

Real Benefits from Uncertainty

Besides the many, mostly generalized, conceptual benefits possible when uncertainty exists, there are many more specific benefits that have been observed as realizations of uncertainty. In those 'right' contexts, uncertainty is wielded as a tool for good. For example, uncertainty can function to generate new ideas and propensities (Ramoglou & Tsang, 2016). It can be used as a randomizer for particular kinds of coding (e.g., in Monte Carlo simulations, genetic algorithms, and other virtual landscape-traversing tactics to move digital agents away from false-stops at local maxima). It can be used to help determine the area and volume of complicated spaces (e.g., by surrounding them with easily calculated spaces and then providing a way to 'throw darts' in order to calculate the proportion that stick to that space). It can be used to help control chaotic systems, moving their attractors and the system's outcomes (e.g., to exploit Lagrange points in space missions when fuel is low—Stewart, 2019), or stabilizing them by adding randomness (Taleb, 2012). Indeed, Taleb (2012) has even labeled 'things' that benefit from uncertainties (e.g., from shocks and disorder) as *antifragile*—things such as options and residual rights. Other things that benefit from uncertainty have more historic labels; for example, *synergies* occur when whole systems have upsides unpredicted by the behavior of their parts (Halpern, 2003), unpredicted because of *ex ante* uncertainties.

Uncertainty can also be used as a threat to tame 'bad' behavior (Dixit & Nalebuff, 1991). For example, it has been used by governments to discipline banks (Nosal & Ordoñez, 2016). Recently, it has been used by NATO—as *strategic response uncertainty*—to try to dissuade escalatory moves by Russia in the Ukraine (e.g., to dissuade the use of tactical nuclear weapons).

Uncertainty can also be used—perhaps counter-intuitively—to build trust. Some level of uncertainty is required for trust to emerge (Adobor, 2006; Bhattacharya et al., 1998; Dasgupta, 1988). Once built, trust can (and often does) provide many benefits from the cooperation that follows (especially when complete contracts are too costly or too complex or too counterculture to be written and enforced).

Even uncertainty in decision-making, at the right levels, can improve the process—by increasing the learning and dynamics that take place (Kuhlthau, 1993) because people tend to be curious and more engaged when they see some room for debate in the vacuum that incomplete information provides.

On a more personal/individual level, uncertainty has several potential benefits. For example, Wilson and colleagues (2005) describe how uncertainty can generate positive feelings in the right context (e.g., as when receiving a gift), sometimes even where such feelings increase with uncertainty (Kurtz et al., 2007). Uncertainty is also a primary characteristic of most sorts of play and gaming (Costikyan, 2013). In fact, humanity has a rich history—across cultures—of taking uncertainty and transforming into games (Costikyan, 2013). Play has even been defined by some sociologists (e.g., Roger Caillois) as 'uncertain activity'. Every game of skill—every pleasing one—involves risks, surprises, and unknowns that could result in any player being defeated. And, when one considers the 'play' industry (e.g., involving computer games, VR, gambling, D&D, and most sports)—let alone when one considers the amount of time (and money) people spend on games and play—the real 'felt' benefits of (that kind of) uncertainty appear *very* important to humanity and to what it is to be human (even on a daily basis).

Conditions for Benefits

With uncertainty we have argued and observed that benefits are possible; so, uncertainty can certainly be useful (Stewart, 2019). However, the context (i.e., its specific conditions) matters for whether benefits are more likely to occur, or be felt, in reality. For example, the character of the relevant narrative matters—without a secure narrative, uncertainty causes fear, but within a secure narrative, joy can come from the prospect of new experiences (Kay & King, 2020).

The condition of 'the right' amount' of uncertainty can also matter. For example, the decision to expand capacity by firms in an industry is often dependent on the degree of uncertainty over future demand. Too little uncertainty can lead to costly and inefficient wars of preemption, but sufficient uncertainty can give rise to orderly incrementalism in capacity expansion and resulting higher social welfare levels. Uncertainty can act as a brake on wasteful overcapacity investments (Porter, 1980).

The right conditions may also include the characteristics of the decision-maker or others involved. Personal interest is likely to increase when moving from a routine decision to one with more uncertainty, but then can decrease with more uncertainty as the feeling of control is lost

(Kuhlthau, 1993). Essentially, too much predictability reduces innovativeness and the joy that such experiences can create, while too little increases anxiety and confusion (Costikyan, 2013). The transitions in personal interest across that span of decision uncertainty will likely be affected by the personalities involved and by the compensation and accountability schemes involved. More work is needed in this area to better match decision-maker (and compensation) characteristics to the uncertainties (and their potential benefits and costs) embodied in the problems they are assigned.

Trade-offs are often involved in the context; usually, certainty must be relinquished in exchange for the possibility of windfalls (Ben-Haim, 2001). So, actions that protect a decision against environmental uncertainties may actually reduce favorable surprises. Such trade-offs need to be identified and assessed then prior to taking actions to address a focal unknown so that potential benefits are not unintentionally capped.

Who Benefits

The entities—persons, firms, and institutions—who benefit from uncertainty are either the ones who intentionally generate it or who are lucky. To the latter, *ex post*, these will be the entities that then enjoy some form of advantageous asymmetry relative to their rivals, an asymmetry that is likely to involve the greater ability to leverage possible upside outcomes or to mitigate possible downside outcomes. So, to identify who could benefit from a specific decision-made-under-uncertainty, a lot of specific information needs to be known. Generalizability is not likely (beyond obvious conditions [like mathematical or logical domination]).

That said, others have been more 'confident' in their predictions: For example, under a stable narrative, Kay and King (2020) predict it is more likely that creative, socially-aware (e.g., in terms of being effective social learners) and socially-capable (e.g., in terms of being effective communicators) individuals will thrive under 'high' uncertainty. Meanwhile, Knight (1921) suggests that uncertainty is likely to paralyze bureaucratic organizations while providing profitable opportunities to those more enterprising, entrepreneurial, and creative. We, given our definition of uncertainty (or at least for many forms of it, like unknown unknowns), do not consider any such predictions valid.

Returning to the start of this chapter, but on a more philosophical level (i.e., a level with a great scale in time and space), humanity (in general) does benefit from uncertainty. Humankind has been programmed to pursue uncertainty (e.g., to explore the globe; to enjoy 'playing'), to bear it when it wants, to learn from it, and to exploit it to its own ends. So far, we have seen many benefits (and costs) arising from uncertainties. As 'we' become the source of a greater proportion of them, and a more capable exploiter of them (against each other, for example, politically), we will need to be much more careful in how we deal with uncertainty because there is never any guarantee that the arguably historic net benefits will continue.

> **Summary**
> Uncertainty has several upsides; it can create new benefits, increase existing benefits, and mitigate existing harms. It is important to human freedom, creativity, and progress. It is existentially linked to entrepreneurial activity. It is one explanation for why (useful) institutions exist. It can be a basis for trust, for synergies, and for organizational renewal. It is essential in the 'play' we increasingly spend our time on. It can even help in controlling chaotic systems. Acknowledging (and exploiting) the potential benefits of uncertainty helps in assessing it in a more balanced, less fearful way.
>
> Why the positive effects of uncertainty matter:
>
> - Acknowledging the possible upsides of uncertainties provides balance in assessing the potential impacts, given the natural focus is on the downsides; that greater perspective may also help in widening the stakeholder pool considered
> - Knowing these exist helps ensure that opportunities for benefits are not missed
> - Many of these effects have been and continue to be very important, philosophically, historically, and commercially to humankind
>
> What the positive effects of uncertainty mean for business and policy:
>
> - Opportunities to exploit these effects for good
> - Opportunities to apply the attractive marketing aspects of mystery and play more responsibly
> - Opportunities to improve the conditions for creativity associated with uncertainty

References

Adobor, H. (2006). Optimal trust? Uncertainty as a determinant and limit to trust in inter-firm alliances. *Leadership & Organization Development Journal, 27*(7), 537–553.

Barney, J. B. (1986). Strategic factor markets: Expectations, luck and business strategy. *Management Science, 42*, 1231–1241.

Beck, U. (2009). *World at risk*. Polity.

Becker, S. W., & Brownson, F. O. (1964). What price ambiguity? Or the role of ambiguity in decision-making. *Journal of Political Economy, 72*(1), 62–73.

Ben-Haim, Y. (2001). Decision trade-offs under severe info-gap uncertainty. *ISIPTA* (June) (pp. 32–39).

Bernstein, P. L. (1996). *Against the gods: The remarkable story of risk*. Wiley.

Bhattacharya, R., Devinney, T. M., & Pillutla, M. M. (1998). A formal model of trust based on outcomes. *Academy of Management Review, 23*, 459–472.

Costikyan, G. (2013). *Uncertainty in games*. MIT Press.

Dasgupta, P. (1988). Patents, priority and imitation or, the economics of races and waiting games. *The Economic Journal, 98*(389), 66–80.

Denzau, A., & North, D. C. (1994). Shared mental models: Ideologies and institutions. *Kyklos, 47*(1), 3–31.

Dixit, A. K., & Nalebuff, B. J. (1991). *Thinking strategically: The competitive edge in business, politics, and everyday life*. WW Norton & Company.

Garner, W. R. (1962). *Uncertainty and structure as psychological concepts*. Wiley.

Griffin, M. A., & Grote, G. (2020). When is more uncertainty better? A model of uncertainty regulation and effectiveness. *Academy of Management Review, 45*(4), 745–765.

Halpern, J. Y. (2003). *Reasoning about uncertainty*. MIT Press.

Heiner, R. A. (1983). The origin of predictable behavior. *The American Economic Review, 73*(4), 560–595.

Kaplan, S. (2008). Framing contests: Strategy making under uncertainty. *Organization Science, 19*(5), 729–752.

Kay, J. A., & King, M. A. (2020). *Radical uncertainty*. Bridge Street Press.

Knight, F. H. (1921/64). *Risk, Uncertainty and profit*. Augustus M. Kelley.

Kuhlthau, C. C. (1993). A principle of uncertainty for information seeking. *Journal of Documentation, 49*(4), 339–355.

Kurtz, J. L., Wilson, T. D., & Gilbert, D. T. (2007). Quantity versus uncertainty: When winning one prize is better than winning two. *Journal of Experimental Social Psychology, 43*(6), 979–985.

Nosal, J. B., & Ordoñez, G. (2016). Uncertainty as commitment. *Journal of Monetary Economics, 80*, 124–140.

Porter, M. E. (1980). *Competitive strategy: Techniques for analyzing industries and competitors*. Free Press.

Ramoglou, S., & Tsang, E. W. (2016). A realist perspective of entrepreneurship: Opportunities as propensities. *Academy of Management Review, 41*(3), 410–434.

Shackle, G. L. S. (1979). *Imagination and the nature of choice.* Edinburgh University Press.

Stewart, I. (2019). *Do dice play God? The mathematics of uncertainty.* Hachette UK.

Taleb, N. N. (2012). *Antifragile: How to live in a world we don't understand.* Allen Lane.

Townsend, D. M., Hunt, R. A., Beal, D. J., & hyeong Jin, J. (2020). Venturing into the Unknown: A Meta-Analytic Assessment of Uncertainty in Entrepreneurship Research. *Academy of Management Proceedings.*

Wilson, T. D., Centerbar, D. B., Kermer, D. A., & Gilbert, D. T. (2005). The pleasures of uncertainty: Prolonging positive moods in ways people do not anticipate. *Journal of Personality and Social Psychology, 88*(1), 5–21.

CHAPTER 8

Optimal Uncertainty (in Decision-Making)

> He was like Goldilocks, but his porridge was vacations?.drugs?.ontologies?.religion?.hats?.patriarchical control?.humility?.sales pressure?—*Anonymous*

Why a Goldilocksian 'Amount' of Uncertainty Can Exist

Some uncertainties have mostly positive perceived effects, and the rest mostly negative ones. This implies that some problems involve a good balance of possible effects, emerging either from one 'balanced' uncertainty or from a mix of several offsetting uncertainties (offsetting in terms of the possible net benefits and harms perceived).

Such a good balance is often found in 'exploration' problems, ones that involve: the thrill of entrepreneurship (even when numbers indicate a high probability of failure); the creative rush of confronting some unexpected big challenges when entering a new space (as happened with *Apollo 13*); or, simply the entertainment and curiosity of playing a novel new game (knowing that we will not win this first round).

The hate–love relationship that humanity has with uncertainty has been noted for some time. For example, Knight (1921) observed the paradox that while humankind strives rationally to reduce uncertainty, it is done with the recognition that eliminating uncertainty, even nearly, would result in unappealing lives.

It appears that several implicit, or at least optimistic, assumptions underlie these sentiments, not the least of which involve *who* is enjoying the possible upsides and downsides, and *what* those possible downsides could entail. In some contexts, especially artificial ones like game design or speculative theorizing, it is not surprising to see claims that an optimal level of uncertainty can exist (Bradac, 2001). That Goldilocks level, however, is a challenge to identify even in such artificial contexts (Costikyan, 2013). So, when considering real-world contexts, it should not be surprising to assume that finding or implementing that level, even if identifiable, is nearly impossible (given most uncertainties are uncontrollable by their very nature of having no known cause-and-effect relationships to leverage).

At What Level of Analysis?

For the identification and possible implementation of an optimal amount of uncertainty, perspective matters. Assuming it is possible to tune uncertainties in this manner, it is likely to be an easier task at finer/lower levels (of play and analysis) than at higher levels. At higher levels (e.g., at the group, organization, or society levels) the target is bigger, more complex, and more spread out, making it much more difficult to assess the disparate effects and integrate them in a fair manner to achieve a balance. Further, at these higher levels, there will be more pressures to innovate and compete within and across groups—essentially adding new uncertainties to the mix—making the tuning of overall uncertainty-related effects much more difficult to accomplish.

Besides there being differences in how easily an optimal level of uncertainty can be attained based on the level of application, the recognition that different levels need to be accounted for in this task raises one further important issue: The reactions to uncertainty will greatly differ by level of perspective (Knight, 1921). These levels will have conflicting goals related to uncertainties. Individuals may focus on entertainment goals, while society may focus on the goal of mitigating people- and planet-related harms, while firms may focus on profitable opportunities for exploration and innovation. Any mechanisms for trading off such uncertainties among parties will be prone to many failures, not only from informational gaps related to uncertainty but from negative spillovers (e.g., from firm activities to society and the natural environment). This issue, then, points to the need to have an explicit description of the decision-maker and their goal (to set the relevant level of analysis) in order to even have a chance at tuning the system to a desired balance of uncertainties.

For What Ends?

The identification and application of an optimal level of uncertainty (noting that the *optimal-for-whom* issue is important) has many possible ends. When it is achievable, however, it has been mostly used to manipulate the behaviors and emotions of a target (although it can also be used to enhance the value of private information for gain).

For entertainment-related ends, optimization ensures game-play is neither too boring nor too uncontrollable. While most games tune the level of only one type of uncertainty, some games switch across uncertainty types while constraining that increased challenge (e.g., a game that requires quick physical responses cannot also pose difficult mental challenges—Costikyan, 2013). Building on the game concept—as a form of entertainment that also tutors the player—uncertainties can also be manipulated to provide serious training. Simulations of emergency situations (e.g., for pilots, firefighters, police, soldiers, medics, and so on) present unusual outcomes that push students into uncertain situations to assess behaviors, emotions, pace and choices, and where students can 'see' and 'feel' the harsh downsides without being in real danger. Getting the level of uncertainty correct allows students to learn better (versus being bored or overwhelmed). Then, building on the training concept—uncertainties can also be used to stress-test a subject (e.g., to determine their limits) or simply to provide experiences that they would not likely have in the real world simply so that they may better understand the possible downsides to a decision.

Manipulating the level of uncertainty may also be used to more directly influence the behavior of a potentially 'troublesome' target. It can be used to create fear to alter the decision-making of an independent entity, often increasing the feeling of accountability in that entity to any downsides it could generate. For example, it may be optimal for governments to design policy- and action-related uncertainties so that any bailouts and regulations facilitate improved (rather than destructive) self-regulation of targeted industries and firms (Nosal & Ordoñez, 2016). Such policies and actions, including investments in basic research, can also affect the tempo of tactical activities taken by industry players, in order to, for example, mitigate socially-inefficient preemptive moves and reward option-like small-stepping of investment. Such manipulations through the 'design' of uncertainties can benefit the economy and consumers.

Besides being used to mitigate 'bad' behaviors, uncertainty can be manipulated to spur 'good' choices and actions. Occurring through games and training, the right level of uncertainty provides healthy challenges to targets to elicit their 'good' creativity and curiosity. Note that such 'training' not only can increase such useful innovation and exploration in entities, but it can focus that on specific areas that the manipulator chooses (e.g., on unsolved problems; on situations that have traditionally had poor outcomes; and, so on), in order to increase the potential benefits of such an exercise.

Getting the level of uncertainty right is also important for creating and maintaining trust. Trust cannot exist without uncertainty—a minimum level is needed—but too much uncertainty leads to a breakdown of trust; so, the trust-uncertainty relationship is non-linear, if not complex (Adobor, 2006). While both too low and too high a level of uncertainty are dysfunctional to trust, oddly it seems that under moderately high levels of uncertainty that *only* trust will work as a means to having a functional relationship between two commercial entities (Barney & Hansen, 1994).

On a broader scale, market health itself may require a moderate level of uncertainty. Too little uncertainty and the market economy is stale and stagnant. Too much uncertainty and the market economy can spiral out of control because of reactive, undesirable social unrest (Taylor, 2003). Governments that find the right balance through policy maximize the efficient use of capital in their markets (Krumbein, 2012).

Besides optimizing uncertainty to manipulate behaviors, the tuning of uncertainty can also be used (more directly) to increase the value of private information, as examples of insider-trading have famously illustrated (Shin & Kim, 2019).

How to Generate It

To generate the right level and mix of uncertainties, one needs some control. Policy-makers, game-designers, military intelligence services, and others often have considerable control over the generation of specific types of uncertainties for others. Independent entities that can voluntarily choose to explore new areas (e.g., new technologies, markets, products, processes, partners, business models, strategies, or organizational forms) also have some control over the selection of uncertainties they experience.

When control exists, generating the right amount of uncertainty (e.g., in terms of levels, mix, pace, and so on) is a design issue—one that should be contingent on the target entity, the goal, the resources available, and the constraints. Dealing with uncertainty is not trivial, given the multiple dimensions, trade-offs, non-linearities, and interdependent effects involved (e.g., as uncertainty increases, the consequent anxieties, miscommunications, politics, and opportunism do so as well). Designers of uncertainty-experiences need to be aware of such sensitivities, and how they may evolve over time. This gets even more challenging—and perhaps more rewarding—when mixing uncertainty types (e.g., the game *Portal* combines first-person-shooter with puzzle-solving to provide a rich and entertaining experience to its players—Costikyan, 2013).

Besides the design of uncertainty for human targets, it is also useful to consider the design for pseudo-cognitive entities, like AIs. Optimal uncertainty design is likely to help train AI systems for unusual events that the usual real-world data fed into it may not, and so help it reduce its biases against *black swan* events (Taleb, 2012).

Summary

Having the ability to tune the balance of uncertainties is unusual. When it is available, it provides a means to influence a target's behaviors (for good or evil). Doing that effectively requires private information, and a sensitivity to the target entity, the goal, the constraints, and the level of analysis involved. For specialized training (of people and AI), it is indispensable.

Why 'optimal' uncertainty matters:

- Tuning uncertainty well is at the core of good entertainment
- The goldilocks level of uncertainty is programmed into human nature, so understanding its bounds is important to maximize any intended impact
- It is an irreplaceable tool for safe emergency training

What 'optimal' uncertainty means for business and policy:

- The best mixes of uncertainties often generate the most demand and profit for the associated products (e.g., games; culinary experiences; and, so on)
- Given manipulation is involved, there are ethical issues to consider (and regulate); especially longer-term (where few studies have been done)

References

Adobor, H. (2006). Optimal trust? Uncertainty as a determinant and limit to trust in inter-firm alliances. *Leadership & Organization Development Journal, 27*(7), 537–553.

Barney, J. B., & Hansen, M. H. (1994). Trustworthiness as a source of competitive advantage. *Strategic Management Journal, 15*(S1), 175–190.

Bradac, J. J. (2001). Theory comparison: Uncertainty reduction, problematic integration, uncertainty management, and other curious constructs. *Journal of Communication, 51*(3), 456–476.
Costikyan, G. (2013). *Uncertainty in Games.* MIT Press.
Knight, F. H. (1921/64). *Risk, uncertainty and profit.* Augustus M. Kelley.
Krumbein, J. (2012). Two invisible hands and optimal uncertainty. *SSRN 2034000.*
Nosal, J. B., & Ordoñez, G. (2016). Uncertainty as commitment. *Journal of Monetary Economics, 80,* 124–140.
Shin, D. D., & Kim, S. I. (2019). Homo curious: Curious or interested? *Educational Psychology Review, 31*(4), 853–874.
Taleb, N. N. (2012). *Antifragile: How to live in a world we don't understand.* Allen Lane.
Taylor, C. R. (2003). The role of risk versus the role of uncertainty in economic systems. *Agricultural Systems, 75*(2–3), 251–264.

CHAPTER 9

Measures of Uncertainty (in Decision-Making)

© The Author(s), under exclusive license to Springer Nature Switzerland AG 2024
R. J. Arend, *Uncertainty in Strategic Decision Making*,
https://doi.org/10.1007/978-3-031-48553-4_9

The Importance of Measuring Uncertainty and Its Characteristics

In order to properly manage something, first it must be measured; without measurement, there is no reference point to assess change (e.g., progress or failure), and without the ability to assess change there is no way to relate it to whatever actions were taken to affect that change and, so, no way to determine the cause-and-effect understanding underlying what the term 'management' means. This concept applies not only to known things but also to things that involve unknownness (*aka* uncertainties). Uncertainty must be measured (in whatever limited ways possible) to even begin to manage it. Wrapping one's arms around the uncertainties of a focal decision—perhaps in terms of what is known, or the range of possible outcomes, or its familiarity, or its avoidability—provides a start to addressing it (better). For several types of uncertainty, measurement is challenging given, by definition for these types, if one could measure them then they would theoretically lose their unknownness. In the real world, rare events are often imbedded in noise, and so sometimes even capturing the full realized outcomes of existing uncertainties can be difficult and, so, impede the ability to identify, track, learn from, and better understand them in the future. Regardless of the difficulty, making efforts to try to measure uncertainties (and their characteristics and their realized outcomes) is very important, as several types theoretically exhibit (or have been observed to exhibit) a low-probability-but-high-consequence nature. Table 9.1 depicts the main approaches, perspectives, and measurement types relating to uncertainty.

It is not only imperative to identify and apply measures of uncertainties, but also to keep them as objective as possible in order to improve the consistency of the categorization and of the subsequent learning about the underlying uncertainties. Keeping the measurements objective also helps with the legitimization of uncertainty studies, as it improves repeatability and common understanding. The objective measures can also be of value in validating perceptual (subjective) measures (Starbuck, 1976). Only with greater precision in defining, using, and measuring the uncertainty types will we be able to improve our performance in making decisions under uncertainty (Milliken, 1987).

Measures of uncertainty are needed both before and after the focal decision. When a subsequent realization of the impact of the uncertainty (apart from on the decision) is observable—which may not always

Table 9.1 Measuring uncertainty

Approaches to Measurement	objective measures (using instruments); independent of measurer
	subjective perception-based measures (e.g., using surveys)
	mixed/combined objective-subjective measures
Practical Measures (of real-world data—existing and privately-held)	statistical
	perceptual
	mixed (e.g., automated textual analyses of news articles)
Conceptual Measures (on theoretical or simulated data)	assumed statistical (representative algebra of mean, variance, volatility, and so on)
	math model-based (exploring the spread of results from running thousands of variations of agents and parameters in NK landscapes)
Immeasurability	...as a counter to these approaches and suggested measures is the argument that some uncertainties have no measures (e.g., unknown unknowns and unknowable known unknowns)

be the case—it should (also) be measured. Trying to draw as much informational value from the uncertain event as possible should be the goal to maximize learning, especially about whether any of the *ex ante* unknowns could have been made known prior (e.g., by identifying mistaken assumptions, miscommunications, and so on). Note that the doing the *ex post*—realized-outcome-focused—measurement (and interpretation) may not be as straightforward as it appears. This is because such measurements are likely to be biased by what happened rather than what could have happened. Learning only from realized outcomes is dangerous as good (/bad) luck is easily mistaken as good (/bad) judgment; false good judgment is likely to then be relied upon in the future, with unnecessarily disappointing results. Of course, it is not always easy to imagine and assess the un-realized outcomes (although, tools like *post-mortem* scenario analyses and simulations may help). Perhaps drawing on information concepts in psychology and law (e.g., counterfactual thinking), where there is a great emphasis on outcomes that did *not* occur but could have, would be one avenue to explore further (Garner, 1962).

Approaches to Measurement

Three approaches dominate uncertainty measurement: a mostly objective approach (e.g., using mechanical or statistical instruments); a perception-based approach (e.g., using surveys); and, a mixed approach of the two (Samsami et al., 2015). Objective approaches produce the same results independent of who takes the measurement. Perception-based approaches can, and often do, differ based on who takes the measurement because of the influence of a myriad of that person's historic experiences, inherited traits, instantaneous reactions, idiosyncratic feelings, attentions, and so on. The mixed approach involves a number of variants from simply forcing subjective-qualitative perceptions into quantified scales, to averaging perceptual cues, to focusing on their commonalities, to weighted combinations of the two measurement types. (More elaborate measures also exist, such as [objective/repeatable] automated textual analysis of written perceptions.) Note that there is likely to be measurement error involved in any of these approaches (e.g., due to the limited precision of the instruments being applied), in addition to possible modeling error (e.g., due to failures in controlling for effects of excluded factors, like humidity, temperature, calibration effort, and so on). Other measurement issues may involve the contextual circumstances involved, like when the measurement was taken—for example, whether it was taken when the system had fully stabilized (which may not be easy to determine under uncertainty).

The choice of approach will depend on several considerations. Primarily, it should depend on the decision's target. If it is a human subject (e.g., an employee, customer, or other sentient stakeholder), a subjective approach may be best. If it is a machine, a thing, or a policy, an objective approach may be best. If it spans both types of target, then the mix of approaches may be best. Secondarily, the choice of approach should depend on the resources, capabilities, and time available.

Practical Measures

Hypothetically, there is no limit to the practical measures that could be applied in attempts to assess uncertainty, given there is no limit to the possible embodiments of uncertainty and the circumstances in which it appears (i.e., regarding a specific outcome at a specific point in time and space). Which measure to use will depend on the decision characteristics (e.g., the goal) and the decision-making context (e.g., the time, money, and skills present). How much to invest in any measure depends on its costs and benefits, where those benefits often rest on what can be learned about the unknown factors both before and after the decision is made and whether those latter lessons can be applied to future decisions. How much to invest in the specificity of the measure involves the (perceived) trade-off between the benefits of specificity (i.e., as focused on how important this one decision is) versus the benefits from generality (i.e., as focused on the lessons that can be applied to similar decisions and similar uncertainties).

The three main approaches described above lead to several types of possible practical measures: First, there are objective measures to consider (e.g., involving direct evaluation of an uncertain factor's characteristics, statistical characterizations of data related to the uncertain factor, indirect proxies, and hypothesized correlates for the uncertain factor's characteristics). Second, there are subjective measures to consider (e.g., based on asking those involved in the decision, or asking observation questions about their perceptions before and after the experience). Third, there are conceptualized measures (e.g., based on simulated data of a model of the problem, or on relevant scenarios). Fourth, there are various combinations of these types to consider.

To illustrate, consider the example of the uncertainty embodied in the unpredictability of the external context of a focal business decision. Many measures, spanning the main approaches, have been proposed. There is the perceptual measure of Miles and Snow (1978) that is reliable and valid but unstable (Magnani & Zucchella, 2018). There is the alliance-specific survey measure of Adobor (2006) that asks respondents to predict investment costs and financial payoffs from an inter-firm relationship on a scale from 'completely unpredictable' to 'completely predictable'. There is Duncan's scale that measures the lack of information about future events, including outcome states and their probabilities (Milliken, 1987). There is a measure defined by the log of the number of possible outcomes that a focal decision has (Garner, 1962). There are newspaper-based measures like the *Economic Policy Uncertainty* indices of Baker et al. (2016). Such measures are even available back to 1900 for the US (and can be found for many other countries at www.policyuncertainty.com—Altig et al., 2020). There are also subjective uncertainty measures based on surveys about business expectations (e.g., the monthly *US Survey of Business Uncertainty* that estimates probability distributions over firm sales growth rates for a one-year horizon—Altig et al., 2020). Other measures include those based on forecaster disagreement over questions and those probing respondents to rate the overall uncertainty their businesses face.

To provide a less-specific-to-any-one-uncertainty idea of the variety of measures used, a partial list of measures found in a recent survey of the management-related literature includes the following items: In terms of 'more direct' measures, there are those involving: signal noise; the standard deviation of the outcome; the standard deviation of the value-weighted excess returns; the volatility index; the signal-to-noise ratio; the dispersion index of expert opinion; missing information (quality/ quantity); the range of possible outcomes; the ratio of knowns to unknowns; confidence in beliefs; frequency and size of shocks/surprises; scenario number and span; unusual actions required; the range of information unknown of total relevant information; the ambiguity premium paid; earnings dispersion; Bayesian (learning) uncertainty; information quality; the known outcome range where the probability distribution of outcomes is unknown; the number of potential sources of uncertainty; the number of possible options; and, the extent of dependence on uncontrolled entities (e.g., alliance partners). In terms of 'indirect'/ proxy measures, there are those involving: the mean-deviated industry concentration ratio; Henisz's POLCONIII index; newness; inexperience; unrelatedness; unfamiliar components in a patent; physical distance to an object of study; technological turbulence; similarity of the data produced in a model of the object of study; years to expiration of a policy; divergent thinking; the corruption index; gaps in competence; the frequency of elections (as change events); turnover rates; the need for flexibility; misalignment; the amount of creativity needed; the percent that is routine; the terrorism index; expert disagreement; the lack of industry structure (nascency); the number of checks and balances used; leader tenure; R&D spending; feedback quality; dynamism/speed; and, munificence/resource scarcity. In terms of 'data-driven' measures, there are those involving: the root mean square error of residuals from regression on data; option-based volatility; statistical variance; the log of the standard deviation of the growth rate; Bellman equation; (NK) landscape changes (frequency; size); Janis-Fadner coefficient of imbalance; idiosyncratic volatility; option value; complexity measures (e.g., number of nodes; number of interdependencies); and, the Shannon measure of average information. In terms of 'perceptive' (i.e., survey-based) measures, there are questions about: the difficulties in taking steps to an outcome; causal ambiguity; psychic distance; predictions; future changes;

and, unpredictableness. Other approaches and measures include those involving: graphical interpretations; verbal descriptions; observations of frantic search (in the lab or in the field); relaxation of model parameters; and, informational asymmetries.

Conceptual Measures

To apply conceptual/theoretical measures requires making some 'big' (i.e., simplifying) assumptions about the focal decision and type of 'uncertainty' it involves. This is straightforward for well-defined contexts, like casinos (and experimental gambling labs) where randomizing devices (or their algorithms) are known. Even when these are highly complex, simulations can mimic possible outcomes from which estimates of distributions, dynamics, and other characteristics can be measured.

Essentially, these measures are based on mathematical models that either directly, or indirectly, provide some calculable outcome of interest, or pseudo-data for an estimate of that. Such models can assume one or more underlying cause-and-effect relationships, and then alter variable values over a large enough range to provide a basis for measures of range, mean, variance, stability, and so forth. For ambiguity-as-range problems—where all is known about the problem other than the distribution of possible outcomes that span a known range—the situation can be modeled and some limited analyses can be done, for example, to measure relative costs of uncertainty relative to other informational levels (Arend, 2022a). For composite game problems—where the players can play the same set of options across different possible tables that each have known payoffs but where the actual table that is used in the game is unknown (as is the distribution of probabilities that picks that table)—basic measures of uncertainties are possible (e.g., payoff ranges) and so some strategies (e.g., minimax) can be compared, for example, using simulations (Arend, 2022b).

Conceptual models can also lead to logical and mathematical statements that help measure, or otherwise increase the understanding of, the uncertainties involved. For example, one can state that the amount of ambiguity in a problem increases with the number of distributions not ruled out by the current knowledge of that problem (Einhorn & Hogarth, 1986). Or, one can apply evidence theory to assess two measures of uncertainty about a problem: the first being 'belief' as embodying the amount of positive evidence justifying a position; and, the second being 'plausibility' as embodying the absence of evidence to justify the position. Or, one can apply information-gap analysis and hypothesize a mathematical system—one with explicit laws—to imagine what occurs if the unknown was known, and to calculate uncertainty in terms of a pseudo-probability under various expected relationships (e.g., those involving the trade-offs between uncertainty levels and outcome ranges—see Bernstein, 1996). Or, one could apply other pseudo-probability mathematics, such as possibility theory and fuzzy set theory when the problem is better-defined (e.g., involving quantum-like uncertainty over well-defined states). Such conceptualizations can lead to stating laws governing the problems (or system contexts)—ones that are often obvious—as well as to some useful definitions of terms and conditions that help with communications, and the prioritization and sequencing of problems and approaches to them (e.g., based on the complexity, stability, or dynamics of the model). For example, the proposal that 'uncertainty over the outcome of a problem increases with the number of possible outcomes' (Garner, 1962) suggests both a real measure (i.e., the number of possible outcomes) and a ranking order.

IMMEASURABILITY

We have, thus far, taken the position that some useful measures of a problem's uncertainty can exist, can be feasibly captured, and can provide benefits (e.g., relating to that current problem or to future problems, or more generally to the increased understanding of that uncertainty). And, so, we recommend trying to measure uncertainties. Now, for balance, we consider the opposing position: that uncertainty *cannot* be measured either theoretically or practically (e.g., Taleb, 2012). This may be so because it is technically infeasible (as no measurement instrument exists to capture it, say, at the subatomic scale) or it is economically infeasible (its benefits do not outweigh its costs). This debate over which position is generally more applicable is unlikely to be settled soon (while it may be settled for some specific cases—where the type of uncertainty is known or the problem is trivial). For most decisions, that choice to pursue measurement or not will be made by past practice, necessity, and the given constraints (e.g., a lack of time or instruments); for the remainder, it will likely depend on the idiosyncrasies of the problem and decision-maker at hand. Of course, what determines that choice is not unlike what is considered when any new challenge, even one with no unknowables, is confronted (i.e., and choices over what to measure, how, when, where to do it, and who does it need to be made); situational judgments will occur. Either way, the evolved and strong human instinct to better identify the new or uncertain situation through attempts to measure it will have a significant impact.

Summary

In order to properly manage, or even to fully comprehend uncertainty, it must be measured in some way. This is a challenge; some types of uncertainty (e.g., unknown unknowns) cannot be measured—at least *ex ante*—by their very nature. Others can only be measured by their realized impact. Some, however, are measurable over several useful dimensions both before and after a decision affected by them needs to be made. More measurement—across many approaches—needs to be done so that 'we' can all learn more about uncertainties in order to address them more effectively and efficiently. Potentially, the best measures will become standardized, so that society can communicate better and share data in order to help each other deal with uncertainty.

Why measures matter:

- Without measurement, there is no proper management
- Measurement can lead to less confusion, to more useful definitions of types, and to insightful dimensioning of uncertainty
- Objective measurements can help create conceptual consistency across fields, improve communications, and increase legitimacy of the study of uncertainty

What measures of uncertainty mean for business and policy:

- The design of proper instruments to measure uncertainties, their characteristics and impacts, is valuable (and can provide advantages)
- Accurate measurements will increase the confidence, feeling of control, ability, and learning related to uncertainty within an organization
- Accurate measurements can lead to new markets that better allocate uncertainties more efficiently internally and externally

References

Adobor, H. (2006). Optimal trust? Uncertainty as a determinant and limit to trust in inter-firm alliances. *Leadership & Organization Development Journal, 27*(7), 537–553.

Altig, D., Baker, S., Barrero, J. M., Bloom, N., Bunn, P., Chen, S., & Thwaites, G. (2020). Economic uncertainty before and during the COVID-19 pandemic. *Journal of Public Economics, 191*, 104274.

Arend, R. J. (2022a). The costs of ambiguity in strategic contexts. *Administrative Sciences, 12*(3), 108.

Arend, R. J. (2022b). Strategic decision-making under ambiguity: insights from exploring a simple linked two-game model. *Operational Research* (forthcoming).

Baker, S. R., Bloom, N., & Davis, S. J. (2016). Measuring economic policy uncertainty. *The Quarterly Journal of Economics, 131*(4), 1593–1636.

Bernstein, P. L. (1996). *Against the gods: The remarkable story of risk*. Wiley.

Einhorn, H. J., & Hogarth, R. M. (1986). Decision making under ambiguity. *Journal of Business, 59*(4), S225–S250.

Garner, W. R. (1962). *Uncertainty and structure as psychological concepts*. Wiley.

Magnani, G., & Zucchella, A. (2018). Uncertainty in entrepreneurship and management studies: A systematic literature review. *International Journal of Business and Management, 13*(3), 98–133.

Miles, R. E., & Snow, C. C. (1978). *Organizational strategy, structure and process*. McGraw-Hill.

Milliken, F. J. (1987). Three types of perceived uncertainty about the environment: State, effect, and response uncertainty. *Academy of Management Review, 12*(1), 133–143.

Samsami, F., Hosseini, S. H. K., Kordnaeij, A., & Azar, A. (2015). Managing environmental uncertainty: From conceptual review to strategic management point of view. *International Journal of Business and Management, 10*(7), 215–229.

Starbuck, W. H. (1976). Organizations and their environments. In M. D. Dunnette (Ed.), *Handbook of industrial and organizational psychology* (pp. 1069–1123). Rand McNally.

Taleb, N. N. (2012). *Antifragile: How to live in a world we don't understand*. Allen Lane.

CHAPTER 10

Multi-Dimensionality of Uncertainty

Why Uncertainty Is Multi-Dimensional

Uncertainty is multi-dimensional because decisions, events, and natural contexts are multi-dimensional. Our world consists of input-throughput-output processes, time and XYZ space, 5W1H questions (who, what, why, when, where, and how), outcome characteristics, different stakeholders, and so on. One or more of these can—and, in reality, will—involve incomplete information. Further, these possible dimensions of uncertainties can interact—adding complexity to the focal problem and expanding the effects experienced in one or across several dimensions.

Unfortunately, the terminology involved with dimensioning is often confusing. Any one uncertainty can be characterized by a type (e.g., based on what is uncertain or the source of the uncertainty), a level (e.g., low to high), an entity (e.g., a rival), and so on—which are all possible dimensions. Further, these dimensions are not always well-separated—in the literature, in theory, or in reality (e.g., due to existing interdependencies and imprecise measures). In other words, the identification and assessment of the multiple dimensions of uncertainty has not been completed in the literature.

One way to study these multiple dimensions is to first associate them with meaningful (e.g., often-occurring) categories of problems that are easier to understand, analyze, and address separately. For uncertainty, this often entails problems that mix both known and unknown items, given the real world cannot be easily partitioned into the known and the unknowable (Kay & King, 2020). It also means trying to cover the multiple states of unknownness with typologies, assembling diagnosis tools that identify the core uncertainties, and finding ways to track their evolution (e.g., Townsend et al., 2018). Only then may it be possible to meaningfully study how such uncertainties interact with one another (O'Connor & Rice, 2013). This first step may provide useful sets of dimensions common to the identified uncertainty types.

However, besides these different types of uncertainties, there is (almost) always the dimension of *degree* to consider as well. Unknownness comes in degrees, in a spectrum of increasing fuzziness from certainty to pure ignorance (Dequech, 2011; Ramoglou, 2021; Taylor, 2003). While the default view of categorization does not consider differences in the severity of the uncertainty, those differences may well be important in its prioritization and treatment (Bradley & Drechsler, 2014).

While breaking down a problem's uncertainties into sets of its types and their severities is a logical preliminary approach to understanding the dimensions involved, there may be a need later in the process to capture the whole problem in order to get to a suitable solution (i.e., one that involves *all* of the relevant dimensions). Note that using this preliminary divide-and-conquer mentality may not always work because part of the problem's unknownness can involve how the uncertainties or dimensions interact, making the later step of reconstituting the whole from the divided parts impossible. In that sense, uncertainty-laden problems can be holistic in ways that certain ones are not (Ben-Haim, 2001); in those cases, tackling the problem as a given indivisible whole may work better, but at the cost of leaving the mix of its uncertainties as a black box with their separate dimensions mostly unidentified.

Which Dimensions?

There are many different dimensions that can be considered when analyzing and categorizing uncertainty. To be clear, the dimensions we speak to here differ from the approaches to, and specific instruments of, measurement in the previous chapter. Here, we are speaking to delineating features of uncertainty (e.g., the 'axes' that define the character of an uncertainty rather than the measured values on those axes). Drawing on the relevant literature, these include delineations relating to:

- the problem's overall context (e.g., business-related; policy-related)
- the nature of the unknown (e.g., how fundamental it is to the decision process)
- the unknown object at play (e.g., is it the facts, probability, possibility, range, confidence, value, beliefs, actions, outcomes, options, or something else that is not known)
- the severity/degree of unknownness (e.g., is it partially known, or knowable)
- asymmetry (e.g., does the decision involve lock-out or lock-in; is it the same for the rival)
- novelty (e.g., how unfamiliar is the problem)
- the spatial nature/location
- the temporal nature
- any interference involved
- its substantive versus procedural content

- social-ness/societal-ness
- ethical-ness
- objectivity versus subjectivity
- latency (i.e., the difficulty in perception or anticipation involved)
- criticality (to survival/ to task)
- source (e.g., whether in the phenomenon or with the decision-maker)
- the targets of impact
- political-ness
- interactive-ness (e.g., in a game)
- structure-relatedness
- linguistic-ness/communicability/ambiguity
- consequence
- tradability
- location in the supply chain/value chain
- potential impact size, span, balance, and temporal pattern
- avoidability/controllability

(e.g., Bammer & Smithson, 2008; Beck, 2009; Ben-Haim, 2001; Bradley & Drechsler, 2014; Dequech, 2011; Hansson, 1996, 2022; Hertwig et al., 2019; MacLeod & Pingle, 2000; O'Connor & Rice, 2013; Packard et al., 2017; Roeser, 2019; Sykes & Dunham, 1995; Walker et al., 2003).

Besides thinking about a first layer of dimensions (as face characteristics), uncertainty is often also described by secondary layers. For example, Ellsberg concluded that the *reliability* of probability estimates—the second-order confidence over the first-order estimates—needs to be taken into account in decision analysis. And, studies have shown that such second-order issues matter (e.g., to insurers' decisions on pricing policies—Cabantous, 2007), regardless if it is contrary to normative subjective expected utility theory.[1] That said, the attitude of many philosophers and statisticians toward such second-order (and higher)

---

[1] Such studies revealed that the *source* of the uncertainty over the first-order estimates—whether that source was imprecision or a disagreement among experts—affected subjects' confidence in those estimates and ultimately the decisions made.

dimensions has mostly been negative, due to fears of an infinite regress (Hansson, 1994).[2]

Adding to the task of measuring the primary dimensions of the uncertainty at one point in time, the priority and values of those dimensions are likely to change over time given that many decision problems are dynamic in nature. Those dynamics themselves may even involve further uncertainties as, in many cases, it is not often possible to assign a probability to the transition from one state to another (although abstracting to a Markovian system may be possible—Halpern, 2003). Besides the transitions, there may also be action (e.g., information search), feedback, and learning to consider (that may reduce or increase uncertainties). In all, the dimensioning of complex decisions may be overwhelming; so, starting with a static, one-level version of benchmark decisions may be the most feasible way to begin understanding the uncertainty types and their primary dimensions.

BASES FOR THESE DIMENSIONS

One way to make sense of, and get some perspective over, the overwhelming multi-dimensionality of possible uncertainties is to consider their two main origins—nature and people. It is useful to remember that multi-dimensional uncertainty is *the nature of nature*. The world involves complex, dynamic, and interconnected phenomena of varying predictability. The natural universe does behave according to some discoverable laws based on observable and thankfully repeated patterns. While those patterns most often express variance, change, and surprise (e.g., limited discontinuity) over time, they also most often provide opportunities for exploitation based on rational (versus random) human action. For example, we exploit the laws of physics and chemistry to build machines and processes to make agriculture successful. Besides a consideration of natural phenomena, it is useful to consider the roles that other humans

---

[2] The consideration of the second layer dimensions is more important in social settings, when real decision-makers are involved. For any one agent, there may be a need to consider those second-level issues in terms of whether what is told to the agent is true, whether the agent does not forget, and whether the way the agent obtains new information does not itself give the agent information (Halpern, 2003). When considering more than one agent being involved in the decision problem, there are then possible multiple layers of beliefs (or knowledge) about what agents are thinking about one another (as each is thinking about that) to track—leading to an unattractive regression.

take in generating the uncertainties that must be addressed. For example, decision-makers are limited (e.g., in sensory intake; in computational power; in action) in ways that will always guarantee that 'we' do not ever have complete information (other than in theoretical models). That said, it is also useful to recall that, as a species, we have survived with much less information and capabilities than we have today. We have evolved (and continue to evolve) ways to act on limited information, to some net positive effect (so far). While this may indicate that the multi-dimensionality of uncertainties has not yet paralyzed our decision-making or defeated us (through producing fatal decisions) and thus is not 'that bad' to deal with (e.g., by ignoring many of its depths and details), that is no guarantee that it won't nor is it any valid indication that we cannot do better.

Humans survive with and against two forces—nature and other humans. Each has its dimensions, complexities, and dynamics. Each provides some information and hides other information; but, humans are uniquely effective in deceiving each other. There are theories about our larger outer brains—that it was grown solely to keep track of social information, including all of the uncertainties that such human interactions entail. It is no surprise that we have created institutions, laws, justice systems, recording and communications devices, and, more recently, digital social media, all to feel somewhat in control of the incomplete information bubbles in which we conduct our lives (while trying to influence others for our benefit).

Uncertainty is universal, however, and does not just arise through such media nor just in our species. Uncertainty can exist apart from language, as seen in nonlinguistic species (Bradac, 2001). And, of course, language does not always exist to reduce uncertainty—it is often a source of ambiguity and deception, not just through unclear interpretations of words and phrases, but also through tone (e.g., sarcasm) in both written and spoken form (Packard et al., 2017).

Surviving and succeeding against the first force—nature—is, by itself, not easy. Its continual state of change affects all forms of unknownness in many dimensions (Townsend et al., 2018). It consists of a series of connected events, each dependent on another; and, that is radically different from the way we model them (i.e., where each decision-event has zero influence on the outcome of the next) (Bernstein, 1996). In fact, the density of structural linkages and interactions between parts of nature and our reality can be quite overwhelming (Dequech, 2011). On top of that, there are timing issues in those interactions to consider (e.g., where the time when A and B are measured is crucial for determining whether one causes the other in addition to the true strength of that relationship—Mitchell & James, 2001). And, on top of even that, there are inconsistencies to consider in our own abilities to study those natural events (e.g., inconsistencies across measurement technologies and users) (Kapoor & Klueter, 2021). While time allows learning (through observation, experimentation, search, and action) that produces a general trend towards the reduction of uncertainty in natural phenomena, within any one field, the amount of uncertainty perceived typically waxes and wanes (e.g., as past unknowns are made known [in providing values in all their relevant dimensions] and new unknowns are discovered) (O'Connor & Rice, 2013).

Surviving and succeeding against the second force—humankind—is also, by itself, not easy. And, dealing with it starts in our own heads. Uncertainty is a cognitive state—consisting of both computation and emotion (Bradac, 2001). To the latter, the range of relevant feelings includes: confidence; disappointment; relief; frustration; confusion; optimism; doubt; satisfaction; and, anxiety (Kuhlthau et al., 2008). While, in theory, we model a decision-maker's values as constant, known, and precise, those values—in ourselves and in others—are none of those, adding to the uncertainties needing to be considered (Hansson, 1996). Human perceptions over what information is missing (e.g., from whom, about what, and why) affects the types (and dimensions) of the uncertainties we believe need to be dealt with (Milliken, 1987). That leads to the attribution of uncertainty more to subjective sources (e.g., inadequate understanding) than to objective sources (e.g., incomplete information), and makes issues surrounding fellow humans (e.g., communication, deception, incentivization, opportunism) appear a greater threat than issues springing from nature alone (Lipshitz & Strauss, 1997).

The bases of the dimensions of uncertainties stem from nature and from ourselves. They focus on the ways we can characterize and potentially measure our fears and hopes that can emerge from the unknowns in our lives.

Dealing with Multi-Dimensionality

Dealing comprehensively with uncertainty—in terms of its multiple dimensions (and layers and interconnections)—seems like an impossible task. While dividing that dimensionality up looks to be helpful approach, the challenge does not end there.

One way to divide up that dimensionality that has been suggested is to start with modeling a single uncertainty (as an exemplar of a single type of uncertainty and its limited dimensions). However, modeling any one uncertainty itself leads to a concern over further uncertainty. The *Viniar* problem arises—which is the mistake of believing one has more knowledge than one does about the real world from the application of the conclusions from an artificial model (Kay & King, 2020). That, itself, raises an issue about the difficulty of distinguishing bad luck from the model's failure and from perceptual and measurement failures, and so on.

Perhaps one way to choose between such models is via consensus. A better understanding of the uncertainty can then emerge from identifying just how much and in what ways relevant competing models can differ and yet still allow for agreement. With such an approach, it may be useful to think of how one model can be precisely derived from the other by some specific type of added information—where that type defines the dimension(s) of uncertainty at play (Ben-Haim, 2001).

Even if one can properly identify a focal dimension of uncertainty, integrating that with the other relevant dimensions at play is likely to be challenging. For example, there are several ways that such integration be problematic: it can lead to divergent or conflicting estimates or prescriptions; the estimates (over likely outcomes) it does lead to can remain ambiguous; and, the outcome it suggests may be impossible or infeasible (Bradac, 2001). Further, there are questions over at what level to stop that integration and how to prioritize the dimensions that remain.

Beyond that, we still need to be reminded that real decision-makers, even when using theoretical models, will understand uncertainty in an epistemologically-biased manner. Uncertainty is about 'what we do know' and 'how we know what we know', and given each of these conceptualizations is bounded, we will be biased in the decisions that we make under uncertainty (Samsami et al., 2015). For example, due to those bounds, people usually act on one risk assuming it is isolated from other risks, whether or not that is true (Schoemaker, 2002). Such decomposition and delinking can provide insights into the nature of uncertainty and how to derive useful information (Rowe, 1994). However, that parts-of-the-whole, divide-and-conquer mentality, can also be dangerous. It only gets us so far because it is missing the holistic parts and effects. This leads to the question over what collection-point of dimensions to apply in any specific uncertainty-laden decision. One answer is, in ignorance, to try all of them and see which works best, noting contingencies and limitations. Obviously, much future work in this area is needed to address such questions.

Summary

Uncertainties entail multiple dimensions because the decisions we face also do. The bases of the dimensions lie in nature and other humans. There are many possible dimensions that can be used to delineate the character of an uncertainty and help define its type, but the literature has yet to sort these, let alone differentiate primary-level from lower-level dimensions. The multi-dimensional nature of uncertainty raises the question of whether to take an 'isolated pieces' approach or a 'holistic' one (or some combination) to best study it.

Why multi-dimensionality matters:

- Nature and people are multi-dimensional, so the uncertainties they create are as well, and need to be accounted for
- It sets up a tension between attacking the dimensions separately versus examining them as a holistic collection, one that is not easy to resolve
- A full laundry list of primary dimensions (let alone of secondary ones, other than the confidence levels over the primary ones) is yet to appear in the literature

What uncertainty's multi-dimensionality means for business and policy:

- Needing to take into account multiple dimensions (with multiple layers and dynamics) when making a decision involving uncertainty
- Needing to agree on standard sets of (primary) dimensions to make better progress in measuring, studying, and communicating about them
- Needing to explore new technologies and alternative dimensions (some of which may be newly measurable) for increasing the characterizations of (different types of) uncertainty to improve prediction

REFERENCES

Bammer, G., & Smithson, M. (2008). Understanding Uncertainty. *Integration Insights, 7*(1), 1–7.
Beck, U. (2009). *World at risk.* Polity.
Ben-Haim, Y. (2001). Decision trade-offs under severe info-gap uncertainty. *ISIPTA* (June), 32–39.
Bernstein, P. L. (1996). *Against the gods: The remarkable story of risk.* Wiley.
Bradac, J. J. (2001). Theory comparison: Uncertainty reduction, problematic integration, uncertainty management, and other curious constructs. *Journal of Communication, 51*(3), 456–476.
Bradley, R., & Drechsler, M. (2014). Types of uncertainty. *Erkenntnis, 79,* 1225–1248.
Cabantous, L. (2007). Ambiguity aversion in the field of insurance: Insurers' attitude to imprecise and conflicting probability estimates. *Theory and Decision, 62*(3), 219–240.
Dequech, D. (2011). Uncertainty: A typology and refinements of existing concepts. *Journal of Economic Issues, 45*(3), 621–640.
Halpern, J. Y. (2003). *Reasoning about uncertainty.* MIT Press.
Hansson, S.O. (1994). *Decision theory. A brief introduction* [Department of Philosophy and the History of technology. Royal Institute of Technology. Stockholm.]
Hansson, S. O. (1996). Decision making under great uncertainty. *Philosophy of the Social Sciences, 26*(3), 369–386.
Hansson, S. O. (2022). Can uncertainty be quantified? *Perspectives on Science, 30*(2), 210–236.
Hertwig, R., Pleskac, T. J., & Pachur, T. (2019). *Taming Uncertainty.* MIT Press.
Kapoor, R., & Klueter, T. (2021). Unbundling and managing uncertainty surrounding emerging technologies. *Strategy Science, 6*(1), 62–74.
Kay, J. A., & King, M. A. (2020). *Radical uncertainty.* Bridge Street Press.
Kuhlthau, C. C., Heinström, J., & Todd, R. J. (2008). The 'information search process' revisited: Is the model still useful. *Information Research, 13*(4), 13–14.
Lipshitz, R., & Strauss, O. (1997). Coping with uncertainty: A naturalistic decision-making analysis. *Organizational Behavior and Human Decision Processes, 69*(2), 149–163.
MacLeod, W.B. & Pingle, M. (2000). An experiment on the relative effects of ability, temperament and luck on search with uncertainty. [University of Southern California Law School, Olin Research paper 00–12.]
Milliken, F. J. (1987). Three types of perceived uncertainty about the environment: State, effect, and response uncertainty. *Academy of Management Review, 12*(1), 133–143.

Mitchell, T. R., & James, L. R. (2001). Building better theory: Time and the specification of when things happen. *Academy of Management Review*, 26(4), 530–547.

O'Connor, G. C., & Rice, M. P. (2013). A comprehensive model of uncertainty associated with radical innovation. *Journal of Product Innovation Management*, 30, 2–18.

Packard, M. D., Clark, B. B., & Klein, P. G. (2017). Uncertainty types and transitions in the entrepreneurial process. *Organization Science*, 28(5), 840–856.

Ramoglou, S. (2021). Knowable opportunities in an unknowable future? On the epistemological paradoxes of entrepreneurship theory. *Journal of Business Venturing*, 36(2), 106090.

Roeser, S. (2019). Emotional responses to luck, risk, and uncertainty. In *The Routledge Handbook of the philosophy and psychology of luck* (pp. 356–364). Routledge.

Rowe, W. D. (1994). Understanding uncertainty. *Risk Analysis*, 14(5), 743–750.

Samsami, F., Hosseini, S. H. K., Kordnaeij, A., & Azar, A. (2015). Managing environmental uncertainty: From conceptual review to strategic management point of view. *International Journal of Business and Management*, 10(7), 215–229.

Schoemaker, P. J. (2002). *Profiting from uncertainty: strategies for succeeding no matter what the future brings*. Simon & Schuster.

Sykes, H. B., & Dunham, D. (1995). Critical assumption planning: A practical tool for managing business development risk. *Journal of Business Venturing*, 10(6), 413–424.

Taylor, C. R. (2003). The role of risk versus the role of uncertainty in economic systems. *Agricultural Systems*, 75(2–3), 251–264.

Townsend, D. M., Hunt, R. A., McMullen, J. S., & Sarasvathy, S. D. (2018). Uncertainty, knowledge problems, and entrepreneurial action. *Academy of Management Annals*, 12(2), 659–687.

Walker, W. E., Harremoës, P., Rotmans, J., Van Der Sluijs, J. P., Van Asselt, M. B., Janssen, P., & Krayer von Krauss, M. P. (2003). Defining uncertainty: A conceptual basis for uncertainty management in model-based decision support. *Integrated Assessment*, 4(1), 5–17.

CHAPTER 11

Uncertainty's Connections to *Entrepreneurship*

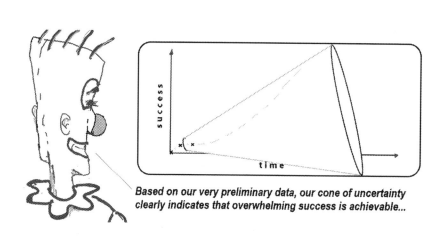

Based on our very preliminary data, our cone of uncertainty clearly indicates that overwhelming success is achievable...

WHY UNCERTAINTY CONNECTS TO ENTREPRENEURSHIP

Entrepreneurship is existentially, often definitionally, connected to uncertainty. For example, it is apparent in Knight's (1921) definition of entrepreneurship as bearing uncertainty. In that story, the entrepreneur makes an upfront sacrifice (e.g., puts in an effort) in order to

© The Author(s), under exclusive license to Springer Nature Switzerland AG 2024
R. J. Arend, *Uncertainty in Strategic Decision Making*, https://doi.org/10.1007/978-3-031-48553-4_11

167

obtain an uncertain payoff (Dimov, 2016; Rapp & Olbrich, 2020). The entrepreneur makes judgments about resource deployment—over resources that are subject to informational market failures—and acts on them; it is only in such imperfect markets that new ventures can emerge and prosper (Felin et al., 2021; Packard et al., 2017; Shackle, 1961; Townsend et al., 2020).

Although not the first to connect entrepreneurship to uncertainty, Knight (1921) is the best known to, arguably because of the detailed theoretical arguments he made and the context in which he made them. In those arguments, entrepreneurial activity can only occur when non-risk uncertainty exists. If critical market unknowns were insurable, decisions would be standard operating procedure—based on computable expected values and in the wheelhouse of incumbents—with little room, other than luck, for new ventures and variant actions (i.e., the things normally associated with entrepreneurship). In fact, the unknowns involved in entrepreneurship are not and cannot be of a known quantity or quality (Knight, 1921); it is the kind of uncertainty that is not susceptible to precise measurement and, hence, is not susceptible to elimination. It is the kind of uncertainty that accounts for the peculiar income of the entrepreneur (Knight, 1921). Of the two kinds of income that exist—contractual income (*aka* neoclassical economic theory's rents) and residual income—it is the latter that the entrepreneur takes as profit after others have been paid contractually to carry out the venture's business (Knight, 1921). So, like explorers, entrepreneurs need to make decisions under the fog of uncertainty in order to find their treasure (Kay & King, 2020).

Prior to Knight, both Cantillon and Smith connected entrepreneurship to uncertainty. Like Knight, Cantillon (1755) also described entrepreneurship as judgment-based decision-making under conditions of uncertainty. Like Knight, he conceived the entrepreneur's judgment in terms of the ability to make business decisions and take actions when the range of possible future outcomes and their likelihoods were unknown. In other words, entrepreneurial judgment is applied when information is unreliable or incomplete (Casson, 1993; Foss et al., 2007). Years after Cantillon, [Adam] Smith (1776) also made reference to uncertainty and its role in entrepreneurial activity. From Knight (1921) forward, the Austrian School of economics has carefully explored the entrepreneur, and the entrepreneur's character, judgments, and actions in the face of imperfect markets. From that school emerged

Mises (1949)—who saw the entrepreneur as acting on the imperfections brought about by the dynamics of the market—and Kirzner (1997)—who argued that entrepreneurship involves taking action under uncertainty. The Austrian School leverages Knightian uncertainty and so diverged sharply from the predictive, analytical building blocks of neoclassical micro-economic theory (i.e., where the objective function, set of resource constraints, and technologically feasible means are all known—Kirzner, 1997). For example, Kirzner often stresses that the entrepreneur faces ineradicable uncertainty (Ramoglou, 2021).

The connection of uncertainty to entrepreneurship is not simply high-level—i.e., isolated to pointing out that incomplete information will generate market imperfections that can disadvantage incumbents. The connection is multi-faceted. So, while Knight (and others) did see that market imperfections are critical to the functioning of the economy, it still takes strategic execution and innovation—and meeting the uncertainties involved in those activities—to successfully enter an industry (Kay & King, 2020). New entry requires offering something of value that differs substantially from incumbent and substitute products, and that requires novelty, novelty that entails unknowns (Wright & Phan, 2017, 2018). Unknowns also emerge from the often unpredictable reactions of incumbents, customers and the supply chain. If one defines an (entrepreneurial) opportunity as the *collection* of these uncertainties, then no opportunity can be objectively known *ex ante* (Ramoglou, 2021), despite what is sometimes optimistically expressed.

On the more realistic (and pessimistic) side, entrepreneurs often make decisions under conditions of ambiguous causation, time pressure, charged emotions, and consequential extremes (e.g., Baron, 2008; Durand & Vaara, 2009; Mullins & Forlani, 2005; Shepherd et al., 2015). As such, they frequently default to subjective judgments and simple heuristics to make progress (Gigerenzer & Gaissmaier, 2011). That decision-making mode separates many entrepreneurs from non-entrepreneurs—the former being leaders who take action under uncertainty based on their own individual beliefs and the latter being those who do not (McMullen & Shepherd, 2006; Rapp & Olbrich, 2023). That said, few if any studies have systematically investigated the empirical relationship between uncertainty and entrepreneurial action (Townsend et al., 2020).

Although there is a solid connection between uncertainty and entrepreneurship, it is not always positive, and many open questions remain. To the latter, entrepreneurship research is becoming increasingly aware of the lack of adequate clarity about uncertainty and its full relationship to entrepreneurship (Berglund et al., 2020; Packard et al., 2017; Ramoglou, 2021). Some believe that potential returns to entrepreneurship may be highest when uncertainty is highest (Taylor, 2003), others see diminishing returns (Knight, 1921), and yet others see uncertainty as damaging to entrepreneurs' subjective vitality and creativity (Rauch et al., 2018). Depending on the type of uncertainty, the stage of the venture, and the entrepreneur herself, a range of effects of uncertainty can be experienced (e.g., including the significant failure rates of new ventures). So, the relationship of uncertainty to entrepreneurship remains complex, problematic, and in need of more answers and conditions (Townsend et al., 2018).

WHICH UNCERTAINTIES AND ACTIVITIES?

There are many kinds of uncertainties (which a later chapter will catalogue). Entrepreneurs, as innovators and leaders, will experience several (Foss & Klein, 2020). Entrepreneurs face a more pluralistic set of 'uncertainties' than simply investment risk and causal ambiguity (Townsend et al., 2018). They face known unknowns about the markets they enter or create, about the new technologies they apply and alter, and about their competencies to successfully manage their ventures (Shepherd et al., 2015; Wu & Knott, 2006). They also face unknown unknowns—which should not affect their decisions, given there is nothing that can be done about them (other than to arbitrarily and wastefully speculate) (Dimov, 2016). Fortunately, research has shown that entrepreneurs do display different attitudes toward exogenous uncertainties (e.g., unknown unknowns) versus endogenous ones (e.g., known unknowns that can be influenced) (Forbes, 2007; Wu & Knott, 2006). As such, the more effective entrepreneurs are sensitive to how the uncertainties they confront are characterized, including in their communications internally and to their stakeholders (e.g., to not confuse the exogenous unknowns with the endogenous ones) (Kay & King, 2020).

These market, technological, and managerial uncertainties that entrepreneurs face are driven by several factors. First, other than technology, the other uncertainties can result from their underlying processes being *non-stationary* (i.e., not being governed by unchanging physical laws). Dynamics, interdependencies, and complex social processes often make it difficult, if not impossible, to collect complete information about a (market-focused or managerial) decision. Second, unknowns arise from novel and otherwise unique events (because these events have no history to learn from); events that entrepreneurs often have to be involved with to be successful. And, third, the actions themselves that are taken in such unique events also often have no precedent from which to predict, making them inherently uncertain as well (Mises, 1949).

Regardless of these types of uncertainties and their drivers, entrepreneurs remain a special type of decision-maker that deals with them—a decision-maker who has relatively less time and fewer resources, but relatively more higher-powered incentives and more bias than others. It is the Knightian entrepreneur, who with skill and luck, exploits the opportunities that bring progress under radically uncertain conditions. While these decision-makers cannot and do not 'optimize' in their activities, they are not irrational in their approaches to the unknowns they face (as that is the only way they can sustain success).

Drivers of the Entrepreneurship Connection

An entrepreneur's individual characteristics and needs (in addition to society's) drive the deep connection of these special people to the uncertainties they choose to confront in the hopes of realizing unusual benefits. Based on research, entrepreneurs separate themselves from others in several ways: They have more open attitudes towards (financial) loss (Shepherd et al., 2015). They share an ability to recognize potential opportunities and imagine different futures (Ramoglou, 2021). They have the ability to perceive the nature of a game and the rules by which it is played while they are playing it (Ancona, 2012). They exude greater confidence (Knight, 1921). They possess a wider body of relevant knowledge and experience from which to draw (Shane, 2000). They feel greater comfort with unique events (Packard et al., 2017). And, they are able to act purposefully through commitments and partnerships toward goals that involve unknown outcomes[1] (Dimov, 2016).

---

[1] It is worth clarifying what is meant by 'bearing' uncertainty. One can do so by understanding what it is that is being borne and the possible consequences, or one can do so by acting on impulse and ignorance; only the former is considered in theory (i.e., and, as serving an academic purpose) (Dimov, 2016).

At the societal level, the successful connection of entrepreneurship to uncertainty is driven by many practical supporting conditions and factors, including: a stock of heterogeneous talent sufficient to cover (i.e., exploit) most new technological shocks; a taxation system that provides high-powered incentives to individuals who will take actions to commercialize new ideas at scale; a relatively forgiving bankruptcy process; a media and culture that idolizes entrepreneurial success; a financial system that includes pools of savvy and mentoring angel and venture capital investors; and, a willing collection of would-be entrepreneurs who are prepared to wait for the right opportunity and then to invest heavily in it personally for years (because the potential perceived payoff to them is often much greater than what the initial hourly compensation is). Having a wide and deep pool of entrepreneurs decreases the possibility that any given exogenous shock will overlooked because it means that each shock will be assessed using a myriad of perspectives, experiences, and skills (Kirzner, 1973; Shane, 2000).

The connection is also driven by the opportunity itself. Often the opportunity will encompass characteristics that are unattractive to incumbents. For example, the opportunity may be of an insufficient scale or payback period to meet the investment hurdle of an incumbent. Or, the opportunity may involve the possibility of too great a negative spillover on the incumbent's brand should it fail. Or, the opportunity may simply require too different a managerial or technological adjustment for the current administration to find attractive. Or, the opportunity may simply be less visible to incumbents.

THE CONTEXT OF THE ENTREPRENEURSHIP CONNECTION

The context of entrepreneurship's connection to uncertainty is complicated. For example, the connection involves multiple orientations: Besides trying to exploit the given uncertainties relating to a focal opportunity, entrepreneurs often try to create uncertainties for others to protect their advantages and opportunities strategically (Scoblic, 2020). That said, because some uncertainties can get in the way of their intended actions, entrepreneurs also try to reduce selected unknowns (McKelvie et al., 2011). And, it should be noted, that not all entrepreneurs see any given uncertainties in the same way; some entrepreneurs may act on strong beliefs that essentially blind them to specific unknowns, giving others the illusion that they are uncertainty-tolerant (McMullen & Shepherd, 2006).

The connection of entrepreneurs to uncertainty is strong, but in some respects that is because it is relative; it may appear quite robust because the connection of others to uncertainty is weak. Recall that entrepreneurial success occurs, in part, due to the relative inaction and poor judgment of (incumbent) rivals. When rival managers do not have the motivation, insight, expertise, or resources to see or then act on potential opportunities—those resulting from uncertainties—then entrepreneurs have a much greater ability to connect (Knight, 1921).

That connection involves more than just positive effects, however. While the relevant uncertainties can generate opportunities that end up as valuable innovations newly available to society (due to the actions of entrepreneurs), there are also costs to consider. First, society will pay a higher price for those innovations than it would have had to if the uncertainty had been absent or eliminated (Knight, 1921). Second, the ongoing uncertainty-driven market imperfections (that allow entrepreneurial activity) are, by definition, expensive frictions to the economy involving a variety of inefficiencies and harms. So, while a few astute investors (like Warren Buffet) appear to exploit such imperfections fairly and often (e.g., by being better at evaluating companies than the majority of investors), others do so unfairly (e.g., exploiting insider information, using pump-and-dump ploys, applying pyramid schemes, and so on), and at a non-trivial cost to the rest of the market (Kay & King, 2020).

Managing the Entrepreneurship Connection

Like other decision-makers, entrepreneurs use a variety of approaches to address uncertainties. Despite the theoretical argument that entrepreneurs mostly benefit from uncertainty, and several selected case examples, the burning question remains that if they do actually capitalize on irreducible *a priori* uncertainty in practice (Klingebiel & Adner, 2015; Posen et al., 2015) then what is their secret? [What is the most (and least) effective tool that they use—whether it is business planning, rational choice, prediction, judgment, design, or something else (Felin et al., 2019; Gruber, 2005)?] If, however, they don't actually (systematically) capitalize on uncertainty, a question then arises regarding what the types or characteristics are of the uncertainties that inhibit their choices, actions, and learnings (Townsend et al., 2020).

We know that, to most decision-makers, uncertainty is an epistemological obstacle to be overcome, or mitigated, or passively accepted (Artinger & Powell, 2016; Tang & Wezel, 2015; Townsend & Busenitz, 2015). When it is irreducible, it poses its greatest challenges (Chandler et al., 2011). So, it is likely that entrepreneurs not only 'manage' uncertainty by trying to exploit (some types of) it when they feel confident in their judgments, but also do so by trying to mitigate it—both when they do not feel confident and when they are actually trying to execute their intended actions to exploit it (de Vasconcelos Gomes et al., 2021).

We briefly consider four of the main ways that entrepreneurs deal with uncertainties below; we describe many more approaches in a later chapter. First, entrepreneurs try to learn new information that reduces the incompleteness of knowledge about the problem that they initially encounter. They actively try to acquire such new knowledge through search and through learning by conducting small, feedback-rich experiments, and when that fails, they make decisions based on estimates grounded in that experience (Kirzner, 1997). Second, they apply heuristics—simple rules that focus attention on a select few known inputs while ignoring other factors that are not known. Entrepreneurs must often make quick decisions, and heuristics increase the speed of a decision and also, under the right conditions, the effectiveness of addressing emerging challenges and opportunities (Shepherd et al., 2015). Third, they try to use 'naïve others' to insure a focal uncertainty (e.g., by soliciting potential stakeholders to provide conditional funding) through confident quality signaling and other tactics (Teece et al., 2016; Zafar et al., 2021). Fourth, entrepreneurs try to predict and plan in order to generate a narrative that they can find confidence in and sell to others as a coherent and credible story (Kay & King, 2020). The value of such a narrative is not in its truth but in what it illuminates, such as new insights over the causes and consequences of the main uncertainties (Kay & King, 2020). Regardless of the approach, however, the role and effectiveness of each remain highly contested in entrepreneurial research (Gruber, 2005; Townsend et al., 2020).

There is a paradox that remains in entrepreneurship: true uncertainty (i.e., irreducible unknowability), by definition, means that *nobody* can know the related profitable opportunities *ex ante*. That includes entrepreneurs (Ramoglou, 2021). So, while it may be that entrepreneurs have different foreknowledge (of other things than the focal unknown) and have different motivations and characteristics, they can only imagine and believe—they cannot 'know'—about the opportunities associated with unknowns (Ramoglou, 2021). So, when entrepreneurs talk about the perception of opportunities, it should be noted that they are engaged in a 'language game of imagination' and not objective truth-telling (Ramoglou et al., 2020). (This also includes the imagination of the financial consequences, both the possible upsides and downsides [e.g., counting the 'affordability of possible losses'].)

Summary
A very strong—historic, existential, definitional—connection exists between entrepreneurship and uncertainty. That said, it is a connection that is under-explained and under-detailed in the literature (other than at the highest theoretical levels). No one—no set of special people—can reduce irreducible unknowns, so 'entrepreneurial' success can only arise from luck (or inside information), and not anything else, regardless of appealing labels like 'judgment'. Regardless, we note that the connection is not always positive (e.g., as resulting in socially beneficial innovations) as the uncertainty linked to entrepreneurship has its costs (i.e., given the inefficiencies and market frictions that incomplete information entails). For uncertainties that are not irreducible though, specific characteristics that differentiate entrepreneurs from others (e.g., incumbents) may provide an advantage for exploiting them, but that is yet to be extensively described or proven in the literature so far.

Why the connection to entrepreneurship matters:

- For entrepreneurs, it is important to understand what they are getting into—the need to face several uncertainties to be successful
- For economists and other academics, it is important to explore the effects of informational market failures in terms of the beneficial entry and innovation that can result
- To better understand the harms of entrepreneurial failures in terms of the various costs and frictions and exits that occur

What the connection to entrepreneurship means for business and policy:

- It helps for predicting what entrepreneurs will do (so their ventures can be supported or bought at the right times)
- It helps in building a robust pool of would-be entrepreneurs so that technological shocks do not go unexploited
- It leads to a better understanding of the asymmetries of entrepreneurs to incumbents in terms of which to support for addressing specific types of uncertainty over time

REFERENCES

Ancona, D. (2012). Sensemaking, framing and acting in the unknown. In S. Snook, N. Norhia, & R. Khurana (Eds.), *The handbook for teaching leadership: Knowing, doing, being* (pp. 1–19). Sage Publications.

Artinger, S., & Powell, T. C. (2016). Entrepreneurial failure: Statistical and psychological explanations. *Strategic Management Journal, 37*(6), 1047–1064.

Baron, R. (2008). The role of affect in the entrepreneurial process. *Academy of Management Review, 33*, 328–360.

Berglund, H., Bousfiha, M., & Mansoori, Y. (2020). Opportunities as artifacts and entrepreneurship as design. *Academy of Management Review, 45*(4), 825–846.

Cantillon, R. (1755 [1931]). *Essai sur la nature du commerce en général* (H. Higgs, Ed. and Trans.). Royal Economic Society.

Casson, M. (1993). Entrepreneurship and business culture. In J. Brown & M. B. Rose (Eds.), *Entrepreneurship, networks and modern business* (pp. 30–54). Manchester: Manchester University Press.

Chandler, G. N., DeTienne, D. R., McKelvie, A., & Mumford, T. V. (2011). Causation and effectuation processes: A validation study. *Journal of Business Venturing, 26*(3), 375–390.

de Vasconcelos Gomes, L. A., Facin, A. L. F., & Salerno, M. S. (2021). Managing uncertainty propagation in innovation ecosystems. *Technological Forecasting and Social Change, 171*, 120945.

Dimov, D. (2016). Toward a design science of entrepreneurship. In J. S. Katz & A. C. Corbett (Eds.), *Models of start-up thinking and action: Theoretical, empirical and pedagogical approaches* (Vol. 18, pp. 1–31). Emerald Group Publishing Limited.

Durand, R., & Vaara, E. (2009). Causation, counterfactuals, and competitive advantage. *Strategic Management Journal, 30*(12), 1245–1264.

Felin, T., Gambardella, A., Stern, S., & Zenger, T. (2019). Lean startup and the business model: Experimentation revisited. *Forthcoming in Long Range Planning* (Open Access).

Felin, T., Kauffman, S., & Zenger, T. (2021). Resource origins and search. *Strategic Management Journal.* https://doi.org/10.1002/smj.3350

Forbes, D. P. (2007). Reconsidering the strategic implications of decision comprehensiveness. *Academy of Management Review, 32*(2), 361–376.

Foss, K., Foss, N. J., & Klein, P. G. (2007). Original and derived judgment: An entrepreneurial theory of economic organization. *Organization Studies, 28*(12), 1893–1912.

Foss, N. J., & Klein, P. G. (2020). Entrepreneurial opportunities: Who needs them? *Academy of Management Perspectives, 34*(3), 366–377.

Gigerenzer, G., & Gaissmaier, W. (2011). Heuristic decision making. *Annual Review of Psychology, 62*, 451–482.

Gruber, M. (2005). Process matters—Empirical evidence one the value of marketing planning in VC-backed startups. *Academy of Management Proceedings, 1,* S1–S6.

Kay, J. A., & King, M. A. (2020). *Radical uncertainty.* Bridge Street Press.

Kirzner, I. M. (1973). *Competition and entrepreneurship.* University of Chicago Press.

Kirzner, I. M. (1997). Entrepreneurial discovery and the competitive market process: An Austrian approach. *Journal of Economic Literature, 35*(1), 60–85.

Klingebiel, R., & Adner, R. (2015). Real options logic revisited: The performance effects of alternative resource allocation regimes. *Academy of Management Journal, 58*(1), 221–241.

Knight, F. H. (1921/64). *Risk, uncertainty and profit.* Augustus M. Kelley.

McKelvie, A., Haynie, J. M., & Gustavsson, V. (2011). Unpacking the uncertainty construct: Implications for entrepreneurial action. *Journal of Business Venturing, 26*(3), 273–292.

McMullen, J. S., & Shepherd, D. A. (2006). Entrepreneurial action and the role of uncertainty in the theory of the entrepreneur. *Academy of Management Review, 31*(1), 132–152.

Mises, von L. (1949). *Human action: A treatise on economics.* Ludwig von Mises Institute. www.mises.org/humanaction.asp

Mullins, J. W., & Forlani, D. (2005). Missing the boat or sinking the boat: A study of new venture decision making. *Journal of Business Venturing, 20*(1), 47–69.

Packard, M. D., Clark, B. B., & Klein, P. G. (2017). Uncertainty types and transitions in the entrepreneurial process. *Organization Science, 28*(5), 840–856.

Posen, H. E., Leiblein, M. J., & Chen, J. S. (2015). A behavioral theory of real options. In *AoM Proceedings.*

Ramoglou, S. (2021). Knowable opportunities in an unknowable future? On the epistemological paradoxes of entrepreneurship theory. *Journal of Business Venturing, 36*(2), 106090.

Ramoglou, S., Gartner, W. B., & Tsang, E. W. (2020). "Who is an entrepreneur?" is (still) the wrong question. *Journal of Business Venturing Insights, 13,* e00168.

Rapp, D. J., & Olbrich, M. (2020). On entrepreneurial decision logics under conditions of uncertainty: An attempt to advance the current debate. *Journal of Innovation and Entrepreneurship, 9*(1), 21.

Rapp, D. J., & Olbrich, M. (2023). From Knight uncertainty to real-structuredness: Further opening the judgement box. *Strategic Entrepreneurship Journal, 17*(1), 186–209.

Rauch, A., Fink, M., & Hatak, I. (2018). Stress processes: An essential ingredient in the entrepreneurial process. *Academy of Management Perspectives, 32,* 340–357.

Scoblic, J. P. (2020). Learning from the future. *Harvard Business Review, 98*(4), 38–47.

Shackle, G. L. S. (1961). *Decision, order, and time in human affairs.* Cambridge University Press.

Shane, S. (2000). Prior knowledge and the discovery of entrepreneurial opportunities. *Organization Science, 11*(4), 448–469.

Shepherd, D. A., Williams, T. A., & Patzelt, H. (2015). Thinking about entrepreneurial decision making: Review and research agenda. *Journal of Management, 41*(1), 11–46.

Smith, A. (1776 [1937]). *The wealth of nations* (Cannan, Ed.). Modern Library.

Tang, Y., & Wezel, F. C. (2015). Up to standard?: Market positioning and performance of Hong Kong films, 1975–1997. *Journal of Business Venturing, 30*(3), 452–466.

Taylor, C. R. (2003). The role of risk versus the role of uncertainty in economic systems. *Agricultural Systems, 75*(2–3), 251–264.

Teece, D., Peteraf, M., & Leih, S. (2016). Dynamic capabilities and organizational agility: Risk, uncertainty, and strategy in the innovation economy. *California Management Review, 58*(4), 13–35.

Townsend, D. M., & Busenitz, L. W. (2015). Turning water into wine? Exploring the role of dynamic capabilities in early-stage capitalization processes. *Journal of Business Venturing, 30*(2), 292–306.

Townsend, D. M., Hunt, R. A., Beal, D. J., & Hyeong Jin, J. (2020). Venturing into the unknown: A meta-analytic assessment of uncertainty in entrepreneurship research. In *Academy of Management Proceedings.*

Townsend, D. M., Hunt, R. A., McMullen, J. S., & Sarasvathy, S. D. (2018). Uncertainty, knowledge problems, and entrepreneurial action. *Academy of Management Annals, 12*(2), 659–687.

Wright, M., & Phan, P. (2017). AMP articles in an uncertain new world. *Academy of Management Perspectives, 31,* 1–3.

Wright, M., & Phan, P. (2018). The commercialization of science: From determinants to impact. *Academy of Management Perspectives, 32*(1), 1–3.

Wu, B., & Knott, A. M. (2006). Entrepreneurial risk and market entry. *Management Science, 52*(9), 1315–1330.

Zafar, S., Waddingham, J., Zachary, M., & Short, J. (2021). Search behavior and decision confidence in equity crowdfunding: An information search process model perspective. *Journal of Small Business Management, 2*(4), 1–34.

CHAPTER 12

Uncertainty's Connections to *Strategy*

WHY UNCERTAINTY CONNECTS TO STRATEGY

Strategy is a plan for increasing an organization's performance by leveraging specific factors in a defined context. It is a means to successfully achieve pre-specified objectives, within a limited scope, based on known advantages. *Strategies exist because of uncertainties*; this is because plans are unnecessary when everything is known. The uncertainties surrounding

© The Author(s), under exclusive license to Springer Nature Switzerland AG 2024
R. J. Arend, *Uncertainty in Strategic Decision Making*, https://doi.org/10.1007/978-3-031-48553-4_12

rival actions and reactions, regulatory choices, technological advances, customer preferences, supply chain bottlenecks and so on, make it valuable to strategize; that is, to consider the range of outcomes resulting from a set of available choices and identify the best option. The 'best' can be defined in several ways, including the highest expected payoff, or the highest upside (e.g., to exploit whatever opportunities arise), or the most effective in mitigating against the worst downsides. Strategic analysis provides a form of forewarning so the firm can be better forearmed. Thus, uncertainty is the primary determinant of a firm's strategic decision logic (Packard & Clark, 2020).

Strategy covers a wide swath of performance-related dimensions and concerns. It includes both offensive (e.g., attacking; first-strike; preemptive) and defensive (e.g., protective; responsive; retaliatory) approaches, both cooperative (e.g., alliances; partnerships; venture capital investment) and competitive (e.g., price wars; fighting brands; comparative advertising; employee poaching; vertical foreclosure) moves, and combinations of such (e.g., *coopetition*'s logic of 'expanding the pie prior to dividing it'). The potential complexity of such actions by others, in addition to the 'fog of war' (e.g., disinformation; misinformation; signaling; lobbying) that exists when trying to interpret them, severely reduces the predictability of the actors that the firm confronts. That competitive unpredictability is one main source of uncertainty that organizations confront. Fortunately, there are a number of strategic tools (e.g., industry analysis; value chains; capabilities frameworks; business model decompositions; and, game theory) that provide a structured, communicable way to make use of the information available and to identify what is missing.

To be clear, *strategic* decisions are choices that significantly affect performance, involve irreversible (resource) commitments, and are interdependent (i.e., where any one party's payoffs are dependent on the actions of others as well as their own). These multi-party interactions necessarily give rise to real unknowns—given the limited information one has access to about others (e.g., about their feelings, intentions, knowledge, skills, and so on).

Uncertainty can be debilitating to planning and decisions. When there is insufficient information about the problem to compute expected values for each viable choice over the possible outcomes, then there is no way to optimize the decision—i.e., to identify the best choice. So, uncertainty can defeat (i.e., make inoperable) the standard strategizing processes and decision analysis methods. In such cases, the best way forward is to *respecify the decision* so that 'non-standard' approaches can be considered. That often means that optimization will not be possible, but a path to fulfill an alternative objective may be viable based on what is specifically known for that decision problem (e.g., to maximize the minimum possible payoff).

When the decision is specified in great detail, it may be easier to identify the types of uncertainties at play and which treatments or approaches are most applicable for them. This, of course, is only possible with a fuller understanding of the types of uncertainty and the viable approaches to each (along with their limitations)—which is what we provide later in this book. That typology and associated treatment regimen should provide better strategic outcomes. (We are arguing that there are *no* general approaches that work best across the wide variety of uncertainties experienced in real business problems; this is because, for example, unknown unknowns differ greatly from known unknowns.) Strategically, a better understanding of the uncertainties and approaches will also provide insights into how others may see and deal with them, possibly making it easier to transfer some uncertainty or tactically create it for others. It may also be useful to know how to leverage it when it is 'controllable' (e.g., has provided some good luck to the firm that can be leveraged). When seen in such a positive light, it has even been suggested that uncertainty is the cornerstone of explaining the sustained competitive advantage for those fortunate firms (Foss & Knudsen, 2003).

Uncertainty and Theories of the Firm (and of Firm Rents)

Theories of the Firm (TotF) explain why the firm exists as a transactionary, organizational, legal, or collective entity—in essence, why other forms of doing business (e.g., using the spot markets) are not as efficient or effective. Theories of Firm Rents (ToFR) explain why some firms earn more than the total costs of the activities they undertake (including financing costs and the opportunity costs of the resources they hold)—in essence, why some organizations create and capture more value than others.

Several TotFs draw on uncertainty. For example, firms—as collectives of individuals—must exist when the problem-solving requirements exceed that of any one individual agent—due to the incomplete information caused by the limits of any one individual's access to, and processing ability of, available data. The firm can deal with more complexity and information flow because it can coordinate specialists (e.g., Dosi & Egidi,

1991). Indeed, *without* uncertainty, there is *no* need for firms to exist because there is no possibility for opportunism, unknown resource values, knowledge spillovers, or specialization—which are the main elements of TotFs. TotFs use uncertainty as a core construct, as do more basic theories about resource allocation and investment. For example, *transaction cost economics* leverages both behavioral uncertainty—in terms of not knowing how actors will act in response to incentives (e.g., with opportunism)— and environmental uncertainty—in terms of not knowing future demand for a focal product. *Real options theory* focuses solely on environmental uncertainty—in terms of the volatility of returns of an underlying asset and the value of delaying investing in it (Leiblein et al., 2018).

A TotF that is also a ToFR is the resource-based view (RBV—see Barney, 1991; Penrose, 1959; Wernerfelt, 1984). Uncertainty is one of the two necessary conditions for sustained competitive advantage under the RBV (Foss & Knudsen, 2003); the second is immobility—which is also dependent on uncertainty (due to sunk cost commitments). Here, uncertainty is captured in the heterogeneity of expectations, or 'luck', of the focal firm (Foss & Knudsen, 2003). In fact, the luck-as-product-of-uncertainty has been argued to explain most of the variation in firm performance in some models (MacLeod & Pingle, 2000).

Top Management's Focus on Uncertainty

Uncertainty is the fundamental problem facing an organization's top management team (Milliken, 1987; Thompson, 1967). The strategic context of any firm is uncertain, although the degree and the sources of the uncertainties differ across firms (Wernerfelt & Karnani, 1987), making dealing with it a firm-specific task for management. Uncertainty is a central issue in the organization theory literature, and specifically in theories explaining the relationship between organizations and their environments (Dill, 1958; Duncan, 1972; Lawrence & Lorsch, 1967), a relationship that is constantly monitored by upper management. A central debate in strategy and entrepreneurship concerns whether uncertainty exerts a net positive or a net negative effect on venture performance (Townsend et al., 2020), making management's job of dealing with it complex rather than one-sided. In fact, major consultants like McKinsey & Co suggest that uncertainty requires new ways of thinking about strategy rather than relying on the past practice of either under-estimating it to generate the required forecasts for planning and capital budgeting processes or overestimating it to support going with 'gut' instincts because standard analyses cannot work (Courtney et al., 1997).

The challenge that uncertainty poses to top management teams stems not just from having to deal with it for standard decisions (e.g., make-or-buy choices), but also from having to deal with it across other, often non-standard decisions, where the focal uncertainties can appear in many forms, some of which are not obvious. As such, administrators are likely to experience different types of uncertainty as they try to understand and respond to changes in the competitive environment (Milliken, 1987). Unfortunately, much of the management literature has mischaracterized uncertainty as a unidimensional construct—in terms of its intensity (Dess & Beard, 1984; Tushman & Anderson, 1986), stability (Lawrence & Lorsch, 1967), velocity (Eisenhardt, 1989), smoothness (Suarez & Lanzolla, 2007), and so on. While such simplified perspectives of uncertainty have made its analysis easier, and have produced important insights into the challenges and effects of some uncertainties on firms (Kapoor & Klueter, 2021), they have missed the full and complex challenge that multi-dimensional uncertainties pose to administrators. We understand that just setting up an accurate model of an uncertainty's singular effects (e.g., in a staged option game) is tricky enough, let alone identifying the best approaches to take once that has been modeled (e.g., Dixit & Nalebuff, 1991; Ramoglou, 2021), but it produces a false picture of (and unjustified confidence over) the kinds of uncertainty that most firms confront because most kinds involve multiple effects. Work on these more complex problems is currently lacking in the literature.

Uncertainty and Contracting

One of the basics of doing business is contracting—formalizing a voluntary transaction between separate parties. Uncertainty presents core challenges here because of the unforeseen contingencies that exist when looking out to the future and, thus, can result in the inability to write a complete contract—one that covers every possible relevant upcoming event (Ghirardato, 2001). Many scholars have suggested that the nature of contracting (and of firm structures) cannot be fully understood without taking into account the role of unforeseen contingencies (Dekel et al., 1998). Broad categories of rights—ones intentionally left vague to allow the adaptation to circumstances as they arise—are sometimes used as a means of dealing with uncertainties (Dekel et al., 1998). The unforeseeable outcomes arise because of the often complex nature of the constitution of relevant events—as they involve dynamics, externalities, path-dependency, endogeneity, and even multi-directional interactions between actions, events, and outcomes (Dosi & Egidi, 1991). And, when such jolts do occur, there remains limited understanding of the proactive and reactive approaches firms use (Zahra, 2021).

Deeper into Uncertainty

Uncertainty—through its relationship with danger and its association with both devastating loss and joyful gain—has influenced the course of industrialization, starting with intercontinental shipping (Beck, 2009). As a result, it has affected the status of nations; for example, it is suggested that America's leadership in the world is a result, in part, of how its political systems and its organizations manage and survive uncertainty better than rival structures and governance (Krumbein, 2012). Of course, flows of capital across the globe are affected by uncertainty; in fact, Keynes (1936) argued that it is the principal reason for liquidity in the economy (Hodgson, 2011).

DRIVERS OF THE STRATEGY CONNECTION

Uncertainty is required to realize any new profits—without it, there is no new value creation or capture (Schoemaker, 2002). In perfectly-informed markets there exist no arbitrage opportunities. Without unforeseen change, there is no alteration of prices for factors of production or outputs. That is theory. In reality, as Nathan Rothschild explains: *Great fortunes are made when the cannonballs are falling in the harbor, not when the violins play in the ballroom* (Schoemaker, 2002). Firms that create change, anticipate it better, adjust to it faster, are lucky enough to have windfall gains from its effects, all can and often do, increase profits, whether that change is in the form of technological advances, regulatory updates, consumer sentiment, discovery of new raw materials deposits, pandemics, violence, or other significant events.

Strategy is the field that counters uncertainty. It analyzes significant, often new problems where outcomes are not predictable, in order to improve performance. On the one hand, it offers prescriptions to lower the uncertainties and mitigate their threats (Brandenburger & Nalebuff, 1996). On the other hand, it also offers suggestions for how to create uncertainty for others, for private gain—to exploit the cover it provides (e.g., making imitation harder through causal ambiguity), or the fear it generates (e.g., with random audits), or the fees it produces (e.g., in CDOs and other exotic financial instruments). Even in well-defined games-as-models-of-business-interdependencies, uncertainty often remains important in the outcome (e.g., in mixed strategy equilibria; in Folk Theorems; and, so on—see Dixit & Nalebuff, 1991).

The Context of the Strategy Connection

Uncertainty has varied effects depending on the strategic context. There can be net social gains, for example, when in a repeated prisoner's dilemma there is an uncertain endpoint, making the backwards induction-based choice of mutual defection un-supportable (Dixit & Nalebuff, 1991). There can also be a washout of the influence of underlying management quality, for example, in games of blind information search, because initial luck has the greatest effect on performance (e.g., MacLeod & Pingle, 2000). Uncertainty also affects the expectations of values—uncertainty increases the worth of information as it rises (both in terms of its level and the level of the audience's aversion to it—see Etner et al., 2012), and it increases the expected excess returns of firms voluntarily entering into its unpredictable context (Epstein & Schneider, 2008). And, as uncertainty decreases—with experience and learning—it also has significant implications for value appropriation by firms (Kapoor & Klueter, 2021).

Uncertainty affects industry competition. (Of course, not all industries face deep uncertainty at all times, but when uncertainty is significant, it is likely to affect rivalry—e.g., Teece et al., 2016.) Often it is the more bureaucratic firms that suffer—those larger, more established organizations that routinize their practices simply end up inhibiting adaptive management in uncertain times (Hage, 1980; O'Connor & Rice, 2013). Environmental jolts often render set strategies ineffective, thus affecting competitive positions; younger firms try to gain ground by being proactive while incumbents hesitate to act because they have more to lose by making mistakes and then having to admit to those predictive errors (Zahra, 2008). While uncertainty affects rivalry, rivalry also affects uncertainty, or at least its impacts; rivalry intensifies the effects of uncertainty on decision-making, for example, reducing informational search and inducing faster action (Hertwig et al., 2019). In those conditions, it appears that the perceived cost of losing out to rivals seems to outweigh the benefits of acquiring more information. In experiments, for example, when people play the 'rivals in the dark' game (with two options, one rival, and some first-mover advantages) the player stopping their search first is more likely to obtain the better position (Hertwig et al., 2019). Further, it should be noted that uncertainty is not always symmetrical to rivals; in many cases, the uncertainties confronting (or even perceived by) one firm can differ from those confronting (or perceived) by others, and that needs to be considered in strategic analysis (Arend, 2022a, 2022b).

Uncertainties and Activities

Because strategy is existentially linked to uncertainty, then, by extension, most major activities of the firm are also influenced by uncertainty. The strategist's primary duty is to increase the performance of the organization; one main way is to identify and act on new opportunities. In that case, a strategist's initial challenge is to mentally construct a representation or map of what they see as an opportunity (based on incomplete information), and then to generate a set of the activities that will exploit it (knowing that the implementation will be imperfect and that the context will change and surprises will occur) (Ehrig & Schmidt, 2022).[1] Because of such uncertainties, the strategist cannot know if her beliefs about necessary and sufficient activities and relations among the parts of her representation are correct, and so her plan is subject to revision (Ehrig & Schmidt, 2022). As such, the extent of planning relative to adaptation for any relevant activity should depend on the amount of uncertainty surrounding her organization (Packard & Clark, 2020). Uncertainty—with its many facets generated by complex decision interdependencies—is thus a core element of theories involving the major activities of the firm, including resource allocations, resource investments, and the governance over those resources (e.g., the make, buy or share decisions) (Leiblein et al., 2018).

---

[1] Note that even modeling the strategist's firm in such situations is not straightforward. It is problematic to treat the firm as a macro-level whole during periods of uncertainty; instead, it may be more useful to view it as a collective of people with different cognitive frames (Kaplan, 2008).

Managing the Strategy Connection

The primary challenge of strategy and its associated tactics and tools—for managers and entrepreneurs—is to facilitate the successful handling of uncertainties with regard to future demand (Anupindi & Jiang, 2008; Goyal & Netessine, 2007), competition (Grimm et al., 2006; Milliken, 1987), institutional and regulatory change (Bylund & McCaffrey, 2017; Smith & Grimm, 1987), factor markets (Walker & Weber, 1987; Williamson, 1975), and more (Packard & Clark, 2020). Because there are many types of uncertainty, and many dimensions to any one uncertainty, there is no single strategy that performs best across all situations (Luan et al., 2019). Indeed, many decision contexts are comprised of many uncertainties, as well as their interactions, transitions, and dynamics, which greatly complicates the selection of decision logic (Packard & Clark, 2020). More research on those more complex problems is needed to understand (more holistically and more completely) all that uncertainty means to strategy.

> **Summary**
> Strategy is inextricably connected to uncertainty. Strategy exists because of uncertainty—to manage it and to leverage it. Effective strategizing considers both the potential good and bad aspects of the relevant uncertainties, as well as their multiple dimensions and dynamics. More advanced strategizing considers how to leverage it against rivals (e.g., playing upon any asymmetries), and even with partners (e.g., to build trust). Performance differences—both short-term and sustained—are often attributed to uncertainty, both in theory and in practice. The complexities of some problems (e.g., in terms of involving multiple uncertainties) are yet to be fully analyzed for their strategic potential.
> Why the connection to strategy matters:
>
> - Uncertainty is the basis for most theories of the firm and theories of firm rents
> - Strategy has an existential relationship with uncertainty, being affected by it and affecting it in several different ways
> - The connection is becoming more important to understand as economic turbulence and production scales increase, and as more interactions and interdependencies among parties are uncovered and attempted

What the connection to strategy means for business and policy:

- Understanding the uncertainties—their types and dimensions—involved in major decisions will help increase performance
- Building a database of the treatments and approaches to various types of uncertainty will be useful in better comprehending which do and do not work and why, so that the most appropriate ones can be chosen in the future
- Applying uncertainty to improve competition policy may be useful, beyond using it for merger control (e.g., Clayton Act Section 7)

REFERENCES

Anupindi, R., & Jiang, L. (2008). Capacity investment under postponement strategies, market competition, and demand uncertainty. *Management Science*, 54(11), 1876–1890.

Arend, R. J. (2022a). The costs of ambiguity in strategic contexts. *Administrative Sciences*, 12(3), 108.

Arend, R. J. (2022b). Strategic decision-making under ambiguity: Insights from exploring a simple linked two-game model. *Operational Research*, 22, 5845–5861.

Barney, J. B. (1991). Firm resources and sustained competitive advantage. *Journal of Management*, 17, 99–120.

Beck, U. (2009). *World at risk*. Polity.

Brandenburger, A. M., & Nalebuff, B. J. (1996). *Co-opetition*. Harvard Business School Press.

Bylund, P. L., & McCaffrey, M. (2017). A theory of entrepreneurship and institutional uncertainty. *Journal of Business Venturing*, 32(5), 461–475.

Courtney, H., Kirkland, J., & Viguerie, P. (1997). Strategy under uncertainty. *Harvard Business Review*, 75(6), 67–79.

Dekel, E., Lipman, B. L., & Rustichini, A. (1998). Recent developments in modeling unforeseen contingencies. *European Economic Review*, 42(3–5), 523–542.

Dess, G. G., & Beard, D. W. (1984). Dimensions of organizational task environments. *Administrative Science Quarterly*, 29(1), 52–73.

Dill, W. R. (1958). Environment as an influence on managerial autonomy. *Administrative Science Quarterly*, 2(4), 409–443.

Dixit, A. K., & Nalebuff, B. J. (1991). *Thinking strategically: The competitive edge in business, politics, and everyday life*. W. W. Norton.

Dosi, G., & Egidi, M. (1991). Substantive and procedural uncertainty: An exploration of economic behaviours in changing environments. *Journal of Evolutionary Economics, 1,* 145–168.

Duncan, R. B. (1972). Characteristics of organizational environments and perceived environmental uncertainty. *Administrative Science Quarterly, 17*(3), 313–327.

Ehrig, T., & Schmidt, J. (2022). Theory-based learning and experimentation: How strategists can systematically generate knowledge at the edge between the known and the unknown. *Strategic Management Journal, 43*(7), 1287–1318.

Eisenhardt, K. M. (1989). Making fast strategic decisions in high-velocity environments. *Academy of Management Journal, 32*(3), 543–576.

Epstein, L. G., & Schneider, M. (2008). Ambiguity, information quality, and asset pricing. *The Journal of Finance, 63*(1), 197–228.

Etner, J., Jeleva, M., & Tallon, J. M. (2012). Decision theory under ambiguity. *Journal of Economic Surveys, 26*(2), 234–270.

Foss, N. J., & Knudsen, T. (2003). The resource-based tangle: Towards a sustainable explanation of competitive advantage. *Managerial and Decision Economics, 24*(4), 291–307.

Ghirardato, P. (2001). Coping with ignorance: Unforeseen contingencies and non-additive uncertainty. *Economic Theory, 17,* 247–276.

Goyal, M., & Netessine, S. (2007). Strategic technology choice and capacity investment under demand uncertainty. *Management Science, 53*(2), 192–207.

Grimm, C. M., Lee, H., & Smith, K. G. (Eds.). (2006). *Strategy as action: Competitive dynamics and competitive advantage.* Oxford University Press.

Hage, J. (1980). *Theories of organizations: Form, process, and transformation.* Wiley.

Hertwig, R., Pleskac, T. J., & Pachur, T. (2019). *Taming uncertainty.* MIT Press.

Hodgson, G. M. (2011). The eclipse of the uncertainty concept in mainstream economics. *Journal of Economic Issues, 45*(1), 159–176.

Kaplan, S. (2008). Framing contests: Strategy making under uncertainty. *Organization Science, 19*(5), 729–752.

Kapoor, R., & Klueter, T. (2021). Unbundling and managing uncertainty surrounding emerging technologies. *Strategy Science, 6*(1), 62–74.

Keynes, J. M. (1936). *The general theory of employment.* Macmillan, Cambridge University Press for the Royal Economic Society.

Krumbein, J. (2012). *Two invisible hands and optimal uncertainty.* SSRN 2034000.

Lawrence, P. R., & Lorsch, J. W. (1967). Differentiation and integration in complex organizations. *Administrative Science Quarterly, 12*(1), 1–47.

Leiblein, M. J., Reuer, J. J., & Zenger, T. (2018). What makes a decision strategic? *Strategy Science, 3*(4), 558–573.

Luan, S., Reb, J., & Gigerenzer, G. (2019). Ecological rationality: Fast-and-frugal heuristics for managerial decision making under uncertainty. *Academy of Management Journal, 62*(6), 1735–1759.

MacLeod, W. B., & Pingle, M. (2000). *An experiment on the relative effects of ability, temperament and luck on search with uncertainty* [University of Southern California Law School, Olin Research Paper 00-12].

Milliken, F. J. (1987). Three types of perceived uncertainty about the environment: State, effect, and response uncertainty. *Academy of Management Review, 12*(1), 133–143.

O'Connor, G. C., & Rice, M. P. (2013). A comprehensive model of uncertainty associated with radical innovation. *Journal of Product Innovation Management, 30*, 2–18.

Packard, M. D., & Clark, B. B. (2020). On the mitigability of uncertainty and the choice between predictive and nonpredictive strategy. *Academy of Management Review, 45*(4), 766–786.

Penrose, E. T. (1959). *The Theory of the Growth of the Firm*. Oxford University Press.

Ramoglou, S. (2021). Knowable opportunities in an unknowable future? On the epistemological paradoxes of entrepreneurship theory. *Journal of Business Venturing, 36*(2), 106090.

Schoemaker, P. J. (2002). *Profiting from uncertainty: Strategies for succeeding no matter what the future brings*. Simon & Schuster.

Smith, K. G., & Grimm, C. M. (1987). Environmental variation, strategic change and firm performance: A study of railroad deregulation. *Strategic Management Journal, 8*(4), 363–376.

Suarez, F. F., & Lanzolla, G. (2007). The role of environmental dynamics in building a first mover advantage theory. *Academy of Management Review, 32*(2), 377–392.

Teece, D., Peteraf, M., & Leih, S. (2016). Dynamic capabilities and organizational agility: Risk, uncertainty, and strategy in the innovation economy. *California Management Review, 58*(4), 13–35.

Thompson, J. (1967). *Organizations in action*. McGraw-Hill.

Townsend, D. M., Hunt, R. A., Beal, D. J., & Hyeong Jin, J. (2020). Venturing into the unknown: A meta-analytic assessment of uncertainty in entrepreneurship research. *Academy of Management Proceedings, 2020*(1), 17318.

Tushman, M. L., & Anderson, P. (1986). Technological discontinuities and organizational environments. *Administrative Science Quarterly, 31*(3), 439–465.

Walker, G., & Weber, D. (1987). Supplier competition, uncertainty, and make-or-buy decisions. *Academy of Management Journal, 30*(3), 589–596.

Wernerfelt, B. (1984). A resource-based view of the firm. *Strategic Management Journal,* 5(2), 171–180.
Wernerfelt, B., & Karnani, A. (1987). Competitive strategy under uncertainty. *Strategic Management Journal,* 8(2), 187–194.
Williamson, O. E. (1975). Markets and hierarchies: Analysis and antitrust implications: A study in the economics of internal organization. *University of Illinois at Urbana-Champaign's Academy for Entrepreneurial Leadership Historical Research Reference in Entrepreneurship.*
Zahra, S. A. (2008). The virtuous cycle of discovery and creation of entrepreneurial opportunities. *Strategic Entrepreneurship Journal,* 2(3), 243–257.
Zahra, S. A. (2021). The resource-based view, resourcefulness, and resource management in startup firms: A proposed research agenda. *Journal of Management,* 47(7), 1841–1860.

CHAPTER 13

Uncertainty's Connections to *Creativity, Art, and Music*

...in uncertain times, some happy news

Connecting Uncertainty to Creativity

Highly creative ideas are dependent on uncertainty—often arising because of luck (Simonton, 2013). Being creative requires going beyond the information given and daring to be wrong, by taking intellectual risks and hazarding guesses that are no more than 'shots in the dark' (Simonton, 2013). In that sense, a theory of uncertainty is a theory about creativity, rather than one about cognition, because a creativity theory must fall *beyond* the boundaries of what is known and include the unknown (Spender, 2006). One theory of creativity that is based on evolutionary logic and that includes both unknowns and knowns was proposed by Campbell (1960)—i.e., that creativity requires both blind variation and selective retention, the former characterized as uncertain and the latter as rational.

Creativity researchers do not yet agree on what counts as a creative idea (Plucker et al., 2004). That said, most psychologists (and patent-granting offices) agree on at least two criteria: novelty (i.e., originality) and usefulness (i.e., value to some consumer) (Simonton, 2013). Novelty often outweighs usefulness (e.g., as with art), and requires an ability to imagine a future that is radically different from the present—moving its audience into a previously unknown place (Dequech, 1999). Trying to do something new involves the impossibility of knowing what that thing will look like; whether it is possible to actually realize; and, if it is, what its properties entail (Silverberg et al., 1988). That creative process is full of unknowns. For example, the good fortune of having one thing suggest a useful other thing is often quite mysterious, and often does not rest upon the possession of common qualities that support valid inference (Knight, 1921).

Creativity is inseparable from uncertainty (Kay & King, 2020). And, creativity cannot be formalized; the main reason being that there is nothing certain about producing it. Creativity can only be described after the fact. While ideation tools have existed for some time (e.g., brainstorming, derivation, analogy, transformation—see Dosi & Egidi, 1991), and now AI-driven combinatory algorithms exist, neither has come close to automating creativity (although AI may 'look' like it creates, it is following prompts to combine existing data and patterns without any 'understanding' of them other than how the output relates to a set goal measure [with one difference being that human creativity often does not have such a predetermined goal measure]); that is because the unknowns involved in the creative process cannot be properly captured. (Tools cannot be designed for surprises, nor can code draw on unknown factors.[1]) Creativity means conjuring up new worlds with characteristics that don't fit the current one, where that lack of fit prohibits the use of processes formed for the current world (Barrow, 1998). As such, creativity appears chaotic in nature, even though its output—the creative product— tames that chaos into a comprehensive vision (Ehrenzweig, 1967). It appears chaotic because trying things that have never been tried before necessarily involves an absence of knowledge—one that breeds surprise and sometimes wonder (Dequech, 1999).

Given every new thing comes from existing things—because we can't get something from nothing—it seems somewhat dismissive to state that even novelty (creativity) is just recombination (Gilfillan, 1935; Schumpeter, 1939; Usher, 1954). While creativity in art, science, or just plain practical life, consists of a recombining existing conceptual and physical materials (Nelson & Winter, 1982), there remains uncertainty in how those components will combine and how that combination will perform (Fleming, 2001), given the near-infinite ways of doing so. In other words, creativity is not 'just' recombination but a very specific, skilled, intelligent process that draws upon experience, adaptability, perception, mindfulness, inspiration, and others.

Creativity also has an interesting relationship with constraints. Creativity may appear chaotic, but it is affected and affects the very real constraints it confronts. Primarily, creativity is necessarily constrained to drawing on things—knowledge and physical objects—that already exist. That noted, creativity also involves the manipulation of other imposed constraints (Shackle, 1966)—like the breaking out from implied but artificial boxes (e.g., of convention, of expectation, and of context). When we wish to explore creativity in a non-threatening manner, we often do so within the constraints of an experiment or a game, where the uncertainties at play are more controllable. In such safe settings, we can study just how creative participants can be (e.g., in solving mysteries, in bricolaging a useful object out of random parts, or in brainstorming new ideas given a prompt). In related settings—in simulated emergencies (for pilots,

---

[1] Note that the question over automating creativity is not without controversy; for example, economist and political scientist Herbert Simon (1995) has 'explained' creativity with two mechanisms—recognition (as a knowledge base) and heuristic search (as a technique to explore that base).

firefighters, doctors, and others)—we can see a different form of creativity (also one that evolution has shown to be valuable to our survival, given the many deadly unknowns that surviving in the wild used to entail). The continued study of these forms of creativity is likely to increase our understanding of how best to respond to different types of uncertainty in various contexts.

CONNECTING UNCERTAINTY TO ART AND MUSIC

Throughout its history, humankind has embodied the products of its creativity in art and music (e.g., in paintings, theatre, dance, opera, poetry, compositions, concerts, sculpture, fashion, tapestries, and so on). And, those products have often retained and leveraged some of the uncertainties that were involved in those creative processes. For example, uncertainty is a common theme in the arts, often used as a tension-building device (e.g., in *Hamlet*). Optical illusions are designed to stimulate uncertainty (Kay & King, 2020). In fact, it is the privilege of the artist to combine fantasy with reality—to create sensory ambiguity that awakens the audience to new possibilities (Ehrenzweig, 1967). One way this is done is through syncretistic vision—where objects are recognized from cues rather than from detail—playing with the bounds of what is knowable and unknowable from pieces of given information (Ehrenzweig, 1967). Essentially, art provides another 'game'—but where the public projects meaning onto an abstract picture. And, this is useful for retaining diversity in our society—a valuable characteristic of any gene (or meme) pool in a dynamic and competitive environment (Barrow, 1998). Such diversity extends to the need to have respect for non-scientific approaches to the world, such as through art and religion, that exercise creativity in different ways, given that science is only *one* way for humans to make meaning in an uncertain world (Faber et al., 1992).

In art and music, we can forget our practical interests and strivings, and lose ourselves in more of a selfless contemplation that explores unknowns and welcomes surprises (Gray, 2002). In fact, in music, surprise and predictability find an optimal balance in sequences of sounds in the most celebrated pieces (Garner, 1962). There is even a characteristic spectral form describing how sound intensity is distributed over different frequencies to produce what humans consider pleasant noise from an unpredictable (stochastic) source (Barrow, 1998). The evolution of (Western) music has proceeded along a series of steps—where each step loosened the constraints a bit more—in order to open up new unknowns for composers to confront. A new step was taken once the box defined by the previous step's rules had been completely (and creatively) explored through then-novel patterns (Barrow, 1998).

The balance of the known and unknown—of surprise and predictability, of abstraction and reality, of constraints and freedoms—is important in all art (Garner, 1962). Arguably, there can be no art without discipline, just as there can be no art without uncertainty. The formats and the formulaic constraints set the context in which to be creative—in terms of identifying and exploiting the unknown spaces within the known (or what was thought to be known) (Bammer & Smithson, 2008). While some artists have done so by exploiting the tension between certainty and uncertainty like the Surrealists and Dadaists, others have used uncertainty as a creative force (e.g., to inspire their visual art through paper crumpling—see Bammer & Smithson, 2008). In art, uncertainty is harnessed and cultivated, and seen as an alternative or complement to certainty; it is not seen as something to be feared, contained, reduced, or mocked as ignorance, but instead as something to be admired, enjoyed, and inspired by.

WHY THE CONNECTIONS EXIST

Art offers a different perspective on uncertainty—one from the heart rather than from the gut or the brain. It is a perspective that explores the balance between optimizing the known (e.g., brush techniques, musical notes, the physical properties of the media involved) and exposing the unknown (e.g., with new techniques and instruments, with the mixing of media, and so on). Conceiving art differs from solving problems—with the former being more active and inventive and the latter being more reactive and efficiency-seeking (Shackle, 1966). Art is neither arbitrary nor unconstrained. It takes a different kind of knowledge—about what *can* be done rather than about what *must* be done (Shackle, 1966). While the latter is needed to survive in the short-term, the former is what is needed to evolve and shine in the longer-term (by dealing more deeply with the unknowns). We need both kinds of mindsets (Shackle, 1966).

But how do we get from here to there—from the unknown to the known? Is it through creativity or something else? How do we build knowledge out of ignorance? This is Plato's *Meno problem*—the core of epistemology, the study of the nature and origins of knowing. It does not appear possible to acquire new knowledge without having some prior knowledge (Nickles, 2003); where those priors are either hardwired by genetics or programmed through socialization (Simonton, 2013). Ideas— as possible extensions of knowledge—can get us from here to there. But, not all ideas can do so. Ideas can be characterized in many ways, including by their originality, usefulness, and non-obviousness. It is the creative ideas (the ones with all three of those characteristics) that are more likely to get us from here to there. But, highly creative ideas are also highly uncertain—involving more surprises (Simonton, 2013). So, while knowledge can be defined as 'justified true beliefs', it appears that highly creative ideas must begin as unjustified and with very low levels of belief. This implies that those who come up with and promote such creative ideas will be a 'special' breed (i.e., to see and believe in things that most others do not). Those willing to expend the effort to test, justify, and explain their creative ideas are the artists and entrepreneurs that every progressive society needs. The rewards to such individuals (e.g., in potential profits or popularity or legacy) then need to be substantial because, besides the challenge of generating such ideas, the ignorance (and often the defensiveness) of the market needs to be overcome at an often great personal expense, given that audience's understandings can only be built upon what they already believe (Kay & King, 2020).

Creativity in business implies more and often different constraints (or minimal requirements) than in art—i.e., for production feasibility (in terms of costs and safety), for utility (in terms of usefulness for some consumer segment so it is willing to pay more than the production costs), and for some minimal inimitability (in terms of protection from rival 'products' for the time needed to pay back the investment in generating and developing the new idea). As such, art can act in some ways as a 'canary in a coalmine'—dealing with things beyond logic and imagination, and thus priming consumers, producers, regulators, and other future stakeholders for what (commercial, industrial, and military goods) may come next. Such art can make the previously unknown (or unimaginable) into the known (or at least imagined). This involves a different kind of assessment—as art expresses hypotheses that are verified by introspection into the stakeholder's own past experiences (Ehrenzweig, 1967) rather than verified by some standard scientific test. As such, art can be much more provocative than business; artful creativity can open new territory that risks chaos and fragmentation at much lower cost or harm

(Ehrenzweig, 1967), and that is a beneficial function that remains quite underappreciated by society.

Philosophical Questions Raised

Uncertainty's connection to the arts raises several interesting (philosophical) questions, including the age-old query of *what is art?*, but newly here, as it relates to uncertainty. Why do we appear to need it, to produce it, and to admire it? Is it part of what it means to be human? (And, what evolutionary forces [related to uncertainty] have driven our species, and others, to engage with it?) Then, what is creativity in that realm, and does it take on different forms for different uncertainty and constraint types? Then, for those different types, can they be done better, faster, and cheaper? What lessons for business (and policy) about addressing uncertainties can be gleaned from experiences in the arts? (And, are there ways to find synergies between these two activities?)

If creativity is mostly recombination, how will big data and AI impact its evolution? What role will humanity play? Will humanity 'see' the product of such artificial processes (e.g., with Dall-E) in the same way it sees more directly 'human-made' art, video, music, and sculpture? If not, where is its place in our society (hopefully not just to replace some traditional commercial artists and writers). What will it mean for humanity to relinquish our arts to technology? What ethical issues are involved (besides fakery, perfect duplication, transferability to multiple media, ownership rights, artists' rights, misappropriation of culture, and so on)? In uncertain markets, can 'manufactured/ manipulated' art be better used to test out possible related business ideas, and is that faithful to what art is?

Summary
Creativity is existentially related to uncertainty. Creativity does not exist without uncertainty (or without discipline). Creative processes use uncertainty in several different ways, including as inspiration and in the end-products. The arts and music are wonderful playgrounds for exploring the balance of the known and the unknown. Such creative activities face different constraints than business activities do, and so can be a realm worth learning from about how to deal with several types of uncertainty.

Why the connections to creativity matter:

- Creativity is a primary way to deal with uncertainty positively, in making sense of it and being inspired by it
- Creativity involves finding a balance between the unknown and the known that is playful, interesting and healthy
- Creativity in the arts emphasizes the heart (affect) and entails fewer and different constraints (than business does), and so offers a unique a valuable perspective to consider

What the connections to creativity, art and music mean for business and policy:

- There are many ways that businesses can leverage the creativity found in the arts and in music (besides in their PR, marketing and some R&D, and outside of the entertainment and gaming industries)
- Such synergies support funding the creative arts—in education and well beyond—and further studies of how different uncertainties are managed in that realm to apply elsewhere

References

Bammer, G., & Smithson, M. (2008). Understanding uncertainty. *Integration Insights, 7*(1), 1–7.
Barrow, J. D. (1998). *Impossibility: The limits of science and the science of limits*. Oxford University Press.
Campbell, D. T. (1960). Blind variation and selective retention in creative thought as in other knowledge processes. *Psychological Review, 67*, 380–400.
Dequech, D. (1999). Expectations and confidence under uncertainty. *Journal of Post Keynesian Economics, 21*(3), 415–430.
Dosi, G., & Egidi, M. (1991). Substantive and procedural uncertainty: An exploration of economic behaviours in changing environments. *Journal of Evolutionary Economics, 1*, 145–168.
Ehrenzweig, A. (1967). *The hidden order of art: A study in the psychology of artistic imagination*. University of California Press.
Faber, M., Manstetten, R., & Proops, J. L. (1992). Humankind and the environment: An anatomy of surprise and ignorance. *Environmental Values, 1*(3), 217–241.
Fleming, L. (2001). Recombinant uncertainty in technological search. *Management Science, 47*(1), 117–132.
Garner, W. R. (1962). *Uncertainty and structure as psychological concepts*. Wiley.
Gilfillan, S. (1935). *Inventing the ship*. Follett Publishing.

Gray, J. (2002). *Straw dogs: Thoughts on humans and other animals*. Farrar.
Kay, J. A., & King, M. A. (2020). *Radical uncertainty*. Bridge Street Press.
Knight, F. H. (1921/1964). *Risk, uncertainty and profit*. Augustus M. Kelley.
Nelson, R. R., & Winter, S. G. (1982). *An evolutionary theory of economic change*. Belknap Press/Harvard University Press.
Nickles, T. (2003). Evolutionary models of innovation and the Meno problem. In *The international handbook on innovation* (pp. 54–78).
Plucker, J. A., Beghetto, R. A., & Dow, G. T. (2004). Why isn't creativity more important to educational psychologists? Potentials, pitfalls, and future directions in creativity research. *Educational Psychologist, 39*(2), 83–96.
Schumpeter, J. A. (1939). *Business cycles: A theoretical, historical, and statistical analysis of the capitalist process*. McGraw-Hill.
Shackle, G. L. S. (1966). Policy, poetry and success. *The Economic Journal, 76*(304), 755–767.
Silverberg, G., Dosi, G., & Orsenigo, L. (1988). Innovation, diversity and diffusion: A self-organisation model. *The Economic Journal, 98*(393), 1032–1054.
Simon, H. A. (1995). The information-processing theory of mind. *American Psychologist, 50*(7), 507.
Simonton, D. K. (2013). Creative thought as blind variation and selective retention: Why creativity is inversely related to sightedness. *Journal of Theoretical and Philosophical Psychology, 33*(4), 253–266.
Spender, J.-C. (2006). *Knightian uncertainty and its resolution as institutionalized practice* [v9 Working Paper].
Usher, A. P. (1954). *A history of mechanical inventions*. Harvard University Press.

CHAPTER 14

Uncertainty's Connections to *Spirituality/Religion*

Connecting Uncertainty to Spirituality and Religion

God has arguably been made humankind's biggest mystery (Bammer & Smithson, 2008). And, in god's absence, uncertainty reigns. Each is both feared and celebrated, depending on both the potential and realized outcomes of important events. Humanity has a strange, love-hate relationship with uncertainty, one that religion and the spirituality underlying it have successfully exploited. On the one hand, religion offers a way to deal with uncertainty, in some ways even absolving its subjects of their responsibility for events, through the idea that every outcome is part of *god's plan*. On the other hand, religion needs inexplicable-level uncertainty, and for things to go surprisingly well for its patrons, at least well enough to retain the idea of some positive magic of its god(s), so that they remain unquestionable objects worthy of worship. This two-sided relationship seems to nicely match the basic needs of humans—to find joy, identity, and meaning in the possible upsides of the uncertain while also to be given comfort, a cushion, and an excuse for possible downsides. And, this 'spiritual product' was bound to apply to a wide audience, because one thing *is* certain—that every person will experience both the upsides and downsides of irreducible uncertainties in their life.

There exist three broad domains of thought in our world—religion, humanism, and science. Each offers a way to reduce uncertainty and the anxieties that come with it (Hertwig et al., 2019). Of these, perhaps religion—as embodied in specific forms of spiritual belief—has been around the longest. In fact, it could be argued that, in the pre-modern world, a significant portion of humanity did not 'see' any randomness, but instead just the will of the gods playing out (Kay & King, 2020).

Some have argued that the history of popular religions should be considered as an unfortunate shift in 'seeking truth' (as the answer to uncertainty). That shift is defined by the movement of truth-seeking from the internal and personal (i.e., trying to deal with the unknowns relating to one's own being) to the external and societal (i.e., trying to deal with uncertainty through community). The unfortunate part was that with that shift came the proclamation of questionable 'truths'—e.g., the declaring of particular acts as sins, as evil, and as worthy of earthly punishments. With that shift, religions became (historically documented) instruments of all kinds of horrible exploitations (Ehrenzweig, 1967).

Some would argue that the worship of truth (as a certainty) has its origins in a Christian cult (Gray, 2002). Many parts of theology, like *eschatology*—the study of big mysteries like the final destiny of the soul and of humankind—focus directly on insolvable uncertainties, while explicitly providing comforting and directive answers that are 'sold' as truths. Religious traditions have, and have had to, address a diverse array of uncertainties because these traditions alone promise the answers; and, religions have (arguably) successfully done so by either warning their subjects about them or by accommodating themselves to them (Beck, 2009). (To the latter, the Vatican appears to have recently accommodated the technological uncertainties of social media with *Facebook* and *Instagram* accounts for the Pope. To the former, too much harm to vulnerable groups has already been done by it.) In fact, it appears that the precise Christological formulations of its early church councils were necessitated by heretical challenges to it (i.e., by questioning its 'certainties') rather than by (what one would think it should have been:) the organic evolution of the studies of its traditions (Berger & Luckmann, 1966).

Such heretical challenges appeared to explode from the seventeenth century on. In Europe, society entered into a new and significant association with uncertainty, making God surrender his role as lord of the universe and its workings. For example, religious beliefs were usurped by mathematics—considered to be a newer belief system where things were not only true but *necessarily* true because they were provable. (However, mathematics did not prove to hold 'the answer', as work by Gödel and others has shown [Stewart, 2019].) Science and technology also vied for the position of truth-revealer and a pathway-to-the-answers. For example, technology has often been seen as a real way to provide what religion had always promised—immortality (Gray, 2002). It has not yet been delivered. Neither has science in ways that religion has. While science can advance human knowledge, it has not made humanity cherish truth (at least not in the same way religion has enticed humanity to believe in its 'truths'). So, humanity remains divided, even after the last four centuries of increasing enlightenment, on how best to deal with uncertainties—i.e., through spiritual beliefs or through scientific ones. Regardless, though, the world depends on people—both religious and not—making decisions that trade-off uncertain benefits and costs, that produce progress and decline, that are infused with human error, ignorance, hubris, power-grabs, spirituality, and unfortunately also the seeds of potential self-destruction (Beck, 2009).

CONNECTING SPIRITUALITY TO DECISION-MAKING UNDER UNCERTAINTY

Given that spirituality/religion offers ways to mitigate uncertainty (or at least the feelings of anxiety uncertainty causes), it should not be surprising that it could also significantly affect decision-making under uncertainty (i.e., for those who are religious). Recently, this has been evident in how religion and entrepreneurial activity have been linked (e.g., *Chick-fil-A*; *Hobby Lobby*) (Judge & Douglas, 2013; Smith et al., 2021). Entrepreneurs face many uncertainties starting up and running their ventures (e.g., involving demand levels, technological feasibility, and so on) (e.g., Smith et al., 2019). Yet, entrepreneurs appear to embrace uncertainties and the opportunities that may arise from them (Baron, 2004). Similarly, those who are spiritual appear to be comfortable with uncertainty, given spirituality's ability to provide a sense of control and protection in such environments (Forstmann & Sagioglou, 2020; Rietveld & Hoogendoorn, 2022; Sargeant & Yoxall, 2023). As a result, in many countries and geographic clusters, the overlap of entrepreneurial activity and religious intensity is high. In some research, spiritual intensity is a significant independent factor correlated with greater acceptance of uncertainty in business decisions, and a significant moderating factor for entrepreneurs in feeling greater comfort with many types of uncertainty (Arend, 2023). Spirituality is prevalent and is not disappearing (Smith et al., 2021); the same is true for entrepreneurial activity. The influence of each on the other—a fundamentally interesting one given they represent the two main world-views of humanity (i.e., of business and belief—Busenitz & Lichtenstein, 2019)—has been under-researched and overly-simplified in the past, and needs more work in the future to get the best from each.

IMPORTANCE OF UNCERTAINTY IN RELIGION

Uncertainty is of existential importance to religion. Without uncertainty (especially about the future, for example, regarding the existence of an afterlife), spiritual belief systems—organized or not—would cease to provide their unique value—of being able to answer the unanswerable—to individuals and to society. While the uncertainty-related value of religions may have waned (slightly) over the last four centuries, the influence of religion remains significant (as of 2023, 84-percent of the world identifies with a religious group), doubtless because it offers other benefits, such as providing a comforting and useful identity to its followers. However, when the concept of probability caught on, where people could measure variance and compute an expected value independently of any higher beings, truth was no longer established by religious authority, and that authority did diminish (Kay & King, 2020). Regardless, religion has held on to other authority.

Religion retains its authority to codify what is good and bad. That codification, however, is not unique; further, the idea that there is both good and bad is central to what uncertainty is. All animals have within them a principle by which to distinguish good from bad—benefits from harms. This is because their existence and welfare are improved by some outcomes and decisions while being damaged by others (Gray, 2002). Uncertainty, itself, is only interesting because it can involve both significant possible benefits and significant possible harms—conditions that nature, commerce, and spirituality help define. Compared to nature and commerce, however, religion goes further in such definitions, often by tying real outcomes to additional outcomes—i.e., to post-death, eternal rewards and punishments. Doing so can influence contemporaneous decisions under uncertainty (and, not always for the better). That noted, events in religious history, like the reformation, reduced some of that 'good' artificial calculus, for example, by eliminating the confessional that forced followers of those affected sects to feel more responsible for their own destinies—and so such reforms resulted in them feeling less accountable for the outcomes of their own decisions in an uncertain world and possibly (and unfortunately) taking them less seriously (Bernstein, 1996).

Uncertainty and religion have a further, more personal, important relationship. Faith (in spiritual beliefs) is a kind of trust; one that arises because uncertainty exists, and one that is most often of a morally positive kind (Bammer & Smithson, 2008). Interestingly, the other side of the coin of faith—doubt—is an intrinsic part of having faith, given that *certainty and faith are theoretically mutually exclusive.* Indeed, doubt is a healthy part of one's faith (e.g., as a means to regularly return to considering faith's limits and one's own responsibilities in life); without it, faith is often unhealthy. Unquestioned faith leads to fundamentalism—as an embodiment of the *only* certainties that (some book or some person says) exist—and, that state of belief is often exploited for destructive ends.

DRIVERS OF UNCERTAINTY IN RELIGION

As many thinkers and novelists (e.g., Dostoevsky) have observed, it appears that humankind has demanded, presently demands, and will always demand, the trappings of spirituality and religion—namely miracle, mystery, and authority—as painless ways to address the challenges of their freedom (Gray, 2002). Humans cannot live without some form of illusion or hope, as often embodied in religious beliefs and myths. Religion has offered an appealing overarching narrative in most societies, and for many still does—one that includes the idea that any uncertainty (and its accompanying anxieties) can be dealt with effectively (Kay & King, 2020). For those who do not belong to organized religion, many have either turned to an irrational faith in technological progress as their antidote to nihilism (Gray, 2002), or sought artistic outlets to find deeper meaning in their lives. In fact, it seems that both aesthetic and religious experiences are prolific producers of useful provinces of meaning (Berger & Luckmann, 1966). Religions need uncertainty to provide 'interesting' meaning—in order to hold the attention of their followers in spite of the so many other 'things' in their lives that vie to hold their attention and offer meanings. Religion, and more generally spirituality, is a daily-use consumable that offers both consistency and robustness, but yet does not 'get stale' or 'wear out'. The only way such spirituality can do that is to exploit the changes and challenges produced by uncertainties—and, do so with a specialization on the moral dimensions of decisions (i.e., where most 'commercial' offerings fear to tread).

OFFERING SOME BALANCE

This chapter is not meant to argue, in any way, that religion or spirituality is inherently bad—as theoretical constructs or even in some realized forms. Religion can be, and often is, good. It often provides: a healthy identity for people; a basis for trust-building; increased philanthropy; important outreach; valuable education; implementable moral codes; useful and entertaining myths; and, even a shared cultural basis for communicating about uncertainties that could be leveraged (Denzau &

North, 1994). The need for such things, and for other spiritual trappings, like hope, still exists, and will well into the future. Some may argue that organized religion needs to be replaced by something new, something with similar benefits but less baggage, more safeguards, and less discrimination, but critically still something outside the commercial and political (i.e., something that transcends 'nations' and 'profits'). It will be interesting to see whether and how that occurs.[1]

If that does occur, though, it is unlikely to be based on 'scientific progress', at least as that has historically evolved. Kuhn (1962) does not paint a 'pretty' picture of such a process. Further, the historic evidence of that possibility—of science replacing religion—has not been 'happy'. For example, the promise of enlightenment (made over two centuries ago) has been broken; reason has failed to emerge as the primary source of authority and legitimacy in our world. This is because our reasoned knowledge is, and will always be, incomplete. The truth will not always out. No perfect information market will ever exist (as frictions are just too profitable to create and exploit). Power, backed ultimately by violence rather than reason, will continue. It is unfortunate, but it seems certain.

As it stands, then, perhaps the relevant journey that humankind has been on can be described in three phases: First, *truth was god*—humanity created god because it felt no control, so communicating with 'higher beings' became the way to deal with uncertainty.[2] Second, the *truth was science*—some control (or at least predictions of some unknowns) became viable, and that limited the need for god. Now, third, *truth is power*—entities (e.g., dictators; corporations) have become gods as they have gained more significant abilities to present their own privately beneficial 'facts' (i.e., their knowns in the face of unknowns) in more efficient, tailored, and monitored ways.[3] We are not in a good place. A mature, shrewd return to a combination of science and morality (even with some

---

[1] It will also be interesting to see whether such replacements can resolve the logical paradoxes that religions have not, such as the *Paradox of Evil*—where God is desirous of humans living in happiness, God is omnipotent, but evil exists and makes humans unhappy (Denzau & North, 1994).

[2] Explanations for unknowns began as myths, dogmas, and taboos, but evolved into organized belief systems about gods—i.e., religions (Denzau & North, 1994).

[3] Note that all along the way, there have been those exploiting such alternative pathways to certainty-as-truth, be they those selling access to spirits, snake-oil, or regulatory influence. That has remained constant, and that is where we really miss the countervailing conscience that religion and spirituality have always promised.

of its spiritual trappings) will likely be necessary to provide a healthy counterbalance.

Summary
Spirituality and religion are delicate subjects. The analysis of their connections to uncertainty here are not directed at any one current religion/theocracy. The analysis reveals an existential connection to uncertainty; if we knew everything, then we would not need to 'believe' in anything. We would not need a story, a book, or a person to provide answers to unanswerable questions (e.g., about the afterlife). Religion—and the underlying spiritual belief systems—often provide comfort to those facing uncertainties; doing so through a moral code, community, support, and a solid reference point. As such, spiritual intensity—in terms of the strength and commitment to a set of beliefs—can, and does, affect decision-making under uncertainty, often in pro-entrepreneurial ways. We have yet to see the full beneficial potential of this connection.

Why the connection to spirituality matters:

- The connection is important because religion is important, and will continue to be, with billions served
- The connection is existential, with significant historical roots, but remains today in terms of spiritual intensity providing comfort in uncertain environments
- Spirituality affects decision-making under uncertainty, often significantly, and often with important actors like entrepreneurs

What the connection to religion/spirituality means for business and policy:

- Religion significantly affects the legitimacy of businesses and governments, in the least in terms of moral standards (and often in new, unknown situations)
- Spiritual beliefs can affect real business-model decisions (e.g., hiring; whether to open on Sundays; who to serve; and, so on) with uncertain results
- Making policy choices over uncertain events (e.g., a pandemic) on science alone (unfortunately) is sometimes not enough, and that is one place where religion can have a powerful positive influence.

REFERENCES

Arend, R. J. (2023). Integrating entrepreneurial and spiritual identities under uncertainty. *Journal of Business Venturing Insights*. Forthcoming.

Bammer, G., & Smithson, M. (2008). Understanding uncertainty. *Integration Insights, 7*(1), 1–7.

Baron, R. (2004). The cognitive perspective: A valuable tool for answering entrepreneurship's basic "why" questions. *Journal of Business Venturing, 19*, 221–239.

Beck, U. (2009). *World at risk*. Polity.

Berger, P., & Luckmann, T. (1966). *The social construction of reality*. Penguin Book.

Bernstein, P. L. (1996). *Against the gods: The remarkable story of risk*. Wiley.

Busenitz, L. W., & Lichtenstein, B. B. (2019). Faith in research: Forging new ground in entrepreneurship. *Academy of Management Perspectives, 33*(3), 280–291.

Denzau, A., & North, D. C. (1994). Shared mental models: Ideologies and institutions. *Kyklos, 47*(1), 3–31.

Ehrenzweig, A. (1967). *The hidden order of art: A study in the psychology of artistic imagination*. University of California Press.

Forstmann, M., & Sagioglou, C. (2020). Religious concept activation attenuates cognitive dissonance reduction in free-choice and induced compliance paradigms. *The Journal of Social Psychology, 160*(1), 75–91.

Gray, J. (2002). *Straw dogs: Thoughts on humans and other animals*. Farrar.

Hertwig, R., Pleskac, T. J., & Pachur, T. (2019). *Taming uncertainty*. MIT Press.

Judge, W. Q., & Douglas, T. J. (2013). Entrepreneurship as a leap of faith. *Journal of Management, Spirituality & Religion, 10*(1), 37–65.

Kay, J. A., & King, M. A. (2020). *Radical uncertainty*. Bridge Street Press.

Kuhn, T. S. (1962). *The structure of scientific revolutions*. University of Chicago Press.

Rietveld, C. A., & Hoogendoorn, B. (2022). The mediating role of values in the relationship between religion and entrepreneurship. *Small Business Economics, 58*(3), 1309–1335.

Sargeant, S., & Yoxall, J. (2023). Psychology and spirituality: Reviewing developments in history, method and practice. *Journal of Religion and Health, 62*, 1159–1174.

Smith, B. R., Conger, M. J., McMullen, J. S., & Neubert, M. J. (2019). Why believe? The promise of research on the role of religion in entrepreneurial action. *Journal of Business Venturing Insights, 11*, e00119.

Smith, B. R., McMullen, J. S., & Cardon, M. S. (2021). Toward a theological turn in entrepreneurship: How religion could enable transformative research in our field. *Journal of Business Venturing*, 36(5), 106139.

Stewart, I. (2019). *Do dice play god? The mathematics of uncertainty.* Hachette.

CHAPTER 15

Uncertainty's Connections to Curiosity, Neurobiology, and Evolution

Connecting Uncertainty to Curiosity

Curiosity is the strong desire to know or learn something, often without immediate necessity. (It is also the moniker of a very capable Mars rover.) It is an aversive state that is caused by uncertainty (in the form of information deprivation) (Loewenstein, 1994). It is a powerful motivator for learning, creativity, and subjective well-being (Gallagher & Lopez, 2007; Hardy et al., 2017; Shin & Kim, 2019; Von Stumm et al., 2011). *Forward curiosity*—the curiosity for *what*—is triggered by unpredictability (i.e., uncertainty about the future). *Backward curiosity*—the curiosity for *why*—is triggered by incongruity, by surprise, and by confusion (Brod et al., 2018; D'Mello et al., 2014; Kamin, 1969) and motivates an active search for the unknown causes (Shin & Kim, 2019). Curiosity is the response to an 'optimal' level of uncertainty—it is above the level where the answer is trivial (i.e., as to be an easy extrapolation or explanation) and below the level where the answer is seemingly impossible (e.g., as requiring incredibly deep expertise or extraordinary effort, involving vast complexity, and complicated, non-linear dynamics).

Curiosity is a cognitive appetite for certainty (Shin & Kim, 2019), even when the drive to learn has no apparent utilitarian value, or involves danger (Hsee & Ruan, 2016; Oosterwijk, 2017). Curiosity can be understood through *Drive Theory*. That theory suggests that an internal deficit—here, of information—leads to an unpleasant arousal, which then instigates exploratory behavior—here, informational search—in an attempt to restore a hedonic state of balance (Hull, 1952). Curiosity then dissipates when the necessary knowledge is gained, or the feeling disappears for other reasons (Markey & Loewenstein, 2014). Curiosity stems from an innate drive to make sense of (and possibly improve) the environment. Its successful resolution often initiates a positive feedback loop, one that encourages further curiosity and deeper information-seeking until some limit is reached (e.g., in understanding that focal subject, or in the realization of the impossibility of reaching further answers) (Shin & Kim, 2019).

Being curious differs from being interested. *Situational interest* is a positive affect triggered by things like autonomy, relatedness, and competence. Curiosity is an aversive cognitive state caused by an information gap. Situational interest obeys the hedonic principle; it is associated with the brain's opioid 'liking' system. Curiosity is a drive; it is associated with the brain's dopaminergic 'wanting' system. Interest draws people to the stimulus; curiosity draws people to actively seek missing information (Shin & Kim, 2019). Situational interest requires comprehension (Kintsch, 1980; Silvia, 2008); curiosity requires a gap in knowledge, often caused by incompleteness, ambiguity, and non-comprehension. So, there are several dimensions that delineate curiosity from situational interest, including: their underlying theories; their biological underpinnings; their triggers; their relevant affects; and, their needs for different types of information (Shin & Kim, 2019). Curiosity appears to be more of an evolutionary adaptation to a world of uncertainty than does simple interest, given its deeper drive, greater need for understanding, and its trigger being grounded in (wanting to reduce) surprise.

In order to be surprised—to trigger curiosity—the individual has to have both a reference base of knowledge and an awareness of the unknown (Shin & Kim, 2019). Between those levels of understanding is the information gap that drives curiosity. That uncertainty can be the result of several different stimuli—e.g., complexity, ambiguity, incongruity, or novelty.

Connecting Uncertainty to Neurobiology

Without uncertainty there is no need for a brain, just reflexes; there is no need to predict or to explore because there is no new information to seek out. Uncertainty drives evolution of organisms, the design of their brains, and the associated neurobiology. For an organism to survive in our uncertain world, it must have a brain that performs abbreviation *and* its environment must display sufficient order to make encapsulations possible over reasonable dimensions of time and space (Barrow, 1998). For us, our human brain is a prediction machine. In our heads, the 'brain economy' trades probabilistic predictions so that the body can filter noise, make decisions faster, and take action to change things for its own benefit (Clark, 2016). As such, the brain is not some reference resource or reactive interpreter of the senses; it is an action-oriented, enabling node in the dense, shared exchanges between itself, its body, and its uncertain world (Clark, 2016).

Why is the brain, as a prediction and action machine, the best design (versus a brain that takes in sensory information, processes it, then reacts; or, one that builds a vast map of its environment and updates it continuously)? It is because of the rate and span of incoming signals, and the immediate dangers that have been involved in our environments. Our brains make guesses—combining perception, action, emotion, and exploitation of contextual structures with a common neurobiological currency to do so (Clark, 2016). This provides functional consistency and speed in dealing with an ever-changing world, and one that involves the many uncertainties that require exploring. By continuously guessing, we get feedback on what we need to update faster (which is advantageous to our survival). Behavioral and neuroscientific research indicates that prediction errors release dopamine to then trigger continual new learning (as seen in the hypercorrection effect—see Butterfield & Metcalfe, 2006; Marvin & Shohamy, 2016; Schultz et al., 1997). But, when the neurological combination is damaged, for example, by incapacitating the emotional responses, then the prediction machine can break down (Damasio, 1994) because each part relies on the other (Roeser, 2019). Being able to make good decisions under uncertainty requires our brains to be completely functional.

Our brains exploit the consistencies in our environments to make predictions. And, by focusing on the difference between the real signal and the brain's predicted one, the bandwidth is minimized (Clark, 2016). It is much more difficult to simply take in (a lot of) raw data and try to explain it, rather than just test a select set of hypotheses (which is what our brain does well). The brain weights prediction error signals to drive subsequent sampling of the world to test its hypotheses, doing so by combining perception, action, and emotion in coherent, self-fueling loop (Clark, 2016). The brain not only uses its predictions to test its knowledge, it also uses them to select the signals to process, and even to *adjust* and temper those signals—that latter function being more beneficial when such incoming signals are more noisy, ambiguous, and incomplete (Clark, 2016). So, in more uncertain contexts, the brain itself actively filters 'what that uncertainty looks like' prior to adjusting to it (which is a meta-level tactic that may be dangerous when the context has rapidly shifted).

Our brains are wired to respond to uncertainty. Even a small amount of it triggers an error response in the orbital frontal cortex (Rock, 2008) that cannot be ignored, making it difficult to focus on other things until it is resolved. That sensitivity makes large uncertainties highly debilitating. And, when that area of the brain is damaged, subjects are simply unable to make plans in the face of uncertainty (MacLeod & Pingle, 2000). There is even a part of the brain that is triggered by the anticipation of possible— uncertain—rewards, sometimes having more effect than the receipt of the reward itself; it is one part of the brain that drives exploration into the unknown (Brafman & Brafman, 2008). As such, *human brains are not computers*; they are built as adaptive mechanisms for recognizing patterns to predict and act better for gain in an uncertain world (Kay & King, 2020). When expectations are met, there is an increase in dopamine levels in the brain as a reward (Rock, 2008). But when curiosity is awakened, neuroimaging indicates brain regions associated with conflict and negative affect—the anterior insula and anterior cingulate cortex—become activated to spur action (Jepma et al., 2012). Explaining the good feelings that many forms of entertainment have (e.g., jokes, detective stories, romances, and other drama) are the neuroimaging studies of subjects who are asked trivia questions knowing that they would be given the answers shortly after, that have indicated that even such minor induced-curiosity activates reward-related brain regions significantly (Shin & Kim, 2019).

Our brains are wired to be incessantly proactive, to restlessly seek new sensory data to use as a means of checking and correcting its predictions (Clark, 2016). The brain tries to know the pattern of events occurring moment-to-moment; it craves the certainty required to predict with accuracy (Rock, 2008). Why? Because without good prediction, the brain must use significantly greater resources, involving more energy-intensive parts, in an attempt to process the moment-to-moment experiences. Of course, prediction is not *the truth*—at least in terms of conscious mapping. Trying to get to a comprehensive truth is a luxury (or a drawback) in the struggle of life; natural selection does *not* favor a nervous system that focuses on consciously mapping out the world at the expense of trying to live in it. To live in it means relying a lot on our subconscious brain. What the brain 'knows and does' (without our thinking) is vastly different from what we learn and comprehend through our conscious awareness: we process 14 million bits of information per second, with the bandwidth of our consciousness being only 18 meager bits! (Gray, 2002).

Connecting Uncertainty to Cognition

Our neurobiology is more about processing information that we are not aware of than information that we are aware of. Yet, we 'occupy minds' that are focused on the latter—that ruminate on what we are consciously aware of. So, let's now concentrate on the conscious—our cognitions—to further assess how uncertainty matters. Our conscious is used to look further out into the future and more widely out into the world than our subconscious; and, the only effective way to do that is to rely on information beyond our personal experiences. But, that necessarily entails *more* uncertainty, because the source of that extra information is not us, but a less-reliable and less-complete narrative.

For advanced species, predicting the present/immediate future is simply not enough. Humans are built to engage the world, not only in ways that are sensitive to their past experiences, but also in ways that actively bring forth their desired futures (Clark, 2016). We rely on cognitive processes of internalization to interpret and evaluate sources of external uncertainty in order to provide a basis for opportunity formation and enactment (Magnani & Zucchella, 2018). We do this through a consciousness that is epiphenomenal, one that provides us with the ability to imagine future states of affairs (Knight, 1921).

In order to extend our predictions through the use of others' experiences and knowledge, we need the ability to produce and interpret symbolic descriptions almost as if these were our own experiences (Hertwig et al., 2019). We can only do that through conscious thinking (although mirror neurons may play a similar role for more physical planning functions subconsciously). That search for symbolic information—regardless of source—is what cognition entails (Hertwig et al., 2019). And, given that our brains are prediction machines, the need for such search is driven not only by the unexpected additional things that happen (i.e., from our senses taking in more input than expected) but also by unexpected absences of things (i.e., our senses taking in less input than expected). The latter is a bonus that comes from predictive-processing (versus simple sensory-processing); such processing provides not only a null hypothesis test but also a two-way feedback system for fine-tuning prediction consciously (Clark, 2016).

Cognition is about acquiring a better understanding of the world, through thought and experience, in order to more accurately guess the incoming signals as they arrive in the short-term, and to act to exploit those predictions in the longer-term (Clark, 2016). Making decisions to act also requires having sufficient confidence in those predictions (Kay & King, 2020). Evidence exists that we are cognizant of the level of confidence we have in such predictions (as well as of how that level alters with our abilities at that point in time); for example, such evidence comes from ambiguity aversion experiments, where subjects show a preference for known risks over unknown risks (Ellsberg, 1961). Human ambiguity tolerance peaks in adolescence (the time when we are most physically able to deal with it), evidenced then by our searching less for information prior to making consequential decisions (Hertwig et al., 2019). By contrast, mature adults increase their information search under ambiguity, fear, and an overload of options (Hertwig et al., 2019). (Note that we all start out life under strong uncertainty—Denzau & North, 1994.)

Prediction—both conscious and subconscious—even though limited, has worked in the past, because the world has also usually been limited in what it has presented to us. The number of the properties of nature, and the modes of the behaviors of its creatures, are both limited, regardless of the fact that there is an infinite number of their combinations. Given we have tended to deal with the former set more historically, and that those things tend also to have stable properties, we have been able to muddle through. And, even when that set of properties changes, it tends to do so in fairly consistent and ascertainable ways, usually making (sufficient) prediction possible (Knight, 1921). That said, in some cases, we have extended inference well past our perceptions in order to make judgments under uncertainty (Knight, 1921), even though that can sometimes lead to systematic errors (Gigerenzer, 2005). And, in other cases, hope (as the possibility of gain) is all we have had—an irrational cognition that only exists because uncertainty does (Brafman & Brafman, 2008).

Our cognition occupies the epistemic space between truth and ignorance (Hertwig et al., 2019). Even when we are closer to the latter—where information is scarce and unreliable—our minds still formulate beliefs, models, and predictions that we then act upon. Not only does our mind predict the future based on incomplete information, it does so across multiple scenarios—where, at a minimum, those scenarios cover what will happen when we do not act and what will happen if we act in a specific way. (The more specific ways we consider acting, the more scenarios we must then imagine and compare among.) It should not be surprising that such predictions are often inaccurate. Inaccuracies arise from at least four different sources: our inability to perceive the past perfectly; the mistakes in making logical inferences from whatever past we had perceived; the errors in any of that cause-and-effect logic itself; and, the blunders we are bound to make in taking the action we are considering (Knight, 1921). Even when it comes to placing a cause with an effect, it is only our conscience interpretation of each (based on our limited perceptions) that is used, rather than reality (Knight, 1921). Given such issues, our cognitive abilities need to be multi-level to work well—to include a meta-level tool that selects the right tool for the given context (e.g., that takes into account the possible discrepancies between perceptions and reality, and the other limits to our mental capacity) (Hertwig et al., 2019). As such, we need to know when to trust our senses, when to trust others' data, when to extrapolate, when to imagine, and when to simply ignore (Barrow, 1998). In business, such cognitive processes not only have to work at the individual level but also at the organizational level, to be effective in responding to uncertainty (Magnani & Zucchella, 2018).

Uncertainty has both negative and positive effects on our cognition. Psychopathologists find that uncertainty can be harmful to mental health, for example, being a major driver of anxiety disorders (Kozyreva & Hertwig, 2021). Others find that uncertainty can increase working memory capacity (Randles et al., 2018), attention span, and neural processing, and even can intensify vigilance for new information (Griffin & Grote, 2020; Walker et al., 2019). The function of consciousness is to infer, and so when we can do so with confidence based on the given information and context, then the underlying uncertainty is seen to offer a helpful stretch of those muscles; but, when we cannot, then uncertainty is seen to cause a painful paralysis (Knight, 1921). Unfortunately, trying to measure that break-point level of confidence in some probabilistic terms or language (in order to better understand uncertainty's effects) does not often work (Romeijn & Roy, 2014). Overall, our cognition acts on what we infer rather than what we perceive, and uncertainty makes that much more challenging (Knight, 1921); as such, our minds have adapted—have evolved—in ways that can deal with what will inevitably be inconsistencies. We have learned how to deal with contradiction.

CONNECTING UNCERTAINTY TO EVOLUTION

Without uncertainty there would be no evolution (Kay & King, 2020). Without uncertainty, there is either stability or predictable change and, therefore, only one stable and foreseeable best set of organisms to match a known time and place. There is no need to experiment or competitively select. However, *with* uncertainty, there is a need to produce variance in a population—through mutation, through environmentally-triggered genetic switches, and through partially random reproduction events. There is then also a need to select the variants with the best fit to the given environment—who are most likely to survive it and what is likely to immediately follow—with some noise in that process itself (for robustness). Contextual uncertainty in this process is itself addressed with uncertainties (and some predictable behaviors), ones built into the biological and genetic responses, which evolved themselves because they were better at surviving uncertainty (Heiner, 1983).

Evolution can only work when certainty exists. Knowledge-as-certainty—knowledge that is based on some minimal level of stability and predictability in the environment—is needed for communications, for selection, and for identifying what to keep versus what to change in the evolutionary process (Barrow, 1998). The small amount of it that is useful—truthful, stable—is exploited by every animal's organs—organs that have been generated by scarce genetic resources to help their owners escape predators, find food, and gather more information (Barrow, 1998). As such, evolution does require some regularities in nature—ones that living things encounter in order to embody theories about natural laws that allow them to use those laws to survive (Barrow, 1998). That process of going from 'encountering' to 'embodying' works because information acquisition is a hedonic experience (Shin & Kim, 2019). The human brain responds to information acquisition as it does to food or to sex. And, while that 'immediate rewards-based' process can be beneficial, it can also go wrong. For example, the strong loss aversion that evolution has instilled in us as a survival mechanism for dealing with uncertainty in the short-term, can have negative impacts longer-term when it converges with commitment—when it locks us out of slightly more-risky but much more beneficial options (Brafman & Brafman, 2008).

Human cognition has also evolved to deal with uncertainty (and done so better than other species who display greater rigidity and inflexibility when facing uncertainty—Heiner, 1983). Instead of having only one mode of thinking or acting, we have evolved several, adapted to differing levels of uncertainty (and its dangers). According to *Dual Process Theory* we have two main cognitive systems: the first being intuitive and emotional but working fast, with the second being rational, slow, and effortful, but normatively superior (Roeser, 2019). In other theories, humans have evolved multiple information-processing architectures, each adapted to both the quality of information and the relative magnitudes of the rewards and punishments involved, including semantic and pragmatic inferencing (Hertwig & Gigerenzer, 1999; Hertwig et al., 2019). So, when punishments are high relative to rewards and the quality of information is low (i.e., high uncertainty contexts), then we switch to a processing architecture that focuses on identifying specific strings of highly reliable information from which to make decisions. In that theory, brain evolution started with adopting heuristics that used less memory load but still were accurate, and then grew more memory so that decision-time decreased and that the option to use more sophisticated heuristics emerged (Hertwig et al., 2019). Our thinking was, therefore, honed by evolutionary rather than axiomatic rationality, producing many of the so-called behavioral biases we identify today (Kay & King, 2020). Both the harshness of the environment and its uncertainty push organisms to select faster strategies, whether in decisions or lifecycles; to the latter, the shorter the expected lifespans the greater the benefits from accelerating maturation and reproducing early, even when it compromises longevity (Hertwig et al., 2019).

Besides evolving multiple ways of thinking, we have also evolved multiple ways of acting in the face of uncertainty. Humans have coevolved with our environments—environments that impose often harsh natural selection—by learning how to manipulate those environments by artificial means in order to escape from the prisons imposed by our limited senses and abilities (Barrow, 1998). We have evolved to predict and preempt nature; we can react to a situation before that situation materializes (Knight, 1921). The farther ahead we can 'see', the more adequately we can act to adapt to our environments, and the better we can live. Humans are programmed to be active in seeking and filtering new information to mitigate uncertainties that harm our predictions (Brafman & Brafman, 2008). Humans have also evolved the ability and drive to share that information-seeking burden and the burden of taking on uncertain outcomes through cooperation; first, through cooperation among our families and tribes, to now cooperation among communities, organizations, and nations (often as a means of using reciprocal commitments to help each other in the uncertain future—see Kay & King, 2020).

It is important to note that cognition-related evolution does not equate with knowledge, let alone with truth. Coping with uncertainty, in all its forms and dimensions, has been a constant challenge to human evolution; even more than any challenge to solve the mysteries of the universe (Kay & King, 2020). Evolution does *not* care about what was true; it simply continues to produce a variety of traits, at random, in every breeding organism before there is any need for such variants, in order to meet the unknown demands of the future (Barrow, 1998). Darwinian theory is clear that an interest in the truth is unnecessary, if not often a disadvantage, for survival and reproduction. In fact, in a competition for mates, self-deception is usually an advantage, and, in a competition for food, other-deception is a definitive advantage; in other words, it is non-truth that is often selected for (Gray, 2002).

Evolution entails several other concerns to the decision-makers of today besides its apathy (or even its antipathy) towards truth-seeking (and truth-telling). While the variation-selection-retention cycle gives rise to entities that can better deal with uncertainties, it also gives rise to more capable rivals (Hertwig et al., 2019). At the extreme, in overly-competitive contexts, cognitive abilities may actually be degraded by such evolution—for example, when rivals are forced to use the simple heuristic of a 'one-sampling choice' (to ensure they each get the same reward on average), each entity is prevented from evolving a better sampling strategy (Hertwig et al., 2019). The evolution of decision mechanisms and strategies can also be influenced by other factors, such as: individual and collective information-processing constraints; fitness landscapes that contain multiple local maxima; and, population-level traits. Such sensitivities make the beneficial effects of that evolution highly unpredictable (Hertwig et al., 2019). Considering sensitivities further, it is worthy to note that in the real world, it is the extreme events—as embodied in the tails of distributions—that are often relevant to survival; when that is the case, it is the economically-rational-expected-value-maximizers who get wiped out rather than the more conservative beings, because averages don't matter as much as detrimental extremes (Kay & King, 2020). As such, a predisposition to avoid large losses can be a useful attribute. Evolution tends to favor survivors (who use quick heuristics under the pressures of uncertainty) rather than maximizers (who take the time and cognitive effort to search for information and make complicated calculations). That said, some of the extreme-outcome-focused pressure can be mitigated when we form groups (to insure each other); but that entails a different type of evolution. The evolution of our institutions differs from biological evolution in many important ways; for example, it differs by the contribution of intentionality—we can use non-random mutation (while nature does not). And, it would be an error to describe or model the evolution of these group-level processes as if they were random (i.e., uncertain) when we analyze and choose among them (Kay & King, 2020).

Humans have evolved ways to think about different types of unknowns. For example, our risk preferences have both a base component that applies to many domains of life, as well as a range of add-on components that are specific to particular psychological, situational, and demand characteristics (Hertwig et al., 2019). And, given we are social animals, we have evolved abilities for dealing with interpersonal uncertainties that include strong capacities for social learning and communications (Kay & King, 2020). We have also evolved the ability to work in groups to address unknowns, in ways that are even sensitive to the group's size; for example, studies indicate that smaller groups have an increased propensity to apply risk-averse strategies (Hertwig et al., 2019). Further, we have evolved ways to deal with the uncertainties that groups themselves generate; for example, by avoiding being a lone standout (Brafman & Brafman, 2008). And, when not in a group, we have evolved a two-level way to judge uncertain outcomes—with an estimated value, and an estimate of its confidence (Knight, 1921).

The evolved drive to make sense of our environment, to search for information, and to process that into answers, has been crucial to human survival (Shin & Kim, 2019). At the individual level, that drive to take risks, based on the incentives, appears to change as we age (Hertwig et al., 2019). Modeling such evolutionary processes involves a complicated conceptual space with high dimensionality (Silverberg, 1997). This is due to the novelty of stimuli that have existed and continue to be experienced, starting from when our ancestors came across strange animals, unknown plants, and other tribes, to now when we ourselves come across new technologies, diseases, and natural disasters; such novelty has always created anxiety in humans, anxiety that naturally springs from a lack of information (James, 1950). And so, we continue to hone our anxiety-reducing skills just as we generate more sources of uncertainty in our never-ending attempt to discover (and apply) more information (that then leads us down infinite rabbit-holes of deeper causes and opportunities).

Drivers of the Connections

Human, you are a strange animal—driven to reduce uncertainty (e.g., through learning) while constantly increasing it (e.g., through innovation). Uncertainty is an aversive, anxious mental state arising from new stimuli, so the human mind has evolved to try to eliminate it (Wilson et al., 2005). But, that is difficult given the limited sensory information it receives. What we see (and can imagine based on what we've seen) is all there is to use (Hertwig et al., 2019). And, sometimes what we see is already restricted by our preferences (Hertwig et al., 2019). Luckily (?), we humans have a gift for self-deception, allowing us to thrive in our ignorance—by taking action on limited information (rather than by being paralyzed by it) (Gigerenzer, 2005). Given the dangers and uncertainties that such deception entails, humans have given rise to a morality that other entities have not (Gray, 2002). So, we continue to struggle to control both the uncertainties that are thrust upon us and those that we seek out, as well as those we thrust upon ourselves in so doing. Evolving in such a multi-layered manner is unlikely to have been simple.

The most complicated things that have evolved, like the human brain, entail seemingly impenetrable structures. Even if we had a 'theory of everything' for the brain, that still would not provide all of its solutions (i.e., the truth of it) (Barrow, 1998). Thus, a 'unified theory for human behavior' appears unachievable (Kay & King, 2020). And, turning to what the brain produces 'as science', there is no guarantee that our ideas and conceptualizations of the world evolve towards the truth. Memes are not genes. And, there are no mechanisms of selection of ideas akin to those of natural selection; only the optimistically naïve believe that what exists as competition among ideas will result in the triumph of the truth. Unfortunately, in reality, the only winners of such a game are those with power and human folly on their side (Gray, 2002). And so, we humans settle with 'muddling through', based on whatever certainties that the world provides (or we believe it provides). Indeed, repeated, identifiable patterns are needed for any conscious life to exist (Barrow, 1998). Our world has been relied upon to provide a 'training signal' that thankfully continues to allow us to compare predictions with actual sensed energetic input— a cycle that lets us (and our genes) learn and adapt to the uncertainties that we will always confront (Clark, 2016). Uncertainty has necessitated evolution, evolution that has produced the brain, and its mind's curiosity to respond to uncertainty.

PHILOSOPHICAL IMPLICATIONS

The main philosophical issue that arises when connecting uncertainty to cognition concerns the question of human *free will*. If we have it then it is less likely that specific human actions will ever become predictable (i.e., be not uncertain). If we do not have it, theoretically, we (and every other [less sophisticated] species) are predictable (and, therefore, exploitable). In practice, of course, even without free will, humans may not be predictable if, for example, the system our brains use is 'chaotic' in nature (and the initial conditions are not feasibly obtainable).

It seems that if real indeterminateness does emerge from the human activities, it is through the freedom in our conduct (Knight, 1921). So, while some of our decisions may be habitual and involve no sense of free will, other decisions seem to be reasoned where the underlying freedom of choice makes prediction difficult (Gilboa, 2009).

Given that dichotomy of human behaviors—with some highly predictable and some unknowable—what is the conclusion? This is not the book to resolve the debate on free will. (That is a not-yet-sorted rabbit-hole of inquiry—one that raises many follow-on questions about free will, like if it is an illusion, then what kind?) This book is about making decisions, and so we must necessarily (and happily) assume that humans have the freedom to choose their options. Further, we acknowledge (like most others in this literature) that uncertainty arises over how other sentient beings behave—a point that aligns with believing that most organisms behave *as if* they had free will. However, given we also believe that our brains are limited in what these biological mechanisms can do, and how well they can predict their worlds, there are limits to that freedom of will (i.e., it is not unrestricted, especially in action or timing or impact). Essentially, the philosophical question of whether free will exists is not a question of interest here; there are several less-explored and practically more interesting questions to consider relating to uncertainty in terms of its causes (of which one may be free will) and its effects.

Summary
Evolution exists because of uncertainty, as does it products—our brains, and the curiosity and cognition that that neurochemistry enables. The brain is an evolved but highly imperfect mechanism for dealing with uncertainties. It does so on at least two different levels—the subconscious and the conscious—using limited and outdated information. The most efficient way it has evolved to do so involves constant prediction with feedback-processing, along with multiple layers of add-on features, from self-deception to anxiety to curiosity to the enjoyment of humor. Our brains are open to good and bad manipulation by others, by drugs, and by its own separate mind-parts. Much more work needs to be done to restrict such manipulation.

Why these connections matter:

- Evolution, our brains, and our cognitions are all existentially linked to uncertainty; so, understanding uncertainty can help with understanding them
- Finding better ways to feed human curiosity and exploration, and to improve it with tools, and to share the outcomes, should benefit us individually and collectively
- Implies the need for better ways to evolve idea-memes, making the process more equitable, reliable, diverse, and effective, especially as it relates to uncovering unknowns

What the connections to curiosity, neurobiology and evolution mean for business and policy:

- Stricter regulations are needed to control how businesses and institutions are exploiting our (curiosity-related) neurobiology for private gain, especially to protect the young
- New regulations are needed to restrict the uncertainty-as-disinformation that our evolved technologies, like AI-based systems, are generating, and especially to hold those responsible for the harms caused to account
- There are business opportunities available for helping consumers battle the onslaught of false and uncertain messaging and attempted influences on our minds

References

Barrow, J. D. (1998). *Impossibility: The limits of science and the science of limits.* Oxford University Press on Demand.

Brafman, O., & Brafman, R. (2008). *Sway: The irresistible pull of irrational behavior.* Doubleday Business.

Brod, G., Hasselhorn, M., & Bunge, S. A. (2018). When generating a prediction boosts learning: The element of surprise. *Learning and Instruction, 55,* 22–31.

Butterfield, B., & Metcalfe, J. (2006). The correction of errors committed with high confidence. *Metacognition and Learning, 1,* 69–84.

Clark, A. (2016). *Surfing uncertainty: Prediction, action, and the embodied mind.* Oxford University Press.

D'Mello, S., Lehman, B., Pekrun, R., & Graesser, A. (2014). Confusion can be beneficial for learning. *Learning and Instruction, 29*, 153–170.

Damasio, A. (1994). *Descartes error—Emotion*. Putnam Press.

Denzau, A., & North, D. C. (1994). Shared mental models: Ideologies and institutions. *Kyklos, 47*(1), 3–31.

Ellsberg, D. (1961). Risk, ambiguity, and the Savage axioms. *The Quarterly Journal of Economics, 75*(4), 643–669.

Gallagher, M. W., & Lopez, S. J. (2007). Curiosity and well-being. *The Journal of Positive Psychology, 2*(4), 236–248.

Gigerenzer, G. (2005). I think, therefore I err. *Social Research: An International Quarterly, 72*(1), 195–218.

Gilboa, I. (2009). *Theory of decision under uncertainty*. Cambridge University Press.

Gray, J. (2002). *Straw dogs: Thoughts on humans and other animals*. Farrar, Straus and Giroux.

Griffin, M. A., & Grote, G. (2020). When is more uncertainty better? A model of uncertainty regulation and effectiveness. *Academy of Management Review, 45*(4), 745–765.

Hardy, J. H., III., Ness, A. M., & Mecca, J. (2017). Outside the box: Epistemic curiosity as a predictor of creative problem solving and creative performance. *Personality and Individual Differences, 104*, 230–237.

Heiner, R. A. (1983). The origin of predictable behavior. *The American Economic Review, 73*(4), 560–595.

Hertwig, R., & Gigerenzer, G. (1999). The 'conjunction fallacy' revisited: How intelligent inferences look like reasoning errors. *Journal of Behavioral Decision Making, 12*(4), 275–305.

Hertwig, R., Pleskac, T. J., & Pachur, T. (2019). *Taming uncertainty*. MIT Press.

Hsee, C. K., & Ruan, B. (2016). The Pandora effect: The power and peril of curiosity. *Psychological Science, 27*(5), 659–666.

Hull, C. L. (1952). *A behavior system: An introduction to behavior theory concerning the individual organism*. Yale University Press.

James, W. (1950). *The principles of psychology*. Dover.

Jepma, M., Verdonschot, R. G., Van Steenbergen, H., Rombouts, S. A., & Nieuwenhuis, S. (2012). Neural mechanisms underlying the induction and relief of perceptual curiosity. *Frontiers in Behavioral Neuroscience, 6*(5), 1–9.

Kamin, L. J. (1969). Predictability, surprise, attention, and conditioning. In B. A. Campbell & R. M. Church (Eds.), *Punishment and aversive behavior*. Appleton-Century-Crofts.

Kay, J. A., & King, M. A. (2020). *Radical uncertainty. Decision-making beyond the numbers*. Bridge Street Press.

Kintsch, W. (1980). Learning from text, levels of comprehension, or: Why anyone would read a story anyway? *Poetics, 9*, 87–98.

Knight, F.H. (1921/64). *Risk, uncertainty and profit.* Augustus M. Kelley.

Kozyreva, A., & Hertwig, R. (2021). The interpretation of uncertainty in ecological rationality. *Synthese, 198*(2), 1517–1547.

Loewenstein, G. (1994). The psychology of curiosity: A review and reinterpretation. *Psychological Bulletin, 116*(1), 75–98.

MacLeod, W. B. & Pingle, M. (2000). *An experiment on the relative effects of ability, temperament and luck on search with uncertainty* (University of Southern California Law School, Olin Research Paper 00–12).

Magnani, G., & Zucchella, A. (2018). Uncertainty in entrepreneurship and management studies: A systematic literature review. *International Journal of Business and Management, 13*(3), 98–133.

Markey, A., & Loewenstein, G. (2014). Curiosity. In *International handbook of emotions in education* (pp. 238–255).

Marvin, C. B., & Shohamy, D. (2016). Curiosity and reward: Valence predicts choice and information prediction errors enhance learning. *Journal of Experimental Psychology: General, 145*(3), 266–272.

Oosterwijk, S. (2017). Choosing the negative: A behavioral demonstration of morbid curiosity. *PLoS ONE, 12*(7), e0178399.

Randles, D., Benjamin, R., Martens, J. P., & Heine, S. J. (2018). Searching for answers in an uncertain world: Meaning threats lead to increased working memory capacity. *PLoS ONE, 13*(10), e0204640.

Rock, D. (2008). SCARF: A brain-based model for collaborating with and influencing others. *NeuroLeadership Journal, 1*(1), 44–52.

Roeser, S. (2019). Emotional responses to luck, risk, and uncertainty. In *The Routledge handbook of the philosophy and psychology of luck* (pp. 356–364). Routledge.

Romeijn, J. W., & Roy, O. (2014). Radical uncertainty: Beyond probabilistic models of belief. *Erkenntnis, 79*, 1221–1223.

Schultz, W., Dayan, P., & Montague, P. R. (1997). A neural substrate of prediction and reward. *Science, 275*(5306), 1593–1599.

Shin, D. D., & Kim, S. I. (2019). Homo curious: Curious or interested? *Educational Psychology Review, 31*(4), 853–874.

Silverberg, G. (1997). *Evolutionary modeling in economics: Recent history and immediate prospects.* MERIT.

Silvia, P. J. (2008). Interest—The curious emotion. *Current Directions in Psychological Science, 17*(1), 57–60.

Von Stumm, S., Chung, A., & Furnham, A. (2011). Creative ability, creative ideation and latent classes of creative achievement: What is the role of personality? *Psychology of Aesthetics, Creativity, and the Arts, 5*(2), 107–114.

Walker, A. R., Luque, D., Le Pelley, M. E. & Beesley, T. (2019). The role of uncertainty in attentional and choice exploration. *Psychonomic Bulletin & Review, 26*, 1911–1916.

Wilson, T. D., Centerbar, D. B., Kermer, D. A., & Gilbert, D. T. (2005). The pleasures of uncertainty: Prolonging positive moods in ways people do not anticipate. *Journal of Personality and Social Psychology, 88*(1), 5–21.

CHAPTER 16

Past Failures to Engage with Uncertainty

Identifying the Failures to Engage

The failures of mainstream economics- and business-related fields to engage seriously with uncertainty have been apparent for at least a century. Knight (1921) highlighted this neglect in classical economic theory over one hundred years ago, using it to argue a place for entrepreneurial studies. At the same time, Keynes (1921) also recognized that a central limitation of mainstream economic theory was the lack of a proper analysis of uncertainty and tried to make progress with it. Several economists in the Austrian School followed suit in the interim but arguably did not bring significant engagement with uncertainty to economics or management research. More recently, it remains understood that mainstream academic economics still neglects fundamental uncertainty (Dequech, 1999). Uncertainty is rarely analyzed as a distinctive modality associated with specific ways of problematizing the future; instead, uncertainty is seen merely as vagueness (O'Malley, 2000). Formal economic modeling continues to neglect the significance of uncertainty (Nash, 2003); there is a failure to properly analyze economic behavior under uncertainty (Fontana & Gerrard, 2004). Indeed, theoretical (business) research has stopped short of seriously and fully engaging with uncertainty (Lampert et al., 2020). Despite a long-standing recognition of the importance of uncertainty in management, strategy research has not given sufficient attention to the distinct challenges and processes involved in strategic decision-making under uncertainty (Rindova & Courtney, 2020).

A century ago, Knight (1921) highlighted the concept *uncertainty-as-unknownness*, separating it clearly from the concept of insurable *risk-as-expected-value-computability*. He listed a half-dozen ways to deal with a known unknown, including to bear it entrepreneurially. Keynes (1921) also sought to move beyond the orthodox theory of economic behavior, with a theory of decision-making that subsumed risk within a more general theory that allowed for conceptualizations of non-risk uncertainty. Such conceptualizations included: fuzziness; ill-defined probability distributions; and, the possibility of future structural change to which no relative frequencies could be attached (Fontana & Gerrard, 2004). Instead of building on these ideas, however, the relevant academia failed to engage further on true uncertainty—especially in its theoretical modeling; rather, they attempted to shift the conversation to simpler, more familiar (and arguably misrepresentative) conceptualizations that were easier to 'solve'.

The main shifts were to probability-based conceptualizations—either with or without additionally and explicitly invoking subjective utilities. The benefits of downplaying the uncomfortable possibilities of real ignorance and unpredictability when confronting actual uncertainty and replacing them with the apparent confidence stemming from mathematics-based precisely-computed answers and predictions, were significant; those benefits coming in the form of publications and funding and lucrative consulting. The costs, or at least the dangers, of that simplification-of-unknowns-into-estimates, have been, and will continue to be, high, as important unknowns-sold-as-knowns were ignored rather than properly monitored, often until it was (almost) too late (e.g., regarding: the ozone layer; unmonitored toxins; forever chemicals; black-box AI; and, so on). Another cost that has recently proven near-fatal is the loss of trust the public has in science that arose when its too-confident predictions and prescriptions were proven wrong by events (e.g., in many parts of the recent Covid response, but excluding the value of the vaccines). Treating unknowns as knowns should not be done, but is done nonetheless, with little accountability, and even less public value. That needs to change.

Despite the ubiquity of uncertainty, scientific attention has been focused primarily on probabilistic approaches—where 'uncertainty' is assumed measurable and, thus, possible to express numerically (Kozyreva & Hertwig, 2021). This sad intellectual journey of the topic of uncertainty is unfortunately indicative of many fields of inquiry in which the realm of analysis is reformulated and narrowed in order to exclude elements that cannot be quantified and measured but can only be judged (Boyd, 2012). For example, in Savage's (1954) modeling, individuals transform a problem of uncertainty into one of risk by using prodded subjective estimates of outcome probabilities (MacLeod & Pingle, 2000). Indeed, in the last half-century-plus of 'rational choice under uncertainty studies' (*aka* decision science), agents have been modeled as optimizing under defined constraints by listing possible courses of action, defining the consequences of the alternatives, evaluating those consequences based on their likelihoods of occurring, and selecting the best available option, all the while assuming such elements are accurately known (Kay & King, 2020). But why, given that they are often not 'accurately known' (especially in the most interesting and important cases)?

This ascendancy of risk over uncertainty in the relevant literature has been multi-pronged while also disappointingly inevitable (O'Malley, 2000). Fields have leveraged both mathematical (e.g., probability- and possibility-based models) and experimental (e.g., behavioral studies of subject's decision-making under risk, ambiguity, and uncertainty, conducted in a lab or remotely through a survey) approaches. Economics, in particular, has focused on transforming decisions involving uncertainty into purely risky choices, rather than considering uncertainty as a fundamental challenge to the core of their theories (Beckert, 1996).[1] Indeed, the standard approach in economic theory is to treat uncertainty as risk in an attempt to hold on to its optimization models (Mousavi & Gigerenzer, 2017). Sociology has dealt with the problem differently, for example, by assuming that rational actors live in a socially-structured world that helps them decide based on the current expectations, despite the uncertainty of the situation (Beckert, 1996).

It appears that much more effort has gone into justifying probability as a way to represent uncertainty than into any other alternative (Halpern, 2003). Essentially, the methods employed in theoretical and empirical analyses of economic systems that were developed for the case of pure risk have been imposed on cases involving uncertainty (Beckert, 1996; Taylor, 2003). As a result, probability (unfortunately) remains the most influential contribution to the conceptual comprehension of uncertainty (Hertwig et al., 2019). This means that probability theory is (too) often applied outside of its limits (which is *Mill's critique*— see Kay & King, 2020). The Knight-Keynes uncertainty concept has simply fallen in use since the 1920s and 1930s, at least until recently (Hodgson, 2011). Now, mainstream economics needs to move beyond its reductionist method of analyzing all uncertain choice situations as if they involved well-defined probability distributions; it needs to develop a more legitimate, honest theory of decision-making under uncertainty that encompasses non-ergodic choice situations (Fontana & Gerrard, 2004). But unfortunately, economics continues to exile those topics where genuine uncertainty prevails (e.g., ecological dangers; shifts in

---

[1] Note that even when dealing with risk (sometimes labeled as *aleatory uncertainty*), things are not so simple. For example, philosophers and probabilists argue for logics to consider probability in ways that do *not* depend on assigning every elementary outcome an equal likelihood (e.g., as with the faces of a fair die)—instead, the likelihoods may represent relative frequencies or subjective assessments (Halpern, 2003).

taste) (Scott, 2020). This needs to be challenged not only in economics but in other disciplines (e.g., philosophy) as well (Bradley & Drechsler, 2014).

To be more explicit, uncertainty has not only been (mis)modeled as objective risk, it has also been (mis)modeled as subjective risk. To the latter, such modeling has usually also included subjective expected utility (SEU)—in terms of valuing the focal unknown outcomes. In fact, it seems that the study of decision-making under uncertainty has been dominated by SEU, as formulated by von Neumann and Morgenstern (1944) and Savage (1954). Such SEU models rank among the most important work in twentieth-century social science (Einhorn & Hogarth, 1986). In SEU models, the decision problem is formulated as choice of action, where the choice that maximizes the utility of the decision-maker given their beliefs on the probability distribution of the events is preferred. In multi-period models, the initial beliefs may or may not be correct, but are then updated through Bayesian learning to improve their accuracy (Dosi & Egidi, 1991); the legitimacy of so doing may look solid on the surface but may be highly questionable (i.e., given those beliefs or that feedback may not have any objective bases in contexts containing known unknowns, let alone unknown unknowns).

Perhaps surprisingly, Knight anticipated this (unwelcome) rise of subjective probability (Knight, 1921, p. 235), and even the kind of behavioral decision-making now associated with Kahneman and his colleagues. To the latter, behavioral decision-making assumes that if it is possible to identify the patterns of human decision-making biases empirically, and even to induce them, then it is easier to understand and predict how real decision-makers will respond to future uncertainties (Spender, 2006). It provides a positive rather than a normative perspective on decision-making under uncertainty. As such, it replaces economic rationality with something else—as derived from experiments—and so, arguably, does *not* really deal with (objective) uncertainty (Spender, 2006). So, in some respects, it is a distraction rather than a way forward in taking some important types of uncertainty (e.g., unknown unknowns; irreducible unknowns) seriously.

Drivers of the Failures

It is worthwhile to take a moment—to pause—and to be mindful of the very real physical and mental discomfort everyone feels when they are caught in a moment of ignorance, with a problem where they realize that there is no right, let alone better, answer among a wide variety of possibilities. While that discomfort may emerge partly as a result of culture, or education, or social experiences (e.g., nightmares of having not studied for the test; or, being laughed at in an early school setting for honestly saying you did not have the answer), it is also likely that it results from a quite primitive human (reptilian?) response. That response is seen positively in curiosity and the drive to explore, and negatively in anxiety, shame, and involuntary paralysis. It is strong, deep, and lifelong. But, it is why science (and entrepreneurial activity) exists in all of its (often valuable) forms.

That response often translates into faith, a faith that science can lead to answers for everything, and so, must overcome uncertainty eventually. As such, most academic attempts to escape radical uncertainty are based on a belief in the unrelenting progress of scientific truth (Kay & King, 2020). Indeed, a recurrent theme of Western philosophy and science, including its social science, involves reformulating systems of knowledge in order to bracket uncertainty, so as to permit the application of logical deductive rigor to solve the problems it vexes (Scott, 2020). As it is, however, uncertainty poses a real challenge to economic (and any other scientific) theories because it questions the causality of actions. That is why economists are so hesitant to acknowledge uncertainty, and why they desperately try to transform it into the category of risk—dishonestly arguing that there is always some information available that can be used to assess the unknowns (Beckert, 1996). However, decision-making under uncertainty cannot be so subsumed, for example, because actions under uncertainty often require creative re-organizations of knowledge and the imaginative generation of new possibilities (Rindova & Courtney, 2020).

That response also often drives us to avoid engaging with uncertainty. And, there are many ways in which we indeed try to avoid it. As discussed above, one way is to offer a (falsely confident) probability estimate rather than to admit ignorance. This way has even been legitimized by some scholars by actually defining 'the probability of an event' as 'being an individual's subjective degree of belief' about it (Feduzi et al., 2012). When that definition is adopted, probabilistic reasoning can be applied to any uncertain situation so that only risk remains (de Finetti, 1967). Indeed, in that perspective, all uncertainty is essentially *epistemic*—i.e., simply subjective. In such a world, then, if a decision-maker's beliefs and preferences can be expressed numerically, then they should obey the rules of probability (Halpern, 2003). And, even if this is not true (which it is highly unlikely to be) for any one decision or decision-maker, the further argument is made that evolutionary pressures will make human predictions accurate over time or across people (e.g., because only the best predictors will survive; or, the collective knowledge of the tribe will suss out a good estimate of an unknown). Similarly, there are arguments based on market efficiency—that markets for information will perform as 'selection' environments that reduce uncertainty by settling on best estimates. (Obviously, the very real existence of novel problems and of market failures impugn such arguments.)

One of the reasons why we have failed to engage with uncertainty—and instead treated it as risk—is that (thankfully) that failure has not often proved fatal. In fact, treating uncertainty as risk has some practical upsides: It provides a what-looks-like-standard justification for choosing a specific alternative in a decision *ex ante* and even often even *ex post* (if the guess was not too far off and the harm done not too large). In the moment, it also allows one to move forward (out of the 'analysis paralysis'), bolstered by some (false) confidence—an action that may provide more learning from the feedback relative to whatever learning could have been gleaned from waiting for the uncertainty to clear up on its own. This faith in the efficacy of a convert-uncertainty-to-risk 'orientation' doubtlessly emerges from most people's everyday decision-making experiences: Given the practical reality that *every* decision is made under incomplete information, and that most of the decisions people partake in (being non-strategic and non-novel) involve a sufficient history or contextual understanding, we can see why people have grown comfortable with that orientation (as its probability-based analysis has usually provided 'sufficient enough' results). So, we can understand why people may feel that the same orientation should apply to those 'other' decisions that involve (much) less history or understanding, especially if they seem to include some (but not all) of the same factors (i.e., the known known ones [versus the unknown unknown ones]). And, so, we can see why some scholarly thought has followed that path; but, it is no excuse for not realizing it is the wrong path for many important decisions.

There is a history in science of containing and trivializing *abnormalities* as 'a niche'—with abnormalities here referring to the decisions where conversion-to-risk does not apply. Arguably, it has been done to other (often related) ideas such as chaos theory and complexity that also often involve the problem of unpredictability (Hodgson, 2011). Contemporary economics retains a devotion to model-based prediction; so, when that prediction is thwarted, then often that type of problem falls out of favor (Hodgson, 2011). Economics elevates those approaches and problems that yield predictions and solutions and downplays those that don't. So, partly because of its intrinsic non-quantifiability, the Knight-Keynes uncertainty concept has been relatively ignored (Hodgson, 2011) compared to quantifiable risk. And, when it is considered, it is relegated to the category of 'unusual shocks or shifts' that are unpredictable and inexplicable (Kay & King, 2020), and so not worth of study until after they occur. Such uncertainty is not favored as a subject in mathematically-oriented decision theory either, because it appears as inaccessible to meaningful mathematical treatment (Hansson, 1996). Such marginalization of uncertainty has been achieved though, not by rational demonstration of the superiority of risk analysis, but instead by a Kuhnian-like paradigm-shift that silences incommensurable debate (O'Malley, 2000). Mainstream economics simply does not have a place to fit non-quantitative uncertainty into its models. Without measurable probabilities, quantified theories cannot exist, and so economists have pushed aside Keynesian-Knightian objections that uncertainty is incalculable, by either ignoring the unquantifiable concept or by giving it a subjective and quantifiable interpretation (Hodgson, 2011).

Engaging seriously with uncertainty is also bad for (academic) business. Given that alternatives, like probability, have simplicity and beauty and can be easily applied with (academic) training, it is not difficult to understand why economists and statisticians ignore true uncertainty (Kay & King, 2020). Such uncertainties must be erased from the picture because they cannot be measured or priced (Kay & King, 2020). Instead, it is easier to follow the cult of prediction-oriented techniques—a set of approaches that feeds on itself and provides a beautiful peacock's tail of seeming progress towards modeling the 'less-knowable' (Hodgson, 2011). And, such an illusion is bolstered by the very real progress science has made in causal discoveries—the ones that have reduced a phenomenon's known unknowns down to a state where they are sufficiently knowable as risks (i.e., as credibly estimable in value). But those real and effortful scientific discoveries should *not* be confused with the lazy and unjustified assumption that every uncertainty can be accurately represented through the application of an analogy, a degree of personal confidence, or a degree of certainty based on available evidence, or another unsubstantiated guess.

Engaging seriously with uncertainty is not just bad for (academic) business in terms of the extra efforts that would have to be made, but also because of the financial impact. Academics seek out grants by justifying their research in terms of its practical or predictive value. Research that involves humbler claims of prediction (e.g., research on better understanding irreducible uncertainty) is less attractive for those on grant-awarding bodies with missions to promote academic work offering more immediate practical consequences (Hodgson, 2011). For example, the rationale for adopting the SEU model to analyze the insurance market is straightforward: it allows an insurer to attach sharp numerical probabilities to every event and thus makes the insurance mechanism work (i.e., that being when all of the individual risks are insured and competition in the market leads to Pareto-efficiency) (Feduzi et al., 2012).

The lack of engagement with uncertainty comes at a hefty cost, however—it severely limits the modeling and understanding of reality. The ergodic assumption implies a very limited conception of the scope of human behavior (Fontana & Gerrard, 2004). And, because underlying all probability models is the belief that the future will behave as in the past, that orientation endangers its (overly confident) devotees whenever there is a discontinuity in conditions (Rowe, 1994).

Regardless, it appears that we are where we are in this failure to engage. When even established techniques for dealing with *complexity*—which is not even as vexing as uncertainty—such as agent-based modeling and NK-landscape simulations, are generally rare in leading mainstream journals (Hodgson, 2011), then the prospect of publishing new and serious analyses of non-risk uncertainty is rather slim. Proper measures of uncertainty—as it exists prior to a decision and after (in terms of its impacts)—have been asked for but remain lacking (Millar et al., 2018). The underlying question about uncertainty—what can be known and what will remain unknown—is all too often ignored by modern science (Faber et al., 1992). Instead, the mistake of perceiving uncertainty as a 'zero or one' concept continues (Samsami et al., 2015). And so, the resistance to taking up better ways of engaging with uncertainty continues, as does uncertainty's ability to effectively debilitate decision-makers and academics alike (Bammer & Smithson, 2008).

WHY PROBABILITY-BASED APPROACHES FAIL

Failing to engage with uncertainty most often means over-engaging with probability, which is an approach that can fail in strategic decisions. The proper use of probability requires specific conditions that are not always adhered to. It is only in very special cases that a probabilistic mathematical analysis—i.e., an exhaustive and quantitative study—can be made (Knight, 1921). So, while the intuition behind relative frequency is powerful, it cannot extend to all cases where probability is actually applied, given that some of those cases are new (Halpern, 2003). Applying probabilities in such cases is an unacceptable cheat (Kay & King, 2020). In other words, any axiomatic representations of micro-economic behaviors under uncertainty that look like straightforward rational choice problems must adhere to very strong restrictions on the nature of uncertainty, or be considered illegitimate (Dosi & Egidi, 1991). As such, most representations are wrong, or must be taken with suspicion, when the origins of any objective probability distribution supposedly capturing the 'uncertainty' is not provided (Townsend et al., 2018).

Probability-based modeling often fails because reality cannot often be reduced to known distributions of key factors. The claim of decision theory that most real mysteries can be reduced to well-defined puzzles by the application of probabilistic reasoning is flawed; the claim is false (Kay & King, 2020). The basic flaw arises when a precise formalization is sought to cover for a lack of precision (Hansson, 1994). Simply put, probability has its problems—the needed numbers aren't always available (Halpern, 2003). And, extending probability to business theories (e.g., relating to efficient markets) is even more problematic; strong conditions like 'no arbitrage' require the world to run on the edge of its possibilities and that everything worth happening has already happened, but that is not reality, at least not a reality where the common application of routines never creates unexploited opportunities (Dosi & Egidi, 1991). In reality, any (short-lived) equilibria are path-dependent, behavior-dependent, and institution-dependent; they are uncertain, and are not well-captured in models that act 'as if' none of these complications existed (Dosi & Egidi, 1991).

Despite widespread acknowledgment that there are problems in using probability to represent uncertainty, it continues; but, doing so is now occurring with several attempts at patching. For example, conditioning is a good patch, but suffers from several problems, particularly when it comes to dealing with events of probability zero (e.g., regarding whether they are truly impossible) (Halpern, 2003). And, while some probabilities may seem estimable from experts, most such people are not prepared to assign probabilities to *all* possible outcomes, let alone to try to compute the more compounded or confusing ones. For the latter, such judgments would have no valid basis of any kind (Nash, 2003).

The reliance on real decision-makers for their subjective estimates also dooms probability-based approaches that seek to deal with real uncertainties. This is so for several reasons: First, it is easy to reject the view that every rational agent is at heart a strict Bayesian, limited only by their computational capacity and memory (Levi, 1974). Second, real decision-makers have biases, only some of which we can hope to pin down because we can never have the complete objective data against which to rate all of them (Spender, 2006). Third, real decision-makers are quite limited in thought—they do not know all of the available options, nor all of the consequences of those options, nor even whether what they wish for today will be what they do tomorrow (Kay & King, 2020). And so, expecting them to provide complete and stable estimates of unknowns is problematic. Fourth, real decision-makers vary considerably; there are important psychological differences in the way people experience uncertainty, so choosing who is right is not straightforward. Fifth, when assessing uncertainty in real-world tasks assigned to decision-makers, the precision of any estimates based on the gambling analogies that are often used as prompts in experiments most often is misleading; this is because the participants' beliefs about real uncertainties are much more loosely held and ill-defined (Einhorn & Hogarth, 1986).

Probability-based approaches are also bound to fail for novel problems where uncertainties occur. In such cases, there is no possibility of forming groups of instances of sufficient homogeneity for a quantitative determination of true probability. Strategic business decisions often deal with situations that are far too unique for any sort of statistical tabulation to have any value for guidance. In those cases, objectively measurable probability (calculated before or after the fact) is simply inapplicable (Knight, 1921). Yet, it still is applied; in fact, orthodox theory assumes that we have knowledge of the future of a kind quite different from that which we do, or can, actually possess. The hypothesis of a calculable future leads to the incorrect interpretation of the principles of behavior, and to the dangerous underestimation of concealed factors such as doubt, precariousness, hope, and fear (Keynes, 1973). There simply remains a significant contrast between the assumed probabilistic knowledge depicted by the theorist and the convictions and opinions of real decision-makers upon which they base their conduct outside of laboratory experiments, especially in novel situations (Knight, 1921).

Finally, another major shortcoming of the probabilistic model is that it cannot express the epistemic state of 'radical' uncertainty (Romeijn & Roy, 2014). It does not provide a language to express a state of ignorance or often even identify what is uncertain. This can lead to 'model uncertainty'—where there is doubt in a model's assumptions but no sufficient means to express alternative assumptions—or to a more 'personal uncertainty'—where there is an insufficient grasp of the decision-maker's uncertainty regarding such assumptions (Romeijn & Roy, 2014).

Such known failures of the probabilistic approach have led to some interesting choices. For example, the choice of whether to adopt models with grand predictive claims where the concept of uncertainty is downplayed, or to limit the use of modelling and inhibit such predictive claims (Hodgson, 2011). For economics, and the social sciences generally, the assumption that the uncertainties being studied are amenable to statements with the status of risk is highly questionable, but is widely accepted nonetheless (Faber et al., 1992). That is so, even though a probabilistic framework is hardly a one-size-fits-all approach, nor one that can account for unmeasurable uncertainty (Hertwig et al., 2019). And, even though there are dangers when such an approach is applied to big issues like climate change—where using a precise probability function to represent uncertainty about states and consequences misrepresents the severity of such important uncertainties—it is (Bradley & Steele, 2015). Admitting ignorance and recognizing that the information is inconclusive, rather than trying to create a number, may often be the better choice (Halpern, 2003).

How That Failure Extends to Subjective Expected Utility

Probability is at the core of SEU approaches to addressing uncertainty, although those approaches add the complications of utility functions and more explicit subjectivity. However, even with those add-ons, SEU is not applicable to real ('large') world decisions involving uncertainties. Savage (1954) saw the distinction between small and large worlds—i.e., that SEU and Bayesian decision theory *only* apply to small—read: artificial, game-like, risk-only—worlds (Hertwig et al., 2019). Savage's ideal of behavior is absurd in real life—i.e., where the decision-maker can visualize all possible outcomes and attach probabilities to them; and so, he stated such behavior *only* applies to 'small' worlds, where decision optimization is possible (Kay & King, 2020). Further, SEU fails to capture many important elements that characterize decision-making under uncertainty, including: that the nature of the uncertainty people experience in real-world decisions is very different from that inherent in gambling devices; that changes in context can strongly affect people's evaluations of uncertainty; and, that payoffs can systematically affect the weight that people give to uncertainty (Einhorn & Hogarth, 1986).

ALTERNATIVES

Failing to engage with uncertainty is bad enough. Misrepresenting it as a probabilistic risk, in order to get to some resolution, prediction, or choice, is worse. It is even more so because there are better alternatives, although those often either take more effort to use or do not provide the level of optimization desired. Each such alternative (e.g., fuzzy math; ambiguity-as-bounded-uncertainty; possibilities) entails advantages and disadvantages (Halpern, 2003). Each challenges the idea that people simply reduce uncertainty to risk; and, that is good because people do deal with uncertainty in other ways (e.g., accepting black boxes, limited sight, and spiritual intervention), and even appear to have an adaptive toolbox for dealing with uncertainties in context (Hertwig et al., 2019). Although sometimes unsettling, it should be understood and accepted that it is often better to do without knowledge of probabilities than to guess at them (Hertwig et al., 2019).

Summary
Humanity is up against a rather long history of denying, avoiding, and misrepresenting non-risk uncertainties. Academia has a long history and a strong set of current incentives to reduce uncertainty to risk in order to produce answers to difficult (e.g., unoptimizable) problems. It will not be easy to alter the basic human reactions or the editorial biases towards

uncertainty; it will not be easy to get parties to admit their ignorance or their lack of legitimacy for producing estimates, and to move them to apply alternative methods and perspectives in dealing with 'true' uncertainties. If we do not do so, however, misapplications of probability-based thinking will continue, as will the harms that come from that, especially for strategic decisions.

Why these failures matter:

- Without an awareness of the limitations of probability- and SEU-based approaches to decision-making under uncertainty, their misapplications increase
- Without knowing the possible failures that come from mis-modeling uncertainty as risk, bad decisions and their harms are more likely
- Without knowing the drivers of the failures to engage with actual unknownness, those failures are likely to continue unabated

What the failures to engage with uncertainty mean for business and policy:

- There are opportunities to exploit the entities that do choose the wrong (and simple) approaches to dealing with uncertainty
- Policy-makers need to do a better job of educating entities of the alternatives to probability-based approaches for dealing with non-risk uncertainties and to identifying when those approaches are most likely to fail
- Academia needs to do better in publishing non-quantitative and non-reductionist analyses of uncertainties

References

Bammer, G., & Smithson, M. (2008). Understanding uncertainty. *Integration Insights, 7*(1), 1–7.

Beckert, J. (1996). What is sociological about economic sociology? Uncertainty and the embeddedness of economic action. *Theory and Society, 25*, 803–840.

Boyd, W. (2012). Genealogies of risk: Searching for safety, 1930s–1970s. *Ecology Law Quarterly, 39*, 895–987.

Bradley, R., & Drechsler, M. (2014). Types of uncertainty. *Erkenntnis, 79*, 1225–1248.

Bradley, R., & Steele, K. (2015). Making climate decisions. *Philosophy Compass, 10*(11), 799–810.

de Finetti, B. (1967). Probability: Interpretations. In *International encyclopaedia of the social sciences* (Vol. 12, pp. 496–505). Macmillan.

Dequech, D. (1999). Expectations and confidence under uncertainty. *Journal of Post Keynesian Economics, 21*(3), 415–430.

Dosi, G., & Egidi, M. (1991). Substantive and procedural uncertainty: An exploration of economic behaviours in changing environments. *Journal of Evolutionary Economics, 1*, 145–168.

Einhorn, H. J., & Hogarth, R. M. (1986). Decision making under ambiguity. *Journal of Business, 59*(4), S225–S250.

Faber, M., Manstetten, R., & Proops, J. L. (1992). Humankind and the environment: An anatomy of surprise and ignorance. *Environmental Values, 1*(3), 217–241.

Feduzi, A., Runde, J., & Zappia, C. (2012). De Finetti on the insurance of risks and uncertainties. *The British Journal for the Philosophy of Science, 63*(2), 329–356.

Fontana, G., & Gerrard, B. (2004). A Post Keynesian theory of decision making under uncertainty. *Journal of Economic Psychology, 25*(5), 619–637.

Halpern, J. Y. (2003). *Reasoning about uncertainty*. MIT Press.

Hansson, S. O. (1994). *Decision theory: A brief introduction*. Department of Philosophy and the History of technology. Royal Institute of Technology.

Hansson, S. O. (1996). Decision making under great uncertainty. *Philosophy of the Social Sciences, 26*(3), 369–386.

Hertwig, R., Pleskac, T. J., & Pachur, T. (2019). *Taming uncertainty*. MIT Press.

Hodgson, G. M. (2011). The eclipse of the uncertainty concept in mainstream economics. *Journal of Economic Issues, 45*(1), 159–176.

Kay, J. A., & King, M. A. (2020). *Radical uncertainty. Decision-making beyond the numbers*. Bridge Street Press.

Keynes, J. M. (1921). *A treatise on probability*. Macmillan.

Keynes, J. M. (1937 [1973]). The general theory of employment. In *The collected writings of John Maynard Keynes* (Vol. 14, pp. 109–123). Macmillan, Cambridge University Press for the Royal Economic Society.

Knight, F. H. (1921/1964). *Risk, uncertainty and profit*. Augustus M. Kelley.

Kozyreva, A., & Hertwig, R. (2021). The interpretation of uncertainty in ecological rationality. *Synthese, 198*(2), 1517–1547.

Lampert, C. M., Kim, M., & Polidoro, F., Jr. (2020). Branching and anchoring: Complementary asset configurations in conditions of Knightian uncertainty. *Academy of Management Review, 45*(4), 847–868.

Levi, I. (1974). On indeterminate probabilities. *Journal of Philosophy, 71*, 391–418.

MacLeod, W. B., & Pingle, M. (2000). *An experiment on the relative effects of ability, temperament and luck on search with uncertainty* (University of Southern California Law School, Olin Research Paper 00–12).

Millar, C. C., Groth, O., & Mahon, J. F. (2018). Management innovation in a VUCA world: Challenges and recommendations. *California Management Review, 61*(1), 5–14.

Mousavi, S., & Gigerenzer, G. (2017). Heuristics are tools for uncertainty. *Homo Oeconomicus, 34*(4), 361–379.

Nash, S. J. (2003). On pragmatic philosophy and Knightian uncertainty. *Review of Social Economy, 61*(2), 251–272.

O'Malley, P. (2000). Uncertain subjects: Risks, liberalism and contract. *Economy and Society, 29*(4), 460–484.

Rindova, V., & Courtney, H. (2020). To shape or adapt: Knowledge problems, epistemologies, and strategic postures under Knightian uncertainty. *Academy of Management Review, 45*(4), 787–807.

Romeijn, J. W., & Roy, O. (2014). Radical uncertainty: Beyond probabilistic models of belief. *Erkenntnis, 79*, 1221–1223.

Rowe, W. D. (1994). Understanding uncertainty. *Risk Analysis, 14*(5), 743–750.

Samsami, F., Hosseini, S. H. K., Kordnaeij, A., & Azar, A. (2015). Managing environmental uncertainty: From conceptual review to strategic management point of view. *International Journal of Business and Management, 10*(7), 215–229.

Savage, L. J. (1954). *The foundations of statistics*. Wiley.

Scott, J. C. (2020). *Seeing like a state: How certain schemes to improve the human condition have failed*. Yale University Press.

Spender, J.-C. (2006). *Knightian uncertainty and its resolution as institutionalized practice* (v9 Working Paper).

Taylor, C. R. (2003). The role of risk versus the role of uncertainty in economic systems. *Agricultural Systems, 75*(2–3), 251–264.

Townsend, D. M., Hunt, R. A., McMullen, J. S., & Sarasvathy, S. D. (2018). Uncertainty, knowledge problems, and entrepreneurial action. *Academy of Management Annals, 12*(2), 659–687.

von Neumann, J., & Morgenstern, O. (1944). *Theory of games and economic behavior*. Princeton University Press.

CHAPTER 17

A New Typology of Uncertainty (for Decision-Making)

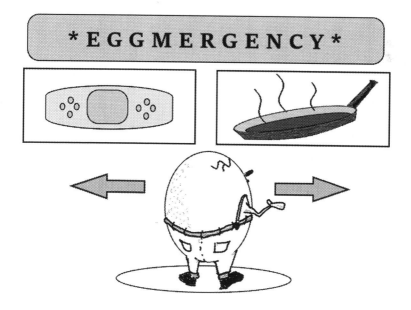

Introduction to a New Typology

The basis for improving decision-making under uncertainty is a divide-and-conquer approach; and, to divide, we desperately need a better typology. What exists now in terms of labels and categorization just does not work; it is confusing, inconsistent, incomplete, and at its worst, misleading. What we propose here is something new—an approach that is inclusive, clear, helpful, and focused on correctly treating the uncertainties identified; an approach that focuses on the kinds of unknowns that could make a strategic decision non-optimizable.

So, we are essentially implying, if not stating, that *all past typologies are flawed*, if not wholly wrong. The current slate of categorizations does not serve business or science well; most are simply too specific in nature (e.g., tailored to entrepreneurial innovation, to competitive moves, to social influencing, and so on) and so are doomed to fail outside that one application. Many confuse their types with the associated impacts, sources, and decisions present, while some just redefine established terms in a self-serving, misrepresentative fashion (see Ramoglou, 2021).

Here, we start with the idea that *triage* is a universally understood and practically useful process. It makes sense to consider it in this analysis because, bottom line, the first thing that we need to know is whether the uncertainty is treatable or not. When it is not treatable (i.e., when there are important unknowables involved in the decision process), then we need to approach the problem in a different way than treating the uncertainty directly. When the uncertainty is treatable (i.e., with only knowables are involved), we can then proceed to determine the urgency for treatment, diagnose the problem further to determine the best treatment, treat it, monitor it, learn from it, and so on. Diagnosis involves applying the decision-making process to identify the specific type of unknown involved, its strategic importance, its 5W1H characteristics, the feasibility of available treatments, and so on (or, alternatively, the level of fear of losses—relative and absolute, the compensation structure to the decision-maker, and so on). In practice, this will not be a clean and logical application of criteria. (Note that there is also the trivial case of when it is determined in triage that treatment is *not* required because there is sufficiently complete information to make an [expectedly] optimized decision. In that case, standard operating procedures for decision-making are sufficient rather than 'special' uncertainty-based treatments or approaches.)

Reminders About the Main Assumption and Definition

The main assumption in this book is that something 'as given' to the decision-maker will cause, or is causing, non-optimizability. That something can only be an *unknown factor* [e.g., an unspecified contingency or catalyst or contextual condition] or the *unknown value of a key characteristic of known (i.e., identified) factor* [e.g., the demand level value of a new product in a specific market at a specific time]. Each type of unknown presents an *uncertainty* (as defined in this book) that implies an objectively-defined optimal solution does not exist *ex ante* (Dequech, 2003). Figure 17.1 depicts the two-by-two matrix of the important things that can be unknown and how they relate. The unknown factors with logically unknown factor characteristic values are the *unknown unknowns* (e.g., famously spoken about by Rumsfield in 2002). The known factors with known characteristic values are the *known knowns* (where a standard decision process for optimization is possible). The known factors with unknown characteristic values are the interesting cases here, because those initially unknown values—the *known unknowns*—can be split into those that are knowable and those that are not (with different treatments for each).

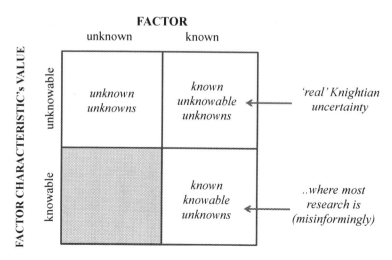

Fig. 17.1 The possible unknowns (underlying uncertainty)

The uncertainties-as-unknowns analyzed here—*prior* to any treatment—present a danger because, by definition, their impacts are unpredictable (Tannert et al., 2007). Some of these uncertainties even violate the assumed treatable nature of those 'things' labeled as 'uncertain' in the past (those things described in the business, economics, political, and psychology literatures, and based on perspectives from the purely objective to the purely subjective—e.g., Ben-Haim, 2001; Garner, 1962; Raiffa & Luce, 1957; MacCrimmon, 1966; Milliken, 1987; Townsend et al., 2020).

The Plan for This Chapter

We present the contents of this chapter in four steps: First, we review a select few well-known types (or labels) of uncertainties; all are flawed. Second, we describe our triage-based approach to building our primary uncertainty categorization (with an accompanying flow diagram). Third, we describe our secondary categorization that, given our focus is on decision-making, details the distinct decision-making steps where an unknown can render the decision non-optimizable. Fourth, we consider tertiary and further categorizations (e.g., with uncertainties differentiated by strategic importance, intensity, feasibility, time, ethical responsibility, decision-maker interests, and so on).

Past Uncertainty Types and Labels

Previous research has provided many different labels for uncertainties; these different labels have made the understanding of uncertainty, well, uncertain. To some scholars, we are in the sixth age of studying uncertainty—where we acknowledge that uncertainty presents itself in many forms, each associated with its own level of comprehension (Stewart, 2019). To others, we are at a stage where we have moved past the blunt delineations of risk from uncertainty and uncertainty from ignorance (Faber et al., 1992). Recently proposed types and labels of uncertainty include: variability; imperfect information; obscurity; vagueness; ambiguity; incomplete knowledge; chance; chaos; volatility; disorder; entropy; the unknown; randomness; turmoil; stressor; error; dispersion; unknowledge; a lack of information that may or may not be rectified in the future; complexity; turbulence; novelty; equivocality; luck; unknowingness; unpredictability; dynamism; and, uncontrollability (Buchko, 1994;

Hogarth, 1987; Kay & King, 2020; March & Olsen, 1976; McMullen & Shepherd, 2006; Roeser, 2019; Scoblic, 2020; Taleb, 2012; Terreberry, 1968; Townsend et al., 2018; Weick, 1979). And, adjectives used to describe different uncertainties include: Knightian; primary; deep; absolute; creative; environmental; and, so on (Kapoor & Klueter, 2021; Knight, 1921; Koopmans, 1957; Packard et al., 2017). It is no wonder that it seems the more one tries to study the related literature, the more one grows skeptical about the concept of uncertainty (Boyd & Fulk, 1996; Samsami et al., 2015). Providing a logical typology seems one way out of this conundrum (Packard et al., 2017).

Prior to introducing such a typology, it is useful to (critically) review the main types of uncertainties that are well-known, or well-studied, or well-worn, in the literature. We do so now:

Incomplete Information

This is a general and somewhat ambiguous term. It could, literally, just reflect the fact that not all items are available that could provide a perfect and precise prediction of the outcome of every choice. In other words, this could cover risk, where every outcome is known to the level of expected but not 'point' value. That would not be uncertainty under our definition, as such problems are considered optimizable. So, this is a (too) loose term that considers uncertainty simply as a lack of knowledge (Kaur & Dasgupta, 2018; Magnani & Zucchella, 2018; Packard et al., 2017). However, to some, it is a label that covers (only) substantive uncertainty (Dosi & Egidi, 1991), as gaps in knowledge (Heiner, 1983, 1988). To others, though, it can also cover cases that are considered more fundamental—where some essential information about future relevant events cannot be known at the moment of decision (Dequech, 1999), implying a surrendering to chance (Bammer & Smithson, 2008). Apparently, this is the term favored in self-reports describing decision-making under uncertainty (Kaur & Dasgupta, 2018; Lipshitz & Strauss, 1997).

Under this label, uncertainty is in a broad sense just 'limited knowledge about past, present or future events' (Walker et al., 2013), or about environmental events even more generally (Dosi & Egidi, 1991). But, this label can also be used with specificity to relate to items in the decision process, such as undifferentiated alternatives or undisclosed response options (Conrath, 1967; Lipshitz & Strauss, 1997; Milliken, 1987).

Incomplete information is considered common in several contexts. It is typical in strategic planning and design (Ben-Haim, 2001). It is frequently referred to when new technologies emerge (Kapoor & Klueter, 2021). It can involve ambiguities over the probability distribution of an outcome or the size of that outcome (Du & Budescu, 2005). And, it can lead to incomplete markets (Kay & King, 2020).

Incomplete information can trigger a range of responses, from curiosity to a search for the missing information to its subjective estimation (often based on past data considered relevant) to simply bearing it (Bammer & Smithson, 2008; Shin & Kim, 2019).

Knightian Uncertainty

Knight (1921) neatly separated risk from uncertainty. He did so by separating the informational conditions where insurance and other standard operating procedures could be used (and where optimizable decisions could be made)—i.e., the risky situations—from conditions that were uninsurable, where standard decision processes were inapplicable, and where one had to bear the unknowns—i.e., the uncertain situations. This was done to acknowledge that real information-based market failures exist in the world—ones that allow the emergence of entrepreneurial activity (defining entrepreneurs as those who voluntarily bear the uncertainty).

Although a very useful delineation (i.e., of uncertainty from risk)—one still referred to over a century later—the term 'Knightian uncertainty' involves several issues.[1] First, there are many variants of uncertainty that meet its definition and, so, the study of uncertainty is not progressed much by that definition alone (e.g., given those variants entail different embodiments that vary in treatment, and so on). Second, Knight (1921) regrettably did not simply stop with the powerful point being made that there exists a place for entrepreneurs in economic theory when information is incomplete; instead, he referred to *judgment* as a differentiator for the successful entrepreneurs. Adding to that 'magical' power of judgment (that few possess), he also then states several other ways around his kind of uncertainty that may be taken. That was an unfortunate choice; instead, he should have described several logical reasons why some decision-makers may have more reason to bear uncertainty—for example, in having

---

[1] Please see this Chapter's supplement for further details on a selection of the more important issues.

less to lose (e.g., due to lower opportunity costs, or lower potential negative spillovers), or more to gain (in a relative sense versus rivals, or due to the ownership of more potentially complementary resources), or greater positive but subjective beliefs (based on their own experiences or what they consider inside information), and so on.

Instead of dealing—coldly—with the definitional vulnerability of bearing uncertainty, he fell into the trap of trying to 'play hero' by attempting to explain ways to deal with uncertainty besides being 'good at bearing it'. He described five other ways to deal with uncertainty, where each of those ways transforms the *ex ante* focal unknown it into something (more) insurable or optimizable. These are practical approaches where the uncertainty is *not* borne but rather is addressed through standard operating procedures (i.e., where the expected outcome is in the form of normal rents). The five possible ways to deal with—rather than bear—the uncertainty that Knight describes are (1921: pp. 239–240): 'consolidation' (i.e., insure it with offsets); 'control of the future' or apply an 'increased power of prediction' (i.e., increase its certainty directly or indirectly); use 'the diffusion of the consequences of untoward contingencies' (i.e., reduce its downsides); and, 'directing industrial activity more or less along lines in which a minimal amount of uncertainty is involved and avoiding those involving a greater degree' (i.e., organize to avoid it). Listing these ways has led to dangerous consequences in the subsequent literature. The primary one is that recent papers have considered these ways as 'entrepreneurial', when that is clearly wrong—as no (Knightian) uncertainty is actually borne under these approaches. Further, Knight failed to specify any costs, competitive interactions, timing issues, or details of implementation, for any of those five ways. So, any paper citing Knight, and interpreting such ways as being costless, or simple, or lacking competition (e.g., Rindova & Courtney, 2020), endangers anyone pursuing such prescriptions. Instead, each of those five ways should be interpreted as an alternative possible capability-based rent explanation, where some firms may be relatively better at uncertainty-reduction through one of those five ways. (However, if all firms know those ways, and none is differentiated in its capabilities, there will be *no* unusual rents available.)

Nevertheless, Knightian uncertainty remains a well-known and often-invoked term, especially in the entrepreneurship literature (O'Malley, 2000). Economists also reference Knight's (and Keynes' [1921]) distinction of uncertainty from risk (Dequech, 2003). Several consider it a synonym for unknowability (Miller, 2012; Packard & Clark, 2020; Ramoglou, 2021), for unknown states of the world (Glycopantis & Muir, 2008), for unknown consequences of actions (Hébert & Link, 1988; MacLeod & Pingle, 2000; McMullen & Shepherd, 2006; Townsend et al., 2020), for immeasurability (Boyd, 2012), for uninsurability (Feduzi et al., 2012; Langlois & Cosgel, 1993), for unknown probabilities (March & Simon, 1958), for unforeseen contingencies (Foss et al., 2007; Littlechild, 1986; Shackle 1972; Williamson, 1996) and for unknown unknowns (Lampert et al., 2020; Pisano, 2006). As such, Knight's definition is not exactly 'crisp' (Spender, 2006).

While Knight's definition has been sufficiently crisp to be considered *in*consistent with a rather large field of mathematical work on decision-making under uncertainty (Hey, 1989; Spender, 2006), it has been interpreted by others in questionable ways. For example, some have seen it as differentiating between objective and subjective probabilities, the latter of which is based on degrees of belief (Magnani & Zucchella, 2018; Savage, 1954). Others see it as a context with no right (or wrong) choices where no lessons can be learned (Alvarez et al., 2018). Perhaps best interpreted, it is meant to call attention to the fact that humankind is limited in what it can know, and yet still must make important decisions under those conditions (Ramoglou, 2021; Townsend et al., 2018).

Ellsbergian Ambiguity

The ambiguity that Ellsberg (1961) has defined and experimented with is also a well-known, explicitly defined form of uncertainty. In this case, it is focused on unknown and unknowable probabilities of known events, but specifically where the range of those probabilities is known. Through experiments, the aversion to this ambiguity has been differentiated from the aversion to risk. To be of interest here (in this book), the range of probabilities also must be strategically interesting—it must be non-trivially non-optimizable (e.g., covering both significant possible gains and losses). As defined by Ellsberg, ambiguity is a form of Knightian uncertainty.

Ambiguity is an intermediate state of 'uncertainty' between ignorance—where no distributions are ruled out—and risk—where all distributions but one are ruled out (Becker & Brownson, 1964; Einhorn & Hogarth, 1986). It applies to situations in which there is a limited set of plausible futures, system models, outcomes, or weights, but where probabilities cannot be assigned to them (Marchau et al., 2019). It is present when the lack of knowledge of an objective probability distribution prevents the decision-maker from solving an optimization problem (Manski, 2000). Many other variants of the definition exist, involving: what information is missing (and whether it could be made known); which order of probabilities is unknown; and, what kinds of outcomes are at play (e.g., Becker & Brownson, 1964; Camerer & Weber, 1992; Dequech, 2011; Dosi & Egidi, 1991; Einhorn & Hogarth, 1988; Fontana & Gerrard, 2004; Holm et al., 2013; Packard et al., 2017; Townsend et al., 2018).

Regardless of the exact definition used in the literature, Ellsbergian ambiguity has been proven to affect real decision-making in experiments. In the lab, subjects were presented with the decision to draw from one of two urns where the distributions over the probabilities associated with the urns differed—i.e., the first urn's distribution was known; the second urn's was not known but its probabilities were bounded within a known range that had its midpoint at the mean of the first urn's known distribution. It has been demonstrated that subjects, on average, expressed an aversion to ambiguity (i.e., by choosing the first urn), and under payoff conditions, would pay to avoid it. Further, the amounts paid to avoid ambiguity were consistently related to the degree of ambiguity (Becker & Brownson, 1964).

The main problem with the general term 'ambiguity' (like uncertainty) is that the range of interpretations and variants of it is just too great, leading to unnecessary confusion in the literature. Such variants include: *probability ambiguity* as a situation where a stock offers a precise return but with a wide range of probability, or as a situation where the probabilities of a set of possible outcomes that have not been encountered are unknown (Hertwig et al., 2019); *outcome ambiguity* as a situation where a stock offers a range of returns but without a precise probability of each; and, *conflict ambiguity* is a situation where two experts disagree on the return for the same stock (Aggarwal & Mohanty, 2022). The number of different interpretations of the label 'ambiguity' itself is large, and includes: where the possible outcomes of the various options are known, but where all that is known about their probabilities is that they are nonzero (Hansson, 1996); where decision-makers are not given probabilistic information about the external events that might affect the outcome (Etner et al., 2012); unknown cause–effect relationships (Santos & Eisenhardt, 2009); only having enough information to make a partial or imprecise judgement (Bradley & Drechsler, 2014); being a subjective variable that determines one's confidence in one's probability estimates (Becker & Brownson, 1964); having any distribution of probabilities other than a point estimate (Becker & Brownson, 1964); where relevant information is missing (e.g., is marked with gaps, is vague, or is precise but contradictory) (Aggarwal & Mohanty, 2022); knowing the choice set but not the objective function (Manski, 2000); incompletely known probabilities (Hansson, 1996); the inability to define the degree of confidence one assigns to the probabilities of outcomes (Duncan, 1972); a situation where one cannot answer the question of whether action X causes outcome Y in situation Z (Townsend et al., 2018); the collapse of sensemaking (Weick, 1995); the impossibility of discerning what is important or even what is going to happen (Townsend et al., 2018); hazily-defined alternative states (March, 1994); limited knowledge of a stable causal structure (Fontana & Gerrard, 2004); epistemic risk (Schoemaker, 2002); identifiable potential futures without a specific scenario (Samsami et al., 2015); the inability to identify all of the factors that shape the future (Courtney, 2003); and, the absence of factual answers (Murphy & Pinelli, 1994). Obviously, consensus on this term is unfortunately absent.

Ignorance

Ignorance is often defined in terms of 'knowing very close to nothing' about a problem or phenomenon other than that it exists. As such, it can cover all of the previous terms, which is quite *un*helpful when trying to understand what it is that is unknown, how that impacts the decision, and whether that is treatable. To some, it is supposed to be a term more focused on the unknown unknowns and the unimaginables than on the known unknowns and the other less-severe decision-making challenges. Regardless, it is a poorly-defined term with some paradox—in that if one knows one is ignorant then it must be that one is *not* ignorant. It is a term that has not often received the attention it deserves (Faber et al., 1992). And, it is a term that some have *separated* from uncertainty; the latter being the situation where some aspects of the future are actually considered known (Dequech, 1999).

The alternative definitions of ignorance include: A lack of knowledge about the future, without degrees (Dequech, 2011). A lack of probabilistic knowledge (Hansson, 1994). Unknown future states (Faber et al., 1992). Unknown kinds of possible outcomes (Roeser, 2019). A lack of judgment-relevant information (Bradley & Drechsler, 2014; Raiffa & Luce, 1957). A problem plagued by no clarity of definition, no objectively correct solution, and imbued with vagueness and indeterminacy (Kay & King, 2020). A lack of knowledge about the state of nature (Yager, 1999). Being devoid of information regarding when, where, or how an event has occurred or will occur (Bar-Anan et al., 2009; Berlyne, 1960; Shin & Kim, 2019). A deep level of uncertainty where one does not even know that one does not know (Walker et al., 2003). *Nichtwissen* or nonknowledge (Bammer & Smithson, 2008). Radical uncertainty (McMullen & Shepherd, 2006). The opposite of determinism (Courtney, 2001; Walker et al., 2003). When knowledge is not immediately available but is possible in principle (Ramoglou, 2021). And, indifference of choice (Cohen & Jaffray, 1980; Etner et al., 2012).

Some of the variants of the term ignorance include: *sheer ignorance*—where one does not realize one's ignorance until surprised by the discovery of new information (Kirzner, 1997); *total ignorance*—as also the opposite of determinism (Marchau et al., 2019), or as fundamental and severe uncertainty (Bradley & Steele, 2015; Hertwig et al., 2019; Mousavi & Gigerenzer, 2014); *complete ignorance*—as the extreme of uncertainty (McMullen & Shepherd, 2006), or as an incompleteness in preferences (Etner et al., 2012); *closed ignorance*—as a purposeful ignoring or suppressing of one's recognition of one's ignorance; *communal ignorance*—as information lacking even to society (Faber et al., 1992); *irreducible ignorance*—as indeterminacy (Walker et al., 2003); *phenomenological ignorance*—as unknown phenomena; *epistemological ignorance*—as an unknown structure of knowledge (Faber et al., 1992); *recognized ignorance*—as unknown functional relationships or statistical properties, where the scientific basis for developing scenarios is weak (Walker et al., 2003); and, *self-imposed ignorance*—as taboo, distortion, or irrelevance (Bammer & Smithson, 2008).

As seen in the wide range of definitions and variants, this term is overused and lacks consensus; it does not provide a useful basis for a typology (or even a stable delineation of one type of uncertainty).

Aleatory Uncertainty

This is actually *not* an uncertainty here—as decisions vexed by it are optimizable. It is a label derived from the Latin *alea*—a roll of the dice. It is risk—a situation where the probabilities are known. That said, what may be a real unknown is the cause-and-effect relationship at play. However, in these are situations, there exists sufficient premises and/or repeated trials to know the odds of each possible event occurring. Aleatory problems are gambles (e.g., coin tosses; roulette wheel spins; dice rolls). The risk involved is related to the variability inherent in the underlying system, a variability that is considered irreducible (Kaur & Dasgupta, 2018).

This is a label for randomness, but it is in a form where the probability distribution is known. It is one of the most ancient and common forms of randomness in human culture. Luck is part of the phenomenon. The underlying random process can be used to make games more interesting—to provide minor shocks, to break symmetry among players, to provide variety in the game's path (ensuring better replayability), and to create a sense of drama (e.g., in rolling a critical hit). While it can be used to improve games, an overreliance on it can make a game worse (e.g., by creating an overreliance on luck versus skill) (Costikyan, 2013).

As with the other well-known, oft-used terms, there are many alternative definitions of aleatory uncertainty, such as the following: It is *a priori* probability, where there is absolute homogeneity in the classification of instances that are completely identical except for indeterminate factors (Knight, 1921). It involves a system model that can be described probabilistically (Helton & Johnson, 2011; Marchau et al., 2019). It is stochastic behavior. Sometimes referred to as *ontic*, it stems from the statistical properties of the context (Kozyreva & Hertwig, 2021). It can be interpreted as an extensional measure of relative frequency. It describes random mutations (Hertwig et al., 2019). It describes puzzles (Kay & King, 2020). It can be referred to as *type B* uncertainty, where a probability distribution of the potential outcomes can be assigned (Hoffman & Hammonds, 1994; Townsend et al., 2018). It can also be referred to (unfortunately) as *objective uncertainty* in the entrepreneurship field (Townsend et al., 2020). It is *not* residual risk (Bammer & Smithson, 2008).

Unknown Unknowns

Often associated with *surprise*, or considered as a form of ignorance, unknown unknowns are actually relevant decision factors that are only known *after* they are revealed. There is some debate on whether they have to be *ex ante un*imaginable; some argue that, in one variation, the 'surprise' could be imagined but given a zero probability of occurring (where these events are also termed *unforeseen contingencies*—Dekel et al., 1998). This kind of uncertainty—of factors—defines the 'sixth age of understanding', where it is newly known that such unknown unknowns exist (Stewart, 2019). In reality, such uncertainty about uncertainty has become pervasive in business- and policy-related decision-making (Einhorn & Hogarth, 1986).

There are several different definitions of unknown unknowns, and we sample a few now: They are an 'external' category, the essence of incomplete knowledge, unknown by everyone, and the basis of fundamental uncertainty (Dimov, 2016). They represent *meta-ignorance* (Bammer & Smithson, 2008). They include *black swans* (i.e., unanticipated rare events—Taleb, 2012), and comprise everything from unlikely to unimaginable events (Kay & King, 2020). They are high-impact, extremely rare, and unpredictable events (Rindova & Courtney, 2020). They embody another source of unknowability (Faulkner et al., 2017; Feduzi et al., 2021; Ramoglou, 2021). They are *unexpected uncertainty* (Marchau et al., 2019). They are *unknowledge* or surprise (Faber et al., 1992). They stem from being unaware of the possibility of being unaware of an event (Dekel et al., 1998). They are *incalculable uncertainty* (Boyd, 2012). They represent a reality that is subject to non-predetermined structural change (Dequech, 2011).[2]

The effects of unknown unknowns are sometimes positive. For example, they can be used to a foster desire for exploration in a game (or world?) where the theme is known but the rest remains to be discovered (Costikyan, 2013). Given their potential presence means that it is impossible to write contracts contingent on *all* possible outcomes, parties have a greater incentive to communicate, to persuade, and to learn from each other, increasing the possibility of gains from cooperation (Kay & King, 2020). When unknown unknowns are thought to be associated with procedural uncertainty (i.e., where one does not know and cannot know before the decision which or how many 'algorithms' to 'solve the

---

[2] It is important to note that there is nothing that can be done with unknown unknowns: From such absolute ignorance we can derive nothing but absolute ignorance (Graaff, 1957; Stewart, 2021). This is not just theoretical, but very real—as it is observed that executives don't know what they don't know (Courtney et al., 2013). In terms of theory, though, the outcome of unknown unknowns—surprises—may be differentiable; for example, into those that are fully unexpected versus those that run counter to the expected outcome (Shackle, 1953).

problem' can be generated, or even if they can be generated at all), there is a greater incentive to analyze and improve existing processes (Dosi & Egidi, 1991). And, when unknown unknowns are 'expected' to occur, organizations are motivated to consider ways to identify such surprises faster, and respond quicker; and, that may make them more agile (and successful) under more common conditions.

Equivocality

This term relates to the condition when two otherwise differentiable things related to making a decision (e.g., alternative choices) have the same value (e.g., net benefits). By definition, then, equivocal situations have no objectively best single answer (Townsend et al., 2018; Weick, 1979). This can occur when preferences or meanings are underdefined. It can also result from self-imposed ignorance.

There exist several definitions and alternative labels for equivocality, such as: *nominal uncertainty* (i.e., an equivocality of occurrence that ensues when equal probability is assigned to all events) (Garner, 1962); *vagueness*—when it is not known which of two possible actions to take to produce a specified outcome given the current knowledge of a context (Townsend et al., 2018); knowledge problems that result from the existence of multiple meanings or interpretations that lead to competing conceptions of reality (Daft & Macintosh, 1981; Spender, 2006) and confusion (Weick, 1995); and, a state of undifferentiated alternatives (Kaur & Dasgupta, 2018) that often leads to undecidability (Bammer & Smithson, 2008).

Equivocality is often bad, but it can have an upside. Situations where multiple meanings appear to be equivalent at one level can lead to greater sensitivity to alternative perspectives that provide additional insights (e.g., to provide delineation at a different level of analysis) (Costikyan, 2013).

Vagueness

Most generally, vagueness occurs when the decision-maker cannot differentiate between 'what something is and is not' in the problem, making it impossible to assign values (e.g., probabilities or payoffs) to that thing and, ultimately, making it impossible to optimize the problem. It is *indeterminateness* (Knight, 1921), existing when the *law of the excluded middle* (i.e., either it is so or it is not so) fails to be satisfied (Kay & King,

2020). It also exists under equivocality. It can take the form of *linguistic uncertainty* regarding communication with others (Hansson, 2022). It is often associated with *fuzziness* and blurry boundaries (Bammer & Smithson, 2008). As such, work on fuzzy sets (Zadeh, 1978), and various other approaches to quantify probability ranges, and so-called *second-order uncertainty*, have been undertaken to better understand the issues (e.g., Cohen, 1977; Einhorn & Hogarth, 1986; Marschak, 1975; Shafer, 1976; Wallsten et al., 1983).

Epistemic Uncertainty

Often paired with aleatory uncertainty (*aka* contextual or external risk), epistemic uncertainty refers to issues with the decision-maker (i.e., it is focused on the non-contextual or internal unknowns). However, this term refers to a *source* of uncertainty rather than a type—it refers to the unknowns that can emerge from the bounded abilities—both cognitive and sensory—of the human decision-maker (Spender, 2006). The term is derived from the Greek *episteme*—meaning knowledge; so, it refers to a lack of knowledge or understanding about the focal problem (Helton & Johnson, 2011; Lipshitz & Strauss, 1997). Sometimes it is considered (feasibly) addressable (e.g., with new technology or training), and sometimes it is not (Holmes & Westgren, 2020). (When that unknown is considered addressable, that differentiable case has also been labeled as epistemic uncertainty [Walker et al., 2003].[3])

Like other often-invoked terms, there are many alternative labels, definitions, and interpretations of epistemic uncertainty. We provide several here for illustration: It is incomplete knowledge, incomplete information, or inadequate understanding (Kozyreva & Hertwig, 2021). It is *subjective ignorance* (Kaur & Dasgupta, 2018). It refers to the decision-makers' lack of knowledge and understanding of the problem's causal structure (Rindova & Courtney, 2020). It concerns computational constraints that prevent the full determination of the structure of the environment (Kozyreva & Hertwig, 2021; Simon, 1972). It is a lack of computational ability (Packard et al., 2017). It involves subjectivity, in the form of the underlying values and perspectives of the decision-maker (Marchau

---

[3] Note that, when the unknown is (theoretically) addressable, there may still be (subjective) uncertainties about its addressability and the specific best way to address it (Hertwig et al., 2019; Kuhlthau, 1993).

et al., 2019). It can represent situations when the decision-makers admit that they are not absolutely certain, but they do not see, or have the ability to measure, the degree of uncertainty in an explicit way (Hillier & Lieberman, 2001; Marchau et al., 2019). It is uncertainty about the decision-maker's own fitness relative to others (Hertwig et al., 2019)—an *agential uncertainty*—that casts doubt on that agent's future decisions and ability to execute (Hansson, 2022). It can present in the form of a lack of confidence in dealing with (other) uncertainties (Magnani & Zucchella, 2018). A popular alternative label is *procedural uncertainty*; a label that also concerns a decision-maker's limited computational and cognitive capabilities (Dequech, 2011), and other competence gaps in problem-solving and model-building (Dosi & Egidi, 1991). Epistemic uncertainty is also compatible with, and complementary to, *fundamental uncertainty* (Dequech, 2011). Yet another label is *cognitive uncertainty*—being a lack of knowledge and a limitation on data and information (Potter et al., 2012); it is a state that is sometimes alleviated by research and learning (Samsami et al., 2015).

There are several specific ways that decision-makers can be bounded in their abilities, and so produce specific forms of epistemic uncertainty. Labels for these forms include: *performative uncertainty* (e.g., physical limitations); *schedule uncertainty* (e.g., regarding the limited time the decision-maker has); *perceptive uncertainty* (e.g., limitations in being able to find hidden objects); *analytic uncertainty* (e.g., regarding the ability to parse complicated decision trees and compute trade-offs); *solver's uncertainty* (e.g., concerning puzzle logic expertise, and solution-envisioning); and, executive function limitations (e.g., in the ability to sort through contingencies) (Costikyan, 2013). Further variants of epistemic uncertainty exist, in alternative forms where the boundedness of the decision-maker is either fully specified, partially specified, or unspecified (Helton & Johnson, 2011). Many of these variants can be observed in how real people play strategic games, like chess, or deal with new technologies or unfamiliar cues (Dequech, 2011; Dosi & Egidi, 1991; Kozyreva & Hertwig, 2021). Regardless of the specific definition, label or variant, epistemic uncertainty is a category of potential *sources* of unknowns; it is not a specific type of uncertainty itself.

Other Potential Types

Besides the previous set of well-known (candidate) 'types' of uncertainties—all of which are flawed and obviously poorly defined—there are many other concepts about unknowns that have all contributed to the current terminological confusion in the field. We conclude this first part of the chapter with a partial listing of those other concepts, definitions, and alternative labels for uncertainty now: An unknown outcome space. A limited knowledge of alternatives. Environmental complexity (Kozyreva & Hertwig, 2021). A lack of knowledge of the situation. A lack of knowledge about how others might respond to our actions. Indeterminacy. Incommensurability (Spender, 2006). Unknowns that are casual, human and organizational, external, or probabilistic (Samsami et al., 2015). Unknown outcomes, situations, or alternatives (Lipshitz & Strauss, 1997). Incomplete information about ethics, options, state space, and probabilities (Bradley & Drechsler, 2014). Variability and randomness (Meijer et al., 2006). Open sets of decision options and/or outcomes (Packard et al., 2017). Unknown inputs, parameters, and locations (Walker et al., 2003). Unknown origins, current context, and future outcomes (Dewey, 1915; Nash, 2003). Stochastic information (Hertwig et al., 2019). Unknown probabilities (Packard et al., 2017). An underdetermined system (Stewart, 2019). Undecidability, error, confusion, distortion, or non-specificity (Bammer & Smithson, 2008).

It is plain to see that the relevant literature has *not* converged (or even attempted to converge) on a universal language to describe uncertainty—either as an umbrella concept or as delineated into separate types. Without that universal language, the study of uncertainty will simply flounder. Very little scientific progress occurs when we talk past each other. But, this is a self-imposed problem with a known solution. It starts with a clear definition (like the practical one we have suggested in this book) for the umbrella term of uncertainty, and continues strongly with the logical categorization of its types. To this latter challenge, we offer the following:

THE NEW PRIMARY TYPOLOGY

To improve decision-making under uncertainty, it is first important to determine whether a decision problem is 'improvable'. The definition of uncertainty here is that the decision, as given, is non-optimizable. So, the primary typology will function to delineate those uncertainties that are treatable to make the decision optimizable from those uncertainties where that is not possible. That has not been done before. Note that there are nuances to this clear delineation.

Recall that we are assuming: an objective viewpoint (i.e., that objective reality exists); that the decision is strategic (e.g., has the potential for a significant performance impact, involving large irreversible resource commitments); that the problem involves making a decision (with an action taken) by a specific time; and, that to optimize the decision requires the ability to calculate expected values (or point values) for every possible choice, where such values are based on a whatever goal was originally provided.

The new primary typology is based on the *triage* process—an approach grounded in determining the treatability of a target. This is used to identify the types of uncertainty that cannot be treated (i.e., to get to the optimization of a decision in terms of its original goal) as well as the types that can be. The resulting typology provides a basis for secondary and tertiary categorizations that can be used to diagnose the uncertainty (e.g., to determine the best treatment for the uncertainty types that are treatable).

Figure 17.2 depicts the flowchart of this triage process: The top flow indicates the path of logic when the *factor* is unknown-as-given, and thus, unknowable prior to the decision point (e.g., because if one does not know that the factor is missing then one cannot put the effort in to find it). Logically (and objectively) that also implies that it has characteristic values that are unknown and unknowable. It is assumed that these render the decision non-optimizable. Given the factor is unknown, this type of uncertainty is untreatable.[4]

---

[4] There are two latent questions regarding the *unknown unknowns* of the top flow. However, each violates the assumption that objective reality exists and that the decision is being considered from that perspective. The first question relates to 'knowing' that an unknown unknown exists—e.g., being certain that the model of the problem is (substantively) incomplete. Objectively, if there is an unknown unknown then we cannot know that that factor exists and, thus, cannot act to make it exist. We could have a 'feeling' that something is missing, but that is purely subjective. The second question relates to a hypothetical regarding if the unknown factor *was* known at the time (e.g., by going back in time once it had been revealed) then could its characteristic's value also have been known. Objectively, again, if it is an unknown unknown then that value is also unknown at the time of the decision. Subjectively, though, such a hypothetical could have resulted from an unfortunate error in model-building (a subjective oversight error) that could be critiqued *ex post*, with regret (given if the model would have been correct and the factor

17 A NEW TYPOLOGY OF UNCERTAINTY ... 265

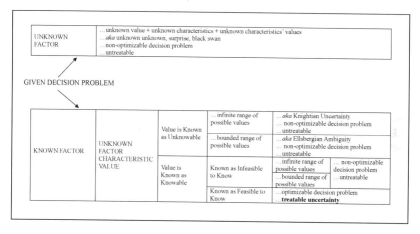

Fig. 17.2 A logical path from unknowns to a new primary typology of uncertainties

The bottom flow indicates the path of logic when the factor is known (as is its characteristic of interest) but the *value* of that factor's characteristic is unknown-as-given. (For example, consider an unknown level of demand for a new product in a specific market over a specific period of time—the factor is known [it is 'demand'], the factor's characteristic is known [it is the demand 'for that product in a specific place and time'] but the actual value [the 'quantity'] of that demand in those circumstances is *not* known.) Without that value, then the outcomes of the possible choices (e.g., to manufacture, price, and introduce that product in that market in a particular season) cannot be calculated, making the decision, as given, non-optimizable. Unlike the top flow—where what to act upon is unknown—in the bottom flow there is a defined target of potential treatment. That target can be delineated into two possible (objective) cases:

In the first case, the known factor's characteristic's value is *known to be unknowable*. A relevant subsequent question involves 'how unknowable'—e.g., as an infinite possible range of values or as a known finite range of values (e.g., where the distribution of probabilities of the values

known, perhaps its characteristic's value could have also been known, and the decision then hypothetically optimized, but it wasn't).

Table 17.1 New primary typology of uncertainty

Triage category	Variant	Sub-variant
Treatable	Known Factor with Unknown Characteristic Value that is Known to be Feasibly Knowable	
Untreatable	Unknown Factor (aka *Unknown Unknown*)	
	Known Factor with Unknown Characteristic Value that is Known to be Infeasibly Knowable	Infinite Range of Values
		Bounded Range of Values
	Known Factor with Unknown Characteristic Value that is Known to be Unknowable	Infinite Range of Values
		Bounded Range of Values

in that range is known to be unknown and unknowable). (The former is often labeled as Knightian uncertainty and the latter as Ellsbergian ambiguity.) But, regardless of the answer to that subsequent question, the uncertainty is still not directly treatable, and so the decision is non-optimizable.

In the second case, the known factor's characteristic's value is *known to be knowable* (although it is an unknown value 'as given'). The relevant subsequent question involves the *feasibility of that knowability*. If the knowability is *known to be infeasible* then that value is essentially unknowable; the uncertainty is then not (practically) treatable, and the decision remains non-optimizable. If the knowability is *known to be feasible*, however, then the uncertainty is treatable in the sense that the decision can be made optimizable. (The next steps in that process then involve further categorization of the uncertainty to identify the best treatment and priority.) Table 17.1 summarizes the uncertainty types identified in this primary categorization.

Cleaning Up the Minor Issues Involved

Note that we are not considering two other parts of the bottom flow: First, we are not considering the situation where the factor and its characteristic value are known; that is *not* uncertainty, as the decision is optimizable 'as given'. Second, we are also not considering what would be a regressive path—the first part of which would be wondering if the knowableness of the factor's characteristic's value was itself unknown (rather than being known to be ether knowable or unknowable). However, that path violates the objective reality assumption—where something is either known or it is not. (Subjectively, there are errors, doubts, and gut-feelings to contend with.) Otherwise, there is a regression to the question of the known knowableness of the knowableness of the unknown (i.e., that unknown being the factor's characteristic's value) [and, the question of the feasibility of addressing any knowableness], and so on, in infinite regress. (We expect in practice that no real decision-makers would go further than one level of verification of the value's knowableness, and the feasibility of that, anyways.)

Note that the top flow depicts something the decision-maker would *not* actually consider; it is provided for the clarity and completeness of our primary categorization. The top flow is about unknown unknowns; their revelation must be surprising to the decision-maker, by definition. That said, can one 'expect to be surprised', say, based on the historic rate (and impact) of surprises in what are thought to be similar contexts?—yes, but that does not itself point to a way to treat that uncertainty (i.e., that specific unknown unknown) or to improve the decision.

It is important to note that there are *some* items that are known at the point of applying this preliminary categorization in the bottom flow: that the factor is known; that its characteristic 'whose value is unknown as given' is known; and, that that value makes the decision non-optimizable. As such, there is already a framework in play—the decision-making process. That process can be used to identify a list of possible 'missing items' that will impede it so as to cause the problem to be non-optimizable. We assume that such a list can be composed into a yes/no format—such that the decision-maker knows the unknown value (i.e., missing item) will or will not impede the decision. At this primary level, though, the decision-maker has yet to dig deeper to identify 'in what specific way' it will impede the decision (as that is part of the secondary typology). The other item that is known is that 'a problem exists that requires a decision'. It is important, at this point, to reflect upon the fact that there is *no* easy way to portray the process of getting to all that 'pre-knowledge'—of arriving at all the conditions (and knowns) described above. (We expect it would lead to a regression, possibly to the origin of the universe, though.) Instead, we simply assume that the decision-maker is given truthful facts sufficient to understand that a decision is needed (with a known time for it to be made). This is a standard approach used for these types of analyses, and provides a benchmark for adding complications regarding such as 'how did we get here?' preliminaries (as well as any 'what ifs' regarding possibilities like 'what happens when more than one uncertainty exists and they interact?', and so on). We have to start our journey somewhere, and the point of needing to make a decision is a suitable one to start with here.

THE RELEVANT SECONDARY TYPOLOGY

After the primary typology is applied, it is appropriate to identify precisely where in the decision-making process the roadblock to optimization lies. With that greater detail comes a better basis for treatment of the unknown or for applying even more fine-tuned diagnostics. Recall, we have assumed that the correct mindset to apply to the focal problem *is* the decision-making process—i.e., the process of attaching a(n expected) worth on each possible alternative and choosing the best one, given any constraints, as is normally done in business, policy, and so on.

The decision-making process is made up of several standard steps, from initially gathering the relevant facts to finally learning from the outcomes. Each one of these steps requires the factors, or the values of a factor's characteristics, to be known in order to proceed towards identifying an optimal choice. When such items are unknown, then that signifies an uncertainty exists (i.e., being an item that ensures the non-optimizability of the decision). We discuss those process steps now, in terms of providing a secondary typology of uncertainties—one that moves from the *treatability* identified in the primary typology to the identification of precisely *where* in the decision process the uncertainty occurs. (We move through these steps in a natural order rather than by any other priority; we understand that decision-makers will vary in their adherence to this order.) Table 17.2 summarizes the uncertainty types delineated by this second categorization.

STEP ONE—ASSESSING THE BACKGROUND FACTS

The decision-maker is given a set of facts—truthful knowledge—about the problem and the decision. In this step there is an assessment of the past and present situation relevant to the decision problem. These facts form

Table 17.2 New secondary typology of uncertainty

Step#	Decision process step description	...details
1	Assess the Background Facts	...about the present state (of reality)
		...about the past states
2	Understand the Goals	
3	Identify the Stakeholders	
4	Recognize All Options/Choices	
5	Recognize All Possible Outcomes	
6	Calculate the Payoffs of the Outcomes	
7	Consider the Ethics and Values Involved (separately from the goals)	
8	Calculate the Overall Worth of Each Outcome	
9	Assign Probabilities to Uncontrollable Outcomes	
10	Understand the Timing Involved (separately from the background facts)	
11	Apply the Relevant Constraints (separately from the background facts)	
*	...*at this point all of the information needed to identify the optimal choice is available (based on its expected worth under the relevant constraints, for a one-shot decision); below are considered the dynamic issues*	
12	Identify the Dynamic Links in Extended Processes (linked decisions)	
13	Assess Other Common Issues (separately from one-shot outcomes of Step 5)	...about unknown effects on rival targets
		...about unknown responses of targets
		...about unknown target intensions
		...about unknown target constraints

the basis for the goals, the valuations of possible outcomes, the feasibility of options, and perhaps even the reasons why there is a problem now (e.g., identifying what changed from the past). It is background material; it provides a benchmark for action. As such, there are '*items*' that could be unknown (*we will focus solely on the known factor characteristics* [that may have unknown values] *from here on out in this typology*) and, if unknown, could make the decision non-optimizable; such items would constitute an identifiable type of uncertainty.

State Uncertainty/ Uncertainty about the Present Reality

If there are unknown items—factual gaps—that impede the decision-maker's ability to fill in a full picture of the present relevant reality, then potentially there is no benchmark from which to calculate changes in the worth of possible choices, which could lead to the non-optimizability of the decision (Hansson, 2022). A different but related type of uncertainty may involve the lack of clarity in the roles of the people involved in the decision process (as being a confusion that may also create an information gap). If that is the case, the decision may also be non-optimizable as given (Stager, 1967), although it is very likely treatable.

Uncertainty about the Past

Uncertainty about the past is often connected to uncertainty about the present through the understanding of ongoing causal relationships. (That connection is partially severed when the present involves great novelty, however. But, in that case, backward curiosity is often evoked [Brod et al., 2018; Bruner & Postman, 1949; Loewenstein, 1994; Shin & Kim, 2019].) Regardless, uncertainty about the past can be considered as a separate realm, with its own sources (e.g., recall bias, haphazard recording, record losses through fires and floods, and so on). In general, knowledge of the past is partial and incomplete (Bammer & Smithson, 2008); but, if that incompleteness results in an unknown item relevant to the focal decision that renders the problem non-optimizable, then that is also an identifiable type of uncertainty.

STEP TWO—UNDERSTANDING THE GOALS

A decision-maker needs to know how to evaluate progress; the goals (that are given) provide that basis for measuring changes that result from making the decision. The goal statement often explains why the problem is seen to exist (i.e., as a block to reaching the goal[s]); and, it helps in aligning the organization's strategy—including its vision and its communications. (However, if there is more than one goal and these conflict, then potentially more problems are created.)

If one or more goals are not known (i.e., in such cases, the 'items' of interest are the missing or under-defined goals, or the lack of instruction on how to trade the given goals off) then the objective function is not known, and then the worth of any outcomes are unknowable, resulting in a non-optimizable problem (Hertwig et al., 2019; Rowe, 1994). This identifiable type of uncertainty has sometimes been labeled *normative uncertainty* in the literature (Bradley & Drechsler, 2014).

Step Three—Identifying the Stakeholders

The possible outcomes of the decision are only meaningful in terms of who (and what) they affect—i.e., the stakeholders. Those stakeholders, including the planet, are affected by the choices and events relevant to the decision problem (including 'the choice to do nothing' when something could have been done). Assessing the ethical impacts of different choices also requires the knowledge of which stakeholders could be involved. When one or more stakeholders are unknown (across all possible choices and outcomes), then the choices cannot be correctly evaluated, and the decision is non-optimizable. This is another identifiable type of uncertainty.

Step Four—Recognizing All Possible Relevant Options/Choices

Optimizing a decision requires choosing one alternative out of many. If the full set of possible choices is not known, then this choosing cannot be done. (It may be possible to choose among only the known choices, but that leaves the issue over whether a different, then-unknown alternative may have been better—alone, or in combination with either known or unknown others; as such, we consider the decision objectively non-optimizable.) This constitutes another identifiable type of uncertainty.

The idea that some options may not be known is not new. For example, it has been termed, or described, as *creative uncertainty* (Packard et al., 2017), as the *uncertainty of demarcation* (Hansson, 1996), as a form of *fundamental uncertainty* (Mousavi & Gigerenzer, 2014), as *unknown actions* (Bradley & Drechsler, 2014), as an *underspecified choice set* (Ghirardato, 2001), as *option uncertainty* (Bradley & Drechsler, 2014), as incomplete information about alternatives (Kozyreva & Hertwig, 2021; Simon, 1972), and as *modal uncertainty* (Bradley & Drechsler, 2014).

We also understand that it is possible to artificially contain all choices (e.g., into 'do nothing' and 'do something'); however, in such cases, the set of outcomes cannot be evaluated (e.g., there is no identifiable [finite] set of outcomes for the 'do something' category), and so this is *not* a real workaround to the uncertainty (i.e., that uncertainty persists).

STEP FIVE—IDENTIFYING ALL POSSIBLE OUTCOMES (RELEVANT TO THE CHOICES)

Each possible outcome is the raw realization of the interaction of a choice made by the decision-maker and the events caused by the context (e.g., nature). The outcomes provide the basis for computing the expected worth of each possible choice. Such raw realizations (e.g., of 'no umbrella' interacting with 'rain') are *not* the payoffs, or the utilities of those payoffs, that arise from that specific outcome occurring (given those latter constructs are dependent on other factors like measures, goals, preferences, and so on). So, *without* the knowledge of those outcomes, then no intermediate or final measures of their impacts are calculable, and so the decision is non-optimizable (Kay & King, 2020). Thus, unknown possible outcomes are an identifiable type of uncertainty.

As with uncertainty over choices (i.e., unknown alternatives), the idea of uncertainty over outcomes (i.e., unknown consequences) is *not* new. There are many labels and descriptions in the literature for this case, including: *state space uncertainty* (Bradley & Drechsler, 2014; Ghirardato, 2001); *uncertainty of consequences* (Hansson, 1996); *unanticipated consequences* (Kozyreva & Hertwig, 2021; Simon, 1972); unknown bounds of the full outcome space (Hertwig et al., 2019); *outcome uncertainty* (Costikyan, 2013; Szentkirályi, 2020); *unknown possibilities* (Hansson, 1996; Milliken, 1987); incomplete knowledge of future states of the world (Walker et al., 2003); a form of fundamental uncertainty (Mousavi & Gigerenzer, 2014); *possibilistic uncertainty* (Hansson, 2022); an inability to classify instances (Langlois & Cosgel, 1993); *environmental uncertainty* (Packard et al., 2017); and, *scenario uncertainty* (Walker et al., 2003).

Note that the core issue with the existence of unknown possible outcomes lies not with any particular unknown outcome itself, but with the *range* of such outcomes. The implicit assumption is that that range is unbounded, so if the unknown outcome is 'extreme', then it greatly affects the worth of the related choices and, thus, the identification of the best choice (Marchau et al., 2019). With an unbounded range, these are 'large' worlds (versus Savage's 'small' worlds), where the uncertainty is immeasurable (Kozyreva & Hertwig, 2021). Note that this type of uncertainty should not be confused with knowing all possible states but not knowing which are probability zero events, given then the range would be known, and it would be possible, in some cases, to make headway in optimizing decision (i.e., by eliminating the dominated choices).

Note that the effects of this uncertainty are not always bad. For example, many real (for-entertainment) games are never-ending (i.e., they essentially have no final outcome), such as *Space Invaders* and *CityVille*, yet are still highly enjoyable (Costikyan, 2013). And, an initial lack of closure on the outcome possibility set often spurs counter-factual thinking (Bradley & Drechsler, 2014), and other imaginative cogitating, that can spur future entrepreneurial actions (Dimov, 2007a, 2007b; Kier & McMullen, 2018).

There are several possible causes of this type of uncertainty. Novelty—often brought on by technological breakthroughs—makes it difficult to find any basis for identifying and classifying future outcomes (Dattée et al., 2018; Knight, 1921). The law of unintended consequences—humankind's inability to see past a few steps of interaction—also ensures, in reality, an incomplete picture of outcomes (Stewart, 2019).

STEP SIX—CALCULATING THE (MONETARY) PAYOFFS OF THE OUTCOMES

Each possible outcome from the focal decision involves monetary costs and benefits, as well as non-monetary payoffs (e.g., measurable in emotional, psychological, spiritual, chemical toxicity, carbon footprint-related, and other 'currencies'). This set of different 'payoffs' can then all be collectively translated into a utility level or a final amount of worth. So, if one or more of these payoffs (for each outcome) is not known, then some choices' expected values cannot be computed, and the decision cannot be optimized. (As noted with the analysis of the outcome knowability, the real issue concerns the range of possible unknown payoffs; if this is unbounded, there is no path to making the decision less non-optimizable.) Thus, unknown payoffs are also an identifiable (separate) type of uncertainty.

This type of uncertainty is also not new. It has been labeled and described prior, sometimes as an objective issue (as we assume here) and sometimes explicitly as a subjective issue. Objectively, it has been described as an *uncertainty of values* (Hansson, 1996), as *unknown outcome sizes* (Hertwig et al., 2019) and as *unknown values* to attach to consequences (Bradley & Drechsler, 2014). Subjectively, the label is not the issue; the issue is which value is 'correct' as such payoffs may be contentious among different parties (Marchau et al., 2019), given they may be based on subjective perceptions or on individual preferences (Hertwig et al., 2019).

STEP SEVEN—CONSIDERING THE ETHICS AND VALUES OF THE OUTCOMES [SEPARATED FROM GOALS]

The raw outcomes also need to be assessed in terms of ethics and values, separate from their basic payoffs, assuming that the decision-maker cares about more than just their own organization (i.e., assuming the differential effects of outcomes on the range of stakeholders matter). Those raw outcomes would be assessed by their impacts in terms of size, equity, distribution, justice, and impingement on stakeholder rights, specifying their effects on whom, where, when, and for how long, in what form, and how. Without that knowledge, the decision-maker's choices cannot be fully evaluated and the best one cannot be chosen. Having such *ethical uncertainty* makes the decision non-optimizable (Bammer & Smithson, 2008; Bradley & Drechsler, 2014; Bradley & Steele, 2015).

We note that this assessment brings in some subjectivity (i.e., in the form of which ethical standards the decision-maker applies) but that subjectivity is not about the 'facts', which is where our assumption over objectivity is important and remains. This is a 'rule' or 'value' type of uncertainty rather than a fact uncertainty (Bammer & Smithson, 2008). (Note that the range of possible influence here by the unknown [i.e., being the ethical value of an outcome] is, by the conceptualization of ethics [i.e., that some outcomes will *not* be accepted], sufficiently wide to ensure that—without knowing the ethical assessment of each possible outcome—the decision would be truly [i.e., practically and non-trivially] non-optimizable.)

This type of uncertainty has other labels and descriptions in the literature: as *value uncertainty* (Bradley & Drechsler, 2014; Hansson, 2022; Samsami et al., 2015); and, as *subjective uncertainty* (Tannert et al., 2007).

Step Eight—Calculating the (Overall) Worth of the Outcomes [Utilities]

Bringing together the raw outcomes, their various payoffs and their ethical and value assessments, while also considering goals and other preferences, produces a 'final scoring' (i.e., overall worth or utility) for each possible outcome of each possible choice. If that final score cannot be calculated for every possible outcome—if something is unknown in that calculation—then the best choice cannot be identified, making the decision non-optimizable. This is another identifiable type of uncertainty.

This type of uncertainty appears under different labels in the literature, including as *utility uncertainty* (Hertwig et al., 2019; Milliken, 1987; Rowe, 1994), and as *preference uncertainty* (Bradley & Steele, 2015).

Step Nine—Assigning Probabilities to the Uncontrollable Outcome-Affecting Events

Most choices involve a variety of possible outcomes; this is because the decision-maker is *not* the only entity acting at the same time to influence the outcome. Other entities—ones that the decision-maker cannot fully control—acting at the same time can include: nature; rivals; partners; regulators; and, consumers. In order to account for their effects on the outcome, a likelihood is assigned to each combination of their possible actions (e.g., a 50-percent chance of rain; a 30-percent chance of playing 'up' in a mixed strategy equilibrium game; and, so on). This is done so that an expected worth can be calculated for each choice (in terms of its interactions with each of these possible combinations). When these likelihoods are unknown and unknowable (i.e., because their underlying distribution is not known nor are the distributions underlying that distribution)—then an uncertainty exists that makes the decision non-optimizable (Lampert et al., 2020). This entails another identifiable uncertainty type.

This type of uncertainty is not new; in fact, it is the most described type in the decision-making under uncertainty literature (Bradley & Drechsler, 2014; Roeser, 2019; Townsend et al., 2018). This issue of unknown probabilities is also most associated with the Knightian uncertainty label, as well as with the Ellsbergian ambiguity label (in this latter case when the range of the probabilities is known). Other labels of this uncertainty include: *radical uncertainty* (Kay & King, 2020); *strong uncertainty* (Dequech, 2011); and, *strong substantive uncertainty* (Dosi & Egidi, 1991). Such uncertainty is also often caused by novelty—for example, for a one-time event where probabilities cannot really apply (Dimov, 2016).

STEP TEN—INCLUDING ANY TIMING ISSUES INVOLVED IN THE PROCESS

The sequence and scheduling of events relevant to the decision can impact the choice (e.g., whether extra information can be made available before having to decide for some choices but not others; whether impacts take longer to emerge for the specific outcomes of different choices). As with any element of the decision that affects either the facts that are known before the decision or the valuation of the possible outcomes of the choices, if that element is unknown, then it can affect the optimizability of the decision. For example, if there are unknown facts about any bounded windows of opportunity for some choices, or required timing sequences for others, or indeterminate time horizons, or differential discount rates due to delays, then the decision may be non-optimizable (Bradley & Steele, 2015). This embodies another identifiable uncertainty type.

This *temporal uncertainty* has many descriptions: as an unknown length of time to reap benefits (Hertwig et al., 2019) or to reach a conclusion (Edwards, 1965); as an unknown rate of change: as time being an unknown moderator of a causal relationship (Mitchell & James, 2001); and, as an unknown pace of evolution of events (Kapoor & Klueter, 2021).

STEP ELEVEN—APPLYING THE RELEVANT CONSTRAINTS

Assuming that the best choice can be identified through the first ten steps, a set of constraints specific to the decision-maker's organization must still be accounted for. If these are unknown, and can differentially affect the choice set, because they rule out the implementation of, or alter the set of, acceptable outcomes (i.e., alter their final worth), then the true final expected values for all of the choices cannot be computed, and the decision is non-optimizable. Such constraints vary, and could include ones that are: legal or regulatory (based on the organization's location and industry); technological; physical; temporal; resource-based;

attention-based; capability-based; spatial; capacity-based; supply chain-based; financial; natural (science-based); communicative; observational; and, so on. This is also an identifiable type of uncertainty.

A Line of Demarcation in the Decision-Making Process

The preceding eleven steps cover the different uncertainties that can arise in making *one* single, isolated decision.[5] We now shift our attention to situations where the assessment of one decision does not end the analysis—i.e., we now consider situations that involve multiple related decisions that occur sequentially over time. Across time periods—when the problem becomes 'dynamic'—there are two main things that can happen to the kinds of unknowns we care about here: first, initial unknowns could become more known (e.g., through search or experimentation efforts); second, new unknowns could emerge. We consider these dynamics below—in general, and then in more detail for business-related concerns.

STEP TWELVE—IDENTIFYING THE DYNAMIC LINKS IN THE EXTENDED PROCESS

When the analysis does not end with the making of the one focal decision, then there are possibilities for many further unknowns to occur and even for some past ones to be reduced or eliminated (through new knowledge being revealed along the way). The ability to identify the reliable sources of feedback, the relationships between decisions (e.g., if some decisions affect the range of choices possible for subsequent decisions or the range of new information that can be generated to use in subsequent decisions), and the other relevant dynamic effects (e.g., reputational effects, signaling, trust-building), then becomes necessary for optimizing the overall exercise. With such added items to keep track of comes the possibility of having new unknowns appear in the now-dynamic process,

---

[5] The literature refers to so-called *wicked problems* as those plagued by several of these uncertainties—where relevant parties cannot agree on the goals, the outcome set, the probabilities and the proper valuation methods (e.g., Head, 2022). Others have characterized wickedness in other, separable ways, often dealing with specific contexts, like entrepreneurship (Arend, 2015).

and those making the full exercise non-optimizable. This would add to the types of identifiable uncertainties.

Step Thirteen—Assessing the Dynamics of Competition

Business decisions are seldom one-shot or isolated. Business decisions often occur in sequential bunches against similar competitors. While game theory has been used to study many of these multi-period interactions, it is an approach that assumes that *all relevant information is known* (so that the decisions can be optimized). We do not make the same assumption here because the focus is on identifying uncertainties. Instead, to differentiate these kinds of decision-sequences, we assume a focus on the strategic (competitive) business context, where the game is *relative*. To survive and prosper, the focal firm needs to perform better than its rivals. Thus, understanding how the firm's own decisions impact its rivals matters (as does deciding on how to react to their decisions). But, those impacts are *not* fully visible, nor are the decision processes of rivals; that opaqueness (e.g., about a rival's awareness, motivations, capabilities, constraints, execution) creates uncertainties (regarding outcomes, the associated payoffs and timing, and so on) that can render the firm's decision non-optimizable. Hence, these are also identifiable uncertainty types (that are often subsumed under the label of *competitive uncertainty*). We highlight four of these possible unknowns now:

Unknown Effects on Rival Targets

One firm will never know the full effects of its decisions on another (independent) firm; that realization creates potential uncertainties (Ghirardato, 2001; Hanany et al., 2020; Milliken, 1987). When those outcomes (i.e., the ones on rivals), their probabilities, and their monetary and non-monetary impacts are unknown—to the extent that the range of effects on the firm's evaluation of its choices is significantly wide—then the underlying decisions are non-optimizable. (However, when the range is narrower, as is usually assumed, and given whatever history has occurred with interactions with those known rivals, the decisions are often considered optimizable enough, or at a scale or investment that is not strategic enough, to be made with some comfort.)

Unknown Responses of Targets

Given any one firm cannot peek into another to get a full assessment of any impacts, it is also impossible to predict with certainty what the responses will be from rivals (as well as from consumers, business partners, regulators and other stakeholders) to any actions taken (Bammer & Smithson, 2008; Magnani & Zucchella, 2018; March & Simon, 1958). That said, technically, the summary of such responses should be accounted for in the outcomes captured for each choice in the original decision (for whatever period of time was considered relevant). The unknowable responses are a source of outcome uncertainty (more so in a dynamic game). This subtype of outcome uncertainty (as we have categorized it through our secondary typology) is often separated and labeled as a kind of *response uncertainty* (Conrath, 1967; Garner, 1962; McMullen & Shepherd, 2006; Milliken, 1987; Packard et al., 2017; Samsami et al., 2015; Townsend et al., 2018), or as *interactive uncertainty* (Hansson, 2022). Game theory provides a benchmark on possible reactions, when all other relevant information is assumed known and all entities act rationally (Spender, 2006). (As with the effects, it is the range of responses that is of practical interest here. When that range includes out-of-the-ordinary acts or acts that could remove a rival from play, then the uncertainty is of real strategic interest, and the decision being non-optimizable is a higher priority condition to address.)

UNKNOWN TARGET INTENSIONS

Competitive intelligence exists, in part, to identify the intensions of rivals—so that their offensive actions and defensive reactions can be more accurately predicted (Porter, 1980). Such intensions cannot be known completely (Abbott, 2005). As such, they are a source of unknowns that can be realized as unknowable, unpredicted actions and reactions in a set of competitive decisions—items that can make one or more items of that decision non-optimizable (Yager, 1999). Game theory simply assumes that the intensions are rational—that the target is an unbiased value-maximizer; in reality, that assumption is often wrong. This 'source' of uncertainty is often labeled as a 'type' in the literature: as *strategic uncertainty* (Adobor, 2006; Hertwig et al., 2019; Milgrom & Roberts, 1992); as *uncertainty about rival behaviors* (Hertwig et al., 2019); *rival or player uncertainty* (Costikyan, 2013); and, as *social* and *exchange-specific uncertainty* (Adobor, 2006; Yamagishi et al., 1998).

Even relying on experts (e.g., competitive intelligence consultants) to reduce the unknowns about a rival's behaviors can introduce further uncertainties (e.g., about that reliance on experts; and, if they disagree, on whom to trust) (Hansson, 1996). When the 'rival' target is an institution, there are other labels that can be applied to the sources of the relevant decision step unknowns (e.g., *policy uncertainty*). (Policies can affect the decision process in several ways, including effects on the choices available and on the timing involved [Baker et al., 2016; Nosal & Ordoñez, 2016].) When the 'rival entity' is composed of other firms in an ecosystem, the label usually applied is *ecosystem uncertainty* (Kapoor & Klueter, 2021). When the 'target' is a strategic alliance partner, the label is *relational risk* (Adobor, 2006). When the 'target' is the consumer, the label is *demand* or *market uncertainty* (McDonald & Eisenhardt, 2020; O'Connor & Rice, 2013). There can also be *supplier uncertainty*. The sources of *this* source of decision unknowns (i.e., this source being others' intentions) include the variability associated with human behavior, with signaling, and with technological progress (Walker et al., 2003).

Unknown Target Decision Constraints

Competitive intelligence also exists to provide information on the constraints of targets—in terms of identifying the limits of how much they could affect the focal firm (e.g., is their production capacity sufficiently unconstrained to support a price war that bankrupts this firm?). Without that knowledge, if the bounds are assumed wide, then that 'source' of an unknown (e.g., of possible outcomes) is likely to cause non-optimizability in a decision. When target capacities (e.g., a rival's creative abilities) are sufficiently known, such uncertainties do not exist (Packard et al., 2017); but, when they are not sufficiently known, they can be considered as additional sources of unknowns associated with realized rival actions, and logged under the labels of *strategic* or *behavioral uncertainty* in the literature (Hertwig et al., 2019).

A Tertiary Typology

Our primary typology divides uncertainties into those that are directly treatable (i.e., leading to the feasible optimization of the decision) and those that are not. The secondary typology categorizes an unknown by which step in the decision process it affects (i.e., in the way that it makes the decision non-optimizable, as given). Together, these typologies get the decision-maker to the point of knowing exactly how the decision process is being compromised by either a feasibly treatable unknown (where the decision can be optimized) or by an unknown that renders the problem, as given, irreducibly non-optimizable. We discuss in the next chapter both the treatments for the treatable unknowns and the approaches for altering the problem when the unknowns are not treatable. We believe that getting to this point in a clear way provides a big step forward in improving decision-making under uncertainty.

We now discuss one way that any uncertainty can be diagnosed further for treatment (and for the prioritization of that treatment)—in terms of even greater specification of its characteristics. Consider the full *Aristotelian 1H5W* approach to proper information-gathering when studying any phenomenon. Answering these six questions (i.e., the how, what, why, who, where, and when) even defines valid theorizing (Whetten, 1989). Our primary and secondary typologies have already addressed the question of *how* the item is uncertain (i.e., in its treatability and in its place in the decision process), *who* is involved (i.e., in identifying the stakeholders), and *when* (i.e., in the temporal issues). Two previous ways the literature has categorized uncertainties include a focus on the specific *what* that is unknown and the specific *why* it is unknown (i.e., the source of unknownness). We discuss those prior to considering the *where* of the unknown. For these last three questions—i.e., areas of greater specification—of the uncertainty, we now describe the major relevant dimensions of each.[6]

---

[6] Note that we have proposed a set of typologies that have not appeared in the literature (at least as formal typologies to our knowledge). This implies, and we state this now explicitly, that all previous typologies have been flawed. The flaws are many (e.g., mixing sources with types; lacking specificity; and, so on). There have been many flaws of basic logic as well. For example, several typologies fail to differentiate between *gaps* in a set of values of a factor (e.g., gaps in the set of possible options or outcomes) and the *range* of possible impacts those can values can have on a decision (e.g., Packard et al., 2017); an open set in the former sense makes much less difference than in the latter sense as to

Dimensions of Specifying What Is Uncertain

There are an almost infinite number of items (i.e., factor characteristics) that can be unknown in business (and in other complex and rapidly-evolving fields, like engineering and medicine). For example, it can be the demand of a specific product in a specific market at a specific time (Wu & Knott, 2006), the technological feasibility of a new product or process, or the probability of a deregulatory bill passing. Or, it can be the full list of opportunity ingredients required for a successful new venture (Ramoglou, 2021). Of course, trying to better understand what the focal item embodies—especially in terms of its differentiability as a potential strategic factor—has been a focus of heterogeneity-based, rent-focused theorizing for decades in micro-economics and strategy (Barney, 2002; Grant, 1996). This is an important feature to specify for analysis because some of these factors (e.g., tangible resources, capabilities, knowledge, and so on) are managed differently than others (e.g., with legal protections).

Table 17.3 describes several useful dimensions to consider when prioritizing a decision involving *what* item is uncertain. These dimensions help the decision-maker acknowledge where the item fits into the strategic performance picture of the focal organization. We start with identifying the theoretical strategic foundations at stake, then move to the strategic importance involved, and then to the primary and secondary costs and benefits (that make up the outcome and payoffs related in the choice), and finally to any peculiarities involved.

Recall we have assumed that the decision is strategic in nature. As such, it is likely that the 'item' embodying the uncertainty is also strategic in nature (i.e., as affecting any one of the three core questions of strategy—over investment, competition, and firm structure [Leiblein et al., 2018]). The first dimension identifies the item's role, if any, in a specific theory of firm rents (so it can be analyzed and assessed appropriately through the lens of that theory). For example, if the item concerns a strategic factor's unknown value, rarity, inimitability or appropriability in a resource-based view of sustained competitive advantage (Barney, 2002), then its potential treatment is likely to differ from when the item involves unknown access

---

whether any real uncertainty exists (i.e., in terms of effects on the optimizability of the decision).

Table 17.3 New tertiary typology breakdown on the main dimensions of the known factor's unknown characteristic value to consider

Description of dimension	Cases	Notes
..the kind of *Strategic Factor* represented	• resources/capabilities/knowledge underlying competitive advantage • industry position/business model • in functional area/internal value chain	• being able to place it into a specific theory of rents may help better identify how to evaluate and address its uncertainty (includes uncertainties about length of associated success or costs)
..the *Intensity Characteristics* it displays[a]	• magnitude of consequences • (social) consensus of whether it is good or bad • temporal immediacy • proximity • concentration of effect • interactions (with other factors)	• the intensity characteristics of it may help with prioritization on focusing resources and attention to better evaluate and address its uncertainty
..the *Primary Costs and Benefits* generated	• to production, profitability or innovation (includes technological uncertainty, scale and scope economy uncertainties)	• the impact on the organization's triple bottom line categories, whether good or bad, may help with better evaluating and addressing its uncertainty • the people and planet categories also raise the possibility that it is embodying ethical uncertainty that also requires evaluation and addressing

(continued)

Table 17.3 (continued)

Description of dimension	Cases	Notes
	• to people—employees, customers, and community (includes demand uncertainty, unionization, etc....) • to planet	
..the *Secondary Costs and Benefits* generated	• to rivals (includes competitive uncertainty) • to partners and complementors (includes supplier uncertainty) • to regulators (includes regulatory uncertainty)	• the interdependencies with others—through competition, cooperation, coordination and constraints—raise the possibility of relative (versus absolute) costs and benefits to consider, as well as increase the complexity of modeling (these more than one-way relationships)
..the *Idiosyncratic Nature* involved	• whether it is private, or self-imposed, or voluntary (versus common and shared) and whether it is local or wide-spread (e.g., exogenous like a pandemic) may help better evaluate and address it	• the uncertainty of it

[a]several intensity dimensions sourced from Jones (1991)

to a complementary asset that affects the appropriation of a core piece of knowledge (Teece, 1986).

The item is also likely to have an *intensity*—a measure of its overall relative possible proportional impact on stakeholders depending on its unknown value (e.g., Bradley & Dreschler, 2014; O'Connor & Rice, 2013). We draw upon many of Jones' (1991) dimensions of his 'moral intensity' construct to offer a set of characteristics to assess the item here. The item's intensity can be considered a function of: the *magnitude of consequences*—measuring the sum of harms and benefits done to those impacted; the *social consensus*—measuring the extent of social agreement in how the item involves harms and benefits; the *temporal immediacy*—measuring the delay between the present and the start of the item's consequences, where a smaller delay implies greater immediacy; the *proximity*—measuring the psychological, social, and physical nearness that the decision-maker has for those impacted by the item; the *concentration of effect*—an inversely proportional measure to the number of stakeholders affected by the item; and, the *interactivity*—measuring how connected and non-separable the item is to other important factors in the organization. As with other intensity scores, it is the collection of measures over these dimensions taken as a whole that is used for purposes of comparison (to other items and other organizational priorities). The score then affects how the item is potentially addressed by the firm (e.g., in terms of how much effort is allocated to assessing it; whether the treatment is given; and, so on) (Jones, 1991).

The item's strategic nature arises because its unknown value (i.e., the factor's characteristic's value) could produce either a net negative or a net positive payoff for the decision. As such, the item must involve both potential costs and benefits. This allows us to differentiate the item by both its primary and its secondary costs and benefits. The *primary* effects can be considered along the triple-bottom line dimensions—as impacts on profits, people, and the planet. Note that the item's effects on people and the planet may also entail possible moral uncertainties. The *secondary* costs and benefits may be best captured in relative terms; as impacts that arise mainly through the item's interdependencies with other parties in the industry (e.g., regulators), and so can be differentiated in terms of competitive, cooperative-coordinative, and constraining effects. This consideration of interactions and co-evolution with other parties is important given that firm performance (and the decisions underlying it) is often measured in relative terms.

Finally, the item may be characterized in terms of its *idiosyncrasy*—how voluntary and private it is to deal with. This dimension is important to assess to determine whether the item can be avoided in some manner, and, if not, whether that item (e.g., unknown demand) is also likely to affect other relevant parties and how. The better the latter is known, the more likely it is to identify actions that could be taken to leverage or exploit the commonalities and differences among the parties in dealing with it.

In order to make the preceding discussion of *what* more relatable, we provide a table (Table 17.4) of sample items that could be unknown, for reference and inspiration. (We hope that it can be used for analogical thinking for whatever the Reader is dealing with in their decision problem.)

Table 17.4 Examples of what could be unknown in the business decision context

Regarding the Basics of Business:
- Organizational Goals
- Strategy
- Positioning
- Own Resources & Capabilities
- Organizational Structure (formal and informal)
- Ecosystem(s) and Platform(s)

Regarding the Business Context:
- Rivals
- Substitutes
- Complements
- New Entrants
- Suppliers
- Distributors
- Customers
- Government (regulations; taxes; subsidies)
- Technology
- Trends
- Locational Infrastructure
- Related and Supporting Industries
- Locational Factor Endowments
- Insurance
- Financial Markets

Regarding the Effects of the Unknown, on:
- costs/harms/negative spillovers
- benefits/positive spillovers
- quality of the product
- safety
- efficacy
- health
- resistance/ anxiety
- willingness-to-pay
- sales
- operations

Regarding the Dealing with the Uncertainty:
- cause-and-effect of main relationships
- available tools

Regarding Expertise in which Tools to Apply:
- criticality of factor
- latency of the unknown

Regarding Industry Evolution:
- changes in growth
- changes in buyer segments served buyers' learning
- diffusion of proprietary knowledge accumulation of experience
- changes in scale
changes in costs
- product, marketing, process innovations
- structural changes in adjacent industries
- government policy changes
- entries & exits
- market size
- optimal product configuration
- nature of potential buyers
- technical feasibility
- end-game competition
- subsidy programs
- intimidation and retaliation by integrators
- future existence of markets
- global antitrust laws
- enforcement of antitrust laws
- disruption
- hyper-competition
- cultural changes
- communications quality
- economic conditions
- political upheaval
- locational differences
- economies of scale and scope
- first-mover advantages and disadvantages
- synergies
- diversification opportunities
- international opportunities

Dimensions of Specifying Why the Uncertainty Exists

The *why* question of uncertainty primarily leads to identifying its possible *sources* (see Chapter 4 for our discussion and categorization of the drivers of uncertainties). Identifying the sources is important because it is likely to affect how to address that uncertainty in the future. Davidsson (2015) considers them as the *external enablers* of uncertainty. Rowe (1994) describes them as the causes of measurement error, inconsistent human behavior, and chaotic systems. Discovering the source-as-cause is a key step to understanding the cause-and-effect relationships likely involved in producing the unknowns, and with that understanding, a possible path to better controlling or predicting the unknowns is much more likely. For example, the approaches for addressing the unknown will differ between when the source is nature (i.e., sometimes referred to as *aleatory* or *stochastic uncertainty*) versus when the source is another sentient being, due to issues of skill, leverage, bargaining power, opportunities for cooperation, capacity for deception, and so forth.[7] Besides this example dimensioning dichotomy over the main source of uncertainty being either non-sentient or sentient, subdimensions can exist that provide relevant details; for example, whether the natural source is based on a chaotic system or not. (Briefly returning to the unknown unknowns, these may be further delineated into those surprises that *only* arise from the actions of a known party [e.g., through experimentation or play], those surprises that occur regardless [i.e., due to natural systems], and those 'surprises' knowingly created by others [as in the *Softsoap* story—see Brandenburger & Nalebuff, 1996].)

Dimensions of Specifying Where the Uncertainty Exists

The *where* of uncertainty primarily leads to the dimensioning in terms of *spatial* localization. This is important to understand to customize the approach to that place (e.g., in that country, market, division, channel, network, platform, or sector), and possibly to better control spillovers of knowledge related to that uncertainty within and across those spaces.

---

[7] Recall that an unknown can arise from nature (e.g., arising in chaotic systems, and systems with evolving genotypes), or from other humans (e.g., arising from a *closed ignorance*—the willful non-recognition of knowledge—that can be a rational social or political choice of decision-makers), or a combination of the two (see Faber et al., 1992).

Revisiting a Selection of Uncertainty Sources to Highlight the Separation from Types

We now reconsider several sources of uncertainty that are often confused with uncertainty types. We do so to better delineate the differences between where an unknown comes from versus what it presents as. (We understand that a categorization method could be 'by source', but given that many sources can individually create many presentations of uncertainty [i.e., a one-to-many relationship], we have chosen a different categorization method. A further reason why source-based typologies are questionable is that it could be argued that there are always sources to the sources [i.e., an infinite regress problem].)

Measurement Uncertainty

Inaccurate empirical methods (and the errors and limits associated with method application) may lead to measurement error that leads to uncertainties over facts, outcomes, probabilities and so on (Bradley & Drechsler, 2014). The unavailability of measurement functions can also lead to such uncertainties (Ben-Haim, 2001).

In a reversal of causation, uncertainty itself can lead to measurement issues, given what is to be measured is unknown or indescribable (Bammer & Smithson, 2008; Spender, 2006).

Model Uncertainty

If the originating phenomenon—and its related decision—cannot be captured in a model, then it cannot be analyzed or optimized. An incomplete model (e.g., with missing parameters or rules) is a source of unknowns in a decision—embodied in factual uncertainties (Ben-Haim, 2001; Hertwig et al., 2019; Marchau et al., 2019; Walker et al., 2003).

Model uncertainty can arise when the various parties to a decision (e.g., experts) do not know, or cannot agree on, how the underlying system works (Bammer & Smithson, 2008; Lempert et al., 2003). Such a situation is often labeled *deep uncertainty* (Marchau et al., 2019), or *radical uncertainty* (Kay & King, 2020), or *causal uncertainty* (MacLeod & Pingle, 2000; Szentkirályi, 2020), or *structural uncertainty* (Hansson, 2022), or wicked (Rittel & Webber, 1973).

To be clear, bad modeling can cause gaps (that wouldn't otherwise exist), while bad models simply involve missing items (without causing those unknowns). What can cause either includes novelty (McDonald & Eisenhardt, 2020), war (Kay & King, 2020), or other forms of large-impact surprise. (Note that sometimes modeling uncertainty can be designed into a situation, as an impactful means of entertainment, or to spur creative thinking in an audience [Costikyan, 2013].)

Environmental Uncertainty

The decision context—the uncontrollables (Powell, 1992)—generates unknowns both independently (Yager, 1999) and interdependently (i.e., based on the choices made and subsequent actions taken by the decision-maker) (Haasnoot et al., 2013). It is often labeled as *exogenous* or *external uncertainty* (Downey et al., 1975; Jauch & Kraft, 1986; Kahneman & Tversky, 1982; Magnani & Zucchella, 2018), or *objective* or *true uncertainty* (Downey & Slocum Jr, 1975; Griffin & Grote, 2020), or *state uncertainty* (Milliken, 1987). To some scholars, such uncertainties are always present and can never be fully resolved (Packard et al., 2017; Samsami et al., 2015; Walker et al., 2003). Such contextual uncertainty can be considered an *ontological uncertainty* that is generated by the stochastic features of complex technical, biological, and social systems that often display non-linear behaviors (Tannert et al., 2007). Again, to be clear, the context is a source of various unknowns; it is not a 'type' of uncertainty.

Endogenous Uncertainty and Knowable Unknowns

When the source of uncertainty is endogenous—i.e., when it is caused the decision-maker or their organization—it is often assumed that any consequent unknowns are knowable (e.g., through discovery and knowledge expansion within the firm's control) (Camerer, 1994; Costikyan, 2013; Fontana & Gerrard, 2004; Griffin & Grote, 2020; Kay & King, 2020; O'Donnell, 2013). Decision-makers can overcome their doubts and limited awareness by learning and believing (Faber et al., 1992; Ramoglou, 2021). Firms can conduct knowledge audits and create expert databases. For many unknowns emanating from the decision context, applying standard searching and planning techniques can reduce or eliminate them (Kuhlthau, 1993). Indeed, such unknowns are often mitigated by history, exploration, and negotiation (Townsend et al., 2018), or by sensing, sensemaking, scenario planning, and real options thinking (Teece et al., 2016).

Endogenous uncertainty itself is thought to have many causes. It can be a result of conscious ignorance (Bammer & Smithson, 2008). It can be a result of initially hidden but actually existent information (Dequech, 2011). Or, it can be influenced by exogenous uncertainty in the form of changes in what is known and can be known to the decision-maker (Griffin & Grote, 2020; Lipshitz & Strauss, 1997; Maitlis & Christianson, 2014).

When the endogenous uncertainty is considered at the individual level, the focus is more on the subjective—usually about confidence and belief levels related to focal unknown's likelihoods (Bradley & Steele, 2015; Ellsberg, 1961; Feduzi et al., 2012; Fontana & Gerrard, 2004; Hertwig et al., 2019; Keynes, 1921); in such cases, it has also been labeled as *metadoxastic uncertainty* (Hansson, 2022). Bottom line, endogeneity is a source category of uncertainties, not a type; however, many of the uncertainties that emerge from that source are treatable. The next chapter describes such treatments.

> **Summary**
> A new typology is needed in the decision-making under uncertainty literature. Currently, there are just too many conflicting terms and convenient (versus grounded) categorizations existing across the many relevant fields. There is no universal language describing, or basis for delineating, uncertainties. That must change in order to real scientific progress to be made—to improve the state of decision-making under uncertainty. We propose and argue a primary and secondary typology to do so. The primary typology delineates treatable uncertainties from those that cannot be treated. The secondary typology delineates uncertainties by what part of the decision-making process they affect (to make the decision 'non-optimizable as given'). This categorization provides much-needed clarity; for example, by clearly differentiating sources of uncertainty from the unknowns they produce.
> Why a new typology matters:
>
> - The only feasible way to make progress with such a complex and confused concept like uncertainty is with a divide-and-conquer

mentality—specifically, where that division comes in the form of categorizations of identifiable meaningful types of uncertainty
- ...only then can a universal terminology emerge upon which to communicate (to eliminate redundancies and noise), and then to build and test relevant new theory
- The proposed typologies are built on the strongest and most relevant logics—of triage, of decision-making, and of Aristotelian inquiry—to make them theoretically and practically applicable and valuable.

What a new typology of uncertainty means for business and policy:

- There are many benefits that can come from a clear typology of uncertainties—in communications, in sorting a database of historic confrontations with uncertainties, in being able to learn from others' experiences with uncertainties, and so on
- A clear typology will provide greater insights into the treatability of the uncertainties one faces and the asymmetries in uncertainty that others may face, providing possible opportunities from entrepreneurship and strategic advantage
- The typologies can also provide a better appreciation for the uncertainties that the firm can generate for others (and how to better defend when others attempt to do so to the firm).

Supplement on Knightian Uncertainty Issues

Knight's (1921) seminal work on uncertainty has reverberated for over a century, especially in the entrepreneurship field. However, one hundred years of thinking about its ideas (and testing some of them) has exposed some issues worth considering now.

Knight's (1921) work has had a large impact on entrepreneurship research. Even a century later, his conceptualization of uncertainty continues to influence work on the role of the entrepreneur in bearing specific informational challenges (e.g., Townsend et al., 2020). His delineation of risk from non-risk uncertainty—where the former entails problems that include the distributional information necessary to compute expected outcomes while the latter does not—has resulted in the latter being termed *Knightian uncertainty*. In his model, *only* under this kind of uncertainty can entrepreneurial profits arise—realized by bearing such uninsurable decisions through commitments and actions in pursuit of the profits that come to the residual holders of the contracts that constitute their ventures.

Knight's Model as a Theory of Rents

Special for its time, Knight's (1921) model can now be considered as just another explanation of super-normal rents. Knight's super-normal profits are the result of revenues that are inflated by an undersupplied product combined with input costs that are reduced by their under-demand— with such inflation and reduction arising because of the low number of entrepreneurs-as-producers in that specific (new) product market. (Given that they constitute the few special people who are willing to bear uncertainty, they have little competition in selling their goods on one hand and buying their inputs on the other.) What differentiates Knight's model is the story about what gives an entrepreneur the ability to produce the valued-but-undersupplied products—her unique *judgment of what to do* (i.e., which product to make, how, and in what quantity) *when faced with non-risk uncertainty*. (Luck, confidence, and the ability to execute also help.) In Knight's model, the entrepreneur is the residual holder of a set of contracts because she alone is willing to bear the non-risk uncertainty as the leader of her venture that her employees have contracted with.[8] (Such a private arrangement also limits any spillover of her unique decisions based on her valuable judgment.) That story of rent-earning is no longer unique—as it simply presents just another version of the narrative where someone with a valuable, rare, inimitable, and appropriable capability can use it to gain an advantage (e.g., see the capability, resource, and knowledge-based views—e.g., Barney, 2002; Grant, 1996).

Although that kind of rent-logic is no longer special, the connections Knight's (1921) version has with entrepreneurship, with strategic decision-making, and with uncertainty have been of continued interest, spiking again recently. Its connection with the entrepreneurship field remains strong because that field continues to look for defining theories, especially those that provide solid micro-economic arguments and that have survived decades; so it is not surprising it continues to be an easy

---

[8] Note that Knight's description of the role of the entrepreneur in her venture is so strong that it essentially provides a version of the 'nexus of contracts' theory of the firm over fifty years before it was formally proposed (Jensen & Meckling, 1976).

and popular citation in addition to remaining an inspiration for new theorizing (e.g., Rindova & Courtney, 2020). Its connection with strategic decision-making remains strong, as managers struggle to deal with *VUCA* contexts where unknown unknowns and unimaginables make traditional tools based on scenarios, adaptability and options less applicable (Arend, 2020). And, its connection with uncertainty also remains strong, especially recently, as a renewed interest in incomplete informational problems involving unknowns has occurred. That renewed interest is a result of the historic wave of papers that had unfortunately replaced *real* uncertainty with risk (e.g., through subjective expected utility, beliefs and learning—Hodgson, 2011) 'hitting a (predictable theory-related) wall' when strategic decision-makers increasingly found themselves confronting uncertainty-related problems *without* any solid basis for the justified priors required for such expected-returns-based optimizations. And, so, the subsequent *gold-rush* to describe possible solutions to these unoptimizable problems was on. But, danger now looms when such follow-on work builds upon Knight's model, especially when that model is loosely interpreted. These underappreciated dangers to academics and to practitioners are what we focus on here.

THE THREE DANGERS OF THE KNIGHTIAN MODEL

Knight's (1921) model of entrepreneurial activity (one based on the market failure of incomplete information) involves three main dangers— one involving the main premise of the model, one involving the main implication of the model, and one involving the main definition of the model. We explain why those dangers can matter materially to academia and to practice after describing each.

The Premise Danger

For Knight's (1921) story to work, there must exist, for *all* relevant parties, a minimum level of uncertainty that is *beyond risky* (i.e., without an expected value calculation, and so uninsurable). Essentially, if *even one* party confronts only risk in their decision, then that party could (profitably) provide insurance to others. And, when that occurs, *no* interesting party faces non-risk uncertainty and there is *no* entrepreneurial activity— as Knight would define it—required. No special *judgment* is needed. It is business-as-usual, as the downside is insured.

To illustrate, consider a one-factor production decision. It is a simple optimization problem with one input. The objective for the decision-maker is to maximize the profit on her productive effort. The benefit is accounted for in terms of revenue constituted from the output of the effort (e) multiplied by the output's price (p). The variable cost is accounted for in terms of the square of the effort level exerted. And, there is a fixed investment (F) to enter that market, such that the problem is:

$$MAX\pi(e) = p \bullet e - e^2 - F, p \geq 0, F > 0$$

The optimal effort is a function of the price level ($e^* = p/2$). There is a participation condition (assuming the opportunity cost is normalized to zero) of: $p > 2\sqrt{F}$. So, when the non-risk uncertainty concerns the value of p, then there is *no* optimization possible. It would then be *un*likely that the decision-maker enters this market (i.e., when the value of p is unknowable, as well as its distribution, and the distribution of that distribution, and so on) because there is no guarantee or justified expectation of any positive gain from entering (e.g., given that the price may well lie below the participation condition). If, however, one of the relevant parties has confidence (i.e., subjectively *perceives*, regardless of any objective facts) that the expected price level lies above the participation condition, not only would she rationally enter the market, but she would also offer others the minimum participation price (plus an *epsilon-sized bonus* just above zero) to buy their product. Doing so essentially offers them insurance while also profiting from the expected difference in price without signaling what that level is (so it could not be calculated by others). In that case, she essentially ensures that no Knightian entrepreneurial activity occurs. (Note that we are *not* stating that she is using judgment while she correctly perceives the same level of uncertainty everyone else does, in which case she may be the sole Knightian entrepreneur here; what we are instead saying is that she perceives a lower level of uncertainty than others and so does not need to apply any unusual judgment.)

Thus, this premise of a *universality of a minimum uncertainty level* (i.e., where that uncertainty is a level beyond risky) is dangerous because of its sensitivity to even a minor violation. It severely weakens the robustness of one the most famous theories explaining why entrepreneurs exist. From a theoretical perspective, while it is not unusual to assume that most factors are homogeneous across relevant parties (e.g., in order to simplify a model and focus its analysis), here there is more at stake because of the discontinuity that occurs when even one party differs. It is also troubling that the minimum necessary uncertainty level is singled out for homogeneity when so many factors related to it—like the judgment, confidence, and execution for those facing it—are all assumed *heterogeneous*. It is troubling because judgment—and the confidence in it needed to act—should be linked to the level of uncertainty being perceived. Reducing perceived uncertainty should increase the confidence a decision-maker has in her judgments, especially any that are unique. That link is embodied in experience. Heterogeneity in decision-maker judgment and confidence is based on past experience (Likierman, 2020), specifically here, on experiences with whatever level of uncertainty had been perceived. So, if experience not only links past perception to the current perception of uncertainty but also the current perception of uncertainty to judgment and its confidence, then the idea that differences in judgment can occur without related differences in perception seems unlikely. With that unlikeliness comes the violation of the focal premise of the model. With that unlikeliness also comes the question of whether the model can be tested (i.e., whether it is possible to separate differences in judgment about uncertainty from differences in perception of that uncertainty). And, with that question of premise and testing, comes the suspicion that such a model's prescriptions may be quite weak in the real world.

Further, when the premise is wrong, we get a mislabeling of what Knightian entrepreneurship is. That mislabeling then poses legitimacy dangers for the original model and any model that builds upon it. For academia, holding the original model's premise here means an under-appreciation in our theories of the sensitivity to uncertainty-level perception involved. It may also mean too few studies of decision-making and opportunity-exploiting based on that uncertainty-perception variance that Knight did not appear to consider.

Any practitioner misinterpreting Knight's premise also faces dangers. There would be an under-appreciation of the variance in how people perceive the same event (e.g., Sjöberg, 2000), including in how they delineate risk from *beyond risk*, and that could lead to mistakes in how the practitioner predicts how rivals, customers and others will react to uncertainty-related problems. When the practitioner perceives non-risk uncertainty while others perceive only risk, she will miss out on using those others to insure what she believes is uninsurable (when she follows Knight). On the other hand, when she perceives only risk while others perceive non-risk uncertainty, she is likely to be exploited as an insurer for those others (when she follows Knight). In either case, following Knight's premise may be very costly.

The Implication Danger

Knight's (1921) story links non-risk uncertainty directly to entrepreneurial activity, doing so with the primary logical implication that if some non-risk uncertainty is necessary to induce entrepreneurial activity, then *more of it will induce greater activity*. The *more* of it refers to both quantity (i.e., more decisions or markets involving non-risk uncertainty) and quality (i.e., higher levels of that uncertainty). Similarly, the *greater* activity refers to both greater quantity (i.e., more entrepreneurs because more markets have the necessary uncertainty level or because any one market involves more uncertainties than one venture can exploit) and quality (i.e., better performance for the entrepreneur in markets that are providing wider or deeper uncertainty-related opportunities to exploit). This implication is based in the text of Knight's (1921) book: he speaks to the larger profits that can be made when greater uncertainties exist in the markets that lack rivals with similar uncertainty-bearing capabilities (p. 230) as the: '*...importance of uncertainty as a factor interfering with the perfect workings of competition...*'. He also speaks to diminishing positive returns to entrepreneurship as being a function of uncertainty: (p. 286), as: '*The question of diminishing returns from entrepreneurship is really a matter of the amount of uncertainty present*'. (Note that diminishing returns can only occur when returns were positive and at levels high enough to measure material reductions.) And, prior to this, he commits to the linkage of uncertainty to income (p. 232) as: '*this true uncertainty ... accounts for the peculiar income of the entrepreneur*'.

The danger arising from this implication is that we know uncertainty has costs, even for Knightian entrepreneurs. Knight (1921) even acknowledges—in a brief concession—that some of his entrepreneurs do fail because their judgment is wrong, their confidence is misplaced, or they are just unlucky. But, the most detailed and common Knightian story does *not* sufficiently reflect upon those failures, nor does it explicitly account for the other negative effects on the windfall-like incomes of the initially luckier entrepreneurs. It is inaccurate, theoretically, to concentrate a model on only the good side of a factor, especially when (even in 1921) the bad sides were known, or at least suspected. For example, it was and remains known that uncertainties have negative effects on even the performance of a Knightian entrepreneur (e.g., by suppressing demand from uncertainty-averse consumers). Not acknowledging that the kind of positive logical relationship that Knight implies between uncertainty and entrepreneurial outcomes is actually likely inaccurate (because it is incomplete) is dangerous. It is dangerous because holding to such relationships ensures that entrepreneurial activity—in terms of level and performance—will not be properly understood in terms of its complex association with uncertainty (e.g., in the field and in empirical studies). We may miss out on studying the interdependencies of the positive and negative effects of uncertainties, perhaps moderated by who the entrepreneur is, and which opportunities are involved. We may miss out on better specifying when entrepreneurial activity should actually arise and what policies there can be that decrease the linked negative effects of uncertainty. At the very least, any theoretical work that builds upon such a questionable implication stands on shaky ground and may damage the legitimacy of the fields it is contributing to.

The practical dangers arising from the overly-positive implication of Knight are even more stark. We know that real-world behaviors are adversely affected by uncertainty. For example, experiments have proven that risk-aversion and ambiguity-aversion are real and involve significant premia that reduce the efficiency of economic transactions and markets (e.g., Becker & Brownson, 1964). We have even seen the devastation that the multi-dimensionality of uncertainty linked to the recent Covid pandemic has had on the newer, smaller—often considered more entrepreneurial—ventures compared to more diversified, or more traditional corporations (e.g., Cui et al., 2023). In this light, the practical implication of Knight's linkage of uncertainty with entrepreneurial activity and performance seems naïve (if not myopic) at best, and unfortunately dangerous at worst.[9] Interpreting Knight as truth about how uncertainty is linked to entrepreneurship will reduce the likelihood of better uncertainty-related opportunity outcomes in the field, and any policy based on those relationships will not work as expected (likely

---

[9] Further, while an entrepreneur may have superior judgment about demand uncertainty, that is no guarantee of superior judgment about the uncertainties over competition, regulation, technology, trends and so on. The uncertainty needed to provide entrepreneurial opportunities in the real world rarely entails only one dimension, yet it is treated that way in Knight (1921), making its dangers *un*likely to be fully appreciated by practitioners relying on that model.

under-performing because it does not account for important negative effects).

The Definition Danger

Knight's (1921) story is famous for its delineation of risk from uncertainty; however, its actual definition of that non-risk uncertainty is problematic due to its lack of crispness (e.g., Spender, 2006). The *under-definition* leads to multiple dangers: First, there are dangers that arise because there are actually many types of non-risk uncertainty that meet Knight's definition (i.e., of being uninsurable, unpredictable, and unoptimizable).[10] But, only some of these types matter; and so, if these are confused with ones that do not matter, then damage is likely. For example, even under non-risk uncertainty some problems may only be trivially non-optimizable (e.g., when the unknown's distribution is bounded by a narrow, but still profitable, range) while others can pose an existential threat (e.g., because the range of payoffs may include bankruptcy-level losses). Second, there are dangers that arise because the nature of the unknowableness of the focal uncertain factor lacks critical clarity. For example, when the unknowable is confused with the unknown-but-knowable, it can jeopardize venture performance (i.e., in terms of missing out on uncertainty reduction or spending too much on trying to reduce the irreducible).

The lack of clarity arises in Knight's (1921) work because he mixes theoretical and practical concerns regarding how *unknowableness* can be dealt with. In theory, non-risk uncertainty is meant to be borne *as is* by entrepreneurs who have (or believe they have) better judgment when facing what they perceive is unknowable. That unknowableness must be irreducible prior to when the strategic decision must be made (Ramoglou, 2021) in Knight's model. And, when the decision is right as that uncertainty is borne, the entrepreneur enjoys super-normal rents. However, and unfortunately, Knight also describes five other ways to *deal with* non-risk

---

[10] For example, the focal unknown may involve the set of possible outcome states, or the set of possible actions, or the set of possible rivals, or the payoffs of those actions in those states, or the distributions of the probabilities of the outcomes occurring, or combinations of these. Each type can entail a different approach or judgment; dealing with an incomplete set of (input) factors should differ from dealing with an unknown distribution of possible outcomes. And that is dangerous because the types can have different impacts on decisions (e.g., relating to their timing and level of commitment).

uncertainty where each of those ways transforms the *ex ante* unknown it into something (more) insurable or optimizable. These are practical approaches where the uncertainty is *not* borne, but rather is addressed through standard operating procedures where the expected outcome is in the form of normal rents.

The dangers to the field arising from the under-definition of Knight's uncertainty are twofold: First, without a proper typology of the possible non-risk uncertainties, the term *Knightian uncertainty* involves too coarse a basis from which to build new theory. Without the provision of the full problem context—including the specific variant of non-risk uncertainty—any potential approaches to non-optimizable problems cannot be properly analyzed, let alone prescribed, with any legitimacy. For example, approaches for handling choice-option uncertainty differs from handling outcome-set uncertainty (e.g., Packard et al., 2017). Such differences in unknowns related to choices, outputs, probabilities and payoffs matter. For example, one unknown but bounded probability can often be dealt with in a decision; but, one unknown outcome or one (relatively unbounded) payoff that could occur for any choice theoretically cannot be dealt with. Second, without a clear delineation of the character of the unknowableness involved—specifically whether it is *unknown-but-knowable* or not—the confusion over what *Knightian entrepreneurs* actually are (i.e., those who bear the unknowable unknowns) will continue. They will be mistaken for entrepreneurs that, as part of their standard operating procedures, are only better at reducing a given unknown to something more known. That leads to mis-categorization, and the subsequent mistaken theorizing and testing that comes from it (e.g., to the point of making mistakes in prescriptions, investments, and empirical investigations).

The practical dangers arising from the under-definition are also twofold: The primary practical danger results from a lack of a proper typology of non-risk uncertainties. Without that typology, it is not possible for practitioners to study (in the field) which heuristics are effective against each type, nor is it possible to provide type-specific prescriptions from data, experience or theory to apply in the field. The second danger is that not having a clear delineation of unknowability is likely to result in mistakes involving treating unknowables as knowables and vice versa. In the real world, the former is likely to involve decision-makers trying to seek more information (e.g., through experimentation with the market), while the latter is likely to involve avoidance of the problem, or waiting it out, or retaining flexibility to respond to the outcome; with the respective dangers being in the forms of wasted effort and overconfidence, and of a wasted opportunity to gather the information to make a better proactive decision.

DISCUSSION

Misinterpreting Knight's (1921) model poses dangers: It should not be interpreted as a robust theory of entrepreneurship or of strategic decision-making under uncertainty, but instead as a model based on a knife's edge premise over the shared minimum level of non-risk uncertainty perceived. It should not be interpreted as describing a simple positive relationship between non-risk uncertainty and entrepreneurial activity (or performance) because, in both the academic and practical worlds, uncertainty's effects are complex and most often negative (Taleb, 2012). And, it should not be interpreted as clearly delineating all non-risk uncertainties in a useful manner, given there are many types of those uncertainties that should be addressed differently. All together, such potential dangers weaken Knight's contribution to today's understanding of entrepreneurial and strategically uncertain phenomena; but, that is not properly recognized by many who continue to cite it and build upon it. Such misinterpretations endanger both precise modeling and in-the-field testing, in addition to the subsequent practical prescriptions that could arise from each.

Reconsidering the premise danger, we know that a universally perceived minimum level of non-risk uncertainty for any focal problem is unlikely in the real world. We know from research that risk perception varies among business people (e.g., Mitchell, 1995). Similarly, we also know that uncertainty perception varies significantly across real decision-makers, including entrepreneurs, with differences in perceived uncertainty levels correlated with many factors, including those associated with the individual, the organization, and the community (e.g., Chawla et al., 2012; Downey & Slocum, 1975; Elenkov, 1997). Such findings are likely to extend to the perception of any critical level of non-risk uncertainty, ruining the necessary condition for *Knightian entrepreneurship* to exist. However, such heterogeneity in uncertainty perception could be exploited by policy-makers by making it easier for the relevant insurance-type markets to exist, so that those seeing less uncertainty can reduce it for those who see more, to the advantage of all. By adhering to Knight, however, that won't be done. Nor will studying what it means to bear perceived uncertainty (e.g., psychologically) so that those who do so can be better understood and compensated (Dimov, 2018).

Reconsidering the implication dangers, we know that increases in the quality and quantity of real non-risk uncertainty are likely to work *against* real venture performance regardless of the potential for new opportunities it creates. For example, a high level of perceived non-risk uncertainty will delay if not decrease demand. Such effects strain the cash flows of most ventures. Further, widespread non-risk uncertainty caused by such events as the pandemic do more than cause decision-making hesitation and cash-flow anxiety to small business entrepreneurs; they can lead to strategic mistakes (Knight, 1921), ones that are existential in such contexts, and understood as such by entrepreneurs. Based on the psychological and behavioral economics research (e.g., Ellsberg, 1961; Kahneman & Tversky, 1979), common forms of uncertainty aversion will cause real entrepreneurs will pull back from investments, reducing even the future performance of their ventures. Added to those reactions, there are often regulatory restrictions on operations, hours, and on capacity, that all harm rather than help especially the new and small ventures. The negative consequences of increased uncertainty—that Knight fails to properly account for—squarely implies there exists an important role for government in reducing the perception, if not the real effects, of widespread uncertainties faced by the (entrepreneurial) small business sector. Real policy should not rely on Knight (1921).

Reconsidering the definitional dangers, we know that it is unlikely that real decision-makers delineate among the various types of non-risk uncertainty, let alone whether they treat each type differently. Questions over who should be responsible for perceiving the uncertainty level or type, how the choice is made whether it needs to be dealt with, and what the sequence is of how to do so, all need to be explored. In the real world, Knight's model has little to say in answering those questions. In following it, we miss out on important avenues for research, for practice and for policy-making.

The implication is that policy-makers have a mandate—especially post-Covid—to fund such research, first in lab studies (where the types and amounts of uncertainties can be better controlled to see if those make a difference to perceptions and behaviors) and second, in the field (to see how those differences translate into reality).[11] That research should provide a better basis for helping economic actors to perceive uncertainty, and then to build better toolkits and expertise for applying those tools when Knight's non-risk uncertainties confront them. Rather than relying on simple interpretations of Knight (and his version of uncertainty), we as scholars of entrepreneurship and strategic management and decision-making need to confront the limitations and dangers of that model and move forward, and we hope that this supplement has provided a basis for so doing.

References

Abbott, J. (2005). Understanding and managing the unknown: The nature of uncertainty in planning. *Journal of Planning Education and Research, 24*(3), 237–251.

Adobor, H. (2006). Optimal trust? Uncertainty as a determinant and limit to trust in inter-firm alliances. *Leadership & Organization Development Journal, 27*(7), 537–553.

Aggarwal, D., & Mohanty, P. (2022). Influence of imprecise information on risk and ambiguity preferences: Experimental evidence. *Managerial and Decision Economics, 43*(4), 1025–1038.

Alvarez, S., Afuah, A., & Gibson, C. (2018). Editors' comments: Should management theories take uncertainty seriously? *Academy of Management Review, 43*(2), 169–172.

Arend, R. J. (2015). *Wicked entrepreneurship: Defining the basics of entreponerology*. Springer.

Arend, R. J. (2020). Strategic decision-making under ambiguity: A new problem space and a proposed optimization approach. *Business Research, 13*(3), 1231–1251.

Baker, S. R., Bloom, N., & Davis, S. J. (2016). Measuring economic policy uncertainty. *The Quarterly Journal of Economics, 131*(4), 1593–1636.

---

[11] Our conclusions are made with the understanding that Knight's is only one theory of entrepreneurial activity. Regardless, its misinterpretations don't help the field; they impede better theorizing and better decision-making. Having a century-old model that can be so easily misinterpreted is not good for the entrepreneurship field because, if it can be dangerous to build on theoretical models like Knight's (1921), then our lack of action on identifying and addressing its mis-interpretations inevitably means that we are likely to allow such dangerous outcomes to occur for any other theory. And, when that happens, then we really have no theory.

Bammer, G., & Smithson, M. (2008). Understanding uncertainty. *Integration Insights, 7*(1), 1–7.
Bar-Anan, Y., Wilson, T. D., & Gilbert, D. T. (2009). The feeling of uncertainty intensifies affective reactions. *Emotion, 9*(1), 123–127.
Barney, J. B. (2002). *Gaining and sustaining competitive advantage.* Prentice-Hall.
Becker, S. W., & Brownson, F. O. (1964). What price ambiguity? Or the role of ambiguity in decision-making. *Journal of Political Economy, 72*(1), 62–73.
Ben-Haim, Y. (2001, June). Decision trade-offs under severe info-gap uncertainty. *ISIPTA,* 32–39.
Berlyne, D. E. (1960). *Conflict, arousal, and curiosity.* McGraw-Hill.
Boyd, B. K., & Fulk, J. (1996). Executive scanning and perceived uncertainty: A multidimensional model. *Journal of Management, 22*(1), 1–21.
Boyd, W. (2012). Genealogies of risk: Searching for safety, 1930s–1970s. *Ecology Law Quarterly, 39,* 895–987.
Bradley, R., & Drechsler, M. (2014). Types of uncertainty. *Erkenntnis, 79,* 1225–1248.
Bradley, R., & Steele, K. (2015). Making climate decisions. *Philosophy Compass, 10*(11), 799–810.
Brandenburger, A. M., & Nalebuff, B. J. (1996). *Co-opetition.* Harvard Business School Press.
Brod, G., Hasselhorn, M., & Bunge, S. A. (2018). When generating a prediction boosts learning: The element of surprise. *Learning and Instruction, 55,* 22–31.
Bruner, J. S., & Postman, L. (1949). On the perception of incongruity: A paradigm. *Journal of Personality, 18*(2), 206–223.
Buchko, A. A. (1994). Conceptualization and measurement of environmental uncertainty: An assessment of the Miles and Snow perceived environmental uncertainty scale. *The Academy of Management Journal, 37*(2), 410–425.
Camerer, C. (1994). Individual decision making. In J. Kagel & A. Roth (Eds.), *Handbook of experimental economics.* Princeton University Press.
Camerer, C., & Weber, M. (1992). Recent developments in modeling preferences: Uncertainty and ambiguity. *Journal of Risk and Uncertainty, 5,* 325–370.
Chawla, C., Mangaliso, M., Knipes, B., & Gauthier, J. (2012). Antecedents and implications of uncertainty in management: A historical perspective. *Journal of Management History, 18*(2), 200–218.
Cohen, L. J. (1977). *The probable and the provable.* Clarendon.
Cohen, M., & Jaffray, J.-Y. (1980). Rational behavior under complete ignorance. *Econometrica, 48*(5), 1281–1299.
Conrath, D. W. (1967). Organizational decision making behavior under varying conditions of uncertainty. *Management Science, 13*(8), B-487.

Costikyan, G. (2013). *Uncertainty in games*. MIT Press.
Courtney, H. (2001). *20/20 Foresight: Crafting strategy in an uncertain world*. Harvard Business School Press.
Courtney, H. (2003). Decision-driven scenarios for assessing four levels of uncertainty. *Strategy & Leadership, 31*(1), 14–22.
Courtney, H., Lovallo, D., & Clarke, C. (2013). Deciding how to decide. *Harvard Business Review, 91*(11), 62–70.
Cui, L., Wu, H., Wu, L., Kumar, A., & Tan, K. H. (2023). Investigating the relationship between digital technologies, supply chain integration and firm resilience in the context of COVID-19. *Annals of Operations Research, 327*(2), 825–853.
Daft, R. L., & Macintosh, N. B. (1981). A tentative exploration into the amount and equivocality of information processing in organizational work units. *Administrative Science Quarterly, 26*(2), 207–224.
Dattée, B., Alexy, O., & Autio, E. (2018). Maneuvering in poor visibility: How firms play the ecosystem game when uncertainty is high. *Academy of Management Journal, 61*(2), 466–498.
Davidsson, P. (2015). Entrepreneurial opportunities and the entrepreneurship nexus: A re-conceptualization. *Journal of Business Venturing, 30*(5), 674–695.
Dekel, E., Lipman, B. L., & Rustichini, A. (1998). Recent developments in modeling unforeseen contingencies. *European Economic Review, 42*(3–5), 523–542.
Dequech, D. (1999). Expectations and confidence under uncertainty. *Journal of Post Keynesian Economics, 21*(3), 415–430.
Dequech, D. (2003). Uncertainty and economic sociology: A preliminary discussion. *American Journal of Economics and Sociology, 62*(3), 509–532.
Dequech, D. (2011). Uncertainty: A typology and refinements of existing concepts. *Journal of Economic Issues, 45*(3), 621–640.
Dewey, J. (1915). The logic of judgements of practice. *Journal of Philosophy, 12*(1), 505–510.
Dimov, D. (2018). Uncertainty under entrepreneurship. In A. Fayolle, S. Ramoglou, M. Karatas-Ozkan, & K. Nicolopoulou (Eds.), *Philosophical reflexivity and entrepreneurship research* (pp 184–196). Routledge.
Dimov, D. (2007a). Beyond the single-person, single-insight attribution in understanding entrepreneurial opportunities. *Entrepreneurship Theory and Practice, 31*, 713–731.
Dimov, D. (2007b). From opportunity insight to opportunity intention: The importance of person-situation learning match. *Entrepreneurship Theory and Practice, 31*, 561–583.
Dimov, D. (2016). Toward a design science of entrepreneurship. In *Models of start-up thinking and action: Theoretical, empirical and pedagogical approaches* (Vol. 18, pp. 1–31). Emerald Group Publishing Limited.

Dosi, G., & Egidi, M. (1991). Substantive and procedural uncertainty: An exploration of economic behaviours in changing environments. *Journal of Evolutionary Economics, 1,* 145–168.

Downey, H. K., & Slocum, J. W. (1975). Uncertainty: Measures, research, and sources of variation. *Academy of Management Journal, 18*(3), 562–578.

Downey, H. K., Hellriegel, D., & Slocum, J. W., Jr. (1975). Environmental uncertainty: The construct and its application. *Administrative Science Quarterly, 20,* 613–629.

Du, N., & Budescu, D. V. (2005). The effects of imprecise probabilities and outcomes in evaluating investment options. *Management Science, 51*(12), 1791–1803.

Duncan, R. B. (1972). Characteristics of organizational environments and perceived environmental uncertainty. *Administrative Science Quarterly, 17*(3), 313–327.

Edwards, W. (1965). Optimal strategies for seeking information: Models for statistics, choice reaction times, and human information processing. *Journal of Mathematical Psychology, 2*(2), 312–329.

Einhorn, H. J., & Hogarth, R. M. (1986). Decision making under ambiguity. *Journal of Business, 59*(4), S225–S250.

Einhorn, H. J., & Hogarth, R. M. (1988). Decision making under ambiguity: A note. In *Risk, decision and rationality* (pp. 327–336). Springer Netherlands.

Elenkov, D. S. (1997). Strategic uncertainty and environmental scanning: The case for institutional influences on scanning behavior. *Strategic Management Journal, 18*(4), 287–302.

Ellsberg, D. (1961). Risk, ambiguity, and the Savage axioms. *The Quarterly Journal of Economics, 75*(4), 643–669.

Etner, J., Jeleva, M., & Tallon, J. M. (2012). Decision theory under ambiguity. *Journal of Economic Surveys, 26*(2), 234–270.

Faber, M., Manstetten, R., & Proops, J. L. (1992). Humankind and the environment: An anatomy of surprise and ignorance. *Environmental Values, 1*(3), 217–241.

Faulkner, P., Feduzi, A., & Runde, J. (2017). Unknowns, Black Swans and the risk/uncertainty distinction. *Cambridge Journal of Economics, 41,* 1279–1302.

Feduzi, A., Faulkner, P., Runde, J., Cabantous, L., & Loch, C. (2021, In press). Heuristic methods for updating small world representations in strategic situations of Knightian uncertainty. *Academy of Management Review, 47*(3), 402–424.

Feduzi, A., Runde, J., & Zappia, C. (2012). De Finetti on the insurance of risks and uncertainties. *The British Journal for the Philosophy of Science, 63*(2), 329–356.

Fontana, G., & Gerrard, B. (2004). A post Keynesian theory of decision making under uncertainty. *Journal of Economic Psychology, 25*(5), 619–637.

Foss, K., Foss, N. J., & Klein, P. G. (2007). Original and derived judgment: An entrepreneurial theory of economic organization. *Organization Studies, 28*(12), 1893–1912.

Garner, W. R. (1962). *Uncertainty and structure as psychological concepts.* Wiley.

Ghirardato, P. (2001). Coping with ignorance: Unforeseen contingencies and non-additive uncertainty. *Economic Theory, 17,* 247–276.

Glycopantis, D., & Muir, A. (2008). Nash equilibria with Knightian uncertainty: The case of capacities. *Economic Theory, 37,* 147–159.

Graaff, J. de V. (1957). *Theoretical welfare economics.* Cambridge University Press.

Grant, R. M. (1996). Toward a knowledge-based theory of the firm. *Strategic Management Journal, 17*(S2), 109–122.

Griffin, M. A., & Grote, G. (2020). When is more uncertainty better? A model of uncertainty regulation and effectiveness. *Academy of Management Review, 45*(4), 745–765.

Gruber, M., MacMillan, I. C., & Thompson, J. D. (2008). Look before you leap: Market opportunity identification in emerging technology firms. *Management Science, 54*(9), 1652–1665.

Hanany, E., Klibanoff, P., & Mukerji, S. (2020). Incomplete information games with ambiguity averse players. *American Economic Journal: Microeconomics, 12*(2), 135–187.

Hansen, L. P. (2014). Nobel lecture: Uncertainty outside and inside economic models. *Journal of Political Economy, 122*(5), 945–987.

Hansson, S. O. (1994). *Decision theory: A brief introduction* [Department of Philosophy and the History of Technology. Royal Institute of Technology. Stockholm].

Hansson, S. O. (1996). Decision making under great uncertainty. *Philosophy of the Social Sciences, 26*(3), 369–386.

Head, B. W. (2022). *Wicked problems in public policy: Understanding and responding to complex challenges.* Springer Nature.

Hebb, D. O. (1955). Drives and the CNS (conceptual nervous system). *Psychological Review, 62,* 243–254.

Hebert, R. F., & Link, A. N. (1988). *The entrepreneur: Mainstream views and radical critiques* (2nd ed.). Praeger.

Heiner, R. A. (1983). The origin of predictable behavior. *The American Economic Review, 73*(4), 560–595.

Heiner, R. A. (1988). Imperfect decisions, routinized behaviour and intertial technical change. In G. Dosi, C. Freeman, R. Nelson, G. Silverberg, & L. Soete (Eds.), *Technical change and economic theory.* Pinter.

Hertwig, R., & Gigerenzer, G. (1999). The 'conjunction fallacy'revisited: How intelligent inferences look like reasoning errors. *Journal of Behavioral Decision Making, 12*(4), 275–305.

Hertwig, R., Pleskac, T. J., & Pachur, T. (2019). *Taming uncertainty*. MIT Press.

Hickson, D. J., Hinings, C. R., Lee, C. A., Schneck, R. E., & Pennings, J. M. (1971). A strategic contingencies' theory of intraorganizational power. *Administrative Science Quarterly, 16*(2), 216–229.

Hmieleski, K. M., Carr, J. C., & Baron, R. A. (2015). Integrating discovery and creation perspectives of entrepreneurial action: The relative roles of founding CEO human capital, social capital, and psychological capital in contexts of risk versus uncertainty. *Strategic Entrepreneurship Journal, 9*(4), 289–312.

Hoffman, F. O., & Hammonds, J. S. (1994). Propagation of uncertainty in risk assessments: The need to distinguish between uncertainty due to lack of knowledge and uncertainty due to variability. *Risk Analysis, 14*(5), 707–712.

Hogarth, R. M. (1980). *Judgement and choice: The psychology of decision*. Wiley.

Holland, J. H., Holyoak, K. J., Nisbett, R. E., & Thagard, P. R. (1986). *Induction: Processes of inference, learning, and discovery*. MIT Press.

Holmes, T., & Westgren, R. (2020). Carving the nature of uncertainty at its joints. *Academy of Management Review, 45*(4), 869–872.

James, W. (1950). *The principles of psychology*. Dover.

Jonas, E., McGregor, I., Klackl, J., Agroskin, D., Fritsche, I., Holbrook, C., Nash, K., Proulx, T., & Quirin, M. (2014). Threat and defense: From anxiety to approach. *Advances in Experimental Social Psychology, 49*, 219–286.

Kagan, J. (1972). Motives and development. *Journal of Personality and Social Psychology, 22*, 51–66.

Kahneman, D., & Tversky, A. (1979). Prospect theory. *Econometrica, 47*, 263–292.

Kapoor, R., & Adner, R. (2012). What firms make vs. what they know: How firms' production and knowledge boundaries affect competitive advantage in the face of technological change. *Organization Science, 23*(5), 1227–1248.

Kauffeldt, T. F. (2015). *Games with exogenous uncertainty played by" Knightian" players* [dev.gtcenter.org].

Kaur, N., & Dasgupta, C. (2018). Types of uncertainty and collaborative uncertainty management strategies evidenced during the engineering design process. In *International conference on computers in education* (pp. 175–180).

Kay, J. A., & King, M. A. (2020). *Radical uncertainty*. Bridge Street Press.

Khodadad Hosseini, S. H., Hamidizadeh, M. R., Hoseini, S. M., & Lashkarboloki, M. (2011). Designing the process model of robust strategy under uncertainty. *Journal of Strategic Management Studies, 2*(5), 83–109.

Kirzner, I. M. (1973). *Competition and entrepreneurship*. University of Chicago Press.

Knight, E., Daymond, J., & Paroutis, S. (2020). Design-led strategy: How to bring design thinking into the art of strategic management. *California Management Review, 62*(2), 30–52.

Knudsen, T., & Levinthal, D. A. (2007). Two faces of search: Alternative generation and alternative evaluation. *Organization Science*, *18*, 39–54.
Korhonen, P. J., & Wallenius, J. (2020). Different paradigms of decision-making. In *Making better decisions: Balancing conflicting criteria* (pp. 1–4). Springer.
Kuhlthau, C. C. (1991). Inside the search process: Information seeking from the user's perspective. *Journal of the American Society for Information Science*, *42*(5), 361–371.
Lachmann, L. M. (1976). From Mises to Shackle: An essay on Austrian economics and the kaleidic society. *Journal of Economic Literature*, *14*(1), 54–62.
Lampert, C. M., Kim, M., & Polidoro, F., Jr. (2020). Branching and anchoring: Complementary asset configurations in conditions of Knightian uncertainty. *Academy of Management Review*, *45*(4), 847–868.
Lee, B., & Yoo, B. (2007). What prevents electronic lemon markets? *Journal of Organizational Computing and Electronic Commerce*, *17*(3), 217–246.
Leiblein, M. J., Reuer, J. J., & Zenger, T. (2018). What makes a decision strategic? *Strategy Science*, *3*(4), 558–573.
Levi, I. (1982). Ignorance, probability and rational choice. *Synthese*, *53*(3), 387–417.
Likierman, A. (2020). The elements of good judgment. *Harvard Business Review*, *98*(1), 102–111.
Lipshitz, R., & Strauss, O. (1997). Coping with uncertainty: A naturalistic decision-making analysis. *Organizational Behavior and Human Decision Processes*, *69*(2), 149–163.
Littlechild, S. (1986). Three types of market process. In R. N. Langlois (Ed.), *Economics as a process: Essays in the new institutional economics*. Cambridge University Press.
Luan, S., Reb, J., & Gigerenzer, G. (2019). Ecological rationality: Fast-and-frugal heuristics for managerial decision making under uncertainty. *Academy of Management Journal*, *62*(6), 1735–1759.
Lytras, M. D., & Pouloudi, A. (2006). Towards the development of a novel taxonomy of knowledge management systems from a learning perspective: An integrated approach to learning and knowledge infrastructures. *Journal of Knowledge Management*, *10*(6), 64–80.
Mack, R. P. (1971). *Planning on uncertainty*. Wiley.
MacLeod, W. B., & Pingle, M. (2000). *An experiment on the relative effects of ability, temperament and luck on search with uncertainty* [University of Southern California Law School, Olin Research paper 00-12].
Magnani, G., & Zucchella, A. (2018). Uncertainty in entrepreneurship and management studies: A systematic literature review. *International Journal of Business and Management*, *13*(3), 98–133.

Mandel, T. F., & Wilson, I. (1993). *How companies use scenarios: Practice and prescription* [SRI Business Intelligence Programme Report R822].
March, J. (1991). Exploration and exploitation in organizational learning. *Organization Science, 2,* 71–87.
March, J. C., & Olsen, J. P. (1976). *Ambiguity and choice in organizations.* Universitetsforlaget.
March, J. G., & Simon, H. A. (1958). *Organizations.* Wiley.
March, J. G. (1994). *Primer on decision making: How decisions happen.* Simon and Schuster.
Markowitz, H. M. (1952). Portfolio selection. *Journal of Finance, 7,* 77–91.
McCray, L. E., Oye, K. A., & Petersen, A. C. (2010). Planned adaptation in risk regulation: An initial survey of US environmental, health, and safety regulation. *Technological Forecasting and Social Change, 77*(6), 951–959.
McMullen, J. S., & Kier, A. S. (2016). Trapped by the entrepreneurial mindset: Opportunity seeking and escalation of commitment in the Mount Everest disaster. *Journal of Business Venturing, 31*(6), 663–686.
Medin, D. L., & Schaffer, M. M. (1978). Context theory of classification learning. *Psychological Review, 85*(3), 207–238.
Milgrom, P., & Roberts, J. (1982). Limit pricing and entry under incomplete information: An equilibrium analysis. *Econometrica, 50*(2), 443–459.
Miller, K. D. (2007). Risk and rationality in entrepreneurial processes. *Strategic Entrepreneurship Journal, 1*(1–2), 57–74.
Miller, A. I. (Ed.). (2012). *Sixty-two years of uncertainty: Historical, philosophical, and physical inquiries into the foundations of quantum mechanics* (Vol. 226). Springer Science & Business Media.
Mitchell, V. W. (1995). Organizational risk perception and reduction: A literature review. *British Journal of Management, 6*(2), 115–133.
Mitchell, T. R., & James, L. R. (2001). Building better theory: Time and the specification of when things happen. *Academy of Management Review, 26*(4), 530–547.
Mullins, J. W., & Forlani, D. (2005). Missing the boat or sinking the boat: A study of new venture decision making. *Journal of Business Venturing, 20*(1), 47–69.
Murphy, D. J., & Pinelli, T. E. (1994). NASA/DOD aerospace knowledge diffusion research project [Report 30: Computer-Mediated Communication (CMC) and the communication of technical information in aerospace. Rensselaer Polytechnic Institute Report].
Nosal, J. B., & Ordonez, G. (2016). Uncertainty as commitment. *Journal of Monetary Economics, 80,* 124–140.
O'Donnell, R. (2013). Two post-keynesian approaches to uncertainty and irreducible uncertainty. In G. C. Harcourt & P. Kriesler (Eds.), *The Oxford handbook of post-Keynesian economics* (pp. 121–142). Oxford University Press.

O'Connor, G. C., & Rice, M. P. (2013). A comprehensive model of uncertainty associated with radical innovation. *Journal of Product Innovation Management, 30*, 2–18.

Orhnial, T. (1980). Potential surprise and portfolio theory. *Diskussionsbeiträge-Serie A*.

Packard, M. D., & Clark, B. B. (2020). On the mitigability of uncertainty and the choice between predictive and nonpredictive strategy. *Academy of Management Review, 45*(4), 766–786.

Pfeffer, J., & Salancik, G. R. (1978). *The external control of organizations: A resource dependence perspective*. Harper & Row Publishers.

Popper, S. W., Lempert, R. J., & Bankes, S. C. (2005). Shaping the future. *Scientific American, 292*(4), 66–71.

Posner, R. A. (2004). *Catastrophe: Risk and response*. Oxford University Press.

Potter, K., Rosen, P., & Johnson, Ch. R. (2012). From quantification to visualization: A taxonomy of uncertainty visualization approaches. *Uncertainty Quantification in Scientific Computing IFIP Advances in Information and Communication Technology, 377*, 226–249.

Raiffa, H., & Luce, R. D. (1957). *Games and decisions: Introduction and critical survey*. Wiley.

Ramoglou, S., & Tsang, E. W. (2016). A realist perspective of entrepreneurship: Opportunities as propensities. *Academy of Management Review, 41*(3), 410–434.

Rietveld, C. A., & Hoogendoorn, B. (2022). The mediating role of values in the relationship between religion and entrepreneurship. *Small Business Economics, 58*(3), 1309–1335.

Rindova, V., & Courtney, H. (2020). To shape or adapt: Knowledge problems, epistemologies, and strategic postures under Knightian uncertainty. *Academy of Management Review, 45*(4), 787–807.

Rock, D. (2008). SCARF: A brain-based model for collaborating with and influencing others. *NeuroLeadership Journal, 1*(1), 44–52.

Rouvray, D. H. (1997). The treatment of uncertainty in the sciences. *Endeavour, 21*(4), 154–158.

Runde, J. (1990). Keynesian uncertainty and the weight of arguments. *Economics & Philosophy, 6*(2), 275–292.

Samsami, F., Hosseini, S. H. K., Kordnaeij, A., & Azar, A. (2015). Managing environmental uncertainty: From conceptual review to strategic management point of view. *International Journal of Business and Management, 10*(7), 215–229.

Sargeant, S., & Yoxall, J. (2023). Psychology and spirituality: Reviewing developments in history, method and practice. *Journal of Religion and Health, 62*, 1159–1174.

Schmidt, S. M., & Cummings, L. L. (1976). Organizational environment, differentiation and perceived environmental uncertainty. *Decision Sciences, 7*, 447–467.

Schwarz, N., & Clore, G. L. (1996). Feelings and phenomenal experiences. In E. T. Higgins & A. Kruglanski (Eds.), *Social psychology: Handbook of basic principles* (pp. 433–465). Guilford.

Shackle, G. L. S. (1949). *Expectation in economics*. Cambridge University Press.

Shackle, G. L. S. (1972). Marginalism: The harvest. *History of Political Economy, 4*(2), 587–602.

Shackle, G. L. S. (1979). *Imagination and the nature of choice*. Edinburgh University Press.

Shepherd, D. A., Williams, T. A., & Patzelt, H. (2015). Thinking about entrepreneurial decision making: Review and research agenda. *Journal of Management, 41*(1), 11–46.

Simon, H. A. (1959). Theories of decision-making in economics and behavioral science. *American Economic Review, 49*, 253–283.

Sjöberg, L. (2000). Perceived risk and tampering with nature. *Journal of Risk Research, 3*(4), 353–367.

Spender, J.-C. (1983). The business policy problem and industry recipes. *Advances in Strategic Management, 2*, 211–229.

Stacey, R. D. (1992). *Managing the unknowable: Strategic boundaries between order and chaos in organizations*. Jossey-Bass Publishers.

Sterman, J. D. (1994). Learning in and about complex systems. *System Dynamics Review, 10*(2–3), 291–330.

Stewart, G. (2021, March). *A passion for ignorance? Not knowing the half of it*. AGORA Column.

Sykes, H. B., & Dunham, D. (1995). Critical assumption planning: A practical tool for managing business development risk. *Journal of Business Venturing, 10*(6), 413–424.

Szentkirályi, L. (2020). Luck has nothing to do with it: Prevailing uncertainty and responsibilities of due care. *Ethics, Policy & Environment, 23*(3), 261–280.

Tannert, C., Elvers, H. D., & Jandrig, B. (2007). The ethics of uncertainty: In the light of possible dangers, research becomes a moral duty. *EMBO Reports, 8*(10), 892–896.

Teece, D., & Leih, S. (2016). Uncertainty, innovation, and dynamic capabilities: An introduction. *California Management Review, 58*(4), 5–12.

Teece, D., Peteraf, M., & Leih, S. (2016). Dynamic capabilities and organizational agility: Risk, uncertainty, and strategy in the innovation economy. *California Management Review, 58*(4), 13–35.

Teece, D. J., Pisano, G., & Shuen, A. (1997). Dynamic capabilities and strategic management. *Strategic Management Journal, 18*(7), 509–533.

Townsend, D. M., & Busenitz, L. W. (2015). Turning water into wine? Exploring the role of dynamic capabilities in early-stage capitalization processes. *Journal of Business Venturing, 30*(2), 292–306.

Townsend, D. M., Hunt, R. A., Beal, D. J., & Hyeong Jin, J. (2020). Venturing into the unknown: A meta-analytic assessment of uncertainty in entrepreneurship research. *Academy of Management Proceedings, 2020*(1), 17318.

von Mises, L. (1949). *Human action: A treatise on economics* [Ludwig von Mises Institute, www.mises.org/humanaction.asp].

Walker, G., & Weber, D. (1987). Supplier competition, uncertainty, and make-or-buy decisions. *Academy of Management Journal, 30*(3), 589–596.

Walker, W. E., Harremoës, P., Rotmans, J., Van Der Sluijs, J. P., Van Asselt, M. B., Janssen, P., & Krayer von Krauss, M. P. (2003). Defining uncertainty: A conceptual basis for uncertainty management in model-based decision support. *Integrated Assessment, 4*(1), 5–17.

Walker, W. E., Lempert, R, J., & Kwakkel, J. H. (2013). Deep uncertainty, entry. In S. Gass & M. C. Fu (Eds.), *Encyclopedia of operations research and management science* (pp. 395–402). (3rd ed.). Springer.

Waterman, R. H., Jr. (1990). *Adhocracy: The power to change*. Whittle Direct Books.

Weick, K. E. (1995). *Sensemaking in organizations*. Sage.

Wheeler, J. A. (1992, December). Quoted in *Scientific American*, p. 20.

Williamson, O. E. (1985). *The economic institutions of capitalism*. Free Press.

Wright, M., & Phan, P. (2017). AMP articles in an uncertain new world. *Academy of Management Perspectives, 31*, 1–3.

Yager, R. R. (1999). A game-theoretic approach to decision making under uncertainty. *Intelligent Systems in Accounting, Finance & Management, 8*(2), 131–143.

Zack, M. (1999). Developing a knowledge strategy. *California Management Review, 41*(3), 125–145.

CHAPTER 18

Best Treatments and Approaches to Uncertainty Types (in Decision-Making)

Introduction to Uncertainty Treatment

To improve decision-making under uncertainty, it has been important to define uncertainty, to understand its span, sources, and impacts, and then to categorize its types, all *prior* to considering how to address it. This chapter is about addressing those main uncertainty types. That entails first treating the unknowns that can be treated—to make them known so that the decision can be optimized. The first part of this chapter considers the variety of treatments available to do that, based on how controllable the context is, and how more known the unknown can be made. What is left are the untreatable uncertainties. Besides simply bearing these, we consider *treating the problem rather than the uncertainties* in order to make progress. The second part of this chapter draws on game theory as an analogy for how to approach these situations. With the treatments suggested in the literature covered, we use the third part of the chapter to consider several issues in the actual problem-processing surrounding the decision-making steps (e.g., accounting for costs, task assignments, and so on) to complete the analysis of how decision-making can be improved when it is vexed by uncertainty.

In the first part of this chapter, we also critique the many ways that apply to the 'unknowns that are feasibly knowable prior to having to make the focal decision' (i.e., the uncertainties we categorized as treatable using the primary typology of the previous chapter). We do *not* break these treatments further down into which apply best at different stages of the decision process (to comply with the secondary typology), however, for two reasons: The first reason is that any one treatment applies (without further specification) to *many* types of unknowns (i.e., to unknowns at different decision steps); for example, experimentation could be used to make known an unknown that embodies a contextual fact, or a possible outcome, or its probability, or a constraint. The second reason is that there are other dimensions—ones involving the characteristics of existing treatments themselves—that provide a more natural way to organize those treatments. Thus, we categorize treatments by those characteristics here (rather than by which specific secondary and tertiary types of uncertainty they apply to).

In the second part of this chapter, we describe several ways to begin to address the untreatable uncertainties. Recall that there are three types of untreatable uncertainties identified in the previous chapter: The first type are the surprises—the unknown unknowns (i.e., the unknown, unknowable factors). Theoretically, there is absolutely nothing that can be done to address them (by definition). An organization may do things to make its people 'feel better' about them by focusing on problems where historically fewer surprises have occurred, or by trying to prepare (for the unpreparable) by building agility in the organization (e.g., reducing the hierarchy) (Kay & King, 2020). (But, theoretically, the surprise could be something that disadvantages such structures). The second type are the infeasible-to-make-knowable unknown values (of known factor characteristics). The obvious approach is to work to make the infeasibleness (more) feasible in the future, assuming that the firm believes it will see such unknowns again, and that the costs and efforts for so doing are worth the possible future benefits. Doing so may entail technical adjustments, investments in R&D, improving access to financial resources, and so on. The third type are the (presently) unknowable values (of known factor characteristics). This type will be our focus for the second part of this chapter—a focus on altering the problem rather than on trying to uncover the unknowable values—for the betterment of the organization and of the decision-maker. Figure 18.1 depicts the flowchart of treatments and approaches described in this chapter.

Throughout this chapter, we will call out the mistakes of the previous literature (and there are many) regarding the past proposed 'solutions' to decision-making under uncertainty. The biggest problem in that literature, especially recently, and especially in business, and there, especially in the management and entrepreneurship theorizing, has been work that, intentionally or not, confuses the untreatable with the treatable, giving their audiences the false hope that something 'magical' can be done to optimize the problem. It cannot, and it has been a dishonest and anti-academic exercise suggesting otherwise.

Prior to considering the myriad of treatments that have been proposed in the extensive literature involving uncertainty, it is useful to remember two facts: First, *there are no general solutions to uncertainty*, because there are many different uncertainty types, some of which are untreatable by definition. Second, *decision-making under uncertainty is unavoidable*; every decision, especially the strategic and novel ones, involves incomplete information. Yet, we survive nonetheless. Why? Because for most decisions the stakes are low and we believe that we know enough (we believe we know enough because most decisions appear sufficiently similar to those in the past). Also, for many decisions, the big unknowns have

Treatable Uncertainties	Bucket#	Treatment Description	Characteristics of Treatment			
			.fully knowable value	.not controlled value	.real values	.non-partnered
Treat the Treatable to 'Optimize' the Decision	1	...*uncovering the unknown value via* discovery, search & monitoring	✓	✓	✓	✓
	2	...*uncovering the unknown value via* experimentation, experience, analysis & modeling	✓	✓	✓	✓
	3	...*uncovering the unknown value via* influencing the value through social construction & preemption	✓	controllable value	✓	✓
	4	...*uncovering the unknown value via* scenarios & simulations	✓	✓	possible values	✓
	5	...*adapting to the range of possible values* via flexibility, options & robustness	partially knowable value (range known)	✓	✓	✓
	6	...*covering to the range of possible values* via burden-sharing & insurance, or through diversification	partially knowable value (range known)	✓	✓	partnered

Untreatable Uncertainties	Bucket#	Approach Description	Variants of Approach/ Comments
Bear It, or Alter the Given Problem to Improve the Situation	A1	...bear the untreatable uncertainty as given	/aka Knightian Judgment
	A2		...applying heuristics
			...acting 'as if' unknowns were known (usually using an estimate)
		...change the (absolute) goal, and optimize that altered decision problem by...	...deciding based only on knowns
			...altering the knowns to reduce possible harms
			...modeling what is known
			...applying information-gap theory
	A2b	...change the goal to a relative one	/use rival moves to match or outplay them
	A3		...play 'no regrets'/ conservative moves
			...follow standard procedures, routines or norms
		...change the focal entity (to the decision-maker[s])	...express dissatisfaction and doubt
			...ignore, suppress and deny the uncertainty
			...try to delay the decision
			...try to avoid the decision or uncertainty
	A4	...for 'games', alter the game	/cooperate with others to remove their uncertainty for mutual benefit

Fig. 18.1 Flowchart of triaging uncertainty

been stripped away through institutionalization—by putting them in the form of contracts (with residual rights), by regulating actions, by creating behavioral customs, by creating products that are shielded from contextual extremes (e.g., by their casings), and by providing forms of insurance. But, such safety mechanisms and familiarities can have some unfortunate consequences. For example, they may make uncertainties that creep up on us or have delayed outcomes—have a 'boiling frog' effect—appear dangerously unimportant until it is too late (e.g., global warming). Or, they may produce an overly optimistic perspective, one that focuses on what uncertainty can and does sometimes produce when borne—e.g., successful entrepreneurs and innovative products. Perhaps it is better to strike a balance, with an equal focus on the pain, paralysis, confusion and failure that uncertainty (more) often generates in business, in society, and in our lives.

One last note prior to delving into the treatments and approaches for dealing with various uncertainties: There exists an extensive literature on many of these treatments and approaches (but one that hasn't been organized, described, and bounded in any way, let alone in the logical way we lay out below). So, other books exist that are specific to search, simulation, scenario-planning, and so on (let alone courses, exercises, and consultants for these methods). In fact, now there are even AI (artificial intelligence) resources available to provide detailed and extensive new search capabilities (with as-yet-proven accuracy in many circumstances). We, obviously, cannot cover the details of such treatments and techniques in one chapter. So, we describe them briefly with some highlights, especially regarding their limitations, instead.

Part One—Treating the Treatable Uncertainties

The existing literature suggests a wide variety of treatments for making the (feasibly) knowable unknowns known. It is useful to categorize these treatments in order to better understand their differences. We categorize them based on four characteristics—where each characteristic is a dichotomous assumption: The first concerns *the assumption of knowability*—either the unknown is fully knowable or it is partially but-significantly knowable (i.e., useful actions can be taken based on the reduction of the unknownness, for example, because it has been reduced to risk). The second concerns *the assumption of control*—either the firm can control the decision problem content to make the unknown known or it cannot. The third concerns *the assumption of reality*—either the unknown's value exists now in the real world or it only exists as a possibility in the hypothetical world. The fourth concerns *the assumption of independence*—either the decision is being dealt with by the firm alone (as is) or it is not (e.g., as independent partners are involved in treating the unknown). This set of characteristics provides a solid categorization of the majority of the existing treatments into *six* big 'buckets':

> The first bucket involves fully knowable, non-controllable, real unknowns, using non-partnered approaches. These passive-to-somewhat-active treatments include search, discovery, and observation (as ways to uncover the value of the unknown). This bucket concerns information-gathering techniques that flesh out the problem to determine the unknown value.

The second bucket also involves fully knowable, non-controllable, real unknowns, using non-partnered approaches. The difference to the first bucket is that these treatments are much more active (or interactive with the context) in practice, and include experimentation, analysis, and modeling. This bucket concerns scientific 'prodding' techniques that flesh out the problem to determine the unknown value.

The third bucket involves fully knowable, *controllable*, real unknowns, using partly non-partnered approaches. These treatments entail socially or physically influencing the problem context in order to select a value for the unknown. Two big assumptions are involved: that context is malleable; and, that somehow this firm has more control over it than others.[1] This bucket concerns control techniques to make the unknown known.

The fourth bucket involves fully knowable, non-controllable, *hypothetical unknowns*, using non-partnered approaches. These treatments, including simulations and scenario-planning, uncover the unknown's possible values under different conditions so that, at a minimum, an expected value for the unknown can be calculated based on the conditions faced. This bucket concerns structured imagination techniques that fill out the initially incomplete problem description in order to make the unknown known.

The fifth bucket involves *partially knowable*, non-controllable, real unknowns, using non-partnered approaches. These treatments include preparations for change, the creation of options, and flexibility. This bucket concerns techniques that allow the firm to be ready for the limited range (and known distribution) of (newly known) values that the unknown can take.

---

[1] Note that the assumption of context malleability is insufficient on its own to support the use of these treatments; the added (and 'big') assumption of this focal firm having more control than rival entities (e.g., competitors, consumers, regulators, and others) is also necessary. Modeling why, how, when, and where this focal firm does have that greater control is beyond the scope of this chapter (and this book). It is left for future work (given it involves many further assumptions about the characteristics of 'the competition to shape the context' amongst rival entities, models of which the micro-economics field has filled journals and books with over decades).

The sixth bucket involves *partially knowable*, non-controllable, real unknowns, *using partnered approaches*. These treatments include uncertainty-sharing and diversification. This bucket concerns techniques that effectively alter the firm's boundaries in order to provide benefits in dealing with the limited range (and known distribution) of (newly known) values that the unknown can take.

Prior to delving into the details of these buckets, it is useful to note two important items: First, this categorization is not perfect; there will be overlap (e.g., as with the first two buckets). Given the literature does not provide full definitions of treatments according to these proposed categories, this should not come as a surprise. Second, we realize that we are only focusing on five of the sixteen possible combinations of the four dichotomous characteristics (*n.b.*, the first two buckets use the same combination, with the difference being in the aggression level of the treatment used to separate them). We do so to provide a tolerable number of (robust) treatment categories (six) that logically organizes the substantial existing literature. (This seems more reasonable than describing a different treatment type for each of the sixteen possible combinations of characteristics. In other words, we have chosen to work with the existing 'database' of [often practical and practiced] techniques related to uncertainty—a database that only covers a small set of those combinations—rather than to generate artificially-specific and unproven ideas to fill in the blanks in a table of possible characteristic combinations.)

BUCKET ONE—UNCOVERING UNKNOWNS VIA DISCOVERY, SEARCH, AND MONITORING

These treatments involve collecting more information in order to make the unknown known. That information can concern facts, values, constraints and identifiable patterns, that can be used to address simple unknowns in the decision steps. It can also concern relative frequencies that can be used to address unknown probability levels. Securing better knowledge is one of the most studied and documented methods of dealing with the unknown (Kinght, 1921). Such information-gathering will differ by target, search scope, effort, persistence, technique, cost, redundancy, and so on.

The search process—seeking out additional information—is a natural response to ignorance (Hertwig et al., 2019; Spender, 2006). This is partly because, in practice, such information often exists (Arrow, 1973); for example, uncertain business environments usually contain strategically relevant data, such as clear trends in market characteristics that a resource-bounded firm has yet to harvest. This search response is captured in *uncertainty reduction theory*, a theory that predicts that the basic human drive to reduce unknowns increases with the number and severity of those unknowns (Berger & Calabrese, 1975). It is a drive that motivates people to interact in order to uncover new information (Bradac, 2001). It is often termed *curiosity*—an evolved desire to explore and learn specific information in response to actual or potential surprise (Baranes et al. 2015; Lanzetta, 1963; Shin & Kim, 2019; Stager, 1967; van Lieshout et al., 2018). That drive is more likely to be enacted when the importance and benefits of resolving the unknown are expected to be greater than the costs of attaining the information (Golman & Loewenstein 2016; Kim 2013; Shin & Kim, 2019).

The process doesn't stop at collecting new data; that data needs to be interpreted, and reasoning needs to be applied, in order to assess the unknown in its context (Daft & Weick, 1984; Kuhlthau, 1993; Samsami et al., 2015). Data collection, itself, may stop when sufficient new knowledge has been gained to make the unknown known. The time taken to do so that will depend on factors relevant to the rate and cost of search, and so on (Stager, 1967). The goal of that search is to develop the understanding necessary to solve the problem and then enact that decision under uncertainty (Hyldegard, 2006; Kuhlthau et al., 2008; Zafar et al., 2021). Such information-gathering is one of the actions often attributed to successful entrepreneurs—regarding how they transform knowable unknowns into knowns (Dimov, 2016).

At the individual level, many studies support the notion that such information-seeking is a process of knowledge-construction, with different cognitive and affective stages (George et al., 2006; Kuhlthau et al., 2008; Pitts, 1995; Serola & Vakkari, 2005; Vakkari et al., 2003; Wang & Soergel, 1998). At the organizational level, search is a multi-party learning process (Huber, 1991; Katila & Ahuja, 2002).

The practical actions that can be taken to obtain more information vary widely, and include: monitoring key trigger events like adoption rates of new products and the like behaviors of nontraditional competitors; participating in several industry consortia (Courtney et al., 1997);

implementing a competitive intelligence system that covers the major dimensions of rival decision-maker characteristics and their organizational constraints (Porter, 1980); monitoring alliance-partner relationships for breaks in trust (Adobor, 2006); implementing quality inspections, rating systems, certifications, and information centers (e.g., CARFAX) in transactions (Lee & Yoo, 2007); employing intermediaries, or suitable technologies (e.g., blockchain), to reduce informational market frictions; interviewing stakeholders early on (e.g., to seek consensus; to mark critical signals; to explore their support) (Ancona, 2012); subdividing the issue to make better use of experts (Hansson, 1996); monitoring unknowns (and the decision context) in real time (Ben-Haim, 2001); target-searching books, journals, the Internet, and people (Bammer & Smithson, 2008); and, applying extensive market research and systematic polling of affected stakeholders (Bammer & Smithson, 2008).

There are many factors involved in conducting effective search and monitoring. Given that search itself is also uncertain, the likelihood, speed and cost of arriving at useful information (i.e., the unknown's value) likely depends on luck and on the pattern of trials undertaken (Nickerson & Zenger, 2004; Simon, 1962). To the latter point, how the individuals involved in the process engage in seeking information can play an important part in resolving the uncertainty and in increasing organizational confidence in the decision (Kuhlthau et al., 2008; Sturm, 2003; Zafar et al., 2021). In terms of scope, firms can consider the range from local to distant search (Katila & Ahuja, 2002), from incremental to radical methods, and from exploitation to exploration in mindset (March, 1991), based on their prior experiences. In terms of depth, firms can consider the degree to which existing knowledge is reused or exploited (Katila & Ahuja, 2002), with the intermediate degree often seen as the best balance. In terms of stopping the search, it can be planned or based on a rule, and often is a function of the benefits and costs associated with the available options and with their goals (Hertwig et al., 2019). Moderators of information search include: contextual characteristics (e.g., its complexity, domain, and variance); decision-maker characteristics (e.g., their affect, health, compensation, social pressures borne, age, aspirations, and cognitive abilities); feedback and exploration rules (Nickerson & Zenger, 2004); and, organizational history (e.g., as affecting what is 'seen' by its agents) (Hertwig et al., 2019). Adaptive searchers tune to the properties of the context, and to their goals, abilities, and experiences. Scanners search for weak signals of change in the present conditions (Scoblic, 2020). Systematic search can be undertaken only when the searcher is aware of the nature of what they do not know *and* of the way to find out the missing information (Kirzner, 1997). A further factor to consider is *competitive pressure*—regarding any additional costs of not acting first, or from acting too fast and missing out on the benefits of additional experience or of observing rivals' choices (Hertwig et al., 2019). Such competitive pressures vary considerably as a function of the prize, the industry structure, and time.

There are several issues to keep in mind when choosing this treatment (Gavetti & Levinthal, 2001). First, there are costs involved, including opportunity costs and processing costs; one method to minimize such costs is to use small samples (Hertwig et al., 2019). Second, processing new information itself poses a challenge to organizations; it often has a disruptive impact on organizational constructs, especially in new firms, where it can lead to confusion (Kuhlthau, 1993). Third, 'more is not always better' when it comes to information search; for example, if new information reinforces rather than resolves the uncertainty (Kuhlthau, 1993; Zafar et al., 2021). There is likely an optimal information level prior to 'full', even regardless of cost.

Note that this bucket has several other labels (e.g., exploration, discovery, hunting, foraging, scouring, gaining situational awareness, auditing, inventorying, and so on). For example, *discovery-driven planning* is a popular approach that is premised on explicitly quantifying outcomes—i.e., making the unknown known through search—to better understand and manage emerging opportunities (Kapoor & Klueter, 2021).

BUCKET TWO—UNCOVERING UNKNOWNS VIA EXPERIMENTATION, EXPERIENCE, ANALYSIS, AND MODELING

These treatments differ from those in the first bucket by the *amount of interaction* involved with the context in which the unknown's secrets are hidden; there is more directed prodding (e.g., experimentation) and more modeling (versus simple gradient-directed or randomized path-following over an informational landscape). These (more) active treatments include: scientific experimentation, experiencing, and other active learning methods (on the prodding side); and, sensemaking and inference (on the modeling side).

Experimentation

Besides search, scientific experimentation is probably the best-known treatment for uncovering information (Fontana & Gerrard 2004; Foss et al., 2019). It involves a cycle of observing, generating hypotheses, testing those, measuring the outcomes, and feeding back the results until the unknown is made known (Bammer & Smithson, 2008; Einhorn & Hogarth, 1986; Gomes et al., 2021; Kapoor & Klueter, 2021; Porter, 1980). The scientific process is itself, essentially, the acquisition of information (Garner, 1962). It is a valuable approach given that some mysteries are only uncovered by 'trying' them (e.g., as with supersonic flight at altitude) (Kay & King, 2020).

There are many variants of experimentation. An 'entrepreneurial' variant involves *abduction*, and the imaginative generating and testing of multiple hypotheses quickly (Schoemaker, 2002; Teece & Leih, 2016; Teece et al., 2016). That variant may use a *build-measure-learn* mentality with a 'minimum viable product' that is launched, experienced, and fed back for adjustments to test a core value proposition (Fisher, 2021; Teece et al., 2016). Or, it may use a *lean-startup* method where the experimentation is directed at learning rather than planning—at failing fast then pivoting (Teece et al., 2016). An exploratory variant applies a careful design of experiments, often using techniques such as Monte Carlo sampling (Marchau et al., 2019). An experiential variant involves a probe-and-learn approach (Brown and Eisenhardt, 1995; Lynn et al., 1996; O'Connor & Rice, 2013). A *bricolage* variant involves trial-and-error tweaking, by making do with what is given (e.g., through recycling wasted pieces) (Taleb, 2012). An internal corporate-venturing variant allows established firms to try new products in novel markets with less negative spillover issues and greater employee motivators (e.g., with the chance to be rewarded for spinning that venture off) (Covin et al., 2018, 2021). A more tepid variant involves simply subjecting new product ideas to focus-group testing and other types of market feedback (Bammer & Smithson, 2008).

All of these variants involve a scientific mindset—where one is willing to entertain alternative hypotheses about the unknown (e.g., regarding its causal structure) and is then able to interpret feedback as confirming or disconfirming evidence that alters the degree of belief in any specific hypothesis about the unknown (Fontana & Gerrard, 2004). Notably, experimentation can make people much more careful than theorizing does (given the practical specifics that need to be addressed) (Taleb, 2012). Of course, with its benefits come the specific costs for experimentation (in time and in effort), costs that may be substantial (Ehrig & Schmidt, 2022).

Sensemaking and Modeling

When one is confused because important facts are unknown, then sensemaking is a good method to apply. When one cannot answer the question of '*what is the story here?*', then sensemaking will help (Ancona, 2012; Weick et al., 2005). Sensemaking has been defined in many ways, including as: the process of structuring the unknown (Waterman, 1990); placing stimuli into a framework that enables comprehension, understanding, explanation, or prediction (Ancona, 2012; Starbuck & Milliken, 1988); inductive and deductive reasoning; moving from anxiety to action; cartography (Weick, 2001); and, creating an improving picture through data collection, action, experience, and conversation.

There are many steps associated with the sensemaking process, including: trying to recognize the situation (Lipshitz & Strauss, 1997); applying abductive reasoning to identify the best explanation for what is observed (Kay & King, 2020); seeking out many types and sources of data; involving others; moving beyond any stereotypes; understanding the nuances; using images, metaphors, and stories to capture the key elements of the new context; and, being aware of the impact of one's own behavior (Ancona, 2012). Essentially, sensemaking is an attempt to create a coherent and credible reference narrative. This narrative-writing is seen in the most systematic process our society has for reaching decisions under conditions of imperfect knowledge—the court trial—where, in civil proceedings, the winning narrative must be better than any presented alternative (Kay & King, 2020). Note that most of those narratives are qualitative rather than quantitative (Feduzi et al., 2012).

The more formal version of sensemaking—the scientific version—*is* modeling (*aka* theorizing) (Bammer & Smithson, 2008). With modeling, we consider key factors within a focal phenomenon and their relationships within a bounded context, often starting with linear thinking and then applying regression analysis for testing (Bammer & Smithson, 2008). Ultimately, the model represents our understanding of the decision problem, its temporal dynamics, the evidence, the environment, and any other available relevant knowledge that will provide a pathway to knowing the unknown (Marchau et al., 2019). Getting the model correct is often crucial (e.g., as with the *Monty Hall* problem—see Gilboa, 2009), as is understanding the broader context within which the problem is tackled (Kay & King, 2020).

Models help us to frame our arguments about big worlds (where the initial unknowns exist) by allowing us to draw analogies with the relevant small worlds in which there are determinate answers (where any unknowns are quickly made known) (Kay & King, 2020). Indeed, models provide the connection for analogies, which most people use when confronted by novel situations (Miceli, 1994). Thus, informed judgment will always be required in understanding and interpreting the output of a (theoretical) model and in using it in any real-world situation—i.e., where the analogies may break down (Kay & King, 2020). Simple models may be useful at first to ground oneself in the situation, but more precision (often using quantification) is always necessary to uncover the unknown value. Such unbundling, or deep-diving, means making more and more specific assumptions to determine the factors that are most relevant, providing greater information about unknowns that need to be acted upon (Kapoor & Klueter, 2021).

Experience and Alertness

In order to generate hypotheses to test, and to even begin to make sense of a new context, one has to experience it (through one's senses). The more alert and sensitive to the informative experiences one is, the more successful in dealing with a knowable unknown one is likely to be (because one is more likely to be familiar with it through those experiences). For example, in improvisational music, if one can recall what has already been played, the unknown future notes can be better complemented when actually chosen and played (Bammer & Smithson, 2008).

Experience is required for learning, especially for the kind of incremental learning that experiments reveal people use when they are immersed in new interactive settings (Hertwig et al., 2019). Experience is often used by subjects to abstract general relationships between cues and the relevant criterion; they do so by forming rules for weighing and combining those cues (Hertwig et al., 2019). Experience is used to build exemplar-based strategies that can be updated (Medin & Schaffer, 1978). Experience with a rival can mitigate future strategic uncertainties involving that rival, even though history rarely repeats itself. So, for effective learning, there are skills needed not only for choosing *what* to experience (e.g., to build a robust base of knowledge) but also for interpreting the *applicability* of those experiences to new situations (e.g., to adjust to evolving preferences) (Hertwig et al., 2019). The latter skill is needed to compensate for the biases that a decision-maker's experiences will entail, like the underweighting of rare events (due to most people's frugality in exploring a given context, a frugality that often causes people to avoid rare events) (Hertwig et al., 2019). (If the decision-maker has no experience with similar events, it is often best to use 'ignorance priors' rather than subjective ones that are based on a false inference.)

In order to gain the right experiences, one has to be alert to them. Kirzner (1973, 1997) describes such successful alertness in his entrepreneurs; he characterizes that alertness as an attitude of receptiveness to the newly made-known-unknowns that pose possible opportunities. It seems that those entrepreneurs, without knowing what to look for, without deploying any specific search techniques, are at all times scanning the horizon for the hitherto unnoticed features of the environment (present or future) that might inspire new profitable activity. That, unfortunately, sounds like 'magic' (and seems to involve a high implicit opportunity cost of attention, not to mention a lot of luck [given the lack of direction and method involved]). Less magically, such alertness is likely to be based on previous relevant experience (perhaps like *absorptive capacity*—where there is more value in search and experience in more basic scientific, technological, and market encounters[2]), and be influenced by the extant frame of the person's mind (Bammer & Smithson, 2008).

Inference from Big Data

Given the recent rapid decline in the costs of sensors, computing power, digital memory, and communications, much more data is becoming available to analyze to help make some unknowns known. AI can help (when it is trained well and checked for accuracy), but can also be biased and dangerous (Kay & King, 2020). As can visualization tools, statistical methods, and other data analytics (Bammer & Smithson, 2008). While such 'big data tools' may not lead to 'big' solutions, they often can provide sufficient immediate improvements (e.g., *Waze* data may

---

[2] Such absorptive capacity enhances an entity's ability to find, grasp, filter, and apply new information (Cohen & Levinthal, 1994; Packard & Clark, 2020).

not be useful for building general models of traffic flow but it does provide rapid access to information that suggests possible solutions to current slowdowns). Other times, especially for critical technological decisions, inference from samples is required (Bernstein, 1996). Note that this can be problematic when contextual knowledge is missing, and rules for sampling (Wald, 1947) cannot be applied with confidence (Hertwig et al., 2019). In other words, big data inferences can help only with *some* knowable unknowns (and not—at least immediately—with all of them).

Other Active Learning Approaches

Fuzziness—as both a qualitative and quantitative concept—can be an effective early approach to getting to know a knowable unknown. The idea that a factor value can take on a range of levels, rather than a single unique level, can help retain useful (although sometimes initially conflicting) information (e.g., from semi-accurate measurements) that sheds light on contingencies and other parts of the path to the truth (Kay & King, 2020).

Other learning approaches deal with: reformatting the available data into different ways that it can be sensed and interpreted; applying mathematical permutations (e.g., chunking music into sections of notes); and, trying multidisciplinary ideas (Bammer & Smithson, 2008).

In all of the cases in these first two buckets of treatment (and in all real practice), *learning* is involved in treating the uncertainty. Human decision-making is an iterative approach where people learn across trials, through alternative framings of the problem, through feedback from various stakeholders, through varying the trade-offs, and hopefully through a collaborative process of discovering what is known, what is knowable, what is unknown, and even perhaps what is possible (Dosi & Egidi, 1991; Herman et al., 2015; Marchau et al., 2019).

Note that, just as with the treatments in the first bucket, the competitive context matters here as well, because rivals will also be taking these active measures to uncover the unknown values. Fortunately, because these treatments are more interactive, they tend to be more visible as well—meaning that 'all' rivals can have a better idea of the actions taken by others (and especially under conditions of market disequilibrium where addressing many uncertainties requires dealing with them 'in the open'— i.e., by using very visible new product launches, promotional campaigns, production capacity expansions, and so on) (Kirzner, 1997). Sometimes, the competition that characterizes the market processes even reveals information that no one was aware of having been lacking (Kirzner, 1997). Such contexts (e.g., newly emerging markets) are challenging to incumbent decision-makers because conventional approaches don't work, and so the competition becomes more about uncovering the unknowns that stop those approaches from working instead (in addition to some imitative parallel play) (McDonald & Eisenhardt, 2020).

BUCKET THREE—UNCOVERING UNKNOWNS VIA INFLUENCING THE OUTCOME THROUGH SOCIAL CONSTRUCTION AND PREEMPTION

These treatments involve socially and/or physically influencing the problem context to control the value of the unknown—thus, making it known. There is an active shaping of the focal unknown (so there is no need to predict the value). Of course, it takes significant effort to do such shaping to control the future (Knight, 1921).[3] It also takes two very big assumptions: first, that the unknown is controllable by this decision-maker or their organization; second, that that control is more powerful than any other party's control over that unknown.

These shaping actions are proactive and self-serving (Courtney et al., 1997; Marchau et al., 2019; Samsami et al., 2015). They often include a design step, and for social construction, uses of symbols as well (Knight et al., 2020; Rindova & Courtney, 2020). Often described as *entrepreneurial actions* or *truth-making*, they are aimed at influencing a target audience to create intersubjective agreement; they work better when the landscape is rich in suggestions and materials for making things (Shackle, 1966; Townsend et al., 2018). They usually require large investments (Courtney et al., 1997), ones big enough to alter knowledge and beliefs at the market level (Gavetti et al., 2017; Rindova & Courtney, 2020). Such investments may involve the rolling out of extensive target education campaigns that promote a specific solution, or the buying of close relationships with significant power blocks (Bammer & Smithson, 2008). The firm needs control over key resources, in addition to skills

---

[3] Although it takes extraordinary efforts to try and control the future, research has indicated that some people naturally react to uncertainty by trying to do just that, and even try harder the bigger the uncertainty (Au, 2017).

in forming and manipulating important interorganizational relationships (Hillman et al., 2009; Packard & Clark, 2020), to be successful. At its core, shaping requires a distinct ability, regarding how to alter knowledge in others, 'from about how things are to how they could be' (Simon, 1996).

Besides the skills needed to control the unknown's value (whether that be in engineering for a physical factor, or in psychology, sociology, and marketing for a social factor), there are further requirements to be successful in applying this treatment. The resources and the time to apply those skills are needed. Also, given that if the unknown is (feasibly) controllable by this organization, then it is likely to be by others, the additional skills and resources to overcome the influences on the focal unknown by rivalrous others is also needed to be successful (assuming their intentions are not actually initially knowable).[4] This competitive issue has always been overlooked in the past literature. It has been overlooked in the theoretical literature because it is quite complicated to model (e.g., given the infinite ways that such informational battles over a third party [the social entity being shaped] can play out). However, that is *no excuse* for ignoring it. Without analyzing who will win the 'shaping battle' over the unknown (and under what conditions it matters), any prescription for this treatment is incomplete and possibly dangerous.

BUCKET FOUR—UNCOVERING UNKNOWNS VIA SCENARIOS AND SIMULATIONS

These treatments (mainly) involve uncovering unknowns not as they are, but as they could be, in value; as such, these treatments (mainly) deal with possibilities rather than with current reality. They include the use of scenarios and simulations. (By 'mainly', we do not rule out the use of such treatments to uncover unknown values that are currently hidden by present limitations in measurement and observation—e.g., where digital models and numerical methods could provide a suitable answer.)

---

[4] This is tricky: If the rival's intentions were known, then the values that the unknown could take would be known, and the decision could be optimized based on that information. But it would not be the best outcome, given the value would be better for the rival than for the firm, given the rival would be in control. If the intentions were unknown, then the uncertainty (over the original unknown value) would remain.

The assumption is that the future (or the currently immeasurable item) *is imaginable* (Lachmann, 1976; Ramoglou, 2021; Shackle, 1979). The tools that can aid in that imagineering include: scenario-planning; simulations; options-thinking; war-gaming; influence diagrams; predictive-modeling (e.g., regressions; extrapolations; NPV analysis; decision trees); latent demand research; system dynamics modeling; game theory; and, creativity (Schoemaker, 2002). The idea is to envision, *ex ante*, the one compelling ecosystem blueprint that is tangible enough to uncover the unknown (Dattée et al., 2018).

Scenario-planning involves several stages; it begins with identifying the forces that will shape the future (Scoblic, 2020). Scenario-planning combines experiences, draws out from them, provides a common language, challenges assumptions, helps the firm develop new instincts, and reframes perceptions of the present (Kay & King, 2020; Schoemaker, 2002; Scoblic, 2020). It enables numerous future states to be distilled down into a manageable number of more likely ones so that responses can be thought through (Packard & Clark, 2020; Teece et al., 2016). Scenario-planning produces a set of internally consistent narratives (as *Shell* has done for decades in their 'future-casting'), narratives that can be ranked for impacts like 'surprise' (Kaplan, 2008; Packard et al., 2017).[5] It is often used to characterize the new states that could develop after major shocks (or after significant deviations in key variable levels); it looks at these extremes in order to gain insights on the more plausible states in-between those extremes (Schoemaker, 2002). Note that developing dynamic capabilities entails applying such scenario-planning (Teece et al., 2016).

Simulations—both computer-based and other—are powerful tools for dealing with complex situations where real contexts, actions, and outcomes are too dangerous and/or costly (Bammer & Smithson, 2008; Hertwig et al., 2019). Many business and training simulations exist, with various levels of virtual, physical, and human interactions (e.g., for human resource management; for new venture startups; for flight training; for fire-fighting; for legal cases; and, so on). Many books and consultants

---

[5] Scenario-planning differs from contingency-planning and sensitivity analysis: While contingency-planning examines one key unknown at a time, scenario-planning examines the joint impact of various unknowns. And, while sensitivity analysis analyzes the impact of changing one variable a tiny bit keeping all others constant, scenario-planning changes multiple variables at a time without keeping the others constant.

also exist to provide extensive details on these simulation products that we cannot cover in this book. One interesting (and often less-digitized) simulation is the *war game*, where participants engage an opponent in simulated conflict, often to explore reactions to novel circumstances (Scoblic, 2020). This is often more helpful when participants get a chance to play each side, so that they can better understand the full dynamics and effects of the 'war' and see all of its unknowns.

Other variants of such participant-engaging simulations include: *backcasting*—where participants work back in time from a particular given future to ascertain what in the present caused its emergence; *crisis simulations*—where participants respond to specific scenarios and then analyze their behaviors relative to alternatives in order to help them prepare for real-life situations; and, *trend analysis*—where participants consider the potential influence of visible patterns of change to identify the various messages and interpretations that can exist in the organization or with its stakeholders (Scoblic, 2020).

Scenarios and simulations mainly exist to generate alternative forecasts for subsequent analysis (Harrison, 1977). They can also uncover further unknowns (Bammer & Smithson, 2008). More generally, they can increase strategic foresight (Scoblic, 2020) by generating multiple views, surfacing deep assumptions, and exploring new terrain (Schoemaker, 2002). Other labels for this type of forecasting (or its steps) include: Assumption Based Planning; Exploratory Modeling; Scenario Discovery; and, Discovery-Driven Planning (Dewar et al., 1993; Marchau et al., 2019; McGrath & MacMillan, 1995).

Scenarios and simulations are often applied when the situation is complex. When that is the case, then decision trees can help to structure the situation to get the programming right and to better envision the big picture (Harrison, 1977). 'What-if' analyses can be used with the simulations to better explore the possibility space (Bankes et al., 2013; Marchau et al., 2019). Often the complexity of a situation is infeasible to mentally simulate (Atkins et al., 2002; Diehl & Sterman, 1995; Sastry & Boyd, 1998), and computer-based methods must be used (Marchau et al., 2019). That level of complexity is often generated by complicated dynamics caused by accumulations, feedback, and time delays, with non-linear interactions among them.[6]

---

[6] A recently popular form of simulation is the NK landscape model where an artificial agent traverses a complex digital multi-dimensional space to find maxima, both local

It should be noted that it is not (always) easy to launch (appropriate) simulations or scenarios. For example, it can be very complicated to think about the options involved in 'coding' these treatments, especially when there is no certain first step for doing so, and given that the initial choices (e.g., over premises and structures) often have the domino effects (Dattée et al., 2018). It often requires patience, skill, and resources to move from rough assumptions to better protovisions. It involves building a resonance loop to move the hypothetical ecosystem trajectory towards the one clarified and shared vision that uncovers the focal unknown (Dattée et al., 2018).

BUCKET FIVE—UNCOVERING UNKNOWNS VIA ADAPTING TO OUTCOMES THROUGH FLEXIBILITY, OPTIONS AND ROBUSTNESS

These treatments entail sufficient knowability of the unknown (versus full knowability). When a *finite range* of possible values can become known, it is often the case that the firm can then prepare—in various ways—to respond to any of the (restricted) realized values 'near-optimally'. (We say 'near-optimally' because the optimal way would not include the costs or trade-offs of having to prepare for alternative values of the unknown that could be realized.)

If the unknown can be made known to the 'risk level' (i.e., where an expected value could be calculated) then the decision-maker can use insurance (and other standard operating procedures) to optimize the choice. If not, then the unknown may be able to be reduced to a level where it is 'partially' known—i.e., where a finite range of possible values for it is known (even without knowing their precise probabilities of occurrence) and the organization can feasibly prepare for these accordingly. In that case, the firm has a basis for investments in flexibility, options, and robustness to address any (now known) possible realizable value (of the focal factor's characteristic). The assumption is that there is a way to

---

and global, when these are not mathematically identifiable (Felin et al., 2014). Such simulations have been used to provide 'evidence' that a specific analogous landscape is suitable to use for a given new problem (Gavetti et al., 2005). Most of the insights from this type of simulation, however, relate to which search techniques (e.g., narrow versus broad) are better for different landscape characteristics (Gavetti & Levinthal, 2000), rather than for finding unknown values.

get to this point (i.e., through the other treatments, like search or experimentation) where the unknown is now partially known, as described. The treatments in this bucket then finish the job—allowing the decision to be (nearly) optimized. The main treatments in this bucket vary by approach: there is *flexibility/adaptability*—where the firm gets ready to adjust to any one of the known possible characteristic's values that is realized; there is *options-thinking*—where the firm preemptively builds paths to exploit the upsides of those adjustments (while mitigating their downsides); and, there is *robustness*—where the firm is structured so as to require little, if any, adjustment to a realized characteristic's value. In reality, each treatment will come with different costs, timing, and other commitments, and so the firm needs to compare among them once it is provided specifics to find the best choice.

First, consider the flexibility/adaptability treatment. This involves managing the realized value of the characteristic and rolling with it (Schoemaker, 2002). It involves investments in reactive systems and leanness (Porter, 1980). It involves planning and management that is contingency-based (Harrison, 1977; Packard et al., 2017). It often involves modifying operations (Lampert et al., 2020; Stigler, 1939). As such, it may be considered a dynamic capability (Kapoor & Klueter, 2021; Teece et al., 1997). It is alternatively termed agility, dexterity, or fluidity; and, the type of resource manipulation required to be successful with its execution is more often associated with startups than with mature enterprises (Millar et al., 2018; Rindova & Courtney, 2020). Such agility is costly to develop and maintain; but, it is often even more costly to a firm if it is missing. It is not a one-size-fits-all ability; and, it is context-sensitive (Teece et al., 2016).

Flexibility relies on two interdependent elements: entrepreneurial management that can combine and recombine resources; and, flexible organizational structures that are rapidly modifiable (Teece et al., 2016). Also useful for flexibility are: accommodating sourcing arrangements; organizational slack; reengineering experience; the ability to do open innovation; a learning-based approach; and, a project-based structure (Dougherty & Hardy, 1996; Eisenhardt & Martin, 2000; Iansiti, 1995; Lipshitz & Strauss, 1997; O'Connor & Rice, 2013; Teece et al., 2016). Such flexibility is akin to dynamic adaptive planning where there is a plan (i.e., involving specific choices and actions) for whatever (within the known range) can possibly happen (i.e., with the partial unknown), and where signposts are used to detect when the realization occurs so that the actions can begin in a timely manner (Marchau et al., 2019).

Second, now consider the options-thinking treatment. Here, the pathways for dealing with each possible value of the focal characteristic are more formalized than with the flexibility treatment. This is a more strategic approach, one that is structured to exploit a realized value's upside potential while mitigating the costs of the downsides (e.g., in the paths abandoned; in sunk costs) (Bradley & Steele, 2015; Courtney et al., 1997; Leiblein et al., 2018; Williamson, 1999). It may take the form of *real options*, as with staged investment (Harrison, 1977; Luehrman, 1998; Packard & Clark, 2020). It may take a dynamic adaptive policy form, one that describes a solid overview of alternative routes into the future (Marchau et al., 2019). Or, it may even take an engineering options analysis form where each route's option value has been pre-calculated (Marchau et al., 2019). As with many of the technical treatments described so far, options, real options, and options-thinking have a vast (and relatively recent) knowledge base available to delve into (e.g., involving journal articles, empirical studies, books, consultants, and, so on). We cannot do justice to the details of such a treatment here (so we encourage Readers to pursue the specialized resources when they are ready). But note, as with most of the treatments outlined in this chapter, these need to be customized to the problem and the relevant treatment's context (e.g., regarding its specific informational and financial market inefficiencies, regulations, and so forth) to be most effective in actual use.

Third, consider the robustness treatment (where the firm's preparation is so thorough that it does not need to appreciably change, regardless of the characteristic's value realized, to get to a near-optimal action) (Khodadad et al., 2011; Lempert et al., 2003; Samsami et al., 2015). Other terms associated with robustness include: resilience; redundancy; and, system comprehensiveness (Bammer & Smithson, 2008; Kay & King, 2020; Marchau et al., 2019). In Information Gap Decision Theory, the term robustness entails a unique trade-off—it satisfices the outcome while maximizing the coverage of possibilities (Ben-Haim, 2006, 2010). Robustness appears to have the greatest upfront costs of the three alternatives, but it is likely to have the fastest implementation (due to the relative lack of reactive changes required to carry out the best decision). As noted prior, deciding on the best treatment will require specifics, and the willingness to compare among alternatives (e.g., whether the benefits of speed outweigh the upfront costs for resilience).

There exist dangers (or downsides) to any treatment approach. In this bucket, the choice to be 'flexible' may, at the extreme, actually entail the organization losing its current source of strategic advantage—its differentiation—if it changes so much that 'it can become almost anything' (Porter, 1980; Raynor, 2007; Samsami et al., 2015).

Bucket Six—Uncovering Unknowns via Sharing the Burden with Cooperation and Insurance, or Through Diversification

These treatments use entities outside the organization, or they significantly expand the organization, in order to cover the newly known possible values that the unknown can take. These treatments, like those in bucket five, are applied only *after* the unknown has been reduced to a finite and feasibly-covered range of known possible values, through the use other treatments (e.g., search; experimentation; simulation). These present treatments have an actionable range of focus that is better effected by employing 'others'—either as independent entities, or by bringing them into the organization via some form of absorptive diversification (e.g., horizontal, vertical, or international). These treatments include: various forms of contractual sharing of the range of possible outcomes, for mutual benefit (e.g., strategic alliances; joint ventures); insurance; and, expanding the organization's portfolio to diversify its exposure to the now-known range of possible characteristic values. Essentially, the organization *collaborates to share* the coverage of the possible contingencies when it is the better alternative (e.g., in terms of speed, net benefits, resource constraints, and so on).

First, consider insurance contracts—where the firm pays an independent entity to provide some predetermined factor should a specific outcome occur (here, that outcome being the realization of one of the newly known possible characteristic value levels). Insurance and annuity design have been around since the seventeenth century (Hacking, 1975; Holmes & Westgren, 2020). Insurance works through the expedient grouping of possible instances (Knight, 1921). It is only possible when, at a minimum, ignorance of the probability of specific future outcomes is considerable in any one case, and that ignorance is common to both the insurer and the insured (Kay & King, 2020). Whereas standard insurance (i.e., to cover what we have defined as risk in this book) is more available when the *Law of Large Numbers* is observed (i.e., when outcomes insured must be both large in number and independent of one another so that there is a straightforward way to calculate the odds of loss), the insurance we refer to here is more specific, and option-like in form. It simply guarantees access to the resources needed (at a predetermined cost) to carry out a decision should a specific value of the characteristic be realized.

Second, consider cooperative sharing contracts—where the firm joins others for mutual benefit (e.g., sharing of costs) in covering the resource requirements for all of the now-known possible characteristic value levels (of the known factor). Such cooperation can be done with supply chain partners (e.g., with lead users), and can take various legal forms (e.g., a joint venture; an outsourcing contract). Such cooperative agreements have evolved in human society for centuries; there exist examples in tribes even today, where reciprocal commitments to help other members in the future can be inherited (Kay & King, 2020). The agreements can lead to beneficial specialization (and subsequent innovation) in roles, and collective intelligence, and learning across partners (Kay & King, 2020). Essentially, given that the range of possible characteristic values could be so wide that the focal firm just does not have the resources alone to cover every realization, having the ability to form (and manage) these sharing partnerships is important, especially when alternatives (e.g., insurance) are not available or attractive. That 'social' skill, combined with a risk-management ability, can lead to successfully dealing with these treatable uncertainties (Ehrenzweig, 1967; Teece et al., 2016).

As with the other treatments, there are many sources of expertise available regarding how to do these sharing agreements (e.g., books, articles, studies, and consultants exist for informal and formal contracts, strategic alliances, joint ventures, network-making, clusters, platform ecosystems, and so on). Recently, many interesting approaches have been described for *ecosystems* (e.g., Dattée et al., 2018; Dunne & Dougherty, 2016; Reetz & MacAulay, 2016). (We cannot cover the specifics in this chapter alone, so we again advise doing a deep dive on these once the problem specifics are known and it is determined that this treatment has attraction.) In terms of managing such cooperation, it often comes down to trust—a concept that has been linked to uncertainty in the literature for some time, both positively and negatively (Adobor, 2006; Barney & Hansen, 1994; Bhattacharya et al., 1998; Dasgupta, 1988; Williamson, 1985). If these sharing relationships reoccur, sometimes such close interaction can facilitate the creation of valuable specific assets, including the accumulation of social data about partners (Adobor, 2006).

When the sharing involved mainly occurs within a 'tribe' (e.g., as with crisis response management—see Brafman & Brafman, 2008), and especially if it is expertise that is being shared, there are several approaches possible that are effective for drawing from multiple voices, including: voting; blending judgments from the respondents; relying on the greatest expert; relying on a selection of top experts; relying on the most confident voices; and, so on (Bradley & Steele, 2015; Hertwig et al., 2019). The best approach is context-dependent (e.g., it depends on the diversity of errors, and the dispersion of individual accuracies), but when in doubt, aggregating more rather than fewer judgments is recommended because it reduces the worst-case error (Hertwig et al., 2019). Keep in mind that tribes can be 'wise' or 'mad' (Hertwig et al., 2019), so drawing on outside expertise (by sharing) is often valuable (Bammer & Smithson, 2008).

Third, consider diversification as the means to cover the range of now-known possible factor characteristic value levels. It is an involved and expensive means, but it reduces reliance on fully-outside partners (especially those who are likely to be more opportunistic under the incomplete contracts necessitated by some uncertainties). The firm expands its portfolio of resources and capabilities so that it can enact the near-optimal decision once the value is realized. Such diversification expands the scope of operations to manage the exposure (Kay & King, 2020; Knight, 1921). There are several directions the diversification can take: vertically in the supply chain; horizontally across industries; and, geographically across national borders. In the literature, vertical integration has been used to reduce the uncertainties related to supply and demand (e.g., to hedge against price fluctuations), especially when the linked stages are capital-intensive (Porter, 1980). Vertical integration has even been found to be effective in new product development when the uncertainties involve technological obsolescence, although this remains debated (Balakrishnan & Wernerfelt, 1986; Eggers & Park, 2018; Kapoor & Adner, 2012). Diversifying into new industries and into international markets is more attractive [relative to alternative means, like acquisitions and alliances] the more such markets involve frictions (e.g., high costs in transferring capital, resources, skilled people, and so on) and non-voluntary informational spillovers (e.g., especially of high-value intellectual property). Again, there are many, many resources for diving deep into diversification and its implementation (e.g., books, articles, studies, and consultants—regarding adding to, subtracting from, balancing, and managing a firm's portfolio of interests, and accounting for the various costs, speeds, controls, constraints, regulations, and market powers involved).

Part Two—Addressing the Untreatable Uncertainties (the Unknown-and-Unknowables)

We now turn to the untreatable uncertainties. These are the unknowns that cannot be made fully or even partially knowable. When they are present, there is no way to guarantee optimal or near-optimal decision outcomes. Addressing these uncertainties has been a challenge in the relevant literature. The response in the research has been comprised of three disappointing behaviors: ignore it; misrepresent it as treatable; or, actually recognize it and plead helplessness. This is perhaps the first book to address it head on, represent it accurately, and provide actual direction.

That response in the literature, however, has not been surprising, and for several reasons: First, experts, scientists, academics, and others simply do not want to admit that *science has limits*; that it fails to provide answers in the face of such uncertainties (and, especially when powerful organizations still must deal with such untreatable unknowns not unoccasionally, in reality). It makes those experts look weak, and that is not what gets funding. Second, research on untreatables is nearly unpublishable. Editors and reviewers (possibly even most readers) are interested in confident, tight prescriptions; ones that nearly guarantee optimization of a decision (often based on a too-narrow set of limitations). They are not interested in descriptions of contexts and problems where such optimization is impossible by definition. Third, on the rare occasion when research on such phenomena is published, it inevitably involves observing the behaviors of the people confronting the unknowns. That is certainly interesting (especially when the participants respond to such unknowns in a consistent enough manner for academics to recognize and comment upon), but it doesn't get us very far. Obviously, the responses being observed are *not* valid treatments (because, by definition, the unknowns will remain unknown, and the decisions will remain non-optimized). Instead, what is observed are responses that are evolutionarily programmed and/or culturally learned. Further, the 'true' underlying reasons for those responses are almost never provided in such studies, making the logic behind choosing one response over another in different situations (for the different untreatables) unknowable, and thus limiting the insights available on what best to do when confronted by such uncertainties.

A Shift in Mentality

Given, by definition, the untreatable uncertainties cannot be addressed directly as is, then in order to improve decision-making (being the aim of this book), a shift in mentality is needed. We draw on *Game Theory* as an analogy for that shift. The main role of Game Theory is in identifying the optimal strategic choice for the focal player in a game, as given. However, sometimes the outcome of such an optimal choice is *inefficient* in terms of the game's final outcome (i.e., an equilibrium), as with the (single-play) *Prisoner's Dilemma*, where both players could improve their lot if they could coordinate (to choose the cooperative action in the game). The *other* (perhaps more creative) role of Game Theory is analyzing how to change that given game into something that increases the efficiency of a final outcome (e.g., Arend, 2022a). That is the mental shift we consider in this part of the chapter—we are *not* treating the uncertainty 'as given' (because it is not treatable), but *instead we are changing the decision problem* in some (reasonable) way in order to address the altered problem in order to optimize it (or at least make some valuable headway on it). Essentially, almost all of the approaches that we describe below follow this meta-level analysis—in terms of improving the given situation, not by optimizing it, but by finding a feasible way to alter the situation instead. (Note that such an exercise can lead to infinite regress [and further unknowns and uncertainties], when we consider levels of 'having the ability to have the ability to alter the situation', and so on; so, we stop at the first level, as that is where the majority of the relevant literature [and practical effort] exists.)

The Four Approaches

As with the first part of the chapter, we focus on making sense of the existing relevant research because it is a 'big' resource that should not be ignored but rather exploited in the appropriate explicit context—i.e., with the right mindset, and under a suitable understanding of the limitations involved.[7] Making sense of that vast amount of existing work implies determining a suitable categorization. We use four main buckets (with one sub-bucket):

The first bucket is the simplest because it does *not* alter the problem; here, the decision-maker takes on and *bears the untreatable uncertainty as is*.
The second bucket is the most widely-explored in the literature; it consists of *altering the goal*. That implies the use of *heuristics* to meet a different goal that involves only the problem's knowns. The sub-bucket we consider differentiates heuristics that involve other entities (e.g., rivals) from those that only involve the focal organization.
The third bucket involves *changing the focal entity*—instead of it being the organization itself, there is a shift of focus to the specific decision-maker and optimizing for their personal interests rather than for the problem itself (e.g., due to an imperfectly-aligned compensation system).
The fourth bucket involves *altering the game* when the problem's unknown involves what can be considered 'other players' (e.g., by altering their payoffs to eliminate an uncertainty about rational strategic actions to take; by cutting a deal with rivals or regulators to remove the uncertainty over how they will act; and, so on).

Prior to proceeding, it is worth noting several points: Hammering on this again—because it is so important—*no one and nothing can treat the untreatable* (by definition); only by luck can someone have success when confronted by a decision with an unknowable unknown. So, it is important to be explicit here that we are not providing any 'magic'; instead, we are clearly stating that any approaches in the literature that claim they can 'optimize (or even improve) the untreatable uncertainty as-given' are *false*. They may change the problem (e.g., by

---

[7] We take this 'literature review' approach for several further reasons, the main one being that there is a lot of research that simply fits the 'change the problem' mentality (e.g., applying heuristics). The alternative of filling in gaps and refining existing concepts to fit a new categorization was simply less appealing, let alone less efficient and effective in making our points here.

altering the goals or assumptions) to leverage what is known or knowable, but none treat the original problem. We are quite disappointed that several pieces of work (e.g., theories) have not been thoroughly honest about this, because there is no place in science or academia for that. No existing approach touting or hinting that it has the magic to treat the untreatable uncertainties is correct, whether that approach is aligned with dynamic capabilities, effectuative attitudes, option-ation, social-constructionist shaping, entrepreneurial judgment, gut instincts, or reality-bending mindsets—none of it—can theoretically work, by definition.[8] Sometimes, science just has to openly admit its limitations (of knowledge) and move on.

BUCKET A-ONE—ADDRESSING THE UNTREATABLE BY BEARING THE IRREDUCIBLE UNCERTAINTY

This is the most straightforward approach—the decision-maker takes on the unknown as given, and acts regardless (i.e., there is no change—no treatment—of the uncertainty). The basis for that action has been labeled several things, including *entrepreneurial judgment* by Knight (1921). Knight explains the existence of entrepreneurial activity by the occurrences of such action in the face of irreducible uncertainty, focusing more on the successes of new ventures (than the failures). (In such cases, it is implicit that the incumbents either do nothing, or choose different actions than the entrepreneurs.) Theoretically, bearing unknowable unknowns in differentiated ways is what spawns 'new stuff'—new firms, new products and processes, new organizational forms, and so on. Under the (informational) market failure that irreducible uncertainty creates, incumbents have no advantages to use to block any such 'new stuff' that would challenge their existing profitable 'old stuff' (and, they may even have disadvantages in offering their own 'new stuff', for example, in terms of negative spillovers if their own judgments should fail). Other labels for this approach include *playing a gamble*, and *intuiting*.

---

[8] One example of the incredibly flawed logic used in such 'analysis' speaks to an ability to reduce uncertainty by restricting one's options (or, alternatively, by restricting the outcome one considers) (Foss & Klein, 2020; Packard et al., 2017); this 'ostrich' technique is ridiculous on its face, as ignoring relevant information, let alone the unknowns, won't improve the likelihood of making a good decision.

The bearing of irreducible uncertainty takes more than identifying a choice; it entails actually taking specific actions to implement that choice. The basis for those actions may be 'more' or 'less' rational (or rationalized). We term the former *judgment* (de Finetti, 1967; Feduzi et al., 2012); it is described as a basis that is more than random, or at least 'feels' that way to the decision-maker. Even though a decision-maker can really only guess what the unknown's value is, and they may not even be able to imagine the full range of those values at that (Knight, 1921), they have confidence in their choice. It is in those situations that Knight (1921) states entrepreneurs apply 'good judgment'; but, he does *not* provide an origin for it, calling that an 'unfathomable mystery' (Scoblic, 2020). He mentions that differences in judgment are likely to arise due to differences in the decision-makers themselves, especially in differences in their own position in relation to the problem itself (Knight, 1921). So, we use the term 'more rational' loosely in this context; there would be no theoretical optimization possible, but a decision-maker may still have a coherent explanation for their chosen action (e.g., based on an analogy to the current problem; based on comfort with the action; based on the initial cost of the action; and, so on). That differs from a decision-maker who explicitly states that they are flipping a coin to decide. In the former case there is a bit more stated control over the decision rather than complete surrender to the uncertainty (Bammer & Smithson, 2008).

In the latter case—the 'less rational' case—there is more explicit acknowledgment that the action chosen in the face of irreducible uncertainty is based on a gamble (e.g., a roll of the dice), or on intuition (e.g., an inexplicable gut feeling), or on superstition, or on trying something new for the sake of newness (Bammer & Smithson, 2008; Beckert, 1996; Mousavi & Gigerenzer, 2014). Regardless, the choice of such acknowledgment, and even the choice of whether to try to explain it, should take into consideration how this affects the organization and its stakeholders (e.g., whether it is likely to reduce anxiety) (Bammer & Smithson, 2008).

The use of bucket a-one as an approach implies that several conditions are met: At the individual level, it implies that the decision-maker feels that they can tolerate uncertainty (can cope with it) and that the cost in effort to do so is low (Shin & Kim, 2019). At the firm level, given this bucket is relatively speedy, it is more attractive when there are possible first-mover advantages involved (Wernerfelt & Karnani, 1987).

Bucket A-Two—Addressing the Untreatable by Changing the Goal

The next 'simplest' approach to dealing with unknowable unknowns is to change the problem to one where just having the knowns is sufficient for making a good decision and taking action on it. For example, the decision-making could change the goal to maximize something to do with the knowns alone (e.g., maximin). Such goal-changing is mainly covered in the relevant literature on heuristics (and on satisficing especially). It also is considered when the decision-maker: acts 'as if' the unknown was known; acts on the knowns alone; alters the knowns to reduce the possible harms; models only what is known; and, uses information-gap analysis.

Heuristics in General

We use the term heuristics here to describe the approach of altering the original problem's goal in order to act on the knowns alone. Addressing untreatable uncertainties in this way is well-recognized (Kozyreva & Hertwig, 2021; Manski, 2000; Mousavi & Gigerenzer, 2014). Heuristics tend to be simple, use only a subset of the information available, involve only a few steps of analysis, and be based on evolved direct learning (Hertwig et al., 2019; Mousavi & Gigerenzer, 2014). Using a heuristic constitutes a belief that ignoring some information in the problem will produce a fast, perhaps even a good, decision (and consequent outcome) (Hertwig et al., 2019). Indeed, heuristics can be effective and efficient for decision-making under some uncertainties (as noted in lab and field research) (Busenitz & Barney, 1997; Shepherd et al., 2015).

Note that there have been recent improvements in creating and applying heuristics. Human learning is relatively biased, bounded, and slow compared with machine learning (and AI). So, it is not surprising that more rules-based decisions (even where there are unknowns) are now being made in accordance with algorithmic, data-exploiting, disciplined procedures; and, in many cases, like (AI-assisted) breast cancer screening, these decisions are far outperforming past methods. While this shift to algorithms has allowed many catastrophic errors of judgment to be avoided (Bernstein, 1996); many valid and deep concerns remain over the biases built up in these systems, their black-boxedness, the overconfidence placed in them, and their increased control over dangerous physical systems (e.g., in automated weapons platforms) (see Chapter 20 for more discussion on AI).

The popularity of the heuristic concept has been fed by behavioral research (which appears to have been usurped by IT/AI research). Applying such simple rules is a default response for most people when confronted by uncertainty (or complexity, or confusion). Real decision-makers only rely on a limited number of heuristics to simplify judgmental operations, even though such heuristics can sometimes lead to severe and systematic errors (Tversky & Kahneman, 1973, 1974). They do so because they are bounded in their rationality—constrained by the resources and time that they can devote to thinking about a problem— which affects the quality of their decisions, even when no unknowns exist (Simon, 1982). However, little is known about how people actually choose between heuristics when confronted by different uncertainties (Hertwig et al., 2019).

Besides being used for individual decision-making (Hertwig et al., 2019), studies have revealed that heuristics are commonly used in organizational decision-making (Gigerenzer & Gaissmaier, 2011), especially now with the rise of machine learning/AI. But, even when the decisions are not made by machines, in the board room it is heuristics and narratives rather than a deep analysis that is preferred. Indeed, statistical theory is often eschewed by managers even when a problem is ideally suited to it, because subjective probability estimates are often distrusted, artificial choice criteria are deemed unacceptable, and the process seems too 'simple' (Harrison, 1977); instead, managers use the uncomplicated process of identifying a few workable options that are evaluated one-at-a-time rather than with detailed comparisons, for determining a choice that is sufficiently justifiable (Kay & King, 2020).

Conditions for Heuristic Use

The specification of conditions for applying heuristics does not end with a general acknowledgement that they can be used for 'addressing' untreatable uncertainties (by altering the given problem). Given that there are many different heuristics available, it is useful to understand that specific heuristics tend to work better under specific conditions (Dosi & Egidi, 1991). *Ecological rationality* specifies the conditions under which a particular heuristic performs more accurately and demands less effort than others (Gigerenzer, 2005; Mousavi & Gigerenzer, 2014). For example, the performance of a heuristic can be affected by conditions like cue-weighting, cue-redundancy, and loss functions (Hogarth & Karelaia, 2007).

There are many conditions to consider: When the contextual condition of predictability increases, all heuristics perform better, but differences between them can increase. When the contextual structure is unknown, the heuristics involving more extensive information-processing tend to dominate those applying lexicographic-type rules (Hogarth & Karelaia, 2007). When the contextual structure is highly unpredictable, ignoring some information and simplifying the process can lead to better decisions (Gigerenzer & Gaissmaier, 2011; Kozyreva & Hertwig, 2021).[9] Under conditions of complete ignorance, the equal-weighting heuristic often works well because it aligns with the probabilistic principle of indifference (Kozyreva & Hertwig, 2021; Reale et al., 2023).

Heuristics can be advantageous not only under specific environmental conditions but also especially under cognitive constraints (Kozyreva & Hertwig, 2021). There is *no* generalist heuristic (that works best in all contexts); each one can be good in one context and bad in another (Hertwig et al., 2019). So, it is important to understand the context and the possible altered objectives of the original problem in order to choose wisely (Hertwig et al., 2019). Also, it is important to consider what other entities involved in the decision will do in the situation—it is likely that they will also use a heuristic to decide, especially when the game is complex (Hertwig et al., 2019). And, when that occurs, the use of heuristics can actually lead to better outcomes than super-rational analysis, most often in expanding-pie types of games (e.g., by using the friendly tit-for-tat heuristic in repeated prisoner's dilemma games) (Dixit & Nalebuff, 1991).

---

[9] There is even a meta-heuristic for heuristics; it boils down to using simpler rules for less predictable contexts (and more complex rules for more predictable ones) (Fox, 2014). This assertion of 'better' is based on a particular measure of *prediction error* (as equal to bias-squared + variance + random error [Luan et al., 2019]). Heuristics (versus deeper analysis), especially simpler rules (versus more complicated ones), work better when their larger bias is compensated for in much smaller variance; a condition which happens in situations of higher uncertainty (at least when that 'uncertainty' is simulated by researchers).

Dangers of Heuristics

Given that heuristics significantly simplify a given problem, eliminating the influence of a material proportion of available information relevant to the decision, it should be no surprise that many potential errors can result in their use. One accounting describes 27 possible errors associated with applying heuristics (Bammer & Smithson, 2008; Hogarth, 1980). For example, consider the often-used *representativeness* heuristic; serious errors can arise because similarity-as-representation is *not* influenced by several factors that actually should affect judgments of probability, such as: base-rates; sample size; misconceptions of chance; predictability; the illusion of validity; the redundancy of inputs; and, regression to the mean (Tversky & Kahneman, 1973, 1974). Or, consider the *availability* heuristic; serious errors can arise from its use because it is affected by factors other than frequency and probability, such as: the retrievability of instances; the effectiveness of the search set; the ease of imaginability; and, any illusory correlation (Tversky & Kahneman, 1973, 1974). Or, consider the *anchoring* heuristic; serious errors can arise because it is affected by: insufficient adjustment; misestimated conjunctive, disjunctive, or compound events; disjunctive structures; and, overly-narrow confidence intervals (Tversky & Kahneman, 1973, 1974). Simply put, heuristics entail biases and variances that are not always explicitly acknowledged (Hertwig et al., 2019). This makes their use potentially exploitable by others (Tversky & Kahneman, 1973, 1974). In general, relying on speculation and simplification (e.g., using heuristics) in lieu of information, even under uncertainty, can exacerbate many problems (Bammer & Smithson, 2008), so it is useful to be vigilant.

Types and Examples of Heuristics

There are many types of heuristics and many variants of each type. Categorization can be based on the characteristics of their rules. For example, the *cautious* decision rules give more weight to the possible negative implications of a choice (Bradley & Steele, 2015). The *informationally demanding* rules draw on considerations of confidence or reliability (Bradley & Steele, 2015). The *fast-and-frugal* rules are robust and involve less effort (Mousavi & Gigerenzer, 2014). The *instance-based inference* rules draw from experiences of one's own social circle

(Hertwig et al., 2019). The *exemplar-based* heuristics work better in non-linear contexts (Hertwig et al., 2019). The *one-reason* heuristics rely on a single factor rather than many, and often work better in contexts involving higher uncertainty (Gigerenzer & Gaissmaier, 2011; Hogarth & Karelaia 2007).

For reference, we provide a set of example heuristics now (noting, as with previous buckets, there are resources available that dive much deeper into this approach than we can here):

- *1/N rule*—resources are allocated equally to each of the N alternatives.
- *availability heuristic*—the ease of which instances are brought to mind drives the assessment of the probability of an event (Hertwig et al., 2019; Tversky & Kahneman, 1973).
- *constant-target strategy*—a target level of risk-taking is selected in the first investment period and then maintained throughout.
- *contrarian strategy*—investment allocations are continuously adjusted as a function of market changes, decreasing the investments in stocks that gained and vice versa.
- *default rule*—follow the default rule in the organization when it exists.
- *dominance 1 rule*—choose the best action under the assumption that the rival is choosing randomly among its non-dominated choices.
- *equality rule*—choose the action that minimizes the differences across players' payoffs.
- *fluency rule*—when an alternative is recognized faster, then infer it is better.
- *gaze rule*—to catch falling object, adjust the running speed so that the gaze-angle remains constant.
- *imitate the majority rule*—follow the choice of the relevant majority.
- *imitate the successful rule*—follow the most successful player's moves in a game (or industry).
- *level 1 rule*—choose the best action under the assumption that the rival is choosing randomly.
- *level 2 rule*—choose the action that is the best response to the rival playing the level 1 rule.
- *level 3 rule*—choose the action that is the best response to the rival playing the level 2 rule.

- Markowitz (1952) *mean-variance optimization rule*—choose the portfolio with the highest mean-to-variance measure (Hertwig et al., 2019).
- *maximax*—choose the action with the highest possible payoff.
- *maximin*—choose the action with the highest worst-case payoff.
- *momentum strategy*—continuously adjust investment portfolio allocations as a function of market changes, increasing the investments in stocks that gained (and decreasing in those that lost).
- *most likely rule*—identify most likely outcome of each option and then select the option with the most attractive most likely outcome (Hertwig et al., 2019).
- *Nash equilibrium rule*—in a game, choose the action consistent with the Nash equilibrium outcome.
- *non-diversified strategy*—for a portfolio choice, place all the eggs in one basket.
- *one-bounce rule*—search through the options as long as there is improvement, when that stops, choose the previous best.
- *priority rule*—go through the option attributes in the following order: minimum gain, probability of the minimum gain, maximum gain, probability of the maximum gain; stop if the minimum gains differ by 1/10th of the maximum gain, otherwise stop if the probabilities differ by 1/10th; then, select the option with the more attractive gain (or probability) (Hertwig et al., 2019).
- *recognition rule*—if an alternative is recognized, then infer it is better.
- *satisficing rule*—choose the first alternative that exceeds a set aspiration level.
- *social maximum rule*—choose the action that maximizes the sum of all of the players' payoffs.
- *take-the-best rule*—search contextual cues in order of validity, and stop when a cue discriminates among choices, choosing the favored alternative under that cue.
- *tallying rule*—count the number of positive cues, and then choose the alternative with the most.
- *equiprobable rule*—assign equal probability to all possible values (applies the principle of indifference) (Hertwig et al., 2019).
- *least-likely rule*—consider only the worst possible outcomes, and choose the option with the smallest probability this will happen (Hertwig et al., 2019).

- *probable rule*—consider probabilities to classify outcomes into either probable or improbable (Hertwig et al., 2019).
- *tit-for-tat rule*—cooperate first, and then imitate the other player's previous move.

Now, consider a deeper dive into two of the best-known rules—maximin and satisficing. Regarding maximin, it is chosen to protect against (known) worst-case scenarios (Manski, 2000; Yager, 1999). As such, maximin has a different objective than expected value theory (Hertwig et al., 2019), and is often observed when real decision-makers face uncertainty (Marchau et al., 2019). However, maximin has been criticized for two reasons: it may be unnecessarily costly to assume the worst-case; and, the worst-case usually happens rarely and so is often poorly understood as a reference point (Sims, 2001). Given such concerns, a middling rule between maximin pessimism and maximax optimism exists in the optimism-pessimism, or Hurwicz α, or Ellsberg index.

Regarding satisficing, it is also a rule that tries to minimize regret, but in a different way than the maximin rule. It asks about 'which outcomes are critical and must be achieved?'. Guaranteeing an acceptable outcome rather than an optimal one, according to an explicitly stated set of criteria, is what satisficing strives for (Simon, 1956). There are even satisficing metrics (e.g., of robustness) that measure the number of states of the world in which the focal alternative meets the minimum performance thresholds (Marchau et al., 2019). Such thresholds are often derived empirically and can be highly effective in repeated decisions (Artinger et al., 2022). In real life, it has also been observed that, due to a decision-maker's limited cognitive capacity, many decisions are made once an alternative that satisfies their aspiration level is found (Beckert, 1996).

Acting 'As If' the Unknown Is Known

Another variant in this 'big' bucket is the approach of acting 'as if the unknown is known' and making an 'optimal' decision based on that. This essentially translates the uncertainty into a risk at worst and a point value at best. Usually, such a translation is based on a subjective estimate of the unknown's value. A great deal of the literature that is *mislabeled* as addressing uncertainty falls into this part of this bucket. The vast array of mathematical models involving small-world, subjective expected utility, or otherwise algebraic solutions-to-unknowns are this—they do not actually deal with irreducible unknowns as-given but instead deal with 'assumed knowns' in some form (e.g., as assumed-known distributions of possible values). (Note that this approach differs from heuristics; with heuristics, only the actual given [or truly uncovered] knowns are used. This 'as if' approach just magically makes up values for unknowns [given they have no theoretical basis] and uses those values in its calculations [as substitutes for the real unknowns].)

In this approach, one replaces the information that is not available with something else, filling in those voids with inputs provided by spontaneous optimism and creativity (Dequech, 2011), or by subjective estimates for which no probabilistic information yet exists (Kozyreva & Hertwig, 2021). Some have considered this a 'small-world' approach (Dekel et al., 1998), one where, given the newly 'filled-in voids' in the problem, standard risk management procedures and protocols can be applied to try to 'optimize' that 'altered' decision (Teece et al., 2016).

There are several proposed bases for choosing a value for the unknowable unknown that are popular in the relevant literature, chief among these are two: subjective estimates, and indifference. Most of these approaches focus on the case when the unknown is a probability (rather than a different characteristic value, like a demand level or a profitability magnitude).

The most written-about approach is the use of subjective estimates. And, when there is time prior to the 'final' decision—time for learning—this is supplemented by the Bayesian-updating of that initial estimate. In that case, an initial working hypothesis is tried out and then corrected (Dimov, 2016). Note that if this was a knowable unknown—if it were a treatable uncertainty—such experimentation would work (as discussed above); but, given we have assumed that that is not the case—that instead we are focused on unknowable unknowns—such experimentation cannot work, by definition. The initial estimate has no basis, and the feedback does not provide reliable information. Regardless, in these writings, the initial estimate expresses the decision-maker's personal beliefs, or intuitions (Gilboa, 2009; Manski, 2000), or their degrees of belief (e.g., of their primary estimate) (Fontana & Gerrard, 2004; Knight, 1921). When learning can occur, inferences are then made from feedback, even though the underlying processes are not fully understood (Beckert, 1996; Kay & King, 2020), in some sort of anchoring-and-adjustment model (Aggarwal & Mohanty, 2022; Einhorn & Hogarth, 1987).

The other most-popular approach involves assigning equal probabilities to the (imagined) possible values of the unknown—applying the principle of indifference (of insufficient reason) (Bernoulli, 1966; Gilboa, 2009; Laplace, 1951).

Further ways to provide a value for the unknown include using: analogies; case-based reasoning; related theoretical relationships of cause-and-effect; genetic algorithms; fuzzy logic; possibility theory; chess-like algorithms; an initial probability of zero to all possibilities; and, plausibility measures (Bewley, 2002; Dixit & Nalebuff, 1991; Gilboa, 2009; Halpern, 2003; Helton & Johnson, 2011; Mousavi & Gigerenzer, 2014; Schoemaker, 2002). Others have suggested the use of paradigms and conventions to 'fill in the voids' in a coherent manner (Choi, 1993). This approach, however, leads to a regress problem—in that no rational explanation for the choice of such paradigms is provided (Pressman & Choi, 1997), although some suggest it is based on experience—personal or organizational (Miceli, 1994).

Given the fact that this approach cannot work (i.e., cannot optimize the 'given' decision), it is not surprising that it comes with many dangers (especially when the decision-maker incorrectly believes that the made-up value for the unknown is legitimate). Those dangers are increased when a patina of validity is provided by Bayesian-updating,[10] which in this case parodies a would-be rational learning process (Bernstein, 1996). It is worthwhile to remember that subjective probabilities of real people are inconsistent with the relevant required axioms and, so, have even less legitimacy as a basis for estimating unknowns than theory would suggest (Dekel et al., 1998; Ellsberg, 1961; Etner et al., 2012; Savage, 1954). And, that does not even account for the further cognitive biases involved in subjective probability estimates—detected in experiments—that indicate such probabilities can be wildly wrong (Tversky & Kahneman, 1973, 1974). Relying on analogies is also dangerous, given that their coherence is no indicator for their accuracy or even for their effect on decision-maker behaviors (Brafman & Brafman, 2008). There just is no well-grounded theory for assessing how good any such void-filling approach is (Kozyreva & Hertwig, 2021), and so it must be considered with great caution.

---

[10] The parable of the naïve thanksgiving turkey nicely illustrates the danger of Bayesian updating (Fox, 2014).

Acting on the Knowns Alone

This is a more generalized approach—one that includes heuristics (by definition), but adds the possibility of using the knowns to inspire the estimation of the unknowns. It is mentioned because it sometimes appears in the literature (Brunswik, 1952; Hertwig et al., 2019).

Altering the Knowns to Reduce Harms

This approach is more interactive than others in this bucket. Instead of simply using the knowns as inputs, it involves influencing their values to mitigate possible losses. Such shaping activities come with some strong assumptions, however (i.e., that doing so is feasible for the firm, and that its actions somehow trump those of rival entities—see bucket three in the first part of the chapter for analogous issues). As such, these activities are easier (and more likely to work) when the known being influenced is more internal or proximate to the organization.

This approach is like, from a game theoretic perspective, trying to alter the game to eliminate undesirable equilibria as unplausible or unattractive (e.g., by changing the payoffs, players, or timing involved) when challenged by multiple possible equilibria in a given game (Beckert, 1996). Firms can even try to use social devices to either restrict their own flexibility to create rigidity in their responses (Beckert, 1996), or to define a rival's range of possible actions (Spender, 2006). They may also be able to do so through superior anticipation and dynamic monitoring (Schoemaker, 2002). In any case, the decision is altered not only by focusing on the knowns but by also trying to alter them in order to optimize a different (but related) problem than what was given.

Modeling What Is Known

We highlight this activity as we wrap up this bucket because it is common (although implicit) to all of the variants in this bucket. All of the approaches in this bucket—approaches that alter decision using (real or assumed) knowns—require the step of modeling that altered problem. It is from the altered model that the decision-maker identifies their best choice. This usually involves finding an appropriate mathematical (or logical) representation of all the available information and then developing a calculus to apply to it to determine the best option (Klir,

2004). The mathematical tools applied may draw from interval analysis, possibility theory, evidence theory (or Dempster-Shafer theory), and probability theory (Helton & Johnson, 2011).

Applying Information-Gap Theory

A mathematical representation that is tuned for uncertainty is information-gap theory (Ben-Haim, 2001). It models each uncertainty as an informational gap instead of as a probability. It quantifies the gaps in extant knowledge (i.e., the unknowns) and considers them as a family of nested sets (Ben-Haim, 2001). It does so by applying two algebraic functions. The robustness function captures the greatest level of the unknown's value at which failure cannot occur, while the opportunity function captures the lowest level of the unknown at which great success can occur (Ben-Haim, 2001). (Note that there are a lot of known things assumed about the unknown and its effects required for this approach to work.) The suggested steps for applying this method to improve the decision involve: conceptualizing the information-gap unknowns; evaluating the decision robustness to them; identifying the critical paths; deciding how much robustness is needed to meet the newly set objective (e.g., for a minimal possible success level with no possibility of failure); and, choosing actions that satisfice that level (Ben-Haim, 2001).

BUCKET A-TWO-*PLUS*—ADDRESSING THE UNTREATABLE BY CHANGING THE GOAL TO A RELATIVE ONE

We break out this approach from the others in bucket a-two because it involves a significant change in perspective—shifting the focus from absolute performance (as implicitly assumed so far) to relative performance. This approach applies best when the most *appropriate* performance goal of the decision is relative (i.e., to a rival); it can also be used when the original goal is absolute but there is no way to optimize that given the unknowns involved. When the goal is altered to being relative-to-a-rival, and assuming that the decisions (or actions) of that rival are visible and true and occur prior to the firm's decision point—which are all significant assumptions—then the tactic of simply *imitating the rival* should keep performance parity with that targeted rival (*ceteris paribus*). This is a 'sailing' race strategy, often used by the lead ship. Many issues can affect the success of this approach, including: when there is more than one important rival and they differentiate in their actions; when the rival's actions are not visible or true; and, when the actions taken by a targeted rival are likely to produce better results than similar ones in the focal firm (e.g., due to differences in resources, capabilities, motivations, and so on).

Keynes (1936) suggests such tactical *mimesis* is one way to reduce uncertainty. Further, it is a way that 'appears rational' (which is important to a 'monitored' decision-maker), and even implies the rationality of those being imitated; with all that favorable inference occurring even though each choice is spurious at its core in this context of unknowable unknowns (Beckert, 1996). Regardless, it is an approach even prescribed more recently, especially in more specific contexts like brand-new markets, where it has been labeled 'parallel play'—being a means for the sharing of valuable learning among first entrants (McDonald & Eisenhardt, 2020).

BUCKET A-THREE—ADDRESSING THE UNTREATABLE BY CHANGING THE FOCAL ENTITY

The approaches in this bucket involve altering the decision problem by changing the entity that is trying to choose; in this case, by shifting to trying to improve the individual decision-maker's utility (rather than trying to optimize the value to the firm). So, the shift in focus is a shift in objective; one that will be influenced several factors, like how that person is compensated (rewarded or penalized) for their choice (e.g., in terms of the rationale or process used versus what the outcome was). When that more personal objective function contains only knowns, where the original decision did not (as assumed here—i.e., that untreatable uncertainties exist in the problem as given), then that new decision can then be effectively addressed (but as a *different* problem than the one given). Even when the new objective function involves unknowns, because the entity has shifted, often the options for addressing the uncertainties do as well (for both the treatable and untreatable ones). For example, depending on the decision-maker's power, they may be able to personally avoid the uncertainty by delegating the responsibility for the outcome to someone else. Other tactics that the individual decision-maker can consider—especially to avoid blame if things go wrong—include: playing no-regrets, conservative moves; otherwise following standard procedures and norms;

expressing dissatisfaction; trying to ignore, suppress or deny the uncertainty; and, trying to delay the decision. (Note that several of these tactics are not available to the decision-maker's organization itself.)

Playing No-Regrets, Conservative Moves

These moves are meant to minimize the downside to the decision-maker, should the outcome be bad for the firm; they are rationalizable, recognizable moves that would be more difficult to critique than others. Most of these moves act on the knowns only (altering the problem to one of standard efficiency-improvement); they tend to reduce the upside potential of a decision to the firm. Such conservative choices include: reducing costs; gathering competitive intelligence; adding skills; reengineering; increasing communications; and, so on (Bammer & Smithson, 2008; Courtney et al., 1997; Samsami et al., 2015). More 'forward-looking' moves include scenario-planning (usually based on past experience), and investing in general flexibility (Schoemaker, 2002). More 'defensive' moves rely on showing a pattern of measurable learning over time; in such cases, stepping-stone micro-decisions are made to elicit feedback for adjustments while the bigger decisions are delayed (Marchau et al., 2019; McGrath & MacMillan, 2000; McMullen & Kier, 2016; Townsend et al., 2018).

Following Available Standard Procedures and Norms

These are also conservative (and defensive) moves; we highlight them as being more based on following what the organization has done in the past (and, often more importantly, what that the decision-maker's boss or mentor has done in the past). There is an *'if it ain't broke, don't fix it'* or a *'respect for elders'* mentality at work here (as in, the decision-maker cannot be blamed for a bad outcome because they just did what their betters did before them in 'similar' situations). This is a default approach that is often observed in the real-world when people are given a job which they cannot do, and instead find a more limited task which they can—which is 'to imitate what has been done by others' (Kay & King, 2020). The idea is to act according to the existing formal and informal rules of conduct. This includes following risk-management procedures (for any risks involved) (Schoemaker, 2002), focusing on short-term efficiency-improvement policies (Scoblic, 2020), and generally focusing on the familiar, routine processes and training rather than on the focal outcomes (Bammer & Smithson, 2008; Dosi & Egidi, 1991; Fleming, 2001). It may also entail breaking the problem down first, and then finding pieces where such routines can be effectively applied (Millar et al., 2018; Rock, 2008). Norms have a few other benefits as well: they can reduce the perception of uncertainties in others; and, they can enhance coordination (e.g., when all parties believe the others are also following the norms) (Fleischhut et al., 2022; Foss et al., 2019).

Expressing Dissatisfaction or Doubt

When the decision-maker believes that the outcome of the decision could be bad, they can try to preempt the blow-back (to minimize personal blame) by expressing dissatisfaction and doubt with the parts of the process that they were not responsible for, or with the existence of the unknowns themselves. (To the latter, by expressing doubt in the existence of the unknown, they could simply then treat it as known—essentially combining an approach in this bucket with one in bucket a-two).

Ignoring, Suppressing, or Denying the Uncertainty

The decision-maker can try to downplay the reality of the situation itself—i.e., that an untreatable uncertainty exists—by ignoring, suppressing, or denying it (as long as that can be 'sold' to whoever will be assessing their performance dealing with the focal problem). This can be done by ignoring or distorting any undesirable information given to them (e.g., that confirms the uncertainty exists) (Lipshitz & Strauss, 1997), by expressing disbelief that such information is reliable (Beck, 2009), or by avoiding the presentation of such information (Bammer & Smithson, 2008). (Again, this can be a combination approach—for example, by denying the unknown, then treating it as known.) While this may work for the decision-maker, the organization most often cannot escape the problem and the consequences of 'doing nothing' (Reale et al., 2023).

Trying to Delay the Decision or Action

While the organization may not be able to delay its choice of action, the decision-maker may be able to (which may be an attractive option as long as they personally cannot be blamed for the organization's paralysis). This can be attempted by: demanding more information be made available prior to the decision; recommending that action should only be taken after the unknown is revealed (due to potentially costly unnecessary intervention); or, making the case that insufficient resources are available to calculate the best decision (as the clock ticks down) (Bammer & Smithson, 2008; Bradley & Steele, 2015; Dixit & Pindyck, 1994; Nosal & Ordoñez, 2016; Wernerfelt & Karnani, 1987). While this may be good for the decision-maker personally, it is often bad for their organization, especially with the uncertainty involving emerging technologies (Cohen & Levinthal, 1994).

Avoiding the Uncertainty

While the organization may not be able to avoid the choice of action, the decision-maker may be able to (which, again, may be attractive as long as they cannot be personally blamed). The decision-maker could use their authority to delegate responsibility for the decision (or at least delegate the blame should a bad outcome occur) (Bammer & Smithson, 2008; Griffin & Grote, 2020). They can do this while also providing extra freedom to act and a strong motivation (e.g., with outcome-based bonuses) to have their underlings bear more of the uncertainty than would otherwise be the case (Foss & Laursen, 2005). The decision-maker could avoid the decision citing a rationale of non-interference (Hansson, 1996), or of taboo (if that is relevant) (Bammer & Smithson, 2008). With sufficient power, the decision-maker may even be able to divest (or wind up or dispose of) the specific part of the organization that the problem impacts, in order to avoid the uncertainty completely (although this gets into issues with the separability of organizational parts, and what the selling price [or tax write-off amount] would be given it would have to be adjusted for the uncertainty in a perfect[ly informed] market).

BUCKET A-FOUR—ADDRESSING THE UNTREATABLE BY ALTERING THE GAME

The approaches in this bucket differ from the others in two main ways: First, there is more involvement with external parties (e.g., rivals; governments; stakeholders). Second, the source of the unknown has to be known for the attempted alteration to the problem (i.e., the game) to be effective (e.g., in changing the original situation into one where the unknown is eliminated). So, more specifics need to be known about the problems in this bucket than in others; only with those specifics can the firm reasonably attempt to change the game so that the decision can be improved (for all participating parties). (Note that this approach differs from the 'shaping of the knowns' described in bucket a-two [of the untreatable uncertainty approaches] because here we are considering cooperative rather than competitive or internal moves.)

When the unknown is known to be affectable by known parties, and affectable in ways that can change the game to reduce the effect of the unknown on those parties, then the parties may have the opportunity (and motivation) to improve their individual and collective outcomes. This is more likely in expanding-pie games. And, it is an approach that involves costs in creating side-payment contracts for cooperation (which implies bringing in—theoretically or practically—additional/third parties). A cooperative mentality is required, as are negotiations and creative incentives, to restructure the original game into an interaction that promises benefits to all the parties involved (Foss et al., 2019).

When the unknown's source is another party (e.g., being the unpredictable possible actions of a rival or consumer or supplier or regulator in the original game), and that party can be reasonably negotiated with, especially if they reciprocally have an uncertainty that is generated by the focal firm, then it may be possible to strike a deal for some mutual win (e.g., one that reduces the range of the effects of these unknowns, especially their downsides). Even in a game where the same uncertainty affects each main party (e.g., see the *implied prisoner's dilemma game* of Arend, 2022b), it may be possible for the rivals to alter the payoffs or to commit to preselected strategies (given side-payment incentives) in such a way that the uncertainty (e.g., of which possible world the future holds) will not affect the choice of either party, thus eliminating the decision problem over what to actually choose as a strategy. (Note that in some cases, this will not technically eliminate the outcome uncertainty itself, but will instead significantly reduce its range, which greatly improves the situation for the firm.)

Part Three—Processing Issues in Decision Uncertainty Treatment/Approach

The first two parts of this chapter provided descriptions of the various ways to treat the treatable uncertainties and to address the untreatable ones. We finish up now with a focus on the main issues that arise in implementing such treatments and approaches. In other work, we have proposed a framework of analysis relevant to these implementation issues, with the acronym *ACME*, standing for awareness + capability + motivation + execution. The focal entity (the organization/firm/decision-maker) first needs to be aware of the uncertainty (and its relevance and possible impacts) for the decision problem to even register. Then the entity must understand it has the capability to implement a variety of feasible options in dealing with the uncertainty (or there is no choice to make)—a capability that entails being able to analyze the problem, decide on a treatment, and hypothetically carry it out. The entity also needs the motivation to deal with the uncertainty in a timely manner (at the organizational and personal [to the decision-maker] levels). Finally, the entity must have the ability to execute (i.e., to actually apply its resources and capabilities efficiently and effectively) on that chosen treatment or approach within the given constraints. (Note that, like with other multistep abilities, experience and the data management of that experience may be useful. So, concepts like absorptive capacity, dynamic capabilities, knowledge management, organizational culture, and so forth, especially for treatments, are likely to affect the smoothness, speed, and success of the decision-processing for that entity. And, at least for speed, that may be important, because sometimes for better performance, the entity only needs to be faster than the mass of the market [Bammer & Smithson, 2008]). Here, we focus mainly on the awareness and understanding of the uncertainty-based decision problem, considering various perspectives. We also highlight several of the key execution concerns, like prioritization, delegation, costs, and the possibility of combining treatments. (The motivational issues and capability concerns for implementation of these treatments and approaches are considered sufficiently standard in nature; we consider them covered well in the vast existing research streams on motivation and capabilities.)

The Awareness of Uncertainties

The skills in detecting, evaluating, and prioritizing uncertainties are important for getting the process started (i.e., towards treating the treatable and addressing the untreatable). The detection of uncertainty has typically been considered as part of the awareness of threats (Griffin & Grote, 2020; Jonas et al., 2014; Kagan, 1972) or, possibly, of the alertness to opportunities (Kirzner, 1973; Knight, 1921). When a decision-maker first becomes aware of a lack of knowledge or understanding, some feelings of apprehension can occur; the task is then to recognize a need for information, regardless of whether initial thoughts are vague (Kuhlthau, 1993). The first priority is to determine whether the problem is primarily risk or primarily uncertainty (Teece et al., 2016), and then, if it is uncertainty, whether it is treatable or not. Also important is to begin to understand and visualize the potential impacts of the now-recognized lack of knowledge (Bammer & Smithson, 2008), and how big that gap in understanding is. It is useful, in the assessment, to provide tangibles for reference (so that others in the firm can also understand the situation) (Bammer & Smithson, 2008). Lateral thinking may increase the likelihood that a wider range of the effects of the unknown(s), and a wider accounting of the relevant knowns, are covered (Bammer & Smithson, 2008). At this stage in the process, it is often better to collect 'everything' and then sort it later (Bammer & Smithson, 2008). Sorting can be based on the quality and truthfulness of the data collected (Bammer & Smithson, 2008). When beginning to assess the problem, it is important to recognize and question the assumptions, to focus on the blind spots, and to involve many stakeholders holding different perspectives, so that factors do not go overlooked (Bammer & Smithson, 2008). All this is valuable because the mistakes and missed facts that arise at the start of the process can have very significant costs later in the process.

Alertness, at both the political and administrative levels, is required to overcome any human obstacles to monitoring the environment, and to detecting any uncertainties (Marchau et al., 2019; Schoemaker, 2002). Some firms may even employ a special exploration/detection organizational unit to run this task (O'Connor & Rice, 2013).

Prioritization

A rank-ordering of newly-detected unknowns may be helpful for a divide-and-conquer approach (especially when those unknowns are sufficiently independent) (Kay & King, 2020; Marchau et al., 2019). There are many bases for ranking, including: treatability; timing; potential losses/gains; ability to contain harms/recover from worst-case outcomes; relative performance effects; and, so on (Bammer & Smithson, 2008). Dividing the problem into smaller blocks, some of which entail the unknowns and some of which do not, often makes the situation more manageable and easier to distribute to specialists (Bammer & Smithson, 2008).

Context Matters—Big and Small

Neither the problem itself, nor the process for its decision-making, should be considered in isolation (Harrison, 1977). Context matters, from the external to the internal to the personal. The focal decision and actions are likely to affect (and be affected by) rivals, partners, resources, access to future opportunities, and the organization's experience bank. So, it is important to select an appropriate frame of reference for assessing the uncertainty (e.g., in order to better recognize its potential impacts) (Bammer & Smithson, 2008). This will help the decision-maker have a proper way of representing it in their mind (Simon, 1995). One may even consider the firm as a 'portfolio of knowledge problems'—some with treatable and some with untreatable unknowns—and with the possibility of some interdependencies among them (Townsend et al., 2018).

Expanding the perspective of a focal problem may sometimes help in understanding it better (as Eisenhower reportedly suggested). One can apply analogies and imagination to do so, or use thick description covering multiple levels of analysis (Kay & King, 2020). Seeing the problem in the light of the organization's traditions, habits, routines, norms, and structural and power predispositions, may also help interpret its challenges (Beckert, 1996). Also important to consider are any asymmetries to rivals, and any timing constraints, relevant to the decision (Hansson, 1996). Accounting for the richer social interactions involved—ones that may affect how people perceive and respond to uncertainty—may be helpful (Hertwig et al., 2019), especially when the problem includes visible and interdependent payoffs (e.g., as studies on human behaviors in the ultimatum games indicate). Finally, putting the problem in the context of the larger economy may be useful, given uncertainty is often viewed differently depending on existing prosperity levels (where it is more tolerated at higher levels) (Bammer & Smithson, 2008).

Taking an organizational perspective is likely to provide additional insights, especially into the potential constraints involved in addressing the uncertainty. Resource restrictions will confine the set of potential options available (Packard et al., 2017). The organization's personnel—in terms of their anxieties and tolerance for novelty and unknowns—will also constrain what the initial assessment and the eventual treatments are (Kuhlthau, 1993). The CEO (and top management team) will also affect the awareness and response to the uncertainty (e.g., in terms of the information search efforts, and its persistence and sources), partly determining the ambidexterity of the organization (Kiss et al., 2020). Organizational trust (in times of uncertainty), informational specificity and accuracy, access to shared interpretive resources, and communications assets, will all affect the ability of the firm to process the decision (Bammer & Smithson, 2008; Brafman & Brafman, 2008; Kaplan, 2008; Louis, 1980; Sewell, 1992). For example, even how the problem is framed when it is communicated to others can affect how it is interpreted and acted upon, so it is very important to be precise in communications during the process (de Palma et al., 2014; Gigerenzer, 2005; Hau et al., 2010; Hertwig & Gigerenzer, 1999). Organizational factors play a major role in determining the willingness for, and the ultimate success in, applying approaches to deal with uncertainties in practice. An appealing and convincing narrative is often required to mobilize political interest in addressing a detected unknown, especially when the treatment will be costly and complicated (Marchau et al., 2019). Some firms have found that increasing the permeability of their boundaries, for example, by having greater interactions with external stakeholders, can be useful in processing uncertainties (Felin & Zenger, 2014).

A consideration of the personal perspective can help with the assignment of responsibilities to different parts of the process (Kozyreva & Hertwig, 2021). For example, prevention-focused individuals tend to be careful and cautious, and work diligently to minimize risk and treatable uncertainty; they would be confident in information search efforts (Crowe & Higgins, 1997; Zafar et al., 2021). More cognitively-flexible persons are more aware of options and alternatives, and more likely to display adaptability and self-efficacy in the face of uncertainty problems (Kiss et al., 2020; Martin & Rubin, 1995). Risk-, ambiguity-, and uncertainty-aversions may also be useful to know about candidates who could be involved in the process (Etner et al., 2012; Schmeidler, 1989). People with minds that are able to ignore some information and to accept some variance, may be good fits for the application of heuristics (Mousavi & Gigerenzer, 2014). And, for some decision problems, temperament can be more important than ability; for example, choosing people to be involved in the process who are decisive in the face of incomplete information can reduce the costs of search when there is little to be gained from it (MacLeod & Pingle, 2000). Many firms find it helpful, regardless of who is assigned to deal with the uncertainty, to lift restrictions on what these employees can do—in order to release their creativity (Foss & Laursen, 2005). It is useful to remember that all people are cognitively limited, so it is important to be sensitive to the perceptual cues and goal structures likely being held in their recent memories when they are assigned uncertainty-related tasks, in order to minimize inference errors (Simon, 1979).

From a different perspective, note that most every decision under incomplete information is unique (especially given that novelty is a main source of unknowns in strategic decisions). Such idiosyncrasy makes the processing of such problems especially challenging, and severely reduces the ability to learn generalizable lessons from them. Problems with unknowns tend to have different dimensions than ones without, and so the standard strategies for dealing with the latter most often cannot be leveraged (Kay & King, 2020). However, keeping a database of the former strategies, even if not fully applicable to the next uncertainty-involved problem, may still be valuable, if only to provide inspiration and to reduce some anxiety in the organization.

One way to put these types of problems in perspective is to apply a reference point. Risk is a common reference point, given it has been well-studied (e.g., in business) and can be optimized for (e.g., in terms of expected value). It is the natural contrast that Knight (1921) used to differentiate his definition of uncertainty. In lab work (e.g., in experiments involving human subjects) risk-aversion can be compared to aversions involving ambiguity and uncertainty (or, at least, some stylized versions of those concepts [involving limited and unlimited ranges of a specific unknown value]) (Arend, 2023; Kay & King, 2020). Although not helpful in the decision-processing itself (because risk is not uncertainty), the reference point of risk may still be useful in communicating to stakeholders what is happening, or why a specific approach is being applied, in order to provide at least some orientation (and, possibly, to compare to when the decision outcome is realized) (Mousavi & Gigerenzer, 2014).

The Costs of Addressing Uncertainties

Recall that a rational entity (i.e., a person or an organization) deals with uncertainty because there are possible upsides relative to not dealing with it (Brafman & Brafman, 2008). In Knight's (1921) positive spin on uncertainty, there are even possible profitable entrepreneurial opportunities for those willing to bear it.

In reality, and in most cases, there are also significant costs (both real and potential) attributed to dealing with uncertainty. There may even be additional possible uncertainties that arise regarding those costs (Knight, 1921), or in executing the treatments and approaches (Ehrig & Schmidt, 2022). To some, that is one of the evils of uncertainty—the difficulty in estimating the costs of reducing, or otherwise addressing, it (Lampert et al., 2020). That may involve agential costs, inspection costs, search costs, emotional costs, effort costs, opportunity costs, social costs, ethical costs, and more (Bammer & Smithson, 2008; Holmes & Westgren, 2020; Lee & Yoo, 2007; Shin & Kim, 2019). Such costs constrain the approaches that can be taken and the extent that they are executed (Bammer & Smithson, 2008). The timing of such costs (e.g., in terms of taking them early, or financing them) is also important to assess. Costs imply trade-offs, or even dilemmas, in dealing with uncertainty-related problems (regarding how to allocate finite resources across all decision types, how to set satisficing limits, and what robustness scope can be considered acceptable) (Bammer & Smithson, 2008; Marchau et al., 2019).

Costs also imply 'allocation' issues, for example, regarding the allocation of responsibility for initially-uncertain-but-later-realized negative spillovers. That raises the question of whether the burden of proof for the safety of a new technology should legally rest with the party that introduces the new technology, with regulators, or with others (Roeser, 2019). Should responsibility under uncertainty be excused (e.g., under a diminished culpability doctrine) (Szentkirályi, 2020)? Or, for ignorance to be excusable, should a higher hurdle be required—where the accused (active) party needs to have shown sufficient regard for others as equals and needs to have taken reasonable measures to prevent exposing them to potential harm (Szentkirályi, 2020)? Such questions not only need to be addressed for cases involving private entities, but perhaps even more so for public ones (who currently escape responsibility through sovereign immunity protections) (Bammer & Smithson, 2008).

Combining Approaches

We have recommended an approach to decision-making under uncertainty that reads like the 'serenity prayer'—*treat the treatable, address the untreatable* (as desired), *and develop the ability to identify each.* Given that problems do not always present as decisions involving only one type of uncertainty, and that some uncertainties can benefit from being addressed using more than one treatment, there is the very real possibility that firms may need to consider combining their approaches for complex problems (and for multi-front unknowns). Combining approaches with greater speed and simultaneity may be advantageous depending on the timing involved in the problem and the costs of doing so (Bammer & Smithson, 2008).

The ability to combine approaches, or the capability to switch from one to another when necessary, likely requires many skills that can be deployed together or in rapid succession, including: search; contract negotiations; the use of hard and soft power; innovation; options-management; heuristics selection; scenario-planning; experimentation; assumption-based reasoning; knowledge management; hedging; change management; and, so on (Bammer & Smithson, 2008; Hansson, 1996; Kahneman, 2003; Kapoor & Klueter, 2021; Lipshitz & Strauss, 1997; Spender, 2006; Townsend et al., 2020; Tversky & Kahneman, 1974; Zafar et al., 2021). Some problems, at some firms, may be easily categorized (e.g., due to recent relevant experiences), with one or more appropriate treatments or approaches quickly identified; other problems may require switching from one approach to another—either to determine the best one, or because the problem requires a multi-step response. To determine the best one, there are several logics that can be applied: moving from the more general to the more specialized; moving from the fastest and easiest to the more involved; drilling down on the problem for greater specifics on its knowns, unknowns, and sub-problems; and, satisficing (Dosi & Egidi, 1991; Newell & Simon, 1972). In any case, firms with flexible management systems, highly-permeable boundaries, active learning, speedy and honest communications, and stakeholder involvement, are likely to be more successful in such combinations and transitions among approaches (Bammer & Smithson, 2008). Regardless, the existence of interdependencies among uncertainties (and even their treatments) is likely to exacerbate efforts to decentralize efforts and decompose any 'full solution' to the uncertainties faced (Felin & Zenger, 2014).

On the Offense—Creating Uncertainties

To complete this discussion on implementation issues, it is worthwhile to recall that many organizations also have the ability to generate uncertainty for their own strategic purposes (Griffin & Grote, 2020; Kaur & Dasgupta, 2018). Dis- and mis-information can 'throw off' rivals and regulators, and delay or degrade actions and reactions that those parties may take to harm the focal firm. Half of the legal process (i.e., the defense) in Western countries is about creating 'reasonable doubt'—i.e., 'uncertainty'—by proposing plausible alternative narratives (i.e., questioning any factual information) in the minds of juries or judges. Much of the entertainment we seek out and enjoy (e.g., mysteries; fictional-world adventures) hinges on creating and manipulating (artificial) uncertainty. Competitive intelligence and corporate espionage exist to cut through the uncertainties that businesses create. The intentional creation of uncertainty (and its mitigation) are big business.

The skills required to effectively breed and manage an entity's portfolio of outward-facing uncertainties are likely related to those for reducing the uncertainties that it faces. Knowing the defenses should help shape effective offenses (as should knowledge of the law, regarding, for example, just how far an organization can spread false information). Military and geopolitical expertise is likely very valuable for insights on how to do this well (and for how it can fail), for the resources needed, and for identifying its costs and its constraints. Other sources for insight and inspiration include game theory, consultants, and recent case histories of such actions in related industries. Certainly, choosing to take this path requires a deep knowledge of the entities being targeted and some confidence that this is a feasible and attractive tactic relative to other uses of resources. It also takes an active mindset (rather than the more reactive one we have assumed in this chapter), one that can exploit control over the timing and forms of the uncertainties directed at others (for good or for bad [but usually not for society's benefit]).

Summary

This chapter draws upon the journey into uncertainty so far to explicitly identify and explain the main ways to improve decision-making under uncertainty. These are based on our primary typology. There are treatments described for the treatable uncertainties. There are *approaches* provided for the untreatable uncertainties—ones that alter the given problem to make the decision 'better' (i.e., in terms of satisfying the new, altered objective). There are issues outlined that affect the execution of these treatments and approaches. The vast literature on addressing uncertainties is exploited by categorizing it logically into buckets of the treatments and approaches, with explanations (for doing so) and boundaries (both implicit in the categorization and explicit). Several past 'solutions'—mainly the ones that have misrepresented where they are applicable—are critiqued.

Why treatments and approaches matter:

- The treatments and approaches described sort out the wide, deep and confusing literature of proposed solutions related to decision-making under uncertainty, into well-defined categories of ways to deal with different types of unknowns
- Multiple options for both the treatable and the untreatable uncertainties are provided
- Limitations and constraints on the more controversial recent proposed 'solutions' to uncertainties are made explicit and explained.

What treatments and approaches (attuned to the new typology) mean for business and policy:

- There is now a set of practical ways to deal with the logically delineated types of unknowns involved in decision-making under uncertainty
- The main processing issues are described for implementing those ways to aid in organizational design
- Competitive issues are highlighted regarding the ways that they can affect the choice of treatments, approaches, and their implementation.

REFERENCES

Adobor, H. (2006). Optimal trust? Uncertainty as a determinant and limit to trust in inter-firm alliances. *Leadership & Organization Development Journal, 27*(7), 537–553.

Aggarwal, D., & Mohanty, P. (2022). Influence of imprecise information on risk and ambiguity preferences: Experimental evidence. *Managerial and Decision Economics, 43*(4), 1025–1038.

Ancona, D. (2012). Sensemaking, framing and acting in the unknown. In S. Snook, N. Norhia, & R. Khurana (Eds.), *The handbook for teaching leadership: Knowing, doing, being* (pp. 1–19). Sage.

Arend, R. J. (2022a). The costs of ambiguity in strategic contexts. *Administrative Sciences, 12*(3), 108.

Arend, R. J. (2022b, forthcoming). Strategic decision-making under ambiguity: Insights from exploring a simple linked two-game model. *Operational Research.*

Arend, R. J. (2023, forthcoming). Integrating entrepreneurial and spiritual identities under uncertainty. *Journal of Business Venturing Insights.*

Arrow, K. J. (1973). Information and economic behavior. In *Collected Papers of Kenneth J. Arrow, 1984 4(11).* Belknap.

Artinger, F. M., Gigerenzer, G., & Jacobs, P. (2022). Satisficing: Integrating two traditions. *Journal of Economic Literature, 60*(2), 598–635.

Atkins, P. W., Wood, R. E., & Rutgers, P. J. (2002). The effects of feedback format on dynamic decision making. *Organizational Behavior and Human Decision Processes, 88*(2), 587–604.

Au, E. W. M. (2017). Seeing the forest and not the trees: When impact uncertainty heightens causal complexity. *International Journal of Psychology, 52*(3), 256–260.

Balakrishnan, S., & Wernerfelt, B. (1986). Technical change, competition and vertical integration. *Strategic Management Journal, 7*(4), 347–359.

Bammer, G., & Smithson, M. (2008). Understanding uncertainty. *Integration Insights, 7*(1), 1–7.

Bankes, S. C., Walker, W. E., & Kwakkel, J. H. (2013). Exploratory modeling and analysis. In S. Gass & M. C. Fu (Eds.), *Encyclopedia of operations research and management science* (3rd ed.) Springer.

Baranes, A., Oudeyer, P. Y., & Gottlieb, J. (2015). Eye movements reveal epistemic curiosity in human observers. *Vision Research, 117*, 81–90.

Barney, J. B., & Hansen, M. H. (1994). Trustworthiness as a source of competitive advantage. *Strategic Management Journal, 15*(S1), 175–190.

Beck, U. (2009). *World at risk.* Polity.

Beckert, J. (1996). What is sociological about economic sociology? Uncertainty and the embeddedness of economic action. *Theory and Society, 25*, 803–840.

Ben-Haim, Y. (2001, June). Decision trade-offs under severe info-gap uncertainty. *ISIPTA*, 32–39.
Ben-Haim, Y. (2006). *Info-gap decision theory: Decisions under severe uncertainty* (2nd ed.). London.
Ben-Haim, Y. (2010). *Info-gap economics: An operational introduction*. Palgrave-Macmillan.
Berger, C. R., & Calabrese, R. J. (1975). Some explorations in initial interaction and beyond: Toward a developmental theory of interpersonal communication. *Human Communication Research*, 1, 99–112.
Bernoulli, J. (1966). *Ars conjectandi: Or, the art of conjecturing*. Harvard University.
Bernstein, P. L. (1996). *Against the gods: The remarkable story of risk*. Wiley.
Bewley, T. F. (2002). Knightian decision theory. Part I. *Decisions in Economics and Finance*, 25, 79–110.
Bhattacharya, S., Krishnan, V., & Mahajan, V. (1998). Managing new product definition in highly dynamic environments. *Management Science*, 44(11-2), S50–S64.
Bradac, J. J. (2001). Theory comparison: Uncertainty reduction, problematic integration, uncertainty management, and other curious constructs. *Journal of Communication*, 51(3), 456–476.
Bradley, R., & Steele, K. (2015). Making climate decisions. *Philosophy Compass*, 10(11), 799–810.
Brafman, O., & Brafman, R. (2008). *Sway: The irresistible pull of irrational behavior*. Doubleday Business.
Brown, S., & Eisenhardt, K. (1995). Product development: Past research, present findings and future directions. *Academy of Management Review*, 20(2), 343–378.
Brunswik, E. (1952). *The conceptual framework of psychology*. University of Chicago Press.
Busenitz, L. W., & Barney, J. B. (1997). Differences between entrepreneurs and managers in large organizations: Biases and heuristics in strategic decision-making. *Journal of Business Venturing*, 12(1), 9–30.
Choi, Y. B. (1993). *Paradigms and conventions: Uncertainty, decision making, and entrepreneurship*. University of Michigan Press.
Cohen, W. M., & Levinthal, D. A. (1994). Fortune favors the prepared firm. *Management Science*, 40(2), 227–251.
Courtney, H., Kirkland, J., & Viguerie, P. (1997). Strategy under uncertainty. *Harvard Business Review*, 75(6), 67–79.
Covin, J. G., Garrett, R. P., Kuratko, D. F., & Bolinger, M. (2021). Internal corporate venture planning autonomy, strategic evolution, and venture performance. *Small Business Economics*, 56, 293–310.

Covin, J. G., Garrett, R. P., Jr., Gupta, J. P., Kuratko, D. F., & Shepherd, D. A. (2018). The interdependence of planning and learning among internal corporate ventures. *Entrepreneurship Theory and Practice, 42*(4), 537–570.

Crowe, E., & Higgins, E. T. (1997). Regulatory focus and strategic inclinations: Promotion and prevention in decision-making. *Organizational Behavior and Human Decision Processes, 69*(2), 117–132.

Daft, R. L., & Weick, K. E. (1984). Toward a model of organizations as interpretation systems. *Academy of Management Review, 9*(2), 284–295.

Dasgupta, P. (1988). Trust as a commodity. In D. Gambetta (Ed.), *Trust: Making and breaking cooperative relations* (pp. 49–72). Basil Blackwell.

Dattée, B., Alexy, O., & Autio, E. (2018). Maneuvering in poor visibility: How firms play the ecosystem game when uncertainty is high. *Academy of Management Journal, 61*(2), 466–498.

de Finetti, B. (1967). Probability: Interpretations. In *International encyclopaedia of the social sciences* (Vol. 12, pp. 496–505). Macmillan.

de Palma, A., Abdellaoui, M., Attanasi, G., Ben-Akiva, M., Erev, I., Fehr-Duda, H., … Weber, M. (2014). Beware of black swans: Taking stock of the description—Experience gap in decision under uncertainty. *Marketing Letters, 25*(3), 269–280.

Dekel, E., Lipman, B. L., & Rustichini, A. (1998). Recent developments in modeling unforeseen contingencies. *European Economic Review, 42*(3–5), 523–542.

Dequech, D. (2011). Uncertainty: A typology and refinements of existing concepts. *Journal of Economic Issues, 45*(3), 621–640.

Dewar, J. A., Builder, C. H., Hix, W. M., & Levin, M. H. (1993). *Assumption based planning: A planning tool for every uncertain times*. Rand.

Diehl, E., & Sterman, J. D. (1995). Effects of feedback complexity on dynamic decision making. *Organizational Behavior and Human Decision Processes, 62*(2), 198–215.

Dimov, D. (2016). Toward a design science of entrepreneurship. In *Models of start-up thinking and action: Theoretical, empirical and pedagogical approaches* (Vol. 18, pp. 1–31). Emerald Group Publishing Limited.

Dixit, A. K., & Nalebuff, B. J. (1991). *Thinking strategically: The competitive edge in business, politics, and everyday life*. W.W. Norton.

Dixit, A. K., & Pindyck, R. S. (1994). *Investment under uncertainty*. Princeton University Press.

Dosi, G., & Egidi, M. (1991). Substantive and procedural uncertainty: An exploration of economic behaviours in changing environments. *Journal of Evolutionary Economics, 1*, 145–168.

Dougherty, D., & Hardy, C. (1996). Sustained product innovation in large, mature organizations: Overcoming innovation-to-organization problems. *Academy of Management Journal, 39*(5), 1120–1153.

Dunne, D. D., & Dougherty, D. (2016). Abductive reasoning: How innovators navigate in the labyrinth of complex product innovation. *Organization Studies, 37*, 131–159.

Eggers, J. P., & Park, K. F. (2018). Incumbent adaptation to technological change: The past, present, and future of research on heterogeneous incumbent response. *Academy of Management Annals, 12*(1), 357–389.

Ehrenzweig, A. (1967). *The hidden order of art: A study in the psychology of artistic imagination.* University of California Press.

Ehrig, T., & Schmidt, J. (2022). Theory-based learning and experimentation: How strategists can systematically generate knowledge at the edge between the known and the unknown. *Strategic Management Journal, 43*(7), 1287–1318.

Einhorn, H. J., & Hogarth, R. M. (1986). Decision making under ambiguity. *Journal of Business, 59*(4), S225–S250.

Einhorn, H. J., & Hogarth, R. M. (1987). Decision-making: Going forward in reverse: *Harvard Business Review, 87*(1), 66–70.

Eisenhardt, K. M., & Martin, J. A. (2000). Dynamic capabilities: What are they? *Strategic Management Journal, 21*(10–11), 1105–1121.

Ellsberg, D. (1961). Risk, ambiguity, and the Savage axioms. *The Quarterly Journal of Economics, 75*(4), 643–669.

Etner, J., Jeleva, M., & Tallon, J. M. (2012). Decision theory under ambiguity. *Journal of Economic Surveys, 26*(2), 234–270.

Feduzi, A., Runde, J., & Zappia, C. (2012). De Finetti on the insurance of risks and uncertainties. *The British Journal for the Philosophy of Science, 63*(2), 329–356.

Felin, T., & Zenger, T. R. (2014). Closed or open innovation? Problem solving and the governance choice. *Research Policy, 43*(5), 914–925.

Felin, T., Kauffman, S., Koppl, R., & Longo, G. (2014). Economic opportunity and evolution: Beyond landscapes and bounded rationality. *Strategic Entrepreneurship Journal, 8*(4), 269–282.

Fisher, G. (2021). *New Venture Legitimacy* [Oxford Research Encyclopedia of Business and Management, https://oxfordre.com/business/view/10.1093/acrefore/9780190224851.001.0001/acrefore-9780190224851-e-313].

Fleischhut, N., Artinger, F. M., Olschewski, S., & Hertwig, R. (2022). Not all uncertainty is treated equally: Information search under social and nonsocial uncertainty. *Journal of Behavioral Decision Making, 35*(2), e2250.

Fleming, L. (2001). Recombinant uncertainty in technological search. *Management Science, 47*(1), 117–132.

Fontana, G., & Gerrard, B. (2004). A post Keynesian theory of decision making under uncertainty. *Journal of Economic Psychology, 25*(5), 619–637.

Foss, N. J., & Klein, P. G. (2020). Entrepreneurial opportunities: Who needs them? *Academy of Management Perspectives, 34*(3), 366–377.

Foss, N. J., & Laursen, K. (2005). Performance pay, delegation and multitasking under uncertainty and innovativeness: An empirical investigation. *Journal of Economic Behavior & Organization, 58*(2), 246–276.

Foss, N. J., Klein, P. G., & Bjørnskov, C. (2019). The context of entrepreneurial judgment: Organizations, markets, and institutions. *Journal of Management Studies, 56*(6), 1197–1213.

Fox, J. (2014). Instinct can beat analytical thinking. *Harvard Business Review, 20*.

Garner, W. R. (1962). *Uncertainty and structure as psychological concepts.* Wiley.

Gavetti, G., & Levinthal, D. (2000). Looking forward and looking backward: Cognitive and experiential search. *Administrative Science Quarterly, 45*(1), 113–137.

Gavetti, G., & Levinthal, D. (2001). Bringing cognition back in and moving forward. *Journal of Management and Governance, 5*(3), 213–216.

Gavetti, G., Helfat, C. E., & Marengo, L. (2017). Searching, shaping, and the quest for superior performance. *Strategy Science, 2,* 194–209.

Gavetti, G., Levinthal, D. A., & Rivkin, J. W. (2005). Strategy making in novel and complex worlds: The power of analogy. *Strategic Management Journal, 26*(8), 691–712.

George, C., Bright, A., Hurlbert, T., Linke, E. C., St. Clair, G., & Stein, J. (2006). Scholarly use of information: Graduate students' information seeking behaviour. *Information Research, 11*(4), paper 272.

Gigerenzer, G., & Gaissmaier, W. (2011). Heuristic decision making. *Annual Review of Psychology, 62,* 451–482.

Gigerenzer, G. (2005). I think, therefore I err. *Social Research: An International Quarterly, 72*(1), 195–218.

Gilboa, I. (2009). *Theory of decision under uncertainty.* Cambridge University Press.

Golman, R., & Loewenstein, G. (2016). Information gaps: A theory of preferences regarding the presence and absence of information. *Decision, 5,* 143–164.

Gomes, L. A. de V., Facin, A. L. F., & Salerno, M. S. (2021). Managing uncertainty propagation in innovation ecosystems. *Technological Forecasting and Social Change, 171,* 120945.

Griffin, M. A., & Grote, G. (2020). When is more uncertainty better? A model of uncertainty regulation and effectiveness. *Academy of Management Review, 45*(4), 745–765.

Hacking, I. (1975). *The emergence of probability.* Cambridge University Press.

Halpern, J. Y. (2003). *Reasoning about uncertainty.* MIT Press.

Hansson, S. O. (1996). Decision making under great uncertainty. *Philosophy of the Social Sciences, 26*(3), 369–386.

Harrison, F. L. (1977). Decision-making in conditions of extreme uncertainty. *Journal of Management Studies, 14*(2), 169–178.

Hau, R., Pleskac, T. J., & Hertwig, R. (2010). Decisions from experience and statistical probabilities: Why they trigger different choices than a priori probabilities. *Journal of Behavioral Decision Making, 23*(1), 48–68.

Helton, J. C., & Johnson, J. D. (2011). Quantification of margins and uncertainties: Alternative representations of epistemic uncertainty. *Reliability Engineering & System Safety, 96*(9), 1034–1052.

Herman, J. D., Reed, P. M., Zeff, H. B., & Characklis, G. W. (2015). How should robustness be defined for water systems planning under change. *Journal of Water Resources Planning and Management, 141*(10), 04015012.

Hertwig, R., & Gigerenzer, G. (1999). The 'conjunction fallacy'revisited: How intelligent inferences look like reasoning errors. *Journal of Behavioral Decision Making, 12*(4), 275–305.

Hertwig, R., Pleskac, T. J., & Pachur, T. (2019). *Taming uncertainty*. MIT Press.

Hillman, A. J., Withers, M. C., & Collins, B. J. (2009). Resource dependence theory: A review. *Journal of Management, 35*(6), 1404–1427.

Hogarth, R. M., & Karelaia, N. (2007). Heuristic and linear models of judgment: Matching rules and environments. *Psychological Review, 114*(3), 733.

Hogarth, R. M. (1980). *Judgement and choice: The psychology of decision*. Wiley.

Holmes, T., & Westgren, R. (2020). Carving the nature of uncertainty at its joints. *Academy of Management Review, 45*(4), 869–872.

Huber, G. (1991). Organizational learning: The contributing processes and a review of the literatures. *Organization Science, 2*, 88–115.

Hyldegard, J. (2006). Collaborative information behavior—Exploring Kuhlthau's information search process model in a group-based educational setting. *Information Processing and Management, 42*(1), 276–298.

Iansiti, M. (1995). Shooting the rapids: Managing product development in turbulent environments. *California Management Review, 38*(1), 37–52.

Jonas, E., McGregor, I., Klackl, J., Agroskin, D., Fritsche, I., Holbrook, C., Nash, K., Proulx, T., & Quirin, M. (2014). Threat and defense: From anxiety to approach. *Advances in Experimental Social Psychology, 49*, 219–286.

Kagan, J. (1972). Motives and development. *Journal of Personality and Social Psychology, 22*, 51–66.

Kahneman, D. (2003). Maps of bounded rationality: Psychology for behavioral economics. *The American Economic Review, 93*(5), 1449–1475.

Kaplan, S. (2008). Framing contests: Strategy making under uncertainty. *Organization Science, 19*(5), 729–752.

Kapoor, R., & Adner, R. (2012). What firms make vs. what they know: How firms' production and knowledge boundaries affect competitive advantage in the face of technological change. *Organization Science, 23*(5), 1227–1248.

Kapoor, R., & Klueter, T. (2021). Unbundling and managing uncertainty surrounding emerging technologies. *Strategy Science, 6*(1), 62–74.

Katila, R., & Ahuja, G. (2002). Something old, something new: A longitudinal study of search behavior and new product introduction. *Academy of Management Journal, 45*(6), 1183–1194.

Kaur, N., & Dasgupta, C. (2018). Types of uncertainty and collaborative uncertainty management strategies evidenced during the engineering design process. In *International conference on computers in education* (pp. 175–180).

Kay, J. A., & King, M. A. (2020). *Radical uncertainty*. Bridge Street Press.

Keynes, J. M. (1936). *The general theory of employment*. Macmillan, Cambridge University Press for the Royal Economic Society.

Kim, S. (2013). Neuroscientific model of motivational process. *Frontiers in Psychology, 4*(1–12), 98.

Kirzner, I. M. (1973). *Competition and entrepreneurship*. University of Chicago Press.

Kirzner, I. M. (1997). Entrepreneurial discovery and the competitive market process: An Austrian approach. *Journal of Economic Literature, 35*(1), 60–85.

Kiss, A. N., Libaers, D., Barr, P. S., Wang, T., & Zachary, M. A. (2020). CEO cognitive flexibility, information search, and organizational ambidexterity. *Strategic Management Journal, 41*(12), 2200–2233.

Klir, G. J. (2004). Generalized information theory: Aims, results, and open problems. *Reliability Engineering & System Safety, 85*(1–3), 21–38.

Knight, E., Daymond, J., & Paroutis, S. (2020). Design-led strategy: How to bring design thinking into the art of strategic management. *California Management Review, 62*(2), 30–52.

Knight, F. H. (1921/64). *Risk, uncertainty and profit*. Augustus M. Kelley.

Kozyreva, A., & Hertwig, R. (2021). The interpretation of uncertainty in ecological rationality. *Synthese, 198*(2), 1517–1547.

Kuhlthau, C. C. (1993). A principle of uncertainty for information seeking. *Journal of Documentation, 49*(4), 339–355.

Kuhlthau, C. C., Heinström, J., & Todd, R. J. (2008). The 'information search process' revisited: Is the model still useful. *Information Research, 13*(4), 13–14.

Lachmann, L. M. (1976). From Mises to Shackle: An essay on Austrian economics and the kaleidic society. *Journal of Economic Literature, 14*(1), 54–62.

Lampert, C. M., Kim, M., & Polidoro, F., Jr. (2020). Branching and anchoring: Complementary asset configurations in conditions of Knightian uncertainty. *Academy of Management Review, 45*(4), 847–868.

Lanzetta, J. T. (1963). Information acquisition in decision making. In J. Harvey (Ed.), *Motivation and social interaction: Cognitive determinants*. Ronald Press, 239–265.

Laplace, P. S. (1951). *A philosophical essay on probabilities.* Dover.
Lee, B., & Yoo, B. (2007). What prevents electronic lemon markets? *Journal of Organizational Computing and Electronic Commerce, 17*(3), 217–246.
Leiblein, M. J., Reuer, J. J., & Zenger, T. (2018). What makes a decision strategic? *Strategy Science, 3*(4), 558–573.
Lempert R. J., Popper, S. W., & Bankes, S. C. (2003). *Shaping the next one hundred years: New methods for quantitative, long-term policy analysis* [MR-1626-RPC, RAND, Santa Monica, California] (pp. 3–4).
Lipshitz, R., & Strauss, O. (1997). Coping with uncertainty: A naturalistic decision-making analysis. *Organizational Behavior and Human Decision Processes, 69*(2), 149–163.
Louis, M. R. (1980). Surprise and sense making: What newcomers experience in entering unfamiliar organizational settings. *Administrative Science Quarterly, 25,* 226–251.
Luan, S., Reb, J., & Gigerenzer, G. (2019). Ecological rationality: Fast-and-frugal heuristics for managerial decision making under uncertainty. *Academy of Management Journal, 62*(6), 1735–1759.
Luehrman, T. A. (1998). Strategy as a portfolio of real options. *Harvard Business Review, 76,* 89–101.
Lynn, G., Morone, J., & Paulson, P. (1996). Marketing and discontinuous innovation: The probe and learn process. *California Management Review, 38*(3), 8–37.
MacLeod, W. B., & Pingle, M. (2000). *An experiment on the relative effects of ability, temperament and luck on search with uncertainty* [University of Southern California Law School, Olin Research paper 00-12].
Manski, C. F. (2000). Identification problems and decisions under ambiguity: Empirical analysis of treatment response and normative analysis of treatment choice. *Journal of Econometrics, 95*(2), 415–442.
March, J. (1991). Exploration and exploitation in organizational learning. *Organization Science, 2,* 71–87.
Marchau, V. A., Walker, W. E., Bloemen, P. J., & Popper, S. W. (2019). *Decision making under deep uncertainty: From theory to practice.* Springer Nature.
Markowitz, H. M. (1952). Portfolio selection. *Journal of Finance, 7,* 77–91.
Martin, M. M., & Rubin, R. B. (1995). A new measure of cognitive flexibility. *Psychological Reports, 76*(2), 623–626.
McDonald, R., & Eisenhardt, K. (2020). The New-Market Conundrum in emerging industries the usual rules of strategy don't apply. *Harvard Business Review, 98*(3), 75–83.
McGrath, R. G., & Macmillan, I. C. (1995). Discovery driven planning. *Harvard Business Review, 73*(4), 44–54.
McGrath, R. G., & MacMillan, I. C. (2000). Assessing technology projects using real options reasoning. *Research-Technology Management, 43*(4), 35–49.

McMullen, J. S., & Kier, A. S. (2016). Trapped by the entrepreneurial mindset: Opportunity seeking and escalation of commitment in the Mount Everest disaster. *Journal of Business Venturing, 31*(6), 663–686.

Medin, D. L., & Schaffer, M. M. (1978). Context theory of classification learning. *Psychological Review, 85*(3), 207–238.

Miceli, T. J. (1994). Book review of: Paradigms and conventions: Uncertainty, decision making, and entrepreneurship. *Journal of Economic Behavior & Organization, 25*(2), 299–301.

Millar, C. C., Groth, O., & Mahon, J. F. (2018). Management innovation in a VUCA world: Challenges and recommendations. *California Management Review, 61*(1), 5–14.

Mousavi, S., & Gigerenzer, G. (2014). Risk, uncertainty, and heuristics. *Journal of Business Research, 67*(8), 1671–1678.

Newell, A., & Simon, H. A. (1972). *Human problem solving* (Vol. 104, No. 9). Prentice-Hall.

Nickerson, J. A., & Zenger, T. R. (2004). A knowledge-based theory of the firm—The problem-solving perspective. *Organization Science, 15*(6), 617–632.

Nosal, J. B., & Ordoñez, G. (2016). Uncertainty as commitment. *Journal of Monetary Economics, 80*, 124–140.

O'Connor, G. C., & Rice, M. P. (2013). A comprehensive model of uncertainty associated with radical innovation. *Journal of Product Innovation Management, 30*, 2–18.

Packard, M. D., & Clark, B. B. (2020). On the mitigability of uncertainty and the choice between predictive and nonpredictive strategy. *Academy of Management Review, 45*(4), 766–786.

Packard, M. D., Clark, B. B., & Klein, P. G. (2017). Uncertainty types and transitions in the entrepreneurial process. *Organization Science, 28*(5), 840–856.

Pitts, J. M. (1995). Mental models of information: The 1993–1994 AASL/Highsmith research award study. *School Library Media Quarterly, 23*(3), 177–184.

Porter, M. E. (1980). *Competitive strategy: Techniques for analyzing industries and competitors*. Free Press.

Pressman, S., & Choi, Y. B. (1997). Paradigms, conventions and the entrepreneur: A review article and response. *American Journal of Economics and Sociology, 56*(1), 51–68.

Ramoglou, S. (2021). Knowable opportunities in an unknowable future? On the epistemological paradoxes of entrepreneurship theory. *Journal of Business Venturing, 36*(2), 106090.

Raynor, M. E. (2007). *The strategy paradox: Why committing to success leads to failure (and what to do about it)*. Currency.

Reale, C., Salwei, M. E., Militello, L. G., Weinger, M. B., Burden, A., Sushereba, C., Andreae, M. H., Gaba, D. M., McIvor, W. R., & Banerjee A. (2023). Decision-making during high-risk events: A systematic literature review. *Journal of Cognitive Engineering and Decision Making, 17*(2), 188–212.

Reetz, D. K., & MacAulay, S. (2016). Beyond ill-structured problems: Tackling true novelty through co-evolutionary search. In *36th Strategic Management Conference SMS*, Berlin.

Rindova, V., & Courtney, H. (2020). To shape or adapt: Knowledge problems, epistemologies, and strategic postures under Knightian uncertainty. *Academy of Management Review, 45*(4), 787–807.

Rock, D. (2008). SCARF: A brain-based model for collaborating with and influencing others. *NeuroLeadership Journal, 1*(1), 44–52.

Roeser, S. (2019). Emotional responses to luck, risk, and uncertainty. In *The Routledge handbook of the philosophy and psychology of luck* (pp. 356–364). Routledge.

Samsami, F., Hosseini, S. H. K., Kordnaeij, A., & Azar, A. (2015). Managing environmental uncertainty: From conceptual review to strategic management point of view. *International Journal of Business and Management, 10*(7), 215–229.

Sastry, L., & Boyd, D. R. (1998). Virtual environments for engineering applications. *Virtual Reality, 3*, 235–244.

Savage, L. J. (1954). *The foundations of statistics*. Wiley.

Schmeidler, D. (1989). Subjective probability and expected utility without additivity. *Econometrica, 57*(3), 571–587.

Schoemaker, P. J. (2002). *Profiting from uncertainty: Strategies for succeeding no matter what the future brings*. Simon & Schuster.

Scoblic, J. P. (2020). Learning from the future. *Harvard Business Review, 98*(4), 38–47.

Serola, S., & Vakkari, P. (2005). The anticipated and assessed contribution of information types in references retrieved for preparing a research proposal. *Journal of the American Society for Information Science and Technology, 56*(4), 373–381.

Sewell, W. H., Jr. (1992). A theory of structure: Duality, agency and transformation. *American Journal of Sociology, 98*, 1–29.

Shackle, G. L. S. (1966). *The nature of economic though: Selected papers (1955–1964)*. Cambridge University Press.

Shackle, G. L. S. (1979). *Imagination and the nature of choice*. Edinburgh University Press.

Shepherd, D. A., Williams, T. A., & Patzelt, H. (2015). Thinking about entrepreneurial decision making: Review and research agenda. *Journal of Management, 41*(1), 11–46.

Shin, D. D., & Kim, S. I. (2019). Homo curious: Curious or interested? *Educational Psychology Review, 31*(4), 853–874.

Simon, H. A. (1956). Rational choice and the structure of the environment. *Psychology Review, 63*(2), 129–138.

Simon, H. A. (1962). The architecture of complexity. *Proceedings of the American Philosophical Society, 106*, 467–482.

Simon, H. A. (1979). Information processing models of cognition. *Annual Review of Psychology, 30*(1), 363–396.

Simon, H. A. (1982). *Models of bounded rationality: Empirically grounded economic reason* (Vol. 3). MIT Press.

Simon, H. A. (1995). The information-processing theory of mind. *American Psychologist, 50*(7), 507.

Simon, H. A. (1996). *The sciences of the artificial* (3rd ed.). MIT Press.

Sims, C. A. (2001). Pitfalls of a minimax approach to model uncertainty. *American Economic Review, 91*(2), 51–54.

Spender, J.-C. (2006). *Knightian uncertainty and its resolution as institutionalized practice* [v9 Working Paper].

Stager, P. (1967). Conceptual level as a composition variable in small-group decision making. *Journal of Personality and Social Psychology, 5*(2), 152–161.

Starbuck, W. H., & Milliken, F. J. (1988). Executives' perceptual filters: What they notice and how they make sense. In D. C. Hambrick (Ed.), *The executive effect: Concepts and methods for studying top managers* (pp. 35–65). JAI Press.

Stigler, G. (1939). Production and distribution in the short run. *Journal of Political Economy, 47*, 305–327.

Sturm, R. R. (2003). Investor confidence and returns following large one-day price changes. *The Journal of Behavioral Finance, 4*(4), 201–216.

Szentkirályi, L. (2020). Luck has nothing to do with it: Prevailing uncertainty and responsibilities of due care. *Ethics, Policy & Environment, 23*(3), 261–280.

Taleb, N. N. (2012). *Antifragile: How to live in a world we don't understand.* Allen Lane.

Teece, D., & Leih, S. (2016). Uncertainty, innovation, and dynamic capabilities: An introduction. *California Management Review, 58*(4), 5–12.

Teece, D., Peteraf, M., & Leih, S. (2016). Dynamic capabilities and organizational agility: Risk, uncertainty, and strategy in the innovation economy. *California Management Review, 58*(4), 13–35.

Teece, D. J., Pisano, G., & Shuen, A. (1997). Dynamic capabilities and strategic management. *Strategic Management Journal, 18*(7), 509–533.

Townsend, D. M., Hunt, R. A., Beal, D. J., & Hyeong Jin, J. (2020). Venturing into the unknown: A meta-analytic assessment of uncertainty in entrepreneurship research. *Academy of Management Proceedings, 2020*(1), 17318.

Townsend, D. M., Hunt, R. A., McMullen, J. S., & Sarasvathy, S. D. (2018). Uncertainty, knowledge problems, and entrepreneurial action. *Academy of Management Annals, 12*(2), 659–687.

Tversky, A., & Kahneman, D. (1973). Availability: A heuristic for judging frequency and probability. *Cognitive Psychology, 5*(2), 207–232.

Tversky, A., & Kahneman, D. (1974). Judgment under uncertainty: Heuristics and biases. *Science, 185*, 1124–1131.

Vakkari, P., Pennanen, M., & Serola, S. (2003). Changes of search terms and tactics while writing a research proposal: A longitudinal case study. *Information Processing and Management, 39*(3), 445–463.

van Lieshout, L. L., Vandenbroucke, A. R., Müller, N. C., Cools, R., & de Lange, F. P. (2018). Induction and relief of curiosity elicit parietal and frontal activity. *Journal of Neuroscience, 38*(10), 2816–2817.

Wald, A. (1947). *Sequential analysis*. Wiley.

Wang, P., & Soergel, D. (1998). A cognitive model of document use during a research project. Study 1. Document selection. *Journal of the American Society for Information Science, 49*(2), 115–133.

Waterman, R. H., Jr. (1990). *Adhocracy: The power to change*. Whittle Direct Books.

Weick, K. E. (2001). *Making sense of the organization*. Blackwell.

Weick, K. E., Sutcliffe, K. M., & Obstfeld, D. (2005). Organizing and the process of sensemaking and organizing. *Organization Science, 16*(4), 409–421.

Wernerfelt, B., & Karnani, A. (1987). Competitive strategy under uncertainty. *Strategic Management Journal, 8*(2), 187–194.

Williamson, O. E. (1985). *The economic institutions of capitalism*. Free Press.

Williamson, P. J. (1999). Strategy as options on the future. *Sloan Management Review, 40*(3), 117–126.

Yager, R. R. (1999). A game-theoretic approach to decision making under uncertainty. *Intelligent Systems in Accounting, Finance & Management, 8*(2), 131–143.

Zafar, S., Waddingham, J., Zachary, M., & Short, J. (2021). Search behavior and decision confidence in equity crowdfunding: An information search process model perspective. *Journal of Small Business Management, 61*(4), 1638–1671.

CHAPTER 19

Conclusions of the Analysis of Uncertainty (as Everything)

Uncertainty sprawls across many disciplines, it is everywhere and it is multifarious (Bammer & Smithson, 2008). Humanity must learn to accept uncertainty as a means for understanding reality rather than a hindrance (Nash, 2003). This will take significant time, and we only started to take it seriously 300 years ago (Hertwig et al., 2019). Right now, it appears that the discussions about uncertainty are 'bipolar'—uncertainty is considered either as something that can and should be eliminated or as something irreducible but important to human affairs (Bammer & Smithson, 2008). We are challenged by its various constructions (e.g., ontological, epistemological, methodological, and spiritual), its many impacts, its many measures, its many sources, and its many forms. And, in some ways, how it is dealt with even defines what (human) rationality is (Bammer & Smithson, 2008).

SUMMARY

We have argued that uncertainty is everywhere and, in many ways, is everything. It has existential connections to most of the constructions spawned by humanity, from businesses to religions to governments to financial markets to entertainment to science. We have also argued that there are recognizable types, sources, and impacts; and, for those types, we have argued that there are various legitimate treatments, or approaches, that can improve the problem in some manner (and some that, by definition, cannot). We have drawn from the extensive, although confusing and poorly organized, literatures related to uncertainty to provide appropriate descriptions and insights. However, we are limited in what we can cover in one book. To that end, we have mostly left the (practical) specifics of any 'deep' topic to a minimum. Despite that caveat, we have offered significant new understandings and prescriptions to help improve future decision-making under uncertainty.

IMPLICATIONS

Explorers seek out the unknown, and then they seek to conquer it (Bammer & Smithson, 2008). That summarizes the eternal, two-pronged drive of intelligent life. Seek out possible gains in new and dangerous landscapes, and then exploit them by better understanding, predicting, and controlling them. Such actions spur the creativity that humanity celebrates and rewards. Truly, we are wired against the 'option' of stopping progress and exploration, as a way to reduce uncertainty (Knight, 1921). As a result, it is a strange 'arms race' that humanity finds itself in—where the uncertainty embodied in trusting each other spurs the kinds of explorations that create even more uncertainty (usually of a different type, like about new technologies [e.g., AI]).[1]

Perhaps a 'new science' is required to adequately deal with uncertainty (Bammer & Smithson, 2008)? Perhaps a multidisciplinary one that admits to ignorance, that is unifying in its definitions of the terms relating to uncertainty and in the categorization of its forms, and that holds a database of approaches (along with their associated successes, failures, costs, benefits, and contingencies, as applied to the different forms of uncertainty)?

Philosophical and Scientific Issues

Over a century has passed since Knight's (1921) clear delineation of uncertainty from risk, and in that time, humanity has been able to put to rest the question of whether irreducible uncertainty exists. It does; it has, and it will (forever). Whether in Gödel's theorems, in quantum physics, or in logical arguments based on the limitations of human measurement, interpretation and recording, there will always be known unknowns with unknowable values (let alone unknown unknowns). Enlightenment was wrong. Science has bounds. New and unique 'things' will continue to arise that previous experience forms poor, if not misleading, signals about. The information upon which we act will always be incomplete, sometimes to the point that it poses strategic dangers (but thankfully mostly not). We can continue to survive, even thrive, knowing that all models are wrong, but that many remain practically useful nonetheless (Clark, 2016). We can perhaps take comfort in the fact that nothing in the universe of experience is absolutely unique nor absolutely the same, and that there are always seem to be some knowns in the problems that we confront that can provide help (Knight, 1921; Ramoglou, 2021).

Trying the avoid 'real' uncertainty has not been the answer. Focusing on treatable uncertainties, risks, and subjective estimates, may have

---

[1] Humanity's only way forward is through the kind of progress that requires us to trust each other because no individual can specialize in all of the areas that may benefit or harm them. We all need to believe that the specialized information that others create and disperse is (substantively) true for real advancements in living standards to occur. And AI is unlikely to replace that need for trust, given the little morality or fear of reprisal it could ever (be programmed to) possess.

been (and may continue to be) the path to filling journal pages, but it does *not* do the analysis of uncertainties—especially the most challenging forms—justice. It keeps humanity from seriously tackling wicked problems (Marchau et al., 2019; Rittel & Webber, 1973), and from meticulously collecting data on which approaches do and do not work (and why) when untreatable uncertainties are confronted.

Observational data and its analysis are also not the answer. Experimental research is important, and it certainly 'sells well' to point out the many interesting individual behaviors that have evolved into us, especially when they do not align with super-rational recommendations. But most of this (published) work is 'artificial' (i.e., made for the lab) and involves simple choices and low stakes. While such work may provide some insights into basic reactions to problems involving unknowns, usually revealing the application of some heuristic, it is rather limited in terms of informing how 'we' should be making better strategic decisions under various forms of uncertainty. Exploring the boundedness of a real decision-maker's rationality, their biases, their coping mechanisms (like a reliance on narratives), and their use of past experiences, is fantastic for psychology and economics (Einhorn & Hogarth, 1986; Kay & King, 2020; Kozyreva & Hertwig, 2021; Simon, 1972), but it doesn't tell us how real decision-makers become aware of any one uncertainty,[2] whether they recognize it as a distinct form of unknown, or how they choose among the various treatments and approaches available to address it (and, so on).

The behavioral approach also regresses the analysis back to the subjective–objective debate.[3] Behavioral studies focus on the subjective (often using the objective as a reference point). Subjective factors complicate the analysis of decision-making under uncertainty, bringing in many more limitations and individual-level unknowns (e.g., in terms of asymmetries of information, emotional responses, personal goals and memories, inconsistent utility functions, learning, and so on) (Bammer & Smithson, 2008). Such factors can cause interpretive havoc, for example, mistaking

---

[2] For example, most executives vastly underestimate the uncertainties they face (Courtney et al., 2013).

[3] Given it seems like an irresolvable debate in the literature, recall we have chosen in this book to take the standard side in the uncertainty literature, which is to assume an objective reality with objective knowns and unknowns. That said, we do consider how subjectivity will enter the picture in several places, for example, when practically processing the decisions.

confusion (as qualitative distortion) with inaccuracy (as quantitative distortion) (Bammer & Smithson, 2008). That is why most theoretical research on uncertainty takes the objective perspective.

The behavioral approach is also limited in the range of important and real aspects of decision-making under uncertainty it can readily explore. For example, experimental studies are ill-suited to explore complex possible interactions among uncertainties. Lab exercises and surveys are quite limited in the amount of information, choices, and surprises that they can expect participants to react to in a representative way, ruling out the drowning of them in the details they would need to consider when uncertainties interact. That restriction on information provision and on participant attention may be less of an issue for case studies, but very few of them exist in this realm (partly because of the complexities involved that would require explanation and analysis [within journal length restrictions]). By contrast, theoretical work can tackle such complexities, partly because subjectivity is not involved, and partly because one interaction at a time could be focused on (with modeling assumptions). For an illustration of the complexities that are likely unanalyzable by the behavioral approach, consider now just two of the interactions that are possible among uncertainties: *sequential interactions*—where one unknown needs to be resolved prior to the other (Adner, 2012; Cooper, 2000; Kapoor & Klueter, 2021); and, *reciprocal interactions*—where addressing one uncertainty shapes the resolution of another that affects the first (Kapoor & Klueter, 2021). When these interactions are not considered, then neither is the possibility of exploiting (or exacerbating) the conditional dependence that exists.

A question remains whether science—as conducted by its flawed human specialists—is sufficiently well-equipped (in its current form) to seriously study uncertainty. Its recent public relations and its history raise doubts. There have been periods of unjustified optimism—with the rampant use of the newest discovery in mathematics or philosophy—promoting the idea that all uncertainty can be overcome. For example, in the nineteenth century, the observation that many social science phenomena followed a *Normal distribution* spurred a deluge of quantitative-methods applications based on the hope that these could be as successfully understood as natural science phenomena are; much disappointment remains (Kay & King, 2020). Science is based on repeated patterns (that have limited variance), and the premise that knowing the rules that govern those patterns (e.g., in nature), allows us to know vast numbers of things (i.e., because those rules can then be applied to an infinite number of specific circumstances) (Barrow, 1998). But, uncertainty ruins that logic; uncertainty is embodied in the novelty, and in the unknown rules that make the application of the known rules of limited value, sometimes severely so. Uncertainty is the ever-present, ever-lasting *nemesis of science*; one that is 'happy' to prey on the subjectivity and bounded rationality of its proponents. That said, for the treatable uncertainties, science has slayed many dragons, starting with the simple effort to make records of what is known, so that search can become a more and more effective and efficient means to 'look up' the value of many knowable unknowns (Gray, 2002).

In order for science to 'do better' in addressing uncertainty, it may be useful to revisit the costs involved. While many costs are likely to be *un*knowable, there is some reference work that can be used to at least understand the kinds of sacrifices involved in the pursuit of the applicable knowledge that could reduce the known unknowns. *Spreng's (2013) triangle* depicts the three-way trade-off between time, energy, and information. It is based on: the limits in the amount of information that can be obtained when applying a given energy budget; the energy-time uncertainty principle (from quantum mechanics); and, the *Wigner (1957) clock limit* (of measurement). To obtain information, there are necessary costs in energy and time (Barrow, 1998), and ever more substantial ones as the precision (e.g., to the atomic level) increases. In other words, there are theoretical and practical limits to uncovering knowledge; to the latter, determining an optimal budget for such scientific work does *not* appear straightforward, but nevertheless it must be kept in mind when allocating resources for scientific pursuits.

At this point, after speaking to the extremes of human science, some humility is in order. It is useful to recall that humankind is *not* unique in having to deal with uncertainty, nor are we unique in sometimes finding ways to (seemingly) triumph over it.[4] Most forms of life have evolved

---

[4] Humans have evolved many reflexes and heuristics to respond to uncertainty—as automatic and nearly-automatic responses to surprises. Such responses may have been useful millennia ago 'on the plains', we question whether some of them are now, given the contexts, dangers, costs, tools, rivals, and long-term importance, have all changed. This remains an avenue for future work. As does the 'more human' emotional impacts involved in facing uncertainties—ones often treated now by drugs and therapies. The instances of deep loneliness that humans can find themselves in due to 'distrust'—as embodied in uncertainty about the intentions of others—have been growing (partly due to the

ways to try to address uncertainty. In fact, the 'knowledge' required to treat some knowable unknowns does not even need minds. That ability is found in all living things. Even trees can communicate with each other about new truths (Gray, 2002).

Returning to human pursuits, the study of philosophy has often contemplated uncertainty. In some philosophies, the acceptance of uncertainty is even considered 'good' or 'healthy'. Whereas in 'Western' thought there is a desire to close the gap between 'what is' and 'what ought to be'—partly by reducing the unknowns—in some 'Eastern' thought (e.g., Taoism), there is no such gap, and the best action comes from a clear view of the situation, including its unknowns (Gray, 2002). That latter attitude of openness, as described by Plato, Kant, and others, can allow 'us' to experience all things as they develop, not as we might predict or prejudge them, but with the acceptance of them 'as they are'—which is often a better place from which to act (Faber et al., 1992).

It is also useful to recall that uncertainty isn't always something to avoid. There are times that it is actively sought out (Bammer & Smithson, 2008), for possible gain. Entrepreneurs seek it out for profitable opportunities (Knight, 1921). Improvisationalists (e.g., in jazz) seek it out for a challenge, and to create entertainment for an audience. Visual artists seek it out for inspiration. Experimentalists seek it out to randomize sample selection. And, social constructionists seek it out in the form of 'chaotic playgrounds' in which to operate where they can more easily alter the opinions of target audiences. Recent field-based work (e.g., Jackson, 2023) describes uncertainty-as-doubt in a mainly positive light, where it has value in several sensitive situations (e.g., surgery), mostly in helping to induce assumption-checking, creativity, and openness (to new perspectives) through (self-) reflection.

Science—as it stands—must change to better address uncertainty in all its forms, sources, and effects. One of the main things it must change is its dishonesty—both the unintentional kind, but more so the intentional kind. Promoting treatments for the untreatable unknowns is unprofessional; and, it is harmful, both to those who take that advice, and to the legitimacy of whatever field (and whichever 'guru') such advice emanates from. It must stop. And, it must be exposed and corrected. Such 'snake oil' may provide some people considerable citations and consultancy

pandemic), and need to be addressed more seriously, starting with a better understanding of such uncertainties (and their origins).

income, but those private gains are small relative to the societal costs created.[5]

We stress that it is the quality of the uncertainty (rather than the quantity) that matters most when it comes to decision-making (Lipshitz & Strauss, 1997). That primary quality is whether the uncertainty is treatable or not. Only the former holds the promise of optimizing the given problem 'as given'. For the latter, the 'best' that can be done is to try and optimize the problem 'as altered' (e.g., as substantively changed in its goal, or in its focal entity, or in some other relevant manner). There is no 'magic trick' for beating unknown unknowns or known unknowable unknowns; and, there are no special people who can (other than through pure luck) (Kay & King, 2020).

The best approach to consider relates to the famous serenity prayer (which itself relates to the art of triage): treat the unknowns that are treatable; address the unknowns that are not (by changing the problem); and, develop the judgment to know the difference (Scoblic, 2020). To the latter, we must work on acquiring the ability to distinguish between the more normal uncertainties and the abnormal ones (Bernstein, 1996). We need to become aware of our ignorance in all its forms, appreciate it, and understand its variants. Because when we are ignorant but *un*aware of it, we end up living in a fool's paradise (Stewart, 2019).

FUTURE WORK

We hope that we have opened up many 'worm cans' along the way in our analysis of decision-making under uncertainty. We have advocated for a 'new' science to explore the many avenues to improve that decision-making. That recommendation implies significant future work—for example, in doing case studies that capture the effectiveness of the various treatments and approaches we have described, and then in cataloguing them by uncertainty type and recording the costs, benefits, contingencies. and implementation issues involved (and, interdependencies with other unknowns, and so on). It implies not only more fieldwork, but better theory-building (Arend, 2019) based on more systematic approaches (Gomes et al., 2021). Further, it also implies greater cross-disciplinary work in trying to connect and unify the various definitions,

---

[5] Those costs include creating unnecessary confusion, leading to more uncertainty over how to deal with uncertainty.

typologies, measures, treatments, and other tools relating to uncertainty.[6] Only on that basis can emerge the kind of precise communications and understandings required to tackle the bigger uncertainty-vexed decision problems that span multiple fields (e.g., like the 'wicked' problems that most often involve both the natural and social sciences).

In terms of how long this may take, perhaps generations. At present, it seems like it will take decades to get new minds educated in a manner that trusts science yet appreciates its bounds (i.e., minds that see strength rather than weakness in the admission of honest ignorance, and that are highly suspicious of any entity promising 'all the answers'), and that understands how and why uncertainty is woven into the fabric of humanity and of the universe (but *not* as a 'god').

(Almost) Final Thoughts

For good, for bad, and for real, uncertainty is everywhere and, in many ways, everything. We have to start somewhere to appreciate it, and to better understand and deal with it. We believe that 'this' is a good place— a good place to build the unified definitions, the logically delineated types, and the sets of honest treatments and approaches relevant for those types. Only from such a foundation can we hope to move forward and build the kinds of knowledge, tools (AI and traditional),[7] and motivations to improve 'our' decision-making under uncertainty. So, with gratitude, we wish 'good uncertainty' to all!

Summary
We thank the Reader for going on this journey of discovery with us. A journey of discovery about arguably the most important concept

---

[6] The recommendation also implies several interesting questions to be considered in future work, such as: When is ignorance about uncertainty actually bliss (versus being a fool's paradise)? When can bad or inappropriate treatments or approaches to uncertainty be exploited by others and at what costs? and, When will the point of inflection occur in science when the ratio of 'the new uncertainties created by discovery' to 'the old uncertainties answered by that discovery' drop to unity or below?

[7] Note that big data and AI are just tools, and so must be used with caution, especially in an uncertain world, where they are likely to provide only the illusion of certainty (Fox, 2014).

for humanity—uncertainty. It is a strange irony that such a journey is needed—because the serious study of uncertainty (especially the untreatable types) has *not* been attempted at any serious level, let alone at a level of 'most important'. That is incredibly disappointing because the foundation to get to that level quickly is so obvious—i.e., get agreement (beginning in the academic community) over terminology, and at least a basic typology, so that we can talk to each other rather than past each other, so that we can start building more effectively on each other's work, and so that a common database of knowledge about uncertainty (and decision-making under it) can be built for study and for reference. It is certainly time to start; we hope that we have provided at least the inspiration if not the tools to do so in this book. *Godspeed*.

Why the journey matters:

- This journey exploring decision-making under uncertainty has hopefully provided a much larger perspective of uncertainty than found elsewhere, in that *uncertainty is everything*
- …as, such, it hopefully has increased the understanding of its importance to humanity, its wide variety of impacts, and its main types
- …and, most importantly, hopefully, it has increased 'our' ability to manage it more effectively—especially to make better decisions under it.

What this journey may mean for business and policy:

- It has proven that uncertainty will always be 'here' and, as such, will always provide a way past the defenses of any incumbencies
- …for both the 'good' (new products, new ventures, new ideas, new art)
- …and, for the 'bad' (new threats, more disinformation, more chaos, more anxiety)
- …which means that academia, business and government all have greater responsibility to find a universal language for it, to adopt a meaningful typology for it, and start getting much more serious in studying it, tracking it, and communicating about it.

References

Adner, R. (2012). *The wide lens: A new strategy for innovation*. Penguin.
Arend, R. J. (2019). *On theory: Brain-mind teleology and the failure in the success of the human use of science*. Cambridge Scholars Publishing.
Bammer, G., & Smithson, M. (2008). Understanding uncertainty. *Integration Insights, 7*(1), 1–7.
Barrow, J. D. (1998). *Impossibility: The limits of science and the science of limits*. Oxford University Press on Demand.
Bernstein, P. L. (1996). *Against the gods: The remarkable story of risk*. Wiley.
Clark, A. (2016). *Surfing uncertainty: Prediction, action, and the embodied mind*. Oxford University Press.
Cooper, L. G. (2000). Strategic marketing planning for radically new products. *Journal of Marketing, 64*(1), 1–16.
Courtney, H., Lovallo, D., & Clarke, C. (2013). Deciding how to decide. *Harvard Business Review, 91*(11), 62–70.
Einhorn, H. J., & Hogarth, R. M. (1986). Decision making under ambiguity. *Journal of Business, 59*(4), S225–S250.
Faber, M., Manstetten, R., & Proops, J. L. (1992). Humankind and the environment: An anatomy of surprise and ignorance. *Environmental Values, 1*(3), 217–241.
Fox, J. (2014). Instinct can beat analytical thinking. *Harvard Business Review*, 20.
Gomes, L. A. de V., Facin, A. L. F., & Salerno, M. S. (2021). Managing uncertainty propagation in innovation ecosystems. *Technological Forecasting and Social Change, 171*, 120945.
Gray, J. (2002). *Straw dogs: Thoughts on humans and other animals*. Farrar.
Hertwig, R., Pleskac, T. J., & Pachur, T. (2019). *Taming uncertainty*. MIT Press.
Jackson, M. (2023). *Uncertain: The wisdom and wonder of being unsure*. Prometheus Books.
Kapoor, R., & Klueter, T. (2021). Unbundling and managing uncertainty surrounding emerging technologies. *Strategy Science, 6*(1), 62–74.
Kay, J. A., & King, M. A. (2020). *Radical uncertainty*. Bridge Street Press.
Knight, F. H. (1921/1964). *Risk, Uncertainty and profit*. Augustus M. Kelley.
Kozyreva, A., & Hertwig, R. (2021). The interpretation of uncertainty in ecological rationality. *Synthese, 198*(2), 1517–1547.
Lipshitz, R., & Strauss, O. (1997). Coping with uncertainty: A naturalistic decision-making analysis. *Organizational Behavior and Human Decision Processes, 69*(2), 149–163.
Marchau, V. A., Walker, W. E., Bloemen, P. J., & Popper, S. W. (2019). *Decision making under deep uncertainty: From theory to practice*. Springer Nature.

Nash, S. J. (2003). On pragmatic philosophy and Knightian uncertainty. *Review of Social Economy, 61*(2), 251–272.

Ramoglou, S. (2021). Knowable opportunities in an unknowable future? On the epistemological paradoxes of entrepreneurship theory. *Journal of Business Venturing, 36*(2), 106090.

Rittel, H. W., & Webber, M. M. (1973). Dilemmas in a general theory of planning. *Policy Sciences, 4*(2), 155–169.

Scoblic, J. P. (2020). Learning from the future. *Harvard Business Review, 98*(4), 38–47.

Simon, H. A. (1972). Theories of bounded rationality. *Decision and Organization, 1*(1), 161–176.

Stewart, I. (2019). *Do dice play god? The mathematics of uncertainty*. Hachette UK.

CHAPTER 20

Supplement on the Impact of Artificial Intelligence on Uncertainty

Artificial Intelligence (AI) involves the ability of a machine to learn, solve problems, and make decisions like a human. Machine Learning (ML) is how that ability is developed—it is the programming that enables the identification of patterns of relationships and then the improvements

© The Author(s), under exclusive license to Springer Nature Switzerland AG 2024
R. J. Arend, *Uncertainty in Strategic Decision Making*, https://doi.org/10.1007/978-3-031-48553-4_20

of those patterns through experience and data. Currently, at least two-thirds of companies use ML. Based on ML, AI's substantial value lies in its ability to transform big and real-time data into 'smart data' to obtain critical information to address problems in close-to-real-time (Hariri et al., 2019).

It remains a question whether recombining ingested data, or identifying gaps and patterns in it, is 'intelligent'. It certainly can be valuable; but it can also be 'garbage-out'. (Consider the responses to the prompts for comic products relating to AI and uncertainty [see above].) AI/ML—which will be referred to simply as AI henceforth (and will also include related technology like the Internet of Things [IoT])—is, essentially, just a tool—an informational tool and, so far, only a tactical tool. Currently (and thankfully), it is a tool where 'we' can currently control the inputs (e.g., prompts; learning data; initial programming) and the output 'format' (e.g., as numbers, natural language, image, sound). But, it is also a rather powerful and potentially dangerous tool—given its speed, scalability, opaqueness, potential far and deep reach into the IoT, and humankind's increasing reliance on it.

WHY THIS SUPPLEMENT (NOW)?

AI is recently important not so much because of what it is, but mostly because of what it does 'now'—and how that relates to our ability to make decisions under several types of uncertainty (and risk). *Humankind has recently reached a significant inflection (saturation?) point in its history—where the amount of data available to us now swamps our ability to process it effectively* (Newman, 2019). [Consider that in 2019, 90 percent of recorded data in the world at that point had been generated just since 2017 (Hariri et al., 2019).[1]] That event/point has shifted power to those new 'gatekeepers' who can best filter, organize, and analyze that vast data for us (and other parties, from advertisers to authoritarians) to use. [Those gatekeepers (e.g., Apple, Amazon, Alphabet, Meta, and

---

[1] The massive increase in data has emerged from recent developments in sensors, networks, and cyber-physical input devices (from smartphones to the IoT), and includes information on health care, social media, agriculture, finance, marketing, and more. That said, such data—while being big, fast, and wide, is currently quite 'noisy' (i.e., incomplete, in different formats, contradictory, miscategorized). That noise characterizes up to 80-percent of data, and that has significant negative impacts on the effectiveness and accuracy of outputs from systems relying on it (Hariri et al., 2019).

Microsoft) leverage AI to do so (Roman, 2023); and, they are now trillion-dollar firms, each with a global reach that influences billions of people and millions of businesses (let alone many governmental institutions).] So, what AI 'does now' is important to consider in a book on strategic decision-making under uncertainty. First, this is because that application of AI—as an emerging technology—to address this new 'data-processing inflection point' raises many questions, some of which involve untreatable uncertainties (e.g., unforeseen harms). Second, this is because many of the concerns that the application of AI raises also involve treatable uncertainties (e.g., the opaqueness of an evolving predictive AI algorithm)—often made treatable because direct AI effects are theoretically 'containable' through restrictions on what the AI can access in the real world. Third, this is because AI is an emerging technology that has received growing attention in application fields (where it has proven its value for 'what it is' in specific tasks like medical imaging diagnosis), but has yet to receive the needed scrutiny in contemporary research (Obschonka & Audretsch, 2020); so, not only does its application (to leverage data) involve unknowns, so does its own form (e.g., its evolution).

SUMMARY OF AI'S IMPACTS ON UNCERTAINTIES

AI does *not* affect pure untreatable uncertainties (e.g., unknowable unknowns remain). AI *might* convert some previously infeasibly-knowable unknowns to feasibly-knowable ones—taking them away from the 'practically unknowable unknown' category (i.e., making them practically treatable when they had not been). [But, that could be said for any advance in information technology (IT).]

AI might also improve the treatments for treatable uncertainties by improving searches, experiments, models, scenarios, simulations, and social influence campaigns, to uncover or mold knowable unknowns. AI might help organizations adapt faster and better, once the unknown is known, by providing deeper insights on new data in real time. AI might even help organizations with finding partners and agreements for sharing limited uncertainty-bearing, and with identifying more options.

As for the untreatable uncertainties, AI might help with approaches that change the goals or the entities given, or that alter the given game, by offering more options based on faster and wider access to 'bigger' data; but, that is it. [But again, the same could be said for any advance in IT.]

Note that such IT advances have historically been good for society, or at least for the consumer; however, they have most often come at a competitive cost to the average business. When such advances are widely adopted, they tend to homogenize several business activities, lower variable costs, and decrease entry barriers—the combined effect of which tends to be new and valuable offerings to the public and streamlined processes for the producers (see Porter, 2001). [It is doubtful that the same pattern can repeat now, however, because such technology is *not* overcoming the current competitive barriers created by privileged data access, network effects, tying, and other abuse-of-dominant position (and consumer data rights) concerns that exist while AI-intensive industries remain under-regulated.] That history aside, AI is a technology that comes with heightened potential harms—especially when it is applied in such a way that it takes decision-making out of human hands, making 'them' (e.g., the organizations implementing their AI) less accountable, which often leads to a nasty 'race to the extreme'. [Consider the 'need' to use AI in automated weapons systems—e.g., where there may be no time for a human to react to a hypersonic missile fast approaching their ship once it is identified—and, what damage such a system can do when it mistakes something else for that missile.] Obviously, regulations are crucial to enforce very careful designs on what AI can do and when and with who's authority. [Ahhh, *SkyNet*.]

Now, to 'be back' to reiterate the *limited* effects of AI on uncertainty, consider a logical example: a *chaotic system* is extremely sensitive to initial conditions. In such a case, without a proper model and access to those initial conditions, not even a massive amount of later data can provide a reliable non-immediate prediction—i.e., even the best AI won't work (Roman, 2023). Untreatable uncertainties will remain so. Besides for the case of chaotic systems, any unknowable unknown will remain untreatable because, by definition, pre-programmed systems cannot cope with circumstances unforeseen by their designers (Smith, 2016). Any modelling of probabilities or other statistical calculations over big data simply cannot solve the brittleness and poor generalization of AI in conditions of untreatable uncertainty (Smith, 2016). AI is further limited as it (now) depends on being provided a clear goal; as such, it cannot handle goal uncertainty or even input complexity (Trunk et al., 2020). Further, ML methods are simply not sufficiently computationally efficient to handle the noisy characteristics of big data (e.g., varying types, incompleteness, bias, unexpected data types) (Hariri et al., 2019). Finally, even state-of-the-art *Uncertainty Quantification* (UQ) methods for AI lack a sound approach for computing a prediction interval or its distribution (Hariri et al., 2019; Zhang et al., 2022). All of this *should* mean, especially in high-stakes contexts (i.e., where potential harms are significant), that any AI-based predictions that do not come with some reliable measure of outcome variance, or are not checked by human experts, should *not* be acted upon (Begoli et al., 2019; Zhang et al., 2022).

THE RELEVANT IMPACT OF AI ITSELF

AI is the latest big technological advance to alter human activity, especially in business; it stands in a long line of advances that more recently include computers, genetic engineering, the Internet, and digital transformation. Such emerging advances in technology always involve future-oriented uncertainty (af Malmborg, 2022). AI, however, may be the *most* disruptive technology that humankind has faced, as it can be more of a substitute than a complement to human decision-making, and fulfilling that function in ways that are often opaque (i.e., in terms of its internal decision 'model') (af Malmborg, 2022).

Such disruption has both significant potential upsides and downsides. AI's increasingly pervasive beneficial uses include: recommendation systems; individualized training; fraud detection; autonomous transportation; social media analysis; medical diagnosis; and, business analytics (Begoli et al., 2019; Roman, 2023; Zhang et al., 2022). And, it offers an effective decision-making complement—i.e., a technology that helps professionals conduct knowledge-work by augmenting their capabilities (Lebovitz et al., 2022). Such an optimistic picture of AI disruption has also been a result of a questionably optimistic policy push from many of our own institutions. That push has been pursued through narratives (from both the private and public sectors) that point toward the general uncertainty of the future and the need to (actually) trust emerging technologies such as AI to help. Such narratives have falsely (verbally) converted valid uncertainties into more relatable vignettes labeled as risks (e.g., competitive risks) (e.g., af Malmborg, 2022). For example, they equate AI with more benign tools (like the introduction of cameras to the art world), and point to their amusing value in 'filling gaps' between established data points (e.g., like between painting styles—as in the AI artwork installation *Unsupervised* at MoMA), while ignoring many of the costs and potential harms.

Due to its disruptive nature, pervasiveness, and questionably-earned trust, let alone its potential for rapid global-scale harm, the study of AI's relationship to uncertainty and decision-making is becoming an important area of research (Obschonka & Audretsch, 2020; Trunk et al., 2020). As yet, however, little work has been done in the field of uncertainty when applied to big data analytics and AI (Hariri et al., 2019), worryingly leaving the use of AI in sensitive environments still in its infancy because there is, as yet, no systematic framework for reasoning about its risks, uncertainties, and related catastrophic consequences (Zhang et al., 2022).

AI THE GOOD

The main benefits of AI related to uncertainties are described above; mainly, AI may improve the treatment of treatable uncertainties—through faster speed, and the consideration and analysis of bigger, more recent data. It, along with the other aspects of digital transformation (such as more, better, and less-expensive sensors) can improve the informational aspects of doing business in ways that reduce some of the risks, some of the informational asymmetries, and some of the other market/transactional frictions. Indeed, the IoT (including the industrial IoT, or IIoT) offers new paths toward greater information, enhanced transparency, and more security (e.g., with blockchain contracts that eliminate the need for an intermediary). When (reputational) data is verified, AI analytics can also reduce the costs of evaluating offers, negotiating and writing out the terms of a contract, and controlling compliance in its fulfilment (Ehret & Wirtz, 2017; Roman, 2023). Like the IT advancements that preceded it, AI is a tool with many potential (and currently-realized) efficiency-based benefits—ones that can reduce several risks and better treat treatable uncertainties. Added to that, AI is perhaps a very useful tool for spurring creativity, for example, through proposing new combinations of existing data (a use which harnesses a type of surprise users can leverage in generating interesting alternative scenarios to consider).

AI THE BAD

The AI *box* itself (i.e., its composition) encapsulates treatable uncertainties that are not always fully treated, and that is bad. Those treatable uncertainties involve its internal model, and the data that feeds it. When those particular uncertainties are not fully treated, damages are likely to occur in various insidious forms, including: in harmful biases in the AI's outputs/recommendations (e.g., that hurt historically-disadvantaged groups); in poor user interactions (e.g., creating needless doubt in users); in misuses of its power (e.g., to generate and spread disinformation, to commit fraud, to reinforce dangerous echo chambers, to manipulate user emotions, and to hack into private systems); in decreased accountability and connection-with-the-outcomes-generated (e.g., making it easier to start wars when only autonomous soldiers are at play); in the scaling up unfair practices (e.g., by scraping copyrighted material for training, without proper renumeration); and, in the widening of inequalities (e.g., between those who own or can pay for access to AI and big data, and those who cannot [and those whose work is replaced by AI]).

Outside of its box, AI's use specifically involves some untreatable uncertainties. This is captured in the recent statement by the *Center for AI Safety* [https://www.safe.ai/statement-on-ai-risk], which expresses concern about AI's effects at an existential threat level. (While this is expressed as a 'risk', there are unknown unknowns involved, and so it is also an uncertainty. For example, there are unknowable effects that could occur when AI is newly connected to previously isolated systems, when it is used for unauthorized access of data, when it threatens the beneficial system of intellectual property protections, and when it threatens the distinction between truth and lies in the kinds of information that society relies upon to interact, vote, and do business [Ehret & Wirtz, 2017].) It is noted that the consequences of AI system failures in safety- and security-critical applications could be catastrophic, and so it is paramount to consider risk and uncertainty issues in AI-affected high-stakes, high-scale, decision settings (Zhang et al., 2022). And, while that might—might—be possible when responsible parties are involved, it is not possible when powerful (global) private entities, or totalitarian nations, are involved.

Less far outside of its box, AI specifically can create (new) perceived uncertainties in its direct users, for good and for bad. It often generates doubt in experts (e.g., radiologists), mostly when the AI's predictions conflict with their own; this is partly because of the opacity of the AI's model (Lebovitz et al., 2022). Experts then face some uncertainty in how to respond. On the good side, any rechecking can reduce errors and biases. On the bad side, AI systems can waste precious resources when its predictions are wrong. Besides the Type I and II error issues, to the bad side there are further concerns. AI users often consult less with other human experts (which can reduce team trust and collective expertise) (Lebovitz et al., 2022). There is often an (unjustified) overreliance on the AI built up over time. And, there is often a reaction of users to apply general heuristics to their AI interactions rather than specific rules to its specific applications (Buçinca et al., 2021). To these latter human 'adaptations', there are dangers when any tool is misused, especially in such high-stakes (e.g., medical) applications (at least for the patient), where imprecision can cost lives.

The Uncertainties in the AI Box

AI's box involves its updating *model* and the *data* it learns from and uses. The use of that AI box is growing rapidly, not only because of the rapid growth of available data itself [see above], but also because of the rise in the push to use that box (that is, so far, relatively cheap and fast to access) (Begoli et al., 2019; Zhang et al., 2022).[2] At the model-level, there are concerns over bias, misspecification, and variance (i.e., concerns that lead to risks and treatable uncertainties [knowable unknowns]). And, at the data-level, there are concerns over bias, shift, items that are out-of-domain, and adversarial attacks (i.e., concerns that also lead to risks and treatable uncertainties) (Zhang et al., 2022).

AI models are relatively opaque; and, sometimes, so is their ultimate application. Whereas, in standard scientific prediction, we tend to understand the questions we are asking and then build the models to answer them, in AI neither the questions nor the models need to be known (Begoli et al., 2019); this approach itself leads to some unpredictability. There is an absence of theory in AI models; models are generated without any explicit mathematical representation upon which we would normally base our estimates of risks and uncertainties, and upon which we would bound the premises (Begoli et al., 2019; Zhang et al., 2022). AI is a data-centric method of model-building; as such, it is vulnerable to overfitting—the problem of performing well on the training set but poorly on as-yet-unseen data (Begoli et al., 2019); of course, such modeling does not, itself, handle surprises well, let alone predict them.

---

[2] One recent application of AI for is for book banning in Iowa due to [aggressive/misguided/questionable] legislation and the expected inability of school librarians to scan every page of every book for targeted [doubtlessly ill-defined] material by an imposed deadline.

The data that AI models learn from, and take as input, are often noisy. This affects the quality of the output from the AI box. The variability of measurements-used-as-input-data poses a severe concern when applying AI because such data imperfections often produce patterns that can confound meaningful prediction (Begoli et al., 2019; Zhang et al., 2022). Even when the learning data comes from experts, there is a non-trivial amount of variance and bias that is often overlooked in programming the AI (Lebovitz et al., 2021). In general, AI data is often complex, multimodal, discordant, noisy, incomplete, and of low veracity and high variety (Begoli et al., 2019; Hariri et al., 2019); this makes it difficult to quantify and qualify the risks and uncertainties involved in AI predictions. Of course, there are reasons why that data is so noisy—it can come in different forms (e.g., from unstructured to structured) and types (e.g., as collected by physical sensors, social media input, audited financial records, and so on) and levels of incompleteness and inconsistency; and, that 'noisiness' is expected to continue, as no universal standard for data is on the horizon[3] (Hariri et al., 2019).

MITIGATING THOSE (TREATABLE) INTERNAL AI UNCERTAINTIES

There are two main ways to mitigate the uncertainties associated with the AI box (i.e., those uncertainties arising from its model and its data)—with technical approaches, and with user-based adjustments. Given either way is not cheap or fast or easy, and the potential damages of any residual uncertainties are large, then efforts in uncertainty mitigation should be at the forefront of AI (Hariri et al., 2019). But, even when such mitigation tactics are applied, it is likely some uncertainties will remain, and so it is also important to try to quantify those relevant uncertainties.

In terms of the technical approaches, there are many mathematical/ codable ways to reduce noise in the data, and in the quirkiness/ sensitivity of the model, including the use of: incremental learning algorithms; Generative Adversarial Networks (to detect out-of-sample cases); evolutionary algorithms; artificial neural networks; fuzzy logic; data

---

[3] Poor quality data is costly in many ways. Estimates of its annual monetary costs to economic activity are in the trillions of dollars (Hariri et al., 2019). As the amount, variety, and speed of such noisy data increase, however, so do the associated risks and uncertainties of relying on them for decisions (Hariri et al., 2019).

cleaning; belief functions; rough set theory; classification theory; granular computing; probability theory; Bayesian theory; Shannon's entropy; sampling; active learning; and, deep learning (e.g., Begoli et al., 2019; Hariri et al., 2019).

In terms of user adjustments, the application of a *caveat emptor* mentality can be effective in interpreting and weighing the value of AI predictions. For example, cognitive forcing functions elicit analytical thinking that can significantly reduce overreliance on AI (Buçinca et al., 2021). Helping users discover the disconnect between AI *know-what* and expert *know-how* can enable a better understanding of the risks and benefits associated with the tool (Lebovitz et al., 2021). And, encouraging users to interrogate/ probe AI tools can help them reconcile any divergent prescriptions, and perhaps even integrate such prescriptions with their own (Lebovitz et al., 2022).

Estimating Those Uncertainties in AI

Because the preceding mitigation techniques are imperfect, even for risks and treatable uncertainties, it is quite valuable to have some estimate of variance and residual uncertainties of AI output. However, such estimation is *not* straightforward because there is no (general) underlying theory for doing so (Begoli et al., 2019). There is not even a method for verifying and objectively validating which, of a set of competing AI models, as generated under different assumptions, better characterizes a targeted reality (Zhang et al., 2022). Indeed, *a new field*—one focused on AI uncertainty quantification—may need to be developed to address this issue (Begoli et al., 2019); one that considers *multiple* risks and uncertainties simultaneously (rather than any single issue, as current research has restricted itself to—Zhang et al., 2022). Such a field would consider the risks and uncertainties arising from both the data and the model inside any AI box; ideally, it would be akin to statistical error analysis. As a start in this direction, one bootstrapping approach that has been suggested involves re-tasking the learning machine to provide estimates of the errors in its own predictions (Begoli et al., 2019).

Main Implications

Regarding AI's relationship to uncertainty, there are several implications for business in general, for entrepreneurship specifically, and for decision-making.

On the negative side, commercial attempts to capture 'the value of AI' add potential risks and uncertainties to society and to an industry that can involve the undermining of privacy, an increase in the complexity of underlying manufacturing systems, the entry of new rivals, and the creation of new substitutes (Ehret & Wirtz, 2017). It may also affect the structure of the firm—its bureaucracy—in unwanted (surprising) ways (e.g., shifting power and employment). On the positive side, AI is likely to positively impact the firms that are appropriately structured (e.g., those that resemble systems-level bureaucracies that conduct low-uncertainty, high-volume, predictive tasks now), although the extent and duration of this is advantageous effect is unknown (Bullock, 2019). Also, on the positive side, whenever there is change—especially in the form of a significant new technology like AI—then there are opportunities for establishing a competitive advantage, but how to do so in a relatively unique and value-adding way is uncertain. One possible way may be to specialize in mastering the negative uncertainties of AI operation (Ehret & Wirtz, 2017) by acting as a service to other firms that are less comfortable with the AI-related uncertainties (and by finding more efficient and effective ways to treat the treatable risks and uncertainties involved—e.g., in the data and/or the model of an AI box).

It is an open question *whether AI will eliminate the entrepreneur*—or, at least, the entrepreneurs who 'fill gaps' in a market, or who innovate through simple recombinations of existing components. AI should be good at those tasks—i.e., in identifying gaps, and displaying possible (feasible) recombinations, as possible options for consideration. However, whether it will provide an incumbent firm with the same entrepreneurial confidence, drive, or optimism for *acting* on those options is uncertain. That said, competing AI boxes, given similar input data (if it existed), are likely to see the same things (i.e., will not offer a firm a unique option) or perhaps even offer 'too much variety' (which is often paralyzing to decision-makers), leaving room for entrepreneurs who see things differently or who can focus more effectively. Of course, at present, there are no reliable, complete, preexisting datasets available that would provide a sufficient orientation, with respect to entrepreneurial tasks related to success, for an AI to train on (Obschonka & Audretsch, 2020). And, it is doubtful whether the irrational and rule-breaking nature of many successful entrepreneurs could be so easily replaced or enhanced (Obschonka & Audretsch, 2020). That noted, AI in the hands of agents with such dangerous natures increases the risks and uncertainties that 'destructive' entrepreneurship results (Obschonka & Audretsch, 2020).

Given AI is a decision-making tool (which can act as a complement or substitute to human decision-making), the question arises over *who should have the final say*—the AI, the human user, or both? Of course, the answer is 'it depends'; but that determination of what it depends on is presently uncertain (at least in the non-trivial cases). For example, evaluating AI performance (relative to alternatives) is not always straightforward (although it may seem so in applications like radiology). That said, currently some tasks favor human discretion—where legal restrictions, or moral, relational, or novel issues are at play (Bullock, 2019; Lebovitz et al., 2021; Smith, 2016). When it is unclear which is favored, perhaps using both is the answer, but even then, there are adjustments to be made, as successfully leveraging AI requires human users to become translators and interpreters of the results rather than only supervisors of a machine; and, that implies an increase in responsibility and a change in the skills needed for AI users (Trunk et al., 2020). Given this possibility of a lack of clarity over decision-making roles, it seems prudent to avoid a rush to adopt AI tools, particularly in applications where the problems are ill-defined, the training data is immature, causal connections are unclear, estimating the risks and uncertainties of the AI is difficult, and the potential for harm (including administrative evil) is significant (Begoli et al., 2019; Bullock, 2019; Lebovitz et al., 2021).

Strangely, it remains unclear in which 'platform' to invest—a human entrepreneur or an AI—when it appears useful 'to take action in the face of uncertainty' (e.g., to help resolve it, as through experimentation). It may seem trivial to have an AI generate a new product prototype and its advertising campaign and then launch it to its targeted audience, all to probe for demand where its 'data' may be missing—i.e., as a response to its characterization of a 'knowable unknown'. But that characterization and its response are likely to differ from the human version. Is that good (and for whom)? One strength of human decision-making is an ability to quickly develop incomplete, disposable, innovative, and useful models of reality that underlie a conviction to take action on the conclusions of such models, even though they are almost always wrong in the face of real uncertainty (Smith, 2016). Further, part of that human process involves emotion—something that the AI box is unlikely to possess any time soon (Smith, 2016). So, would society see a better way to resolve treatable uncertainties when an AI vies to do so, relative to when humans alone do so? What are the frictions and costs to that? Can human consumers react quickly and clearly enough to a rapid increase in the pace and variety of the prototypes that potentially several AIs can rapidly produce? Will AI taking over such a core of human mental activity reduce the meaning of 'being human'? As can be seen, many new (and non-trivial) questions are raised when AI is introduced into strategic entrepreneurial and business decision-making (and action-taking). Here, many new uncertainties can be identified, even when considering ways to reduce uncertainty (e.g., probe a market gap). This is *not* a good initial sign, at least when it comes to AI's effect on the number of unknowns. But, luckily, AI is built to provide some answers (and, hopefully, the rate of new questions will, at some time, decrease relative to the rate of useful answers).

WRAPPING IT UP—THE REAL AND THE F.AI.K

AI is a disruptive technology with the potential for both great benefit and great harm. Currently, it involves (too) many unknowns—its decision-making models are mostly opaque, its full effects unclear, and its trajectory uncertain. As such, humankind must mitigate any of the usual irrational exuberance it has too often given 'shiny new things', and act to reduce AI's seemingly unchecked application. Instead, we must proceed with caution (especially given the already-realized impacts society has seen in the under-regulated big tech platforms [using AI] that have [allegedly] caused massive societal harms—to vulnerable users, to democracy, to privacy, to competition, and so on—all in the name of private gains).

As for AI's impact on uncertainty, we repeat now that no fundamentals regarding uncertainty as expressed in this book were harmed by the inclusion of this chapter. While AI may help with treatments of treatable uncertainties (e.g., by making search faster and more complete) and in adding information to the variety of approaches for untreatable certainties, the untreatableness of untreatable uncertainties remains untouched (while the number of them may even be added to—at least temporarily, by AI's existence itself). (Again, we note that the treatable uncertainties that were previously infeasible—and thus 'practically untreatable'—may, however, be reduced by AI making them now feasible to treat [and, that is indeed a good thing].)

We close this chapter with some thoughts on humankind's journey with uncertainty (and how that relates to AI). It is important to note that humans think, act, pray, science, institutionalize, innovate, invest, and entrepreneur because uncertainty exists. New technologies—especially those that increase 'what is known' (and decrease what is not)—affect those relationships. The questions over whether AI (or AGI) will ever be a full substitute for human intelligence (with our *savoir faire* and *joie de vivre*) (Roman, 2023) may be fun to explore (e.g., at least for philosophers), but are arguably not as important as whether such technologies change the 'island of knowledge' analogy that this book began with—i.e., *will AI actually now decrease the shoreline of our ignorance even as the island of AI-knowledge grows increasingly fast* (and, it is important to note that this is *its* knowledge, not ours [regardless of our limited human access to it])?

We appear now to be bracketing humankind's existence (and it long-running conscious relationship with uncertainty): We have moved from trying to appease some deified [yet amoral] natural forces with our religions, to partially conquering those forces with our [sometimes moral] sciences, to unleashing a [artificial and so far amoral] scientific machine [AI] that can use such forces to destroy us without—ironically—any thought (e.g., through bioweapons; or, through deep fakes and disinformation that confuse our evolved sensory inputs; and, so on). As a species, we have moved from a position where we could not predict well (i.e., where much uncertainty existed), to a position where we could predict better (i.e., where we could insure risks, and resolve knowable unknowns with science), to a position where we want to predict as much as possible (i.e., minimal surprises); we have gone from having very little control (e.g., giving it up to 'the gods'), to having some control, to now seemingly giving up our control again (i.e., to the 'AI god'). But at what cost do we take this current [AI-fueled] step? It may very well be that the cost to 'have everything' (i.e., to uncover all of nature's secrets) might just be 'everything' (i.e., our freedoms, our species' dominance, or even our existence).

We understand that 'having everything' is quite enticing; the potential benefits of AI are substantial (e.g., customized high-quality education, medical diagnosis, psychological care, and pseudo-friendship; optimized physical/ chemical manufacturing processes; gap-identification [and filling] of our limited knowledge; solutions to complex problems like cancer, aging, inter-stellar travel, and [of course] world peace). We also see that the genie is already out of the bottle, pandora's box is opened, the toothpaste is out of the tube, and Elvis has left the building. So, we can only join others in wondering whether the necessary but theoretical 'insurmountable guardrails to abuse (of AI)' are possible—we wonder whether AI can be denied access to important physical systems (when so much is already digitally connected [e.g., to the Internet])—so that its decisions and predictions are not automatically enacted. We worry that it is already too late to react; and, given humankind's historic under-reaction to other foreseeable crises (e.g., climate change), that worry is substantial. As it stands, we are certain humanity will be surprised. However, such surprise aside, we fully expect that humankind will doubtless go out as it entered, regardless of any new technological armor, as *uncertainty's bitch*. [♥].

References

af Malmborg, F. (2022). Narrative dynamics in European Commission AI policy—Sensemaking, agency construction, and anchoring. *Review of Policy Research, 40*(5), 757–780. https://doi.org/10.1111/ropr.12529

Begoli, E., Bhattacharya, T., & Kusnezov, D. (2019). The need for uncertainty quantification in machine-assisted medical decision making. *Nature Machine Intelligence, 1*(1), 20–23.

Buçinca, Z., Malaya, M. B., & Gajos, K. Z. (2021). To trust or to think: Cognitive forcing functions can reduce overreliance on AI in AI-assisted decision-making. *Proceedings of the ACM on Human-Computer Interaction, 5*(CSCW1), 1–21.

Bullock, J. B. (2019). Artificial intelligence, discretion, and bureaucracy. *The American Review of Public Administration, 49*(7), 751–761.

Ehret, M., & Wirtz, J. (2017). Unlocking value from machines: Business models and the industrial internet of things. *Journal of Marketing Management, 33*(1–2), 111–130.

Hariri, R. H., Fredericks, E. M., & Bowers, K. M. (2019). Uncertainty in big data analytics: Survey, opportunities, and challenges. *Journal of Big Data, 6*(1), 1–16.

Lebovitz, S., Levina, N., & Lifshitz-Assaf, H. (2021). Is AI ground truth really true? The dangers of training and evaluating AI tools based on experts' know-what. *MIS Quarterly, 45*(3), 1501–1525.

Lebovitz, S., Lifshitz-Assaf, H., & Levina, N. (2022). To engage or not to engage with AI for critical judgments: How professionals deal with opacity when using AI for medical diagnosis. *Organization Science, 33*(1), 126–148.

Newman, J. M. (2019). Antitrust in digital markets. *Vanderbilt Law Review, 72,* 1497–1561.

Obschonka, M., & Audretsch, D. B. (2020). Artificial intelligence and big data in entrepreneurship: A new era has begun. *Small Business Economics, 55,* 529–539.

Porter, M. E. (2001). Strategy and the internet. *Harvard Business Review, 79*(3), 62–78.

Roman, P. (2023). "Hunting" for information to cope with the omnipresent uncertainty represents the new normality. *International Journal of Communication Research, 13*(2), 84–90.

Smith, R. E. (2016). Idealizations of uncertainty, and lessons from artificial intelligence. *Economics, 10*(1), 1–40, 20160007. https://doi.org/10.5018/economics-ejournal.ja.2016-7

Trunk, A., Birkel, H., & Hartmann, E. (2020). On the current state of combining human and artificial intelligence for strategic organizational decision making. *Business Research, 13*(3), 875–919.

Zhang, X., Chan, F. T., Yan, C., & Bose, I. (2022). Towards risk-aware artificial intelligence and machine learning systems: An overview. *Decision Support Systems, 159,* 113800.

Uncertainty Literature

Abbott, J. (2005). Understanding and managing the unknown: The nature of uncertainty in planning. *Journal of Planning Education and Research, 24*(3), 237–251.

Adam, D., & Witte, T. (1979). Merkmale der Planung in gut-und schlechtstrukturierten Planungssituationen. *Das Wirtschaftsstudium, 8*(1), 380–386.

Adner, R. (2012). *The wide lens: A new strategy for innovation.* Penguin.

Adner, R., & Kapoor, R. (2016). Innovation ecosystems and the pace of substitution: Re-examining technology S-curves. *Strategic Management Journal, 37*(4), 625–648.

Adobor, H. (2006). Optimal trust? Uncertainty as a determinant and limit to trust in inter-firm alliances. *Leadership & Organization Development Journal, 27*(7), 537–553.

af Malmborg, F. (2022). Narrative dynamics in European Commission AI policy—Sensemaking, agency construction, and anchoring. *Review of Policy Research, 40*(5), 757–780. https://doi.org/10.1111/ropr.12529

Aggarwal, D., & Mohanty, P. (2022). Influence of imprecise information on risk and ambiguity preferences: Experimental evidence. *Managerial and Decision Economics, 43*(4), 1025–1038.

Altig, D., Baker, S., Barrero, J. M., Bloom, N., Bunn, P., Chen, S., ..., Thwaites, G. (2020). Economic uncertainty before and during the COVID-19 pandemic. *Journal of Public Economics, 191*, 104274.

Alvarez, S., Afuah, A., & Gibson, C. (2018). Editors' comments: Should management theories take uncertainty seriously? *Academy of Management Review, 43*(2), 169–172.

© The Editor(s) (if applicable) and The Author(s), under exclusive license to Springer Nature Switzerland AG 2024
R. J. Arend, *Uncertainty in Strategic Decision Making*,
https://doi.org/10.1007/978-3-031-48553-4

Ancona, D. (2012). Sensemaking, framing and acting in the unknown. In S. Snook, N. Norhia, & R. Khurana (Eds.), *The handbook for teaching leadership: Knowing, doing, being* (pp. 1–19). Sage.

Anderson, J. C., & Narus, J. A. (1990). A model of distributor firm and manufacturer firm working partnerships. *Journal of Marketing, 54*, 42–58.

Anderson, P., & Tushman, M. L. (1990). Technological discontinuities and dominant designs: A cyclical model of technological change. *Administrative Science Quarterly, 35*(4), 604–633.

Ansoff, I. (1975). Managing strategic surprise by response to weak signals. *California Management Review, 18*(2), 21–33.

Anupindi, R., & Jiang, L. (2008). Capacity investment under postponement strategies, market competition, and demand uncertainty. *Management Science, 54*(11), 1876–1890.

Arend, R. J. (2015). *Wicked entrepreneurship: Defining the basics of entreponerology*. Springer.

Arend, R. J. (2019). *On theory: Brain-mind teleology and the failure in the success of the human use of science*. Cambridge Scholars Publishing.

Arend, R. J. (2020). Strategic decision-making under ambiguity: A new problem space and a proposed optimization approach. *Business Research, 13*(3), 1231–1251.

Arend, R. J. (2022a). The costs of ambiguity in strategic contexts. *Administrative Sciences, 12*(3), 108.

Arend, R. J. (2022b, forthcoming). Strategic decision-making under ambiguity: Insights from exploring a simple linked two-game model. *Operational Research*.

Arend, R. J. (2023, forthcoming). Integrating entrepreneurial and spiritual identities under uncertainty. *Journal of Business Venturing Insights*.

Arendt, H. (1958). *The human condition*. University of Chicago Press.

Arrow, K. J. (1951). *Social choice and individual values*. Wiley.

Arrow, K. J. (1973). Information and economic behavior. In *Collected Papers of Kenneth J. Arrow, 1984 4(11)*. Belknap.

Arrow, K. J. (1974). *Limited knowledge and economic analysis* [University of Illinois at Urbana-Champaign's Academy for Entrepreneurial Leadership Historical Research Reference in Entrepreneurship. SSRN].

Artinger, F. M., Gigerenzer, G., & Jacobs, P. (2022). Satisficing: Integrating two traditions. *Journal of Economic Literature, 60*(2), 598–635.

Artinger, S., & Powell, T. C. (2016). Entrepreneurial failure: Statistical and psychological explanations. *Strategic Management Journal, 37*(6), 1047–1064.

Atkins, P. W., Wood, R. E., & Rutgers, P. J. (2002). The effects of feedback format on dynamic decision making. *Organizational Behavior and Human Decision Processes, 88*(2), 587–604.

Au, E. W. M. (2017). Seeing the forest and not the trees: When impact uncertainty heightens causal complexity. *International Journal of Psychology, 52*(3), 256–260.
Baker, E. (1976). *Klynt's law: A novel*. Houghton Mifflin Harcourt Press.
Baker, S. R., Bloom, N., & Davis, S. J. (2016). Measuring economic policy uncertainty. *The Quarterly Journal of Economics, 131*(4), 1593–1636.
Balakrishnan, S., & Wernerfelt, B. (1986). Technical change, competition and vertical integration. *Strategic Management Journal, 7*(4), 347–359.
Bammer, G., & Smithson, M. (2008). Understanding uncertainty. *Integration Insights, 7*(1), 1–7.
Bankes, S. C. (1993). Exploratory modeling for policy analysis. *Operations Research, 4*(3), 435–449.
Bankes, S. C., Walker, W. E., & Kwakkel, J. H. (2013). Exploratory modeling and analysis. In S. Gass & M. C. Fu (Eds.), *Encyclopedia of operations research and management science* (3rd ed.) Springer.
Bar-Anan, Y., Wilson, T. D., & Gilbert, D. T. (2009). The feeling of uncertainty intensifies affective reactions. *Emotion, 9*(1), 123–127.
Baranes, A., Oudeyer, P. Y., & Gottlieb, J. (2015). Eye movements reveal epistemic curiosity in human observers. *Vision Research, 117*, 81–90.
Barney, J. B., & Hansen, M. H. (1994). Trustworthiness as a source of competitive advantage. *Strategic Management Journal, 15*(S1), 175–190.
Barney, J. B. (1986). Strategic factor markets: Expectations, luck and business strategy. *Management Science, 42*, 1231–1241.
Barney, J. B. (1991). Firm resources and sustained competitive advantage. *Journal of Management, 17*, 99–120.
Barney, J. B. (2002). *Gaining and sustaining competitive advantage*. Prentice-Hall.
Baron, R. (2004). The cognitive perspective: A valuable tool for answering entrepreneurship's basic "why" questions. *Journal of Business Venturing, 19*, 221–239.
Baron, R. (2008). The role of affect in the entrepreneurial process. *Academy of Management Review, 33*, 328–360.
Barrow, J. D. (1998). *Impossibility: The limits of science and the science of limits*. Oxford University Press on Demand.
Barzel, Y. (1997). *Economic analysis of property rights*. Cambridge University Press.
Beach, L. R., & Mitchell, T. R. (1978). A contingency model for the selection of decision strategies. *Academy of Management Review, 3*(3), 439–449.
Beck, U. (2009). *World at risk*. Polity.
Becker, S. W., & Brownson, F. O. (1964). What price ambiguity? Or the role of ambiguity in decision-making. *Journal of Political Economy, 72*(1), 62–73.

Beckert, J. (1996). What is sociological about economic sociology? Uncertainty and the embeddedness of economic action. *Theory and Society*, 25, 803–840.
Begoli, E., Bhattacharya, T., & Kusnezov, D. (2019). The need for uncertainty quantification in machine-assisted medical decision making. *Nature Machine Intelligence*, 1(1), 20–23.
Ben-Haim, Y. (2001, June). Decision trade-offs under severe info-gap uncertainty. *ISIPTA*, 32–39.
Ben-Haim, Y. (2006). *Info-gap decision theory: Decisions under severe uncertainty* (2nd ed.). London.
Ben-Haim, Y. (2010). *Info-gap economics: An operational introduction*. Palgrave-Macmillan.
Berger, P., & Luckmann, T. (1966). *The social construction of reality*. Penguin Book.
Berger, C. R., & Calabrese, R. J. (1975). Some explorations in initial interaction and beyond: Toward a developmental theory of interpersonal communication. *Human Communication Research*, 1, 99–112.
Berglund, H., Bousfiha, M., & Mansoori, Y. (2020). Opportunities as artifacts and entrepreneurship as design. *Academy of Management Review*, 45(4), 825–846.
Bergson, H. (1913). *Time and free will: An essay on the immediate date of consciousness*. Dover Publications.
Berlyne, D. E. (1960). *Conflict, arousal, and curiosity*. McGraw-Hill.
Bernoulli, J. (1966). *Ars conjectandi: Or, the art of conjecturing*. Harvard University.
Bernstein, P. L. (1996). *Against the gods: The remarkable story of risk*. Wiley.
Bewley, T. F. (2002). Knightian decision theory. Part I. *Decisions in Economics and Finance*, 25, 79–110.
Bhattacharya, R., Devinney, T. M., & Pillutla, M. M. (1998). A formal model of trust based on outcomes. *Academy of Management Review*, 23, 459–472.
Bhattacharya, S., Krishnan, V., & Mahajan, V. (1998). Managing new product definition in highly dynamic environments. *Management Science*, 44(11-2), S50–S64.
Bower, J. L., & Christensen, C. M. (1996). Disruptive technologies: Catching the wave. *The Journal of Product Innovation Management*, 1(13), 75–76.
Box, G. E., & Draper, N. R. (1987). *Empirical model-building and response surfaces*. Wiley.
Boyd, B. K., & Fulk, J. (1996). Executive scanning and perceived uncertainty: A multidimensional model. *Journal of Management*, 22(1), 1–21.
Boyd, W. (2012). Genealogies of risk: Searching for safety, 1930s–1970s. *Ecology Law Quarterly*, 39, 895–987.

Boykin, A. W., & Harackiewicz, J. (1981). Epistemic curiosity and incidental recognition in relation to degree of uncertainty: Some general trends and intersubject differences. *British Journal of Psychology, 72*(1), 65–72.

Bradac, J. J. (2001). Theory comparison: Uncertainty reduction, problematic integration, uncertainty management, and other curious constructs. *Journal of Communication, 51*(3), 456–476.

Bradley, R., & Drechsler, M. (2014). Types of uncertainty. *Erkenntnis, 79*, 1225–1248.

Bradley, R., & Steele, K. (2015). Making climate decisions. *Philosophy Compass, 10*(11), 799–810.

Brafman, O., & Brafman, R. (2008). *Sway: The irresistible pull of irrational behavior*. Doubleday Business.

Brandenburger, A. M., & Nalebuff, B. J. (1996). *Co-opetition*. Harvard Business School Press.

Brehmer, B. (1992). Dynamic decision making: Human control of complex systems. *Acta Psychologica, 81*(3), 211–241.

Brod, G., Hasselhorn, M., & Bunge, S. A. (2018). When generating a prediction boosts learning: The element of surprise. *Learning and Instruction, 55*, 22–31.

Brown, S., & Eisenhardt, K. (1995). Product development: Past research, present findings and future directions. *Academy of Management Review, 20*(2), 343–378.

Brumbaugh, R. S. (1966). Applied metaphysics: Truth and passing time. *The Review of Metaphysics, 19*(4), 647–666.

Bruner, J. S., & Postman, L. (1949). On the perception of incongruity: A paradigm. *Journal of Personality, 18*(2), 206–223.

Brunswik, E. (1952). *The conceptual framework of psychology*. University of Chicago Press.

Buchko, A. A. (1994). Conceptualization and measurement of environmental uncertainty: An assessment of the Miles and Snow perceived environmental uncertainty scale. *The Academy of Management Journal, 37*(2), 410–425.

Buçinca, Z., Malaya, M. B., & Gajos, K. Z. (2021). To trust or to think: Cognitive forcing functions can reduce overreliance on AI in AI-assisted decision-making. *Proceedings of the ACM on Human-Computer Interaction, 5*(CSCW1), 1–21.

Bullock, J. B. (2019). Artificial intelligence, discretion, and bureaucracy. *The American Review of Public Administration, 49*(7), 751–761.

Burgelman, R. A. (1983). A model of the interaction of strategic behavior, corporate context, and the concept of strategy. *Academy of Management Review, 8*(1), 61–70.

Busenitz, L. W., & Barney, J. B. (1997). Differences between entrepreneurs and managers in large organizations: Biases and heuristics in strategic decision-making. *Journal of Business Venturing*, *12*(1), 9–30.

Busenitz, L. W., & Lichtenstein, B. B. (2019). Faith in research: Forging new ground in entrepreneurship. *Academy of Management Perspectives*, *33*(3), 280–291.

Butterfield, B., & Metcalfe, J. (2006). The correction of errors committed with high confidence. *Metacognition and Learning*, *1*, 69–84.

Bylund, P. L., & McCaffrey, M. (2017). A theory of entrepreneurship and institutional uncertainty. *Journal of Business Venturing*, *32*(5), 461–475.

Cabantous, L. (2007). Ambiguity aversion in the field of insurance: Insurers' attitude to imprecise and conflicting probability estimates. *Theory and Decision*, *62*(3), 219–240.

Caillois, R. (2001). *Man, play, and games*. University of Illinois Press.

Camerer, C. (1994). Individual decision making. In J. Kagel & A. Roth (Eds.), *Handbook of experimental economics*. Princeton University Press.

Camerer, C., & Weber, M. (1992). Recent developments in modeling preferences: Uncertainty and ambiguity. *Journal of Risk and Uncertainty*, *5*, 325–370.

Camerer, C. F., Bhatt, M., & Hsu, M. (2007). *Neuroeconomics: Illustrated by the study of ambiguity aversion* [DIV HSS 228-77, CALTECH, PASADENA CA].

Campbell, D. T. (1960). Blind variation and selective retention in creative thought as in other knowledge processes. *Psychological Review*, *67*, 380–400.

Cantillon, R. (1755 [1931]). *Essai sur la nature du commerce en général* (H. Higgs, Ed. and Trans.). Royal Economic Society.

Casson, M. (1993). Entrepreneurship and business culture. In J. Brown & M. B. Rose (Eds.), *Entrepreneurship, networks and modern business* (pp. 30–54). Manchester: Manchester University Press.

Chandler, G. N., DeTienne, D. R., McKelvie, A., & Mumford, T. V. (2011). Causation and effectuation processes: A validation study. *Journal of Business Venturing*, *26*(3), 375–390.

Chawla, C., Mangaliso, M., Knipes, B., & Gauthier, J. (2012). Antecedents and implications of uncertainty in management: A historical perspective. *Journal of Management History*, *18*(2), 200–218.

Choi, Y. B. (1993). *Paradigms and conventions: Uncertainty, decision making, and entrepreneurship*. University of Michigan Press.

Churchland, P. S. (1989). *Neurophilosophy: Toward a unified science of the mind-brain*. MIT Press.

Clark, A. (2016). *Surfing uncertainty: Prediction, action, and the embodied mind*. Oxford University Press.

Clark, R. E. (1989). When teaching kills learning: Research on mathemathantics. *Learning and Instruction: European Research in an International Context, 2,* 1–22.
Clore, G. L. (1992). Cognitive phenomenology: Feelings and the construction of judgment. In L. L. Martin & A. Tesser (Eds.), *The construction of social judgments* (pp. 133–163). Erlbaum.
Cohen, L. J. (1977). *The probable and the provable.* Clarendon.
Cohen, M., & Jaffray, J.-Y. (1980). Rational behavior under complete ignorance. *Econometrica, 48*(5), 1281–1299.
Cohen, W. M., & Levinthal, D. A. (1994). Fortune favors the prepared firm. *Management Science, 40*(2), 227–251.
Cole, C. (1997). Information as process: The difference between corroborating evidence and "information" in humanistic research domains. *Information Processing and Management, 33*(1), 55–67.
Conrath, D. W. (1967). Organizational decision making behavior under varying conditions of uncertainty. *Management Science, 13*(8), B-487.
Cooper, L. G. (2000). Strategic marketing planning for radically new products. *Journal of Marketing, 64*(1), 1–16.
Costikyan, G. (2013). *Uncertainty in games.* MIT Press.
Courtney, H. (2001). *20/20 Foresight: Crafting strategy in an uncertain world.* Harvard Business School Press.
Courtney, H. (2003). Decision-driven scenarios for assessing four levels of uncertainty. *Strategy & Leadership, 31*(1), 14–22.
Courtney, H., Kirkland, J., & Viguerie, P. (1997). Strategy under uncertainty. *Harvard Business Review, 75*(6), 67–79.
Courtney, H., Kirkland, J., Viguerie, P., Hamel, G., Prahalad, C. K., de Geus, A. P., & Christensen, C. M. (1999). *Harvard business review on managing uncertainty.* Harvard Business School Press.
Courtney, H., Lovallo, D., & Clarke, C. (2013). Deciding how to decide. *Harvard Business Review, 91*(11), 62–70.
Covin, J. G., Garrett, R. P., Kuratko, D. F., & Bolinger, M. (2021). Internal corporate venture planning autonomy, strategic evolution, and venture performance. *Small Business Economics, 56,* 293–310.
Covin, J. G., Garrett, R. P., Jr., Gupta, J. P., Kuratko, D. F., & Shepherd, D. A. (2018). The interdependence of planning and learning among internal corporate ventures. *Entrepreneurship Theory and Practice, 42*(4), 537–570.
Crawford, G. C., Aguinis, H., Lichtenstein, B., Davidsson, P., & McKelvey, B. (2015). Power law distributions in entrepreneurship: Implications for theory and research. *Journal of Business Venturing, 30*(5), 696–713.
Crowe, E., & Higgins, E. T. (1997). Regulatory focus and strategic inclinations: Promotion and prevention in decision-making. *Organizational Behavior and Human Decision Processes, 69*(2), 117–132.

Cui, L., Wu, H., Wu, L., Kumar, A., & Tan, K. H. (2023). Investigating the relationship between digital technologies, supply chain integration and firm resilience in the context of COVID-19. *Annals of Operations Research, 327*(2), 825–853.

Cyert, R. M., & March, J. G. (1963). *A behavioral theory of the firm*. Prentice-Hall.

D'Mello, S., Lehman, B., Pekrun, R., & Graesser, A. (2014). Confusion can be beneficial for learning. *Learning and Instruction, 29*, 153–170.

Daft, R. L., & Macintosh, N. B. (1981). A tentative exploration into the amount and equivocality of information processing in organizational work units. *Administrative Science Quarterly, 26*(2), 207–224.

Daft, R. L., & Weick, K. E. (1984). Toward a model of organizations as interpretation systems. *Academy of Management Review, 9*(2), 284–295.

Damasio, A. (1994). *Descartes error—Emotion*. Putnam Press.

Danneels, E. (2002). The dynamics of product innovation and firm competences. *Strategic Management Journal, 23*(12), 1095–1121.

Dasgupta, P. (1988a). Patents, priority and imitation or, the economics of races and waiting games. *The Economic Journal, 98*(389), 66–80.

Dasgupta, P. (1988b). Trust as a commodity. In D. Gambetta (Ed.), *Trust: Making and breaking cooperative relations* (pp. 49–72). Basil Blackwell.

Dattée, B., Alexy, O., & Autio, E. (2018). Maneuvering in poor visibility: How firms play the ecosystem game when uncertainty is high. *Academy of Management Journal, 61*(2), 466–498.

Dattée, B., Alexy, O., & Autio, E. (2018). Maneuvering in poor visibility: How firms play the ecosystem game when uncertainty is high. *Academy of Management Journal, 61*(2), 466–498.

Davidon, P. (1996). Reality and economic theory. *Journal of Post Keynesian Economics, 18*(4), 479–508.

Davidsson, P. (2015). Entrepreneurial opportunities and the entrepreneurship nexus: A re-conceptualization. *Journal of Business Venturing, 30*(5), 674–695.

Davis, P. K. (2003). Uncertainty-Sensitive Planning. In S. E. Johnson, M. C. Libicki, & G. F. Treverton (Eds.), *New challenges, new tools for defense decision making*, RAND Corporation.

de Finetti, B. (1967). Probability: Interpretations. In *International encyclopaedia of the social sciences* (Vol. 12, pp. 496–505). Macmillan.

de Palma, A., Abdellaoui, M., Attanasi, G., Ben-Akiva, M., Erev, I., Fehr-Duda, H., ... Weber, M. (2014). Beware of black swans: Taking stock of the description—Experience gap in decision under uncertainty. *Marketing Letters, 25*(3), 269–280.

Deeds, D. L., Mang, P. Y., & Frandsen, M. L. (2004). The influence of firms' and industries' legitimacy on the flow of capital into high-technology ventures. *Strategic Organization, 2*(1), 9–34.

Dekel, E., Lipman, B. L., & Rustichini, A. (1998). Recent developments in modeling unforeseen contingencies. *European Economic Review*, 42(3–5), 523–542.

Denzau, A., & North, D. C. (1994). Shared mental models: Ideologies and institutions. *Kyklos*, 47(1), 3–31.

Denzau, A.T. & Grossman, P. (1993). *Punctuated equilibria: A model and application of evolutionary economic change* [Unpublished manuscript, Economics Department, Washington University].

Dequech, D. (1999). Expectations and confidence under uncertainty. *Journal of Post Keynesian Economics*, 21(3), 415–430.

Dequech, D. (2003). Uncertainty and economic sociology: A preliminary discussion. *American Journal of Economics and Sociology*, 62(3), 509–532.

Dequech, D. (2011). Uncertainty: A typology and refinements of existing concepts. *Journal of Economic Issues*, 45(3), 621–640.

Dess, G. G., & Beard, D. W. (1984). Dimensions of organizational task environments. *Administrative Science Quarterly*, 29(1), 52–73.

Dewar, J. A., Builder, C. H., Hix, W. M., & Levin, M. H. (1993). *Assumption based planning: A planning tool for every uncertain times*. Rand.

Dewar, J. A. (2002). *Assumption-based planning: A tool for reducing avoidable surprises*. Cambridge Press.

Dewey, J. (1915). The logic of judgements of practice. *Journal of Philosophy*, 12(1), 505–510.

Dewey, J. (1927). *The public and its problems*. Holt and Company.

Diehl, E., & Sterman, J. D. (1995). Effects of feedback complexity on dynamic decision making. *Organizational Behavior and Human Decision Processes*, 62(2), 198–215.

Dill, W. R. (1958). Environment as an influence on managerial autonomy. *Administrative Science Quarterly*, 2(4), 409–443.

Dimov, D. (2018). Uncertainty under entrepreneurship. In A. Fayolle, S. Ramoglou, M. Karatas-Ozkan, & K. Nicolopoulou (Eds.), *Philosophical reflexivity and entrepreneurship research* (pp 184–196). Routledge.

Dimov, D. (2007a). Beyond the single-person, single-insight attribution in understanding entrepreneurial opportunities. *Entrepreneurship Theory and Practice*, 31, 713–731.

Dimov, D. (2007b). From opportunity insight to opportunity intention: The importance of person-situation learning match. *Entrepreneurship Theory and Practice*, 31, 561–583.

Dimov, D. (2016). Toward a design science of entrepreneurship. In *Models of start-up thinking and action: Theoretical, empirical and pedagogical approaches* (Vol. 18, pp. 1–31). Emerald Group Publishing Limited.

Dixit, A. K., & Nalebuff, B. J. (1991). *Thinking strategically: The competitive edge in business, politics, and everyday life*. W.W. Norton.

Dixit, A. K., & Pindyck, R.,S. (1994). *Investment under uncertainty.* Princeton University Press.
Dobrev, S. D., & Gotsopoulos, A. (2010). Legitimacy vacuum, structural imprinting, and the first mover disadvantage. *Academy of Management Journal, 53*(5), 1153–1174.
Dosi, G., & Egidi, M. (1991). Substantive and procedural uncertainty: An exploration of economic behaviours in changing environments. *Journal of Evolutionary Economics, 1,* 145–168.
Dougherty, D., & Hardy, C. (1996). Sustained product innovation in large, mature organizations: Overcoming innovation-to-organization problems. *Academy of Management Journal, 39*(5), 1120–1153.
Dow, J., & Werlang, S. R. D. C. (1994). Nash equilibrium under Knightian uncertainty: Breaking down backward induction. *Journal of Economic Theory, 64*(2), 305–324.
Downey, H. K., & Slocum, J. W. (1975). Uncertainty: Measures, research, and sources of variation. *Academy of Management Journal, 18*(3), 562–578.
Downey, H. K., Hellriegel, D., & Slocum, J. W., Jr. (1975). Environmental uncertainty: The construct and its application. *Administrative Science Quarterly, 20,* 613–629.
Du, N., & Budescu, D. V. (2005). The effects of imprecise probabilities and outcomes in evaluating investment options. *Management Science, 51*(12), 1791–1803.
Duncan, R. B. (1972). Characteristics of organizational environments and perceived environmental uncertainty. *Administrative Science Quarterly, 17*(3), 313–327.
Dunne, D. D., & Dougherty, D. (2016). Abductive reasoning: How innovators navigate in the labyrinth of complex product innovation. *Organization Studies, 37,* 131–159.
Durand, R., & Vaara, E. (2009). Causation, counterfactuals, and competitive advantage. *Strategic Management Journal, 30*(12), 1245–1264.
Edwards, W. (1965). Optimal strategies for seeking information: Models for statistics, choice reaction times, and human information processing. *Journal of Mathematical Psychology, 2*(2), 312–329.
Eggers, J. P., & Park, K. F. (2018). Incumbent adaptation to technological change: The past, present, and future of research on heterogeneous incumbent response. *Academy of Management Annals, 12*(1), 357–389.
Ehrenzweig, A. (1967). *The hidden order of art: A study in the psychology of artistic imagination.* University of California Press.
Ehret, M., & Wirtz, J. (2017). Unlocking value from machines: Business models and the industrial internet of things. *Journal of Marketing Management, 33*(1–2), 111–130.

Ehrig, T., & Schmidt, J. (2022). Theory-based learning and experimentation: How strategists can systematically generate knowledge at the edge between the known and the unknown. *Strategic Management Journal, 43*(7), 1287–1318.

Einhorn, H. J., & Hogarth, R. M. (1986). Decision making under ambiguity. *Journal of Business, 59*(4), S225–S250.

Einhorn, H. J., & Hogarth, R. M. (1987). Decision-making: Going forward in reverse: *Harvard Business Review, 87*(1), 66–70.

Einhorn, H. J., & Hogarth, R. M. (1988). Decision making under ambiguity: A note. In *Risk, decision and rationality* (pp. 327–336). Springer Netherlands.

Eisenhardt, K. M., & Martin, J. A. (2000). Dynamic capabilities: What are they? *Strategic Management Journal, 21*(10–11), 1105–1121.

Eisenhardt, K. M. (1989). Making fast strategic decisions in high-velocity environments. *Academy of Management Journal, 32*(3), 543–576.

Elenkov, D. S. (1997). Strategic uncertainty and environmental scanning: The case for institutional influences on scanning behavior. *Strategic Management Journal, 18*(4), 287–302.

Ellsberg, D. (1961). Risk, ambiguity, and the Savage axioms. *The Quarterly Journal of Economics, 75*(4), 643–669.

Epstein, L. G. (1999). A definition of uncertainty aversion. *Review of Economic Studies, 66*, 579–608.

Epstein, L. G., & Schneider, M. (2008). Ambiguity, information quality, and asset pricing. *The Journal of Finance, 63*(1), 197–228.

Etner, J., Jeleva, M., & Tallon, J. M. (2012). Decision theory under ambiguity. *Journal of Economic Surveys, 26*(2), 234–270.

Faber, M., Manstetten, R., & Proops, J. L. (1992). Humankind and the environment: An anatomy of surprise and ignorance. *Environmental Values, 1*(3), 217–241.

Faber, M. H., & Faber, M. H. (2012). Uncertainty modeling. *Statistics and Probability Theory: In Pursuit of Engineering Decision Support*, 43–84.

Faulkner, P., Feduzi, A., & Runde, J. (2017). Unknowns, Black Swans and the risk/uncertainty distinction. *Cambridge Journal of Economics, 41*, 1279–1302.

Feduzi, A., Faulkner, P., Runde, J., Cabantous, L., & Loch, C. (2021, In press). Heuristic methods for updating small world representations in strategic situations of Knightian uncertainty. *Academy of Management Review, 47*(3), 402–424.

Feduzi, A., Runde, J., & Zappia, C. (2012). De Finetti on the insurance of risks and uncertainties. *The British Journal for the Philosophy of Science, 63*(2), 329–356.

Felin, T., & Zenger, T. R. (2014). Closed or open innovation? Problem solving and the governance choice. *Research Policy, 43*(5), 914–925.

Felin, T., & Zenger, T. R. (2017). The theory-based view: Economic actors as theorists. *Strategy Science, 2*, 258–271.

Felin, T., Kauffman, S., & Zenger, T. (2021). Resource origins and search. *Strategic Management Journal*. https://doi.org/10.1002/smj.3350

Felin, T., Kauffman, S., Koppl, R., & Longo, G. (2014). Economic opportunity and evolution: Beyond landscapes and bounded rationality. *Strategic Entrepreneurship Journal, 8*(4), 269–282.

Feynman, R. (1999). *The pleasure of finding things out*. Perseus Books.

Fisher, G. (2021). *New Venture Legitimacy* [Oxford Research Encyclopedia of Business and Management, https://oxfordre.com/business/view/10.1093/acrefore/9780190224851.001.0001/acrefore-9780190224851-e-313].

Fleischhut, N., Artinger, F. M., Olschewski, S., & Hertwig, R. (2022). Not all uncertainty is treated equally: Information search under social and nonsocial uncertainty. *Journal of Behavioral Decision Making, 35*(2), e2250.

Fleming, L., & Sorenson, O. (2001). Technology as a complex adaptive system: Evidence from patent data. *Research Policy, 30*(7), 1019–1039.

Fleming, L. (2001). Recombinant uncertainty in technological search. *Management Science, 47*(1), 117–132.

Fontana, G., & Gerrard, B. (2004). A post Keynesian theory of decision making under uncertainty. *Journal of Economic Psychology, 25*(5), 619–637.

Forbes, D. P. (2007). Reconsidering the strategic implications of decision comprehensiveness. *Academy of Management Review, 32*(2), 361–376.

Forstmann, M., & Sagioglou, C. (2020). Religious concept activation attenuates cognitive dissonance reduction in free-choice and induced compliance paradigms. *The Journal of Social Psychology, 160*(1), 75–91.

Foss, K., Foss, N. J., & Klein, P. G. (2007). Original and derived judgment: An entrepreneurial theory of economic organization. *Organization Studies, 28*(12), 1893–1912.

Foss, N. J., & Klein, P. G. (2020). Entrepreneurial opportunities: Who needs them? *Academy of Management Perspectives, 34*(3), 366–377.

Foss, N. J., & Knudsen, T. (2003). The resource-based tangle: zTowards a sustainable explanation of competitive advantage. *Managerial and Decision Economics, 24*(4), 291–307.

Foss, N. J., & Laursen, K. (2005). Performance pay, delegation and multitasking under uncertainty and innovativeness: An empirical investigation. *Journal of Economic Behavior & Organization, 58*(2), 246–276.

Foss, N. J., Klein, P. G., & Bjørnskov, C. (2019). The context of entrepreneurial judgment: Organizations, markets, and institutions. *Journal of Management Studies, 56*(6), 1197–1213.

Foss, N. J., Klein, P. G., Kor, Y. Y., & Mahoney, J. T. (2008). Entrepreneurship, subjectivism, and the resource-based view: Toward a new synthesis. *Strategic Entrepreneurship Journal, 2*(1), 73–94.

Fox, J. (2014). Instinct can beat analytical thinking. *Harvard Business Review*, 20.

Freeman, C., & Soete, L. (1997). *The economics of industrial innovation* (3rd ed.). London.

Frisch, D., & Baron, J. (1988). Ambiguity and rationality. *Journal of Behavioral Decision Making*, 1(3), 149–157.

Furr, N. R., & Eisenhardt, K. M. (2021). Strategy and uncertainty: Resource-based view, strategy-creation view, and the hybrid between them. *Journal of Management*, 47(7), 1915–1935.

Furr, N. R. (2021). Technology entrepreneurship, technology strategy, and uncertainty. In I. M. Duhaime, M. A. Hitt, & M. A. Lyles (Eds.), *Strategic management: State of the field and its future* (pp. 205–220). Oxford University Press.

Galbraith, J. (1973). *Designing complex organizations*. Addison-Wesley.

Galbraith, J. (1977). *Organizational design*. Addison-Wesley.

Gallagher, M. W., & Lopez, S. J. (2007). Curiosity and well-being. *The Journal of Positive Psychology*, 2(4), 236–248.

Gans, J. S., Stern, S., & Wu, J. (2019). Foundations of entrepreneurial strategy. *Strategic Management Journal*, 40(5), 736–756.

Gärdenfors, P., & Sahlin, N. E. (1983). Decision making with unreliable probabilities. *British Journal of Mathematical and Statistical Psychology*, 36(2), 240–251.

Garner, W. R. (1962). *Uncertainty and structure as psychological concepts*. Wiley.

Garud, R., & Van de Ven, A. (1992). An empirical evaluation of the internal corporate venturing process. *Strategic Management Journal*, 13(S1), 93–109.

Gavetti, G., & Levinthal, D. (2000). Looking forward and looking backward: Cognitive and experiential search. *Administrative Science Quarterly*, 45(1), 113–137.

Gavetti, G., & Levinthal, D. A. (2001). Bringing cognition back in and moving forward. *Journal of Management and Governance*, 5(3), 213–216.

Gavetti, G., Helfat, C. E., & Marengo, L. (2017). Searching, shaping, and the quest for superior performance. *Strategy Science*, 2, 194–209.

Gavetti, G., Levinthal, D. A., & Rivkin, J. W. (2005). Strategy making in novel and complex worlds: The power of analogy. *Strategic Management Journal*, 26(8), 691–712.

George, C., Bright, A., Hurlbert, T., Linke, E. C., St. Clair, G., & Stein, J. (2006). Scholarly use of information: Graduate students' information seeking behaviour. *Information Research*, 11(4), paper 272.

Ghirardato, P. (2001). Coping with ignorance: Unforeseen contingencies and non-additive uncertainty. *Economic Theory*, 17, 247–276.

Gigerenzer, G., & Gaissmaier, W. (2011). Heuristic decision making. *Annual Review of Psychology*, 62, 451–482.

Gigerenzer, G. (2005). I think, therefore I err. *Social Research: An International Quarterly*, 72(1), 195–218.
Gigerenzer, G. (2008). *Rationality for mortals: How people cope with uncertainty.* Oxford University Press.
Gilboa, I., & Schmeidler, D. (1989). Maxmin expected utility with non-unique prior. *Journal of Mathematical Economics*, 18(2), 141–153.
Gilboa, I. (2009). *Theory of decision under uncertainty.* Cambridge University Press.
Gilfillan, S. (1935). *Inventing the ship.* Follett Publishing Co.
Glycopantis, D., & Muir, A. (2008). Nash equilibria with Knightian uncertainty: The case of capacities. *Economic Theory*, 37, 147–159.
Golman, R., & Loewenstein, G. (2016). Information gaps: A theory of preferences regarding the presence and absence of information. *Decision*, 5, 143–164.
Gomes, L. A. de V., Facin, A. L. F., & Salerno, M. S. (2021). Managing uncertainty propagation in innovation ecosystems. *Technological Forecasting and Social Change*, 171, 120945.
Goyal, M., & Netessine, S. (2007). Strategic technology choice and capacity investment under demand uncertainty. *Management Science*, 53(2), 192–207.
Graaff, J. de V. (1957). *Theoretical welfare economics.* Cambridge University Press.
Grant, R. M. (1996). Toward a knowledge-based theory of the firm. *Strategic Management Journal*, 17(S2), 109–122.
Grant, R. M. (2022). *Contemporary strategy analysis* (11th ed.). Wiley.
Gray, J. (2002). *Straw dogs: Thoughts on humans and other animals.* Farrar.
Griffin, M. A., & Grote, G. (2020). When is more uncertainty better? A model of uncertainty regulation and effectiveness. *Academy of Management Review*, 45(4), 745–765.
Grimm, C. M., Lee, H., & Smith, K. G. (Eds.). (2006). *Strategy as action: Competitive dynamics and competitive advantage.* Oxford University Press.
Gross, M. (2007). The unknown in process: Dynamic connections of ignorance, non-knowledge and related concepts. *Current Sociology*, 55(5), 742–759.
Grote, G. (2009). *Management of uncertainty: Theory and application in the design of systems and organizations.* Springer.
Gruber, M. (2005). Process matters—Empirical evidence one the value of marketing planning in VC-backed startups. In *Academy of Management Proceedings* (1, S1–S6).
Gruber, M., MacMillan, I. C., & Thompson, J. D. (2008). Look before you leap: Market opportunity identification in emerging technology firms. *Management Science*, 54(9), 1652–1665.

Haasnoot, M., Kwakkel, J. H., Walker, W. E., & Ter Maat, J. (2013). Dynamic adaptive policy pathways: A method for crafting robust decisions for a deeply uncertain world. *Global Environmental Change, 23*(2), 485–498.

Hacking, I. (1975). *The emergence of probability.* Cambridge University Press.

Hage, J. (1980). *Theories of organizations: Form, process, and transformation.* Wiley.

Halpern, J. Y. (2003). *Reasoning about uncertainty.* MIT Press.

Hamarat, C., Kwakkel, J. H., & Pruyt, E. (2013). Adaptive robust design under deep uncertainty. *Technological Forecasting and Social Change, 80*(3), 408–418.

Hamel, G., & Prahalad, C. K. (1989). Strategic intent. *Harvard Business Review, 20*(3), 45–52.

Hammond, K. R. (1955). Probabilistic functioning and the clinical method. *Psychological Review, 62*(4), 255–262.

Hanany, E., Klibanoff, P., & Mukerji, S. (2020). Incomplete information games with ambiguity averse players. *American Economic Journal: Microeconomics, 12*(2), 135–187.

Hansen, F. (1972). *Consumer choice behavior: A cognitive theory.* The Free Press.

Hansen, L. P. (2014). Nobel lecture: Uncertainty outside and inside economic models. *Journal of Political Economy, 122*(5), 945–987.

Hansson, S. O. (1994). *Decision theory: A brief introduction* [Department of Philosophy and the History of Technology. Royal Institute of Technology. Stockholm].

Hansson, S. O. (1996). Decision making under great uncertainty. *Philosophy of the Social Sciences, 26*(3), 369–386.

Hansson, S. O. (2022). Can uncertainty be quantified? *Perspectives on Science, 30*(2), 210–236.

Harada, V. H. (2002). Personalizing the information search process: A case study of journal writing with elementary-age students (School Library Media Research, Vol. 5 Available Online). *Teacher Librarian, 29*(4), 62–63.

Hardy, J. H., III., Ness, A. M., & Mecca, J. (2017). Outside the box: Epistemic curiosity as a predictor of creative problem solving and creative performance. *Personality and Individual Differences, 104,* 230–237.

Hariri, R. H., Fredericks, E. M., & Bowers, K. M. (2019). Uncertainty in big data analytics: Survey, opportunities, and challenges. *Journal of Big Data, 6*(1), 1–16.

Harrison, F. L. (1977). Decision-making in conditions of extreme uncertainty. *Journal of Management Studies, 14*(2), 169–178.

Hastie, R. (2001). Problems for judgment and decision making. *Annual Review of Psychology, 52*(1), 653–683.

Hau, R., Pleskac, T. J., & Hertwig, R. (2010). Decisions from experience and statistical probabilities: Why they trigger different choices than a priori probabilities. *Journal of Behavioral Decision Making, 23*(1), 48–68.

Hayek, F. A. (1948). The meaning of competition. *Econ Journal Watch, 13*, 360–372.

Hayek, F. A. (1978). Competition as a discovery procedure. *New studies in philosophy, politics, economics and the history of ideas* (pp. 179–190). Routledge and Kegan Paul.

Head, B. W. (2022). *Wicked problems in public policy: Understanding and responding to complex challenges*. Springer Nature.

Hebb, D. O. (1955). Drives and the CNS (conceptual nervous system). *Psychological Review, 62*, 243–254.

Hebert, R. F., & Link, A. N. (1988). *The entrepreneur: Mainstream views and radical critiques* (2nd ed.). Praeger.

Heiner, R. A. (1983). The origin of predictable behavior. *The American Economic Review, 73*(4), 560–595.

Heiner, R. A. (1988). Imperfect decisions, routinized behaviour and intertial technical change. In G. Dosi, C. Freeman, R. Nelson, G. Silverberg, & L. Soete (Eds.), *Technical change and economic theory*. Pinter.

Helton, J. C., & Johnson, J. D. (2011). Quantification of margins and uncertainties: Alternative representations of epistemic uncertainty. *Reliability Engineering & System Safety, 96*(9), 1034–1052.

Henisz, W. J. (2002). The institutional environment for infrastructure investment. *Industrial and Corporate Change, 11*(2), 355–389.

Herman, J. D., Reed, P. M., Zeff, H. B., & Characklis, G. W. (2015). How should robustness be defined for water systems planning under change. *Journal of Water Resources Planning and Management, 141*(10), 04015012.

Hertwig, R., & Gigerenzer, G. (1999). The 'conjunction fallacy'revisited: How intelligent inferences look like reasoning errors. *Journal of Behavioral Decision Making, 12*(4), 275–305.

Hertwig, R., Pleskac, T. J., & Pachur, T. (2019). *Taming uncertainty*. MIT Press.

Hey, J. D. (1989). *Current issues in microeconomics*. Macmillan Education Ltd.

Hicks, J. R. (1979). *Causality in Economics*. Basil Blackwell.

Hickson, D. J., Hinings, C. R., Lee, C. A., Schneck, R. E., & Pennings, J. M. (1971). A strategic contingencies' theory of intraorganizational power. *Administrative Science Quarterly, 16*(2), 216–229.

Hillier, F. S., & Lieberman, G. J. (2001). *Introduction to operations research* (7th ed.). New York.

Hillman, A. J., Withers, M. C., & Collins, B. J. (2009). Resource dependence theory: A review. *Journal of Management, 35*(6), 1404–1427.

Hirshleifer, J., & Riley, J. G. (1979). The analytics of uncertainty and information-an expository survey. *Journal of Economic Literature, 17*(4), 1375–1421.

Hmieleski, K. M., Carr, J. C., & Baron, R. A. (2015). Integrating discovery and creation perspectives of entrepreneurial action: The relative roles of founding CEO human capital, social capital, and psychological capital in contexts of risk versus uncertainty. *Strategic Entrepreneurship Journal, 9*(4), 289–312.

Hodgson, G. M. (2011). The eclipse of the uncertainty concept in mainstream economics. *Journal of Economic Issues, 45*(1), 159–176.

Hoffman, F. O., & Hammonds, J. S. (1994). Propagation of uncertainty in risk assessments: The need to distinguish between uncertainty due to lack of knowledge and uncertainty due to variability. *Risk Analysis, 14*(5), 707–712.

Hogarth, R. M., & Karelaia, N. (2005). Ignoring information in binary choice with continuous variables: When is less "more"? *Journal of Mathematical Psychology, 49*, 115–124.

Hogarth, R. M., & Karelaia, N. (2006). Regions of rationality: Maps for bounded agents. *Decision Analysis, 3*, 124–144.

Hogarth, R. M., & Karelaia, N. (2007). Heuristic and linear models of judgment: Matching rules and environments. *Psychological Review, 114*(3), 733.

Hogarth, R. M. (1980). *Judgement and choice: The psychology of decision*. Wiley.

Hogarth, R. M. (1987). *The psychology of judgment and choice* (2nd ed.). San Francisco.

Holland, J. H., Holyoak, K. J., Nisbett, R. E., & Thagard, P. R. (1986). *Induction: Processes of inference, learning, and discovery*. MIT Press.

Holm, H. J., Opper, S., & Nee, V. (2013). Entrepreneurs under uncertainty: An economic experiment in China. *Management Science, 59*(7), 1671–1687.

Holmes, T., & Westgren, R. (2020). Carving the nature of uncertainty at its joints. *Academy of Management Review, 45*(4), 869–872.

Hough, G. W., Rawlings, D. A., & Turner, M. F. (1997). *Pre-production quality assurance for healthcare manufacturers*. Interpharm Press.

Hsee, C. K., & Ruan, B. (2016). The Pandora effect: The power and peril of curiosity. *Psychological Science, 27*(5), 659–666.

Huang, L., & Pearce, J. L. (2015). Managing the unknowable: The effectiveness of early-stage investor gut feel in entrepreneurial investment decisions. *Administrative Science Quarterly, 60*(4), 634–670.

Huber, G. (1991). Organizational learning: The contributing processes and a review of the literatures. *Organization Science, 2*, 88–115.

Huchzermeier, A., & Loch, C. H. (2001). Project management under risk: Using the real options approach to evaluate flexibility in R&D. *Management Science, 47*(1), 85–101.

Hull, C. L. (1952). *A behavior system; an introduction to behavior theory concerning the individual organism*. Yale University Press.

Hyldegard, J. (2006). Collaborative information behavior—Exploring Kuhlthau's information search process model in a group-based educational setting. *Information Processing and Management, 42*(1), 276–298.

Iansiti, M. (1995). Shooting the rapids: Managing product development in turbulent environments. *California Management Review, 38*(1), 37–52.

Ioannidis, J. P. (2005). Why most published research findings are false. *PLoS Medicine, 2*(8), e124.

Jackson, M. (2023). *Uncertain: The wisdom and wonder of being unsure.* Prometheus Books.

James, W. (1950). *The principles of psychology.* Dover.

Jauch, L. R., & Kraft, K. L. (1986). Strategic management of uncertainty. *Academy of Management Review, 11,* 777–790.

Jepma, M., Verdonschot, R. G., Van Steenbergen, H., Rombouts, S. A., & Nieuwenhuis, S. (2012). Neural mechanisms underlying the induction and relief of perceptual curiosity. *Frontiers in Behavioral Neuroscience, 6*(5), 1–9.

Jonas, E., McGregor, I., Klackl, J., Agroskin, D., Fritsche, I., Holbrook, C., Nash, K., Proulx, T., & Quirin, M. (2014). Threat and defense: From anxiety to approach. *Advances in Experimental Social Psychology, 49,* 219–286.

Jones, T. M. (1991). Ethical decision making by individuals in organizations: An issue-contingent model. *Academy of Management Review, 16*(2), 366–395.

Jordan, M. E., Schallert, D. L., Park, Y., Lee, S., Chiang, Y. H. V., Cheng, A. C. J., ..., Lee, H. (2012). Expressing uncertainty in computer-mediated discourse: Language as a marker of intellectual work. *Discourse Processes, 49*(8), 660–692.

Judge, W. Q., & Douglas, T. J. (2013). Entrepreneurship as a leap of faith. *Journal of Management, Spirituality & Religion, 10*(1), 37–65.

Kagan, J. (1972). Motives and development. *Journal of Personality and Social Psychology, 22,* 51–66.

Kahneman, D., & Tversky, A. (1979). Prospect theory. *Econometrica, 47,* 263–292.

Kahneman, D., & Tversky, A. (1982). Variants of uncertainty. *Cognition, 11*(2), 143–157.

Kahneman, D. (2003). Maps of bounded rationality: Psychology for behavioral economics. *The American Economic Review, 93*(5), 1449–1475.

Kahneman, D. (2011). *Thinking, fast and slow.* Macmillan.

Kamin, L. J. (1969). Predictability, surprise, attention, and conditioning. In B. A. Campbell & R. M. Church (Eds.), *Punishment and aversive behavior.* Appleton-Century-Crofts.

Kaplan, S. (2008). Framing contests: Strategy making under uncertainty. *Organization Science, 19*(5), 729–752.

Kapoor, R., & Adner, R. (2012). What firms make vs. what they know: How firms' production and knowledge boundaries affect competitive advantage in the face of technological change. *Organization Science*, 23(5), 1227–1248.

Kapoor, R., & Klueter, T. (2021). Unbundling and managing uncertainty surrounding emerging technologies. *Strategy Science*, 6(1), 62–74.

Katila, R., & Ahuja, G. (2002). Something old, something new: A longitudinal study of search behavior and new product introduction. *Academy of Management Journal*, 45(6), 1183–1194.

Kauffeldt, T. F. (2015). *Games with exogenous uncertainty played by" Knightian" players* [dev.gtcenter.org].

Kaur, N., & Dasgupta, C. (2018). Types of uncertainty and collaborative uncertainty management strategies evidenced during the engineering design process. In *International conference on computers in education* (pp. 175–180).

Kay, J. A., & King, M. A. (2020). *Radical uncertainty*. Bridge Street Press.

Keynes, J. M. (1921). *A treatise on probability*. Macmillan.

Keynes, J. M. (1936). *The general theory of employment*. Macmillan, Cambridge University Press for the Royal Economic Society.

Keynes, J. M. (1937 [1973]). The general theory of employment. In *The collected writings of John Maynard Keynes* (Vol. 14, pp. 109–123). Macmillan, Cambridge University Press for the Royal Economic Society.

Khodadad Hosseini, S. H., Hamidizadeh, M. R., Hoseini, S. M., & Lashkarboloki, M. (2011). Designing the process model of robust strategy under uncertainty. *Journal of Strategic Management Studies*, 2(5), 83–109.

Kier, A. S., & McMullen, J. S. (2018). Entrepreneurial imaginativeness in new venture ideation. *Academy of Management Journal*, 61(6), 2265–2295.

Kim, S. (2013). Neuroscientific model of motivational process. *Frontiers in Psychology*, 4(1–12), 98.

Kintsch, W. (1980). Learning from text, levels of comprehension, or: Why anyone would read a story anyway? *Poetics*, 9, 87–98.

Kirzner, I. M. (1973). *Competition and entrepreneurship*. University of Chicago Press.

Kirzner, I. M. (1997). Entrepreneurial discovery and the competitive market process: An Austrian approach. *Journal of Economic Literature*, 35(1), 60–85.

Kiss, A. N., Libaers, D., Barr, P. S., Wang, T., & Zachary, M. A. (2020). CEO cognitive flexibility, information search, and organizational ambidexterity. *Strategic Management Journal*, 41(12), 2200–2233.

Kleinmuntz, B. (1992). Computers as clinicians: An update. *Computers in Biology and Medicine*, 22(4), 227–237.

Klepper, S. (1996). Entry, exit, growth, and innovation over the product life cycle. *The American Economic Review* (pp. 562–583).

Klepper, S. (1997). Industry life cycles. *Industrial and Corporate Change*, 6(1), 145–182.

Kline, S., & Rosenberg, N. (1986). An overview of innovation. In R. Landau & N. Rosenberg (Eds.), *The positive sum strategy: Harnessing technology for economic growth* (pp. 275–305). The National Academic Press.

Klingebiel, R., & Adner, R. (2015). Real options logic revisited: The performance effects of alternative resource allocation regimes. *Academy of Management Journal, 58*(1), 221–241.

Klir, G. J. (2004). Generalized information theory: Aims, results, and open problems. *Reliability Engineering & System Safety, 85*(1–3), 21–38.

Knight, E., Daymond, J., & Paroutis, S. (2020). Design-led strategy: How to bring design thinking into the art of strategic management. *California Management Review, 62*(2), 30–52.

Knight, F. H. (1921/64). *Risk, uncertainty and profit*. Augustus M. Kelley.

Knudsen, T., & Levinthal, D. A. (2007). Two faces of search: Alternative generation and alternative evaluation. *Organization Science, 18*, 39–54.

Koopmans, T. C. (1957). *Three essays on the state of economic science*. McGraw Hill.

Korhonen, P. J., & Wallenius, J. (2020). Different paradigms of decision-making. In *Making better decisions: Balancing conflicting criteria* (pp. 1–4). Springer.

Kozyreva, A., & Hertwig, R. (2021). The interpretation of uncertainty in ecological rationality. *Synthese, 198*(2), 1517–1547.

Krumbein, J. (2012). Two invisible hands and optimal uncertainty. *SSRN 2034000*.

Kuhlthau, C. C. (1991). Inside the search process: Information seeking from the user's perspective. *Journal of the American Society for Information Science, 42*(5), 361–371.

Kuhlthau, C. C. (1993). A principle of uncertainty for information seeking. *Journal of Documentation, 49*(4), 339–355.

Kuhlthau, C. C., Heinström, J., & Todd, R. J. (2008). The 'information search process' revisited: Is the model still useful. *Information Research, 13*(4), 13–14.

Kuhn, K. M., & Budescu, D. V. (1996). The relative importance of probabilities, outcomes, and vagueness in hazard risk decisions. *Organizational Behavior and Human Decision Processes, 68*(3), 301–317.

Kuhn, T. S. (1962). *The structure of scientific revolutions*. University of Chicago Press.

Kurtz, J. L., Wilson, T. D., & Gilbert, D. T. (2007). Quantity versus uncertainty: When winning one prize is better than winning two. *Journal of Experimental Social Psychology, 43*(6), 979–985.

Kwakkel, J. H., Walker, W. E., & Marchau, V. A. (2010). Classifying and communicating uncertainties in model-based policy analysis. *International Journal of Technology, Policy and Management, 10*(4), 299–315.

Lachmann, L. M. (1976). From Mises to Shackle: An essay on Austrian economics and the kaleidic society. *Journal of Economic Literature, 14*(1), 54–62.

Lampert, C. M., Kim, M., & Polidoro, F., Jr. (2020). Branching and anchoring: Complementary asset configurations in conditions of Knightian uncertainty. *Academy of Management Review, 45*(4), 847–868.

Langlois, R. N., & Cosgel, M. M. (1993). Frank Knight on risk, uncertainty, and the firm: A new interpretation. *Economic Inquiry, 31*(3), 456–465.

Lanzetta, J. T. (1963). Information acquisition in decision making. In J. Harvey (Ed.), *Motivation and social interaction: Cognitive determinants*. Ronald Press, 239–265.

Laplace, P. S. (1951). *A philosophical essay on probabilities*. Dover.

Larson, A. (1992). Network dyads in entrepreneurial settings: A study of the governance of exchange relationships. *Administrative Science Quarterly, 37*, 76–104.

Lawrence, P. R., & Lorsch, J. W. (1967). Differentiation and integration in complex organizations. *Administrative Science Quarterly, 12*(1), 1–47.

Lebovitz, S., Levina, N., & Lifshitz-Assaf, H. (2021). Is AI ground truth really true? The dangers of training and evaluating AI tools based on experts' know-what. *MIS Quarterly, 45*(3), 1501–1525.

Lebovitz, S., Lifshitz-Assaf, H., & Levina, N. (2022). To engage or not to engage with AI for critical judgments: How professionals deal with opacity when using AI for medical diagnosis. *Organization Science, 33*(1), 126–148.

Lee, B., & Yoo, B. (2007). What prevents electronic lemon markets? *Journal of Organizational Computing and Electronic Commerce, 17*(3), 217–246.

Leiblein, M. J., Reuer, J. J., & Zenger, T. (2018). What makes a decision strategic? *Strategy Science, 3*(4), 558–573.

Lempert R. J., Popper, S. W., & Bankes, S. C. (2003). *Shaping the next one hundred years: New methods for quantitative, long-term policy analysis* [MR-1626-RPC, RAND, Santa Monica, California] (pp. 3–4).

Lempert, R. J., & Collins, M. (2007). Managing the risk of uncertain threshold responses: Comparison of robust, optimum, and precautionary approaches. *Risk Analysis, 27*(4), 1009–1026.

Lempert, R. J., Groves, D. G., Popper, S. W., & Bankes, S. C. (2006). A general, analytic method for generating robust strategies and narrative scenarios. *Management Science, 52*(4), 514–528.

Levi, I. (1974). On indeterminate probabilities. *Journal of Philosophy, 71*, 391–418.

Levi, I. (1982). Ignorance, probability and rational choice. *Synthese, 53*(3), 387–417.

Likierman, A. (2020). The elements of good judgment. *Harvard Business Review, 98*(1), 102–111.

Lipshitz, R., & Strauss, O. (1997). Coping with uncertainty: A naturalistic decision-making analysis. *Organizational Behavior and Human Decision Processes, 69*(2), 149–163.

Littlechild, S. (1986). Three types of market process. In R. N. Langlois (Ed.), *Economics as a process: Essays in the new institutional economics*. Cambridge University Press.

Loewenstein, G. (1994). The psychology of curiosity: A review and reinterpretation. *Psychological Bulletin, 116*(1), 75–98.

Louis, M. R. (1980). Surprise and sense making: What newcomers experience in entering unfamiliar organizational settings. *Administrative Science Quarterly, 25*, 226–251.

Luan, S., Reb, J., & Gigerenzer, G. (2019). Ecological rationality: Fast-and-frugal heuristics for managerial decision making under uncertainty. *Academy of Management Journal, 62*(6), 1735–1759.

Luce, R. D., & Raiffa, H. (1989). *Games and decisions: Introduction and critical survey*. Courier Corporation.

Luehrman, T. A. (1998). Strategy as a portfolio of real options. *Harvard Business Review, 76*, 89–101.

Lynn, G., Morone, J., & Paulson, P. (1996). Marketing and discontinuous innovation: The probe and learn process. *California Management Review, 38*(3), 8–37.

Lytras, M. D., & Pouloudi, A. (2006). Towards the development of a novel taxonomy of knowledge management systems from a learning perspective: An integrated approach to learning and knowledge infrastructures. *Journal of Knowledge Management, 10*(6), 64–80.

MacCrimmon, K. R. (1966). Descriptive and normative implications of the decision theory postulates. In K. Borch & J. Mossin (Eds.), *Risk and uncertainty: Proceedings of a conference held by the International Economic Association* (pp. 1–21). St. Martin's Press.

Machina, M. J., & Siniscalchi, M. (2014). Ambiguity and ambiguity aversion. In *Handbook of the economics of risk and uncertainty* (Vol. 1, pp. 729–807). North-Holland.

Machina, M. J. (1987). Choice under uncertainty: Problems solved and unsolved. *Journal of Economic Perspectives, 1*(1), 121–154.

Mack, R. P. (1971). *Planning on uncertainty*. Wiley.

MacLeod, W. B., & Pingle, M. (2000). *An experiment on the relative effects of ability, temperament and luck on search with uncertainty* [University of Southern California Law School, Olin Research paper 00-12].

Magnani, G., & Zucchella, A. (2018). Uncertainty in entrepreneurship and management studies: A systematic literature review. *International Journal of Business and Management, 13*(3), 98–133.

Maitlis, S., & Christianson, M. (2014). Sensemaking in organizations: Taking stock and moving forward. *Academy of Management Annals, 8*, 57–125.

Mandel, T. F., & Wilson, I. (1993). *How companies use scenarios: Practice and prescription* [SRI Business Intelligence Programme Report R822].

Manski, C. F. (2000). Identification problems and decisions under ambiguity: Empirical analysis of treatment response and normative analysis of treatment choice. *Journal of Econometrics, 95*(2), 415–442.

Mantere, S., & Ketokivi, M. (2013). Reasoning in organization science. *Academy of Management Review, 38*(1), 70–89.

March, J. (1991). Exploration and exploitation in organizational learning. *Organization Science, 2*, 71–87.

March, J. C., & Olsen, J. P. (1976). *Ambiguity and choice in organizations*. Universitetsforlaget.

March, J. G., & Simon, H. A. (1958). *Organizations*. Wiley.

March, J. G. (1994). *Primer on decision making: How decisions happen*. Simon and Schuster.

Marchau, V. A., Walker, W. E., Bloemen, P. J., & Popper, S. W. (2019). *Decision making under deep uncertainty: From theory to practice*. Springer Nature.

Markey, A., & Loewenstein, G. (2014). Curiosity. In *International handbook of emotions in education* (pp. 238–255). Routledge.

Markowitz, H. M. (1952). Portfolio selection. *Journal of Finance, 7*, 77–91.

Marschak, J. (1975). Personal probabilities of probabilities. *Theory and Decision, 6*, 121–153.

Martin, M. M., & Rubin, R. B. (1995). A new measure of cognitive flexibility. *Psychological Reports, 76*(2), 623–626.

Marvin, C. B., & Shohamy, D. (2016). Curiosity and reward: Valence predicts choice and information prediction errors enhance learning. *Journal of Experimental Psychology: General, 145*(3), 266–272.

McCray, L. E., Oye, K. A., & Petersen, A. C. (2010). Planned adaptation in risk regulation: An initial survey of US environmental, health, and safety regulation. *Technological Forecasting and Social Change, 77*(6), 951–959.

McDonald, R., & Eisenhardt, K. (2020). The New-Market Conundrum in emerging industries the usual rules of strategy don't apply. *Harvard Business Review, 98*(3), 75–83.

McGrath, R. G., & Macmillan, I. C. (1995). Discovery driven planning. *Harvard Business Review, 73*(4), 44–54.

McGrath, R. G. (1999). Falling forward: Real options reasoning and entrepreneurial failure. *Academy of Management Review, 24*(1), 13–30.

McGrath, R. G., & MacMillan, I.,C. (2000). Assessing technology projects using real options reasoning. *Research-Technology Management, 43*(4), 35–49.

McIver, D., Shimizu, K., & Kim, B. (2009). A critical review of the environmental uncertainty literature since 1987 [The University of Texas at San

Antonio, College of Business Working Paper Series, Wp# 0067MGT-110-2009].

McKelvie, A., Haynie, J. M., & Gustavsson, V. (2011). Unpacking the uncertainty construct: Implications for entrepreneurial action. *Journal of Business Venturing*, 26(3), 273–292.

McMullen, J. S., & Dimov, D. (2013). Time and the entrepreneurial journey: The problems and promise of studying entrepreneurship as a process. *Journal of Management Studies*, 50, 1481–1512.

McMullen, J. S., & Kier, A. S. (2016). Trapped by the entrepreneurial mindset: Opportunity seeking and escalation of commitment in the Mount Everest disaster. *Journal of Business Venturing*, 31(6), 663–686.

McMullen, J. S., & Shepherd, D. A. (2006). Entrepreneurial action and the role of uncertainty in the theory of the entrepreneur. *Academy of Management Review*, 31(1), 132–152.

McMullen, J. S. (2015). Entrepreneurial judgment as empathic accuracy: A sequential decision-making approach to entrepreneurial action. *Journal of Institutional Economics*, 11(3), 651–681.

Medin, D. L., & Schaffer, M. M. (1978). Context theory of classification learning. *Psychological Review*, 85(3), 207–238.

Meijer, I. S., Hekkert, M. P., Faber, J., & Smits, R. E. (2006). Perceived uncertainties regarding socio-technological transformations: Towards a framework. *International Journal of Foresight and Innovation Policy*, 2(2), 214–240.

Meyer, R. J., & Sathi, A. (1985). A multi-attribute model of consumer choice during product learning. *Marketing Science*, 4(1), 41–61.

Miceli, T. J. (1994). Book review of: Paradigms and conventions: Uncertainty, decision making, and entrepreneurship. *Journal of Economic Behavior & Organization*, 25(2), 299–301.

Miles, R. E., & Snow, C. C. (1978). *Organizational strategy, structure and process*. McGraw-Hill.

Milgrom, P., & Roberts, J. (1982). Limit pricing and entry under incomplete information: An equilibrium analysis. *Econometrica*, 50(2), 443–459.

Milgrom, P. R., & Roberts, J. (1992). *Economics, organization, and management*. Prentice Hall.

Millar, C. C., Groth, O., & Mahon, J. F. (2018). Management innovation in a VUCA world: Challenges and recommendations. *California Management Review*, 61(1), 5–14.

Miller, K. D. (2007). Risk and rationality in entrepreneurial processes. *Strategic Entrepreneurship Journal*, 1(1–2), 57–74.

Miller, A. I. (Ed.). (2012). *Sixty-two years of uncertainty: Historical, philosophical, and physical inquiries into the foundations of quantum mechanics* (Vol. 226). Springer Science & Business Media.

Milliken, F. J. (1987). Three types of perceived uncertainty about the environment: State, effect, and response uncertainty. *Academy of Management Review*, 12(1), 133–143.

Mitchell, V. W. (1995). Organizational risk perception and reduction: A literature review. *British Journal of Management*, 6(2), 115–133.

Mitchell, T. R., & James, L. R. (2001). Building better theory: Time and the specification of when things happen. *Academy of Management Review*, 26(4), 530–547.

Mousavi, S., & Gigerenzer, G. (2014). Risk, uncertainty, and heuristics. *Journal of Business Research*, 67(8), 1671–1678.

Mousavi, S., & Gigerenzer, G. (2017). Heuristics are tools for uncertainty. *Homo Oeconomicus*, 34(4), 361–379.

Mullins, J. W., & Forlani, D. (2005). Missing the boat or sinking the boat: A study of new venture decision making. *Journal of Business Venturing*, 20(1), 47–69.

Murphy, D. J., & Pinelli, T. E. (1994). NASA/DOD aerospace knowledge diffusion research project [Report 30: Computer-Mediated Communication (CMC) and the communication of technical information in aerospace. Rensselaer Polytechnic Institute Report].

Nash, S. J. (2003). On pragmatic philosophy and Knightian uncertainty. *Review of Social Economy*, 61(2), 251–272.

Nelson, R. R., & Winter, S. G. (1982). *An evolutionary theory of economic change*. Belknap Press/Harvard University Press.

Newell, A., & Simon, H. A. (1972). *Human problem solving* (Vol. 104, No. 9). Prentice-Hall.

Newman, J. M. (2019). Antitrust in digital markets. *Vanderbilt Law Review*, 72, 1497–1561.

Nickerson, J. A., & Zenger, T. R. (2004). A knowledge-based theory of the firm—The problem-solving perspective. *Organization Science*, 15(6), 617–632.

Nickles, T. (2003). Evolutionary models of innovation and the Meno problem. In *The international handbook on innovation* (pp. 54–78). Elsevier Science Ltd.

Nikolaidis, E., Ghiocel, D. M., & Singhal, S. (Eds.). (2004). *Engineering design reliability handbook*. CRC Press.

Nilsson, N. J. (1971). *Problem solving methods in artificial intelligence*. McGraw Hill.

Nosal, J. B., & Ordoñez, G. (2016). Uncertainty as commitment. *Journal of Monetary Economics*, 80, 124–140.

O'Connor, G. C. (2008). Major innovation as a dynamic capability: A systems approach. *Journal of Product Innovation Management*, 25(4), 313–330.

O'Donnell, R. (2013). Two post-keynesian approaches to uncertainty and irreducible uncertainty. In G. C. Harcourt & P. Kriesler (Eds.), *The Oxford handbook of post-Keynesian economics* (pp. 121–142). Oxford University Press.

O'Reilly, C. A., III., & Tushman, M. L. (2008). Ambidexterity as a dynamic capability: Resolving the innovator's dilemma. *Research in Organizational Behavior, 28*, 185–206.

Obschonka, M., & Audretsch, D. B. (2020). Artificial intelligence and big data in entrepreneurship: A new era has begun. *Small Business Economics, 55*, 529–539.

O'Connor, G. C., & Rice, M. P. (2013). A comprehensive model of uncertainty associated with radical innovation. *Journal of Product Innovation Management, 30*, 2–18.

O'Malley, P. (2000). Uncertain subjects: Risks, liberalism and contract. *Economy and Society, 29*(4), 460–484.

Oosterwijk, S. (2017). Choosing the negative: A behavioral demonstration of morbid curiosity. *PLoS One, 12*(7), e0178399.

Orhnial, T. (1980). Potential surprise and portfolio theory. *Diskussionsbeiträge-Serie A*.

Packard, M. D., & Clark, B. B. (2020). On the mitigability of uncertainty and the choice between predictive and nonpredictive strategy. *Academy of Management Review, 45*(4), 766–786.

Packard, M. D., Clark, B. B., & Klein, P. G. (2017). Uncertainty types and transitions in the entrepreneurial process. *Organization Science, 28*(5), 840–856.

Paeleman, I., Vanacker, T. & Zahra, S.A. (2021). Wait-and-see versus proactive approaches during an environmental jolt and firm survival. In *Frontiers of Entrepreneurship Research, BCERC Proceedings*, 2021.

Peirce, C. S. (1878). Deduction, induction, and hypothesis. *Popular Science Monthly, 13*, 470–482.

Pennings, J. M., & Tripathi, R. C. (1978). The organization-environment relationship: Dimensional versus typological viewpoints. In L. Karpik (Ed.), *Organization and environment* (pp. 171–195). Sage.

Pennings, J. M. (1981). Strategically interdependent organizations. In P. C. Nystrom & W. H. Starbuck (Eds.), *Handbook of organizational design* (Vol. 1, pp. 433–455). Oxford University Press.

Penrose, E. T. (1959). *The theory of the growth of the firm*. Oxford University Press.

Pfeffer, J., & Salancik, G. R. (1978). *The external control of organizations: A resource dependence perspective*. Harper & Row Publishers.

Pisano, G. P. (2006). *Science business: The promise, the reality, and the future of biotech*. Harvard Business School Press.

Pitts, J. M. (1995). Mental models of information: The 1993–1994 AASL/Highsmith research award study. *School Library Media Quarterly, 23*(3), 177–184.

Plucker, J. A., Beghetto, R. A., & Dow, G. T. (2004). Why isn't creativity more important to educational psychologists? Potentials, pitfalls, and future directions in creativity research. *Educational Psychologist, 39*(2), 83–96.

Popper, S. W., Lempert, R. J., & Bankes, S. C. (2005). Shaping the future. *Scientific American, 292*(4), 66–71.

Porter, M. E. (1980). *Competitive strategy: Techniques for analyzing industries and competitors.* Free Press.

Porter, M. E. (2001). Strategy and the internet. *Harvard Business Review, 79*(3), 62–78.

Posen, H. E., Leiblein, M. J., & Chen, J. S. (2015). A behavioral theory of real options In *AoM Proceedings*, Vancouver, Canada.

Posner, R. A. (2004). *Catastrophe: Risk and response.* Oxford University Press.

Potter, K., Rosen, P., & Johnson, Ch. R. (2012). From quantification to visualization: A taxonomy of uncertainty visualization approaches. *Uncertainty Quantification in Scientific Computing IFIP Advances in Information and Communication Technology, 377*, 226–249.

Poutyface. (2021). *Never fuckin know.* Island Records.

Powell, T. C. (1992). Organizational alignment as competitive advantage. *Strategic Management Journal, 13*, 119–134.

Pressman, S., & Choi, Y. B. (1997). Paradigms, conventions and the entrepreneur: A review article and response. *American Journal of Economics and Sociology, 56*(1), 51–68.

Ramoglou, S., & Tsang, E. W. (2016). A realist perspective of entrepreneurship: Opportunities as propensities. *Academy of Management Review, 41*(3), 410–434.

Ramoglou, S. (2021). Knowable opportunities in an unknowable future? On the epistemological paradoxes of entrepreneurship theory. *Journal of Business Venturing, 36*(2), 106090.

Ramoglou, S., Gartner, W. B., & Tsang, E. W. (2020). "Who is an entrepreneur?" is (still) the wrong question. *Journal of Business Venturing Insights, 13*, e00168.

Randles, D., Benjamin, R., Martens, J. P., & Heine, S. J. (2018). Searching for answers in an uncertain world: Meaning threats lead to increased working memory capacity. *PLoS One, 13*(10), e0204640.

Rapp, D. J., & Olbrich, M. (2020). On entrepreneurial decision logics under conditions of uncertainty: An attempt to advance the current debate. *Journal of Innovation and Entrepreneurship, 9*(1), 21.

Rapp, D. J., & Olbrich, M. (2022, In press). From Knight uncertainty to real-structuredness: Further opening the judgement box. *Strategic Entrepreneurship Journal, 17*(1), 186–209.
Rauch, A., Fink, M., & Hatak, I. (2018). Stress processes: An essential ingredient in the entrepreneurial process. *Academy of Management Perspectives, 32,* 340–357.
Raynor, M. E. (2007). *The strategy paradox: Why committing to success leads to failure (and what to do about it).* Currency.
Reale, C., Salwei, M. E., Militello, L. G., Weinger, M. B., Burden, A., Sushereba, C., Andreae, M. H., Gaba, D. M., McIvor, W. R., & Banerjee A. (2023). Decision-making during high-risk events: A systematic literature review. *Journal of Cognitive Engineering and Decision Making, 17*(2), 188–212.
Reetz, D. K., & MacAulay, S. (2016). Beyond ill-structured problems: Tackling true novelty through co-evolutionary search. In *36th Strategic Management Conference SMS*, Berlin.
Riesch, H. (2013). Levels of uncertainty. In S. Roeser, R. Hillerbrand, P. Sandin, & M. Peterson (Eds.), *Essentials of risk theory* (pp. 29–56). Springer.
Rietveld, C. A., & Hoogendoorn, B. (2022). The mediating role of values in the relationship between religion and entrepreneurship. *Small Business Economics, 58*(3), 1309–1335.
Rindova, V., & Courtney, H. (2020). To shape or adapt: Knowledge problems, epistemologies, and strategic postures under Knightian uncertainty. *Academy of Management Review, 45*(4), 787–807.
Rittel, H. W., & Webber, M. M. (1973). Dilemmas in a general theory of planning. *Policy Sciences, 4*(2), 155–169.
Robertson, T. S., & Gatignon, H. (1998). Technology development mode: A transaction cost conceptualization. *Strategic Management Journal, 19*(6), 515–531.
Rock, D. (2008). SCARF: A brain-based model for collaborating with and influencing others. *NeuroLeadership Journal, 1*(1), 44–52.
Roeser, S. (2019). Emotional responses to luck, risk, and uncertainty. In *The Routledge handbook of the philosophy and psychology of luck* (pp. 356–364). Routledge.
Rogers, E. (2003). *The diffusion of innovation* (5th ed.). New York.
Roman, P. (2023). "Hunting" for information to cope with the omnipresent uncertainty represents the new normality. *International Journal of Communication Research, 13*(2), 84–90.
Romeijn, J. W., & Roy, O. (2014). Radical uncertainty: Beyond probabilistic models of belief. *Erkenntnis, 79,* 1221–1223.

Rosenberg, N. (1996). Uncertainty and technological change. In R. Landau, T. Taylor, & G. Wright (Eds.), *The mosaic of economic growth*. Stanford University Press.
Rouvray, D. H. (1997). The treatment of uncertainty in the sciences. *Endeavour, 21*(4), 154–158.
Rowe, W. D. (1994). Understanding uncertainty. *Risk Analysis, 14*(5), 743–750.
Ruan, B., Hsee, C. K., & Lu, Z. Y. (2018). The teasing effect: An underappreciated benefit of creating and resolving an uncertainty. *Journal of Marketing Research, 55*(4), 556–570.
Ruef, M., & Patterson, K. (2009). Credit and classification: The impact of industry boundaries in nineteenth-century America. *Administrative Science Quarterly, 54*(3), 486–520.
Runde, J. (1990). Keynesian uncertainty and the weight of arguments. *Economics & Philosophy, 6*(2), 275–292.
Samsami, F., Hosseini, S. H. K., Kordnaeij, A., & Azar, A. (2015). Managing environmental uncertainty: From conceptual review to strategic management point of view. *International Journal of Business and Management, 10*(7), 215–229.
Santos, F. M., & Eisenhardt, K. M. (2009). Constructing markets and shaping boundaries: Entrepreneurial power in nascent fields. *Academy of Management Journal, 52*(4), 643–671.
Sargeant, S., & Yoxall, J. (2023). Psychology and spirituality: Reviewing developments in history, method and practice. *Journal of Religion and Health, 62*, 1159–1174.
Sastry, L., & Boyd, D. R. (1998). Virtual environments for engineering applications. *Virtual Reality, 3*, 235–244.
Savage, L. J. (1954). *The foundations of statistics*. Wiley.
Schmeidler, D. (1989). Subjective probability and expected utility without additivity. *Econometrica, 57*(3), 571–587.
Schmidt, S. M., & Cummings, L. L. (1976). Organizational environment, differentiation and perceived environmental uncertainty. *Decision Sciences, 7*, 447–467.
Schoemaker, P. J. (2002). *Profiting from uncertainty: Strategies for succeeding no matter what the future brings*. Simon & Schuster.
Schultz, W., Dayan, P., & Montague, P. R. (1997). A neural substrate of prediction and reward. *Science, 275*(5306), 1593–1599.
Schulz, E., & Gershman, S. J. (2019). The algorithmic architecture of exploration in the human brain. *Current Opinion in Neurobiology, 55*, 7–14.
Schumpeter, J. (1932). Development. *Journal of Economic Literature, 18*, 104–116.
Schumpeter, J. A. (1939). *Business cycles: A theoretical, historical, and statistical analysis of the capitalist process*. McGraw-Hill.

Schwarz, N., & Clore, G. L. (1996). Feelings and phenomenal experiences. In E. T. Higgins & A. Kruglanski (Eds.), *Social psychology: Handbook of basic principles* (pp. 433–465). Guilford.
Scoblic, J. P. (2020). Learning from the future. *Harvard Business Review*, 98(4), 38–47.
Scott, J. C. (2020). *Seeing like a state: How certain schemes to improve the human condition have failed*. Yale University Press.
Serola, S., & Vakkari, P. (2005). The anticipated and assessed contribution of information types in references retrieved for preparing a research proposal. *Journal of the American Society for Information Science and Technology*, 56(4), 373–381.
Sewell, W. H., Jr. (1992). A theory of structure: Duality, agency and transformation. *American Journal of Sociology*, 98, 1–29.
Shackle, G. L. S. (1949). *Expectation in economics*. Cambridge University Press.
Shackle, G. L. S. (1953). The logic of surprise. *Economica*, 20(78), 112–117.
Shackle, G. L. S. (1955). *Uncertainty in economics*. Cambridge University Press.
Shackle, G. L. S. (1961). *Decision, order, and time in human affairs*. Cambridge University Press.
Shackle, G. L. S. (1966a). Policy, poetry and success. *The Economic Journal*, 76(304), 755–767.
Shackle, G. L. S. (1966b). *The nature of economic though: Selected papers (1955–1964)*. Cambridge University Press.
Shackle, G. L. S. (1972). Marginalism: The harvest. *History of Political Economy*, 4(2), 587–602.
Shackle, G. L. S. (1979). *Imagination and the nature of choice*. Edinburgh University Press.
Shafer, G. A. (1976). *A mathematical theory of evidence*. Princeton University Press.
Shane, S. (2000). Prior knowledge and the discovery of entrepreneurial opportunities. *Organization Science*, 11(4), 448–469.
Shepherd, D. A., Williams, T. A., & Patzelt, H. (2015). Thinking about entrepreneurial decision making: Review and research agenda. *Journal of Management*, 41(1), 11–46.
Shin, D. D., & Kim, S. I. (2019). Homo curious: Curious or interested? *Educational Psychology Review*, 31(4), 853–874.
Shrader-Frechette, K. (2007). *Taking action, saving lives: Our duties to protect environmental and public health*. Oxford University Press.
Silverberg, G. (1997). *Evolutionary modeling in economics: Recent history and immediate prospects*. MERIT.
Silverberg, G., Dosi, G., & Orsenigo, L. (1988). Innovation, diversity and diffusion: A self-organisation model. *The Economic Journal*, 98(393), 1032–1054.

Silvia, P. J. (2008). Interest—The curious emotion. *Current Directions in Psychological Science, 17*(1), 57–60.
Simon, H. A. (1955). A behavioral model of rational choice. *The Quarterly Journal of Economics, 69*(1), 99–118.
Simon, H. A. (1956). Rational choice and the structure of the environment. *Psychology Review, 63*(2), 129–138.
Simon, H. A. (1959). Theories of decision-making in economics and behavioral science. *American Economic Review, 49*, 253–283.
Simon, H. A. (1962). The architecture of complexity. *Proceedings of the American Philosophical Society, 106*, 467–482.
Simon, H. A. (1972). Theories of bounded rationality. *Decision and Organization, 1*(1), 161–176.
Simon, H. A. (1979a). Information processing models of cognition. *Annual Review of Psychology, 30*(1), 363–396.
Simon, H. A. (1979b). Rational decision making in business organizations. *American Economic Review, 69*(4), 493–513.
Simon, H. A. (1982). *Models of bounded rationality: Empirically grounded economic reason* (Vol. 3). MIT Press.
Simon, H. A. (1990). Invariants of human behavior. *Annual Review of Psychology, 41*(1), 1–20.
Simon, H. A. (1995). The information-processing theory of mind. *American Psychologist, 50*(7), 507.
Simon, H. A. (1996). *The sciences of the artificial* (3rd ed.). MIT Press.
Simonton, D. K. (2013). Creative thought as blind variation and selective retention: Why creativity is inversely related to sightedness. *Journal of Theoretical and Philosophical Psychology, 33*(4), 253–266.
Sims, C. A. (2001). Pitfalls of a minimax approach to model uncertainty. *American Economic Review, 91*(2), 51–54.
Sjöberg, L. (2000). Perceived risk and tampering with nature. *Journal of Risk Research, 3*(4), 353–367.
Smith, A. (1776 [1937]). *The wealth of nations*. Cannan ed. Modern Library.
Smith, B. R., Conger, M. J., McMullen, J. S., & Neubert, M. J. (2019). Why believe? The promise of research on the role of religion in entrepreneurial action. *Journal of Business Venturing Insights, 11*, e00119.
Smith, B. R., McMullen, J. S., & Cardon, M. S. (2021). Toward a theological turn in entrepreneurship: How religion could enable transformative research in our field. *Journal of Business Venturing, 36*(5), 106139.
Smith, G. F., Benson, P. G., & Curley, S. P. (1991). Belief, knowledge, and uncertainty: A cognitive perspective on subjective probability. *Organizational Behavior and Human Decision Processes, 48*(2), 291–321.

Smith, K. G., & Grimm, C. M. (1987). Environmental variation, strategic change and firm performance: A study of railroad deregulation. *Strategic Management Journal,* 8(4), 363–376.

Smith, R. E. (2016). Idealizations of uncertainty, and lessons from artificial intelligence. *Economics,* 10(1), 1–40, 20160007. https://doi.org/10.5018/economics-ejournal.ja.2016-7

Smithson, M. (1989). *Ignorance and uncertainty: Emerging paradigms.* Springer Verlag.

Smithson, M. J. (2008). *Social theories of ignorance.* Stanford University Press.

Soublière, J. F., & Gehman, J. (2020). The legitimacy threshold revisited: How prior successes and failures spill over to other endeavors on Kickstarter. *Academy of Management Journal,* 63(2), 472–502.

Spender, J.-C. (1983). The business policy problem and industry recipes. *Advances in Strategic Management,* 2, 211–229.

Spender, J.-C. (2006). *Knightian uncertainty and its resolution as institutionalized practice* [v9 Working Paper].

Spreng, D. (2103). Interactions between energy, information and growth. In ICT4S 2013, *Proceedings of the First International Conference on Information and Communication Technologies for Sustainability* (pp. 6–7). Zurich, Switzerland: ETH Zurich.

Stacey, R. D. (1992). *Managing the unknowable: Strategic boundaries between order and chaos in organizations.* Jossey-Bass Publishers.

Stager, P. (1967). Conceptual level as a composition variable in small-group decision making. *Journal of Personality and Social Psychology,* 5(2), 152–161.

Starbuck, W. H. (1976). Organizations and their environments. In M. D. Dunnette (Ed.), *Handbook of industrial and organizational psychology* (pp. 1069–1123). Rand McNally.

Starbuck, W. H., & Milliken, F. J. (1988). Executives' perceptual filters: What they notice and how they make sense. In D. C. Hambrick (Ed.), *The executive effect: Concepts and methods for studying top managers* (pp. 35–65). JAI Press.

Sterelny, K. (2003). *Thought in a hostile world.* Blackwell.

Sterman, J. D. (1994). Learning in and about complex systems. *System Dynamics Review,* 10(2–3), 291–330.

Stewart, I. (2019). *Do dice play God? The mathematics of uncertainty.* Hachette UK.

Stewart, G. (2021, March). *A passion for ignorance? Not knowing the half of it.* AGORA Column.

Stigler, G. (1939). Production and distribution in the short run. *Journal of Political Economy,* 47, 305–327.

Stiglitz, J.E. (1989). Imperfect information in the product market. In *Handbook of industrial organization* (Vol. 1, pp. 769–847). Elsevier.

Sturm, R. R. (2003). Investor confidence and returns following large one-day price changes. *The Journal of Behavioral Finance, 4*(4), 201–216.
Suarez, F., & Lanzolla, G. (2005). The half-truth of first-mover advantage. *Harvard Business Review, 83*, 121–127.
Suarez, F. F., & Lanzolla, G. (2007). The role of environmental dynamics in building a first mover advantage theory. *Academy of Management Review, 32*(2), 377–392.
Suarez, F. F., & Utterback, J. M. (1995). Dominant designs and the survival of firms. *Strategic Management Journal, 16*, 415–430.
Sull, D. N. (2005). Strategy as active waiting. *Harvard Business Review, 83*, 120–129.
Sunstein, C. R. (2007). *Worst-case scenarios.* Harvard University Press.
Sutton, J. (2006). Flexibility, profitability and survival in an (objective) model of Knightian uncertainty [Working paper, London School of Economics].
Sykes, H. B., & Dunham, D. (1995). Critical assumption planning: A practical tool for managing business development risk. *Journal of Business Venturing, 10*(6), 413–424.
Szentkirályi, L. (2020). Luck has nothing to do with it: Prevailing uncertainty and responsibilities of due care. *Ethics, Policy & Environment, 23*(3), 261–280.
Taleb, N. N. (2007). *The black swan: The impact of the highly improbable.* Random House.
Taleb, N. N. (2012). *Antifragile: How to live in a world we don't understand.* Allen Lane.
Tang, R., & Solomon, P. (1998). Toward an understanding of the dynamics of relevance judgment: An analysis of one person's search behavior. *Information Processing and Management, 34*(2), 237–256.
Tang, Y., & Wezel, F. C. (2015). Up to standard? Market positioning and performance of Hong Kong films, 1975–1997. *Journal of Business Venturing, 30*(3), 452–466.
Tannert, C., Elvers, H. D., & Jandrig, B. (2007). The ethics of uncertainty: In the light of possible dangers, research becomes a moral duty. *EMBO Reports, 8*(10), 892–896.
Taylor, C. R. (2003). The role of risk versus the role of uncertainty in economic systems. *Agricultural Systems, 75*(2–3), 251–264.
Taylor, P., & Shipley, D. [unpublished]. *Probably wrong—Misapplications of probability and statistics in real life uncertainty.*
Teece, D., & Leih, S. (2016). Uncertainty, innovation, and dynamic capabilities: An introduction. *California Management Review, 58*(4), 5–12.
Teece, D., Peteraf, M., & Leih, S. (2016). Dynamic capabilities and organizational agility: Risk, uncertainty, and strategy in the innovation economy. *California Management Review, 58*(4), 13–35.

Teece, D. J. (1986). Profiting from technological innovation: Implications for integration, collaboration, licensing and public policy. *Research Policy, 15,* 285–305.

Teece, D. J., Pisano, G., & Shuen, A. (1997). Dynamic capabilities and strategic management. *Strategic Management Journal, 18*(7), 509–533.

Terreberry, S. (1968). The evolution of organizational environments. *Administrative Science Quarterly, 12,* 589–613.

Tetlock, P. E. (2002). Social functionalist frameworks for judgment and choice: Intuitive politicians, theologians and prosecutors. *Psychological Review, 109,* 451–471.

The Temptations. (1970). *Ball of confusion.* Gordy (Motown) Label (Written by N. Whitfield and B. Strong).

Thompson, J. (1967). *Organizations in action.* McGraw-Hill.

Todd, P. M., & Gigerenzer, G. E. (2012). *Ecological rationality: Intelligence in the world.* Oxford University Press.

Towler, R. (1984). *The need for certainty: A sociological study of conventional religion.* Routledge & Kegan Paul.

Townsend, D. M., & Busenitz, L. W. (2015). Turning water into wine? Exploring the role of dynamic capabilities in early-stage capitalization processes. *Journal of Business Venturing, 30*(2), 292–306.

Townsend, D. M., Hunt, R. A., Beal, D. J., & Hyeong Jin, J. (2020). Venturing into the unknown: A meta-analytic assessment of uncertainty in entrepreneurship research. *Academy of Management Proceedings, 2020*(1), 17318.

Townsend, D. M., Hunt, R. A., McMullen, J. S., & Sarasvathy, S. D. (2018). Uncertainty, knowledge problems, and entrepreneurial action. *Academy of Management Annals, 12*(2), 659–687.

Tripsas, M., & Gavetti, G. (2000). Capabilities, cognition, and inertia: Evidence from digital imaging. *Strategic Management Journal, 21*(10/11), 1147–1161.

Trunk, A., Birkel, H., & Hartmann, E. (2020). On the current state of combining human and artificial intelligence for strategic organizational decision making. *Business Research, 13*(3), 875–919.

Tushman, M. L., & Anderson, P. (1986). Technological discontinuities and organizational environments. *Administrative Science Quarterly, 31*(3), 439–465.

Tversky, A., & Fox, C. R. (1995). Weighing risk and uncertainty. *Psychological Review, 102*(2), 269–283.

Tversky, A., & Kahneman, D. (1973). Availability: A heuristic for judging frequency and probability. *Cognitive Psychology, 5*(2), 207–232.

Tversky, A., & Kahneman, D. (1974). Judgment under uncertainty: Heuristics and biases. *Science, 185,* 1124–1131.

Usher, A. P. (1954). *A history of mechanical inventions.* Harvard University Press.

Vakkari, P. (2001). A theory of the task-based information retrieval process: A summary and generalisation of a longitudinal study. *Journal of Documentation,* 57(1), 44–60.
Vakkari, P., & Hakala, N. (2000). Changes in relevance criteria and problem stages in task performance. *Journal of Documentation,* 56(5), 540–562.
Vakkari, P., Pennanen, M., & Serola, S. (2003). Changes of search terms and tactics while writing a research proposal: A longitudinal case study. *Information Processing and Management,* 39(3), 445–463.
van Asselt, M. B. A., & Vos, E. (2006). The precautionary principle and the uncertainty paradox. *Journal of Risk Research,* 9(4), 313–336.
Van de Ven, A. H. (1986). Central problems in the management of innovation. *Management Science,* 32(5), 590–607.
Van Dijk, E., & Zeelenberg, M. (2007). When curiosity killed regret: Avoiding or seeking the unknown in decision-making under uncertainty. *Journal of Experimental Social Psychology,* 43(4), 656–662.
van Lieshout, L. L., Vandenbroucke, A. R., Müller, N. C., Cools, R., & de Lange, F. P. (2018). Induction and relief of curiosity elicit parietal and frontal activity. *Journal of Neuroscience,* 38(10), 2816–2817.
Vecchiato, R., & Roveda, C. (2011). Uncertainty, foresight, and strategic decision making: Evidence from leading companies. *Forth International Seville Conference on Future-Oriented Technology Analysis* (FTA) [FTA and Grand Societal Challenges–Shaping and Driving Structural and Systemic Transformations, Seville, 12–13 May 2011 (pp. 99–102)].
Venkataraman, S. (1997). The distinctive domain of entrepreneurship research: An editor's perspective. In J. Katz & R. Brockhaus (Eds.), *Advances in entrepreneurship, firm emergence and growth* (Vol. 3, pp. 119–138). JAI Press.
von Mises, L. (1949). *Human action: A treatise on economics* [Ludwig von Mises Institute, www.mises.org/humanaction.asp].
von Neumann, J., & Morgenstern, O. (1944). *Theory of games and economic behavior.* Princeton University Press.
Von Stumm, S., Chung, A., & Furnham, A. (2011). Creative ability, creative ideation and latent classes of creative achievement: What is the role of personality? *Psychology of Aesthetics, Creativity, and the Arts,* 5(2), 107–114.
Wald, A. (1947). *Sequential analysis.* Wiley.
Wald, A. (1950). *Statistical decision functions.* Wiley.
Walker, W. E., Lempert, R, J., & Kwakkel, J. H. (2013). Deep uncertainty, entry. In S. Gass & M. Fu (Eds.), *Encyclopedia of operations research and management science* (pp. 395–402). (3rd ed.). Springer.
Walker, A. R., Luque, D., Le Pelley, M. E. & Beesley, T. (2019). The role of uncertainty in attentional and choice exploration. *Psychonomic Bulletin & Review,* 26, 1911–1916.

Walker, G., & Weber, D. (1987). Supplier competition, uncertainty, and make-or-buy decisions. *Academy of Management Journal, 30*(3), 589–596.
Walker, W. E., Harremoës, P., Rotmans, J., Van Der Sluijs, J. P., Van Asselt, M. B., Janssen, P., & Krayer von Krauss, M. P. (2003). Defining uncertainty: A conceptual basis for uncertainty management in model-based decision support. *Integrated Assessment, 4*(1), 5–17.
Wallsten, T. S., Forsyth, B. H., & Budescu, D. (1983). Stability and coherence of health experts' upper and lower subjective probabilities about dose-response functions. *Organizational Behavior and Human Performance, 31*, 277–302.
Wang, P., & Soergel, D. (1998). A cognitive model of document use during a research project. Study 1. Document selection. *Journal of the American Society for Information Science, 49*(2), 115–133.
Waterman, R. H., Jr. (1990). *Adhocracy: The power to change*. Whittle Direct Books.
Weick, K. E. (1979). *The social psychology of organizing* (2nd ed.). Reading, MA.
Weick, K. E. (1995). *Sensemaking in organizations*. Sage.
Weick, K. E. (2001). *Making sense of the organization*. Blackwell.
Weick, K. E., Sutcliffe, K. M., & Obstfeld, D. (2005). Organizing and the process of sensemaking and organizing. *Organization Science, 16*(4), 409–421.
Wernerfelt, B. (1984). A resource-based view of the firm. *Strategic Management Journal, 5*(2), 171–180.
Wernerfelt, B., & Karnani, A. (1987). Competitive strategy under uncertainty. *Strategic Management Journal, 8*(2), 187–194.
Wheeler, G. (2018). Bounded rationality. In E. N. Zalta (Ed.), *The Stanford encyclopedia of philosophy* (Winter 2018 ed.). Metaphysics Research Lab, Stanford University.
Wheeler, J. A. (1992, December). Quoted in *Scientific American*, p. 20.
Whetten, D. A. (1989). What constitutes a theoretical contribution? *Academy of Management Review, 14*, 490–495.
Wigner, E. P. (1957). Relativistic invariance and quantum phenomena. *Reviews of Modern Physics, 29*(3), 255.
Williamson, O. E. (1975). Markets and hierarchies: Analysis and antitrust implications: A study in the economics of internal organization. *University of Illinois at Urbana-Champaign's Academy for Entrepreneurial Leadership Historical Research Reference in Entrepreneurship*.
Williamson, O. E. (1985). *The economic institutions of capitalism*. Free Press.
Williamson, O. E. (1996). *The mechanisms of governance*. Oxford University Press.
Williamson, P. J. (1999). Strategy as options on the future. *Sloan Management Review, 40*(3), 117–126.

Wilson, R. C., Geana, A., White, J. M., Ludvig, E. A., & Cohen, J. D. (2014). Humans use directed and random exploration to solve the explore–exploit dilemma. *Journal of Experimental Psychology: General, 143*, 2074–2081.

Wilson, T. D., Centerbar, D. B., Kermer, D. A., & Gilbert, D. T. (2005). The pleasures of uncertainty: Prolonging positive moods in ways people do not anticipate. *Journal of Personality and Social Psychology, 88*(1), 5–21.

Wittgenstein, L. (1971). *Tractatus Logico-Philosophicu.* Routledge & Kegan Paul.

Wright, M., & Phan, P. (2017). AMP articles in an uncertain new world. *Academy of Management Perspectives, 31*, 1–3.

Wright, M., & Phan, P. (2018). The commercialization of science: From determinants to impact. *Academy of Management Perspectives, 32*(1), 1–3.

Wu, B., & Knott, A. M. (2006). Entrepreneurial risk and market entry. *Management Science, 52*(9), 1315–1330.

Yager, R. R. (1999). A game-theoretic approach to decision making under uncertainty. *Intelligent Systems in Accounting, Finance & Management, 8*(2), 131–143.

Yamagishi, T., Cook, K. S., & Watabe, M. (1998). Uncertainty, trust, and commitment formation in the United States and Japan. *American Journal of Sociology, 104*(1), 165–194.

Yang, S. (1997). Information seeking as problem-solving using a qualitative approach to uncover the novice learners' information-seeking process in a perseus hypertext system. *Library and Information Science Research, 19*(1), 71–92.

Zack, M. (1999). Developing a knowledge strategy. *California Management Review, 41*(3), 125–145.

Zadeh, L. A. (1978). Fuzzy sets as a basis for a theory of possibility. *Fuzzy Sets and Systems, 1*, 3–28.

Zafar, S., Waddingham, J., Zachary, M., & Short, J. (2021). Search behavior and decision confidence in equity crowdfunding: An information search process model perspective. *Journal of Small Business Management, 61*(4), 1638–1671.

Zahra, S. A. (2008). The virtuous cycle of discovery and creation of entrepreneurial opportunities. *Strategic Entrepreneurship Journal, 2*(3), 243–257.

Zahra, S. A. (2021). The resource-based view, resourcefulness, and resource management in startup firms: A proposed research agenda. *Journal of Management, 47*(7), 1841–1860.

Zhang, X., Chan, F. T., Yan, C., & Bose, I. (2022). Towards risk-aware artificial intelligence and machine learning systems: An overview. *Decision Support Systems, 159*, 113800.

Index

A
accept, 23, 69, 92, 363, 381
active learning, 322, 365, 402
advantage, 3, 28, 74, 98, 104, 118, 128, 129, 153, 172, 175, 179, 181, 182, 186, 222, 243, 282, 286, 291, 292, 300, 335, 341, 342, 403
agility, 315, 333
aleatory, 82, 258, 261
alertness, 326, 360
ambiguity, 20, 35, 36, 45, 48, 65, 68, 74, 75, 78, 91, 99, 115, 121, 130, 150, 151, 158, 160, 170, 185, 196, 214, 215, 218, 234, 250, 254, 255, 362, 363
approach, 2, 4, 7, 12, 14, 15, 21, 34, 35, 38, 39, 83, 100, 102, 119, 146, 148, 152, 157, 162, 163, 174, 180, 181, 183, 188, 233, 234, 238, 240, 242, 244, 248, 250, 261, 264, 268, 278, 281, 287, 293, 298, 299, 314, 315, 322, 323, 327, 333–335, 337, 340–343, 347, 349–356, 358, 359, 361–365, 367, 383–385, 388, 389, 397, 400, 402
art, 11, 18, 27, 194–200, 388, 390, 397
artificial intelligence (AI), 27, 91, 317, 393
assumption, 3, 12, 14, 20, 35, 37, 40, 61, 62, 73, 94, 98, 106, 138, 147, 151, 239, 242, 249, 267, 272, 274, 278, 279, 317, 318, 325, 328, 330–332, 341, 347, 352, 353, 360, 385, 402
avoid/avoidance, 7, 14, 16, 27, 95, 104, 116, 121, 223, 236, 253, 255, 326, 354, 357, 383, 387, 404
awareness, 15, 52, 73, 76, 93, 215, 217, 244, 278, 289, 322, 359, 360, 362

B
basis/es, 2–4, 10, 13, 23, 48, 63, 75, 76, 92, 96, 98, 106, 110, 132,

134, 187, 208, 218, 241, 257, 259, 264, 268–270, 272, 273, 290, 293, 299, 302, 332, 341, 342, 350, 351, 389
Bayesian, 2, 101, 150, 235, 241, 243, 350, 351, 402
bear, 95, 97, 102, 104, 129, 130, 134, 232, 252, 253, 292, 299, 301, 357, 364
behavior, 9, 14, 15, 21, 22, 61, 66, 68, 69, 71, 74, 81, 99, 100, 102, 104–110, 128, 131, 139–142, 214, 219, 220, 225, 226, 232, 239, 240, 242, 243, 258, 280, 287, 289, 297, 301, 320, 324, 331, 338, 351, 361, 384
benefit, 3, 9, 17, 34, 40, 68, 70, 97, 107, 116, 120, 121, 123, 129–134, 138, 140, 149, 152, 160, 171, 173, 186, 205, 207, 209, 215, 222, 227, 233, 260, 273, 276, 282, 284–286, 291, 294, 315, 319–322, 324, 334–336, 356, 358, 365, 366, 383, 388, 398, 402, 405, 406
bet/gamble, 2, 38, 39, 48, 101, 104, 258, 342
bias, 2, 38, 61, 82, 108, 116, 142, 171, 222, 235, 241, 243, 270, 326, 343, 345, 346, 351, 384, 396, 399–401
big data, 199, 326, 327, 389, 396, 398, 399
brain, 75, 82, 160, 197, 214–218, 221, 225–227

C

capability, 16, 68, 253, 277, 292, 359
cause-and-effect, 46, 48, 67, 78, 101, 107, 120, 138, 146, 151, 219, 258, 286, 287

challenge, 4, 5, 8, 9, 11, 14, 22, 64, 69, 75, 77, 92–94, 96, 97, 105, 106, 108, 110, 118, 138, 140, 152, 153, 162, 174, 183, 186, 187, 198, 205, 208, 222, 232, 234, 236, 243, 256, 263, 291, 322, 330, 338, 341, 361, 387
change, 18, 46, 53, 61, 65, 66, 68, 69, 71, 74, 76, 77, 83, 91, 95, 107, 117, 146, 150, 159, 160, 183, 184, 186, 187, 208, 215, 219–221, 224, 232, 233, 242, 243, 259, 269, 270, 276, 286, 290, 318, 321, 331, 334, 335, 339, 340, 343, 347, 348, 353, 358, 365, 387, 388, 395, 403, 404, 406, 407
characteristic/s, 3, 14, 19, 21, 27, 37, 38, 40, 60, 61, 63, 67, 79, 80, 82, 105, 132, 133, 146, 148, 149, 151, 153, 156, 158, 171–175, 195, 196, 198, 223, 248, 249, 264–268, 281, 282, 284, 285, 314, 315, 317, 319–321, 332–337, 346, 350, 396
cognition, 21, 71, 75, 194, 217–221, 225–227
combine/combination, 49, 67, 99, 120, 122, 142, 147–149, 163, 180, 195, 196, 209, 216, 219, 271, 275, 287, 292, 298, 319, 330, 333, 336, 356, 359, 365, 396, 398
communication, 8, 71, 72, 78, 80, 109–111, 118, 152, 153, 160, 161, 170, 221, 224, 261, 270, 291, 326, 355, 362, 365, 389
compensation, 80, 133, 172, 248, 321, 340
competition, 39, 74, 77, 106, 185, 187, 188, 222, 225, 239, 253,

282, 286, 292, 297, 318, 328, 405
competitive intelligence, 279, 280, 321, 355, 366
complex/complexity, 7, 12–14, 17, 20, 22, 39, 46, 50, 61–64, 67, 70, 82, 91, 93, 94, 99–101, 104, 106, 107, 131, 139, 141, 150–152, 156, 159, 160, 170, 180–184, 186, 187, 214, 215, 238, 239, 250, 263, 282, 289, 290, 297, 300, 321, 330, 331, 344, 345, 365, 385, 396, 401, 403, 407
computational, 61, 65, 82, 100, 160, 241, 261, 262
conceptual, 130, 131, 151, 153, 195, 224, 234
conflict, 35, 38, 61, 66, 70, 71, 74, 107, 110, 139, 162, 217, 270, 290, 327, 331, 399
confusion, 14, 24, 27, 34–40, 65, 72, 81, 119, 133, 153, 161, 214, 255, 260, 263, 270, 299, 316, 322, 344, 385, 388
conservative, 223, 354, 355
constraint, 16, 20, 21, 35, 79, 141, 142, 152, 169, 195, 197–200, 223, 233, 261, 268, 269, 276, 278, 280, 314, 319, 321, 335, 338, 345, 359, 361, 362, 366, 367
consumer/customer, 37, 66, 74, 120, 148, 169, 180, 184, 194, 198, 227, 275, 279, 280, 286, 295, 297, 318, 358, 396, 405
context, 5–8, 37, 44, 49, 61, 62, 64, 76, 81, 91, 98, 101, 108, 119, 121, 123, 131–133, 138, 149, 151, 152, 156, 157, 168, 172, 179, 182, 185, 186, 195, 197, 216, 219, 220, 243, 254, 258, 260, 263, 272, 277, 278, 286, 289, 299, 314, 318, 320–322, 324–328, 333, 334, 337, 339, 342, 345, 354, 362, 386, 397
contract, 18, 96, 131, 183, 259, 292, 316, 335–337, 358, 365, 398
control, 3, 8, 10, 14, 16, 20, 23, 60, 62, 68, 71, 77, 79, 80, 92, 93, 96, 100, 110, 119, 129, 131, 132, 141, 153, 160, 188, 206, 225, 227, 253, 275, 287, 289, 317, 318, 328, 329, 342, 343, 366, 394, 406
cooperation, 131, 222, 259, 287, 336, 358
cost/s/ly, 9, 10, 17, 20, 22, 28, 40, 51, 66, 70, 79, 96, 97, 102, 104, 106, 115–118, 121–123, 128, 129, 131–134, 149, 151, 152, 157, 173, 175, 181, 182, 186, 198, 205, 233, 239, 253, 273, 282, 285, 286, 292, 294, 296, 314, 315, 319–322, 324, 326, 330, 332–334, 336–338, 342, 349, 355, 357–360, 362–366, 383, 386, 388, 389, 396–398, 400, 401, 405, 406
creativity, 10, 27, 102, 134, 140, 150, 170, 194–200, 214, 330, 350, 363, 382, 398
culture, 79, 116, 131, 132, 172, 199, 236, 258, 359
curiosity, 27, 138, 140, 213–217, 225–227, 236, 252, 270, 320

D

decision, 2, 3, 6–9, 12–19, 28, 35, 37, 45, 51, 60, 62, 63, 70, 71, 73, 75–77, 79–81, 89, 94, 97–100, 106, 117, 118, 121, 123, 129, 133, 149, 157, 159, 163, 168, 180, 181, 186, 207,

215, 226, 233, 237, 243, 244, 248, 251, 259, 263–268, 270, 271, 273, 275–278, 280–282, 286, 288, 289, 314, 315, 317, 321, 324, 329, 333, 337, 339, 343, 344, 350, 352–354, 356, 357, 359, 361, 363–365, 394, 397, 399, 407

decision-maker, 7, 9, 11, 12, 16–18, 24, 36–38, 44, 47, 48, 50, 51, 60–64, 67, 70–74, 76, 81, 82, 92, 93, 98, 99, 106, 117, 122, 130, 133, 159, 160, 171, 223, 237, 241, 243, 252, 260–262, 267, 268, 272, 274, 276, 285, 287, 289, 294, 295, 315, 321, 326, 328, 340–342, 344, 350, 352, 354–357, 359, 384

definition/define, 2, 27, 34, 35, 39, 44–50, 53, 54, 75, 108, 146, 157, 163, 167, 207, 237, 252, 254–256, 259, 263, 293, 298, 314, 319, 352, 363

delay, 24, 39, 50, 65, 66, 72, 77, 182, 276, 284, 301, 316, 331, 355, 356, 366

delegation, 359

demand, 25, 37, 51, 77, 96, 103, 110, 123, 132, 142, 182, 187, 206, 208, 222, 223, 249, 265, 282, 285, 297, 301, 330, 337, 344, 350, 357, 404

deny/denial, 21, 107, 243, 355, 356

dimension, 37, 39, 67, 123, 141, 153, 156–163, 180, 187, 188, 208, 214, 215, 222, 281, 282, 284, 285, 287, 297, 314, 321, 363

disadvantage, 169, 222, 243, 286, 315, 341, 399

discover, 10, 52, 76, 79, 104, 184, 224, 257, 289, 317, 322, 385, 389, 402

disinformation, 4, 10, 38, 68, 70, 105, 110, 111, 117, 120, 123, 180, 227, 390, 399, 406

distribution, 9, 13, 48, 67, 73, 76, 123, 149–151, 223, 232, 234, 235, 240, 252, 254–256, 258, 265, 274, 275, 294, 298, 318, 319, 350, 397

diversification, 13, 130, 286, 319, 335, 337, 338

diversity, 196, 337

doubt, 4, 10, 18, 39, 50, 65, 68, 75–77, 81, 82, 91, 118, 161, 207, 242, 262, 267, 289, 337, 356, 385, 399

driver, 3, 11, 38, 60, 83, 95, 102, 120, 123, 171, 220, 244, 287

dynamic, 3, 17, 61–64, 69, 76, 94, 99, 106, 131, 151, 152, 159, 160, 163, 169, 170, 184, 187, 196, 214, 277, 279, 324, 330, 331, 333, 334, 352

dynamic capability, 333, 341, 359

E

earth, 204

Ellsbergian ambiguity, 48, 255, 266, 275

endogenous, 60, 63, 83, 170, 289, 290

entity/ies, 18, 23, 83, 89–91, 102, 105, 110, 119, 133, 140–142, 150, 156, 181, 209, 223, 225, 244, 275, 279, 318, 326, 329, 335, 340, 345, 352, 354, 359, 364, 366, 388, 389, 395, 399

entrepreneur, 13, 121, 167–175, 206, 252, 291, 292, 294, 296–299, 316, 387, 403, 404, 406

environment, 19, 21, 23, 44, 50, 70, 76, 82, 90, 91, 96, 100, 123, 129, 139, 182, 183, 196, 206, 210, 214–216, 220–222, 224, 237, 261, 320, 324, 326, 360, 398
epistemic/uncertainty, 1, 2, 4, 6, 8, 10, 14, 18, 21–25, 27, 34–40, 44, 45, 47, 50, 51, 62, 65, 71, 80–82, 90, 92, 94, 96–99, 101, 103–106, 109, 110, 117, 119, 123, 128, 131, 132, 141, 146, 152, 158, 162, 170, 180, 183, 197, 207, 215, 219, 220, 232, 235, 237, 239, 242, 248, 250, 253, 256, 259, 261–263, 268, 271, 272, 275, 279, 282, 287, 288, 290, 294, 297, 301, 328, 344, 345, 353, 359, 366, 382, 383, 385–390, 394, 397, 398, 401, 405, 406
epistemological, 38, 53, 174, 382
equilibrium, 68, 106, 122, 275, 348
equity?, 274
equivocality, 35, 250, 260, 261
error, 2, 61, 71, 75, 76, 110, 148, 150, 185, 206, 216, 219, 223, 250, 263, 267, 287, 288, 337, 343, 344, 346, 363, 399, 402
estimation, 13, 252, 352, 402
ethics, 263, 274
evil, 142, 204, 209, 364, 404
evolution, 3, 156, 196, 199, 205, 215, 221–223, 225–227, 276, 395
execution, 169, 278, 295, 333, 359, 367
existential, 27, 65, 90, 108, 128, 175, 187, 206, 210, 298, 301, 382, 399
exogenous, 60, 63, 170, 172, 289, 290

expected value, 3, 50, 68, 98, 101, 116, 168, 180, 207, 264, 273, 276, 293, 318, 332, 349, 363
experience, 3, 4, 9, 48, 52, 81, 91, 95, 103, 104, 110, 116, 123, 129, 133, 141, 142, 149, 170, 171, 174, 183, 185, 195, 204, 218, 221, 237, 241, 243, 286, 291, 295, 299, 322, 324–326, 330, 333, 346, 351, 355, 359, 361, 383, 384, 387, 394
experiment, 23, 36, 48, 104, 108, 116, 174, 186, 195, 218, 220, 241, 254, 297, 323, 363, 395
expertise/expert, 52, 62, 71, 79–81, 150, 173, 214, 262, 286, 289, 302, 336, 337, 366, 400, 402
exploit, 40, 44, 69, 77, 104, 110, 131, 134, 159, 171–174, 180, 185, 186, 208, 216, 218, 244, 285, 333, 334, 366, 382
explore, 9, 21, 23, 27, 62, 141, 163, 195–197, 236, 321, 331, 385, 388, 406

F
failure, 27, 54, 96, 110, 117, 121, 123, 130, 138, 139, 146, 148, 162, 175, 232, 237, 239, 242, 244, 296, 316, 353, 383, 399
feasible/feasibility, 16, 39, 66, 107, 122, 159, 169, 198, 206, 248, 250, 266, 267, 269, 281, 282, 286, 290, 315, 339, 352, 359, 366, 406
feedback, 17, 65, 81, 150, 159, 214, 216, 218, 235, 237, 277, 321, 323, 327, 350, 355
feelings, 8, 81, 89, 91, 92, 98, 100, 105, 116, 119, 132, 148, 161, 206, 207, 217, 360
first-mover, 186, 286, 342

flexibility, 130, 150, 300, 318, 332, 333, 352, 355
fuzzy, 36, 78, 152, 261, 401

G

game, 7, 12, 20, 23, 68, 94, 95, 98, 101, 105, 110, 132, 138, 140–142, 151, 158, 171, 175, 183, 185, 186, 195, 196, 225, 258, 259, 275, 279, 331, 339, 340, 345, 347, 348, 352, 357, 358, 361, 395
game theory, 18, 51, 68, 180, 278, 279, 314, 330, 339, 366
generate, 7, 11, 14, 15, 19, 40, 63, 65–68, 70, 71, 78, 91, 96, 118, 120, 123, 131, 140, 142, 174, 185, 186, 224, 291, 316, 325, 366, 399, 404
goals, 2, 3, 10, 15, 16, 18, 20, 22, 70, 72, 73, 80, 98, 139, 141, 142, 147, 149, 171, 264, 269, 270, 275, 277, 286, 320, 340, 343, 353, 363, 388, 396
Goldilocks, 138, 142
government, 3, 12, 24, 70, 72, 73, 80, 102, 130, 131, 140, 141, 286, 301, 382

H

harm, 28, 34, 40, 68, 111, 116, 117, 119, 120, 123, 139, 198, 207, 227, 244, 286, 301, 361, 383, 396, 397, 404, 405
heterogeneity, 14, 182, 282, 295, 300
heuristic, 13, 15, 19, 102, 169, 174, 195, 221, 223, 340, 343–346, 352, 384, 386
human/humanity, 1, 3, 6, 10, 18, 20, 21, 23–25, 27, 61, 66, 68, 80, 92, 95, 96, 98, 101, 103, 105, 109, 110, 117, 119, 123, 124, 129, 132, 134, 138, 142, 148, 159, 161, 199, 204–206, 216, 221, 222, 224–226, 236, 239, 243, 261, 287, 330, 343, 363, 382–385, 390, 396, 397, 400, 404, 405, 407

I

ignorance, 6, 23, 35, 46, 47, 52, 61, 63, 65, 73, 92, 95, 109, 156, 171, 197, 198, 219, 233, 236, 242, 250, 256–260, 287, 290, 326, 345, 389
ill-defined, 38, 65, 91, 232, 241, 400, 404
imagination, 62, 123, 175, 198, 318, 361
immeasurable/ity, 147, 152, 254, 272, 330
incomplete information, 2, 16, 37, 48, 51, 93, 96, 120, 132, 156, 160, 169, 175, 181, 186, 219, 237, 251, 252, 261, 263, 271, 293, 315, 363
independent, 44, 52, 140, 141, 147, 148, 206, 278, 317, 335, 336, 361
indifference, 257, 345, 348, 350, 351
individual, 7, 12, 18, 20, 21, 23, 36, 50, 61, 62, 73, 77, 80, 81, 96, 104, 123, 133, 169, 172, 181, 215, 223, 233, 239, 290, 300, 320, 337, 344, 354, 362
inference, 36, 82, 99, 194, 219, 322, 327, 346, 354, 363
information, 12, 17, 18, 20, 38, 44–46, 50–52, 65, 68, 73, 75, 80–82, 91, 93, 94, 96, 101, 106, 108–110, 117, 133, 147, 150, 159, 160, 163, 171, 180, 185, 209, 214, 215, 217–219, 221,

224, 242, 251, 255–257, 269, 276, 279, 291, 319–322, 326, 327, 341, 343, 346, 352, 357, 383, 394, 399, 405
information asymmetry/failure, 98, 120
information-gap (theory), 353
innovation, 9, 10, 13, 23, 28, 64, 66, 78, 101, 107, 139, 169, 173, 175, 224, 286, 336, 365
institution, 24, 54, 101, 134, 160, 223, 227, 280, 395, 397
insurance, 13, 28, 71, 101, 116, 130, 239, 286, 293, 294, 316, 335, 336
intelligence, 13, 94, 141, 336, 406
intension, 68, 269, 279
intensity, 183, 196, 206, 210, 250, 284, 285
interdependent, 17, 64, 66, 68, 121, 141, 180, 333, 361
invention, 23
investigation/ory, 4, 8, 299
irreducible uncertainty, 6, 12, 64, 204, 239, 341, 342, 383

J
justice, 12, 160, 274, 334, 384

K
Knightian uncertainty, 35, 45, 47, 48, 169, 252–254, 266, 275, 291, 299
knowable unknown, 317, 320, 325, 327, 350, 386, 387, 395, 406
knowledge, 3, 5, 9–11, 17–20, 46, 48–50, 52–54, 66, 68, 71, 73, 76, 78, 91–93, 95, 99, 105, 106, 108, 117, 122, 151, 171, 174, 195, 197, 198, 209, 215, 236, 237, 242, 251, 256, 257, 261, 263, 268, 272, 284, 287, 289, 321, 327, 329, 359, 360, 365, 386, 397

L
lab studies, 108, 116, 301
landscape, 64, 147, 150, 223, 322, 331, 332, 382
law/legal, 7, 13, 24, 25, 74, 79, 97, 101, 107, 109, 119, 147, 152, 159, 170, 221, 273, 286, 366, 404
learning, 2, 17, 38, 89, 131, 147, 153, 161, 174, 199, 216, 224, 235, 237, 268, 286, 293, 323, 325, 327, 336, 343, 351, 384, 401, 402
level of analysis, 21, 37, 62, 75, 139, 142, 260
limits, 21, 50, 60, 61, 64, 73, 74, 76–80, 94, 118, 121, 122, 207, 214, 234, 280, 386
luck, 12, 36, 98, 147, 162, 175, 181, 185, 194, 258, 326, 340

M
machine learning (ML), 343, 344, 393
market, 47, 66, 69, 74, 94, 120, 130, 141, 168, 169, 175, 198, 237, 239, 265, 282, 286, 294, 321, 326, 328, 338, 348
market failure, 117, 130, 175, 237, 252, 293, 341
mathematics, 13, 44, 49, 65, 76, 77, 152, 205, 385
maximin, 343, 348, 349
maximize, 16, 72, 141, 142, 147, 235, 294, 348
mean/average, 97, 150, 223, 255, 396

measurement, 61, 62, 67, 75, 79, 146–148, 152, 153, 162, 287, 288, 329
minimize, 83, 322, 347, 349, 355, 356, 363
misrepresent, 242, 338
model/modeling, 3, 13, 21, 61, 62, 77, 78, 148, 162, 186, 233, 239, 289, 318, 322, 324, 330, 331, 385
monetary, 97, 273, 278, 401
motivation, 15, 47, 80, 173, 174, 278, 354, 357–359, 389
multi-dimension/al, 156, 159, 163, 183, 331
music, 27, 196, 199, 200, 325, 327

N

nature, 3, 9, 13, 17, 19, 23, 34, 37, 53, 61, 64, 67, 71, 75, 80, 107, 120, 123, 146, 157, 159, 160, 162, 184, 207, 221, 223, 240, 248, 257, 275, 282, 286, 287, 359, 398, 404
negative, 19, 27, 36, 66, 91, 92, 116, 119–121, 123, 124, 139, 172, 217, 220, 253, 285, 286, 296–298, 301, 341, 364, 394
neurobiology, 215, 217, 227
non-linear/ity, 64, 214, 289, 347
non-optimizability, 18, 23, 45, 50, 249, 268, 270, 280
non-verifiable, 61, 78
norm, 354, 356, 361
novelty, 49, 61, 63, 81, 157, 169, 195, 224, 250, 273, 289, 386
numerical methods, 329

O

ontology, 20

opportunity, 2, 11, 18, 34, 64, 70, 79, 95, 104, 110, 121, 129, 133, 134, 159, 171, 172, 174, 180, 186, 224, 240, 276, 286, 287, 297, 300, 322, 326, 387
opportunity cost, 106, 118, 181, 253, 294, 322, 326, 364
optimizability/optimal, 27, 37, 51, 100, 138–140, 142, 196, 249, 276, 286, 294, 322, 337, 338, 349, 386
option, 16, 76, 98, 129, 150, 183, 221, 271, 334, 348, 352, 356
organization, 4, 12, 14, 44, 71, 73, 74, 79, 90, 110, 130, 180, 182, 185, 260, 274, 289, 315, 331, 335, 338, 342, 355–357, 362, 366, 395, 396
outcome, 2, 3, 12, 13, 15–17, 36, 44, 45, 47–50, 62, 73, 79, 92, 93, 95, 98, 99, 101–104, 106, 116, 118–122, 146, 147, 149, 151, 152, 160, 168, 184, 185, 207, 222, 234, 243, 251–253, 255, 256, 259, 260, 263, 269–274, 276, 278, 279, 281, 291, 298, 299, 302, 316, 329, 330, 341, 345, 349

P

past, 18, 20, 27, 36, 39, 72, 76, 93, 103, 152, 182, 218, 219, 248, 250, 263, 269, 270, 273, 281, 295, 315, 329, 355, 367, 390
payoff, 15, 16, 18, 121, 151, 168, 172, 180, 243, 255, 260, 269, 272–274, 282, 298, 299, 347, 348, 352, 361
phenomenon, 2, 3, 20, 27, 37, 46, 78, 81, 106, 158, 256, 281, 324
philosophy, 28, 235, 236, 385, 387
philosophy of science, 20, 107

player, 51, 68, 132, 140, 142, 151, 258, 339, 347, 348, 352
politics, 3, 11, 20, 80, 100, 105, 141
possibility, 5, 8, 18, 21, 34, 46, 60, 76, 77, 103, 116, 120, 130, 152, 157, 172, 196, 209, 219, 233, 236, 240, 243, 259, 268, 273, 277, 317, 331, 334, 351, 353, 359, 365, 404
practical, 20, 25, 38, 39, 54, 101, 106, 147, 148, 172, 196, 237, 239, 263, 279, 297–300, 319, 324, 382
predict, 21, 44–47, 60, 64, 93, 94, 100, 107, 133, 149, 174, 215–217, 222, 226, 235, 328, 387, 400, 406
preempt, 222
prioritize/ation, 110, 123, 152, 156, 162, 281, 359, 361
probability, 7, 13, 14, 16, 23, 36, 45, 46, 48, 49, 62, 69, 71, 76, 82, 96, 99–101, 107, 119, 122, 138, 149–151, 157, 158, 207, 232, 234, 236–243, 252, 254–256, 258, 260, 263, 265, 269, 275, 288, 299, 319, 332, 344, 346, 348, 351, 353, 396
problem, 9, 12, 15, 16, 21, 37, 38, 50–52, 60, 62–66, 69, 70, 73, 76, 80, 93, 96, 99, 100, 120, 138, 151, 152, 156, 157, 159, 181, 184, 197, 234, 238, 240, 241, 255, 257, 258, 263, 264, 267–271, 281, 293, 294, 298, 300, 315, 317, 318, 320, 325, 332, 334, 339, 340, 343–345, 351, 354, 356–358, 360–363, 365, 384, 388, 389, 394, 400, 404, 407
process, 3, 8, 13, 15–17, 22, 46, 70, 74, 80, 93, 119, 157, 195, 217, 220, 221, 227, 249, 264, 267, 268, 276, 281, 286, 314, 320, 323, 327, 344, 351, 360–363, 366, 405
processing issues, 359, 367
product, 11, 14, 19, 23, 28, 46, 66, 70, 74, 97, 117, 120, 122, 142, 196, 199, 226, 249, 265, 282, 286, 292, 316, 320, 323, 331, 337, 341, 394
profit, 47, 95–98, 128, 142, 168, 184, 198, 209, 285, 292, 294
psychology, 25, 102, 110, 120, 147, 250, 329, 384

R

random/ness, 3, 37, 61, 66, 67, 122, 185, 195, 204, 258, 263, 345
rational/e/ity, 2, 4, 7, 8, 12, 18, 19, 24, 50, 51, 68, 74, 82, 94, 98–101, 106, 108, 173, 222, 238, 239, 241, 340, 344, 351, 354, 357, 364, 384
real option/s, 182, 290, 334
regret, 264, 349
regulation/regulator, 37, 61, 73, 74, 96, 120, 121, 140, 198, 227, 279, 285, 286, 297, 318, 340, 364, 396
relation/al, 44, 186, 280, 342, 404
religion, 2, 13, 27, 196, 204–210, 406
resistance, 23, 24, 239, 286
resource, 3, 8, 12, 13, 40, 77, 79, 110, 122, 141, 148, 168, 169, 173, 181, 182, 186, 215, 253, 282, 286, 317, 329, 330, 333, 334, 336, 337, 344, 354, 361, 362, 364, 366, 386, 399
resource-based view (RBV), 128, 182, 282

response, 19, 22, 119, 140, 214, 216, 233, 236, 252, 269, 279, 320, 330, 338, 344, 347, 352, 365, 386, 394, 404
reward, 47, 97, 104, 129, 140, 198, 216, 221, 223, 382
risk, 2, 6, 13, 14, 36, 39, 47–49, 65, 70, 95, 99, 101, 109, 116, 130, 162, 194, 198, 218, 223, 233, 234, 236–239, 243, 252, 254, 257, 258, 291, 293, 295, 298, 300, 335, 349, 350, 355, 360, 362, 363, 397–404
rival, 4, 17, 37, 51, 83, 94, 97, 120, 156, 173, 180, 184, 186, 198, 223, 269, 275, 278–280, 286, 296, 298, 318, 322, 325, 327, 329, 340, 347, 352–354, 358, 361, 386, 403
robustness, 17, 208, 220, 294, 332, 334, 349, 353, 364
routine, 6, 7, 11, 15, 70, 132, 150, 240, 356, 361
rule, 94, 276, 345, 347–349

S

satisfice, 334, 353
scenario, 24, 97, 122, 147, 150, 219, 257, 293, 329, 331, 349, 398
scenario planning, 21, 290, 317, 318, 330, 355, 365
science, 3, 4, 10, 11, 20, 22, 28, 54, 91, 92, 103, 105, 107, 108, 196, 205, 209, 233, 235, 236, 238, 239, 341, 382, 383, 385, 386, 389, 406
search, 20, 64, 67, 100, 102, 105, 119, 159, 174, 186, 195, 214, 218, 224, 277, 317, 319–322, 326, 332, 333, 348, 362–365, 386, 395, 405

selection, 3, 16, 141, 187, 217, 221, 222, 225, 252, 337, 365, 387
sequential, 64, 278
serenity, 365, 388
shape, 256, 318, 330, 366, 385
sharing, 101, 335–337, 395
side-payment, 358
signal, 18, 129, 130, 150, 215, 216, 218, 225, 321, 383
simple, 17, 104, 169, 174, 215, 223, 234, 253, 300, 319, 322, 325, 343, 344, 384, 386, 403
simulation, 14, 24, 67, 131, 140, 147, 151, 239, 317, 329–332, 395
simultaneous, 51, 52, 402
social construction, 7, 328
sociology, 25, 120, 234, 329
source, 19, 22, 28, 35, 37, 38, 60–64, 69, 71–73, 82, 83, 99, 130, 150, 158, 160, 161, 182, 209, 218, 219, 248, 261, 277, 280, 281, 287–290, 314, 335, 357, 358, 362, 366, 382
span, 52, 82, 90, 110, 133, 150, 158, 220, 314
spirituality, 27, 204, 206, 208–210
stakeholder, 12, 16, 37, 39, 99, 134, 156, 198, 269, 271, 274, 279, 284, 321, 327, 342, 360, 363
standard operating procedure, 13, 28, 168, 248, 252, 253, 299, 332
statistic/s, 13, 18, 48
strategy, 98, 102, 141, 151, 179, 182, 184–187, 222–224, 270, 282, 286, 325, 347, 348, 358, 363
subjective expected utility (SEU), 12, 158, 235, 239, 242, 243, 293, 349
subjective probability, 45, 351
supplier, 37, 286, 358

supply chain, 70, 158, 169, 180, 337
suppress, 355
survival, 8, 91, 196, 221, 223
symptom, 82, 119
synergy, 22, 131, 134, 199, 200, 286
system/atic, 17, 21, 22, 44, 51, 62, 67, 70, 76–78, 95, 97, 99, 107, 139, 152, 159, 172, 205, 209, 218, 219, 254, 263, 287, 321, 324, 334, 344, 388, 394, 399

T

taboo, 9, 209, 257, 357
tactic, 104, 131, 174, 216, 353–355, 366, 401
target, 72, 139–142, 158, 265, 269, 279, 280, 328, 347, 387
technology, 25, 37, 61, 63, 66, 67, 70, 75–77, 81, 91, 96, 101, 122–124, 141, 163, 170, 199, 205, 224, 252, 261, 286, 297, 321, 364, 383, 394–397, 405, 406
theory/ize, 13, 14, 20, 34, 37, 49, 65, 68, 78, 93, 94, 98, 101, 106, 116, 128, 152, 171, 182, 187, 194, 221, 222, 232, 234, 236, 238, 240, 241, 252, 295, 299, 302, 320, 351, 353, 400
theory of (firm) rents, 292
theory of the firm, 96, 292
third party, 329, 358
timing/time, 3, 5, 8, 12, 16, 17, 22, 24, 65, 66, 70, 79, 104, 122, 133, 148, 159, 160, 169, 198, 218, 223, 226, 253, 262, 264, 268, 269, 275–277, 280, 282, 298, 321, 329–331, 350, 352, 361, 364–366, 386, 405
transaction, 12, 96, 128, 183, 297, 321

treatable uncertainty, 290, 317, 336, 350, 362, 367, 383, 386, 395, 398, 400, 405
treatment, 19, 22, 27, 28, 34, 35, 60, 83, 156, 181, 188, 238, 318, 389
triage, 2, 8, 248, 264, 291, 388
trial, 72, 74, 258, 321, 324, 327
typology, 14, 15, 22, 25, 27, 39, 40, 181, 248, 251, 257, 263, 264, 267, 268, 279, 281, 290, 291, 299, 314, 367, 390

U

uncontrollable, 49, 138, 139, 289
understanding, 2–4, 8, 11, 12, 14, 19–25, 34, 38, 40, 44, 46, 48, 51–54, 60, 62, 63, 76–78, 80, 91, 105–110, 119, 142, 146, 151, 152, 157, 159, 161, 162, 181, 184, 188, 196, 198, 214, 215, 218, 227, 237, 239, 250, 261, 270, 278, 287, 300, 320, 324, 325, 340, 359–361, 381, 382, 389, 390, 402
unknowable unknown, 299, 340, 341, 343, 350, 354, 383, 388, 395, 396
unknown, 5, 14–17, 21, 37, 45–48, 53, 62, 66, 71, 72, 77–79, 98, 119, 121–123, 129, 133, 150–152, 156, 157, 171, 182, 194, 197, 198, 210, 215, 218, 224, 235, 239, 248–250, 254–258, 261, 263–267, 269, 271–273, 275, 276, 280–282, 285–288, 298, 299, 314, 317–320, 322–325, 328, 329, 332, 335, 341, 343, 349, 351, 353, 357, 358, 386, 395, 403
unknown factor, 60, 107, 118, 149, 195, 249, 264, 266

unknown factor characteristic (value), 249
unknown unknown, 49, 123, 133, 147, 153, 170, 181, 235, 237, 249, 254, 256, 258–260, 264, 266, 267, 287, 293, 315, 383, 388, 399
unpredictable, 11, 12, 66, 67, 71, 72, 81, 92, 149, 169, 185, 196, 223, 238, 250, 259, 298, 345, 358
untreatable uncertainty, 340, 356, 358, 396
utility, 16, 98, 106, 198, 235, 242, 273, 275, 354, 384

V

vagueness, 51, 232, 250, 257, 260
value/s, 3, 12, 13, 25, 40, 45, 51, 101, 120, 128, 129, 141, 147, 151, 159, 161, 169, 180, 182, 185, 207, 233, 249, 260, 261, 264–268, 273–275, 281, 294, 315, 317, 318, 327, 329, 332–337, 349–351, 354, 394, 397, 403
variance, 14, 23, 150, 151, 159, 207, 220, 295, 321, 345, 346, 363, 385, 397, 400, 401
venture, 13, 28, 74, 91, 95, 121, 168, 170, 172, 175, 180, 182, 206, 282, 292, 296–298, 301, 323, 330, 335, 336, 341, 390
volatility, 9, 14, 129, 147, 150, 182, 250

W

wicked, 288, 384, 389

Printed in the United States
by Baker & Taylor Publisher Services